JÜRGEN HABERMAS

NEW DIRECTIONS IN CRITICAL THEORY

NEW DIRECTIONS IN CRITICAL THEORY

General Editors: Robyn Marasco and Antonio Vazquez-Arroyo

New Directions in Critical Theory presents outstanding classic and contemporary texts in the tradition of critical social theory broadly construed, drawn from new work in the Global South as well as Frankfurt School, French, Italian, South Asian, and other sources. The series aims to renew and advance the program and praxis of critical social theory, with a particular focus on theorizing contemporary struggles around gender, race, sexuality, class, colonialism, and globalization and their complex interconnections.

The series was founded by Amy Allen in 2007. She remains on its advisory board.

Hierarchies at Work: Race, World-Systems, and Legal Distribution, edited by Karen Engle and Neville Hoad

Love Troubles: A Philosophy of Eros, Federica Gregoratto

Regenerative Politics, Emma Planinc

The Political Clinic: Psychoanalysis and Social Change in the Twentieth Century, Carolyn Laubender

Critical Theories of Anti-Semitism, Jonathan Judaken

Subaltern Silence: A Postcolonial Genealogy, Kevin Olson

Contesting the Far Right: A Psychoanalytic Critical Theory Approach, Claudia Leeb

Another Universalism: Seyla Benhabib and the Future of Critical Theory, edited by Stefan Eich, Anna Jurkevics, Nishin Nathwani, and Nica Siegel

Fascist Mythologies: The History and Politics of Unreason in Borges, Freud, and Schmitt, Federico Finchelstein

Selected Writings on Media, Propaganda, and Political Communication, Siegfried Kracauer, edited by Jaeho Kang, Graeme Gilloch, and John Abromeit

Crisis Under Critique: How People Assess, Transform, and Respond to Critical Situations, edited by Didier Fassin and Axel Honneth

Praxis and Revolution: A Theory of Social Transformation, Eva von Redecker

Recognition and Ambivalence, edited by Heikki Ikäheimo, Kristina Lepold, and Titus Stahl

For a complete list of books in the series, please see the Columbia University Press website.

JÜRGEN HABERMAS

Public Intellectual and Engaged Critical Theorist

PETER J. VEROVŠEK

Columbia University Press
New York

Columbia University Press
Publishers Since 1893
New York   Chichester, West Sussex
cup.columbia.edu

Copyright © 2026 Columbia University Press
All rights reserved

Cataloging-in-Publication data is available from the Library of Congress.
ISBN 9780231213028 (hardback)
ISBN 9780231213035 (paper)
ISBN 9780231559683 (epub)
ISBN 9780231565264 (PDF)

Cover design: Milenda Nan Ok Lee
Cover art: Talal Nayer

GPSR Authorized Representative: Easy Access System Europe,
Mustamäe tee 50, 10621 Tallinn, Estonia, gpsr.requests@easproject.com

For Anja, Hanah, and Dora

Contents

Preface ix

Introduction: Habermas the Public Intellectual 1

1. Mediating Theory and Practice 31
2. The Journalistic Years, 1951–1955 54
3. At the Institute for Social Research, 1956–1959 92
4. A Partisan Professor in the Student Movement, 1960–1971 129
5. Retreat to Starnberg, 1971–1982 156
6. Return to the Public Sphere, 1983–1992 180
7. A Turn From Germany to Europe, 1993–2009 217
8. The Colonization of Politics by Economics, 2010–2020 248

Conclusion: The Last Public Intellectual?, 2021–2025 278

Notes 311

Bibliography 381

Index 409

Preface

On the morning of June 7, 2024 I was on the S-Bahn commuter rail, traveling from central Munich to the suburb of Starnberg, one of the wealthiest towns in Germany. Upon my arrival, I headed down the stairs from the platform. Although the lake, with the morning sun reflecting gently off its glistening surface, beckoned to my right, I headed left toward the exit that leads to the town itself. At the top of the stairs—just as we had agreed—stood Jürgen Habermas, dressed in khakis, a red polo shirt and a charcoal blazer.

For someone like me, who has devoted so much time and energy to studying the life and work of the most important philosopher of the postwar era, it was a surreal moment. While I had been in the same room with him a few times before, standing in front of Habermas and having him shake my hand and greet me with the words, "*Ah, Herr Verovšek, schön, Sie kennenzulernen,*" was overwhelming, to say the least. I felt the need to pinch myself as I sat beside him as he drove me to his house—just a few weeks before his ninety-fifth birthday—in his small, dark gray Peugeot. Discussing philosophical issues while sitting on the couch in his living room under Günter Fruhtrunk's modernist painting dedicated to Theodor Wiesengrund Adorno, with short breaks for *Kaffee und Kuchen* every couple of hours, was without a doubt the highlight of my professional life. The story of my meeting with Habermas is one that I will proudly share not only with my colleagues and students for the rest of my life, but hopefully also with my grandchildren someday.[1]

I never would have thought to embark on this research without the inspiration that Jürgen Habermas, both the philosopher and the public intellectual, has provided to me and so many others over the years. I am incredibly grateful to him for his work and for the personal support he showed me—both by granting me access to his papers and by spending more than eight (!) hours discussing my work with me at his home, surrounded by books and memorabilia from his long and illustrious career. The fact that he was willing and able to do this for a young(ish) colleague like me speaks not only to his intellectual generosity, but also to his readiness to support and assist a generation of scholars who could be grandchildren.

My visit with Habermas has a long backstory. In many ways, this project dates back to the spring of 2008, when I took a course on "Rethinking Sovereignty" co-taught by my *Doktormutter*, Seyla Benhabib, and Robert Post at the Yale Law School. In a session devoted to exploring sovereignty and nation-building in the European Union (EU), we discussed a number of Habermas's political writings on Europe, which had appeared with increasing frequency over the previous years. I had already been introduced to Habermas by Amy Allen, one of my undergraduate advisors and the longtime editor of the series in which this book appears, during my time at Dartmouth College. Given my preexisting interest in Habermas's work—which Amy had not only sparked but also nurtured, despite her more skeptical reading of it—and my proficiency in German, Seyla suggested that I write my seminar paper on the relationship between Habermas's political theory and his public-facing writings on the EU. That paper, which later became the basis for my first peer-reviewed academic publication (and forms the backbone of the seventh chapter of this book), served as the inspiration for this project more than a decade later.[2]

While Habermas played an important role in my doctoral dissertation on the role of memory in the origins and development of European integration, the idea of writing a book focused on the relationship between his philosophical work and political writings remained in the back of my mind. After completing my PhD, I spent a number of years on contingent teaching contracts while turning my dissertation into a book, ulitmately published as *Memory and the Future of Europe: Rupture and Integration in the Wake of Total War*.[3] It was not until I arrived at the University of Sheffield in the UK to take up my first permanent (tenure-track) position as a lecturer (assistant professor) in the Department of Politics that I could even begin to consider taking on a second book project. Although I had a number of other ideas, I kept coming back to the possibility of writing an intellectual biography of Habermas as a public intellectual. Explaining the close connection between Habermas's philosophical ideas and his efforts to spur democratic deliberation on important issues as an engaged public intellectual became increasingly important to me through conversations with my colleagues at Sheffield—especially Matt Sleat and Ed Hall, two prominent proponents of political realism, a strain of contemporary political thought I engage with in chapter 1.

Habermas is usually regarded by members of this movement as the paradigmatic representative of "mainstream liberalism," an approach that they disparage as a quietist form of applied ethics that has nothing to do with what they call "real politics." In response to these realist critiques, I found myself repeatedly having to explain that, while Habermas does indeed reject the idea that philosophy can be directly applied to politics (what I refer to in this book as "the separation thesis"), he has nonetheless translated the practical implications of his philosophy for key political issues through his frequent interventions in the West German public sphere (what I have come to call the "theoretical continuity thesis").

In the fall of 2018, with the support of Matt and Ed, as well as my other colleagues in the Political Theory Research Group—Alasdair Cochrane and Luke Ulaş—I put together a proposal for a British Academy Mid-Career Fellowship. This funding, which was awarded later that year, bought me out of my teaching and administrative duties for the entire 2019–20 academic year. This financial support allowed me to spend two full semesters reading Habermas's writings and conducting research in the Habermas Archive (*Vorlass*) at the Johann Christian Senckenberg University Library in Frankfurt am Main. Habermas generously granted me access to his papers, and the archivists, Oliver Kleppel and Mathias Jehn, provided invaluable assistance while I was conducting my research. Rainer Forst, with whom I had previously spent a year on a DAAD (*Deutsche akademische Austauchdienst*) fellowship during my Ph.D., helped me to obtain housing and an academic community at the Forschungskolleg Humanwissenschaften in Bad Homburg, just outside of Frankfurt.

In addition to those already mentioned, I have accumulated a number of other debts over the five years it took to research and write this book. I am particularly grateful to Roman Yos, who, when I emailed him out of the blue in the winter of 2019, helped me to gain access to a number of Habermas's early newspaper articles that I had been unable to locate myself. While I cannot detail—or even necessarily remember—everyone who offered helpful comments and advice during the many presentations of elements of this project, of those not already mentioned, the following individuals (in no particular order) all played a role in its completion: Gordon Finlayson, Benjamin Schupmann, Gabriele De Angelis, Peter Gordon,

Max Pensky, Simone Chambers, Kenneth Baynes, Verena Erlenbusch-Anderson, Matthew Longo, Paul Linden-Retek, Igor Shoikhedbrod, Brian Milstein, James Ingram, Alexander Livingston, David Ingram, Javier Burdman, Bill Scheuerman, Jensen Sass, Janosch Prinz, Michael Frazer, Samuel Bagg, Christopher Meckstroth, Eduardo Mendieta, Thomas Fossen, Miriam Ronzoni, Liam Shields, Richard Child, James Pattison, Thomas A. McCarthy, Bryan Garsten, Christian Volk, Peter Rožič, David Lebow, Onur Bakiner, Kimberly A. Lowe, Krysztof Kedziora, William Outhwaite, Patrick O'Mahony, Roderick Condon, Gerard Delanty, Matthew Specter, Jon Catlin, Hille Hacker, Rüdiger Görner, Andrew Hines, Tim Christiaens and Markus Patberg. I would also like to thank my research assistant at the University of Groningen, Carla Goltings, for her invaluable assistance in formatting the footnotes and compiling the bibliography. My sincerest apologies to those I have inadvertently forgotten.

On February 2, 2024, I was able to hold a workshop on a full draft of this book manuscript at the Normative Orders Research Cluster of Goethe University Frankfurt. My sincerest thanks to Rainer Forst, who not only hosted and co-funded this event (with the assistance of his assistant, Sonja Sickert), but was also actively engaged in the constructive discussions on all of the chapters over the course of that very long and intellectually stimulating day. It was also Rainer who sent Habermas my draft book manuscript, thus setting the stage for our meeting in June 2024.

This event would not have been possible without the financial contributions I received from my new intellectual home, the University of Groningen—both from Jan van der Harst, the recently retired head of the Chair Group on the History and Theory of European Integration, who generously donated some of his research funds to me, as well as from the Groningen Research Institute for the Study of Culture. I owe a great intellectual debt of gratitude to Thomas Biebricher, Roman Yos, Eva Buddeberg, Maeve Cooke, Till van Rahden, Peter Niesen, Vivienne Matthies-Boon, Regina Kreide and Martin Saar for their invaluable comments on the individual chapters. Thomas Gregerson also read the manuscript and provided many helpful bibliographic references, along with more general notes. I am likewise grateful to the other participants who spent the day helping me improve this book.

Coming full circle, I would like to thank Amy Allen, who was the editor of New Directions in Critical Theory when I first pitched this project to her, and Wendy Lochner, the philosophy editor at Columbia University Press, for their assistance in seeing this book through to completion. Ben Kolstad managed the project; Marcella Munson did a wonderful job copyediting the manuscript. Talal Nayer most generously drew the image for the cover of this book for me based on a photograph of Habermas working in the medium of the published word, doing "what one can do from one's desk (*was man so vom Schreibtisch aus tun kann*)" to improve the quality of democratic debate in the public sphere.[4]

While Habermas provided me with many notes correcting various *Tatsachenfehler* that had crept into an earlier draft of the manuscript, this is not an authorized biography, and any remaining errors are mine and mine alone. Despite my admiration for him and his work, I also know that Habermas disagrees with some of the interpretations I put forward in this book. I can only hope that his remarkably generous comment—that "as an observer, you perhaps see this better (*Vielleicht sehen Sie das besser als Beobachter*)"—indeed proves true, at least occasionally.

Finally, I could not have completed this project without the unwavering support of my wife, Anja, and the patience of my two young daughters, Hanah and Dora. Anja shouldered much of the burden at home while I was away conducting research and presenting my work at various conferences, and Hanah and Dora provided a welcome distraction from the stresses and insecurities that come with completing a project like this. *Hvala za vse!*

JÜRGEN HABERMAS

Introduction

Habermas the Public Intellectual

Jürgen Habermas is one of the—if not *the*—most important philosophers of the postwar era. His writings on the public sphere and his development of the theoretical paradigm of communicative action set him apart in a discipline that is characterized by increasing specialization and retreat into siloed subfields. The concept of the public sphere (*Öffentlichkeit*), which forms the basis of his "talk-centric" conception of modern democratic politics, lies at the heart of his broad-ranging interdisciplinary philosophy, which is guided by the issue of "how a fragile and until now repeatedly disrupted social coexistence (*bisher immer wieder zerreißendes soziales Zusammenleben*) can succeed."[1]

In keeping with his commitment to open debate as the fundamental basis of political legitimacy, Habermas has also engaged extensively in the key social and political debates of his time. In doing so, he has sought to act as "an engaged public intellectual in the very same 'political public sphere' that he theorized as a philosopher."[2] In fact—as I argue in this book—his political commitments and active engagement in public debate have both motivated and shaped his theoretical work in important ways (and vice versa), leading him to take up issues that he might not otherwise have addressed, and to do so in ways he might not otherwise have considered. As a result, I contend that while the distinction between the different parts of his opus should be acknowledged, Habermas's political writings ought to be treated as an integral part of his work, alongside his contributions as a philosopher and sociologist.

Although he has "devoted as much energy and passion to his work as a public intellectual as to his philosophical work," the existing secondary literature is problematic insofar as it focuses on the latter to the detriment of the former.[3] This "peculiar imbalance on the side of theory that has characterized Habermas's reception in English-speaking countries" is due—at least in part—to the fact that, for the majority of his career, his public engagement has been oriented primarily toward the (West) German context.[4] Although he has expanded his scope in recent decades to address the issues faced by Europe and the increasingly globalized world more generally, Habermas has been a key figure in the democratic public sphere of West Germany (the Federal Republic of Germany [FRG]) for its entire existence to date. His work "is part of the dramatic intellectual reconstruction of the post-war period that enduringly liberalized and Westernized German politics."[5] Starting with his widely publicized attack on Martin Heidegger for failing to apologize for his collaboration with the Nazis in 1953; through the Historians' Dispute (*Historikerstreit*) about the meaning of the Nazi past in the mid-1980s; and including his interventions regarding Germany's unique responsibilities during the Eurozone crisis following the Great Recession of 2008 and Germany's foreign policy in the wake of Russia's 2022 full-scale invasion of Ukraine—to name just a few of the most prominent examples—Habermas has been a key figure in almost every important debate in the Federal Republic (FRG) since its foundation in 1949.

Despite the fact that he has been publicly recognized as the "teacher of Germany (*Praeceptor Germaniae*)," the "conscience of society," and "Europe's leading public intellectual," broad strains of contemporary scholarship condemn his philosophical system for its supposed lack of a clear relation to politics.[6] While some critics accuse Habermas of ignorance toward "real politics" because his philosophy is not directly "connected to practical interventions," others interpret him as a "German Rawls"—that is, a mainstream, status quo, quietist, apathetic liberal whose philosophy is a form of "applied ethics."[7] Still other readers tar Habermas as a universalistic "bureaucrat of pure reason" whose work displays no understanding of the agonistic, local, particular, and conflictual nature of the political.[8]

By focusing on his contributions to debates in the broader public sphere—rather than his philosophical and sociological publications, which have been well covered elsewhere—this book pushes back against what I see as a fundamental misreading of Habermas's project, both philosophically and politically. In doing so, I highlight the relationship between Habermas's journalistic interventions and his theoretical oeuvre, a distinction that is often either elided or overlooked in the existing literature. My basic thesis is that Habermas's political writings must be read alongside his academic work in order to make sense of his project, both within scholarship and in the political realm. Rather than simply attempting to put his theoretical ideals into practice or molding his philosophy to fit his political commitments, I propose a more nuanced picture of Habermas as a thinker whose work is the result of a constant mediation between theory and practice, of a dialectical learning process (*Lernprozess*) in which neither component enjoys primacy. In this sense, although the theories Habermas develops as a philosopher are indeed universalistic, they are complemented by the contextualism of his writings as a public intellectual, which for most of his career have focused on "one particular mission . . . helping the norms of universal reason to prevail in Germany, the land of the Counter-Enlightenment, and educating [his] compatriots to democracy."[9]

Although it is true that the mature Habermas seeks to distinguish between his roles as an academic philosopher and a nonexpert public intellectual, his commitment to what I call "the separation thesis" does not mean that his politically engaged interventions are completely divorced from his philosophical work. On the contrary, in line with my "theoretical continuity thesis," I show that the political positions Habermas defends are in line with his philosophical commitments, even if they flow from them in a mediated, rather than a direct manner. Although Habermas's philosophical works, which are presented in a difficult "Prof.-Jargon," appear to have little connection to the "visible desire to speak in public" and the "surprisingly high tolerance of conflict [displayed] by such a quietly working scholar," I argue that the two separate roles that Habermas takes on are ultimately part of a consistent whole.[10]

One important implication of my argument is that Habermas's social and political interventions, many of which have been republished in the twelve volumes of his *Kleine politische Schriften* ("short political writings"), must be read alongside his philosophical work. Given this commitment, in this book I narrow my focus to Habermas's understudied and public-facing texts and speeches, many of which have never been republished or translated for an international audience. Where such comparison is fruitful or necessary, I then place them into conversation with his theoretical work. As a result, this book aims to make at least an initial step toward rectifying the current imbalance in the reception of his thought between his political and his academic works.

In addition to highlighting the necessity of reading Habermas's philosophical works alongside his public-facing contributions, my argument also responds to the growing literature on public intellectuals and the public role of scholarship more generally. More specifically, I engage with the growing literature demanding that political theory speak to policymakers and have a direct "impact" on policy.[11] In opposition to these trends—as well as calls from epistemic democrats, who argue that experts should take on a greater place in government and governance—Habermas follows Immanuel Kant and Max Weber in seeking to ford what Wendy Brown refers to as the "moat between academic and political life." Habermas drops a number of drawbridges to connect these separate domains so that scholarship can "inform political struggles and help to develop their potentials or illuminate their weaknesses" while also being informed by the historical complexity revealed by these same struggles. However, he strictly "distinguishes the place where values are struggled for from the place where they can be queried and analyzed, doubted, taken apart, reconsidered."[12]

On the one hand, what I am calling his separation thesis seeks to ensure the democratic equality of all citizens by protecting the public from scholars, who seek to exert their academic authority in the public realm. In contrast to much of the contemporary philosophical literature, which endorses such interventions by those who presumably know better, Habermas maintains that everyone must be accorded an equal opportunity to participate in politics. While few citizens ever actually stand for election, in line with Habermas's discursive conception of democratic legitimacy (and the theoretical continuity thesis), he argues that all individuals—including noncitizens—in modern democracies are called to participate "in the weighting of competing public opinions," either tacitly, by following debates in the public sphere, or through the conscious articulation of a position in these same informal deliberations.[13] On the other hand, this proverbial moat is also designed to protect academics from political interference, thus preserving both their pedagogical *Lehrfreiheit* (freedom to teach) as well as their broader academic freedom in both research and the internal governance of the university. This ensures the integrity of teaching and research while also enabling "faculty to speak as citizens in the public square without professional sanction."[14]

Although politically engaged intellectuals should play a role in public policy, I argue (following Habermas) that it is foolish to demand that all scholars engage in these activities, given that "the temperaments required for success in these two enterprises of scholarship and politics are distinct."[15] This is not to say that there are no individuals capable of fulfilling both of these tasks while also maintaining the boundary between them. Although this cannot be expected of all academics, I present Habermas as the paradigmatic example of such a *"bidimensional* being," who, in the words of Pierre Bourdieu, is able to call "into question the classical alternative of pure culture and political engagement."[16]

Building on his early scholarship—especially his first monograph, *The Structural Transformation of the Public Sphere* (1962)—as well as his mature legal and political theory, I argue that Habermas's philosophical arguments regarding the central place of the public sphere in modern democratic politics are generally consistent with his work as a public intellectual. I buttress this argument using his personal papers, which are stored in the Habermas Archive (Habermas Vorlass, or HV) at the Johann Christian Senckenberg University Library in Frankfurt am Main. Bringing these different primary sources together, I not only tie his activities as an engaged intellectual to his philosophical ideals but also show how his political commitments and public-facing work often motivate his philosophy (and vice versa). This book thus not only emphasizes these understudied texts and debates but also links them to the scholarship on Habermas, resulting in a novel interpretation of his thought that is both more comprehensive and more complete.

In the rest of this introduction I lay the foundations for the rest of the book. The first section introduces Habermas's understanding of the role of philosophy in modern democratic life, which in turn provides the foundation for his conception of the public intellectual. In the second, I compare Habermas's academic and political writings, focusing on differences in tone, style, and argumentation. The third analyzes how he positions himself in the public sphere by considering *when*, *how*, and *where* he chooses to intervene in political affairs while still maintaining his professional status and reputation as a philosopher. The fourth section presents important themes that consistently appear in his work as a public intellectual. Chief among these, I argue, is his sustained effort to urge his fellow citizens to remember and learn from the painful legacy of the Nazi past. Following a brief methodological note, I conclude by outlining the overall structure of the book and summarizing the chapters that follow.

PHILOSOPHY IN MODERN DEMOCRATIC LIFE

Although Habermas builds on the "unfinished project" of the Enlightenment and champions the force of rational argumentation, he also consistently emphasizes his belief that philosophers and other intellectuals have no special insight into or privileged position in public affairs.[17] Instead, as I detail in chapter 1 on Habermas's mature conception of the relationship between theory and practice, public intellectuals should serve as mediators between specialized spheres of knowledge and everyday conversations, speaking to fellow citizens from a perspective of common sense informed by scholarship. On this view, philosophers intervening in the public sphere should "see themselves as translators of abstract knowledge and ideas into more concrete terminology." They thus serve as "competent chairpersons in the ongoing decision-making process that is cultural renewal."[18]

In light of this commitment, Habermas argues that in an increasingly globalized, pluralistic, and multicultural world, as public intellectuals philosophers can claim no epistemic priority for the arguments they present to the broader reasoning public, since "philosophy is a fallibilistic enterprise and does not endow intellectuals who use their philosophical insights with any legitimacy that goes beyond their qualification as citizens."[19] While philosophers have certain advantages—such as not having to rely on public commentary for their livelihood and being accustomed to thinking about the big picture—Habermas argues that the people at large remain the ultimate arbiter of the claims presented in the public sphere. Building on this foundation, I interpret his political writings as an attempt to apply insights from his philosophy—as well as his own political beliefs—to his political community as a fellow citizen "when current events are threatening to spin out of control—but then promptly, as an early warning system."[20]

Much like the famed American sociologist C. Wright Mills, Habermas gives such social critics acting in the public sphere two basic tasks: "to turn personal troubles and concerns into social issues and problems open to reason . . . [and] to combat all those forces which are destroying genuine publics and creating a mass society."[21] Although public intellectuals draw on their professional reputations and the moral authority earned through past engagements, the power and legitimacy they command are not solely based on their expertise. On the contrary, "the courage of conviction, as the necessary precondition for speaking in defiance of the established powers and the public, also contributes to public intellectuals' special authority."[22] More generally, Habermas ascribes five "unheroic virtues" to such figures:

— a mistrustful sensitivity to damage to the normative infrastructure of the polity;
— the anxious anticipation of threats to the mental resources of the shared political form of life;

— the sense for what is lacking and "could be otherwise";
— a spark of imagination in conceiving of alternatives;
— and a modicum of the courage required for polarizing, provoking, and pamphleteering.[23]

Although intellectuals can get worked up about many different issues, their fundamental task is to expand "the democratic imagination and civic sensitivity of citizens and their leaders alike."[24]

The role of the public intellectual thus gives Habermas an outlet to express his own ideas and his not infrequent indignation at political developments in Germany, in Europe, and around the world, in a way that is clearly separated from his academic research. "It is this capacity to get irritated" by current events, he argues, "that turns scholars into intellectuals."[25] Moreover, this same "irritation" can also spill over into an intellectual's scholarly work, as I argue it often does in Habermas's case—most notably in his critiques of other theorists in the *Philosophical Discourse of Modernity* (1985).

That being said, the role of the public intellectual is not limited to giving increasingly specialized scholars a political voice; the Socratic "gadfly" also plays a crucial "public role in the context of a liberal political culture—namely, as the 'guardian of rationality'" in the public sphere.[26] Much like Václav Havel, Habermas also sees public intellectuals as figures who engage in "thinking in general terms about the affairs of this world and the broader context of things." Given the increasing globalization and multiculturalism that define politics and society at the start of the twentieth century, it makes sense that those "who are most keenly aware of these interconnections, who pay the greatest regard to them, [and] who take the most responsible attitude toward the world as a whole" would play a role in shaping public debate about its future.[27]

Habermas also agrees with the Palestinian postcolonial theorist and fellow social critic, Edward Saïd, who points out that, while not usually affiliated with political parties, the "intellectual is not really a neutral figure." Instead, through responsible action, creativity, and courage, they help uphold the values of a free and deliberative democracy by taking on "the role of 'democracy's helpers,'" working to improve the tone and quality of public debate.[28] Building on what Habermas refers to as their "avantgardistic instinct for relevances," the public intellectual thus "self-consciously rejects the contemplative ideal of withdrawal and detachment, and is vitally concerned to 'make a difference,' 'to take a stand,' to 'help society.'"[29]

To a certain extent public intellectuals are like weather vanes: their interventions "tell us about the strength and direction of the prevailing political wind." However, Habermas's broad influence means that, in many cases, he "has also helped to make the weather," using his political writings to channel the existing political turbulence in ways that "shift the terms of debate."[30] Thus, in addition to advancing his theoretical commitments by helping to transform the nascent public sphere of the nascent West German state—which was "democratic in name only"—"into something that engaged citizens could work with" by expanding "the role of the civic-minded burgher," he has also made himself impossible to ignore. As a recent observer points out, "Whatever their politics, Germany's policymakers have always had to take Jürgen Habermas seriously."[31] In recent decades, this has become increasingly true for the rest of Europe as well.

ACADEMIC PUBLICATIONS VERSUS PUBLIC INTERVENTIONS

Although the distinction between Habermas's theoretical research in philosophy and sociology—aimed at developing an understanding (*Verstehen*) of social and political interaction at an abstract level—and his politically oriented praxis as a public intellectual, where he intervenes in ongoing debates in the public sphere, is analytically clear, the close connections between the themes that he addresses in these different areas of his work result in many marginal cases. Additionally, the structure of the German media landscape, along with Habermas's relatively limited publication of essays in academic journals, makes this task even more difficult. Whereas publishing industries abroad typically maintain a clear distinction between academic, peer-reviewed journals and public-facing forums, this boundary is less defined in the German-language context.

For example, early in his career, Habermas frequently published in *Merkur*.[32] Although its subtitle, "German Journal for European Thought," makes it sound like a scholarly outlet, its editors explicitly reject this classification, stating that it "is not an academic journal, although many of its contributors are based at universities." Some of Habermas's contributions to this self-described "cultural journal" are clearly political commentaries, including reprints of political debates in the public sphere, such as his exchange of letters with the German political scientist Kurt Sontheimer regarding the Left's connection to the domestic terror attacks of the 1970s (see chapter 5). However, others are more academic contributions to themes within European thought.³³ The fact that *Merkur* also "stands for the introspective search for the reasons underlying the moral and political catastrophe" of Nazism only made this outlet more attractive to Habermas, despite what he describes as the "conservative impulses" of its editors.³⁴

The *Blätter für deutsche und internationale Politik* (*Journal for German and International Politics*) holds a similar position in the German public sphere. It claims to be "the most widely read German language political journal," which in the words of the Protestant theologian Karl Barth represents "an island of reason within a sea of nonsense." While its articles contain citations, it brings together academia and political intervention while also ensuring "journalistic standards of good readability and comprehensibility."³⁵ Both of these journals are well suited to the public intellectual precisely because they are difficult to categorize and cut across the usual divide between academic and public-facing outlets.

One promising way to conceptualize the distinction between academic research and political interventions is not so much through genre, but through style and tone. The difficult, broadly inaccessible nature of Habermas's theoretical prose is one of the most common critiques of his philosophy, as "he often writes in a subtle academic language, drawing upon the specialized vocabularies of the liberal arts and sciences." By contrast, many readers have observed that the prose of Habermas's political writings "is more easily digested than the sweeping vision of the synthetic major works."³⁶ Additionally, whereas his academic contributions certainly do not suffer from an "inability to antagonize (*Gegnerschaftsunfähigkeit*)," in his public commentaries he occasionally even displays a "compulsion to hostility (*Verfeindungszwang*)."³⁷

As a result of the choices he makes about where to publish—and in marked contrast to the "sociologese" of "the sweeping vision of [his] synthetic major works," where Roger Scruton's uncharitable observation that "tedium is . . . a vehicle of an abstract authority" may contain a grain of truth—Habermas's political writings are "more easily digested" and "less technical and more colloquial."³⁸ These different styles are not an accident, but the result of conscious choice.

On the one hand, Habermas argues that linguistic persuasion has no place in his social and political theory, which should be evaluated according to prevailing disciplinary standards of reason and argumentation. On the other, Habermas the public intellectual "us[es] arguments sharpened by rhetoric, [to] intervene on behalf of rights that have been violated and truths that have been suppressed, reforms that are overdue and progress that has been delayed."³⁹ As a result, he frequently engages in polemic and personal confrontation in his public-facing texts. This is consistent with his belief that the public sphere must be defined by "robust manifestations" of conflict. As he notes in a 2020 interview, "I see no reason to wrap angry citizens in gauze (*Wutbürger in Watte zu packen*)."[40]

For example, in rejecting one of Habermas's early essays in 1955 due to objections from the staff of the *Frankfurter Allgemeine Zeitung* (FAZ), his editor Karl Korn writes that "your uncommonly difficult diction (too difficult for the newspaper setting) makes understanding your essay accessible only to a small part of our readership."[41] However, he also notes that in certain cases Habermas's arduous prose is "an advantage (*ein Vorteil*)," as "this style protects you from [the objections of] every Tom, Dick, and Harry (*schirmt Sie gegen Krethi und Plethi ab*)."[42] As a result, at first glance it appears that Habermas's use of polemical rhetoric might help to separate his academic research from his public interventions. However, this is hardly a reliable method, since a number of his more theoretical writings are quite polemical as well. While the lectures on the *Philosophical Discourse of Modernity* are the most prominent example of Habermas making strongly rhetorical claims in his philosophical writings, it is hardly the only one.[43]

Another consequence of the different audiences to which his theoretical and political work is oriented is a distinction in the form and medium of presentation. Habermas presents most of his research either as books or academic articles. These forums are governed by peer review, where other members of the profession act as a jury, judging whether the arguments meet the accepted standards of the discipline.[44] By contrast, his political writings often take the form of essays published in the feuilleton pages of German-language newspapers, which present a mix of cultural criticism, storytelling, and intellectual conversation. This not only allows Habermas to reach a broader audience among the reading public; it also allows him to ask big questions that transcend his professional work as a philosopher and sociologist. Following his mentor at the Frankfurt School, Theodor Adorno, Habermas makes use of the essay so that he can take on the role of the "critic who addresses ultimate questions while dealing with specific, frequently marginal issues."[45]

The easiest way to resolve the dilemma of classification would simply be to follow Habermas's own division of his work. Since 1980, Habermas has released twelve collections of "short political writings," which reproduce political commentaries, interviews, and speeches relating to various controversies he has engaged in within the public sphere. In line with his own self-understanding of the different roles he plays as a teacher, researcher, and public intellectual, it is clear that Habermas "chose to publish them under a separate and distinct title in order to underline the distinction between the role of the professor dedicated to his theory and the intellectual engaged in his society."[46]

The first four editions (I–IV) of this series, which were released as a single volume in 1980, cover Habermas's early work starting in the 1950s. The subsequent collections, contained within the monochromatic covers (red, green, purple, or orange) of the *Kleine politische Schriften* series published by Suhrkamp Verlag, with which Habermas has been affiliated since the publication of the German edition of *Knowledge and Human Interests* (1968), have appeared more frequently. These later volumes are usually devoted to a specific debate (for example, the Historians' Dispute) or seminal event (e.g., German unification) that drew the attention of Habermas the public intellectual.[47]

Although I draw extensively on the essays brought together in the "short political writings," my source base is not limited to these republished texts. First, although many of Habermas's otherwise hard-to-find essays have been reprinted in one form or another, these collections leave out many interesting contributions. Second, despite their title, the short political writings also occasionally include texts that Habermas admits are actually "more strictly academic contributions."[48]

The precise status of these contributions is further complicated by the publication strategy employed by Suhrkamp. Initially, Habermas's preferred publishing house put his philosophical works in their academic series (Suhrkamp wissenschaft) and his "Short Political Writings" in the Edition Suhrkamp. However, this distinction was elided once Europe became Habermas's main public focus following the fall of the Berlin Wall. Most notably, Habermas's *Crisis of the European Union* (2011)—clearly a political commentary—was published with a hybrid cover design, outside both series. Finally, although Habermas has continued to engage in public debate on new issues that have arisen since the onset of the Eurozone crisis in 2010, he has made it clear that the twelfth volume of his *Kleine politische Schriften* devoted to this issue will "presumably (*voraussichtlich*)" be the last in the series.

As a result of these considerations—and as I demonstrate throughout this book—in practice it is often difficult to separate his theoretical and political writings, as themes and arguments from one often blend into the other. This illustrates that Habermas is more inclined to sacrifice the separation thesis in favor of theoretical consistency than the reverse. I therefore focus more broadly on the texts in which Habermas addresses controversies of general interest within the broader social, cultural, and political public sphere—not exclusively on the critical role that the public sphere plays in his philosophical writings.[49]

Additionally, although I highlight the compatibility between Habermas's theoretical and public-facing works, I also argue—unlike other scholars who have examined his political writings—that it is important to respect Habermas's own attempts to maintain a clear separation between these two parts of his oeuvre.[50] For example, I follow Robert Holub's study of Habermas as a "critic in the public sphere" in highlighting the dialogical, debate-based nature of much of his work. However, I depart from Holub and much of the existing literature by focusing specifically on the political discussions Habermas has engaged in as a public intellectual, rather than on the theoretical controversies that have defined his academic career.[51]

This emphasis on Habermas the public intellectual and on the dialogical relationship between his political activism and his philosophical work separates my approach from other commentaries on his work. Even though Stefan Müller-Doohm's authoritative, encyclopedic biography also touches on these issues, it does not focus on them.[52] Finally, covering all of Habermas's long career, from his early journalism of the 1950s to his more recent writings on international politics and the EU, allows me to simultaneously build on the work of scholars whose work focuses on particular periods of Habermas's career, such as Roman Yos's treatment of "the young Habermas," while also transcending their more focused contributions.[53]

HABERMAS'S POSITIONING IN THE PUBLIC SPHERE

Habermas is deeply aware of the importance of how he locates himself and his writings, both in terms of his academic work and as a public intellectual working within the media landscape of postwar West Germany, as well as within the broader transnational European public sphere after 1989.[54] To a certain extent, of course, how he is seen and the features attributed to him as a "positioned party" depend on the viewpoints and interpretations of his interlocutors as well as those of the public at large.[55] Keeping this in mind, my examination of *when, how,* and *where* Habermas has chosen to engage in politically salient debates demonstrates that he has actively sought to situate himself as an independent, authoritative intellectual voice of the Left who speaks out when fundamental democratic values are threatened by contemporary events.

To start, the incisiveness of Habermas's interventions and his timing both play an important role in his success. In certain cases, especially later in his career, he has used his stature—a recognition that he was able to achieve in part due to the underdeveloped nature of the West German public sphere in the immediate postwar period—to elevate existing arguments into full-blown controversies. Far more often, however, he has ignited new controversies about issues that were previously "hidden under the blanket (*unter der Decke gehalten*)" through contributions that captured the attention of the reading public and inspired (often indignant) replies from his opponents.[56]

This is certainly evident in Habermas's first major, attention-grabbing intervention in 1953, when he criticized Martin Heidegger for reprinting a lecture series originally delivered in 1935 without removing a favorable reference to the "inner truth and greatness" of National Socialism, and called on him to apologize and clarify his relationship to Nazism and the Third Reich.[57] Similarly, his critique of the conservative historian Ernst Nolte's revisionist interpretation of the Nazi past in July 1986 transformed what was initially a minor issue of interest primarily to professional historians into a heated political dispute within the German public sphere (see chapter 5).[58] Because Habermas often assumes the role of instigator, his public interventions typically unfold on his terms, allowing him to choose and define the discursive framework.

An additional advantage of this choice is that it allows Habermas to better balance his academic *Beruf* (profession or vocation) with his activities as a public intellectual and social critic, which he refers to as his *Nebenberuf*—his "secondary vocation" or "side hustle." His efforts to maintain this balance—often prioritizing his primary profession, or "anchor job," particularly during the 1970s (see esp. chapter 5)—are clearly evident in his correspondence. There, he frequently declines requests from mass media outlets to comment on the latest public scandal or further defend his position, noting, "I am pressured from all sides to do this and that, but in the end I still have my job (*Beruf*)." This is often followed by the promise that he will be in touch "when current events seem to require me to make my opinion known."[59] In this sense, Habermas is part of what Bruce

Robbins refers to as "the conceptual relocation of intellectuals *within* rather than outside occupations" that occurs over the course of the twentieth century, which allows them "to achieve vocationally 'contented lives' without sacrificing political consistency."[60]

Second, Habermas controls his positioning through the *type of media* in which his work appears. Interestingly, although he is aware of the power of radio and television—for example, his mentor at the Institute for Social Research, Theodor W. Adorno, used the former to great effect after his return to Germany in the 1950s[61]—Habermas is never seen "on screen," and his voice is seldom heard "on the airwaves." This is certainly not due to any lack of opportunity. On the contrary, an examination of the correspondence in the Habermas Vorlass makes clear that he had ample invitations to appear in both forms of "new media" throughout his career, invitations that he almost always declined.[62]

Although Habermas occasionally excuses himself due to his "work overload (*Arbeitsüberlastung*)"[63]—this relates to his aforementioned need to balance his *Beruf* and *Nebenberuf* as well—more often he responds to such invitations by asking the producers of the program in question "to regard it as my personal idiosyncrasy (*persönliche Idiosynkrasie*) that I have inhibitions regarding television screens." Such responses are common even in cases where it is clear that he is tempted to accept. For example, Habermas was undoubtedly attracted by the opportunity to participate in an hour-long discussion on the UK's Thames Television's program "Something to Say" with Hannah Arendt, a thinker he admires and had met in person on at least three different occasions during his stay as the Theodor Heuss Visiting Professor in Philosophy at the New School for Social Research in New York in 1967.[64] Despite his desire to meet Arendt again and engage in discussion with her, Habermas, in declining, asks the producer for understanding regarding "my refusal, which most certainly has no snobbish motives."[65]

At other times, however, he makes it clear that there is more at play in his rejection of the role of the "media intellectual (*Medien-Intellektueller*)," which Adorno had pioneered in West Germany.[66] For instance, in turning down an invitation to participate in a documentary on the state of contemporary philosophy in West Germany, Habermas notes that this opportunity is not attractive enough to tempt him "to depart from my principle (*Grundsatz*) of not appearing on television. This may be an idiosyncrasy, but one must also live with those."[67] The reasons for this deeper principle are visible in *Structural Transformation*, where Habermas argues that "the published word" is the "decisive mark" of the public realm.⁶⁸ This medium is crucial because it can be broadly shared and enables rational, considered argumentation.

By contrast, Habermas contends that spoken exchanges—whether in person, on the radio, or on television—are less effective and tend to distract from the rational core of public argument, since they rely more on appearance and allow individuals to obfuscate through tone, emotional appeals, and the like. In his understanding, therefore, the public sphere "is not a space of viewers or listeners but an arena in which speakers and interlocutors exchange questions and answers. Rather than everyone else's gaze being focused on the celebrity, an exchange of opinions and reasons takes place."⁶⁹ In other published works, he has also connected this preference to his cleft palate, noting that "my speech impediment may also explain why I have always been convinced of the superiority of the written over the spoken word," since the "written form disguises the taint of the spoken word."⁷⁰

Whatever the reasons, it is clear that Habermas's preference for the written over the spoken word places him at a distinct positional disadvantage in the modern public sphere, which is increasingly defined by audiovisual media. For instance, in his historical typology of intellectuals, Régis Debray distinguishes three main phases: the age of the academic (1880–1930), the era of publishing (1920–1960), and the time of the media intellectual (from 1968 on).⁷¹ During this final period, a new type of public intellectual has emerged: "one who appears on television rather than writes," though for Habermas such an individual would not seem to qualify as a public intellectual, given his commitment to the written word.⁷²

Although Habermas's career began at the very end of the era of publishing, he maintained his loyalty to this model at the time when the rise of radio and television—followed later by the Internet—had already brought about the appearance of the "media intellectual."⁷³ By refusing to participate in this process "on principle," Habermas thus put himself at a distinct disadvantage. The fact that he has maintained such a high profile throughout the postwar period despite this self-imposed impediment is remarkable and attests to his ability to break through the increasing noise and visual focus of the public sphere in the postwar period.

Finally, in addition to *when* and *how*, Habermas's choices about *where* to position himself—i.e., in which concrete publications—are also important. What is incredible, at least from an Anglo-Saxon perspective, is how much of his early journalism consists of reviews of scholarly works and academic conferences—content that major West German newspapers were prepared to publish, often with an honorarium or other form of payment (sometimes quite generous). This openness to scholarly content is due in large part to a historical artifact of the German broadsheet that I briefly mentioned above: the feuilleton.

This feature originated in Paris around 1800 as a supplement to the news, emerging at the height of the salon and coffeehouse public sphere that Habermas theorizes in *Structural Transformation*. It presents a mix of cultural criticism, storytelling, and intellectual conversation that has no real equivalent in the Anglo-American tradition, and it remains a mainstay of all major German newspapers.[74] Given its historical origins, the feuilleton is thus one of the few remaining pieces of what Habermas calls "the bourgeois public sphere," which "tamed the Leviathan of the absolutist state" by giving birth to a self-conscious, politically informed, and critical public.[75]

Most of Habermas's political writings originally appear in this forum. The feuilleton is important not only because it provides him with an outlet for his political writings, but also because it allows him to fulfill his vocation as a public intellectual by engaging in public debate "using arguments sharpened by rhetoric, [to] intervene on behalf of rights that have been violated and truths that have been suppressed, reforms that are overdue and progress that has been delayed." Although Habermas rarely addresses the concept or the role of the public intellectual in his social and political theory, it is no accident that his first major treatment of this topic comes in a speech devoted to Heinrich Heine, whose political journalism in the early nineteenth century marked him out as a "protointellectual" and "midwife of a political public sphere" that would develop in Germany only after his exile to Paris.[76] Interestingly, Heine is often referred to as the "father of the feuilleton" in Germany, a fact that further confirms the central place of this institution in the German-speaking public sphere.[77]

Habermas's years working as a journalist before Adorno brought him to the Institute for Social Research in 1956 played an important role in preparing him for his activities as a public intellectual, as Habermas was familiar with the structure of the West German mass circulation media and of the importance of cultivating relationships with well-placed editors (see chapter 2). In his early career, Habermas did not have the benefits of the "privileged *parcours*" that comes with "team membership" in a prominent intellectual network.[78] Despite this disadvantage, he notes that he was "tremendously privileged (*ungeheuer privilegiert*)," because editors of leading German media outlets at the time were willing and eager to receive contributions from young authors like himself.[79]

However, before 1956 Habermas still had to send his writings to editors without the benefit of an introduction beforehand. The extent to which he was an unknown quantity in his early career is visible in the correspondence surrounding his journalism, which reveals the "backstage" of how he sought to position himself in the media landscape.[80] For example, in 1953 Habermas sent a draft of "Mit Heidegger gegen Heidegger denken" (Thinking with Heidegger Against Heidegger), which ended up being his first major publication, to Korn, who was the head of the FAZ's Feuilleton page at the time and was known for giving young authors like the twenty-three-year old Habermas a publishing platform. Korn, who later became known as "the great discoverer and implementer of the German *Feuilleton*," reacted enthusiastically to this submission.[81] He opens his reply to Habermas's unsolicited manuscript with the words, "And if I am interested in your article!" However, he immediately follows this exclamation by asking who Habermas is, given that "if we publish this article, there will likely be a violent bruhaha (*würde es wohl einen gewaltigen Wirbel geben*)." Since he will have to defend the piece as its publishing editor, Korn notes that he needs more information on its author before he can commit to printing Habermas's intervention.[82]

This initial exchange—and the successful publication of Habermas's attack on Heidegger for not apologizing for his active collaboration with the Third Reich—signaled the beginning of a long-standing partnership between Habermas and Korn. During this period Habermas continued to publish his political writings in other outlets as well, including the *Süddeutsche Zeitung*, with its progressively liberal and social democratic orientation, and the aforementioned *Handelsblatt*, in order to maintain his independence. However, despite placing occasional texts elsewhere, he maintained a close relationship with the FAZ through the 1960s. Indeed, until the conservative historian of Nazism Joachim Fest became its coeditor and took over the Feuilleton in 1973, Habermas observes that the FAZ "embodied a piece of the spiritual tradition of the liberal middle class in Germany."[83]

Immediately after his arrival Fest confirmed the paper's new direction by firing Habermas's friend, Karl-Heinz Bohrer, the literary editor of the FAZ, with whom Habermas had also worked closely.[84] In response to what he saw as this "selling out of the best traditions of the old *Frankfurter Zeitung*," Habermas refused to publish in the FAZ for the duration of Fest's editorship.[85] Instead, he shifted his political writings to other publications, including the *Frankfurter Rundschau* and the *Süddeutsche Zeitung*, as well as the weekly *Die Zeit*, which was his preferred forum for public engagement for much of the post-Cold War period. When the new editor of the Feuilleton, Frank Schirrmacher, sought to bring him back to the FAZ after the unification of Germany in 1989, Habermas was not tempted in the least, noting that he would prefer to limit "his role to that of a reader." He defended his decision by observing that he "notes with interest the unashamedly pro-fascist articles of your correspondent in Rome, a right-wing radical defense of Carl Schmitt's 'imperative of homogeneity,' and the exculpation of Gentile, the fascist political philosopher, by a former PCI [*Partito Comunista Italiano*] intellectual—this is the yield of just a few days."[86]

Habermas's choice to move to *Die Zeit* is particularly interesting in the context of the development of the leading media of the public sphere in West Germany. Immediately following the end of the war, this weekly had a reputation as a "national-conservative (*nationalkonservativ*)" outlet. For example, in 1964 the editor of its Feuilleton page, Rudolf Walter Leonhardt, wrote to Habermas, noting that publishing one of his texts was part of "a ten-year effort, to obtain the best collaborators for this paper." However, Leonhardt noted that Habermas had not made this process easy: "You apparently have some strong reservations, be it against the ZEIT or against me personally."[87]

In response to this complaint, Habermas writes, "My wife claims that I rail against (*schimpfe*) everyone. Given this assumption, I cannot entirely rule out the possibilities that there have also been opportunities to scold you as well." However, after publishing a text in *Die Zeit* in 1964, Habermas also notes that it is possible that in Leonhardt "a miserable author has found a brilliant director."[88]

The effects of these changes to the political landscape of West Germany's newspaper industry are evident not only in where Habermas chooses to publish but also in which outlets his interlocutors choose to respond. Before Fest's takeover, Habermas's conservative opponents, including Heidegger in 1953, had replied to his provocations in the FAZ with articles in *Die Zeit*.[89] However, by the early 1970s this dynamic had flipped, with *Die Zeit* taking up a more liberal position in the media landscape as the FAZ moved to the right.[90] As a result, Habermas's targets often responded to his attacks in *Die Zeit* with articles in the FAZ (for instance, this is the dynamic of the Historians' Dispute of the 1980s).

Finally, in connection to *where* Habermas chooses to publish, it is difficult to draw a clear line separating Habermas's engaged political writings from his academic research in philosophy and sociology. In part, these problems of classification stem from the greater openness of German newspapers to academic debates compared to similar media elsewhere, especially in the Anglo-Saxon world, as my description of the institution of the feuilleton makes clear. As a result, many of Habermas's publications in wide-circulation broadsheets—which, based on their placement, appear to be interventions in the public sphere—actually read more like academic book or literature reviews than typical newspaper articles. This highlights a broader challenge in classifying and separating Habermas's political writings from his academic research.

AN AGENT OF MEMORY IN THE PUBLIC SPHERE

In the previous section I sought to answer a number of questions regarding *when*, *how* and *where* Habermas positions himself as a public intellectual, highlighting his privileged time of birth, which allowed him to put his personal imprint on the nascent, underdeveloped public sphere of the newly created West Germany, his keen sense of timing, his ability to generate debate despite his aversion to the increasingly dominant "new media" of radio and television, and his choices about where to place his interventions in public debate in order to maintain his status as a dominant, but also independent voice of the intellectual left. In addressing these issues, I consciously avoided the question of *why*. Assessing Habermas's success as a public intellectual is difficult and likely due to a number of different factors, including his affiliation with the Frankfurt School and a measure of good fortune as well as some of the other reasons I detailed above.

In addition to these aspects, Habermas's success as a public intellectual is also surely due to his talent for generating labels that both capture the public's attention and goad his opponents into engaging with him. A good example is his reference to the historians who sought to "normalize" West Germany's relationship to the Third Reich by arguing that the gas chambers were merely a response to the atrocities of the Soviet Union that "the curtain should finally be brought down (*ein Schlussstrich sollte endlich gezogen werden*)" on the Nazi past as "new conservatives," a label that they rejected despite their affiliation with the center right Christian Democratic parties.[91] Even members of the German reading public who have never read Habermas's philosophical worked are familiar with many of his key theoretical concepts, such as "the unforced force of the better argument (*der zwanglose Zwang des besseren Arguments*)," "communication free of domination (*herrschaftsfreie Kommunikation*)," "constitutional patriotism (*Verfassungspatriotismus*)," and the "colonization of the lifeworld (*Kolonialisierung der Lebenswelt*)," since they also appear in his public-facing writings. These ideas thus serve as "advertising slogans (*Werbeslogans*)" for Habermas and his work, both as an academic and as a public intellectual.[92]

Finally, and in my view most importantly, is his choice of subject matter. Although his contributions to political debates address a large range of issues, from education, welfare, banking and fiscal policy, the fact that his interventions in these subject areas are almost always rooted in problems related to the touchy subject of postwar Germany's relationship to the *Nazizeit* surely plays an important role in Habermas's success as a public intellectual. In addition to serving as a key to explaining his success as a public intellectual, these issues of memory and collective identity are also a crucial component of *why* Habermas chooses to undertake this public-facing work, instead of just focusing on his highly successful academic career. The decision to engage in public debate is thus inextricably linked with Habermas's "own self-understanding as a citizen in a democratic republic [that] had to incorporate its double past: that of the Holocaust, of course, but also the older positive legacy of the *Aufklärung* that had briefly taken form in the Weimar Republic."[93]

One of the basic presuppositions of this book that Habermas's desire to participate in the public sphere is rooted in his own experiences of Nazism and his "fear of a political relapse." Habermas has admitted that the resources he draws from his own remembered past have "continued to spur my scholarly work."[94] I argue that the same is true of his political writings. Understanding Habermas's interpretation of his own memories of the Third Reich thus not only reveals the political core of his interventions as a public intellectual, but also the political foundations of his academic social and political theory. Although he distinguishes between these two aspects of his work as part of a broader "role-differentiation" that he assiduously seeks to maintain, it is my contention that reading them together reveals the continuity of his work as an attempt to come to terms with Germany's "unmastered past" in order to build a better political future.[95] It is this focus on an "active remembrance—working through [*aufarbeiten*] the past and hoping for a better future" that motivates Habermas's work as a public intellectual, who acts as the "the public conscience of political culture" in West Germany.⁹⁶

While such a project may seems somewhat too simple or obvious for the leading philosopher of postwar Europe, Habermas was well aware of how quickly and easily a country could slide into totalitarianism on the basis of his own biography. Born in 1929 Habermas's family passively adapted to the Nazi regime, with his father joining the NSDAP (*Nationalsozialistische Deutsche Arbeiterpartei* or National Socialist German Workers' Party) for practical reasons. Although Habermas was not enthusiastic about joining the Hitler Youth, he did so in order to fit in the rest of his classmates, noting that he was "politically unenlightened" at the time and was "living in the dark politically (*in politisch Dunklen Zustand*)."⁹⁷ When he learned of the atrocities of the Third Reich through radio broadcasts of the Nuremberg Trials and documentaries from concentration camps at local theaters after the war he observed that world was turned upside down: "all at once we saw that we had been living in a politically criminal system." Looking back that moment of rupture, he notes that "the rhythm of my personal development intersected with the great historical events of the time . . . which then further determined my thinking."⁹⁸

Habermas drew two crucial lessons from the caesura of 1945. Firstly, he observed how easily Germany had slipped into the totalitarian regime of the Third Reich, that is, into "a normality which afterwards proved to be an illusion."⁹⁹ This rapid normalization of criminality only reinforced the need for critical voices in the public sphere able to sound the alarm when political proposals threaten democratic norms and the rights of certain members of society by highlighting the "unjust social relations or pathologies that take root inconspicuously in social life."¹⁰⁰ The memory of how easily the Weimar Republic slid down the slippery slope of far-right populism into totalitarianism therefore serves as a warning and a lesson for the present. As a public intellectual, Habermas therefore often presents himself as a mnemonic agent who highlights how the "twentieth century puts at risk its future by not learning from—by badly forgetting—its own disaster."¹⁰¹

Secondly, reflecting back on "the experience of 1945 and after," Habermas also notes that in addition to the horrors of the past, collective memories of Europe's experience of total war also show something else, "namely that things got better. Things really got rather better. One must use that as a starting-point too."¹⁰²

In this sense, the lessons of the past are not only negative, but can also be put to use as Arendtian "new beginnings" that make communicative "action in concert" possible once more. As a memory entrepreneur, Habermas's public-facing texts are therefore devoted to safeguarding this progress by ensuring that postwar politics and society continue to be defined by "the better traditions of our history, a history that is not unexamined but instead appropriated critically."[103]

A NOTE ON METHODOLOGY

Before I proceed, I would like to briefly clarify how I approach the topic of Habermas's public works. Although methodology has become an increasingly important issue across the humanities and social sciences, political theorists have been reticent about engaging in these debates. However, this reluctance is problematic, since "the choice is not between having a method and not having one, but rather between deciding to think about method or simply carrying on unreflectively."[104]

In reflecting on these issues, I would like to start by making clear what this book is *not*: a historically contextualized study of Habermas's public-facing work that places the primary emphasis on these texts as historically specific responses to the particular circumstances of that time and place. While following Quentin Skinner and the Cambridge School in such an enterprise surely would provide interesting insights, I have chosen a different tack.[105] This rejection has nothing to do with Skinner's "hopelessly inadequate" and "seriously inaccurate" 1982 assessment of Habermas's work in the *New York Review of Books*, a mistreatment that remains a low-point in the Anglophone reception of Habermas to this day.[106] On the contrary, it is rooted in my conviction that such an approach is inappropriate to my subject matter (as well as to my subject), as it severs social and intellectual history from issues of forward-looking, contemporary concern. In retrospect, even Skinner himself has expressed "regret" for having "treat[ed] the past as a separate realm" in his methodological writings, noting that he now recognizes that how "we used to think about our moral and political concepts may be ... helpful to our current purposes."[107]

Instead, in line with Habermas's own commitment to the idea that claims made in a specific context for a particular purpose can still have context transcending meaning, I locate my work within the broader "turn to the present" in the history of social and political thought.[108] This work is "presentist" in two senses: not only does it focus on texts from the recent past produced by a contemporary figure; it also uses this material to better understand problems associated with the present. This approach allows me to use historical material to engage with important contemporary philosophical and hermeneutical issues.[109] Thus, in addition to making the argument that interpreters of Habermas should treat his academic and public facing works as equally important and mutually constitutive parts of his *oeuvre*, I also draw on his historical interventions in public debates to reflect on the place of the philosopher in modern democratic life.

Rather than focusing on the meaning of these texts in their specific temporal and geographic context, I approach Habermas's interventions in social and political debate with the goal of exploring a number of different issues from a presentist perspective. These include: (1) how his mature conception of the public intellectual developed over time; (2) what treating this material as a central and integral part of his overall project means for how we interpret his academic work as a philosopher and sociologist; and (3) what both his theoretical reflections on the relationship between philosophy and politics as well as his long track record of engagement in social and political debate can teach us about the philosophical problem of theory and practice.

In addition to the three main aims enumerated above, in the first few chapters I also use Habermas's interventions in the public sphere to mediate his relationship to the first generation of critical theory. I am particularly invested in pushing back on the "hardened partisans of both camps . . . [who] believe that there can be no reconciliation" between Habermas and his predecessors in the Frankfurt School, particularly Adorno and Marcuse. By contrast, I argue that exploring the nexus between philosophical problems and public expression of political commitment reveals "a continuity that is often missed by critics who insist on the chasm between the first and second generations of critical theory."[110] This requires me to speculate on issues of influence and to identify areas of philosophical overlap between figures operating in different political, temporal and geographic contexts.

Finally, just like the approach associated with the Cambridge School, my methodological choices have downsides of their own. While studying the life and thought of a living individual is already difficult, this issue is amplified when working in the personal archive where the "subject is a *life and work in progress.*"[111]

For instance, my approach raises both issues of archival permission and difficulties associated with having to assign meaning to events before the subject's death.[112] In particular, there is something strange, almost voyeuristic about reading through someone's private correspondence. While this material can provide interesting insights, it also offers something of a strangely intimate but at the same time limited view the subject's life and times, as the material is often one-sided, lacking clear context and occasionally even indecipherable.

As I result of the private letters Habermas most generously gave me access to in the Special Collections (*Spezialsammlungen*) section at the University Library in Frankfurt am Main, I often felt like I was looking at Habermas through something of a *Schlüssellochperspektive*, observing his life as something of a peeping Tom peering through "the keyhole of a door," even though I had obtained his explicit permission to do so. It is most certainly not my goal to revel in making the intimate public or to engage in psychological speculation about the subject of this work. That being said, I do occasionally pull quotations from Habermas's private correspondence in cases where what he writes speaks to the philosophical issues or public stances he has taken that are relevant to my discussion.[113]

This point brings me back to the issue of historical and temporal context. On a narrower level, in relation to his correspondence, this raises the issue of the identities of Habermas's epistolary counterparts and the concrete issues they are addressing. While I provide some basic information about who Habermas is writing to in cases where I quote from such private correspondence (either in the main text or in a note), I will not go into great detail on these individuals and their relationship to Habermas. Instead, I will focus on what Habermas's comments say about the issue under discussion and how they relate the broader issues that guide this study.

More generally, given both my focus and the fact that this has already turned into a longer book than I had initially planned to write, I do not devote much space to the broader social and political context of the debates in which Habermas was intervening. As I have already point out, this book is a work of political theory and intellectual biography, not a Cambridge School intellectual history or a socio-political history of West Germany. Instead, I focus my analysis on the arguments Habermas makes in his public-facing texts.

Despite my critique of the approach he pioneered, I agree with Skinner that insisting "on the autonomy of the text itself as the sole necessary key to its own meaning" is problematic.[114] However, given my own (non-German) background as well as my education in the tradition of critical theory associated with the Frankfurt School, I can make more of a contribution to both contemporary debates on the role of scholarship in public life and to the literature on Habermas by reconstructing the arguments he presents in these understudied, untranslated and difficult to locate texts, rather than on reconstructing their broader context.[115] As a result, I have made the decision to sketch only the most general contours of the broader social and political context in favor of providing the reader with more direct quotations from Habermas's political interventions. In light of this presentist focus I focus in on some particularly important issues and debates in each chapter. However, given the fact that many of these texts are still relatively unknown in the literature, I have decided to still provide at least a brief overview of all of the political interventions Habermas made in each period, in case other scholars are interested and want to follow up on any particular text in greater detail.[116]

LOOKING FORWARD

The chapters that follow flesh Habermas's career as a public intellectual and demonstrate the many ways in which Habermas's political commitments affect his academic work and vice versa. Preceding my substantive analysis of Habermas's political writings, Chapter 1 evaluates the intellectual division of labor Habermas seeks to maintain between his academic work and his political interventions. Although critics of Habermas, many of whom advocate for a closer relationship between philosophy and "real" politics, attack him for being an idealist whose theory is ignorant of and apathetic toward practice, I argue that he not only has an account of political transformation—i.e. of "how to get from there to here"—but that he also seeks to realize his ideas in practice by increasing the quality of public debate through his interventions as a public intellectual. In order not to undermine academic research or participatory, complicated internal logics of political life, I outline Habermas's account of philosophy as a form of thought that is independent from practice but that also allows the theorist to intervene in politics as a public intellectual, who claims no epistemic priority of other participants in democratic debate.

Following this exposition of Habermas's mature account of the relationship of theory and practice, Chapter 2 begins my chronological presentation of his activities as a public intellectual, which also demonstrates how this understanding of the role of the public intellectual developed over the course of Habermas's career. It focuses on years he spent working as a freelance journalist after completing his Ph.D. During this period, he reported on various academic debates and published a number of other articles on the enduring legacy of Nazism in West Germany, culminating in his 1953 attack on Heidegger for his unwillingness to apologize for his collaboration with the Nazi regime. In fact, it was a series of essays that Habermas wrote on continuities between West Germany and the Third Reich that initially attracted Theodor W. Adorno's attention. Adorno subsequently took Habermas under his wing and in so doing resurrected his academic career by giving him an affiliation with the famous Institute for Social Research (*Institut für Sozialforschung*). While this journalistic work does not reflect Habermas's mature understanding of the philosopher as public intellectual, it shows how deeply-seated his desire to intervene in the public sphere really is.

In Chapter 3, I take up Habermas's activities during his initial stay at the Institute from 1956–59, as well as the circumstances surrounding his departure. In working through the public-facing essays that Habermas produced during this period, I highlight the overlooked importance of Habermas's reading of the German *Staatslehre* (state or constitutional theory). I argue that this material and Habermas's early political interventions explain his early and continuing commitment to the priority of the legislature over the executive and judicial branches, because it is the institution that is most responsive to opinion-formation in the public sphere. Finally, I show how these ideas underpin the theoretical arguments presented in the *Structural Transformation* (1962) and set the stage for his attempts to democratize the university in the 1960s.

Chapter 4 starts by detailing Habermas's connection with the Marxist political scientist Wolfgang Abendroth, who sponsored his Habilitation after it was rejected by Horkheimer. It covers the period defined by the German student protests of the 1960s. Using Habermas's public writings—as well as private correspondence and other archival materials—this chapter explores both Habermas's support for the students and his eventual break with them for their "left fascism" (a comment he immediately regretted) and for what he saw as their misguided belief that West Germany was in a pre-revolutionary situation. Although Habermas had not yet formulated the legal philosophy eventually presented in *Between Facts and Norms* (1992), his castigation of the student movement provides important insights into his theories regarding the boundaries that extra-parliamentary political movements must respect in a constitutional democracy.

I argue that it is no accident that Habermas's philosophical research turns to the relatively non-political analysis of language precisely at the time of his retreat from the public sphere more generally. His private correspondence reveals that an offer to join his the physicist Carl Friedrich von Weizsäcker as a co-director of the Max Planck Institute for the Study of the Scientific-Technical World in Starnberg, came at precisely the right time. Chapter 5, which covers this period, shows that this move represented a break not only physically, as Habermas left Frankfurt for a second time, but also intellectually, as the 1970 Gauss Lectures he delivered at Princeton University on the "linguistic foundation of sociology" represent a shift in his intellectual interests from social theory to linguistic philosophy.

However, although Habermas's activities as a public intellectual decline during this period, he cannot avoid getting involved with a number of debates, including the aforementioned exchange of letters regarding the role of the left in fueling domestic terrorism in West Germany. Building on archival sources, I also show how Habermas used his professional stature and reputation to help organize protests on behalf of unorthodox Marxist scholars of the "Praxis School" in Yugoslavia (especially the so-called "Belgrade eight") and of the "Budapest School" in Hungary (in particular, Ágnes Heller and Ferenc Fehér). He was also quickly drawn back into the politics of higher education, as the faculty at Ludwig Maximilians-University in nearby Munich denied him an honorary appointment in the Philosophy Department due to their continued perception of him as a left-wing radical despite his break with the student movement.

Chapter 6 then addresses some of Habermas's most (in)famous and well-known interventions in the public sphere over the meaning of the past and of German unification. It is during this period, after seesawing between the extremes of partisan professorship in the 1960s and retreat from the public sphere in the 1970s, that Habermas's mature notion of the *Nebenberuf* of the public intellectual finally comes into view, as Habermas develops and fully embraces the separation thesis. Although Habermas enjoyed being able to focus on research during the 1970s, he found his administrative duties in Starnberg onerous and missed teaching students. He therefore resigned from the Max Planck Institute in 1981 after completing the manuscript for his two-volume *Theory of Communicative Action*.

His 1983 return to Frankfurt also signaled his reemergence as the leading public intellectual and moral authority of West Germany. His political writings during this period center on two major controversies: (1) the so-called "Historians' Dispute" (*Historikerstreit*) over conservative attempts to "normalize" the atrocities of the Third Reich, and; (2) the "unification debate" (*Vereinigungsdebatte*) that followed the fall of the Berlin Wall and the collapse of communism in 1989. While his interventions raise many different issues, I argue that in both cases Habermas opposition is rooted in his rejection of conservative Chancellor Helmut Kohl attempts to intervene in the German politics of memory through an executive-led, administrative process that left no room for public debate about the issues at stake. Habermas's political writings in this period therefore signal that he is still committed to his reading of the *Staatslehre* and his emphasis primacy of the legislature. This interpretation is supported by *Between Facts and Norms* (1992), the major theoretical work Habermas was writing at this time, in which he roots legal and political legitimacy in the openness of the democratic institutions of will-formation to debates in the public sphere.

In Chapter 7 I address Habermas's growing interest and intellectual involvement in European and global affairs, which marks a move away from the traditional Germanic focus of his work as a public intellectual. Since his retirement from the Goethe-University in Frankfurt in 2004, he has continued to intervene in debates in the public sphere. Although he also engaged in disputes over cloning, genetic engineering and freedom of the will in 1998 and regarding the public use of religion in 2001, most of his contributions have focused on the implications of growing globalization and the multiculturalism that comes with it. While he is interested in the political effects of what he calls "postnational constellation," as a committed European most of his substantive interventions have focused on the development of the European Union (EU).

The place of political integration beyond the nation-state in his thought—which originates in his public-facing works—speaks to a number of his theoretical interest, including those on the future of human nature and on the continuing role of religion in public life. This chapter demonstrates that the example of the EU reveals an ongoing process of adjustment. I argue that these developments, which Habermas seeks to bring together through an approach that he calls "meeting halfway" (*Entgegenkommen*), demonstrates how his political commitments influence his philosophical work and how he seeks to bring these two aspects of his work into harmony with each other.[117]

Chapter 8 focuses on the global financial crisis, which started in 2008, and its effect on the relationship between politics and economics at the start of the twenty-first century. The so-called "Great Recession" highlighted the increasing tension between democracy and late capitalism, as international market forces demonstrated their capacity to dictate policy to formally sovereign political communities. As a result of his preexisting opposition to the takeover of political life by the forces of power (administration) and money (economics), which he laid out in the *Theory of Communicative Action* (1981), Habermas's recent political interventions have forcefully addressed the dangers he associates with the overexpansion of functional systemic forces, as well as the broader instrumentalization of reason that they promote. These political developments—which are central to his public commentaries in this period—also drive his newfound theoretical interest in international law, which defines much of his philosophical work at this time.

Given his existing interest in the EU, Habermas tackles these issues by discussing the flaws in the EU's response to this crisis, which relied too much on economic thinking. He builds on the crisis of the Eurozone to show how postnational integration can help "politics to catch up to economics" by allowing peoples around the world to take control of their destinies away from impersonal market forces. I also use this example to argue that Habermas shares Karl Marx's commitment to combatting naturalized views of economics and material reproduction as a forces that lie outside of human control.

While his arguments are powerful, I argue that in explicitly embracing his role as the *Staatsphilosoph* (state philosopher) of the more powerful, more democratic EU that he would like to bring into being, Habermas has actually violated the separation thesis, which is a key pillar of his understanding of the public intellectual. In particular, at certain points he allows himself to get drawn into representing explicit political positions—even doing so on stage with politicians—rather than merely commenting on them in order to improve the quality of public debate. Additionally, instead of simply analyzing the implications of existing proposals and ensuring that minority voices are heard, during this period he also outlines a positive political program, complete with a blueprint for a reformed EU. By moving beyond the role of an external critic, I argue that Habermas actually violates his own mature understanding of the boundary or moat that should separate theory and practice.

Finally, in addition to bringing my chronological outline of Habermas's political writings up to 2025 (when this book was completed), the conclusion returns to the issues of theory and practice highlighted in this introduction and chapter 1. Building on the preceding discussion, I show how both his political writings and his theoretical work are the result of a *constant mediation* between theory and practice, a dialectical learning process (*Lernprozess*) in which Habermas the public intellectual is constantly interacting with Habermas the philosopher and theoretical sociologist. While some political philosophers who favor direct engagement with politicians and the policy process have attacked Habermas for his lack of engagement with "real" politics, I argue that Habermas's approach of working through debates in the public sphere as a public intellectual is more respectful of the autonomy and decision-making ability democratic societies, as it respects the equality of all citizens as potential participants in public politics discourse.

In addition to bringing the narrative full circle, in the conclusion I also reflect on the future of the Habermasian public intellectual at a time when the public sphere has increasingly moved onto the internet. Through an examination of the Habermas's interventions addressing Russia's full-scale invasion of Ukraine, which began on February 24, 2022, and Israel's assault on Gaza following Hamas's terrorist attack of October 7, 2023, I argue that the basic conditions that made it possible for the classic public intellectual to emerge have been lost. Drawing on Habermas's own reflections on these changes in his 2022 *A New Structural Transformation of the Public Sphere and Deliberative Politics* (*Ein neuer Strukturwandel der Öffentlichkeit und die deliberative Politik*), it seems unlikely that any figure in the future will be able to use the written word, published in the leading media of the public sphere, to shape public discourse as powerfully as Habermas was has been able to do over the course of the long career of public engagement.[118]

This argument may seem to undercut the rationale for studying Habermas as a public intellectual. However, while it may no longer be possible to follow Habermas's solution to these problems, I think that we still can learn something from Habermas about the kind of temperament that is required to conduct oneself with such passion, precision, and conviction as a philosopher in the public sphere. Of all the scholars of the past century, Habermas may rank among the most responsible, not simply for his philosophical work, but for his contributions to questions of politics both in Germany and beyond. I therefore conclude that his development of both his theory and his practice of the public intellectual is still a valuable source of insights for philosophers who want to engage in public affairs in the new context of the digital public sphere. In this sense, Habermas the public intellectual still has as much—if not more—to teach us than Habermas the philosopher and theoretical sociologist.

CHAPTER 1

Mediating Theory and Practice

In this chapter, which precedes my chronologically organized treatment of Habermas's work as a public intellectual, I evaluate the division of labor Habermas maintains between his academic work and his political interventions.[1] In recent years, debates in social and political theory, as well as in the history of political thought, have been reinvigorated as philosophers have shown increasing interest in the relationship between theory and practice. For example, a group of self-styled "realists," supporters of "democratic underlaboring," and public philosophers—to name just a few of the most prominent strands in this "applied turn"—have called on philosophy to engage more directly with politics, either by developing a more agonistic "*political* political theory" or by seeking to influence government directly through engagement with policymakers, participation on policy committees, and similar efforts.[2] Although these commentators frequently attack Habermas for being an idealist whose theory neglects practice, I argue that he not only offers an account of political transformation—i.e., of "how to get from there to here"—but also provides a theoretically consistent means of aligning his political commitments with his philosophical ideals by enhancing the quality of public debate through his interventions as a public intellectual.

I thus contest the claim that Habermas's theoretical system must be drawn out "into a 'real' world from which [his work] otherwise remains isolated." On the contrary, I argue that Habermas has already performatively "refute[d] the objection that the theory of communicative action is blind to institutional reality" through his interventions as a public intellectual.[3] Moreover, as the subsequent chapters document, Habermas and his political commitments stand in a mediated yet dialectical relationship with his philosophical work: although each can stand on its own (the separation thesis), they are internally consistent (the theoretical continuity thesis), with the latter driving the former at some points and the former driving the latter at others.

Despite this interplay, Habermas has sought to ensure that theory "does not sabotag[e] thinking and thereby itself."[4] This commitment is driven by his conviction that "at best," contemporary abstract social theories "can make us more sensitive to the ambivalences of development. . . . Persistent thinking is certainly not enough, but without it you don't get very far."[5] By introducing what he calls a "role separation" between his work as an academic and as a public intellectual, he connects theory to practice in a mediated, indirect way that ensures they remain consistent with each other and also respects the internal presuppositions of these different spheres of modern life.

I begin this chapter by briefly reflecting on the changing role of scholarship in society during the development of modernity. Next, I outline Habermas's relatively constrained view of "what theories can accomplish" and his understanding of the relationship between theory and practice.[6] In the third part, I engage with Habermas's mature vision of the role of public intellectuals, drawing on his reading of the history of social and political thought, and situate his interpretation of their calling within his broader philosophical framework. Fourth, I examine how Habermas engages in public debate as a public intellectual, focusing on how this differs from realist proposals and the model of theorist as democratic underlaborer. I conclude this chapter by reflecting on how Habermas's theoretical understanding and practical engagement as a public intellectual situate him within the theoretical tradition of the Frankfurt School.

THE CHANGING PLACE OF SCHOLARSHIP IN MODERNITY

By linking his philosophical work to the pressing social and political issues of his day, especially in his native Federal Republic of Germany, Habermas places himself firmly within the tradition of the history of social and political thought. After all, almost none of the individuals represented in the philosophical canon—much less the canon of social and political thought—"was a cloistered scholar or university professor detached from the real world of politics."[7] On the contrary, until the last two centuries, many were directly engaged in the politics of their time.

For instance, Plato himself made at least three trips to Sicily to advise the tyrants of Syracuse. Aristotle was the tutor of Alexander the Great, a role not unlike that of Thomas Hobbes, who served as tutor to the exiled royal court during the English Civil War. Similarly, Niccolò Machiavelli was in the Florentine foreign service for a time and helped create his city-state's citizen militia. John Stuart Mill, for his part, spent most of his career as a colonial administrator for the semi-sovereign East India Company; for a time he was even responsible for its relations with the princely states. Jean-Jacques Rousseau took a more direct political role in writing constitutions for Poland and Corsica, while Alexis de Tocqueville and Edmund Burke actually served as legislative representatives in the French National Assembly and British Parliament, respectively.

Over the course of the nineteenth century, however, philosophers moved away from this desire to "influence public policy more directly by acting as advisers to governments and members of think tanks, government commissions, and policy committees," preferring instead to act as external critics of the state and society at large.[8] This change is tied to the development of independent scientific research in the aftermath of the Enlightenment. The creation of the modern university gave individuals interested in the *Wissenschaften*—the sciences broadly conceived—the opportunity to pursue scholarship "organized in special[ized] disciplines in the service of self-clarification and knowledge of interrelated facts" as a paid vocation.[9] This played an important role in the transition away from direct engagement, which spurred the rise of what conservatives often refer to derogatorily as "tenured radicals."[10]

This change solved the problem of how philosophers could earn a living doing philosophy (and academic work more broadly). The onset of the Enlightenment also created a reading public newly interested in affairs of state, as political decisions increasingly affected private economic interests amid the rise of capitalism and expanding global trade. While some of these newly professionalized academics followed Max Weber in pursuing research grounded purely in its "internal presuppositions"—that is, "the rules of logic and method," where "what is yielded by scientific work is important in the sense that it is 'worth being known' "— others took up the example of Immanuel Kant, who argued that "as a scholar, [the individual] is completely free as well as obliged to impart to the public all his carefully considered, well-intentioned thoughts on the mistaken aspects" of public policy.[11]

As an inheritor of both Kant's tradition of Enlightenment thinking and the Weberian Marxism of the Frankfurt School, Habermas is inherently sympathetic to these opposing approaches. However, his mature understanding of the political role of philosophy is also shaped by a third factor: the widespread collaboration of German intellectuals with the Nazi regime. While some passively participated in the process of *Gleichschaltung* (coordination), which led to the dismissal of Jewish professors and the reorganization of curricula, others actively worked to align the university with the totalitarian project of the Third Reich. These efforts not only dismantled the barriers Weber had drawn between science and politics; they also broke with Kant's ideal of the scholar, who "publicly voices his thoughts on the impropriety or even injustice" of policies adopted by the state.[12]

Most notably, the influential philosopher Martin Heidegger, whose work had captivated Habermas during his time as a student, abandoned any pretense of scientific objectivity or the critical stance typically associated with scholarship. Instead, as the newly installed Nazi-approved rector of the University of Freiburg in 1933 he called for a "*völkische* Wissenschaft" devoted to "bringing about *the total transformation of our German existence [Dasein]* . . . embodied in the National Socialist State."[13] While Habermas does not abandon his Kantian duty to publicly adopt a "'critical' stance" against "notions of scientific and technological progress directed by the state," the collaboration of academics and intellectuals with the Nazis made him wary of what he saw as a recurring tendency—especially among *German* philosophers—to be drawn into an "intellectual romance with fascism" via a broader "seduction of unreason" directed against modernity and the Enlightenment.[14] In this sense, while he thinks that public intellectuals can and should embody a form of moral authority as critics in the public sphere, he rejects the idea that they can claim any authority—moral or otherwise—directly in their professional role as philosophers.

While Habermas continues to believe that philosophy is "supposed to play a public role in the context of a liberal political culture," social and political theory has, over the course of the postwar period, come to be seen increasingly as a purely scholarly pursuit concerned with such questions as the structure and cohesiveness of human communities, the origins of legitimacy, and the nature of justice.[15] In part, the rise of these increasingly abstract, supposedly timeless questions surely reflects a disenchantment with the uncomfortable association of many intellectuals with Nazism, fascism, communism and other forms of totalitarianism during the first half of the twentieth century. Additionally, in their effort to create a disciplinary canon capable of offering general answers to enduring political problems, many social and political theorists retreated from engagement with real politics, preferring instead to focus on questions that could be addressed conceptually and had no direct policy implications.[16]

This dominant conception of political philosophy treats theory "as a map" that highlights the salient features of social and political life in an abstract but systematic manner, with the primary goal of producing scientific knowledge. In this context, social and political philosophy is not necessarily quietist and may develop important analytical tools that "enable us to see what to do" in concrete situations, but such practical applications "are not precipitates of a theory in any straightforward way."[17] Habermas does not disagree with this assessment of what social and political philosophy should be. He does, however, believe that it needs to be supplemented by a conception of the Kantian scholar as engaged citizen—one who publicly seeks to "sharpen our vision for the kinds of problems that can be solved through collective action."[18] For him, participating in political discourse as a public intellectual is an expression of his post-1945 conviction that *things had to get somewhat better, and that it was up to us whether the world would change for the better.*[19]

Habermas is hardly the only social and political theorist to express reservations about the apolitical tenor of philosophy after the war. While calls for greater political engagement have waxed and waned, they have grown steadily louder in the final decade of the twentieth century and the opening decades of the twenty-first. Within mainstream social and political theory, there is growing support for the theorist to assume the "limited and modest" role of a "democratic underlabourer," who "is specially equipped to help her fellow citizens make their political choices" by both clarifying the implications of existing proposals and "offer[ing] arguments and justifications of her own."[20] Alongside this thin view, a "ragtag band" of self-styled "realists" has advanced a thicker conception of social and political philosophy as an "effective source of orientation or a guide to action."[21] By challenging the standard approach to social and political theory, proponents of both positions have sharpened an internal methodological divide "between truth seeking and democratic responsiveness."[22]

Although realists explicitly reject discursive understandings of politics "of the kind envisaged by Habermas," I argue that they fundamentally misunderstand and mischaracterize his work because they do not pay sufficient attention to the symbiotic relationship between his philosophical and political writings.[23]

By treating his thought as a form of "political moralism" and "ideal theory" detached from the dynamics of actual political life, these critics fail to understand the relatively narrow scope Habermas assigns to philosophy, ignore his understanding of the relationship between theory and practice, and overlook his many political interventions as the leading public intellectual of the Federal Republic.[24] As a result, they are unable to appreciate the extent to which Habermas's theoretical development over the course of his career is a response to real-world events and his political participation therein.

Similarly, although the underlaborer model is more modest, I argue that by granting theorists special authority over their fellow citizens based on their training "in particular skills," including the ability to "assess and examine arguments about values," this approach allows theorists to surreptitiously "supplant or short circuit the democratic process, not contribute to it."[25] The same problem haunts advocates of public philosophy, who "start with a reasonably well-worked out philosophical theory which one then applies to the world." Habermas contends that the goal is not "to work out which position in the debate is correct" in the abstract, as most philosophers intervening in politics are wont to do, but instead to enrich public debate, even if it turns out that philosophers "don't have an answer for everything."[26]

Habermas's mature distinction between the roles of the theorist as academic researcher and as public intellectual seeks to overcome these difficulties by offering an account that defends theory as a truth-seeking enterprise while also permitting the theorist to participate in the political public sphere *as a public intellectual*—and *not* as an expert, a point to which I shall return. While Habermas does associate the theoretical enterprise with the traditional academic model of truth-seeking, he does not think "that one can complete the work of ethics first, attaining an ideal theory of how we should act, and then in a second step . . . apply that ideal theory to the action of political agents."[27]

Such a description does not fit Habermas, given the important role his political interventions play in shaping his theoretical ideas. He also argues that under the complex conditions of the modern world—divided into differentiated spheres of life, each governed by its own internal logic—philosophy can no longer claim to offer "a theory that's supposed to be able to solve all of life's problems." While abstract reflection is still important in ensuring that we do "not to lose the connections in the move from one discourse to another," he notes that it "does not provide instructions for action."[28]

Although he denies that modern philosophy can be directly "action-guiding" and does not assign it a "specific place in the political and policymaking process"—as the underlaboring model does—Habermas does not completely sever theory from practice (a position consistent with what I refer to as the theoretical continuity thesis).[29] Instead, he is committed to the idea that philosophy has much to offer society at large. Yet under modern conditions, Habermas argues, the theorist can only intervene in political debate in the role of an intellectual who "broadens the spectrum of relevant arguments in an attempt to improve the lamentable level of public debates."[30] Although raising the quality of discourse in the public sphere as a public intellectual fulfills the *desiderata* of his theoretical conception of democratic legitimacy and thus falls in line with his broader philosophical commitments, this conception does not claim to be action-guiding; "instead, theory informs the scope of viable forms of practice, enabling us to address the type(s) of practice likely to succeed" without claiming any normative authority over fellow citizens in the public sphere.[31]

In line with his social and political philosophy, Habermas mediates the divide between scholarly research and political relevance through a division of roles, each governed by different norms and expectations. As a professional philosopher or sociologist, the theorist operates within a context where "the production of research and knowledge follows accepted methodological rules" as part of its search for truth. As a citizen, however, the philosopher can also assume "the role of the public intellectual who intervenes where the apparatus has become unable to extricate itself," alerting the broader public to concrete problems in contemporary social and political debate.[32]

Habermas himself exemplifies how one can occupy both of these distinct roles—academic theorist and public intellectual—while keeping them analytically distinct. This chapter therefore examines how his distinction between these roles allows him to defend the truth-seeking model of philosophy (and of the sciences more broadly) while also engaging in concrete social and political debates in a manner that is responsive to the public and respectful of democratic norms of equality and popular decision-making. In this way, this chapter sets up the narrative of this book by clarifying the connection between Habermas's theoretical and political works, as well as his broader understanding of the proper relationship of theory to practice. As a result, it lays the groundwork for my argument that his political writings must both be *distinguished from*, yet also *read alongside*, his academic works.

THE ROLE OF THE PUBLIC INTELLECTUAL

Habermas has devoted much of his philosophical and sociological career to developing a normative ideal of justification based on "the unforced force of the better argument." In his first book, the *Structural Transformation of the Public Sphere* (1962), he introduces a model of democratic legitimacy based on the bourgeois public sphere that emerged in seventeenth- and eighteenth-century Europe, where individuals from different social classes met and engaged in rational debate on issues of public interest. Thirty years later, in *Between Fact and Norms* (1992), he builds on this foundation by arguing that reasoned debate in the informal public sphere of civil society can justify the authority of democratic law, which is produced by legislators in the formal, institutional public sphere. Taken together, these two works yield a discourse theory of democratic legitimacy based on the quality of deliberative "opinion-formation," which must then be filtered into the legal procedures of "will-formation" within the constitutional state (*Rechtsstaat*).

Since newspapers, television, and radio—as well as more recent developments like the internet and digital social media—act as intermediaries between the "weak" publics of everyday argumentation and the "strong" decision-making publics within state institutions, Habermas highlights their importance as the "filter-bed" that shapes the flow and direction of public discourse.[33] He is particularly concerned about the ability of market forces and political agents to illicitly influence the public deliberation that is supposed to occur when free and equal citizens exercise their power of reasoning through public discussion. He argues that such "colonization of the lifeworld" occurs when strategic interests are allowed to influence manipulate public opinion through the mechanisms of selection, presentation, agenda-setting and issue framing.

Since the end of the Cold War, Habermas's work has increasingly warned against the potentially dangerous "media power of private corporations."[34] The growth and consolidation of mass corporate media—driven by the profit motive rather than a commitment to public debate—has led the informal political public sphere to be "characterized by at least two crosscutting processes: the communicative generation of legitimate power on the one hand and the manipulative deployment of media power to procure mass loyalty, consumer demand, and 'compliance' with systematic imperatives on the other."[35] By undermining the normative ideals embedded in existing public spheres, these developments pose a fundamental threat to the democratic legitimacy of contemporary politics.

Despite the normative implications of his legal and political philosophy, Habermas resists drawing a direct line between theory and practice. On the contrary, he warns his readers "not to expect any more or anything different from theories than what they can achieve—and that's little enough."[36] Although he does not believe that research must be completely objective and value-free, Habermas shares Weber's skepticism of "'scientifically' pleading for practical and interested stands" under the conditions of modernity, where "the various value spheres of the world stand in irreconcilable conflict with each other."[37] As an institutionalized profession pursued within the modern university, he rejects the idea that philosophy—or any other science—can access eternal truths universally valid for everyone from a Archimedean "view from nowhere" (this is one of Habermas's favorite expressions, which he often quotes in English).

By contrast, Habermas argues that philosophy, as a modern form of research, is engaged in the pursuit of "scientific truth as a form of truth which can be defined only in terms of methodological research."[38] As a result, it is defined by an intellectual division of labor that reflects the existence of different spheres of life. He concludes: "one has to talk about philosophical questions philosophically, sociological questions sociologically, political questions politically. One has to know which discourse one is operating in and what tools one is employing."[39]

Habermas's interpretation of philosophy as a theoretical enterprise oriented toward truth (*Wahrheit*) and understanding (*Verstehen*) builds closely on Weber's methodological writings. In light of the modern separation of value spheres, each of which operates—and must be understood—according to its own internal logic, Habermas denies the possibility of "offering a theory that's supposed to be able to solve all of life's problems." Instead, he argues, "to get anything out of theoretical work, you have to follow it for its own sake." Scientific theories can, at best, "make us more sensitive to the ambivalences of development: they can contribute to our ability to understand the coming uncertainties."[40]

From Habermas's perspective, therefore, realist calls for theory to provide direct "normative guidance about how we should act in the real world" are dangerous because they necessarily elide the distinction between theory and practice.[41] More specifically, such unmediated attempts to fulfill Karl Marx's watchword of "philosophy becoming practical" fail because they assume that theory is "capable of thinking not only the totality that is hypostatized as the world order, but the world-historical process as well." In the aftermath of what he calls "Weber's austere insight into the disintegration of objective reason," Habermas argues that theory is no longer "capable of identifying the subjects who will establish this unity practically and of showing them the way."[42]

Although philosophers like Raymond Geuss accuse Habermas of creating "ideal theory of how we should act, and then in a second step . . . apply[ing] that ideal theory to the action of political agents," Habermas explicitly rejects this model. He argues instead that "decisions for the political struggle cannot at the outset be justified theoretically and then be carried out organizationally."[43] In contrast to this straightforward two-step approach, he instead divides the relationship between theory and practice into three separate functions: 1) the development of theories based on true statements that "can stand up to scientific discourse"; 2) the identification of social actors and movements who can build on these insights through the "organization of processes of enlightenment"; and 3) the "selection of appropriate strategies . . . [for] the conduct of the political struggle."[44]

Within this process, philosophers occupy a privileged position only in the first step, in which they engage in disciplinarily governed theoretical research oriented toward truth. As a result, Habermas argues that theory "effects change precisely by remaining itself," and not by engaging in practice.[45] Although social and political theory seeks to understand the theoretical preconditions for the second stage as well, Habermas argues that it cannot intervene directly, since the process of enlightenment must be based on "consensus aimed at in practical discourse, among the participants" if it is to reflect their use of practical reason rather than mere rhetorical or ideological compulsion. Finally, he notes that "the political struggle can only be legitimately conducted under the precondition that all decisions of consequence will depend on the practical discourse of the participants—here too, and especially here, there is no privileged access to truth."[46]

Habermas's objection to models of political practice that treat members of society as passive objects "whose eyes are to be opened by the social theorist" leads him to reject not only the realist approach but also the idea that theory can offer "orienting action-guidance," as the model of the democratic underlaborer proposes.[47] In contrast to Leninist interpretations of the philosopher as the vanguard of revolution, he instead argues that theorists "must never imagine the addressees of social theory, or even society itself, as a subject writ large" whose desires and interests can be assumed or identified from the outside. On the contrary, Habermas notes that at this third stage "there are only participants." Given his conviction that "[t]here can be no theory which at the outset can assure a world-historical mission . . . for the potential sacrifices," it is not at all surprising that Habermas rejects calls for political philosophy to transform itself into "something like the 'realist' view, to put it slightly differently, to neo-Leninism."[48]

Habermas's constrained understanding of the role that the theorist can and should play in politics is informed by personal experience. As a student in the 1950s, he was disappointed to discover how many leading German thinkers, including Carl Schmitt, Martin Heidegger, and his own *Doktorvater*, Ernst Rothacker, had not only cooperated with the Nazi regime, but also actively participated in the removal of Jewish faculty and publicly supported Adolf Hitler's policies (see chapter 2). This lack of judgment was, for Habermas, evidence of a *déformation professionnelle* that led these thinkers to believe they could use Hitler as a vehicle to realize their theoretical ideals by "leading the *Führer*" (*den Führer führen*).[49] Following Theodor Adorno, who writes disdainfully of the "elitist desires for authority" (*elitären Herrschaftswünsche*) displayed by these intellectuals, Habermas insists that German theorists have given up whatever right they ever had to serve as "teachers of the nation."[50]

Despite the particularities of the German historical experience, Habermas also thinks that modern philosophers *in general* have lost any special claim to expertise, due to the differentiation of value spheres diagnosed by Weber. As a result, he argues that philosophy can no longer operate in the magisterial mode associated with Kant and Hegel. Nevertheless, he maintains that it still has an important role to play in mediating between academic disciplines and everyday experience. Renouncing its Enlightenment-era claim to be the final arbiter and judge of knowledge, this new form of "postmetaphysical thinking" acts as a "stand-in" or "interpreter," helping to translate the specialized, technical insights of other sciences into the discourse of everyday life. Habermas notes:

> In the discourse of modernity, [philosophy] must respect the autonomous logics of the differentiated 'value spheres' (Max Weber) of science and technology, law and morality, and art and art criticism, just as it must respect the autonomy of any discipline within the science system. But because it *reconstructs* the rational core of these pre-existing cultural and social structures, it becomes 'multilingual' in a way which qualifies it to play the role of an *interpreter* in the public sphere who mediates between the expert cultures and between the latter and the lifeworld.[51]

He therefore contends that "the postmetaphysical philosopher lacks any privileged intuitions or intellectual instruments of his or her own."[52] As the term postmetaphysical suggests, this conception of the philosopher's role is closely related to Habermas's Weberian view of philosophy's relationship to the other academic disciplines. He writes: "Whereas [natural and social] science focuses exclusively on an object domain, philosophy keeps its eye at the same time on the insight provided by a corresponding learning processes, that is, on what the knowledge we have acquired about the world (including the human being as another entity in the world) means 'for us.'"[53]

Even though it is reduced "to elucidate[ing] the nature of situations in which people have the choice to redefine the rules and regulations by which they live," theory, for Habermas, can still contribute to practice by "systematically considering the interrelations between different social value spheres." While the engaged critical theorist may be tempted to short-circuit this process by moving directly from ideals to their realization, Habermas argues that such an approach is anachronistic given the challenges and complexity of contemporary society: "Before we can engage in attempts to mediate theory and practice toward any end, we must ensure that each problem has been examined and pursued in terms of its inner logic."[54]

In contrast to realist calls for a more direct relationship between theory and practice—as well as to the democratic underlaborer model, which assigns theorists a privileged role in the policy process—Habermas argues that "the question of whether a specific 'practice' advances a certain goal cannot be decided beforehand, within the context of even the most complex theory." The aim of theory is, rather, "to make explicit a potential that already exists in contemporary society."[55] As an academic enterprise oriented toward truth, theoretical reflection can assist practice only insofar as it informs the scope and conditions of possibility for social and political change.

Habermas's realist critics often claim that he engages in a project of "ideal theory" that "tries to construe discussion on the model of a highly idealized conception of what purely rational or scientific discussion is."[56] However, because his approach refers "only to the normative contents that are *encountered* in practice, which we cannot do without," it sidesteps the debates between ideal and nonideal theory that dominate contemporary methodological discussions. Pushing back against realist accusations that his theory is based on "an idealized version of a Socratic dialogue," Habermas clarifies, "I never say that people *want* to act communicatively, but that they *have to*" because there "are elementary social functions that can only be satisfied by means of communicative action." Rather than outlining the ideal conditions for communication as a utopian end-state based on full compliance, or examining how discourse actually functions as a result of partial adherence within a transitional theory, Habermas seeks instead to reconstruct the internal normative presuppositions that underpin linguistic communication and are therefore necessary and "constitutive for sociocultural forms of life."[57]

Although Habermas limits philosophy's scope, denies the theorist a special role in policymaking, and confines social and political theory to analyzing the "complex network of social value spheres characterized by different 'inner logics,'" this does not preclude theorists from engaging in social and political debates.[58] On the contrary, he argues they have an important role—but not as underlaboring or realist authorities "connecting political reality and political theory." Rather, they should act as public intellectuals "limited to mobilizing the relevant issues, information and arguments for public disputes" so that their fellow citizens can "make their own more or less rational decisions in the voting booth in the light of competing opinions."[59]

From Habermas's perspective, the theorist as public intellectual is neither an idealist philosopher laying out blueprints for a future that simply needs to be realized, nor a democratic underlaborer "argu[ing] about the ideas and values that politicians ought to draw on in responding to the world."[60] He also rejects the model of the public philosopher who believes that the "purpose of political theory is to diagnose practical predicaments and to show us how best to confront them" by engaging directly in policy and policymaking.[61] Instead, the public intellectual is a critic of existing proposals who "cannot rely on anything except the strength and precision of his or her arguments, and must renounce all other forms of authority and narcissism."[62]

MEDIATING THEORY AND PRACTICE

In contrast to his contemporary critics, who hold that social and political theory must have direct implications for "discussions of the practicalities of political action and choice," Habermas argues that the academic search for truth should remain separate from the social and political interventions of public intellectuals, who seek to contribute to democratic legitimacy by raising the quality of debate in the public sphere.[63] Although this is not "the kind of division of labor in which one thing has nothing to do with the other," Habermas has sought to ensure that these two functions remain separate as different forms of intellectual activity. Responding to critiques of his political engagement—as well as inverse accusations from scholars who defend the truth-seeking model of academic research that he is too involved in politics—Habermas observes, "What annoys me terribly, what gets to me, is the aggressiveness of people who do not see the role-differentiation in me."[64]

Habermas's conception of the proper roles of the academic theorist and the public intellectual, respectively, is best understood when situated within the history of political thought, especially the ideas of Immanuel Kant, Max Weber, and Michel Foucault. Drawing on Kant's famous 1784 distinction between the public and private use of reason, Habermas as public intellectual sees it as his duty (*Pflicht*) "*as a man of learning* addressing the entire *reading public*" to "use his own reason and speak in his own person" in the service of the enlightenment of society as a whole.[65] As a *private* citizen, who neither speaks for an administrative body or organization nor in order to further his own personal economic interests, Habermas follows Kant in retaining the right to make *public* use of his reason in order to influence the *public* process of collective will-formation.

However, as a teacher in the seminar room and as a professional academic—i.e., as a state official employed at a public university (although the same would apply to researchers working in private institutions of higher education who are governed by the same codes of professional ethics)—Habermas argues that he is bound by the rules and norms that govern this particular value sphere. In "acting on a commission imposed from outside" and "employed by the government for public ends," philosophers and sociologists are limited to the use of their *private* reason as *public* servants, whose job it is to both engage in research oriented towards truth (a process that is governed by disciplinary norms of peer review) and to educate students in line with their contract.[66] While academic researchers can still voice their political opinions as a *private* citizens acting in the *public* sphere, they have no right to impose their ideas on students in the classroom, where they are contracted to engage in a pedagogical function drawing on *private* reason. As Keith Haysom observes, "Habermas retains from Kant not only the abstract radicalism of his moral universalism, but also the essentially conservative desire to separate public and private, theory and practice, for fear of their mutual corruption and contamination."[67] This principle is what I call the separation thesis.

Despite his adoption of these classical Kantian categories, Habermas does not buy into the Weberian notion that its status as a science means that social and political theory should have nothing to do with politics. On the contrary, he challenges Weber's "complete division of labor" between scientific knowledge and political decision-making by insisting that despite the increasing separation of value spheres, reason conceptualized in terms of the "unforced force of the better argument" still has a role to play in social and political life.[68] Habermas thus "insist[s] upon the analysis and rational discussion of the relationship between available techniques and practical decisions, which [are] completely ignored in [Weber's] decisionist model."[69]

In light of these philosophical and methodological commitments, he argues that philosophers can engage in public affairs only as public intellectuals, whose task is to help combat the manipulation of democratic discourse by spin doctors, interest groups, and political parties, all of which contribute to the "neutralization of citizens (*Neutralisierung der Staatsbürger*)."[70] This position explains Habermas's sustained focus on the media's role in mediating between informal debates in civil society and the formal public sphere of institutions vested with decision-making powers. The dominant actors in this intermediate space are media opinion leaders as well as those who wield systemic forces of power and money, including political actors who hold administrative power, directors of economically influential firms, and heads of media corporations that compete for public attention in order to sell advertising. Given the potential for public opinion to be manipulated, Habermas maintains that politically and financially unaffiliated intellectuals play a key role in ensuring that the strategic competition for media power (and the profits it brings!) does not overshadow the communicative generation of legitimate power.

Because their livelihood is governed by "professional involvement in contexts of meaning that have an autonomous logic of their own," public intellectuals retain the ability to "speak truth to power," enjoying what Habermas calls the "privilege of having to deal with public issues only as a sideline."[71] Since they intervene in public life not as part of their Weberian *Beruf* (vocation) but rather as a *Nebenberuf* (secondary calling), Habermas contends that public intellectuals are strategically "able to get worked up about critical developments while others are still absorbed in business as usual."[72] In this sense, by stepping outside their professional "academic public sphere," public intellectuals become part of what Karl Mannheim, using a term he borrowed from Alfred Weber, called "*freischwebende Intelligenz*" ("the socially unattached intelligentsia" or, more literally, "free-floating intelligence").[73]

However, just as he seeks "to separate the role of the intellectual as clearly as possible from that of the scholar and the academic teacher," Habermas also differentiates the public role of the expert from that of the social critic.[74] He initially introduces this distinction in a 1989 interview in which he observes that "intellectuals today are no longer just writers or philosophers like Sartre and Adorno, but also experts, who know something about economics, questions of health or atomic energy." Such expert intellectuals "are more necessary than ever [*notwendiger denn je*]" given the increasing expansion and specialization of the bureaucratic and economic systems that ensure material reproduction (a phenomenon already noted by Weber). However, Habermas sees these experts as fundamentally different from public intellectuals, given that they speak from a position of subject competence that can be questioned by "counter-experts," rather than as public intellectuals—as "someone who feels responsible, regardless of lack of competence [*kompetenzfrei*], for things that matter not just to them personally."[75]

This distinction is related to a similar thought voiced by Michel Foucault, who differentiates between the general and the specific intellectual. The former "speaks in the name of the universal, takes the side of humanity, reason, or truth and seeks to represent all those excluded from the circuits of public debate." By contrast, the latter acts as a "savant or expert" by seeking to "provide instruments of analysis, to locate lines of weakness, strong points, positions where the instances of power have secured and implanted themselves, [by providing] a topological survey of the battlefield."[76] In other words, whereas experts provide technical details on specific problems, public intellectuals are called upon to take stands on important moral issues, acting as what Pierre Bourdieu has called "defenders of the universal."[77]

Habermas adopts this understanding from his French colleagues, observing that the public intellectual is "not in demand as an expert. She [is] supposed to have the courage to take normative stances and the imagination to adopt novel perspectives without losing an awareness of her own fallibility."[78] However, he also departs from Francophone interpretation in important ways. For example, Foucault argues that for the expert or specific intellectual, "there can be no question for me of trying to tell them [i.e., the citizens] 'what is to be done.'" Conversely, in this model the public or general intellectual is explicitly allowed to take substantial stands on important social and political issues, as long as she is able "to explain the moral point of view, and—as far as possible—justify the claim to universality of this explanation."[79]

Habermas reverses this argument. Rather than barring experts from taking specific stands on issues, he argues that they can do so because the positions they take are presumably based on their professional knowledge of the Weberian "inner logics" of their particular field of research. As a result, they may be able to provide suggestions on how to best meet the internal demands of the sphere of life they specialize in without violating their scientific objectivity involved in the search for truth. By contrast, because public intellectuals play the role of a "dilettante who questions the demarcation lines between various realms and provokes through his or her very lack of expertise," they cannot base their opinions on scientific claims to knowledge.[80]

The result is that the public intellectual appears in social and political debate primarily as a critic of existing discourses—not as an advocate, but as a defender of the feedback loop "between an informed elite discourse and a responsive civil society," between opinion- and will-formation, in which "the generative flow of communication is from the periphery to the center." Public intellectuals therefore play a key role in the agenda-setting function of the informal public sphere by helping to ensure that the public opinions emerging from this anarchic communicative realm have "benefited from information, thoughtfulness, and the exchange of ideas." While they may occasionally take partisan stances—as many of Habermas's own interventions undoubtedly do—this is only a problem when these positions become "detached from civil society inputs and can no longer claim to be responding to a flow of information from the periphery to the center."[81] As politically engaged citizens, social critics serve, in Habermas's words, as "the medium and intensifier of a democratic will."[82]

In this sense, the primary function of the Habermasian public intellectual is to make sure that marginalized voices, opinions and arguments are heard. While public intellectuals have no claim to authority in the public sphere, they are called on to reframe issues by holding elite experts, administrators, lobbyists, media personalities, politicians, and other actors with access to power and money accountable for drowning out underrepresented individuals and groups affected by the issues under discussion. In this sense, the public intellectual acts as a "discourse agent whose activity appeals to the *moral* or context-transcendent normative dimension of public discourse; as a tradition-smashing agent of Enlightenment modernity, a supporter of principles of universal justice and right, of critical debate and democratic rule, with a deep suspicion concerning conventional identities and traditions of all kinds."[83]

MODELS OF THEORETICAL ENGAGEMENT

These considerations on the role of the public intellectual bring me back to contemporary critiques of Habermas that take him to task for failing to recognize that "Wissenschaft must be connected with a realm of potential action."[84] Although Habermas agrees that academic research in social and political theory should relate to debate in the public sphere, his account of the public intellectual highlights their role as facilitators of discussion and amplifiers of voices that should be heard (but in practice usually are not), rather than as political agents or underlaborers, who see "real" politics as a matter of "differential choice," and therefore provide arguments in favor of "opting for A *rather than* B."[85] While Habermas defends the right of the political theorist to intervene in public debate as a citizen and as a public intellectual, he argues that scholars betray their professional vocation if they delude themselves into believing that theory "can facilitate better, more effective political action on its own."[86]

Habermas's understanding of the relationship between theory and practice—mediated through the distinct roles of the social and political theorist on the one hand, and the public intellectual on the other—not only differs from realist approaches (whose proponents have, unfairly, focused much of their ire on Habermas), but also from the ideal of the theorist as a democratic underlaborer. This model calls on academic philosophers to utilize their professional skills—"[the] making of careful distinctions, [demonstrating] an understanding of how to assess and examine arguments about values, [conveying] arguments for and against political principles" in order to play a "clarificatory role" in public debate while also "offer[ing] arguments and justifications" with substantive content that will allow their "fellow citizens to decide whether they want to accept them."[87]

The underlaborer model "limits the role of the political theorist to speaking to and with her fellow citizens; she does not seek also to speak on their behalf."[88] In this respect, it bears some similarity to Habermas's understanding of the social and political theorist as a public intellectual. However, in contrast to this approach, Habermas's theorist-as-public intellectual does not act as a "philosopher-investigator" seeking to formulate a positive position or proposal that can be labeled legitimate, nor as an expert offering "a general theoretical perspective, informed by public views, which can provide guidance when special interests collide."[89]

On the contrary, given his historically informed awareness of the professional deformations of the philosophical profession in regards to politics, as well as his radically participatory and open conception of the democratic public sphere, Habermas rejects both the idea that "the theorist's job is to defend her own views" and the notion that she has "authority to tell us *what is actually legitimate for us here and now.*"[90] By drawing a hard line between the voice of the truth-oriented theorist and the critical, engaged public intellectual, Habermas objects to the idea, defended by both realists and proponents of underlaboring, that "political theorists need to be genuine participants in public debate" qua theorists. Rather than ensuring that academic arguments are accessible to "the tribunal of each person's understanding" in the broader public, as the democratic underlaborer model proposes, Habermas insists that the relationship between theory and practice must be characterized by a more distinct division of roles designed to prevent theory from degenerating into mere ideological advocacy.[91]

In large part, this is due to his conviction that such practice increases "the likelihood [that] each individual challenge [i.e. theory and practice] to be met effectively will be severely impaired."[92] There are at least two reasons for this. First, theory and practice are both worse off when they are too readily conflated, as they are guided by fundamentally different orientations. As Hannah Arendt points out in the German version of her essay "Truth and Politics," "The philosopher who intervenes in public is no longer a philosopher, but rather a politician; he no longer seeks truth, but power (*Macht*)."[93] Whereas academic work must follow the inner logic of truth-seeking, practical political interventions are contingent and oriented toward the successful operationalization of power.

Second, these two activities address distinct audiences, as I discussed in the introduction. As a philosopher and sociologist, Habermas directs his research toward those "who have a professional interest in the foundations of social theory."[94] By contrast, in his activities as a public intellectual, he takes up issues that concern not only specialized academic audiences but society at large—often extending beyond the borders of his native Germany. Habermas clearly chooses topics that "lie close to his heart" (*Herzanliegen*) in his political writings. While these exert a strong influence on his theoretical development—as I show in the forthcoming chapters—his systematic theoretical work also "follows the dynamic of its own problems" in important respects.[95]

The emotional interest Habermas displays in his political writings thus contrasts with the quasi-Weberian objectivity of his scientific research. This is visible in how he presents his arguments differently depending on the situation. For example, during a visit to Harvard University, Habermas spoke to students studying his work at the Committee on Degrees in Social Studies, where I also taught after completing my PhD. In the question-and-answer session that followed, one student commended him for the clarity of his presentation and his comments on the political situation, then asked why his theoretical texts were so dense given his ability to formulate his ideas so lucidly. Habermas replied that, as a German philosopher, he had lost the right to use rhetoric in support of his ideas because of the taint of Nazi collaboration that hung over the discipline. As a citizen, however, he still felt a duty to address his fellow citizens as clearly and persuasively as possible when current events threatened either the fundamental rights or lives of individuals from underrepresented groups.[96] In this sense, the role separation he introduces between his philosophical work and his writings as a public intellectual are matched by a "role-based prose (*Rollenprosa*)" as well.[97]

As a result of his understanding of the role differentiation that philosophers must respect between their academic work and their political convictions, Habermas rejects both realist calls for theorists to engage more directly with politics, and the democratic underlaborer model, which seeks to direct "attention towards evidence about the forms in which, and conditions under which, the arguments of political theory are comprehensible to a wider public."[98] Instead, in his view "there is no 'royal path' to mediating theory and practice."[99] By separating the role of the theorist as truth-oriented researcher from that of the public intellectual as engaged citizen, Habermas instead creates a model in which theorists can serve as public critics—calling attention to rights violations and giving voice to those whose views are otherwise drowned out in the cacophony of the chaotic public sphere—while still acknowledging "the healthy implications of the differentiation of value spheres noted by Weber."[100] Although Habermas "consider[s] it impossible to map [*unmittelbar abzubilden*] theoretical positions directly onto party-political ones," this arrangement not only allows the practical "void left by Habermas the philosopher [to be] filled by Habermas the intellectual," but furthermore enables Habermas's political commitments to influence his philosophy in a consistent manner.[101]

CONCLUSION

The modern, largely quietist approach to social and political theory as an academic enterprise has come under increasing attack in recent years. While realist critics of ideal theory have called for theory to be action-guiding both in form and content, practical philosophers within the mainstream tradition instead advocate an underlaboring model, in which social and political theorists use their skills in normative argumentation to clarify existing proposals and offer their own solutions to contemporary problems. In contrast to both models, Habermas proposes a more mediated relationship between theory and practice—one that seeks to preserve the internal logics of these Weberian value spheres while allowing theorists to engage in the public sphere as public intellectuals. Their role, in this view, is to help ensure that the views generated within the "communicative circuit between center and periphery" do not generate strategically manipulated public opinion but instead produce the kinds of legitimate, deliberatively-generated *reflected public opinions* that his theoretical model of democratic legitimacy requires.[102]

Although in his mature account he advocates and practices a strict role separation between his theoretical reflections and practical interventions, reading his scholarly research and political writings alongside each other also shows how "Habermas's work as a public philosopher and as a public intellectual merge."[103] He thus seeks to bring his political commitments into harmony with his philosophical presuppositions without concluding that theory must speak directly to "real" politics or allowing the theorist to claim authority over other participants in the public sphere, as the underlaboring model requires. As a public intellectual, Habermas seeks to combat the "colonization of the lifeworld" by the internal, nondiscursive logics of markets and state power—which he diagnoses in his social and political theory—by performatively "show[ing] that communicative power is as influential on political culture as the steering power of political administration and money."[104]

The key point for my argument is that Habermas does not engage in the public sphere qua theorist but as a public intellectual and fellow participant, aiming to improve the quality of public debate by acting as a critic of existing patterns of discourse. Theoretically, he is convinced that, despite their depoliticizing tendencies, "democracies need active participation of citizens in public life" in order to fulfill the requirements of legitimate political authority.[105] From this perspective—and in keeping with Adorno's frequent appearances on television and radio after his return to postwar West Germany—Habermas's activities as a public intellectual serve as an example of what participation in a functional democratic public sphere should look like.[106]

Although Max Horkheimer, as the director of the Institute for Social Research (*Institut für Sozialforschung*), famously claimed that critical theory differed from traditional approaches by arguing that the theorist's "activity is the construction of the social present," the Frankfurt School has had a fraught relationship with practice from the start.[107] Despite Horkheimer's assertion that the theorist must be "a force within [society] to stimulate change," the project of critical theory started in the 1920s as an attempt within the Marxist tradition to understand why emancipatory practice had not occurred during the interwar crisis and why a revolutionary subject had failed to emerge.[108] In this sense, its turn to Freudian psychoanalysis, ideology critique, and the analysis of mass culture were attempts to interpret the world theoretically rather than to change it in practice; these all reflect the Frankfurt School's conviction that "critical reflection on what went wrong is the order of the day, and, thus, it is to theory, not to praxis, that we have to turn."[109]

Habermas's understanding of the contemporary situation is based more on a Weberian analysis of the separation of the world into irreconcilable value spheres with their own inner logics than on a Marxist diagnosis of "the given historical conditions in which one has to act."[110] Although Habermas is committed to the idea that theory must seek understanding (*Verstehen*) guided by a truth-seeking orientation, this does not mean that his "position has the *actual* effect of . . . diverting attention from the actual social context" as his realist critics would have it.[111] Nor is it a sign that his "form of critical theory apparently abandons the aim of fundamental social change."[112] On the contrary, I argue that understanding the relationship between Habermas the theorist and Habermas the public intellectual reveals that although his philosophical writings seek to "comprehend society without changing it," this practical lacuna is filled by his political writings, where he seeks to stimulate rational debate in the public sphere in line with his political commitments.

Reflecting on critical theory's fraught relationship to practice, I want to conclude this chapter by suggesting that Habermas's attempt to develop a form of practice compatible with his philosophical ideas—without relinquishing theory's orientation to truth or claiming greater knowledge and authority over others in practice—is his attempt to make good on the Frankfurt School's claim to offer "a theory dominated at every turn by a concern for reasonable conditions of life."[113] Although many interpreters argue that Habermas does not fit into this theoretical tradition, my basic thesis is that attending to Habermas's interventions in the public sphere demonstrates precisely that "the famous 'Frankfurt School' of critical social theory seems an excellent fit for Habermas's reformed vision of a socially committed, interdisciplinary philosophy."[114] In this sense, I agree with Stefan Müller-Doohm's assessment that the "intransigence Habermas displays in his public political interventions is a crucial reason why he is still counted as a member of the circle around Horkheimer and Adorno."[115]

I turn to these issues in the next chapter, which begins my chronological presentation of Habermas's public-facing work. There, I examine how Habermas's journalism attracted Adorno's interest and led to the resurrection of his academic career, which he had abandoned after completing his PhD. I focus particularly on how Habermas's early career as a freelance journalist set the stage for his arrival in Frankfurt and the continuity between the basic themes in his public-facing work and the philosophical writings he produced after rejoining academia in 1956 at Adorno's invitation and behest. Although at this point Habermas had not yet formulated the separation thesis or his mature conception of the public intellectual, he was already working to ensure that his public commentaries expressed theoretical continuity with his philosophical work.

CHAPTER 2

The Journalistic Years, 1951–1955

Chapter 1 laid out Habermas's mature understanding of the role of the public intellectual and how it differs from that of the academic philosopher. With that foundation in place, this chapter begins my chronological presentation of his public-facing work. After briefly detailing his early life and years as a student, I turn my focus to the early 1950s—the years he spent working as a freelance journalist after completing his PhD. During this period, Habermas reported on various academic debates and published a number of articles on the state of democracy and the enduring legacy of Nazism in the West German Federal Republic, most notably his 1953 attack on Heidegger for his unwillingness to apologize for—or substantively address—his collaboration with the Nazi regime. Indeed, Habermas's concerns about the persistent continuities between postwar West Germany and the Third Reich, clearly present in these early newspaper articles, run like a red thread through his entire oeuvre.

The early Habermas texts I draw on in the coming pages are not readily available in German, much less in English, as the vast majority have not been republished or translated.[1] This source base thus breaks new ground for the reception of Habermas's work, especially in the non-German speaking context.[2] Beyond their significance for the history of twentieth-century social and political thought, these texts also shed light on the relationship between Habermas and Adorno.

More specifically, these writings—which prompted Adorno to invite a young freelance journalist to join him at the Institute as his personal assistant in 1956—highlight important shared interests that predate their first meeting and foreshadow their later collaboration and friendship. My reading of Habermas's early work reveals three key thematic areas of overlap between his early ideas and Adorno's work: 1) the effects of technology on both work and consumption;

2) concern about enduring social and political continuities between the Third Reich and the early West German Federal Republic; and 3) a turn to art and culture as possible sources of liberation and critique.

In light of these considerations, Habermas's early journalism has crucial implications for how we conceptualize his relationship to Adorno and, more generally, his connection to the first generation of the Frankfurt School. Of course, it is impossible to say that Adorno influenced Habermas before 1956. Quentin Skinner rightly points out that "the conditions sufficient, or at least necessary, for the proper application of the concept" of influence include "that B is known to have studied A's works" and "that B could not have arrived at the relevant doctrines independently."[3] The former is unclear (Habermas has suggested he encountered some of Adorno's writings before 1956, although he has never stated it definitively), while the latter is certainly possible. Fortunately, I am not making an argument based on the concept of influence. Instead, the evidence I present in this chapter demonstrates the existence of some common themes and interests that may help explain why Adorno quickly agreed to take Habermas under his wing at the end of the period covered by this chapter.

This insight is based on a contemporary analysis of Habermas's writings from before 1956. However, in line with the presentist approach I laid out in the introduction, I argue that it has retroactive significance, as it helps to clarify why Habermas later described Adorno as having "played an electrifying role (*eine elektrisierende Rolle gespielt*) for me."[4] This claim may appear as an example of the "mythology of prolepsis," which is based on a "conflation of the asymmetry between the significance an observer may justifiably claim to find in a given historical episode and the meaning of that episode itself."[5] While it is clear that neither Habermas nor Adorno could have been aware of the significance their collaboration would later have, the evidence I present below also makes it clear that they both did view this episode as significant at the time, albeit for different reasons.

This argument is not meant to downplay the significant differences between Habermas's mature critical theory and Adorno's negative dialectics. However, I argue that these later divergences only serve to highlight the importance of Habermas's journalism as a crucial resource for understanding his early attempts to engage in political debates in the public sphere—a desire that would eventually lead him to develop his conception of the public intellectual—as well as his relationship to Adorno and the Frankfurt School more generally. This is particularly important given the tendency in a certain part of the literature on the

Frankfurt School to set Habermas against his mentor by arguing that critical theory is " 'better off' insofar as it is 'closer to Adorno . . . than to Habermas.' "6

The chapter is organized as follows. I begin with a brief overview of Habermas's early life and university studies, including his first public-facing publications. After completing his PhD, Habermas chose to become a freelance journalist rather than pursue an academic career—a path he had not seriously considered at the time.7 The second part focuses on the texts he produced during his three-year career as an independent reporter. The third section is devoted to Habermas's break with Heidegger, which marks his entry into the German public sphere. I then explain how and why Adorno invited Habermas to join him at the Institute in 1956, thus paving Habermas's path into academia. The conclusion reflects on the relationship between Habermas's early journalism and his later understanding of the role public intellectuals should play in modern democratic life.

EARLY LIFE

Jürgen Habermas was born in Düsseldorf in the Weimar Republic on June 18, 1929, just before the onset of the Great Depression. He spent most of his childhood in the small industrial town of Gummersbach, east of Cologne. Although generally healthy, Habermas was born with a cleft palate, which, despite multiple surgeries, left him with a noticeable speech impediment. As he later recalled, this handicap not only "awakened the feelings of dependence and vulnerability and the sense of the relevance of our interactions with others," but also made him deeply aware of both the social nature of human beings and how the "subjectifying gaze of others" is mediated through language. In one of the few autobiographical reflections that Habermas has published, he notes that his "nasal articulation and distorted pronunciation" affected his early life as a schoolboy because "other people did not understand me very well" and this often meant that "they responded with annoyance or rejection."8

Looking back on his childhood, Habermas himself has speculated about the effect of this deformity on his thought and on his obsession with communication as the basis of social and political life. While his understanding of the public sphere is not dissimilar to the "public realm" of "words and deeds" theorized by Hannah Arendt, Habermas's conception of *Öffentlichkeit* is defined neither as a "space of appearances" nor "of viewers or listeners"; rather, it is "an arena in which speakers and interlocutors exchange questions and answers," where "an exchange of opinions and reasons takes place." In this sense, Habermas's commitment to "the published word" as the "decisive mark" of the public sphere can be understood as a product of his personal experience of how the "written form disguises the taint of the spoken word."[9]

Politically, Habermas's earliest memories were defined by the dictatorship of the Nazi party, which came to power in 1933. Support for National Socialism was high in his hometown. Although his father, Ernst Habermas, was a national conservative, he became a member of the National Socialist Party almost immediately after Hitler's *Machtergreifung* (seizure of power) and later even joined the Wehrmacht—he was stationed in northern France from 1941 until the end of the war—just as he had volunteered to fight in the First World War. At age ten, Habermas duly joined the Hitler Youth, in accordance with the law, though he did not enjoy its militarism or the macho culture it fostered. To avoid some of these aspects—and reflecting his childhood ambition to become a doctor—he managed to have himself placed into medical training rather than the otherwise compulsory military service expected of teenagers at the time.[10] In February 1945, as part of the so-called "final battle (*Endkampf*)" for Germany, Habermas was called up to fight for the Wehrmacht. Fortunately, as he later recalled, "I was somewhere else ... on that night the military police came to look for me. Then, thank God ... the Americans came."[11]

While Habermas escaped military service, both his father and his older brother, Hans-Joachim, fought in the war and spent time as US prisoners of war in its immediate aftermath. While there is no evidence that either were believers in the racist ideology of the Third Reich, Habermas notes that his home was typical in terms of its "bourgeois adaptation to the political environment" of the time.[12] Despite his own emphasis on open communication, Habermas never seems to have engaged his father in dialogue about his actions during the *Nazizeit*. Although he later recognized that "[b]ecause we cannot know how we ourselves would have acted, a certain restraint in moral judgement [is warranted] when it comes to the mistakes of our own parents," he did make it clear in a 1955 letter to Hans Paetschke, one of his editors at *Merkur*, "that my father and I do not agree on political matters."[13]

Like many in his generation, Habermas experienced 1945 as a decisive rupture, both personally and politically: "Overnight, as it were, the society in which we had led what had seemed to be a halfway normal everyday life and the regime governing it were exposed as pathological and criminal." Although he had the "good fortune of a late birth (*die Gnade der späten Geburt*)," which meant that he could not be held to bear personal responsibility for the crimes of Nazism, Habermas took what he would later refer to as the "caesura (*Zäsur*)" of 1945 as a sign not only that "[a]fter the revelations concerning Auschwitz, nothing could be taken at face value," but also that "my cohort had the opportunity to learn without reservation from the Nuremberg war crimes trials."[14]

The revelations of 1945 thus trigged the kind of need for self-reflection in Habermas, "without which I would hardly have ended up in philosophy and social theory."[15] In the aftermath of the war—and as a result of his reflections on it—Habermas gave up on his plans to study medicine.[16] Toward the end of high school, he instead began to consider becoming a journalist who would write "with a sense of the topicality about the urgent problems of the day." However, he ultimately decided to pursue a degree in philosophy because "I was captured by the enthusiasm for existentialist philosophy at the time."[17] When he made this choice he could not have foreseen that his disappointment with the German intellectual establishment's lack of reflection on their own complicity with the Nazi regime would lead him to abandon his philosophical career in favor of journalism.

UNIVERSITY YEARS AND BREAK WITH HIS PROFESSORS

Habermas's decision to study philosophy was also influenced by Peter Wingender, his father's brother-in-law, who was also one of Habermas's teachers at the Gymnasium (high school) in Gummersbach. His uncle not only nurtured the young Habermas's growing interest in the subject by suggesting further reading but also prepared his nephew-in-law for his intake interview with Professor Nicolai Hartman at the Georg-August University in Göttingen.[18] Although Habermas described himself as already "highly politicized" at the time, his undergraduate studies in philosophy, with minors in history, psychology, literary studies and economics, offered him little opportunity to bring his interests inside and outside the classroom together in what he later described as the "at once elitist and apolitical self-image of the German universities."[19]

Looking back on his time as an undergraduate, Habermas recalls, "My studies were characterized by a dichotomy between my philosophical and my political convictions."[20] Despite this disconnect, his time at the university allowed him to familiarize himself with the main currents of academic philosophy, including the tradition of German idealism. However, his professors only covered topics that allowed them to steer clear of current sociopolitical issues and questions about the recent past. Although Habermas later became known for his social and political thought, he notes that "I did not know the word 'Gesellschaftstheorie' [social theory] at the time; it was to remain foreign to me throughout my studies," including during his semester abroad in Zurich in 1950 and after later transferring to the university in the West German capital, Bonn.[21]

Fortunately, Habermas was able to find many other outlets for his political activism outside the university. He arrived in Göttingen in 1949, just as territories occupied by the Western powers were being reformed into postwar West Germany. This was an exciting time for Habermas, who describes himself as a product of American "reeducation," for whom " 'democracy,' not Anglo-Saxon liberalism, was the magic word."[22] Although it was fully absent from his academic studies, he was still able to engage his political interests: "I visited election campaign rallies and encountered practically all the figures who later entered Adenauer's cabinet or played some other important role."[23]

While the events surrounding the founding of the Federal Republic were certainly exciting, Habermas's political hopes were quickly dashed. In light of the recent past—marked by the Great War, the interwar crisis and the *Nazizeit*—he was dismayed by the nationalistic character of postwar German politics. Although he viewed the creation of West Germany, with its new Basic Law (*Grundgesetz*) grounded in respect for human dignity and the protection of fundamental human rights violated by the Nazi regime, as an opportunity for a new beginning, Habermas feared this chance was being squandered by the desire for a return to normalcy and the communicative silencing (*kommunikatives Beschweigen*) of the recent past. While he later came to appreciate the politics of "binding to the West (*Westbindung*)" pursued by the new chancellor and the Christian Democrats, at the time "the continuity of social elites and cultural prejudices through which Konrad Adenauer marshaled consent for his policies was stifling. There had been no break with the past, no new beginning in terms of personnel, no change in mentality—neither a moral renewal nor a revolution of political mindset."[24]

Habermas initially shared his political disenchantment with his wife, Ute Wesselhoeft, whom he met at university. However, since his philosophical work at the time did not provide an outlet for his frustrations, he soon began to write articles for public consumption, reviving his interest in writing journalistic pieces "in reaction to the day" (*aus dem Tag heraus*).²⁵ In a 2019 interview, Habermas notes that, as a high school student, he had already published a number of film and play reviews for the local edition of the *Kölner Stadt-Anzeiger*.²⁶ Unfortunately, neither I nor any other researcher has been able to locate copies of these texts.

The first available text by Habermas, which Till van Rahden recently discovered in Hans-Ulrich Wehler's papers in the *Deutsche Literaturarchiv* (the German Literary Archive) in Marbach, dates back to 1951. It was published in the second issue of *Schwarz auf Weiß* (*Black on White*), the newspaper of his high school in Gummersbach. His article, which appeared under the title "Is our Generation Modern?," appeared bearing this tag line: "From among the circle of our youngest alumni, a budding journalist sends us this 'INCITEMENT TO A CONVERSATION.'"²⁷

In this piece Habermas notes that certain historical events—most often wars—affect such a broad swath of individuals that it becomes possible to speak of a new generation.²⁸ He then compares his cohort, which experienced World War II as adolescents, to the generation that lived through the Great War. That interwar generation confronted the historical break they had experienced by "affirming the fact that they had been uprooted." Moreover, in seeking to come to terms with the past, they had sought to "clear the building site from rubble," metaphorically speaking, and had "become wet in the process. After all, they had no roof."

By contrast, Habermas accuses his generation of being too conformist and "uncritical," resulting in a "search for security in traditional forms of community (*Gemeinschaftsformen*)." Instead of confronting the homelessness of the German tradition after the horrors of Auschwitz and the Holocaust, he berates his peers for seeking to build themselves a new home built of "illusions handed down on matchboxes (*aus den Streichholzschachteln überlieferter Illusionen*)." While he sees some benefits in the individualistic pacifism of his cohort, he diagnoses them with "exhaustion and flight from the world (*Erschöpfung und Weltflucht*)." Continuing with his earlier metaphor, he notes: "We leave that building site unused and prefer to rent the attic of the old house. We want to have our peace and quiet and a private hobby while others do the work. . . . At best, we read the paper and get angry." He concludes that the "great failure of our generation" in comparison with that shaped by World War I is "that we cannot set alight and recast the old tracks, institutions and conventions."²⁹

Habermas was particularly concerned with how his cohort—and German society at large—related to Germany's historical and cultural traditions in the aftermath of the rupture of Nazism. This worry was closely connected to his long-standing "interest in dramatic literature, in Georg Kaiser, Hasenclever, Wedekind and, of course, Sartre, [who] served a mediating function" between his philosophical studies and political interests.[30] The connections Habermas drew between these areas can be seen in can be seen in "Against the Moral-Pedagogical Arrogance of Cultural Criticism," a short opinion piece he published in 1952. Reflecting on the meaning of German culture after 1945, he observes that it is "a truism that we live by appropriating our traditions. However, for those who have still not noticed it . . . another truism should be repeated: Goethe and Hegel have been dead for over a hundred years."

While he acknowledges the provisional nature of his reflections, and the "arrogance of assuming that we already hold the truth in our hands," he also observes that postwar Germans have the advantage of finding themselves in a position in which "our discomfort drives us to give an account of the constitution of our world and our being within it." Thus, he observes that "no time demands greater caution regarding the practical solutions offered by tradition and a greater openness in terms of that which is seen as a solution in the first place" than the present, which he sees as a kind of post-crisis "transitional stage, from whose probing movements a new historical answer can spring."[31] While he offers no solutions to this problem, it is clear that he is sympathetic to Arnold Gehlen's anthropologically based critique of humanity's relationship to technology.

This essay is by no means Habermas's first engagement with issues of culture and cultural criticism in his public-facing work. Indeed, several of his publications as a student address theater and the performing arts, since "discussions about dramaturgy were the medium in which to discuss political questions at a higher level of generality" for Habermas at this time.[32] A good example of this is a series of reviews he wrote for the *Frankfurter Allgemeine Zeitung*, which marked his debut in this most prestigious of German daily newspapers. The first, entitled "Gottfried Benn's New Voice," reviewed *The Voice Behind the Screen* (*Stimme hinter dem Vorhang*), recently published by the winner of the 1951 Georg Büchner Prize in German language literature.[33]

Although Habermas admired Benn's work, he was wary of its political implications. Benn had been appointed head of the poetry section of the Prussian Academy in 1933, signed a vow of personal allegiance to the Führer (the so-called *Gelöbnis treuester Gefolgschaft*), and even defended the Nazi regime by arguing that under Hitler "German workers are better off than ever before."[34] Although

Benn turned away from the Nazis after the Night of the Long Knives (also known as Operation Hummingbird [*Unternehmen Kolibri*]), Habermas remained suspicious of the emphasis Benn's work placed on abstract notions like style as the source of historical truth. He saw this as a form of escapism that seeks to hide an "antisocial and antihumanitarian catechism in the absolute form." Habermas's debut article in the *FAZ* thus reveals his desire to use art as a way to reflect on the present, not to abstract from it. Moreover, while he admires Benn's existentialism, he criticizes it for legitimating indifference rather than care for the other.[35]

In August, Habermas also published a review of the fourth annual student theater festival in Erlangen. He was particularly impressed by the foreign student groups, whose performances "dominated" the festival. However, as the title—"Academic Summer Retreat in Erlangen?: International Student Performances Without Courage"—makes clear, he was critical of the lack of broader social commentary in the shows. Rather than merely encouraging the students to "play a bit of theater (*halt ein wenig Theater spielen*)," he urged them to "passionately make the stage into a forum in which they can make a statement (*die Bühne mit Leidenschaft zu dem Forum zu machen, auf dem sie aussagen können*)."[36]

In "Audio Drama's Defect Is its Opportunity" and "The Acoustic Stage," the other two reviews Habermas published in the *FAZ* in 1952, he explores the critical potential of radio theater (*Hörspiel*). In the first, he notes that "radio dematerializes and generalizes. But this automatized abstraction is precisely the productive deficiency that defines the superiority of radio over stage and film." Habermas is particularly taken by this new form's ability to catch listeners unaware in their daily lives: "The cry (*Appell*) from the ether ambushes us in the kitchen and living room. It is an intrusion into the defenseless intimacy of the private sphere. This is possibly the first contact that forms beyond the aesthetic experience (*Erlebnis*)—something like the experience (*Erfahrung*) of the numinous that emerges from the heart of technology."[37]

The second piece continues Habermas's reflections on the critical potential of this new technology to break through the bourgeois individualism of the postwar Federal Republic, which he had criticized in his critiques of his own generation's escapism. He observes that the "allure of the audio drama clearly lies in the fact that compared to the now somewhat lifeless action stage (*Aktionsbühne*) of our large houses (*Großen Häuser*), the acoustic stage of the radio has the advantage of being a necessary forum and not a retrospective afterthought (*nachträglicher Schauplatz*)."[38] Taken together, these three *FAZ* publications from 1952 show

Habermas's appreciation for art as a form of social criticism, a subject Adorno tackles in his posthumously published *Aesthetic Theory* (1970).[39]

These reviews also testify to Habermas's interest in how theater can create a "third place (*dritter Ort*)," between real life and the performance, through which the "stage regains its original stage-like character." Instead of allowing the audience to escape from their real lives into the world of the performance, he favors techniques that break the fourth wall—like direct address or Bertold Brecht's practice of having his characters break into song to interrupt the action—which ensure the audience remains critically engaged rather than passive objects of entertainment.[40] For example, in his review of the play "The Three Masks (*Die drei Masken*)," Habermas takes Egon Vietta to task for failing "to make the location of the players [such] a platform."[41] This was a common critique Habermas levelled against directors who stopped halfway, rather than completing the task of creating this "third place," as seen in the plays of Brecht and Sartre.[42] Much like Adorno, whose chapter on the "Culture Industry" from the *Dialectic of Enlightenment* he apparently read during his studies, Habermas wants art to lead not to complacency, as it so often does in the form of mass entertainment, but to critique.[43]

Habermas's aesthetic interests were not limited to radio and literature. In January 1953, for example, he wrote a piece on the "Musical Style of Film," prompted by a lecture given by the French director Jean Mitry. The talk was cosponsored by the *Cercle français* and the Bonn film club, which Habermas had cofounded at the university. In his review, Habermas writes approvingly of the way Mitry gives his productions a "rhythmic structure" by "coupling the moving pictures with a piece of music."[44] Later that month, he published two reviews of a series of puppet shows presented in Bonn. Writing in the *FAZ* under the title "The Irony of Block and Plaster Heads," he expresses appreciation for the "comic effects" and "expressivity" of this form of performance art and urges readers "to take puppet plays seriously, so that we can have fun watching them."[45] In a review of a second cycle of shows at the same venue, featuring two-hundred-year-old puppets from Szechuan, Habermas describes their "restrained colors" as "moving stained glass."[46]

While Habermas's interest in aesthetics is evident, the question of technology most occupied him during this early period, particularly because it allowed him to bring his philosophical interests to bear on contemporary developments. For example, in "The Moloch and the Arts," published in the *FAZ* in 1953, Habermas reported on a meeting of the Association of German Engineers and an exhibition of industrial design in Stuttgart. Given his infatuation with Martin Heidegger at the time, it is not surprising that Habermas sought to "unmask the legend of technical expediency" by pushing back against the way that "bare, impersonal, faceless" technical products "make people into strangers in their own world because their purposes are subordinated to the authority technical intelligence itself." He ends by asking "how this dreadful state of affairs regarding technology can be dealt with through artistic design." Although Habermas does not have an answer to this rhetorical question, his critique of the dominance of technological means that "dictate to us what has to be considered as useful" over actual human goals echoes Horkheimer and Adorno's earlier critique of instrumental reason and may indeed later have served as a point of theoretical connection with Adorno.[47]

The other important influence on Habermas at this time was his doctoral supervisor in Bonn, the philosophical anthropologist Ernst Rothacker. In December 1953 Habermas used a lecture delivered by his *Doktorvater* at the Academy of Fine Arts in Munich to reflect on art as a possible source of liberation, especially insofar as handicrafts were able to absorb elements of modern art into the process of technical production. In Habermas's reconstruction, Rothacker concluded his lecture with this thought: "In a situation that is determined and endangered by the social, political, moral and spiritual hypertrophy of the technical apparatus, art is once again called upon to banish demons, collect happiness and release knotted feelings." Habermas concludes his review, published as "On the Healing Power of Art" in the *FAZ*, by asking his teacher, "Will the art of finding images not only be able to bring about liberation if these 'images' 'correspond' to the current situation and even bear the features of their technical origin?"[48] He seems to imply that, while art is tasked with keeping human intuitions intact by uniting feelings and images, it can do so only if it both reflects the increasingly technical world and resists it by incorporating a humanist style that transcends mere functionality.[49]

During this initial period, Habermas is clearly still finding his public voice. While his writings engage in some social and political commentary, he is clearly not (yet) working as a public intellectual. Neither, however, are these works really those of a classical journalist. Instead, these early articles and reviews are an outlet for his social and political interests, which occur alongside but clearly are separate from his studies. These two areas, however, would soon come together in a piece that both marked Habermas's entry into the nascent West German public sphere and forced him to rethink some of his basic philosophical positions and commitments.

PUBLIC ATTACK ON HEIDEGGER

My brief overview of Habermas's first public-facing journalistic publications documented his critique of postwar West Germany's failure to engage with the recent past, his worries about the development of modern technology, and his turn to art as a source of liberation. These early commentaries also highlight the impact of Heidegger—whom Habermas would later call "the Great Influence (*Die große Wirkung*)"—on his early thought.[50] This influence is evident in his review of the *Philosophie der Gegenwart* (translated as *Major Problems in Contemporary European Philosophy, from Dilthey to Heidegger*) by Ludwig Landgrebe, who had been one of Edmund Husserl's last assistants before the founder of phenomenology was forced to resign his position due to his Jewish heritage, and who was greatly influenced by Heidegger.[51]

In this article, published under the title "In Light of Heidegger" in the culture section of the *FAZ* in 1952, Habermas argues that both the "glory and disaster" of Western thought "found its conclusion in the technology of modern times." He praises Landgrebe for placing the "question of Being" at the center of Western philosophy, for the "brilliant didactics" of his presentation of Heidegger's work, and for his rejection of French existentialism, whose "self-empowerment of the subject" as "completely autonomous" is incompatible with Heidegger's system. Habermas notes that instead of fighting against technology and seeking to "dominate (*bewältigen*)" it, "a more original conversion is necessary: humanity has to bring itself into a listening attitude toward things and learn to let them be instead of mastering them." While he was clearly still operating under Heidegger's spell, Habermas's conclusion that reason must also set certain limits on what is technically possible and most economically efficient is also compatible with Horkheimer and Adorno's critiques of instrumental reason.[52]

In contrast to his famous attack a year later, this text demonstrates not only the extent to which Habermas saw himself as a follower of Heidegger but also how limited the discussion of Heidegger's Nazism was in the West German public sphere. The same holds true for Benn and Gehlen, both important touchstones for Habermas during this period. Reflecting on their influence on his own thought in a later interview, Habermas notes: "Nobody told us about their past. We had to find out step by step for ourselves. It took me four years of studies, mostly just accidentally looking into books in libraries, to discover what they had been thinking only a decade and a half ago."[53]

Habermas's turn away from Heidegger was precipitated by his friend Karl-Otto Apel, who was working as an assistant to Rothacker while Habermas was still a student. They quickly developed a friendship based on their shared interest in the philosophy of language, which Apel encouraged Habermas to pursue. In fact, as Habermas tells it, it was Apel who brought about the collision of "two intellectual universes"—namely, "my left-leaning political convictions" and "what I was learning in philosophy courses"—when "Apel handed me a copy of Heidegger's *An Introduction to Metaphysics* hot off the press." Apel drew his attention to a passage Heidegger had reproduced verbatim from his 1935 lectures praising the "inner truth and greatness" of National Socialism. This moment marked a crucial intellectual turning point for Habermas, since "[u]ntil then, Heidegger had been my most influential teacher, if only from a distance."[54]

Habermas's attempt to come to terms with this revelation about Heidegger's lack of remorse for his support of the Nazis resulted in "Thinking with Heidegger Against Heidegger," the first major debate that Habermas incited in the German-language public sphere.[55] In the opening lines of this polemic, Habermas observes, "We are concerned here with the philosopher Martin Heidegger not as philosopher, but as a political personality." Although he recognizes that Heidegger is a great thinker—in this role he even compares him to a Hegelian "world historical individual" who "cannot be measured by moral standards"—he is concerned "not with his influence not upon the internal discussion of scholars, but upon the development of excitable and easily enthused students" like himself. To the extent that Heidegger "fosters an interpretation of genius that has the consequence of political destruction," Habermas argues that the "guardians of public criticism rightly may enter the scene."[56]

This initial statement shows that, even at this early stage, Habermas was already reflecting on the distinct roles scholars can play in society. In this respect, one can see this bifurcation as foreshadowing the distinction Habermas later develops between the philosopher and the public intellectual, outlined in chapter 1. After all, in his words, professors are "not only scholars who are concerned with public-political issues from the viewpoint of an academic observer. They are also participating citizens."[57] It is at this level that his disappointment with Heidegger becomes most apparent.

However, Habermas's critique is not confined to this. In addition to his objections to "the fatal linking of a heroic call to 'creative violence' with a cult of sacrifice," he also challenges Heidegger's devaluation of the German intellectual as a "mandarin who devalued 'intelligence' in favor of 'spirit,' 'analysis' in favor of 'authentic thought,' and wanted to reserve the esoteric truth for 'the few.' "[58] By contrast, while Habermas denies that Nazism was an "inevitable outgrowth of the German tradition," he argues that a formal, honest reckoning with the past was necessary to "explore those dispositions [at the core of the German tradition] that could lead, in a period of decay, to fascism."[59]

While Habermas is irritated by Heidegger's attack on the egalitarian spirit of the Enlightenment, visible in his praise for the "heroic individual," "the mighty one... who dares his entire essence" compared to "the timid one who seeks agreement, compromise, and mutual support [Versorgung]," he is truly offended by "the Nazi philosopher's denial of moral and political responsibility for the consequences of the mass criminality," which he simply dismisses "as a mere reflex of a higher destiny that had 'led him astray.' "[60] At this stage, Habermas is still sympathetic to Heidegger's postwar critique of technology but notes that Heidegger's support for the highly mechanized, efficient and instrumentally rationalized Nazi regime shows that Heidegger's "intent to overcome technologized life was falsified in its actual execution." As a result, Habermas concludes, "It appears to be time to think with Heidegger against Heidegger."[61]

After sharing the finished text with Wesselhoeft, Habermas sent it to Karl Korn at the *FAZ*. Korn reacted enthusiastically to this unsolicited manuscript in a letter dated June 16, 1953, but asked the young author for more information about his identity. This was important to Korn, since he anticipated having to defend Habermas during the "huge brouhaha (*gewaltigen Wirbel*)" that would inevitably follow the publication of the polemic.

Korn also offered Habermas some editorial feedback, advising him to tone down some of his more inflammatory remarks about Heidegger. Korn noted that Heidegger "neither perpetrated nor helped, nor did he legitimize" mass murder. He also found Habermas's title—"The Fascist Credo"—too denunciatory as well. He observed that even with these revisions, "everything you wanted to say remains, and remains incredibly severe." In an apparent acknowledgment that Heidegger had brought this on himself, Korn concluded, "But someone who pleaded for severity cannot act surprised if one day he encounters severity as well."[62]

In response to Korn's editorial notes, in the published version of "Mit Heidegger gegen Heidegger denken," which appeared on almost a whole page of the

FAZ's "Pictures and Times (*Bilder und Zeiten*) supplement on 25 July 1953, Habermas changed his polemical words into a critique of the "variability"—later referred to as the "turn (*Kehre*)" in the Heidegger scholarship—that he diagnoses in Heidegger's philosophical appeals from before 1945 and after.[63] The passage in question now reads, "Thus today Heidegger speaks of care [*Hut*], remembrance [*Andenken*], guardianship [*Wächterschaft*], grace [*Huld*], love, intimation [*Vernehmen*], [and] resignation [*Ergeben*], where in 1935 he demanded the violent act."[64]

As Korn had predicted, the publication of Habermas's attack on Heidegger for his failure "to admit his error with so much as *one sentence*" indeed caused a "huge brouhaha."[65] Heidegger himself did not deign to respond to Habermas, although we know that he did read the article. In a letter to his wife in August 1953 Heidegger wrote that he had "deliberately not picked up a newspaper" following this attack.[66] In a 1971 letter to former student and lover, Hannah Arendt, he also refused to have one of his texts republished in a volume she was editing because it "include[es] a text by 'Habermas,' who is now republishing his juvenile polemic published in the *FAZ* years ago."[67]

Instead of replying himself, Heidegger left the task to one of his followers, Christian Lewalter, whose defense in *Die Zeit* Heidegger subsequently endorsed in a letter to the editor. While conceding that it would indeed be contemptible for Heidegger "to rehabilitate the vile system of National Socialism philosophically, much less metaphysically," Lewalter attacks Habermas, arguing that "it would also be vile to impute such infamy to Heidegger without convincing evidence." He notes that Heidegger's political silence after 1934 made such an accusation untenable, and that seeking proof in a "lecture about metaphysics, that is, about the most abstract of all topics and the most remote from politics," is a fool's errand.[68]

The day after Lewalter's attack Korn jumped to his young author's defense with an editorial response in the *FAZ* entitled "Why Does Heidegger Stay Silent?" In it, he defended Habermas from published allegations of "baseness, dishonesty, malice, a mania for persecuting others (*Verfolgungssucht*) and—oh, the particular horror!—Marxism." While Heidegger might consider it below his dignity to engage with a twenty-four-year-old student, Korn notes that in his text "the student H. expressed not only his weariness, but the impatience of his entire generation."[69]

One month later, Korn gave Habermas the opportunity to weigh in on the controversy he had started as part of a full-page *FAZ* broadsheet of reader comments under the heading "Necessary Discussion about Heidegger (*Notwendige Diskussion über Heidegger*)." In his short response, Habermas rebutted Lewalter's accusation that he had made too much out of a single sentence in a text about metaphysics, noting that he would not have mentioned it if Heidegger's comments did "not follow directly from the lecture itself." From the context, Habermas concludes that Heidegger must have seen Nazism as a solution to—in his words—the "tragic clash of technology and man (*tragischen Zusammenprall von Technik und Mensch*)." If that was not Heidegger's view in both 1935 and 1953, Habermas argued, then he should never have allowed the lecture to be reprinted.[70]

In passing, Habermas—identified only as a "student from Bonn" in the biography that accompanied his published reply—also let it be known that his teacher was the "most esteemed (*hochverehrten*) Erich Rothacker," thus indirectly pushing back on accusations that he was a neo-Marxist whose attack on Heidegger was politically motivated. This was a shrewd move, as the philosophers in the *FAZ*'s readership at the time would have been aware of Rothacker's own collaboration with the Nazi party.

Rothacker himself appears to have been deeply unsettled by Habermas's passing comment, summoning Habermas into his office soon thereafter. Since they did not have regularly scheduled supervision meetings, Habermas was unsure what the meeting was about—even after it was over. It was Wesselhoeft who later guessed that Rothacker had been sounding him out to see if he was next on Habermas's hit list (he wasn't).[71] This impression was reinforced later that year, when Rothacker, in a *FAZ* piece on his hopes for the future, made clear his aversion to any public reckoning with his past: "I am sixty-five years old and would like to live in a country under such circumstances as would enable me to bring my research to a close without being offended and disturbed."[72]

While Habermas never publicly attacked Rothacker, he was under no illusions about the fact that "the intellectual vanguard of the old regime" had "with a few exceptions . . . survived denazification unharmed." That these old German professors "felt immune to criticism from others and saw no reason to be critical of themselves . . . kept alive fears of a relapse into the authoritarian patterns of behavior and elitist intellectual habits of a pre-democratic Germany," which in his case "persisted even into the early 1980s."[73] Given his political interests—and the fact that he did not think that an academic career was a realistic option for him—Habermas decided to pursue a career as a freelance journalist.

70 The Journalistic Years, 1951–1955

CAREER AS A FREELANCE JOURNALIST

Rothacker was not the only Bonn academic in Habermas's orbit who had been closely associated with National Socialism. Oscar Becker, the other full professor of philosophy at the university, was an avowed "Germanic-Nordic racist" who had been banned from teaching after the war but reinstated in 1951.[74] It was, ironically, a course Becker taught on the philosophy of Friedrich Wilhelm Joseph von Schelling that introduced Habermas to the thinker who would ultimately be the subject of his doctoral dissertation. Given that both of his professors at Bonn had been "intellectual giants of the 'Thousand-Year Reich'" who had not made any attempt to "philosophically reflect on the horrors of war which they had directly or indirectly experienced," it is hardly surprising that Habermas grew disillusioned with the idea of uniting his theoretical and political interests within postwar academic philosophy.[75] As Habermas would later recall in speaking of the institution of the German university at the time, "they were all Nazis there (*da waren alle Nazis*)."[76]

In 1954, Habermas completed his dissertation, *The Absolute and History: On the Ambiguity in Schelling's Thought*. Written in only nine months, the work focuses on Schelling's texts from 1809 and 1821, in which the philosopher develops his speculative "ages of the world" as a way to probe the relationship between God, the world, and humanity. Although Heidegger's notion of fundamental ontology was a crucial reference point for Habermas in this work, he concludes that despite Schelling's stated desire to break from the homocentric model in with the ego has priority over nature, Schelling ultimately remains trapped in the philosophy of the individual subject that he, like Heidegger, wishes to overcome.[77]

Ultimately, Habermas decided not to pursue an academic career, even though his dissertation had been graded as an *opus egregium* (glorious work) by his examiners.[78] Instead, he revived his earlier ambition to work as a journalist, offering commentary on important themes and developments in postwar German politics, culture, and society. This fact may explain—at least in part—why Habermas never published his dissertation.[79] Other likely contributing factors were Habermas's own lack of confidence about his conclusions, given that he had completed the work with very little supervision, and the fact that this text marks the end of the initial phase of his work before his near-total break with Heidegger and Heideggerian thinking. Additionally, given the success of his attack on Heidegger and his growing apprehension about the politics of West Germany, he might also have seen this as a choice to prioritize his politics over his scholarship. In this way, the choice was less a retreat from academia than a deliberate shift toward shaping public debate.

While devoting the next couple of years to his journalistic work, Habermas never fully abandoned his philosophical pursuits. In fact, Rothacker supported his application to the German Research Foundation (*Deutsche Forschungsgemeinschaft*, DFG) for a two-year grant to fund a project on the concept of ideology. This support not only kept the door to academia open but also supplemented his otherwise irregular income, which depended on selling articles to various newspapers.[80] The money was welcome, as Wesselhoeft, now Habermas's wife, had given birth to their first child, Tilmann, on May 17, 1956. This financial cushion meant that Habermas could pursue his journalism "according to my own inclination," at least to a certain extent.[81] While Habermas never denied his connection to his *Doktorvater* and even contributed to a *Festschrift* of essays in Rothacker's honor in 1958, it is also clear that he "did not see himself as a pupil of Rothacker in the sense of a faithful adherent."[82]

While Habermas's writings as a freelance journalist are wide-ranging, they consistently display a keen and abiding interest in the state of democracy in the nascent West German Federal Republic. His first truly political commentary appeared as a letter to the editor published on August 13, 1953, in the independent newspaper *Der Fortschritt*, titled "Democracy on the Butcher's Block."[83] In this piece, Habermas criticizes many key aspects of parliamentary democracy, including election by list, vote whipping and party discipline more broadly. He contends that these "extra-parliamentary" practices take legislative power away from the people's representatives by ensuring that the chamber's agenda is "controlled by the party apparatus and economic interest groups" instead of the members of parliament themselves. As a result, instead of serving as space for deliberation, as he believes democratic legitimacy requires, "Parliament becomes a cabinet of mirrors, where the members of parliament straddle each other in oratorical idleness (*im rednerischen Leerlauf spreizen*)."[84]

This Madisonian, predominantly negative understanding of the influence of political parties reflects Habermas's disillusionment with parties across the political spectrum of early West Germany. It also reveals his regard for the United States not only as a source of democratic ideas but as a model of good democratic practice at a time when the lack of party discipline meant that bipartisan "elastic" and "case-by-case majorities" were still common in Congress. While

Habermas accepts that representation is a necessary aspect of democracy in modern societies—where most citizens lack the time to engage in politics on a full-time basis—he argues that MPs should be selected through "public rhetorical contestation (öffentlichen Streitgespräch)" in an agonistic manner on the basis of "the binding rules of speech (im Rahmen verbindlicher Sprachregeln)," rather than "by appointment behind closed doors."[85]

While this early text foreshadows Habermas's later emphasis on public debate and his prioritization of the legislature as the guardian of democracy, the concept of a participatory informal public sphere of opinion formation that channels its conclusions into the legislature is not yet present. Instead, at this point he emphasizes deliberation within formal institutions and the fact that MPs must be able "to make decisions personally." Interestingly, he presents the way students make decisions in their internal "parliamentary forum" as an example of good democratic practice. This testifies to his longstanding interest in student politics, which will come to the fore in his public engagement in the 1960s. In words that echo his pessimistic conclusions in *Structural Transformation of the Public Sphere* (1961), he notes: "We no longer believe in the public superiority of the better argument . . . Rather we believe in the public superiority of the influential individual."[86]

While this letter to the editor focuses on the behavior of democratic political elites, Habermas's early journalism also demonstrates a growing interest in the political participation of everyday citizens. In " 'Without Me' on the Index," published in early 1955, Habermas furthers his critiques of the ruling parties for preventing the youth from expressing their opinions "in a socially relevant way." He also links his generation's political apathy to the rapid and superficial manner in which denazification was carried out, noting that "it is not dates of birth, but responsiveness that separates the minds."[87]

This piece was Habermas's contribution to a broader debate centered on the slogan "Without Me," used to mobilize opposition to Chancellor Konrad Adenauer's plan to rearm West Germany—a precondition for its accession to the North Atlantic Treaty Organization (NATO). While Adenauer and the rest of the ruling class saw youth opposition as a product of "the money the communists had spent on propaganda," Habermas argues that these reservations are rooted in a "mentality shaped by the special experiences of the totalitarian system and its collapse." Although this temperament often manifested as a retreat into private life—a tendency Habermas condemned—it also offered opportunities to those willing to dig into the "crumbly soil of a taboo past." Insofar as it signaled a "desire for a new and clean order with the insight into the unique opportunity of 1945," Habermas saw "Without Me" as an opportunity to move into a future where "nationalism has lost its vigor" and where European integration can be based on more than just a reflexive anti-communism dictated by geopolitics and "our commitment to world history."[88]

Habermas eventually published this piece in the *Deutsche Studentenzeitung* (German Student Newspaper). He had first sent it to Korn at the *FAZ*. Korn's initial reaction was positive; in his reply he wrote, " 'Without Me' made a similarly strong impression on me as your Heidegger essay did back then."[89] However, since "Ohne mich" was "really a political article," Korn, as the editor of the Feuilleton, noted that he could not take responsibility for publishing it on his own. After consulting Paul Sethe, one of the *FAZ*'s postwar cofounders and a critic of Adenauer's foreign policy, the final verdict was: "Very interesting; but impossible, of course."[90]

While Korn invited Habermas to write a new, more "fluently and more comprehensively formulated" article focusing on his generation's reserved attitude to politics, Habermas instead offered his "hot iron" to *Süddeutsche Zeitung*, which he noted was "generally 'braver' than the *FAZ* anyway."[91] However, he was turned down there as well. While the *Deutsche Studentenzeitung*—where the article ultimately appeared—was a smaller outlet, it served Habermas's purpose. The publication not only cemented his interest in student politics but also brought his name to the forefront of campus debates across the country, among both students and faculty, generating numerous letters to the editor in the paper's next edition.[92]

In "The Masses—This Is Us," a text he published in the *Handelsblatt*, Habermas seeks to rehabilitate the idea of the masses as a positive political force. While acknowledging their successful manipulation by Hitler—who saw the masses as "sluggish and cowardly (*träge und feige*)" despite their outsized support for his movement—Habermas rejects this "fallacy about the masses," as he put it in an article published a month later in the *Wiesbadener Kurier*. Pushing back against the "poison of human contempt," he argues that the masses could be more than passive objects of technical control and "social facilitation." After all, "Propaganda does not make us into the masses; we belong to the masses because we jump together to the propagandistic shepherd's pipe."[93]

Recovering a positive conception of the masses as a political force with personal responsibility and initiative would require more focus on "the educational influences on the masses" to filter any "deformed elements." Even more importantly, it requires that bourgeois citizens realize that elites include them in this concept as well: "The masses should not be confused with a mob of raw, rundown fools. The masses—they are not the others; the masses—this is us: solid, well-dressed citizens . . . not at all as uniform as we are said to be from every corner of the world." While many parties and politicians focus on manipulating the masses, Habermas argues that a truly progressive, democratic movement could win power by "focusing less on the organization of machines and more on the organization of people."[94] This focus on popular participation and on the "organization of people" anticipates many of the arguments about the communicative nature of politics Habermas will later make as well.

His growing interest in mass politics is also evident in a report Habermas wrote on an experiment about national stereotypes conducted in 1951 with students in Berlin by the Psychological Institute of Humboldt University. Published in the *Handelsblatt* under the title "Two Hundred Characteristics for Fourteen Peoples," this article also provides evidence that even at this early stage Habermas was already aware of Walter Lippmann's scholarship, as he mentions Lippmann's 1922 book on *Public Opinion* in passing. Habermas breathes "a sigh of relief" at the conclusion that such "ungrounded conceptions (*unbegründete Vorstellungen*)" are not as strongly or as widely held as is often thought. However, he is concerned by the negative views many students hold of minorities as well as the "ideological origin (*Herkunft*)" of prejudices held against "peoples behind the 'Iron Curtain' " in the now-communist east.[95]

Habermas addressed similar issues in the *FAZ* soon thereafter in a piece entitled "For and Against Testing: Opposing the Spirit of Contempt for Mankind." In this article, which was occasioned by the increasing use of psychological examinations in various industries, he came out strongly against the utility of the kind of "human engineering" (English in original) enabled by tests that measure individuals against predetermined, standardized scales that can "only determine how the subject behaves with regard to this or that thing," but cannot "really get at the essence of who the person is." According to Habermas, instead of revealing individual characteristics, such investigations only fulfill "the requirements of institutions and machines that need human material suitable for their functions"[96]

This conclusion is notable in light of existing methodological debates, where Habermas defended a position in line with the tradition of Gestalt and holistic psychology against contemporary quantitative methods imported from the United States. While his opposition to objectification is clear, his defense of continuity within German psychology is potentially problematic given his reservations about the role that the discipline and its representatives (including Philipp Lersch, Albert Wellek, and Rothacker) had played during the *Nazizeit*.[97] That said, his other publications—including the aforementioned article on national stereotypes, where Habermas reflects on the effects of 1945 on such prejudices—as well as his later association with Adorno and the Frankfurt School during the later Positivism Dispute (*Positivismusstreit*) help to allay these concerns.[98]

The correspondence contained within the Habermas Archive (Vorlass) also provides evidence for Adolf Frisé's early support for Habermas's journalism, as does the fact that he frequently published in the Düsseldorf-based *Handelsblatt*, where Frisé was the cultural editor. In "Nine Years Under the Microscope: Germany's Intellectual Development Since 1945," Habermas presents an "attempt to take stock (*Versuch einer Bilanz*)" of the situation. Although he acknowledges the "German miracle," especially in the realm of economics, Habermas notes that it "has no real luster. We live more with the feeling of a missed chance."[99]

The ostensible reason for this article was *Merkur*'s publication of an almanac, edited by Hans Paeschke and Wolfgang von Einsiedel, entitled *The German Spirit Between Yesterday and Tomorrow* (*Deutscher Geist zwischen Gestern und Morgen*). However, this merely served as a vehicle for Habermas to address how German intellectuals had failed to confront their own past. In this respect, Habermas once again compares the sterility of postwar Germany to the "explosive and idea-rich (*ideenreich*) twenties" following the Great War. He bemoans the enduring "reign (*Herrschaft*) of grand old men" who "confidently preserve the European educational tradition ... without allowing for any true confrontation." Fortunately—in Habermas's view at least—this "gerontology" is increasingly being confronted by a younger generation that is ready and able "to resist totalitarianism not only in its consequences, but also in its intellectual origins."[100]

Most of the twelve pieces Habermas published in the *Handelsblatt* during this period dealt with similar themes relating to business and economics—not surprising, given the paper's headquarters in the heart of Germany's industrial Ruhr region. Although he had not yet begun to systematically read Marx, certain Marxist themes are clearly visible in his description of the alienating effect of automation on the labor process. For example, in "The Unskilled Worker Becomes a Trained Engineer," published on May 14, Habermas reflects on the negative consequences of "professional redeployment through technology (*Berufsumschichtung durch die Technik*)." While work on a modern assembly line requires more education than in the past, this form of labor—dictated by the speed of the conveyor belt—robs employees of the ability to use their "technical skills (*fachliches Geschick*)" for self-expression: "This externally regulated form of labor dictated by mechanized production eliminates both the possibility of 'working on the entire product' and the scope (*Spielraum*) for working according to tradition and personal style: the worker can no longer 'express himself' in his work."[101] Instead of finding meaning in the fruits of personal labor, as previous generations of craftsmen could, modern engineers are tasked only with overseeing the process of production itself and repairing machinery when necessary.

In June, Habermas wrote a pair of pieces for the *Handelsblatt* on the state of modern bureaucracy. Expanding his earlier reflections, he argues that just like for blue collar workers, the work of a white collar manager is also increasingly "tied to the technical nature of the production process." The manager is the main "instrument" of this transformation and personifies "the impersonal power of the modern bureaucracy," which has been rapidly expanding even as the number of workers has remained the same. In an important modification of Marx's theory of capital, Habermas argues that contemporary society is witnessing a "seizure of power (*Machtübernahme*)," as the owners of the means of production have increasingly ceded control of their capital to managers, on whom they now also depend.

While this phenomenon is most visible in the private realm, similar developments are also discernable in public administration, where the ministerial bureaucrat plays a similar "objectivizing, formalizing . . . ethically neutralizing" role to the company manager. Foreshadowing his later critique of the bureaucratized welfare state in *Legitimation Crisis* (1973), Habermas is particularly concerned that this will lead to "rule (*Herrschaft*) by experts" at the expense of democratic political control. He concludes, "They [i.e., bureaucrats] belong to the 'State' or to the 'Company,'" noting that, given the rapidly increasing size and power of the administrative apparatus, "it will be difficult in the future to control the bureaucracy (both within state administration and in the economic realm)."[102]

This article, published on July 7, is followed by a second on the twenty-fifth, entitled "Officials (*Beamte*) Must Have Imagination (*Phantasie*)," in which Habermas reflects on how "internal checks" might address or "cure" the "weaknesses of bureaucracy" laid out above. At the turn of the century, Max Weber had already analyzed how calculation and specialization enabled gains in efficiency through hierarchically organized bureaucracy. The problem is that these gains came at the price of a loss of meaning and social cohesion, since such systems replace social relations between individuals with functional relations between offices and therefore operate "[w]ithout regard for persons."[103]

In light of this problem, Habermas asks whether "the indisputable advantages of rationalization cannot be isolated from the weaknesses and dangers inherent in it." In considering how to reassert control over bureaucracies and their managers—both in business and within the state—he focuses on the characteristic that bureaucrats share with workers: the inability to "personally express themselves" in their labor, which is increasingly regimented and governed by external rules. In contrast to ethical neutrality and distance, Habermas wants "to descriptively fill the abstract 'process' " of rule by reminding civil servants that "a face, a family, an existence lies behind every address." In this way he aims "to bind officials ethically and substantively" so that bureaucracy can function in a "socially meaningful" manner.

Habermas therefore calls on bureaucrats to develop "an inner distance to the organization," otherwise known as "civil courage (*Zivilcourage*)," that will allow them to work in the interests of concrete individuals, not that of the abstract, arbitrary (*willkürlich*) system. He argues that this can be achieved through the deployment of imagination (*Phantasie*), which can help the bureaucrat understand the actual situation—not just the case—of the person standing before them. Concretely, such a change would require officials to consider not only the internal correctness of their decisions, but also their "social effects." Such a procedure would allow "the expert maneuvers of the bureaucracy, which can hardly be controlled 'from the outside,' to gain a corrective 'from the inside.' "[104] While it is unclear if Habermas had read Herbert Marcuse's 1941 reflections on the "social implications of modern technology," his conclusions bear some similarity to Marcuse's earlier speculation that "the public bureaucracy can be a lever of democratization" insofar as it can protect "the people from the encroachment of special interests upon the general welfare."[105]

Habermas's continuing interest in music is also visible during this period. Bringing this topic into conversation with the business and economic interests of the readership of the *Handelsblatt*, in "Like on a Saturday Afternoon" (1954) Habermas examines the role of music in the workplace. He is particularly interested in how it is deployed to combat "fatigue, boredom, weariness and nervousness." While working to music and labor songs predates industrialization, the difference today is that the rhythm of work "is determined by the beat of machines." Although attempts to take advantage of the "obvious economic benefits of work music" have spread throughout the economy, "this alienation of work music from work becomes evident where it is intended to stimulate intellectual work, which is by its nature unrhythmic—in offices and at universities."[106]

Even though Habermas is writing for a business audience, he still attempts to provoke thought by undercutting conformist, instrumental treatments of art as a means of extracting more from workers. In addition to his worry that using song in this way inhibits truly " 'listening' to a piece of music," he fears that it undercuts music's emancipatory potential. While he observes that employers are becoming increasingly aware of music's ability to tap new "reserves in modern, technically mediated work," Habermas also hopes that "sources of power are still hidden in the secret connection [between work and music] today."[107]

The connections Habermas draws between the increasing deployment of background music in postwar workplaces and the latent critical potential of art not only signals affinities with Adorno that predate their meeting and collaboration but also testify to his ability to apply philosophical concepts to almost any aspect of social life, even though he claims not to have been aware of "social theory" at this point. For example, in 1954 Habermas used a summer road trip in his family's 1936 Opel—which the family called *Grauchen* ("little gray")—as an opportunity to reflect on contemporary culture as "something like a hermeneutic science (*Geisteswissenschaft*)" that requires "the constant translation of foreign texts, the anticipation of foreign worlds, styles, manners and quirks."[108]

Habermas's reflections, spurred by his recent acquisition of a driver's license, were published in the *FAZ* in November as "Driving: The Person Behind the Wheel." While Habermas recognizes the advantages in speed and efficiency enabled by driving, he also notes the alienation that this "overdetermined" and "externally regulated" mode of transport—which "turns the ground into a track and the landscape into an area"—brings about. This argument echoes the points made by Marcuse, who later became Habermas's close friend, in 1941 when he reflected on the role that the highway plays in "subordinating [the driver's] spontaneity to the anonymous wisdom which ordered everything for him." While driving has much critical potential, it is increasingly turning into "a single-purpose instrument." As a result, Habermas fears that "the car will lose not just the earth underneath but also its grip on the surface; what remains will be the 'driving lane.' "[109]

He also maintains his interest in both theater and film during this period, using them to further his critiques of the forgetfulness of postwar German society.[110] For example, in a highly polemical review of Viktor Tourjansky's film *Morgengrauen* (*Daybreak*), published by the *Süddeutsche Zeitung* at the beginning of October 1954, Habermas criticizes the "carefree attitude of a restoration that ignores facts and experiences" by "presenting the defeat in 1945 as on a par with a lost tennis match." In contrast to the silences and active forgetting of his father's generation, which was currently in power, Habermas notes the "sublime sensitivity of the younger generation vis-à-vis the inhumane consequences of collective processes." He argues that "the officially maintained mental attitude [*Bewußtseinslage*] of rehabilitation will coincide with reality again" only once this younger cohort is listened to and allowed to "find a contemporary and creative, in any case an appropriate answer."[111]

Given his academic background, Habermas also reviewed major publications and produced reports on debates at major conferences related to his research interests for leading newspapers in the FRG. In 1954, for example, he published his reactions to a number of different works, including Helmut Plessner's *Between Philosophy and Society* (*Zwischen Philosophie und Gesellschaft*), Johannes Flügge's *The Ethical Foundation of Man* (*Die sittlichen Grundlagen des Geistes*), Hans Lipps's *The Reality of Man* (*Die Wirklichkeit des Menschen*), and Bruno Brehm's *The Clone: Humanity, Animals, Dreams and Machines* (*Das Ebenbild. Menschen, Tiere, Träume und Maschinen*), as well as the German translation of Aldous Huxley's *The Doors of Perception*.[112]

In 1955, he published three more reviews. The first addressed a book by the American businessman John Diebold, entitled *Automation: The Advent of the Automatic Factory* (1952), which had recently appeared in German translation. While this review appeared in the *FAZ* in January, it is clear that Habermas had already read it and was thinking about it in 1954, as he draws on Diebold's insights about the Second Industrial Revolution in "The Dialectic of Rationalization," which appeared in mid-1954. However, whereas Diebold was optimistic about the potential of automation to "shorten the work week" as fewer laborers are needed to do the necessary "supervisory or skilled maintenance work" demanded by the automated factory, Habermas is much more skeptical about the social effects of these developments (I address this in detail below).[113]

The second, titled "The Come Back [sic] of German Sociology" ("come back" appears in English in the original), was a review essay examining Arnold Gehlen and Helmut Schelsky's *Sociology: A Text- and Handbook for Modern Social Studies*, as well as the *Dictionary of Sociology* edited by Wilhem Bernsdorf and Friedrich Bülow.[114] The authors of the former—both of whom used sociology and anthropology to think about the effects of technology in ways reminiscent of Rothackerls philosophical anthropology—were particularly important reference points for Habermas. This is evident in the fact that in 1956 Habermas also reviewed Gehlen's *Primordial Man and Late Culture* (*Urmensch und Spätkultur*). While Habermas appreciates Gehlen's attempt to bring institutions into his anthropological understanding of man as "a being defined by collected instincts, surplus drives and world-openness (*instinktenbundenes, antriebsüberschüssiges und weltoffenes Wesen*)," he is skeptical of Gehlen's attempts to apply this individualistic model to social criticism, i.e., to the contemporary "decay (*Zerfall*) of institutions."[115]

Finally, in 1955 Habermas reviewed the German Catholic philosopher Bernhard Lakebrink's new book on *Hegel's Dialectical Ontology and the Thomistic Analectic*.[116] These book reviews served many purposes. From a purely practical standpoint, these publications—along with his other articles—helped Habermas put food on the table after his doctoral stipend ran out. In the early 1950s it was possible to earn a living as a freelance journalist since newspapers paid authors a fee for all articles they published, and even quasi-academic outlets like *Merkur* gave their contributors an honorarium.[117] As Habermas pointed out in an exchange with Hans Paeschke, his editor at the aforementioned journal, his financial situation meant that "I have to pursue my journalism not only according to my own inclination; it is also subject to economic calculation."[118]

In addition to helping him pay the bills, these book reviews allowed Habermas to maintain a foothold in disciplinary debates and higher education more generally. When possible, he also reported on major academic meetings for the press.[119] For example, that summer Habermas attended a meeting of sociologists organized by the aforementioned Schelsky, who held a professorship at the University of Hamburg at the time. The other attendees—including Helmuth Plessner, Heinrich Popitz, Hans Paul Bahrdt, Karl Martin Bolte and Ralf Dahrendorf—were mostly young scholars who had come together not only to present their work but also to reflect on the academic climate of the time and their chances of obtaining full-time university positions.[120]

This meeting was important because Habermas would go on to develop close relationships with a number of other participants, including Schelsky, Plessner, and Dahrendorf. In what may reflect either Habermas's view of the meeting's importance or his need for money, he wrote two reports of this small conference—one for the *Handelsblatt*, the other for the *FAZ*. In the latter, entitled "Up-and-Coming Sociologists Introduce Themselves," he noted an increasing "rationalization of higher education (*Rationalisierung der Hochschulpraxis*)," in which outsiders like himself who were "formerly the heart of the university, will only be 'allowed in' with difficulty" as the entire system was increasingly organized "as a ladder with rungs... according to seniority."[121]

Habermas's report also reflects his dismay that the next generation of young sociologists seemed to ignore important questions about class conflicts within society, which he took as evidence of "a conformist attitude towards the compulsions and attainments of technological progress."[122] These conclusions help to explain why Habermas would later be willing to take an unpaid position as Adorno's assistant: it would allow him to pay his dues and get his foot on the academic ladder. They also show that Habermas's interest in the organization of higher education, which come out most strongly in his activist stance in the 1960s, has deep roots in his thought.

In October of that same year Schelsky invited Habermas to attend a workshop organized by *Der Bund* in Wuppertal, in which he reported that the "impulses of the immediate postwar years, namely the striving for spiritual and social renewal, still lives." The focus of this ninth meeting of "The Association" was "The Consumption of Culture and the Culture of Consumption (*Kulturkonsum und Konsumkultur*)."[123] This theme spoke to Habermas's interests and he even delivered a paper of his own titled "Notes on the Imbalance (*Mißverhältnis*) Between Culture and Consumption." While the original manuscript does not survive, Habermas published a paper under this title in *Merkur* in 1956.[124] In the later, reworked version of this argument he contends that the "externally controlled system of habits of consumption" create a "simple representation of the status quo on the surface and a prohibition on making the real transparent in terms of its possibilities."[125]

His report for the *Handelsblatt* focuses on the controversy that erupted at the height of the conference between those, "who conservatively believed in a stable balance between good and bad and therefore simply attributed the demonstrable damage [of contemporary developments] to the 'functional mode of industrial society,' and those on the other side who still had enough utopian spark to search for radical methods of healing." Although Arnold Gehlen was the key representative of the former position, Günther Anders, whose paper set off the dispute, was the leader of the latter. Habermas does not explicitly take sides in this debate. However, his articles makes clear that his sympathies lay with Hannah Arendt's first husband, who argued that the "deforming effects of radio and television" extended to factual reporting about court proceedings, parliamentary debates, and soccer matches. As a result of the cutting and editing necessary for media broadcasts, "the customer obtains realistic templates in place of reality and becomes incapable of forming real experiences."[126]

This meeting also allowed Habermas to cement his relationship with Paeschke, whom he met in person for the first time in Wuppertal.[127] The fact that he became a frequent contributor to *Merkur*—the "German Journal for European Thought"—in its aftermath provides further evidence that Habermas was not prepared to completely cut ties with academia. In fact, in 1955 Habermas's journalistic production declined by more than half, as he began to write more articles for this quasi-academic journal. Fortunately, he was able to make good use of the research he conducted for his public-facing work, as the articles published in *Merkur* during this period often drew on themes Habermas had already explored in his journalism.

In 1954, Habermas published his first—and probably most influential—early article in *Merkur*. Entitled "The Dialectic of Rationalization: On Pauperism in Production and Consumption," it is one of the few articles from this period that has been republished, albeit in a pirated, unauthorized edition.[128] Although it is a scholarly rather than a journalistic or public-facing political article, it is important because it draws together and builds on ideas from his journalism on the sociology of labor and industrial relations. It also represents Habermas's first substantive, scholarly engagement with Karl Marx's critique of capitalism and drew the attention of influential scholars in Germany to the young thinker. While he agrees with Marx that modern, routinized, increasingly automated forms of production drive the alienation of worker, Habermas argues that Marx's framework overlooks the crucial role consumption plays in this process of estrangement. More specifically, Habermas argues that "the pauperism of industrial labor is infectious and carried over to mass consumption."[129]

Habermas uses the term pauperism (*Pauperismus*) in this context to designate the class-based nature of the material, spiritual, cultural and intellectual impoverishment produced by "machine culture" on both the supply (production) and demand (consumption) sides of market relations. His empirical starting point is the observation that increases in material prosperity and standards of living are accompanied by ever greater alienation—not only in the workplace but also at home. While the effects of automation were initially restricted to production, where they turned artisans who once created entire products themselves into overseers (*Überwachter*) of machines, similar "hygienic processes" of specialization and "technological rationalization" gradually spread throughout the entire economy via both vertical and horizontal integration of companies. Finally, in a third step of "social rationalization," the introduction of "scientific management" was applied to management through "Human Relations," as well as to the state and society as a whole, where everyone had to learn and behave in line with "*the one best way*."[130] Using a phrase copied almost verbatim from the aforementioned study of music in the workplace, "Like on a Saturday Afternoon," Habermas concludes that in all areas of life "our world is determined by the beat of machines."[131]

The results of the contagion of machine culture become visible precisely in the spread of pauperism from production—where it creates the conditions for greater material well-being—to consumption, where its effects are expressed as "insecurity, helplessness, forlornness (*Verlorenheit*), depression, and disorientation." The basic problem, according to Habermas, is that it is hard for workers to break the alienated habits ingrained in them during eight-hour workdays during their free time. Although they try to separate work from the rest of their lives through the idea that "'life' first begins with free time, begins at home," this separation is unsustainable, as the pathologies of production infiltrate their existence outside of work through their participation in consumption. What Marx refers to as this "dual life" of individuals is unsustainable, because the need to sell the mass goods produced in the workplace leads to an increasing "mobilization of needs (*Bedarf*)" in which "artificially stimulated needs (*Bedürfnisse*) take the place of customs."[132]

This highlights the connection between work and needs, between pauperism and consumption. Habermas traces this to the desire for a broader, socially enforced need to "*keep up with the Jones* [sic, original in English]," which demonstrates the falseness of desires stimulated by the need to consume. As workers lose "the proper relation to 'things' ('*Dinge*')," which "takes away their face" and makes things into "anonymous factors" used for benefit and exchange, people increasingly begin to regard one another in a very non-Kantian manner—as things or tools, mere means to their own ends. The result is a "creeping alienation . . . [that]

originates simply in the fact that all contacts, first physical and then essential, become brittle."[133]

Habermas would later observe that "The Dialectic of Rationalization" already contained "the kernel of much of what I later came to write in *The Theory of Communicative Action*."[134] For example, his point about the migration of machine culture—and the processes of rationalization it entails—is reminiscent of the arguments he would later make about the "colonization of the lifeworld" by systems of power and money that operate with independent logics of their own.[135] While economics and administration—two preoccupations that appear repeatedly in his freelance journalism—are not illegitimate per se, they become pathological when they overstep their boundaries and "infect" all areas of life.

While the technological rationalization of production was originally meant to "to create space for that which develops independently [autochthonously] and not automatically," in the "Dialectic of Rationalization" Habermas already concludes that its overexpansion into culture, society, politics, and leisure has the opposite effect. His later argument about the need to protect the lifeworld—i.e., the space of social and cultural reproduction—from colonization by the anonymous, autopoietic (self-reproducing) forces of the system is thus anticipated by his 1954 claim that "what is necessary is clearly a kind of equilibrium between forms of rationalization that each limit the other in opposing directions." It is only by blocking off certain areas of life from the "machine culture" of rationalization that humanity can prevent the "instrumental (*zweckrationale*), controlled operations" from becoming "perverted into totally aimless action."[136]

The fact that Habermas references instrumental rationality (*Zweckrationalität*) in this article not only demonstrates his familiarity with Max Weber, who popularized this term, it also signals certain preexisting affinities to Adorno and the rest of the Frankfurt School, which was also preoccupied with the spread of instrumental reason to all areas of life. In a similar argument that Habermas could not have been familiar with at this time, Adorno also observes that "human needs are not natural but historical, the products of class rule."[137] However, Habermas's substantial debt to Heidegger and Rothacker is more clearly visible at this early stage. For example, Habermas references Rothacker's notions of lifestyle (*Lebensstil*) and stance/posture/attitude/bearing (*Haltung*) to criticize how the West has elevated and exported a valorization of "making available (*Verfügbarmachen*)" around the world.[138]

Habermas explicitly notes that he is using the word thing (*Ding*) in a Heideggerian sense to designate objects that "get lost . . . when they degenerate into simple 'orderable inventory,' " becoming "inconspicuous and devoid of any *Dasein* of the own."[139] His analysis of how the objects of production and consumption turn into mere "things" recalls Heidegger's analysis of the impoverished existence of objects that are merely "present-to-hand (*zuhanden*)," used by forgetful, unaware individuals as equipment, rather than being allowed to "shine forth" in their actual Being (*Dasein*) as by individuals who are aware of their real, ontological existence and treat them as "present-at-hand (*vorhanden*)" in their actual being.[140] In Habermas's words, such *zuhanden* objects "allow the person, who is using them, to forget, that they actually are something."[141]

This text, which appeared in *Merkur* in August 1954, was not the first that Habermas had sent to this outlet. However, while his previous submissions had been rejected, this time both Joachim Moras and Hans Paetschke reacted enthusiastically, with the latter assuring Habermas that "we see in your work one of the most intensive contributions that have reached us recently."[142] In fact, this text marked the beginning of a long and fruitful relationship between Habermas and Paetschke, who worked as his primary editor at the journal that was Habermas's primary outlet for academic articles through the 1960s.

"The Dialectic of Rationalization" generated quite a ruckus after its publication—much more so than any of Habermas's later contributions to *Merkur*. For example, Schelsky wrote to Habermas in December to express his interest in Habermas's argument. In January of that same year, Schelsky had published a piece summarizing the latest scholarship on technical progress, so he was familiar with the topic. While he noted that "it is difficult to deal with these issues in writing," he was eager to have a conversation with Habermas about it at the earliest opportunity.[143] His interest in Habermas's piece might well have been a result of the fact that despite their differing theoretical foundations, both "recognize a system-theoretical approach as legitimate and indispensable for an understanding of modern society, but at the same time insist on the necessity of other approaches as well."[144]

Although it was never published, Schelsky later wrote a "Response to Jürgen Habermas," which runs over 160 pages. In it, he engages with the dichotomy between the human being and the system described above—a theme central to Habermas's later thought. Schelsky sees this valorization of concrete community, contrasted with an abstract, undertheorized conception of society, as highly problematic. Noting the affinities between this position and that of Adorno, he concludes:

> If there is something like a "Frankfurt School" of "critical theory" at all, then this identification of a bourgeois-romantic with a Marxist-humanist critique of contemporary time would have to be considered one of its characteristics; we would need to emphasize, though, that Habermas formulated this position very early on and before he had any contact with "Frankfurt," although it allowed him to make "Frankfurt" his home later.[145]

Schelsky was not the only established intellectual so struck by Habermas's argument that he wrote to *Merkur*'s editors inquiring about their young author.[146] On February 24, 1955, Moras wrote to Habermas to inform him that "Mr. Adorno has just told us in a letter that your essay on the dialectic of rationalization has been of great interest to him, and although he does not agree with the basic position, he found that some aspects were presented in an extraordinarily original and productive way."[147]

Although Habermas would later deny that his argument was influenced by the *Dialectic of Enlightenment*, noting that his reading of the chapter on the "Culture Industry" had "only tacitly . . . directed and enriched" his work, there are distinct similarities between the two, even though they draw on very different sources.[148] Perhaps the biggest difference is that while Horkheimer and Adorno locate the problems of instrumental reason deep in the Enlightenment and in European civilization going back to ancient Greece, Habermas's argument is somewhat more optimistic. He concludes: "Not prophets and better people, but the general contemporary recognition of insights is needed to put an end to this socially irrational process and its inherent pauperism."[149]

Although Habermas never followed up on Adorno's inquiry to Moras, at the end of 1955 Frisé, his editor at the *Handelsblatt*, saw his potential and offered to put him in touch with Adorno. When Habermas responded with "a halfhearted 'yes, if you like,'" Frisé took the initiative and approached Adorno. To his surprise, Adorno was already aware of Habermas and immediately expressed his interest in meeting the young Habermas.[150]

At Frisé's urging, on December 13, 1955, Habermas wrote to Adorno, thanking him for suggesting that he apply for an open entry-level position in sociology at

Würzburg—an opportunity Habermas had described in a previous article as part of the university's "lower middle class." Although Habermas did end up applying, he notes, "I would prefer to complete my education together with experienced researchers. What I want to do is to make a connection . . . to empirical social research."[151] He concludes by asking Adorno for his advice, on how he might achieve this goal.

Adorno's eagerness is visible in the fact that he responds on December 14, 1955, likely the same day he received Habermas's letter. He immediately takes up Habermas's request by inviting Habermas to join him at the Institute for Social Research (*Institut für Sozialforschung*) in a "vocational placement," even though no paid position was currently open. Such a post would allow Habermas to educate himself in "empirical social research" with the goal of obtaining full-time employment, which would require Horkheimer's agreement as director. Before concluding by once again praising Habermas's essay on "pseudo-consumption (*Scheinkonsum*)," Adorno immediately asks Habermas to come and visit him at the Institute on Friday, January 6 and even offers to cover Habermas's travel costs from Bonn.[152]

While there is no record of Habermas's first meeting with Adorno on January 6, 1956, it apparently went well. Based on the correspondence contained within the Habermas Vorlass, it appears that Adorno gave Habermas a manuscript copy of his "On the Problem of the Family," to which Habermas responded in a letter dated January 15. Habermas opens his commentary on Adorno's theses—which brings together themes from the Institute's 1936 *Studies on Authority and the Family*—by noting that he agrees with Adorno's argument that "the apparent regeneration of the family conceals an actual regression."[153]

However, Habermas continues by noting that in his opinion the crisis of the family is not just due to the "pressure of the war and its consequences," but also to "reprivatization" of the family, which is no longer "the power center of survival." Combined with the growing "mistrust of the abstract organization of a highly rationalized and increasingly unmanageable society," the increasing push for individual consumption (described in the "Dialectic of Rationalization"), and a weariness of with politics and other collective enterprises (visible most notably in the popular slogan "Without me [*Ohne mich*]"), the result is that groups of all kinds, including the family, are increasingly being pulled apart. The fact that Habermas is able to draw on so many of the arguments from his various journalistic publications in expressing "my interest in your work" to Adorno highlights

88 *The Journalistic Years, 1951–1955*

the preexisting affinities in their interests and conclusions—affinities that are often overlooked.[154]

After exchanging a few more letters, on January 20 Habermas agreed to join Adorno at the Institute, where he would become Adorno's first personal assistant. While this position was initially unpaid, Habermas could—at least initially—rely on his scholarship from the German Research Foundation to study the concept of ideology.[155] Adorno also proposed several projects for Habermas at the Institute, including commissions, such as a review of the recent literature on Schelling that would include a Marxist component. Habermas agrees, noting that he is prepared to take on this project since "over the last six months I have consumed—more than enjoyed—the Marxist primary literature on a great scale."[156] He also highlights his excitement about joining the research team at the Institute after the relative isolation of his time as a freelance correspondent. After all, "even and especially if every now and then you get lost in journalism, you are still basically quite isolated."[157]

A few days later, on January 26, Adorno finally replied to Habermas's letter and his decision to come to the Institute. "I am happy from the bottom of my heart that you are coming and I sincerely hope that our relationship will be productive and will live up to its full potential. I also informed Mr. Horkheimer of our connection and he is as pleased as I am."[158] On February 15, 1956, Habermas arrived at the Institute for Social Research, thus beginning his apprenticeship in both empirical social research and critical theory. While this did not signal the end of his work as a journalist, it was the first step toward bringing his political and philosophical interests together. Yet his mature conception of the relationship of theory to practice—as well as of the public intellectual as such—is still a long way off.

CONCLUSION

This chapter focused on Habermas's university studies and his time as a freelance journalist. After presenting a brief biography of his early life and student years, I detailed not only the topics and themes he addressed in his early journalism but also how this work helped attract the attention of Adorno at the Institute in Frankfurt. Since these texts are largely unknown and have, for the most part not been republished, they offer a valuable new perspective on Habermas's early intellectual development.

This material is also important because a powerful strand in the literature on the Frankfurt School pits "the 'good' Adorno against the 'bad' Habermas," portraying the latter's revisions to the former's approach to critical theory as "an insidious ruse."[159] By contrast, my reading of Habermas's earliest publications reveals three key philosophical interests that he shares with Adorno: 1) a concern about technology in work and consumption, 2) fears regarding the continuities between the FRG and the *Nazizeit*, and 3) a turn to art and culture for liberation and critique. My interpretive argument, which draws on texts Habermas produced before his first meeting with Adorno in 1956 and highlights the importance of this meeting for both at the time, does not "foreshorten the past" but instead enriches our understanding of it while also increasing our understanding of the present.[160]

As a result, within the presentist methodology guiding this study, it is clear that Habermas's journalism from 1951 to 1956 holds important, often overlooked implications for how we conceptualize his relationship to Adorno and the rest of the Frankfurt School. These texts are particularly valuable for elucidating why Habermas was drawn to Adorno (and vice versa). The material presented in this chapter also demonstrates why it is a mistake to link Habermas's work primarily to Horkheimer's or to accuse him of having "modeled [his philosophy] on Horkheimer's view of critical theory."[161] While the late Horkheimer opposed Habermas's activism, Adorno supported him as an academic seeking to engage in debates in the public sphere, as the following chapter will make clear.[162]

Although Habermas's journalism was clearly important to both his later academic work and his subsequent political activities, these public-facing texts differ from his later public interventions in a number of important respects. Most notably, unlike the public intellectual—who pursues social criticism in the public sphere as a *Nebenberuf* (secondary vocation) and can claim the "privilege of having to deal with public issues only as a sideline" due to financial independence—Habermas in 1954 and 1955 wrote at least partly out of "economic calculation," the money from his ideology scholarship notwithstanding.[163] Since journalism was his *Beruf* during this period, these pieces—although they are public-facing and appear in many of the same outlets as Habermas's later political writings—cannot truly be considered the work of a public intellectual.

In this sense, Habermas's journalism represents an important stage in his career that predates the separation thesis, allowing for significant overlap between his academic interests (which were, in a sense, his *Nebenberuf* at this time) and his work for a broader audience. This position stands in marked contrast to much of the existing literature, which regards these early writings as irrelevant because they predate his connection to the Frankfurt School. Habermas has contributed to this oversight by referring to his early journalistic works as "youthful sins," most likely because many engage Heideggerian themes and predate his turn toward social theory. However, despite this characterization, this chapter has shown that the seventy articles Habermas wrote before joining the Institute are crucial to the intellectual history of critical theory. They not only explain how Habermas came to be associated with the Frankfurt School, but also reveal the intellectual affinities that led Adorno to hire Habermas as his personal assistant in 1956.[164]

Despite the important differences between his journalism and later writings as a public intellectual, interesting parallels emerge between these two stages of Habermas's work. Thematically, many of his core interests remain the same: his emphasis on and support for student politics and the importance of public participation in politics, critique of the dangerous legacies of Nazism in postwar West Germany, rejection of nationalism, and interest in the politics of memory, to name just a few. More generally, in contrast to those who see Habermas as a quietist, apolitical thinker whose work "finds peace within itself" and thus "has nothing to do with critical theory," his early journalism and its thematic connections to his later theoretical work reveal that this is not the case.[165]

For example, Stefan Müller-Doohm, Habermas's biographer and one of the few scholars to engage with some of these texts, contends that "in his early journalistic work, he was hesitant to draw political conclusions or to make political statements."[166] My detailed engagement with these texts in this chapter challenges this conclusion. On the contrary, as I have shown, Habermas's newspaper articles on collective memory, trauma, work, technology and consumption in the early to mid-1950s frequently contain strong political statements and often address explicitly political topics. Moreover, these texts demonstrate how Habermas sought to integrate his political and philosophical interests from the very beginning of his career.

Building on the arguments presented here, the next chapter traces the development of Habermas's public engagement during his initial tenure at the

Institute. Freed from the financial pressures that had compelled him to produce journalistic texts regularly to support his young family, his public-facing publications slow considerably. Nevertheless, he continues to think about the relationship between theory and practice, albeit from a more academic perspective. As I will show, it is during this period that Habermas begins to think philosophically *about* the public sphere and its role in modern democratic life. This project culminates in the publication of *The Structural Transformation of the Public Sphere* in 1962 and sheds light on his activist tendencies more broadly—tendencies that also explain his departure from the Institute in 1959 due to Horkheimer's opposition. This next period thus not only sets the stage for his later interventions as a public intellectual but also for his academic career as a theorist of the public sphere and for his mature philosophical understanding of the relationship between theory and practice.

CHAPTER 3

At the Institute for Social Research, 1956–1959

As documented in the previous chapter, Adorno's invitation for Habermas to join him at the Institute for Social Research in Frankfurt am Main arrived at a pivotal moment, both personally and professionally. Habermas had initially "wanted to be done with philosophy (*mit der Philosophie Schluss machen wollte*)" after finishing his PhD, since this path did not seem able to offer him the opportunity to "fulfill my interest in the enlightenment of our situation" in West Germany. The opportunity to work with Adorno rekindled his philosophical engagement and prompted him to seriously consider the possibility of pursuing a university professorship for the first time.[1] In the wake of this move, Habermas's journalistic production understandably declined as he focused increasingly on academic work, which also helped secure external grants to fund his unpaid position in Frankfurt.

Despite the fact that he was now engaged in his on-the-job training in sociology, Habermas maintained a keen interest in the political, cultural, and social development of the early Federal Republic of West Germany. As he later reflected, "I consider it a lucky circumstance that, back in the 1950s and 1960s . . . [I] experienced the most important period in postwar German history in Frankfurt and Hesse [the *Bundesland* in which Frankfurt am Main is located] in a climate of compressed contemporaneity."[2] Although Habermas notes that these controversies took place "in a milieu that was intellectually stimulating and irritating in equal measure," he concludes, "In retrospect, these were the most intense years of my adult life."[3]

As Jewish émigrés who had been forced to leave their homelands and later chose to return, Horkheimer and Adorno stood at the center of debates "over the orientation that the political mentality of the Federal Republic should take."[4]

Beyond their broader significance for West Germany, Habermas observes, "After their return to the homeland that had expelled them, Jewish emigrants became irreplaceable teachers for a younger generation." In a statement that summarizes his view of the German cultural and philosophical heritage after 1945, he notes, "Who if not those who had been 'racially discarded' . . . could have developed a sharper sensibility for the dark elements . . . of our morally corrupt traditions?"[5]

Before I proceed, I would briefly like to reflect on the social and political context of the West German public sphere in the mid-1950s. By the 1980s, Germany had become known for its open memory culture and vibrant public sphere—in part due to Habermas's own activism—but this was not the case in the 1950s. As Habermas notes in *Structural Transformation*, which he was writing during this period, although Kant and other German thinkers were crucial in developing the concept of publicity and the public sphere, the historically divided German territories did not have a strong tradition of "parliamentary life" in the nineteenth century. Consequently, "the public's rational-critical debate of political matters took place predominantly in the private gatherings of the bourgeoisie."[6] While open and democratic debate did take place during the interwar years in the liberal Weimar Republic, the practices established during this brief interlude were quickly quashed by twelve years of Nazi dictatorship and the country's subsequent occupation and division.

In light of these considerations, the public sphere that Habermas was inserting himself into in the 1950s "was perhaps democratic in name only." While the West German Basic Law established the foundations for an open public sphere, the main political players prioritized anti-communism and the rebuilding of state capacity in the geopolitical context of the early Cold War, rather than on the creation of a democratic culture. As a result, in its early years the Federal Republic's public sphere was defined more by its silences and a clear "*cordon sanitaire* around Nazi crimes," which was maintained in both the private and the public spheres.[7]

These broader cultural trends were reinforced by the fact that the leading media in postwar Germany were dominated by individuals who had supported the Nazi regime. Certain figures, including Karl Jaspers, Dolf Sternberger, and Hannah Arendt—as well as Adorno himself—indeed condemned the indifference of the Germans public to their historical responsibility and expressed concern over the continuities between the fascist past and the supposedly democratic present in the late 1940s and 1950s.[8] However, as Habermas himself experienced during his studies, most professors sought to conceal and suppress their activities under the Third Reich.

These intellectuals were supported in this endeavor by publishers and editors of newspapers and cultural programs, many of whom had themselves been collaborators. In fact, in 2025—long after his death in 2002—it emerged that Siegfried Unseld, the long-time publisher of Surhkamp Verlag, with whom Habermas worked closely and which has published the vast majority of his work, had himself been a member of the Nazi Party. When asked for his reaction, Habermas noted that he was unaware of this but also questioned whether "this circumstance really plays a role in assessing this man's life's work."[9] Although this example shows that it often took even longer for the details of individual cases to emerge, it was not until the 1960s that democratization and collective memory emerged as subjects of broad public debate.

As I documented in the previous chapter, Habermas's reaction to this state of affairs is clearly visible in a number of his journalistic works. In this sense, his decision to become a journalist is in line with his later observation that it is "this capacity to get irritated which turns scholars into intellectuals."[10] After arriving at the Institute, Habermas fully embraced the opportunity to explore the "variant of Hegelian Marxism developed further in the 1920s with the help of Max Weber's sociology of bureaucracy," a tradition revived in Germany by "the Frankfurt Institute of Social Research, in the final analysis in the person of Adorno." Building on his 1953 attack on Heidegger and his growing skepticism toward the dominant currents of phenomenology, existentialism, and philosophical anthropology that had survived the Nazi *Gleichschaltung* (coordination) of the German university system, Habermas credits these Jewish exiles who had been "magnanimous enough to return to the country that had driven them out" for helping him to learn how "to distinguish the traditions that are worthy of being continued from a corrupt intellectual heritage." As a result, he argues that "the political culture of the old Federal Republic owes the hesitant progress it made in civilizing its attitudes in good, perhaps decisive, part to Jewish emigrants."[11]

The philosophical tradition Habermas encountered at the Institute was not only based on texts he had never before encountered and untainted by the historical legacies of National Socialism; it also carried "academic controversies [that] also had political connotations from the beginning."[12] As a result, Habermas enjoyed the freedom to pursue scientific topics related to his political interests. Whereas previously he had "found the key to modernity in the visual arts, especially painting," his affiliation with the Frankfurt School opened "a new universe . . . a world of completely unexpected, fascinating colors and shapes that revolutionized my previous perception of the world."[13]

In retrospect—and for the purposes of this study—Habermas's initial stay at the Institute between 1956 and 1959 is important for two main reasons. First, working with Adorno allowed Habermas to observe how his new mentor helped build the public sphere of the newly created West Germany by using "the reputation of his scientific position to vehemently warn the public of the afterlife of national socialism." Despite the generational divide that separates Adorno as "the philosopher of the holocaust [sic]" from Habermas's "post-holocaust philosophy," Müller-Doohm points out that for both, "the catastrophic history of the century of extremes is the background that informs their philosophy" and their broader intellectual practice.[14] In this sense, it is hardly an exaggeration to say that during his time with Adorno at the Institute, Habermas was introduced to the role of the public intellectual—a new perspective that would allow him to move beyond his previous identity as a journalist.

Second, by allowing him to think about the same themes in both his political and his academic writings, the tradition of critical theory gave Habermas the tools he needed to think sociologically and philosophically *about* the public sphere and its role in modern democratic life; he was no longer "just" a journalist writing *for* the general reading public. As he would later point out, "Critical social theory offered me a perspective from which I could embed the emergence of American, French, and English democracy, and the repeated failure of attempts to establish democracy in Germany, in the larger context of social modernization."[15] Both in terms of its theme and its substantive arguments, Habermas's first major academic project following his doctoral dissertation—*Structural Transformation of the Public Sphere* (1962)—was thus driven in important ways by his preexisting political concerns. This book, which Habermas recently noted has "remained my most successful to date," is a powerful example of a case in which Habermas's political interests and engagement drive him to develop important themes in his philosophical work.[16]

Although Habermas's production of political writings decreases during this period, it does not stop completely. In working through the public-facing essays that he did produce, I highlight the overlooked importance of Habermas's early thought on democracy, his critiques of the memory politics of West Germany and the importance of his reading of the *Staatslehre* (state or constitutional theory) for his later development. I argue that this material—together with Habermas's early political interventions—helps explain his consistent commitment to prioritizing the legislature over the executive and judicial branches, since the legislature is the institution most responsive to the rational opinion-formation of regular citizens within the public sphere.[17] I conclude by reflecting on how Habermas's activist tendencies and interest in public engagement led to his departure from Frankfurt in 1959 due to objections from Max Horkheimer.

In contrast to Adorno, who supported Habermas as both an academic and a public intellectual, Horkheimer saw Habermas's desire to affect actual social and political change as dangerous given the political climate of the early Cold War. As a result, Habermas was forced to leave the Institute in 1959. Fortunately, he continued to receive Adorno's support and was starting to make a name for himself more generally, which enabled him to advance his academic career (his *Hauptberuf*)—a precondition for his *Nebenberuf* (secondary vocation) as a public intellectual.

ARRIVAL AT THE INSTITUTE

After arriving at the Institute for Social Research in February 1956, Habermas initially continued to publish journalistic articles. His decision to join Adorno, who spoke "with the voice of a victim in the land of the perpetrator," was at least partially driven by the "conviction that a philosophical explanation of the historical origins of fascism and totalitarianism could most likely be found there." As a result, Habermas's writings at this time continue to engage with West Germany's silencing of the recent past.[18]

In the context of this commitment, Habermas chose to review Margret Boveris's *Betrayal in the Twentieth Century* (*Verrat im 20. Jahrhundert*) for the *German University Newspaper*. In her book, Boveris—who had worked for newspapers affiliated with the Third Reich during World War II and had accepted the Nazi War Merit Medal (*Kriegsverdienstmedaille*) in 1941—sought to relativize the idea of treason by arguing that the labels of hero and traitor were merely the caprice of the "wheel of history (*Rad der Geschichte*)." Understandably, Habermas was not convinced by this argument, seeing it as representative of a "militant anti-Enlightenment" attitude that he associated with "young conservatives (*Jungkonservativen*)."[19]

He also continued to publish in *Merkur*. Most of these pieces are reviews of philosophical and sociological literature that drew his interest.[20] For example, in light of his new affiliation, Habermas took the opportunity to review Walter Dirks and Max Horkheimer's edited volume *The Responsibility of the University*. He highlighted Horkheimer's conclusion that students should be taught to "practice a combination of critical examination of the facts and productive imagination (*Phantasie*)," which does not have to "wait for the initiative for action, including for political action, to come from others. Every theory contains an affective moment."[21] While Habermas's activist tendencies—especially in regard to student politics—would later bring him into conflict with Horkheimer, this publication makes it clear that he was trying to connect his thought to that of the entire Frankfurt School —and not just that of Adorno—during this period.[22]

As a result of his new affiliation, Habermas also began to engage more substantively with both psychoanalysis and Sigmund Freud, a central figure for the Frankfurt School. He was given the opportunity to immerse himself in this material during a lecture series commemorating Freud's centenary, hosted by the Institute in collaboration with Alexander Mitscherlich, a Heidelberg-based psychoanalyst who would later become the first director of the Sigmund Freud Institute in Frankfurt. On May 7—just one day after the opening event held on Freud's one hundredth birthday—Habermas published the first in a series of reviews, titled "Freud—the Enlightener." Writing in the Frankfurter Allgemeine Zeitung (*FAZ*), he highlighted the importance of the event for both Germany and Frankfurt, especially given that Freud had been driven out of the city and declared *persona ingrata* by the Nazis soon after receiving the Goethe prize in 1930. Habermas further noted the presence of both the President of West Germany, Theodor Heuss, and the *Bundesland* (province) of Hessen, Georg August Zinn, at this event and praised the presentations of the two organizers and the analyst Erik H. Erikson on the psychoanalytic method.[23]

A week later, Habermas published a shortened version of his initial report in the Basel-based *National-Zeitung* under the title "Germany Rehabilitates Freud." This piece, written for a foreign audience, highlighted the fact that he considered it to be "one of the most difficult and not always dignified tasks" of West Germany "to clarify its relationship to its own historical past, especially through those men whose image a confused tradition has blurred or which political narrow-mindedness has defaced."[24] These "brilliant lectures," which Habermas later described as having "broke[n] like an intellectual flash flood from a foreign world over the early Federal Republic," made a great impression on him and in his opinion "provided initial sparks for momentous advances in the political culture of the Federal Republic."[25]

Over the course of this event, Habermas would go on to publish reports on the lectures given by two other notable attendees: René A. Spitz, one of the pioneers of infant psychology; and Eduardo Krapf, a researcher who had been deported from both Nazi Germany and Peronist Argentina and who proposed a collaborative relationship between psychoanalysis and Christianity. Habermas concluded his series with a final piece on the contributions by Franz Alexander, Hans Zulliger, and Herbert Marcuse.[26] While this final essay mentions all three figures, and Alexander's observation regarding the "banning of psychoanalysis in totalitarian states" confirms Habermas's thesis about the importance of these lectures for the postwar West, it is nevertheless Marcuse who takes center stage.[27]

Habermas reports that his first meeting with Marcuse was "a revelation" for a number of reasons. First, Marcuse brought "the political aspect" of the current situation into his theoretical lecture in a way that showed Habermas how his own political and philosophical interests could be combined. As Habermas would later point out, "Marcuse was the only one [of the first generation of the Frankfurt School] who held fast (*festhalten*) to the old theory—even politically."[28] Second, Marcuse made this political connection through an analysis of the paradox of the present, where rising production and consumption were accompanied by the feeling of loss and scarcity. He resolved this issue, which was also a key concern of many of Habermas's own journalistic publications as well as of the "Dialectic of Rationalization," by arguing that increasing libidinal repression had resulted in a new form of domination (*Herrschaft*) that caused individuals "to behave in a world of abundance as in a world of want."

Finally, Marcuse provided Habermas with the theoretical combination he had been searching for since his days as a student, i.e., "that miraculous transformation of an early Marxist philosophy of history into the vocabulary of Freud's teaching."[29] In particular—and in contrast to his earlier comment to Adorno regarding the fact that he "consumed, rather than enjoyed" Marx—Marcuse's interpretation was an inspiration for Habermas. Despite the love of literature visible in his early journalism, Habermas is now able to say that "I was more interested in Marx and Engels than Tolstoy."[30] This change of heart is also visible in a seventy-page

"Report on the Philosophical Discussion of Marx and Marxism" published by Habermas in the *Philosophischer Rundschau*.[31]

This realization not only resulted in a life-long friendship with Marcuse; it also provided Habermas with the inspiration for his later *Knowledge and Human Interests* (1968) in which he identifies the self-reflection enabled by psychoanalysis as a possible source of liberation from the contemporary condition.[32] For Habermas, this conference—and Marcuse's lecture in particular—demonstrated the effect that "the intellectual translation of scientific work can have on public discourses."[33] His attempts to identify the proper approach for such translation would include a number of other models until he finally developed his notion of the public intellectual in the early 1980s.

EDUCATION POLICY AND POSTWAR ACADEME

Habermas continued to write for newspapers throughout his career, but his journalistic output begins to taper off after 1956. During his time at the Institute, Adorno—who was himself one of the leading public intellectuals of West Germany—provided Habermas with a model for integrating his philosophical and political interests.[34] Although Habermas's self-understanding at this time was still divided between the roles of academic and journalist, Adorno demonstrated that it was possible to pursue both roles concurrently.[35]

Habermas's return to academic life meant that, although he no longer had to publish for the public sphere to support himself and his young family, he continued to engage in public debate in ways that were theoretically consistent with his burgeoning philosophical work. During this period, he published two essays addressing education policy in West Germany. The first, a long essay published in *Merkur* in March 1957, was titled "The Chronic Sickness of University Reform (*Das chronische Leiden der Hochschulreform*)." It was based on an externally funded study, "The University and Society (*Universität und Gesellschaft*)," conducted at the Institute with Adorno as the principle investigator. Adorno's influence, both philosophical and political, is evident in how "Habermas synchronized scientific and academic developments with social developments."[36]

Interestingly, this is the first of Habermas's public essays to be reprinted in volume 1 of the *Kleine politische Schriften*, which was devoted to the issue of

"Reform in Schools and Higher Education (*Schul- und Hochschulreform*)." The second essay, originally published in *Der Monat* in 1959 under the title "The Conservative Spirit and its Modernist Consequences: On the Reform Plan for the German School," appears in this 1981 volume as well. The fact that Habermas chose to republish these texts in the first edition of his "short political writings" testifies to the fact that he saw these publications—at least retrospectively—as the beginning of his career as a public intellectual.[37]

In "The Conservative Spirit and its Modernist Consequences," Habermas responds to a plan for the reform of the education system produced by the Ministry of Culture.[38] By extending the period before children are segregated based on ability and tracked into vocational or classical secondary schools, this proposal sought to enact what Habermas calls "the liberal principle of performance selection (*das liberale Prinzip der Leistungsauslese*)" and to ensure that "contemporary education" provides students with better "orientation in the modern world," to quote the report itself. Although Habermas applauds the higher level of education this plan would offer to all students, the majority of whom would no longer automatically be considered "vocational students per se," he also bemoans the fact that this "social progress" comes "at the price of a 'realistically' reduced level of education" for all.[39]

Habermas objects to the traditional system of tracking by ability on two levels. To start, he notes that this system places a heavy burden on teachers, who are responsible for determining which students would be allowed to proceed to the *Gymnasium* (high school) and which would be relegated to vocational schools. Given the great effects this decision will have on the lives of the pupils, especially those from the lower classes—both in terms of their future economic earnings and well as their social status—he highlights his fear that this "responsibility of unusual proportions (*Verantwortung ungewöhnlichen Ausmaßes*)" will not only be "be a burden to the discerning, but [also] a temptation to the prejudiced (*Vorurteilsvollen*)." Relatedly—and given the limited number of places available in high schools—he is dismayed by this proposal's overt attempt to refocus the German school system away from the broader goal of educating children and instead toward the explicit goal of ensuring a steady supply of workers for the capitalist labor market. Citing Helmut Schelsky, he expresses his dismay at the fact that schools are becoming "allocation offices within a forced economy of social opportunities (*Zuteilungsämtern in einer Sozialchancen-Zwangswirtschaft*)."[40]

From this perspective, Habermas worries that the proposed reforms underestimate the effects of social class in shaping the opportunities for students to demonstrate "giftedness (*Begabung*)." As he points out, while the number of families that are able to create a positive educational environment is already small for economic reasons, the fact that an even greater number "have no social connection with the bourgeois tradition" means that they may pass up the opportunity for further schooling for their children, even if it is offered. He also fears that the attempt to align education with the modern world by turning toward mathematics and the natural sciences is due less to the actual needs of the time and more to the fact that certain professional associations have turned into a "powerful pressure group that has replaced the better arguments."[41]

This insight sets up Habermas's conclusion. The rapid growth in labor productivity, which has significantly reduced the necessary labor time, means there is no justification for the government to channel large numbers of students into vocation schools so they can begin working at the age of fourteen or fifteen.[42] On the contrary, this development should increase the time available for the education of all students. Moving from the economic to the political perspective, Habermas argues that the inherent structural instability of mass democracy (*Massendemokratie*) "makes the raising of general educational standards a social necessity." After all, educated citizens are a necessary precondition for a democracy like the FRG to "be able to reproduce itself as a democracy in the long term."[43]

Whereas this piece addresses primary and secondary education, in the "Chronic Sickness of University Reform," Habermas pushes back against attempts by both the state and the labor market to curtail the university's independence.[44] The essay's starting point is the need to reverse the cooptation of institutions of higher education to serve the needs of the Third Reich and its state-administered economy. After the fall of the Nazi regime, many professors who had been returned to their positions, such as Karl Jaspers, argued for "the renewal of its original spirit (*der Wiedererneuerung ihres ursprünglichen Geistes*)" by rehabilitating the German university's original nineteenth-century ideals focused on the formation (*Bildung*) of the bourgeois individual. Turning away from the functional and ideological appropriation of the university by the previous regime, such proposals focused on creating a program of "general education (*studium generale*)" or liberal arts. These suggestions were driven not only by a desire to leave the recent past behind, but also by the conviction that an educational approach focused on the character of the individual could serve as a defense against the kind of mass politics that had brought Hitler to power in the first place.

However, as Habermas points out, these early, idealistic plans "to give back to the university its character-forming capacity (*Bildungsfähigkeit*) and political responsibility ... in order to establish and maintain a democratic society" were soon superseded by the imperatives of West Germany's public administration and the newly privatized economy. Rather than reflecting the university's core elements—academic freedom and the integration of teaching and research—Habermas instead argues that reform in higher education is institutionalized as a "never-ending process of reform (*Dauerreform*)" based on short-term measures driven by the need for efficiency and utility. In light of these developments, "the university reproduces what could be seen as its own inner contradictions" through ever-greater disciplinary specialization, bureaucratization, and "scholastification (*Scholarisierung*)."[45] The result is that science becomes an end in itself, with no connection to the lives of its students or practitioners.

Despite the differences between the postwar reforms carried out in the democratic Federal Republic and those in the communist German Democratic Republic, Habermas notes that education has been subordinated to bureaucracy in both. Although this rationalization brings the university into line with other contemporary institutions, he argues that making the university respond to bureaucracy—whether private (economic) or public (the state)—threatens to "sterilize" the "critical substance" of education. While the conservative, feudal structures of the university indeed seem out of place in the modern world, it is—paradoxically—precisely these anachronistic elements that can help to preserve the original intentions of education by "carving out non-administrative reserves (*Reservate*) for freedom."[46]

This argument foreshadows Habermas's pessimistic conclusions regarding the dangers posed by the state's cooption of the public sphere in *Structural Transformation* (1962) and of the "colonization of the lifeworld" by the forces of power (state administration) and money (market forces) in the *Theory of Communicative Action* (1981). In this early version, Habermas contends that the concentration of capital and rise of economic planning have led to "once-separate spheres of 'the state' and of 'bourgeois society' ... being pushed into each other (*sich ineinander schieben*)." The implication is clear: "This interdependence" (*Verflechtung*) destroys the relative autonomy of the 'cultural sectors' ... from which science and the university obtained a certain degree of freedom of movement (*ein gewisses Maβ an Bewegungsfreiheit*)."⁴⁷

What is to be done in response to the "statification of society (*Verstaatlichung der Gesellschaft*)" and accompanying "socialization of the state (*Vergesellschaftung des Staates*)" is less obvious, especially as these processes work against each other such that it is increasingly difficult undertake any meaningful action whatsoever. The university—like all other institutions—increasingly finds itself caught in the double bind of having to satisfy the needs of both the state and the economy to ensure its survival. Habermas is particularly wary of the increasing need for science to be directly "applicable," as this need for economic or political utility means that its findings are put into practice without any scientific guidance. As a result, the need for "applicability (*Praktikabilität*)" not only "increases the paradoxical alienation of theory from practice," but also estranges scientific research from the individual's ideal of living a meaningful life filled with purpose.⁴⁸

While proposals for the revival of the humanities and the liberal arts like those presented by Karl Jaspers seek to push back against these tendencies, Habermas argues that they fail to address the basic, systemic problems that subtend the broader "neutralization of science." Dealing with these issues would require a fundamental transformation of the modern model of the university, that space in which "research becomes a public service and teaching becomes mere instruction." A retreat to the university's past is not sufficient. Instead, what is needed is active engagement with the actual purpose of the university. This requires more than the reflection of "each specialized science on its own foundations," but instead a broader consideration of the consequences of science for the life of the individual, which will then also allow it "to criticize its relationship to social reality," to "recover their links with living, purposive practice."⁴⁹ Bringing the essay back full circle, Habermas concludes that what is needed is not a new, pluralistic understanding of scholarship, but the realization that "theory reconciled with practice does not content itself with practicability." In his view, only such an approach can prevent "the university becoming the site of rector's addresses for a second time—speeches reminiscent of the academic power seizures of 1933."⁵⁰

The final line of Habermas's text not only sets out what he thinks is at stake in higher education reform; it is also a direct reference to Martin Heidegger's "Rectoral Address," which he delivered upon assuming the rectorship of the University of Freiburg after Hitler's seizure of power. In "The Self-Assertion of the German University," Heidegger presents himself as the "Rector-Führer," who would oversee the university's *Gleichschaltung* with the Nazi regime. In the words of the postwar Allied denazification commission, Heidegger's text—with its praise of Hitler, positive references to the *Führerprinzip*, and appeals to the authenticity of military and labor service—"placed the great prestige of his scholarly reputation. . . . in the service of the National Socialist Revolution, thereby [making] an essential contribution to the legitimation of this revolution in the eyes of educated Germans."[51]

Given the context and argument of Habermas's text, it is clear that he sees Heidegger's collaboration with Hitler as a classic example of how the university must resist calls to become "practical" by allowing itself to be coopted by the state and economic forces. Instead of giving in to their "elitist desires for authority" (Adorno) by serving "teachers of the nation," Habermas instead argues that the role of scholars and scientists in political life should be confined to that of the critic.[52] It is only in this way that the university can maintain its status as a reservoir of freedom and thought in the increasingly administered and rationalized modern world.

As I detailed in the previous chapter, in 1953 Habermas published an essay in the *FAZ* criticizing Heidegger—his former philosophical mentor—for his unapologetic collaboration with the Nazi regime. During his initial tenure at the Institute, Habermas continued to engage critically with Heidegger and his problematic legacy. This is unsurprising, as Habermas not only shared Adorno's concerns regarding the intellectual and political continuities of the Nazi regime with the Third Reich, but also the worry that, in Heidegger's "jargon of authenticity"—to borrow the title of Adorno's 1964 book—"the concept of the existential is placed in the service of irrationalism, of the rejection of rational argumentation, of discursive thought as such."[53]

Habermas's continued interest in Heidegger is also visible in two texts he produced during this period. The first, published in the *FAZ* in 1959 under the title "The Great Influence: A Timely (*chronistische*) Note on Martin Heidegger's 70th Birthday," was also republished in the German edition of Habermas's *Philosophico-Political Profiles*, alongside his original critique of Heidegger's publication of his *Lectures on Metaphysics* from 1935 to 1953.[54] Unlike his first piece, in which Habermas explicitly addressed Heidegger as a political personality and not as a philosopher, this time around Habermas instead focuses on the academic sphere, starting his review with the following observation: "In the framework of the modern university, Martin Heidegger is the most influential philosopher since Hegel." While he also notes Heidegger's retreat from academic life and the fact that he has become a popular speaker among "captains of industry" and other "managerial types," Habermas focuses on the varied and profound "academic influence of Heidegger from the margins."[55]

Habermas's theoretical disagreement with Heidegger—despite his status as a Heideggerian during his student days—is visible from the start. In a sentence that acknowledges both the ambitious, alluring scope of Heidegger's project and what Habermas views as the inherent authoritarian tendencies of this "prophetic thinker" who places himself at a "distinction of rank" above others, Habermas writes that while Heidegger challenges his reader "into a view that stretches out over the epochs of the world . . . he is expected to follow down untrodden paths rather than being afforded the mutuality of conversation." Given the emphasis the young Habermas has already started placing on open communication and discourse, this observation leads to his devastating thesis about Heideggerianism: "Communication does not belong to the basic vocabulary of this philosophy."[56]

In the remainder of this anti-laudatio, Habermas unfolds his argument by tracing not only the failure of *Being and Time* (1929), which remains incomplete because Heidegger refused to acknowledge that the thinking Being (*Sein*) of *Dasein* can only be ontologically grounded by recognizing "the thoroughly historical character of truth, which proceeds from the world of humans as its open horizon." Instead of interpreting this failure of his "first philosophy (*Ursprungsphilosophie*)" as a sign that he needed to turn his attention to "the history of this situation, to the development of the social life context," Heidegger instead moves in the opposite direction, toward a history of Being. This inward turn leads not only to the "'subjective' ossification" of Heidegger's thought after his "*Kehre* (turning)," but it also deprives itself of any concept of normativity.[57] Summing up his critique, Habermas expresses his dismay at the way Heidegger has been "reimported" into West Germany—via Jean-Paul Sartre and French thought more generally—as a progressive thinker ("A Heidegger renaissance born of the spirit of the Resistance—what a source of misunderstandings!"). He further concludes that the very fact Heidegger is considered great "sheds light on why our relationship to greatness is a broken one."[58]

Habermas's second engagement with Heidegger during this period, entitled "An Alternative Myth of the 20th Century," was published soon thereafter in the *Frankfurter Hefte*.[59] The essay offers a review of two works—the German philosopher Walter Bröcker's *Dialectic, Positivism and Mythology*, and the German psychoanalyst Peter Fürstenau's *Heidegger: The Structure of his Thinking*—in order to address the state of contemporary philosophy. Habermas opens the review by noting that philosophy "no longer represents the knowledge of its time." Instead, it is reduced to outlining the logic of the other sciences and serving as a foundation for knowledge (from the perspective of logical positivism) or to imparting education (from a humanistic point of view). In any case, in line with Habermas's later conception of the limited scope of "what theory can accomplish," he notes that in the twentieth century philosophy has become "one discipline among others" practiced at the university.[60]

In his review, Habermas outlines how Bröcker tries to escape from the limitations on contemporary philosophy by once again giving it the power to think about "the world as a whole (*im Ganzen*)," without the limitations of having to take the findings of the specialized, empirical sciences into account. Bröcker accomplishes this by rehabilitating the concept of myth through an active rebuilding of philosophy's connection to poetry, especially via Homer and Hölderlin. The problem, as Habermas points out, is that this move can only be justified through adherence to "blind authority"—namely, the authority of Heidegger, who argues without justification that such poetry gives access to the truth about the world. Instead of taking this route of re-mythologization, Habermas instead follows Fürstenau, who critiques Heidegger's "destructive thinking" for robbing philosophy of the "social foundation of its construction." The result is a form of theoretical thinking that "responds to the newly developed sciences by reworking their empirical findings philosophically."[61] Although brief, the review demonstrates both the extent to which Habermas has freed himself from Heidegger's thrall and the early development of his concept of philosophical thinking—one that is not only compatible with but also draws upon the empirical, especially social, sciences.

In addition to his early critique of Jaspers's proposals for the rehabilitation of the German university, Habermas also engages more broadly with Jaspers's legacy during this period. For example, in 1956 he wrote two reviews of books by Karl Jaspers. Just before his move from Bonn to Frankfurt, at Karl Korn's behest, Habermas published an extended review of Jaspers's interpretation of Schelling in *Greatness and Fate* (*Größe und Verhängnis*). In this commissioned piece, Habermas critiques Jaspers's focus on Schelling's "genius as a magician (*Zauberer*), not a philosopher." Responding to his editor's request, Habermas highlighted the contemporary "fight between the Heideggerians and Hegelians over Schelling." However, rather than taking a side, he instead sought "a third, dialectical approach to 'transcendence,' that is more than just 'illuminating' and yet also not 'gnostic.' "[62] That said, his second piece, a review of the third edition of Jaspers' *Philosophy*, makes it clear that Habermas still thought highly of his work, which was also of interest to Adorno. In his correspondence, Habermas notes that if he had been familiar with both his writings and those of Jaspers, "it would have made it very difficult for me to do my own modest work, if not completely impossible."[63]

These reviews form the background for a more thorough engagement with Jaspers' work in 1958. This essay, in which Habermas compares Jaspers favorably to Heidegger, was also later republished in *Philosophico-Political Profiles*, a study of public personalities (and not just philosophers) in West Germany.[64] In "Jaspers and the Figures of Truth," a genuine laudatio that Habermas published in honor of his subject's seventy-fifth birthday, the contrasts to Heidegger are immediately clear. Rather than retreating from the world and the historical character of truth, Jaspers embraces the fact that truth "cannot be established rationally in an unequivocal way that is binding for all . . . the intention of complete tolerance with the mood of unconditional resoluteness." Instead of seeking a form of monological leadership through prophesy, as Heidegger did, Jaspers evaluates philosophical ideas by "whether they hinder or promote communication; this is their highest criterion." For Habermas, it appears as though these two contrasts alone are enough to explain both Jaspers' active opposition to the Third Reich and Heidegger's active collaboration with it.[65]

As these biographical essays make clear, Habermas's engagement with the works of prominent German academics in this period were shaped by their behavior under the previous regime and their contemporary meaning for the Federal Republic. This is also evident in Habermas's interaction with Helmut Plessner during this period—especially in his review of *Die verspätete Nation* (*The Belated Nation*), the title of Plessner's 1959 book, which alludes to a widely used historical term referring to Germany's late unification; it only became a nation-state in 1871.[66] Plessner, who had returned to Germany after seventeen years in exile following his forced resignation from his professorship in Cologne in 1933 due to his Jewish ancestry, was a prominent and "clean" exponent of philosophical anthropology—an approach Habermas knew through his doctoral work under the "stained" Ernst Rothacker.

The legacy of the Third Reich figures prominently in this review. Habermas reflects on "the borders within us (*Grenzen in uns*)" that had developed, as the unified prewar German tradition was now "broken," divided between the newly recognized German-Jewish tradition that the Nazis had expelled and the now indelibly tarnished "pure" intellectual history that the Third Reich had promoted and whose contemporary exponents had collaborated with Hitler's dictatorship. For Habermas, the postwar reappropriation of the former offered the necessary opportunity to engage in "a catch-up learning process (*eines nachholenden Lernprozesses*)" that would force the FRG to reevaluate what it meant to be German after Auschwitz.

This essay followed another in which Habermas sought to clarify both his intellectual and personal relationship to (philosophical) anthropology, a field with which he was associated due to his connection to Rothacker.[67] Habermas's interest in this topic was shaped primarily by the tensions between the philosophy of history (which Herder, Kant and Marx argued operated with a progressive logic of its own) and humanity's supposedly stable, unchanging anthropological "nature." While Habermas's contribution to the philosophical dictionary edited by the German philosopher Alwin Diemer in 1958 was clearly shaped by issues with which "I had occupied myself with . . . [s]ince my schooldays," the structure and authors he engages with signal that it is also an attempt to wrestle with the implications of the "broken" German tradition after 1945.[68]

Habermas starts his entry by defining anthropology as a discipline that "deals with the natural history of man and his "extraction" from necessity (*seiner 'Abstammung' von den Sog*)." Consequently, philosophical anthropology—a field that builds on the empirical findings of this empirical discipline but nevertheless remains bound to philosophical rules of logic, metaphysics and ethics—reflects on the meaning and importance of the discipline for "the essence of humanity (*das Wesen des Menschen*)." The entry continues by briefly summarizing the various canonical thinkers' engagements with issues of philosophical anthropology. However, on this initial point he immediately cites Plessner, whom he credits as one of the founders of this approach, to argue that it is this self-understanding of his own essence that is important for man, not its mere facticity. The result of this insight is that "people understand themselves differently based on historical and social situation."[69]

Still building on Plessner, Habermas concludes that "if this is so . . . then humanity has many essences," not one eternal, stable and inescapable nature. This insight is confirmed by the fact that philosophical anthropologists are also human beings and cannot engage in this research without also reflecting on their own nature. As a result, this approach not only "shows what is, but also inescapably (*unvermeidlich*) shows something of what could be." Later in the review Habermas also credits Plessner with moving philosophical anthropology "away from principles and substances towards *Structures*."[70] Taken together, Plessner's work thus not only highlights the impact of external conditions on the anthropological situation of humanity at a given time and place, but also shows how the individual is caught in an "eccentric position," as "the human being must bridge the distance between the condition of existing as a body (*zuständlicher Leibexistenz*) and objective physical existence (*gegenständlicher Körperexistenz*)."[71]

At this point—roughly in the middle of the text—Habermas turns to Arnold Gehlen, whose work defines the second half of the encyclopedia entry. Given his views regarding the reciprocal relationship between Heidegger's philosophy and his totalitarian politics, the fact that "phenomenologically speaking, Gehlen's determinations (*Bestimmungen*) correspond step-by-step to the determinations of Heidegger's analysis of Dasein" is the first sign that Habermas is wary of Gehlen's conclusions. In particular, Habermas is skeptical of the conservative position implied by "Gehlen's attempt to deduce human nature, including his 'culture,' exclusively from his practical need to cope with life (*Lebensbewältigung*)." Habermas sees this theory based on "invariants" as overly "dogmatic," especially when it is present as value-free social science.[72]

By contrast, Habermas notes that Plessner had already realized that "an anthropology like Gehlen's, which includes only action (*Handlung*), leaves no space for verbal communication (*Ausdruck*)." Plessner demonstrates that communication enables more than just the realization of functional goals, allowing for the creation of meaning (*Bedeutung*), with the examples of laughter and crying. This leads Habermas to a more general critique of the concept of "authenticity (*Echtheit*)"— here he most likely has Heidegger in mind—as well as of anthropology more generally, insofar as it speaks ontologically in universal categories. In this context Habermas praises Rothacker for developing a comparative cultural anthropology that avoids "Gehlen's naïveté." However, while this comment reflects Habermas's background, his conclusion advocates for Marcuse's synthesis of psychoanalysis and sociology as a model for the alliance that philosophical anthropology should forge with the culturally and historically determined social sciences.[73]

This encyclopedia entry is not a form of public engagement directed at the public sphere. Nevertheless, Habermas's critique of the way Gehlen develops his scientific work based on conservative assumptions in order to later transpose these into conservative political positions reveals several things: first, that Habermas is thinking seriously about the relationship between scientific research and politics; and second, that his own reservations regarding the political positions of figures like Heidegger and Gehlen are working their way into his scientific analyses. This piece, with its emphasis on linguistic communication and the importance of culturally and historically specific lifeworlds (*Lebenswelten*) in shaping how individuals experience the world also foreshadows how Habermas's philosophical work will develop in the coming decades.[74] Finally, it signals his continued attempt to come to terms with Rothacker's politics and his legacy.

Habermas's complicated relationship to Rothacker is also visible in his decision to contribute to a *Festschrift* in his *Doktorvater*'s honor in 1958, in line with academic convention. However, despite this sign of "personal loyalty," the essay itself does not engage with Rothacker's work.[75] Instead, in "Notes on the Relationship Between Work and Free Time" Habermas returns to Marx in order to critique the very concept of "free time," which he argues is anything but free. On the contrary, he argues that "free time" is an "ideology" that only has the "appearance of individually disposable time," as it is actually still "to a large extent determined by the level of development (*Entwicklungsstand*) and the concrete form of industrial work." Building on Friedrich Pollock's 1955 study of the potential of automation, Habermas expresses the hope that the masses of workers might be able to take advantage of a reduction of labor time to participate in political life. In an argument that foreshadows his later work on the public sphere, Habermas notes that it is only through active participation in political debate and civil society that regular citizens can hope to gain some modicum of "control of the execution of political power."[76]

Although these essays deal with issues from the academic sphere, they clearly indicate that Habermas is still motivated by what he sees as the incomplete reckoning with "the recent past (*jüngsten Vergangenheit*)." This interest was not confined to the university, but also to postwar west German society more generally. As Habermas notes in an essay he published in May of 1957, the very fact that the Third Reich was still being discussed as the "recent" past, despite the fact that more time had passed since its fall than it had been in power, testifies to its continued importance for German society and politics.[77]

Habermas's piece, entitled "The Biographical Veil," analyzes a film about the death of Gustav Stresemann, the longtime foreign minister of the Weimar Republic, who had sought the reconciliation of Germany and France after the Great War and whose death opened the way for Hitler's rise to power. While it is clear that Habermas admires Stresemann, he is critical of political biography as a genre that "sanctions a view of history as a natural process" and therefore makes it seem inevitable. For this film, the message seems to be "Stresemann dies and the SA marches (*Stresemann stirbt und SA marschiert*)." The realization of the film itself also "has an apologetic effect"; it narrows the circle of responsibility for Hitler's dictatorship to a small group of insiders, while simultaneously absolving the masses, who "do not even appear" before the camera, of any culpability whatsoever.[78]

The review also highlights Habermas's continued interest in consumer culture. He ends the review by noting that this film is the result of a "growing interest in biography on the part of consumers." Habermas speculates that this is due to a desire to see great individuals undertake great deeds at a time when the social and economic system has increasingly resulted in the "abolition of the responsible subject (*Aufhebung des mündigen Subjekts*)." This conclusion links Habermas's commentary on the Stresemann film to two other publications on consumer culture that he was working on at the time. It also shows that his Marx-inspired interest in the role of consumers in modern culture, politics, and society carried over from his journalistic years into his early academic career.

The first of these two publications, a short report entitled "Can Consumers Play?," was published in *FAZ* in April 1957.[79] This piece builds directly on some of Habermas's earlier essays discussed in the previous chapter, including "Dialectic of Rationalization." It extends Habermas's critique of Marx for overlooking the extent to which consumption in individuals' free time—not just labor during the working day—"is determined from the outside (*fremdbestimmt*) by the technical-bureaucratic apparatus." It also relates to his growing interest in education policy, as he takes the growth in production and the decline in necessary labor time as evidence that "our labor-orientated educational system will not be appropriate to our future situation."

What is new in this piece is Habermas's engagement with the concept of play (*Spiel*). By this, he is not referring to speech act theory or the philosophical concept of language games, but rather to the idea that the concept of play allows individuals to break out of the standard circle of production and consumption by "giving things their own meaning" in ways that do not conform to economically determined logics. Yet with the rationalization of the economic system and its expansion into all areas of life, our modern "consumption society leaves no room for play." For Habermas, this is also connected to the fact that modern social and economic theories themselves have no genuine conception of "free time." Instead, free time is defined purely negatively as time spent not working, and it is integrated into the system through the function of consumption. Although Habermas appreciates the emancipatory potential of play—citing Adorno's remark that play allows "jovial refusal [to take] the place of pain (*joviale Versagung an die Stelle des Schmerzens*)" and observing, "The playing man is the redeemed man (*Der spielende Mensch ist der erlöste*)"—he ultimately concludes that in the modern world play is reserved for the gods.

The second piece is a more academic treatment in which Habermas reviews *On the Consumer Front: A Provisional Appraisal of Modern Culture* (*An der Konsumfront: Zwischenbilanz des modernen Lebens*, 1957), by the Austrian writer Karl Bednarik.[80] Although Bednarik exposes many of the deficiencies of modern mass culture, in "Criticism of consumption—specifically for consumption (*Konsumkritik—eigens zum Konsumieren*)," Habermas remains unconvinced by his vivid but impressionistic comparisons of nylon stockings to the atom bomb. In the end, he argues, "Bednarik creates connections where there are none, in order to cover up those that are and are correct." Rather than "leading to understanding," he argues that the result is a form of "pseudo-understanding" based on "ready-made conclusions."[81]

Similarly, Habermas rejects Bednarik's optimistic conclusion that humanity's cultural heritage and potentialities offer individuals a way out by allowing them to differentiate between value and nonvalue in their private lives. On the contrary, for him this move is characteristic a popular but deficient form of moralistic sociological analysis—or a form of "religious existentialism," as Habermas refers to it at the end of his review—that "relieves itself of its own critical responsibility by making the individual responsible for what the burden of conditions makes of him."[82] This is part of Habermas's more general criticism of the *Konsumkritik*, which he sees as conformist in the worst sense insofar as it "avoids both the historical view of the old conservatives and the revolutionary view of the young conservatives." In addition to marking Habermas's first use of the term *Jungkonservativen*, which he famously applied to Michel Foucault in 1981, this review also marks his first application of the term "refeudalization"—a key concept in *Structural Transformation*—which he notes was unnecessary for people like Bednarik, who "found that the present was actually feudal enough."[83]

While Habermas's journalistic output becomes somewhat less frequent during this period, its tenor and tone do not fundamentally change. On the contrary, although his work is united by certain themes and ideas, his academic and political writings largely exist in parallel. Bringing them together will first require Habermas to develop a theory of the public sphere. This was his primary academic undertaking in this period.

BUILDING TOWARDS A CONCEPT OF THE PUBLIC SPHERE

In addition to these public interventions on education policy and the legacies of Nazism in postwar West German academe, Habermas—demonstrating his commitment to the theoretical continuity thesis even at this early stage—also published a number of pieces on contemporary political debates in West Germany during his initial stay at the Institute. This development signals an important shift in Habermas's public-facing work. While the quantitative decline in his newspaper publications shows that public engagement has gone from being his primary to his secondary vocation, the fact that a growing number of these articles addressed to the broader reading public explicitly address political issues is a sign he was starting to develop what he would later describe as a "willingness to have an effect on political debates," which he notes "constitutes an essential characteristic of the intellectual."[84]

Habermas's increasing interest in social criticism—and the public sphere as such—is visible in a short text he published in April 1957 entitled "Coping with Abstraction . . . (*Der Abstraktion gewachsen sein . . .*)." Habermas starts the piece by reflecting on how few individuals in the FRG know what the acronym NATO (North Atlantic Treaty Organization) stands for or what the hydrogen bomb is, much less how either works—indeed, few understand what the dials on their radio do even though they use them every day. This leads Habermas to reflect on how the growing abstraction of everyday life into increasingly complex, rationalized structures and systems means that no one fully understands how or why they work. Even bureaucrats within the state bureaucracy do not grasp the full implications of their work.[85] As Habermas later notes in a short piece reviewing a study of the effects of bureaucratic forms of labor on workers, published in the *Süddeutsche Zeitung* in September 1958, the problem in an era of increased automation is that "the leeway (*Spielraum*) for superiors to command is getting smaller and smaller." This points to a broader issue for both the private sphere of industry and the state: "bureaucracy, with its hierarchical structure, is stuck in the manufacturing period and has lagged behind the demands of industrial society."[86]

These initial observations bring Habermas to his main point. In an argument that foreshadows the bleak analysis of the second half of *Structural Transformation*, he notes that these general trends are accompanied by a "breakdown of the public sphere (*Zerfall der Öffentlichkeit*)," a space in which individuals could previously meet with other to discuss and understand issues of societal import. Now, however, "the barriers between the sphere of intimacy and of the public have fallen." The resulting privatization of the public sphere is matched by the politicization of the private, as individuals can only understand political events like the Hungarian Revolution of 1956 from the perspective of their biographical interest in the fate of Imre Nagy. While it is unclear how he thinks that this can be achieved, Habermas ends by calling for the institutions of society to be once again be put under the control of people so that what occurs no longer does so "above our heads, but with the will and awareness (*Wille und Bewußtsein*) of the majority."[87]

While this conclusion presages the direction of Habermas's philosophical work and his growing interest in strengthening both the quality of debate in the public sphere as well as its ability to exert control over political decision-making as a public intellectual, the opening lines of this piece also highlight Habermas's increasing concern about the geopolitical situation at the start of the Cold War. In linking the issue of the bomb to the public sphere, Habermas is following Karl Jaspers, "who after 1945 had advocated for the democratization of West German society like few others."[88] In 1958, Jaspers had also published the text of a radio program he gave entitled, *Die Atombombe und die Zukunft des Menschen* ("The Atom Bomb and the Future of Humankind").[89]

The aforementioned Carl Friedrich von Weizsäcker was also a key participant in this debate. Although he had been involved in the Nazi attempt to obtain a nuclear bomb during the Second World War, after the war he became a staunch opponent of nuclear armament. This led Weizsäcker, with whom Habermas would later co-direct the Max Planck Institute for the Research of Living Conditions in the Modern World, to join seventeen other leading German physicists in signing the Göttingen Manifesto on April 12, 1957, which opposed Adenauer's attempts to arm the newly constituted West German *Bundeswehr* (Federal Army) with tactical nuclear weapons.

In "The Veiled Terror," published in the *Frankfurter Hefte* in 1958, Habermas reflected on a text that Weizsäcker had published in *Die Zeit* that same year entitled "Living with the Bomb."[90] Although Weizsäcker had concluded that nuclear armament made no sense for Germany, Habermas is compelled to write his own response due to the accusation that Weizsäcker had not adequately accounted for the doctrine of graduated deterrence. According to US Rear Admiral Anthony Buzzard, this doctrine called on the West to develop "small" atomic bombs "since our [the West's] conventional forces are unable to withstand the vast Communist conventional forces without the tactical use of nuclear weapons." This doctrine thus sought to differentiate between "massive retaliation" using "large" hydrogen bombs (H-bombs) that would result in the destruction of the entire world and the tactical use of smaller atomic bombs (A-bombs) that could be used "without provoking the strategic use of hydrogen weapons."[91]

In his analysis, Habermas critiques the doctrine of graduated deterrence. He starts by noting that it is based on game theory, which—using the assumptions of logical positivism—presupposes that both players are operating with the same "'cultural self-understandings,' which are not self-evident elsewhere, for example in Russia." Habermas also doubts that escalation would stop with the use of small nuclear weapons once the taboo on non-use has been broken, especially in a situation that would be seen by both sides as a "battle of life and death (*Kampf auf Leben und Tod*)." As a result, he concludes that all approaches to living with the bomb can only work if they realize what they already assume: the necessity of disarmament. After all, "In the shadow of large weapons, you can no longer carelessly frolic around (*unbekümmert tummeln*) with the small ones, as if they didn't exist."[92]

During this period Habermas also became engaged in the "Fight Against Nuclear Death (*Kampf dem Atomtod*)," launched in March 1958 by the social democratic politician Walter Menzel, and joined an associated protest associated with this campaign in Frankfurt.[93] In the wake of this event, Habermas wrote "Agitation Is the Citizen's Primary Duty (*Unruhe erste Bürgerpflicht*)," the text of a speech he delivered at a student protest against the stationing of atomic weapons in West Germany, held at the Römerberg in central Frankfurt.[94] Its publication in the Frankfurt student newspaper shows that Habermas was already deeply involved with student politics during his first stay at the Goethe University. In an attempt to further spur public debate, Habermas's piece appeared alongside a contribution by Franz Böhm, the former rector of the university and an MP from the Christian Democratic Union (CDU), in which the latter argued in favor of atomic rearmament and accused the students (and Habermas) of not understanding the political situation.

The title of Habermas's piece, where he argues that "it is no longer possible to prevent war by preparing for war" and bemoans the euphemisms being used to "sell A- and H-bombs to the people," reverses a famous public notice issued by Graf von der Schulenberg-Kehnert in the aftermath of the battles of Jena and Auerstedt in 1806: "keeping calm (*Ruhe*) is the citizen's first duty."[95] In contrast to the passivity of this old adage (*Sprichwort*), Habermas instead returns to his calls for greater contestation and democratic participation in public life, visible in some of his early journalism. For instance, he criticizes the conservative government of Chancellor Konrad Adenauer of practicing "a politics of faits accomplis," in which "everything is decided for the people, but nothing together with the people."[96]

By contrast, Habermas notes that the students and their supporters are the ones "bringing plebiscitary elements into the political life of the Federal Republic." He once again decries the fact that party discipline and the whip mean that decisions are reaching in smoke-filled back rooms rather than on the floor of the Bundestag, as one would expect in a "representative democracy in the classical sense," where members of parliament are "free to vote as they will and only responsible to their conscience." In a passage that shows he is already thinking about the place of higher education and the public intellectual in political life, he also notes that while "the university as a corporation should maintain its political neutrality," it can "only remain a cradle (*Hort*) of the freedom of conscience so long as members can openly voice their political convictions."[97]

Stefan Müller-Doohm argues that in contrast to Habermas's early journalism—a corpus characterized by Müller-Doohm as one in which Habermas "was hesitant to draw political conclusions or to make political statements"—by the late 1950s "Habermas really began to show his true political colours" during "the debate over the rearmament of the Federal Republic."[98] While I have already documented my disagreement with the first part of this statement in the previous chapter, I agree with the second. While Müller-Doohm is right that rearmament was a crucial issue that acted as a "trigger" for Habermas, his emerging self-definition as a public intellectual during this period—as well as the close proximity he had to students as a result of his appointment at the Institute—both contributed to his gradually more confident and active political engagement.

It is also important to realize the extent to which Habermas was putting himself on the line—not only by speaking out so vocally against rearmament, but also by attacking Böhm and the Christian Democrats in print. Böhm was not only the former rector of the university (a position Horkheimer had held from 1951 to 1953) and a prominent representative for the CDU in the Bundestag; he also sat on the executive committee of the Institute's foundation. Given Habermas's limited job security at the Institute, taking on such a powerful figure was hardly wise. Doing so also further alienated Habermas from Horkheimer, who—consistent with the Institute's longstanding policy of adopting an "obscuring, Aesopian language" to avoid unnecessary political conflicts—did not want himself or the Institute involved in political debates.[99] For his part, Habermas was no fan of Horkheimer, whom he criticizes for his politically "overly cautious maneuvering (*übervorsichtliches Taktieren*)."[100]

In addition to these public activities, Habermas was also active as a scientific researcher during this time. One of the first assignments Adorno gave Habermas after his arrival at the Institute was to write the theoretical introduction for a study of political attitudes at the university, entitled *Students and Politics*. Funded by an external grant from the German government, this study "was to take its place in the tradition of great empirical research projects carried out by the Institute of Social Research," including *The Authoritarian Personality* and *Studies on Authority and the Family*.[101] It also continued Habermas's own early exploration of a radical "idea of democracy" inspired by his introduction to the Frankfurt School and motivated by his growing interest in how citizens could reclaim influence over politics amid increasing administration and the personalistic "politics of strength" exemplified by the way Adenauer sought to "rule in our [i.e., the people's] name."[102]

While it is not a political writing addressed to the public sphere, "On the Concept of Political Participation (*Über den Begriff der politischen Beteiligung*)," which Habermas drafted in 1958 (though it was not published until 1961), is important for my argument, as it provides important insights into the development of the concept of the public sphere that would culminate four years later in *Structural Transformation*. Taken together with evidence from his various political and journalistic engagements, it also establishes a link showing that this philosophical theory of the public sphere was inspired and motivated by Habermas's political commitments. In this sense, it is a good example of how the ideas Habermas defends in his political and journalistic writings work their way into his academic work without simply subordinating one to the other in a direct, unmediated fashion.

In his theoretical introduction to this study, Habermas lays the foundation for a "sociological inquiry into the political consciousness of Frankfurt students."[103] While its tone, empirical analysis of qualitative data, and phenomenological approach make clear the influence that Adorno already had on Habermas over the previous two years, Habermas also brought many new elements to critical theory, including an active engagement with the concept of democracy.[104] Whereas in previous studies conducted under the aegis of the Institute democracy "had been a concession to research clients and the prevailing situation," Rolf Wiggershaus points out that Habermas not only took democracy seriously but also "invested it with radical content" and "made into an explicit standard of measurement."[105]

Unlike much of the German scholarship on democracy, which was still engaged in debates stemming from the internal German philosophical tradition (discussed in greater detail below), during his stay at the Institute Habermas sought to familiarize himself with the American literature on democracy. That is not to say he agreed with it. In contrast to leading American scholars—including Morris Jones, David Riesman, and Nathan Glazer—who saw democracy as a mechanism for ensuring a stable social equilibrium, in his theoretical introduction to the empirical studies ultimately published as *Student and Politics*, Habermas argues that popular rule "is fundamentally premised on the idea of participation."[106] In making this argument, Habermas clearly staked out a position that opposed both the growth of the administrative state and the institutional empowerment of the executive and judicial branches at the expense of the legislature, which was increasingly influenced by party politics and lobbying. The result was a society that "functionalizes its citizens increasingly to serve various public purposes, but privatizes them in their consciousness," thus producing "unpolitical citizens within what is actually a political society."[107]

Far from telling students to focus on their studies, he encouraged them to make their voices heard, as they had in the rearmament debate. For Habermas, postwar West Germany could either continue down the path toward becoming a technocratic, depoliticized welfare state, or it could change course and develop into a genuine, participatory democracy. While his later analysis in *Legitimation Crisis* (1973) seems to indicate that he thought the former had occurred, in the late 1950s he still believed that citizens acting through civil society and the public sphere could force the Federal Republic to take their views into account through "extra-parliamentary actions," an idea that would become politically important during the student protests of the late 1960s (also addressed in the next chapter).

Habermas's earnest, radical approach to democracy was unique for the Frankfurt School, as was his "systematic treatment given to studies in political science and constitutional law by 'bourgeois' scholars."[108] In this sense "On the

Concept of Political Participation" was a crucial part of Habermas's "on-the-job" training in political science, a field that was quite weak in the early Federal Republic. Because this "auxiliary science" engaged directly with contemporary affairs, it was deeply affected by the Nazi seizure of all areas of life through their policy of coordination.[109]

The underdeveloped status of political science (*Politikwissenschaft*) at this time is also signaled by the fact it did not yet exist as an independent discipline in West Germany. Instead, questions of political legitimacy were debated within a field known as the *Staatslehre* or the *Staatsrechtslehre*, whose origins date back to G. W. F. Hegel's *Elements of the Philosophy of Right* (1820). Although often translated as "state theory" and "constitutional theory" (literally "teaching on state law"), this field was organized around the German concept of the "*Staat*." Although usually rendered as "state," this word can also refer to "government" or "nation," More specifically, *Staat* refers to an organized form of community that aspires to "a higher grade of moral quality than *Gesellschaft* (society)."[110]

This field of study is aptly named, as it reflected predominant views within German society in which the "state was thought to be an end in itself, and was thus seen as dissociated from the individual and society."[111] For Habermas, this was an utterly inappropriate course of action given the crimes recently committed in the name of the state. As a result, he sought to find ways to break out of the narrow strictures of the academic study of politics in postwar West Germany, while also retaining some connection to the basic contours of the German debate so that he could engage in dialogue with other researchers in his homeland. This also allowed him to express his "vital desire to controversially pair intellectual traditions," as one of his later assistants, Ulrich Oevermann, described his mentor's approach.[112] The fact that Habermas—a product of postwar political "reeducation"—looked to US politics at the time is notable, as older scholars in the tradition of the *Staatsrechtslehre* "reacted reservedly to the change of political system in 1945."[113]

The debates within the *Staatslehre* after 1945 were interesting and diverse, yet schematically speaking they can be divided into three main "schools," each of which celebrate a different branch of government as its preferred "guardian of the constitution." The first, originating in the writings of the Nazi jurist Carl Schmitt and propagated by Werner Weber and Ernst Forsthoff, roots sovereignty in "the executive, which is essentially active." Because this branch consists of a single individual, its occupant "decides what constitutes an exception" in order to defend the political order in times of crisis.[114] As Frieder Günther points out—and this was what worried Habermas most about this particular approach—"Here the strong continuity in personnel with the *Staatsrechtslehre* of the 'Third Reich' again becomes obvious."[115]

The second, associated with Rudolf Smend, sought to protect the constitutional order by emphasizing the rule of law and the safeguarding of fundamental rights by emphasizing the positivism of the written statute and the power of judicial review.[116] Unlike the Schmitt School, this approach "proved to be more flexible and adaptable to the new constitutional position" of postwar west Germany, as well as its *Bindung* to both the politics and political ideas of the West.[117] The establishment of the strong *Bundesverfassungsgericht* (Federal Constitutional Court) in the Basic Law was crucial for this approach and allowed its supporters to refute the more traditional German view held by Schmitt's adherents, "who argued that the Court may not interfere with the largely unrestrained competence of the executive" to make political decisions. This line of thought, which built much more on the tradition of legal review exemplified by the practices of the US Supreme Court, was troubling for Habermas because it gave political parties "the role of a 'partial constitutional organ'"[118] As Habermas's argument in chapter 1 makes clear, this position was unacceptable and undemocratic from his perspective.

Finally, the third approach, which built on the writings of Hermann Heller and Wolfgang Abendroth, emphasized popular sovereignty expressed through the will-formation of a democratically elected parliament. In the latter's words, democratic values and their concretization must always come "from the people and not the jurists."[119] While he rejected the judicial focus of Smend, Habermas did agree that "the interpretation of the constitution had to be determined by taking values into consideration" as part of the legislative process.[120] Habermas's turn to the public sphere was also influenced by Otto Kirchheimer, Karl Loewenstein, and the so-called Freiburg School which sought to "remove the traditional German *étatisme* conclusively" from German constitutional thinking by importing Anglo-American ideas about civil society and the political community as possible alternatives to the *Staatrechtslehre*'s obsession with the state as a *Rechts-* or *Justizstaat*.[121] Horst Ehmke's emphasis on the need to develop a "consensus of the reasonable and righteous minded" within society bears some similarity to Habermas's later ideas about the role of the public sphere in democracy.[122]

Although Habermas draws on all three strands in his analysis of "On the Concept of Political Participation," his earlier essays on democracy make it clear that he favors an approach that roots democracy in the legislature. Unlike the other two schools, this strand treats the people as republican "coauthors" of the law, rather than mere objects of its authority. It is also consistent with Habermas's early theoretical commitment to the idea that democratic participation is the only a guardrail against totalitarianism and dictatorship, both of which seek a "neutralization of the citizens (*Neutralisierung der Staatsbürger*)" that turns members of the polity into passive subjects of rule or domination (*Herrschaft*).[123]

Habermas's attraction to Abendroth's approach is rooted not only in its social democratic heritage, to which he was politically sympathetic, but also in the fact that the other two schools were tainted by their association with National Socialism. This connection is particularly clear in the case of Schmitt, who joined the Nazi party and even served as president of the Association of National Socialist Jurists (*Nationalsozialistischer Rechtswahrerbund*). Schmitt's endorsement of Hitler's *Machtergreifung* (seizure of power) through his declaration of a "state of exception," his role in legitimating the totalitarian *Führerprinzip*, and his refusal to participate in the postwar denazification process made Habermas suspicious. In Habermas's mind, Schmitt had an "aura of something conspiratorial and initiatory around him" and his students after the war.[124]

Although Smend refused to collaborate with the National Socialists and was forced to renounce his academic chair in Berlin, his view of judges as neutral interpreters of statutory law allowed jurists who had collaborated with the Third Reich to argue that they had had no choice but to implement the Nazi legal order. In the words of Gustav Radbruch, the former Minister of Justice in the Weimar Republic, "Positivism, with its conviction 'law is law' [*Gesetz ist Gesetz*], actually made the German class of jurists [*Juristenstand*] defenseless against laws of an arbitrary and criminal content."[125] Although German jurists sought to overcome this problem by returning to theories of natural law to ground the fundamental protection of "human dignity" rooted in the *Grundgesetz*, Habermas remained skeptical of "the notion that judges and professional jurists should monopolize the interpretation of the constitution." On the contrary, he worried that Smend's approach placed political power "beyond the reach of any democratically legitimated legislator."[126]

His early emphasis on the importance of participation and his decision to root sovereignty in the legislative branch demonstrates that "Habermas has always been a democrat first and a liberal second."[127] This is particularly visible in *Structural Transformation*, which builds on what he sees as the "forgotten idea of the rule of the people in the form of direct democracy."[128] Habermas sought to concretize this claim by developing an account of democratic legitimacy based on informed discussion and reasoned agreement, rather than institutional divisions of power, majoritarian elections, or mechanisms of fair aggregation. By highlighting the crucial role that "communicative processes of opinion- and will-formation that precede voting," Habermas produced a "talk-centric" rather than "vote-centric" notion of democratic legitimacy.[129]

Although written in 1958, Habermas's conceptual essay on political participation, along with the broader empirical analysis on which is was based (also authored by Habermas), was published three years later as *Student und Politik*.[130] When it finally appeared in 1961 it did so without the imprimatur of the Institute. Rather than being included in the series "Frankfurt Contributions to Sociology" published by the *Europäischer Verlagsanstalt*, it instead appeared on its own with Luchterhand Verlag, which would later also publish *Structural Transformation* in 1962.

The reason for both of these developments were the strident objections of Horkheimer, which ultimately led to Habermas's departure from the *Institut für Sozialforschung*. Although Adorno went to bat for his young assistant, calling "On the Concept of Political Participation" a "tour de force," Horkheimer stuck to his position.[131] Horkheimer recognized that Habermas "probably has a good, or even brilliant, career as a writer in front of him." However, he was convinced that with his overt leftist political activism "he [Habermas] would only cause the Institute immense damage."[132] In fact, in his view Habermas was proof that "one can spend . . . a long time with us [in the Institute], without broadening his experience regarding social reality in the slightest, without even contemplating the present with understanding (*mit Verstand über die Gegenwart nachzudenken*)."[133]

Horkheimer's understanding of the relationship between theory and practice at this time was very different from the one he espoused earlier in his career. Most notably, in his programmatic essay on the differences between "Traditional and Critical Theory" (1937) Horkheimer argues that theory should seek to have a practical impact on society by serving as a "a critical, promotive factor in the development of the masses" by combatting the capitalist ideology that keeps "most men" from recognizing their true interest in emancipation. In contrast to Marx, who thought that theory had the potential to induce social transformation the near future, Horkheimer is more skeptical, arguing that social conditions at the time meant that the prospects for truly transformative action at the mass level were slim. As a result, he argues that theory must go underground, where it can be preserved by "small groups of men" until more favorable historical circumstances come about.[134]

During the course of World War II, Horkheimer's view of the relationship between theory and practice became even more pessimistic. In *Dialectic of Enlightenment*, based on transcripts of a series of conversations held with Adorno while in exile in California in 1944, Horkheimer concluded that critical theory should abandon its links to action, as its emancipatory message would most likely be corrupted by the same ideological processes that created the all-encompassing domination the world was undergoing at the time. As a result of his experiences—the First World War, the Third Reich, the Second World War, exile in Switzerland and America, and of his return to the early FRG, which would probably better be described as post-Nazi rather than democratic—Horkheimer abandoned his faith in revolutionary politics. Following his return to Germany after the end of the war, Horkheimer's position hardened even further given a number of factors, including the anti-communist political climate of the early Cold War, the overwhelmingly conservative, even stifling political climate in the newly created West German state, and his fears that the government would impede the work of the Institute, when it had barely managed to survive its exile during the *Nazizeit*.

As he confessed to Adorno in 1958, "What apparently needs to be defended today certainly appears to me not to be the sublimation [*Aufhebung*] of philosophy through revolution, but what remains of bourgeois civilization."[135] In these circumstances, he argued that all theory could do was to reflect on and give expression to "the self-surrender by reason of its status as a spiritual substance."[136] Unlike Habermas, a reformist product of postwar "reeducation," who sought to translate the utopian impulses he had gleaned from the Frankfurt School into a plea for the greater democratization of the Federal Republic, Horkheimer was convinced that "nothing very positive is to be expected from political changes."[137]

This skeptical, perhaps even resigned position was very different from the reformist position that defines Habermas's political engagement throughout his entire career. Habermas shared Horkheimer's skepticism about the utility of revolutionary thinking, but unlike the director of the Institute, whose lived experience (*Erlebnis*) made him skeptical of democracy's ability to resolve the pathologies of the contemporary world, Habermas had faith in the possibilities presented by the postwar democratic *Rechtsstaat* (his many critiques of West Germany in practice not withstanding). Adorno "publicly voiced his commitment to democracy, contributed to public policy-making in the area of criminal law reform and participated actively in public rallies again the emergency laws." By contrast, Horkheimer was skeptical that meaningful change was possible in the postwar situation.[138]

In this sense in it clear that "Horkheimer took the principle of the message in a bottle [*Flaschenpost*] seriously."[139] Conversely, while Habermas would later draw on Adorno's methods, arguing that they could ground a "radical reformism" that really had the potential to change society for the better, during this period he sought to achieve such gradual changes primarily by participating in social movements as an activist. Unfortunately, such political engagement was incompatible with Horkheimer's view of the situation and his desire the ensure that the Institute remained not only a-political, but in many respects also anti-political.

DEPARTURE FROM THE INSTITUTE

Although Habermas does not believe that theory can be translated into practice in any direct way, these two areas of his work clearly impact each other. The problem, as Müller-Doohm points out, is that in the young, newly opened, post-Nazi public sphere of the early Federal Republic, Habermas was left "without a role model" whose approach to theory and practice he could readily follow or copy.[140] This is not to say that he was the first philosopher to assume the mantle of the public intellectual in West Germany. On the contrary, thinkers including Karl Jaspers as well as the political scientist and journalist Dolf Sternberger—in addition to Adorno himself—had previously done so. While it would take until the 1980s for Habermas to develop his mature conception of the public intellectual, his desire for such a role was already visible in his 1953 article on Heidegger, where he spoke of the important political role played by "the guardianship of public criticism (*die Wächterschaft der öffentlichen Kritik*)."[141]

In addition to being enabled by his encounter with critical theory, Habermas's development from a journalist "with a sense of the topicality about the urgent problems of the day" to an academic and public intellectual was decisively shaped by the time he spent as Adorno's assistant in Frankfurt.[142] It was, after all, "Adorno who created a new role [for the public intellectual] through his specific kind of public use of reason" in the years of the Federal Republic.[143] However, based on what I have already said, it is also clear that both Habermas's political engagement and his desire to maintain a relationship between theory and political praxis played a key role in both Horkheimer's rejection of *Student and Politics* (as well as *Structural Transformation*) and the fact that Habermas was forced to leave the Institute in 1959, despite Adorno's continued support.

Unlike later commentators, who see him as an apolitical ideal theorist, Horkheimer immediately realized that Habermas was not only a deeply political individual, but also that his leftist political views clearly impacted on his scientific work. As a result, long before he developed his conception of the public intellectual, Habermas was already translating the insights of his academic work into political programs by calling on the public to participate in democratic political life by engaging in public discourse and making their voices heard so that "all decisions of consequence . . . depend on the practical discourse of the participants."[144] While he was writing "On the Concept of Political Participation," Habermas notes that he felt that he had no choice but to also participate in the student movement.[145]

It was precisely the connection between his academic work and his activism that was decisive for Horkheimer, who was a very calculating, politically-aware, and perhaps overly cautious thinker.[146] As Müller-Doohm points out, the "eventful" relationship between Horkheimer and Habermas is a "story in itself, whose unfathomable aspects are open only to speculation." This murky picture is due in large part to the fact that few archival sources of this conflict survive, a problem enhanced by Habermas's general reticence to discuss the details of what happened. However, it is clear that these differences were deep-seated and that Horkheimer was skeptical of the "dialectical Mr. H."—as he referred to Habermas in his correspondence with Adorno—from the start.[147]

At first these problems were not about politics. On the contrary, it was Habermas's published reports on the 1956 Freud lecture series at the university that initially drew Horkheimer's disapproval. In what Habermas reports was their first actual conversation, Horkheimer voiced his unhappiness at the fact that Habermas had downplayed the "the role of the Institute for Social Research as the main organizer of the event." Habermas was shocked by this, both as a result of the " 'us and them' pattern underlying this criticism," but also due to the fact that despite his published critiques of traditional authoritarian structures, Horkheimer apparently "seemed to think that he could tell his collaborators what they were to say in their own publications."[148]

While Habermas's shock is understandable, it also testifies to the fact that he had not had the chance to read many of Horkheimer's older texts at this time, such as the inaugural lecture Horkheimer gave upon assuming the directorship of the Institute. After all, in "Tasks of an Institute" (1931) the new director had already made it clear that he did not see himself as leading "a collegial administration," but rather believed in a "dictatorship of the director."[149] This attitude contrasted significantly with that of Adorno. In fact, after arriving at the Institute Habermas was shocked by the dependence Adorno displayed vis-à-vis Horkheimer. As a result, he "felt that he had to defend the sensitive Adorno against the demonstrations of superiority coming from the older director of the institute."[150]

The relationship between Habermas and Horkheimer further deteriorated soon thereafter. In 1956, Hans-Georg Gadamer, a leading figure in philosophical hermeneutics and co-founder of the new postwar journal *Philosophische Rundschau*, asked Habermas to write a review essay on contemporary movements in Western Marxism. Habermas, who had already published a shorter essay on entitled "Perspectives on Marx" in *Merkur* in 1955, accepted this "appealing (*reizvoll*)" commission.[151] In his letter to Gadamer he noted that he was already "to a certain extent (*einigermaßen*)" prepared for the assignment given that he had already been engaging with this primary literature on Marx in the last half year, even though he had "consumed rather than enjoyed it."[152] Habermas's "Literature Review of the philosophical discussion of Marx and Marxism" focused on Marx's concepts of revolution and reification.[153] Gadamer was pleased with the contribution, noting that Habermas "was obviously positively inclined towards fundamental Marxist ideas, but who avoided all political judgement and limited himself to the conceptual analysis of the Marx literature in question."[154]

While this is not a political writing directed to the public sphere, it is important because of Horkheimer's reaction. In a letter to Adorno, Horkheimer paned Habermas's understanding of revolution, noting that he treats the concept as "a kind of affirmative idea, a finite absolute, an idol, which thoroughly falsifies what we mean by critique and critical theory," which is based on an awareness of "of the futility of the thought of salvation [*Rettung*] through revolution." Connecting this reading of the essay to Habermas's political activities, Horkheimer expresses his fear that Habermas's Marxism—Habermas describes his own political attitude at the time as "anti-anti-communism"—plays into the hands of both "the gentlemen in the East" and "of the potential fascists within." Although he recognizes Habermas's talent, Horkheimer argues that he "is blinkered, despite all cleverness, and lacks *du bon sens*." He concludes by asking Adorno to fire Habermas, since "we may not allow the truly careless attitude of this assistant to ruin the institute."[155]

In this case, Adorno was able to push back on Horkheimer's demands. He did so again in 1958, when Horkheimer rejected Habermas's "On the Concept of Political Participation" for similar reasons. However, the director's attitude to Adorno's assistant and what Habermas would later refer to as Horkheimer's "radically pessimistic fundamental convictions [hidden] behind an armor of fear and tactical adaptation" meant that he had little future at the Institute.[156] Fortunately, Gadamer thought highly enough of Habermas to help him obtain a scholarship from the German Research Foundation (*Deutsche Forschungsgemeinschaft*), which would enable him to work on his Habilitation—the second doctorate required for eligibility for professorial posts in the German academy—full time. There is a certain irony to this, given that Gadamer's affiliations to the Nazi party during the previous regime made him a less likely ally than Horkheimer given Habermas's politics and his views on the past. However, in order to secure a place for himself in academia, Habermas was willing to accept help wherever he could get it. As a result, he decided to leave the Institute in July of 1959 to take up the "existence of a scholarship holder."[157]

CONCLUSION

This chapter documented the transformation of Habermas from a freelance journalist to an academic philosopher and sociologist with a "secondary vocation" as a critical, public intellectual. Although his return to the academy as his "primary vocation" means that Habermas the bulk of his work is academic and thus seeks "effects change precisely by remaining itself," this does not mean that his strong political convictions disappeared or are no longer important for his work.[158] On the contrary, Habermas's introduction to critical theory, with its ambition to produce "a theory dominated at every turn by a concern for reasonable conditions of life" enabled Habermas to start to combine his theoretical and political interest in a way that the bourgeois, quietistic philosophy he had learned from his previous teachers, all of whom were tainted by their association with National Socialism, had made impossible.[159]

Habermas's political commitments are visible in all of the work he produced during this period. In his public writings, he addresses issues related to the West German lack of commitment to working through the legacies of the Nazi period in its early years, the importance of true educational reform, the dangers of rearmament. He also voices his opposition to the silencing of true political debate within the Federal Republic, which he sees as a *Kanzlerdemokratie* (Chancellor democracy) that leaves little space for debate within the *Bundestag* (parliament), much less within the public sphere more generally. These political commitments are also visible in the academic works he produces in this period, which focus on citizen participation. His reading of the *Staatslehre* bolsters this argument by highlights the legislative branch as a true carrier of democratic life and values.

In light of the fact that Habermas "had the same critical attitude to many things as Adorno himself," it is not surprising that he gravitated to Adorno rather than Horkheimer.[160] Unlike Adorno, who took on an active role as a public intellectual in the nascent public sphere of the postwar FRG, writing and speaking on the radio about a number of issues related to education, politics and culture in the wake of Auschwitz, Horkheimer was much more reticent. Whether this reluctance was part of a broader conservative turn, an extension of the quietism that he had practiced to ensure the safety of the Institute during his time in exile in the US, or a reflection of the broader mistrust he felt towards Germany and the striking social, political and cultural continuities between the Third Reich and the early Federal Republic, is an open question. What is clear is that Habermas's overt leftist activism—as well as his attempt to bring theory and practice together in his work—resulted in a clash with the Institute's director. The fact that Habermas sought political inspiration for his philosophical work—and vice versa—as well, led to conflicts that required him to leave the Institute and continue his career elsewhere.

Although Habermas had successfully obtained funding to complete *Structural Transformation of the Public Sphere*—and still had Adorno's support—he still needed to find a German professor to sponsor his *Habilitation*. While Adorno theoretically could do so on his own without the director's permission, he was unwilling to cross Horkheimer in this way. Habermas's search was not easy, especially given his activism and strong political positions. Many older, more conservative professors were understandably wary of employing a young radical like Habermas, who might call them out for their accommodation to the previous regime, despite Gadamer's support. Fortunately, Habermas found both a political and an academic ally in Wolfgang Abendroth at the University of Marburg, to whom he ultimately dedicated *Structural Transformation* when it appeared in print in 1962.

CHAPTER 4

A Partisan Professor in the Student Movement, 1960–1971

The mature Habermas is often criticized for "domesticating" critical theory. This reproach points to his development of an allegedly "neo-idealist" linguistic paradigm of philosophy, which replaced the supposedly more engaged, Marxist approach of the first generation of the Frankfurt School.[1] However, as the conclusion to the previous chapter showed, Habermas was forced to leave the Institute for Social Research precisely because of his overt political activism and his attempts to put his theoretical commitments into practice—a desire that clashed with the practical resignation of Horkheimer, who was too politically cautious and calculating for Habermas's taste.[2] More specifically, the director of the Institute pushed Habermas out (at least in part) because the young academic sought to bring theory and practice together. This all occurred before the moment that most defines Habermas's career as an engaged political actor: his association with the student movement of the 1960s. Ironically, at the height of the protests in 1968—some of which Habermas actively participated in—he had not only been back in Frankfurt for four years but also occupied Horkheimer's old professorial chair (with Horkheimer's blessing and support, no less).

Despite Horkheimer's concerns in the late 1950s, Habermas's realist critics are correct that he "is no passionate revolutionary," as evidenced by his break with the students over what he described as their voluntaristic approach—underpinned by the belief that they could create a revolutionary situation in West Germany through an act of will. That said, interpretations of Habermas as a quietist figure who is "is not a passionate anything" also miss the mark.[3] Although he did not agree with the students all—or even most—of the time, in line with what I have called the theoretical continuity thesis, Habermas stood up for his philosophical commitments by actively and passionately engaging with the students throughout the 1960s, even when he disagreed with their ideas and the actions they ultimately undertook.

This support—and Habermas's general encouragement of student participation in politics—testifies to his belief that the student movement was an important contribution to the still-nascent democratic public sphere of postwar West Germany. However, he also drew a line in the sand by disagreeing with their revolutionary diagnosis of the situation and their acceptance of the need for violence. Although he could have been, in the words of one of his colleagues at the time, "the charismatic ringleader (*Anführer*) of the student movement," Habermas rejected this role by publicly voicing his disagreements with them.[4] As Ulrich Oevermann, one of his assistants during this period, points out, "Habermas was exceptionally courageous at the time. He stuck his neck out for everyone else. At teach-ins he . . . stood up and spoke his mind. . . . It was not easy, and at the time it was very brave."[5]

As the previous two chapters have shown, Habermas's commitment to writing for the popular press "in reaction to the day (*aus dem Tag heraus*)" dates back to his adolescence.[6] As he notes in 1964, "My interests . . . extend to philosophy and sociology, and a little, of course, to time-critical (*zeitkritische*) and political issues."[7] Initially, Habermas scratched his political itch by working as a freelance journalist.

After arriving at the Institute, however, Adorno introduced him to the idea of "'committed sociology' as practiced in Frankfurt."[8] This approach not only got him in trouble (with Horkheimer) at the end of the 1950s but also again in the late 1960s, when he broke with the student movement. Although he had worked hard to create within the Socialist German Students' Union (*Sozialistische Deutsche Studentenbund*, or SDS) the kind of democratic politics that could combat the decline of broader public sphere he had diagnosed in *Structural Transformation of the Public Sphere*, by the end of the 1960s it was clear that "his own experience with an attempt to create a critical public within an organization was not encouraging."[9]

Although *Structural Transformation* is clearly part of Habermas's philosophical oeuvre, it had political aims as well. In retrospect, Habermas notes that he wrote the book in order to analyze the potentially "dangerous . . . inherent weaknesses" of the West German Federal Republic.[10] It also played an important role in elevating Habermas's public stature, as it was "one of the most influential books for the incipient oppositional movement at German universities," which helped to define "a generation of West German radicals."[11] However, despite its importance, it is also clear that the more radical elements within the *Außerparlamentarische Opposition* (extraparliamentary opposition, or APO) led by the student movement wanted to go well beyond discursive forms of opinion-formation. Instead of engaging in the proverbial "long march through institutions" that Habermas had advocated in the final pages of *Structural Transformation*, they wanted to engage in actual revolution.

The current chapter traces Habermas's intellectual journey toward this conclusion through the 1960s, culminating in his second departure from Frankfurt. This first part (1959–1963) covers his habilitation in Marburg (though he was still living in Frankfurt at the time) and his first professorship at the University of Heidelberg. This period is defined by his relationship with Wolfgang Abendroth, the Marxist political scientist who offered Habermas a lifeline after he was forced out from the Institute for Social Research in 1959. Although Habermas initially approached several other professors, it was Abendroth who saved Habermas's academic career by sponsoring *Structural Transformation* as his habilitation.

Abendroth also inspired the form that Habermas's public engagement took during this period—an approach Habermas referred to the model of the "partisan professor" in a 1966 laudation, where he compared Abendroth favorably to the unorthodox Marxists of the Praxis School in Yugoslavia, whom he had befriended during this period. In contrast to the separation thesis that Habermas would adopt in the 1980s, Abendroth's approach emphasized the theoretical continuity between academic work and political activism.[12] Although Habermas rejects the application of this label to himself, I argue that, from the external perspective of the observer, it best describes his interaction with the student movement of the 1960s.[13]

The next two parts of the chapter cover Habermas's second stay in Frankfurt as Horkheimer's successor from 1964–1971. During this period, Habermas initially continued to act as an overtly political academic who, despite his sympathies for the students, also subjected their ideas to critical scrutiny. However, as the final section documents, the decline of his relationship with the student movement followed his 1967 accusation that some of its leaders were engaging in "left fascism"—an overly polemical remark intended to highlight his fear that the violent leftist actionism of the students, seemingly grounded in the belief that they could change society through sheer force of will, had inadvertently borrowed a key characteristic of National Socialism. His critique of the student leadership's decisionistic belief that they could conjure a revolutionary situation out of thin air ultimately played a key role in his second departure from Frankfurt, as well as from the public sphere and from his role as a partisan professor—the subject of the following chapter.

HABILITATION AND FIRST PROFESSORSHIP

Horkheimer's rejection of *Structural Transformation* forced Habermas to look elsewhere for someone to sponsor his habilitation. Initially, Habermas contacted Helmut Schelsky and Helmuth Plessner, both of whom reluctantly turned down his request in order to promote internal candidates at their own universities. After this, he sought to revive his journalistic career; Habermas even approached Karl Korn about getting a job as a journalist at the *FAZ*. Korn, however, rejected his request, telling him, "You belong in the academy (*Sie gehören in der Wissenshaft*)." In fact, it was Korn who suggested that Habermas contact Wolfgang Abendroth, the only openly Marxist professor of political science in Germany at the time, even though the two had no prior relationship. Fortunately for Habermas, after speaking on the phone—which was unusual at the time—Abendroth expressed his willingness to take him on by acting as his *Habilitationsvater*, primarily "for political reasons (*aus politischen Gründen*)."[14]

Initially, this association was one of convenience. Habermas continued to live in Frankfurt and only sat in on one of Abendroth's seminars.[15] While this arrangment allowed Habermas to maintain his relationship with Adorno, he quickly developed a deep appreciation for Abendroth, whom he would later describe as a "very important influence on me."[16] In contrast to Adorno's more restrained engagement with contemporary affairs as a public intellectual, Abendroth was openly affiliated with the left wing of the Social Democratic Party of Germany (*Sozialdemokratische Partei Deutschlands*, or SPD) and "was at home in the milieu of the workers' movement." Like Adorno—and in stark contrast to Heidegger, Rothacker, and so many other postwar German academics—Habermas also admired the fact that Abendroth was afflicted "by the failing of being unable to forget the Nazi period (*hatte den Fehler, die Nazi-Zeit nicht vergessen zu können*)."[17] Habermas also notes that Abendroth's "reformist side appealed to me."[18]

As a key contributor to the *Staatslehre* or the *Staatsrechtslehre* (state/constitutional theory, or more literally, "teaching on state law"), the field that preceded the development of political science (*Politikwissenschaft*) in West Germany, Abendroth argued that the Bundestag was the ultimate guarantor of the constitution (outlined in my more detailed discussion of these debates in chapter 3). In contrast to Carl Schmitt, who rooted sovereignty in "the executive, which is essentially active," and Rudolf Smend, who championed the judicial branch's ability to protect fundamental rights through judicial review, Abendroth argued that democratic values and their concretization must come "from the people and not the jurists," i.e., from the only elected branch of government that could claim to directly express popular sovereignty: the legislature.[19] Given his leftist social-democratic beliefs, Abendroth combined this commitment with the Marxian conviction that "the people" could only exercise their sovereignty if their basic material needs had been met. As a result, he argued that the democratic state had to also be a social welfare state. In a speech he later gave on the centenary of Abendroth's birth, Habermas credits him with helping the German people realize "that the welfare state is a condition for the legitimacy of the democratic state based on the rule of law."[20]

Politically speaking, Abendroth also supported Habermas's connection to the student movement, thus helping him to make a "vital contribution . . . to the development of an intellectual left" within the SDS. In 1959 the SPD fundamentally transformed itself by expunging the last hint of Marxism from its party manifesto, thus abandoning the aim of communism. These changes, adopted at an extraordinary meeting of the party conference in Bad Godesberg, generated massive protests within the SDS, whose members were more militant than the SPD leadership, with which the socialist student organization was formally affiliated.

The students—and Habermas—perceived the SPD's new stance as too accommodating to the existing capitalist system. By contrast, the SDS and its supporters sought to preserve a genuinely socialist alternative without falling prey to the dogmatic, authoritarian, party-centered orthodoxy that defined the communist regimes behind the Iron Curtain. To support the students in what they saw as a betrayal of the fundamental socialist principles of the SPD, Abendroth, Habermas and a number of other like-minded intellectuals founded the Association of Socialist Sponsors of the Friends, Sponsors, and Former Members of the SDS (*Sozialistische Förderer-Gesellschaft der Freunde, Förderer und ehemaligen Mitglieder des SDS*). The SPD's party executive sought to quell what it saw as a rebellion against its leadership by declaring membership in this society incompatible with membership in the SDS.[21]

Habermas's work alongside Abendroth in defending the students against the party leadership cemented him as a key leader of the left and an ally of the student movement. This status was underscored when Habermas delivered the plenary lecture at the SDS student conference in Frankfurt on October 4, 1962. Yet the tensions that would later lead to his break with the movement were already evident, as at this event Habermas already warned the students against the dual temptations of "both seeking to act as the intellectual cadre of a new party or to become professional revolutionaries."[22]

Habermas's direct engagement in politics and with the SPD was not limited to his support of the SDS. On the contrary, during this period he interacted directly with Willy Brandt, who became the first social-democratic chancellor of West Germany in 1969. The first of these meetings occurred in 1963, when Brandt was still the mayor of West Berlin. In October of that year Habermas was invited to participate in the Science and Politics Discussion Group (*Gesprächskreis Wissenschaft und Politik*) organized by the Friedrich-Ebert-Stiftung, a foundation affiliated with the SPD.[23]

Although Habermas saw himself as a partisan academic who never "placed [himself] outside the framework of the student movement," in his report written after his meeting with Brandt he explicitly rejected the idea that science (*Wissenschaft*) could be directly applied to politics.[24] On the contrary, he observed that when academics met with the SPD, they did not represent "science" as such, but instead were merely present in their capacity as "intellectuals friendly to the SPD (*SPD-freundlicher Intellektuellen*)." Habermas noted that the only service such intellectuals can provide in their capacity as researchers is by doing studies that will provide the main opposition party in the FRG with the same kind and quality of information that government ministers receive.[25]

A second meeting occurred in 1970 after Brandt had already become chancellor.[26] This interaction was part of a conference on the topic "*Eigentum verpflichtet* (Property/Ownership Entails Obligations)," which was designed to help the SPD think about its policies toward the ownership of private property in the wake of Bad Godesberg. Habermas wrote to Brandt following the meeting and said, "I am convinced that the government you lead is the best we have yet had in this country; it deserves our confidence." However, he also expresses his worry that "tactical, electoral considerations (*wahltaktische Überlegungen*)" were causing the SPD to abandon the core commitments of social democracy. In regard to the topic of the meeting, he notes that the SPD must remain committed to changing the "existing system of private property," rather than merely trying to work within it.[27]

Despite the fact that Habermas overtly supported the SPD and Brandt himself, his biographer Stefan Müller-Doohm notes that this "did not keep him from openly criticizing the opportunistic behaviour of the SPD."[28] The ambivalence visible in Habermas's attitude toward the party despite his identification with social democracy is characteristic of his relationship to other movements and institutions aligned with his political sympathies. In addition to the student movement, this is also clear in his broader views of postwar West Germany. On one level—unlike the first generation of the Frankfurt School—Habermas believed in constitutional democracy and in the potential of the Basic Law (*Grundgesetz*) that the Allies had imposed on West Germany at its creation in 1949. However, as he wrote in an article published by the cultural journal *Magnum* in 1961, he was also scared that the existing West German political class, led by Chancellor Konrad Adenauer, was turning the FRG into an "elective monarchy (*Wahlmonarchie*)" where "decisions are not publicly discussed by citizens," but instead are decided by "great men" who use "scientifically led marketing" to "replace the immediate relationship of the individual with politics."[29]

That said, Habermas was also not blind to the achievements of West Germany. Writing to Leszek Kołakowski in 1970 when he was trying to convince the dissident Polish scholar of Marxism to take up Adorno's old chair in Frankfurt, Habermas notes, "I am one of the intellectuals on the left who has continually observed, criticized, and in many cases fought against the inner development of postwar Germany with great anxiety (*Unbehagen*)." However, despite his concerns—and to his great surprise—he also observes that "in the last few years the Federal Republic has, in comparison to America and France, for example, become a liberal country."[30]

This self-critical attitude was also visible in Habermas's response to the *Spiegel* affair of 1962, which erupted when the editor of Germany's leading political magazine, along with several of its journalists, were arrested on dubious—arguably even unconstitutional—grounds for allegedly revealing state secrets in an article critical of NATO. In the wake of this event, Habermas joined a number of his colleagues at the University of Heidelberg in noting how worrying these developments were in light of "[t]he absence of democratic continuity in Germany, the memory of the decline of the Weimar Republic, and the ensuing rupture in our tradition of the rule of law during the Hitler era."[31] This critical intervention had the desired effect, as it helped to rally the public against the coalition in power, ultimately forcing the chancellor, Konrad Adenauer, to form a new cabinet after the collapse of his government. As Habermas would later note, this was further evidence of the democratic success of West Germany, as "the force of social integration that lay in a public" had demonstrated its power effecting "a change in attitude through argument," i.e. embodying the ideal of discursive democratic legitimacy that Habermas had presented in *Structural Transformation*.[32]

Habermas also continued to write journalistic articles. Following this incident, he published a piece in the *Blätter für deutsche und internationale Politik* arguing for an "abstention from military calculations, which, in the light of the nuclear stalemate now reached between East and West, can neither produce the correct result nor correspond to political requirements in a time of easing tensions." However, while he was happy to comment on these issues in the public sphere, during this period he started to move away from direct engagement with the political system. As a result, he declined an invitation to discuss these issues with Adenauer's successor, Ludwig Erhard, at an event devoted to the topic "Germany from an Internal and External Perspective (*Deutschland aus innerer und äußerer Sicht*)."³³

Habermas's pacifistic tendencies are also evident in his review of Armin Mohler's book analyzing the foreign policy of the French president Charles de Gaulle. Habermas rejects Mohler's positive assessment of the state and of traditional policies based on the balance of power in the face of nuclear weapons. In light of the Third Reich and the horrors of Hiroshima and Nagasaki, Habermas observes, "The violent substance of a potentially unrestrained self-assertion of sovereign states against each other has lost its barbarian innocence." Interestingly, this article marks the first instance that I have been able to locate of Habermas using the terms *Weltinnenpolitik* ("global domestic politics") and *Weltöffentlichkeit* ("global public sphere"), both of which would become common in his later work as a philosopher and public intellectual.³⁴ The term *Weltinnenpolitik*, which would come to play an important role in both his philosophical and his public-facing work after the fall of the Wall in 1989, was initially popularized by the German physicist and philosopher, Carl Friedrich von Weitzsäcker, with whom Habermas would co-direct a Max Planck Institute in the 1970s.³⁵

In July 1963 Habermas also published a polemic in *Merkur* against "moral rearmament," a term he saw as a conservative excuse for an attack on homosexuals and other minorities based on "the model of anti-Semitism."³⁶ However, in a piece published later in 1964, he also rejected the idea that the mere "presence of Auschwitz" resulted in an "identity in substance between politics and crime." Of course, this is not to say that Habermas thought that Auschwitz was unimportant politically; on the contrary, he thought that maintaining its presence in German collective memory was crucial, concluding that "if no dread remains, [then] the monsters return."³⁷

Some of his articles from this period consisted of play reviews or addressed other issues in the realm of culture, demonstrating his continued interest in the aesthetic.³⁸ He also published a number of public interventions on important German thinkers, many of which first appeared in *Merkur* and were later republished in the German edition of his *Philosophical-Political Profiles*.³⁹ Despite his strong interest in both domestic and foreign policy, however, Habermas declined the opportunity to write a regular international press review column for *Merkur* for fear that it would distract him from his academic work.⁴⁰

After obtaining his habilitation in Marburg in 1961—a process that was far from smooth despite Abendroth's support—Habermas became a *Privatdozent* with a *venia legendi* (permission to lecture), which made him eligible for a professorship in Germany. Much to Habermas's own surprise, he immediately received a *Ruf* (call) to an extraordinary (*ausserordentliche*) professorship in philosophy in Heidelberg.⁴¹ This offer had been instigated by Hans-Georg Gadamer, a phenomenologist closely associated with Heidegger, who knew and respected Habermas as a conversation partner their time together in Frankfurt.

Gadamer's invitation was rooted in his conviction that the addition of Habermas would give his faculty a dimension that it lacked.⁴² For his part, Habermas was worried about the potentially conservative tendencies of Gadamer's philosophical approach due to its emphasis on tradition. He was also wary about returning to philosophy, a discipline he thought that he had left behind. However, he notes that to his own surprise that reading Gadamer's recently published *Truth and Method* (1960) "helped me find my way back into academic philosophy" following a period when he had been focused more on sociology and social theory.⁴³

During this time Habermas also maintained his interest in university politics and published a number of interventions on the topic, in addition to the more academic publication of *Student und Politik: Eine soziologische Untersuchung zum politischen Bewußtsein Frankfurter Studenten* (1961), the study of Frankfurt students that had led Horkheimer to push Habermas out of the Institute in 1959. For instance, in 1962, Habermas wrote a short article reflecting on the political role of student groups in the wake of the construction of the Berlin Wall. While Habermas clearly affirms the right and desirability of student participation in public affairs, he was more pessimistic about what they—as well as "every other knowledgeable (*nonnale*) citizen"—can actually achieve in the contemporary situation.⁴⁴

However, in a line that foreshadows his later concerns about the decisionism of the student movement, he also hopes that they will not respond to this "limited scope of action (*Aktionsspielraum*)" by resorting to "the use of plastic bombs

(*Umgang mit Plastikbomben*)." While it may be frustrating and slow, he encourages the students to focus their attention on where they can be most effective, i.e., on the "democratization of higher education" through university governance and participation in the internal processes of "opinion-formation within the political parties, whose academic future (*Nachwuchs*) they represent."[45]

The next year Habermas published "On the Social Transformation of Academic Education" in *Merkur* based on a talk that he had delivered in Berlin in January 1963. In opposition to Schelsky and what could be seen as the other techno-optimists of the time, Habermas was wary of the effects of technological progress on the lives of individuals and communities.[46] In his view, given the changes wrought by technology in the twentieth century, the university needed to shift away from its traditional Humboldtian association with the formation of bourgeois character (*Bildung*). He argued that it should instead devote itself to the task of helping students (as well as society at large) "translate scientifically reified ... relationships back into the network of lived relations."

Based on this conviction, Habermas contends that education can and should be political insofar as it ensures the "return of the power of technical control (*Verfügung*) to the consensus of acting and negotiating citizens" in the democratic public sphere.[47] In making this point, he again pushes back on the idea that scientific research must be divorced from praxis. This statement also foreshadows his mature view of the role of philosophy as a "stand-in" or "interpreter" that helps to translate scientific developments into the everyday lives—or "lifeworlds (*Lebenswelten*)"—of individuals.[48]

During this period, Habermas was also involved in a debate over the proper approach to the social sciences within postwar West German sociology. Although it stretched on through the mid-1960s, the so-called "Positivism Dispute" (*Positivismusstreit*) started in 1961 at a meeting of the German Society for Sociology (Deutsche Gesellschaft für Soziologie) on the "The Logic of the Social Sciences (*Die Logik der Sozialwissenschaften*)" in Tübingen. Karl Popper and Adorno used this opportunity to present their approaches—positivism and critical theory, respectively—as the proper way of grounding knowledge in the social sciences. Given my focus on Habermas's political writings for the public sphere, I will not discuss this dispute in detail, as—unlike his erstwhile mentor at the Institute for Social Research—"Habermas does not appear to be overly distressed at the political implications of positivist research."[49]

In fact, a mere decade later, Habermas would dismiss the entire controversy as "outdated (*überholt*)."⁵⁰ What is important here is that, despite the circumstances surrounding his departure from the Institute, Habermas vocally and unreservedly supported Adorno's position vis-à-vis Popper, thus "remov[ing] any doubts as to whether he should be considered a member of the Frankfurt circle."⁵¹ In the meantime, Horkheimer had also overcome his reservations regarding the "dialectical Mr. H." In part, this appears to be due to the fact that *Structural Transformation*, far from furthering a revolutionary agenda that Horkheimer rejected, ultimately presented "a defense of the liberal promise of the equal participation" in public affairs.⁵² This is important, as it helps explain why Habermas received a call (*Ruf*) to return to the Goethe University to take up Horkheimer's chair in 1964.

A PARTISAN PROFESSOR IN FRANKFURT

Although his position at Heidelberg was formally "extraordinary (*ausserodentlicher Professor*)"—a rank below full professor but nonetheless permanent and secure—Habermas's professorship there provided him with a stable academic appointment. Nonetheless, in 1964 he received two separate calls (*Rufe*) for professorial chairs: one from Berlin, followed shortly thereafter by another from Frankfurt, the latter of which was open due to Horkheimer's retirement. Despite his previous reservations, Horkheimer now fully supported Adorno in arguing that Habermas was best suited "to combine theoretical sociology and philosophy" in the way that his chair required, noting that of all the possible candidates, Habermas was the only "individual of distinction."⁵³ Horkheimer, having gotten wind of Berlin's offer, wrote to Habermas in February 1963 encouraging him "only to decide to go to Berlin if Adorno's and my wish [to have you receive a call from Frankfurt], of which you know, is not fulfilled (*nicht in Erfüllung geht*)."⁵⁴

At first glance, this should have been an easy decision; it was not. Although Horkheimer had overcome his objections to "the dialectical Mr. H," Habermas was still deeply wounded by what had happened. Although Horkheimer had already passed the directorship of the Institute for Social Research to Adorno, Habermas immediately made clear that if he came to Frankfurt he did not want to take up the directorship of the Institute for Social Research that normally would have accompanied Horkheimer's chair. Although he ultimately chose to accept Frankfurt's offer, in explaining his departure from Heidelberg to Gadamer, he noted, "I believe that I am acting in my interests, although I am not completely certain of it; I only know that I am deciding against my feelings (*gegen meine Sympathien entscheide*)."[55]

Writing to Adorno, Habermas notes that he made the decision to return to Frankfurt "primarily (*vor allem*) in order to be able to work in intellectual collaboration (*geistigem Austausch*) with you as my teacher."[56] Meanwhile, in his correspondence with Horkheimer, Habermas writes, "I am aware that succeeding you in your chair (*Lehrstuhl*) is a great honor."[57] However, despite this flattery, it is clear that he had not forgiven Horkheimer. Habermas's conflicted feelings vis-à-vis the longtime director of the Institute are visible in the fact that while he wrote a laudatio for Adorno's sixtieth birthday and immediately published an obituary for him after his death in 1969, Habermas refused multiple invitations to write anything for Horkheimer following his passing in 1973, noting the fact that he was still "too polemical a participant." He was also convinced that Horkheimer himself "would not want me to do so," since they had "never had a friendly relationship."[58] In fact, it was not until the anniversary marking Horkheimer's ninetieth birthday, thirteen years after his death, that Habermas first agreed to write an appreciation of him and his work.[59]

Following his return to Frankfurt in 1964, Habermas found himself "torn between academic work and political practice."[60] During this period, building on both *Structural Transformation* and his research for *Student und Politik*, Habermas continued to develop his concept of political participation (*politische Beteiligung*), which was based on the dialectical insight that participation was only possible in a society where responsible citizens took part in the transformation of administrative power into rational authority. This understanding of the necessity of participation in a rational society—combined with the dim view that Habermas took of the possibilities for "the people" to exercise any real influence on Chancellor Adenauer's *Wahlmonarchie*—led him to call for "extra-parliamentary actions" by members of mass and civil society organizations, who could thus put pressure on political elites from the outside.[61]

This research agenda, visible in a number of academic monographs Habermas produced during this period, including *Theory and Practice* (1963), *Toward a Rational Society* (1968), *Technology and Science as Ideology* (1968) and *Knowledge and Human Interests* (1968), was also taken up by the student movement. Most notably, his theoretical commitment to street action outside the institutions of the state inspired the students to conceive of themselves as a wing of the "extra-parliamentary opposition." Habermas's commitment to Abendroth's model of engagement as a "partisan professor" made him a natural ally of the students during this period.

This alliance was further cemented by Habermas's continued commitment to both the reform and democratization of higher education. Theoretically speaking, Habermas's collaboration was important, as it cemented his diagnosis of the rise of a new form of politics no longer rooted in issues of material reproduction, but in which conflicts instead "arise in areas of cultural reproduction, social integration, and socialization" and "are manifested in sub-institutional, extra-parliamentary forms of protest."[62] Habermas's classification of the students within the category of "new social movements"—alongside the women's movement, the environmental movement, the peace movement, among others—is important, as he uses it to signal his growing belief that classic Marxist policies are no longer sufficient to drive change under the conditions of late capitalism. This foreshadows Habermas's later break with the students; while many of the leaders of this movement were inspired by communist revolts in the third world, Habermas's diagnosis signals his growing skepticism regarding the potential of revolutionary politics in places like postwar West Germany.

Politically, Habermas's interaction with the SDS and the student movement more generally also confirmed his conviction that "without social movements, nothing moves (*ohne soziale Bewegungen bewegt sich nichts*)."[63] Reflecting on the legacy of 1968 from a distance of twenty years, Habermas notes its remarkable success in changing "the definition of what is political," particularly in regard to relations between the sexes, where increasingly "private needs have been politicized." He even expresses surprise that this liberalizing, postmaterialist "march through the institutions has reached even the Christian Democratic party," which in the 1980s was forced to give "some remarkable twists to traditional family and youth policies, at least in their outward appearance."[64]

As I have documented in the previous chapters, Habermas had a longstanding commitment to university reform. In 1965, shortly after his return to Frankfurt, he had the opportunity to make an extended study visit to the United States for the first time. The trip included stops in New York, Ann Arbor, Chicago, and California. Habermas had been invited on this trip—organized by the Institute for International Education in Washington, DC—by the *Studienbüro für politische Bildung* (Study Council for Political Education). In his final report on it, Habermas notes that he was able to "observe the political behavior [*politische Verhalten*] of professors and students at a crucial moment. Criticism of the government's foreign policy decisions about Vietnam and Santo Domingo had led to new forms of academic opposition (the teach-in) precisely during the weeks of our visit."[65] He was given the opportunity to observe the beginnings of the "free speech movement" on American college campuses and even met Mike Rossman, one of the future leaders of the students in Berkeley, "who first confronted me with these 'crazy new ideas,' I called them back then."[66] Based on this experience, which familiarized Habermas with new protest tactics adopted at American universities—such as the "sit-in"—he later defended German students when they adopted similar forms of civil disobedience to ensure their voices were heard.[67]

During this period, Habermas's correspondence reveals that he was frequently asked to speak at discussions organized by the SDS; he almost always accepted. For example, in 1966 Habermas gave an address at the Conference of Universities (*Universitätstage*) in Berlin. In it, he responded to a series of recommendations for the reorganization of German higher education issued earlier that year by the Science Council (*Wissenschaftsrat*). The proposed changes were designed to streamline education by limiting the duration of study (to four and a half years), restricting students' ability to change their major more than once, and curbing openness in postgraduate studies, which would require special permission. In so doing, the reforms would not only have severely limit the right to higher education by deregistering students who took too long to complete their studies; they would have also replaced the liberal "academic freedom" of the German university system—which grants students great liberty to organize their studies as they wish—with what Habermas derisively labeled the "institutionalized planning of academic freedom (*institutionalisierten Planung der akademischen Freiheit*)."[68]

The more general problem that Habermas sees with these proposals to streamline the university to make it more practical and easier to administer, however, is that it focuses on "the mastering technically usable knowledge (*Beherrschung technisch verwertbaren Wissens*)" at the expense of "processes of personal formation (*persönlicher Bildungsprozesse*)" that enable critique of the existing state of affairs. Such critique is especially important given the growing technical complexity of modern life, which means that "we can no longer afford an unreflective implementation of scientific information into the context of the social practice of life."[69] In his view, the practical consequences of scientific technological progress could only be controlled "through the lens of reflection," which was the basis of the classical education preserved in the university system.[70]

As a "long-term partner in discussions with the SDS," he was also often solicited to contribute to various student publications.[71] In November 1966 he took advantage of such an opportunity to comment on the SPD's decision to join in a *grosse Koalition* (grand coalition) with the CDU. Perhaps most problematic was the fact that this new government would include Franz Josef Strauss as Minister of the Treasury despite his central role in the suppression of the press during the aforementioned *Spiegel* affair.

Writing in the student magazine *discus*, Habermas notes, "We have reason to fear the new government. . . . What is known of its plans so far suggests not so much that the safety of democracy will be ensured during a state of emergency as that a state of emergency will be imposed on democracy."[72] Habermas reiterated these concerns in an open letter he cosigned with Irving Fetscher, Ludwig von Friedeburg, and Alexander Mitscherlich. Speaking at a panel discussion, Habermas also notes that this arrangement threatens the basic principles of parliamentarism and those governing the interaction between informal and institutional public spheres, since "if nine-tenths of all MPs belong to the governing parties, then conflicts are resolved to the exclusion of the public."[73]

This intervention clearly demonstrates Habermas's engagement with party-political developments in Germany. Most of his political writings from this period, however, relate to the student movement. For instance, in January 1967 he delivered a lecture at the University of Berlin, later published in *Merkur* under the title "The University in a Democracy: Democratization of the University." Although Habermas recognizes the important role the university plays in preparing students for the job market and in ensuring both the production and transmission of "technically exploitable knowledge," he also notes that as a social institution it has at least three further responsibilities: ensuring that its graduates possess the nontechnical "soft" skills they need to succeed in their careers, safeguarding the cultural traditions of society, and shaping "the political consciousness of its students." While many conservates oppose this final task, Habermas notes that it has always been present. However, the German university system has traditionally fostered a political consciousness "of loyalty to state authority," which he links to the passivity of the middle classes during the Third Reich.[74]

While Habermas notes that after 1945 the German system of higher education had devoted itself to "educating the citizens of the university to become reliable citizens of the new democratic order," he fears that the this period is coming to an end as reforms from the *Wissenschaftsrat* and government more generally are seeking to cut the university's "ties to the political, public realm."[75] In response, Habermas encourages the students not "to accept the existence of an opposition between a university aiming at professional specialization and one aiming at external politicization"; both can be brought together within a democratic form of decision-making that aims at "rationalizing decisions in such a way that they can be made dependent on a consensus arrived at through discussion free from domination."[76] For Habermas, this is important not only because such communicative, critical discussion is a key skill that students have to learn, but also because students themselves are citizens and thus have the right to claim their place in the democratic community of co-decision-makers. This applies not only to politics at large but also to university governance, in which Habermas encourages students to participate alongside junior faculty and professors.

BREAK WITH THE STUDENTS

In June 1967 the protest movement gained new momentum with the killing of one of its members, Benno Ohnesorg, by a plainclothes policeman during a demonstration against the Shah of Iran. In the wake of this event, Habermas was one of only four professors to be invited to speak at a conference organized in Ohnesorg's honor in Hanover. In his talk, Habermas decries the fact that in response to the student protests the "organs of the state have sought to limit participation rights of students," rather than listening to them as fellow members of the public sphere involved in the democratic process of opinion-formation. He interprets this unwillingness to listen as a sign that the "inner construction of [our] political parties is authoritarian" and calls on the students "to compensate for these deficiencies ... in the interpretation and implementation of our social and democratic constitution."[77]

Although Habermas classifies "the intellectual as part of the unorganized extra-parliamentary opposition" alongside the students, he also warns against overreacting to the terrorism with which they were confronted. In particular, in light of the difficulties of translating theory into practice, he highlights the "disparity between criticism and the chances of implementing this criticism" to dissuade students from actionistic attempts to change the world at any cost through the force of will alone. In particular, he cautions them against "provoking a transformation of the indirect violence of institutions into manifest violence," as this would actually harm the students' attempts to "draw attention to our arguments, which we believe are the better ones."[78] In this sense, Habermas agrees with Adorno that actionistic violence merely serves to reinforce the violence of the system underpinning existing social conditions.[79]

These warnings, which many in the audience perceived as castigations, provoked a strong reaction among the students. For example, Rudi Dutschke, a leader of the movement, accused Habermas of killing "the subject to be emancipated with his senseless objectivism."[80] Rather than working through democratic institutions, as Habermas called for, he instead encouraged them to seek out alternative forms of action, without excluding the possibility of violence. Although Habermas had left the meeting (as had Dutschke) and was on his way to his car, he spontaneously returned to deliver a final denunciation of what he saw as the "voluntaristic ideology developed by Dutschke," which he likened to "left fascism."[81]

This statement marked a key turning point in Habermas's relationship with the student movement—and with the left more generally. He later recalled that "the leadership of the SDS stopped being able to speak to me unreservedly."[82] Writing to Adorno at the time, Plessner reported that "Habermas came back ... depressed."[83] Habermas immediately regretted expressing himself in this way, noting that he "was speaking in a clearly hypothetical context."[84] He also clarified his use of this polemical term in a letter to Hans Paetscke, his editor at *Merkur*, noting, "It is fascism, when one thinks that one no longer has to argue."[85]

Interestingly, despite the rift that it caused between Habermas and the student movement in general, he and Dutschke soon patched up their differences. For instance, after the student leader was severely injured by an assassin in 1968, Habermas supported his application to the German Academic Exchange Service (*Deutsche Akademische Austauschdienst*, or DAAD) to study at Boston University.[86] Additionally, "much to Rudi Dutschke's satisfaction," he later retracted his formulation of "left fascism" completely.[87] Upon Dutschke's death in 1979 from long-term complications related to the 1968 assassination attempt, Habermas wrote a laudatio praising the fact that Dutschke was "inspired by the idea of a radically democratic, noninstrumental politics, a politics that depends on forms of organization rendered fluid through communication (*kommunikativ verflüssigte*)."[88]

The fact that Habermas felt the need to do this is noteworthy, as his correspondence from the period immediately following his divisive remark comparing the student movement to fascism reveals that he actually received considerable support from other academics. For instance, Plessner shared his view of the "student Maoists," in whom "fascism discovers its opportunity on the left."[89] Opinion among Habermas's assistants was divided: Oscar Negt accused him of bourgeois ambivalence, while Claus Offe maintained that "Habermas did not say anything wrong on June 9, 1967 in Hanover." In defending this position, Offe notes "the perverse preparedness [of the students] to use violence in the name of determination . . . of a kind with which we are otherwise familiar only from fascists—but this time it came from the left. Habermas was deeply repulsed by this. He considered this interpretation of the situation off the mark. And rightly so."[90] Similarly, Joschka Fischer, another student radical who would become foreign minister as the leader of the Green Party and who attended Habermas's seminars in Frankfurt in the 1960s, also noted that the accusation of left fascism "hit the mark at the time."[91]

Habermas continued to reflect on these same themes at a lecture he gave at the Goethe House in New York later that year, which occurred during his visit to the New School for Social Research as the Theodor Heuss Visiting Professor. In his talk, entitled "Student Protest in the Federal Republic" and attended by Hannah Arendt, Habermas compared the mobilizations in the United States and France to the movement in his native country. Sadly, I have not been able to find any record of Arendt's response to Habermas's talk, a version of which he later published in the *FAZ*.[92] Addressing his American audience, Habermas starts by noting that "the Free University [Freie Universität in West Berlin] is the Berkeley of West Germany," and is "leading the struggle against the majority of professors," who are conservative and do not want to give the students a say in faculty governance or recognize their rights to free speech on the grounds of the university.[93]

Although the protests initially addressed these intra-university issues, he observes that they soon expanded to broader social and political disputes, such as the status of Berlin as a divided city and the Vietnam war. As a result, "For the first time in the history of the Federal Republic of Germany, students are playing a political role that must be taken seriously." Sociologically speaking, Habermas roots this broader mobilization in the fact that this generation is not only the first "whose memory is not determined by the Nazi period," but also emerges from the experience of mass democracy in West Germany. In light of these political developments, especially the *Wirtschaftswunder* (economic miracle), they therefore do not understand why "an economy of poverty is preserved [by the economic and political elites] under conditions of a possible economy of abundance." Habermas endorses student attempts to repoliticize issues that had previously been struck from the political agenda and silenced by the conservative gatekeepers of the public sphere; he even recognizes that given the situation in West Germany, "protest itself must assume the form of provocation, of going beyond the legitimate rules of the game."

He nevertheless rejects both the "new actionism" of the movement's more radical elements, which he feels leads to "fruitless violent acts," and "the worldview of the new anarchism borrowed from Mao and Castro."[94] He thereby draws a clear line between legitimate *activism* outside of formal parliamentary institutions of the state on the one hand, and *actionism* on the other. Following Adorno, Habermas defines the latter as a kind of pseudo-activity, a kind of "hustling, bustling busyness (*Betriebsamkeit*)," which is underpinned by the false belief that it is possible to "rescue enclaves of immediacy in the midst of a thoroughly mediated and rigidified society."[95]

In his introduction to a podium discussion of the "Role of the Student in the APO [*Außerparlamentarische Opposition*, or extra-parliamentary opposition]" after his return to Frankfurt in 1968 Habermas celebrates the success of the student movement in "changing the domestic political situation in the Federal Republic" by helping "to politicize issues that had previously been off-limits for discussion." He also praises the students for their "attempt to develop an extraparliamentary veto power" to make up for the lack of a real opposition in the Bundestag since the onset of the grand coalition. He is also enthused by their admittedly utopian desire to democratize an industrial society increasingly defined by technology and bureaucratization. While Habermas also appreciates the "personal identification" many students exhibit with the third world, he warns them against "drawing suggestive but misleading parallels and making false transmissions the basis for action."[96]

In a statement that serves as a good summary of his general position vis-à-vis the more radical students, Habermas observes, "We are not on the verge of a revolution, neither today nor tomorrow." Insofar as some of the leaders of the movement believe this to be the case, then Habermas argues that their diagnosis is mistaken, as they have failed to account for the different circumstances in the FRG and the dependent nations of the Third World. Instead of "abandoning the basis of legitimacy of our constitution," in the reformist manner that he absorbed from Abendroth, Habermas encourages the left "to realize the intentions of the Basic Law"—West Germany's constitution—instead of reducing "tangible reforms . . . to a pretext for action for action's sake."[97]

This position is also a reflection of Habermas's generational position vis-à-vis the students.[98] Unlike Dutschke and the other radical leaders of this movement, who had no personal recollection of the Nazi past, his own memories of the Third Reich shaped both his philosophy and his politics in important ways.[99] As a result, Habermas reacted strongly against the students' frequent use of the term *fascist* to describe West Germany. Although he was also a critic of the Federal Republic and had reacted against the use of state power in the *Spiegel* affair, Habermas notes that in his view "the left-wing students had a rather clichéd notion of fascism" that failed to take into account that "in spite of everything, the *Bundesrepublik* was one of the six or seven most liberal countries in the world." Reflecting back on this time, Habermas notes, "It was difficult for me to find an audience for such statements, which were intended to introduce a sense of historical proportion."[100]

This perspective testifies to the importance of collective memory for his thought and the weight of his accusation of "left fascism," as well as to the fact that Habermas was already starting to conceive of himself as something of an intellectual gadfly. Though he had not yet formulated his fully-fledged conception of the public intellectual, his public commentaries—which often angered all sides—were already leading some to call him "the Socrates of the Federal Republic."[101] Despite his differences with the students, Habermas repeatedly noted the importance of "science's (*Wissenschaft*) reflection on its political responsibilities," when he and other politically active professors were attacked by conservative politicians, such as the CDU's Minister of Science, Gerhard Stoltenberg, in the Bundestag.[102] Habermas also defended the students in their campaign against Springer, one of the largest and most conservative "publishing conglomerates (*publizistische Großunternehmen*)," whose publications were particular critical of the student movement. In particular, Habermas condemned the sensationalist "smear campaign (*Stimmungsmache*) against the students" being waged by the popular tabloid *Bildzeitung*, which he argued had provoked the reactionary political response to the students by the political system.[103]

Although the SDS had distanced itself from Habermas, the fact that he was still influential among other student groups can be seen in the fact that he was invited to address the Union of German Students (*Verein Deutscher Studentenschaften*, or VDS), which was meeting the Frankfurter Mensa on June 1, 1968. In this talk—delivered in the wake of the university occupation and a violent police intervention—Habermas developed five theses about the student movement. He added a sixth to the text that was later published in both the *Frankfurter Rundschau* and *Der Spiegel*.

Although the title, "The Phantom Revolution (*Scheinrevolution*) Eats Its Children," reveals Habermas's critical perspective on the actions of the SDS, he begins by praising the student movement as an important progressive force within the otherwise rather staid, reactionary politics of postwar West Germany. In his first thesis, he identifies "the immediate goal of the student protest [a]s the politicization of the public sphere."[104] In the second, he also lauds its use of techniques of civil disobedience to challenge the technocratic *Kanzlerdemokratie* implemented by Adenauer. Given his arguments about the nature of democratic legitimacy in *Structural Transformation* and against technocracy in *Legitimation Crisis* (1968), both theses situate the student movement within Habermas's evolving theoretical framework.

The third thesis reveals the influence of Freudian Marxism that Habermas had absorbed from Adorno (and Marcuse during his visits to Frankfurt) during his time at the Institute. In contrast to the leaders of the SDS, who saw themselves as driven by the same economic factors motivating their allies and role models in the third world, Habermas instead locates the sources of their action in the social-psychological realm. Unlike revolutionary movements in the third world—which indeed arise from the kinds of materialist struggles over wealth redistribution that Marx had anticipated—he notes that, as a relatively privileged group in one of the wealthiest countries in the world, the students (most of whom do not have to work to survive) are not truly driven by economic necessity. On the contrary, their protest is motivated by a "new sensibility" that leads them to confront the unjust nature of rewards and achievements under capitalism.

These first three theses serve as a diagnosis of the student movement; the next two present Habermas's basic critique. In the fourth, he argues that following the precepts of orthodox Marxism, the students have adopted a false interpretation of contemporary affairs. For example, he notes that the state's intervention in the economy has not only undermined Marx's crisis theory by helping to stabilize capitalism—giving the workers a stake in the *status quo*—but has also undermined Marx's expectations about class struggle by ensuring that political conflict between the proletariat and the bourgeoisie remains latent and is negotiated within the political system rather than outside it through revolutionary means.

This is important because, as Marx himself recognized in a quotation frequently cited by Adorno, "What is to be done ... depends, of course, wholly and entirely on the actual historical circumstances in which action is to be taken."[105]

Fifth, Habermas argues that, as a result of these misunderstandings, the students confuse reality with appearance (*Schein*), and symbols with what was really happening. This is most evident in the fact that they had been deceived into thinking that occupying a university—a symbolic act—was equivalent to a coup d'état or the storming of the Bastille. He contends that, rather than rallying society to the student's cause, such confrontational actions instead isolate them and undermine the ability of those who share their goals to achieve them through the democratic process. This point not only brings Habermas's Abendrothian reformism to the fore but also highlights his tendency to interpret the movement though the lens of civil disobedience, where it "is necessary to comprehend the exclusively symbolic character of an act of protest, even when that act oversteps the bounds of the legally permissible."[106]

In the sixth thesis, which Habermas added to the published version of his text, he encourages the students to abandon their confrontational tactics in favor of an approach that is more in line with the situation at hand. Instead of overestimating their own power and equating any resistance from the state with fascism, they should learn to mobilize forces within the public sphere to stimulate change within the existing democratic system. As he writes in a letter to Günter Grass, "I would like to say explicitly that in a situation like the present one, I consider playing at revolution not only nonsense but dangerous, especially for liberal socialism." In a line that foreshadows his mature conception of the public intellectual, he concludes "I increasingly see my task as simply expressing what I think I discern (*zu erkennen glaube*), without any consideration on any side whatsoever (*ohne irgendwelche Rücksichten nach irgendeiner Seite*)."[107]

While Habermas saw this intervention as an internal critique, many students in the charged atmosphere of the time saw him as a traitor—abandoning the implications of his own leftist convictions when they threatened to undermine his bourgeois position. This included a number of Habermas's assistants, who even penned a volume under the title, *The Left Answers Jürgen Habermas*.[108] Regardless of the accuracy of Habermas's diagnosis, two things are clear. First, his contributions to the student movement clearly demonstrate that he was committed to stimulating change through the public sphere's ability to "besiege" the existing democratic institutions of the FRG, as opposed to actual revolution.

Second, his diagnosis of the SDS and its tactics should not be seen merely as political writings detached from his philosophical concerns but must instead be interpreted "as part of an ongoing theoretical debate he had been conducting with the Marxist tradition."[109]

Habermas's engagement with the students was not purely rhetorical. On the contrary, he came into direct confrontation with them several times during this period. For instance, on November 14, 1968 Hans Imhoff, a leading activist from Frankfurt, interrupted Habermas's class and attempted to give an inaugural lecture himself. Habermas tried to engage him in open debate, but Imhoff refused. Habermas ultimately suspended the lecture when Imhoff began mocking him by imitating the nasal intonation of Habermas's speech, a result of his cleft palate. Although involved in many tense and uncomfortable interactions with the students, Habermas later recalls, "I felt hurt only once, when Mr. Imhoff aimed below the belt."[110]

Overall, however, Habermas took pride in the fact that he did not seek to "evade responsibility (*Flucht aus der Verantwortung*)" when confronted with protesters with whom he disagreed. On the contrary, "unlike some other colleagues, I tend to stand by my views politically and scientifically even in situations of conflict. If I had wanted to make myself more comfortable, I would have gone either to Constance or to UNESCO in Paris in 1968," both of which offered an opportunity to escape the politically charged atmosphere in Frankfurt during this period.[111] However, unlike his friend and colleague Ralf Dahrendorf, who chose to stand for office in local elections in Stuttgart in order "to formulate a radical position more than just journalistically," Habermas maintained status as an engaged intellectual seeking to change politics by transforming debate in the public sphere, rather than by becoming a politician himself.[112]

In December 1968, the students occupied the Department of Sociology in Frankfurt. In response, the rector of the university, Walter Rüegg, made plans to clear the building, informing Habermas the day before. When the police arrived the next morning they found the building empty.[113] Evidently someone—mostly likely Habermas himself—had tipped the students off to the forthcoming raid.[114]

Throughout this period, Habermas continued to hold his classes. While he was generally sympathetic to them, in a "statement to the students" he published on December 12 he opposed their attempts to undermine "the scientific enterprise as such (*Wissenschaftsbetrieb als solches*)," clarifying that attacks on "science tied to discussion based on the principle of non-domination . . . make enlightened political action impossible."[115] In a discussion paper he wrote for a seminar he held two days later, Habermas highlighted the necessity of keeping science and politics separate: political action can only be measured by "the effectiveness of the acts to which it gives rise," whereas "scientific procedures are measured against standards that. . . . guarantee the progress of knowledge."[116]

Despite their worries about the fanaticism of some of the student leaders, both Adorno and Habermas supported the movement in its early stages. Going against his usual reserved temperament, in May 1968 Adorno had even joined a demonstration calling for the abolition of the emergency laws passed by the Grand Coalition of the CDU and SPD, later even calling for a general strike to achieve this end. As a result, "he was even more astounded to have become a target of the protests."[117]

On January 31, 1969, upon finding the Sociology Department locked, seventy-six students entered the Institute's building and occupied it. Despite his previous support for the movement, when these students refused his entreaties to leave, Adorno—acting in his role as director of the Institute—felt that he had no choice but to call the police, who arrested all seventy-six occupiers.[118] Habermas was working from home on that Friday morning, and was unaware of what was happening until the Institute's secretary called to inform him of the situation. Unfortunately, he recalls that "my spontaneous advice to the directors, 'No police,' came too late."[119]

This incident caused a great furor. It also led to a break within the first generation of the Frankfurt School, as Marcuse, who had become one of the leading "ideologues of the cultural revolution (*Ideologen der Kulturrevolution*)" in the United States, took his erstwhile colleagues to task for betraying the students they had inspired.[120] Although Habermas defended Adorno, who was completely overwhelmed by the situation, he also sought to mediate the dispute and overcome the "breakdown in communication (*Kommunikationsstörungen*)" that it had brought about between Marcuse and "Max the Great and Teddy the wholly Other (*Max der Große und Teddy der ganz Andere*)," as Habermas refers to Horkheimer and Adorno in one of his letters to Marcuse.[121]

During this period, Habermas was also involved in the public debate surrounding the drafting of a new law to govern higher education in Hessen, the state where Frankfurt am Main is located. In it, Habermas defended the principle of democratization, arguing that the committees making academic decisions should be open to everyone involved in teaching and research (not just full professors), while broader issues related to politics within the university should be subjected to open discussion and a process of democratic will-formation that included the students as well as the public at large.[122] In light of both the lack of a real "working through (*Durcharbeitung*)" of the *Nazizeit* among the older generations and the "cliched understandings" of fascism that he saw as driving the more radical elements of the student movement, Habermas was convinced that the university system had to do more to draw a clear line between the past and the present. In this sense, for him, "the development of a truly democratic *Volkspädagogik* was, in the spirit of Adorno, a task of 'education after Auschwitz,' " the title of one of Adorno's most famous essays.[123] These lobbying efforts show that Habermas remained committed to the cause of university reform even after the his break with the SDS, as well as the occupations of the Sociology Department and the Institute for Social Research.

CONCLUSION

In the first two sections of this chapter, I documented Habermas's engagement with the student movement in the early 1960s. The final part then examined Habermas's break with the students. Although he continued to work with certain parts of this movement after 1967, it is clear that the breakdown in this relationship had a significant impact on him. Whereas Habermas had always welcomed the fact that his political activism was divisive and made him "a red flag for the conservatives," his alienation from the left and the APO, which he had helped to inspire, was a probably a greater blow than he would like to admit.[124]

For example, in a letter to Karl-Heinz Bohrer, his friend and editor at the *FAZ*, Habermas expresses exasperation with the whole situation vis-à-vis the student movement, noting, "Drawing attention for these political things makes me want to vomit (*find ich es zum Kotzen*), since I think that I have earned it more with my theoretical books."[125] More generally, Habermas became increasingly skeptical of the "committed sociology" he had sought to practice during the 1960s.[126] Although he continued to oppose pure "academicism" and remained committed to the idea that sociology and philosophy should bear "a relation to [the] critique of the times," in a 1971 radio broadcast for *Hessischen Rundfunk*—one of the few documented appearances Habermas made on the radio—he argued that this relation must be "indirect," rather than the more "direct" approach he had taken with the students.[127] As he notes in a letter to Rudolf Walter Leonhardt, his editor at *Die Zeit*, "I never leave the level of argumentation in my teaching; and the form of my pedagogical activities (*Lehrtätigkeit*) protects me from even inadvertently encouraging students to blur the self-evident line between argumentation and agitation."[128]

As a result of these considerations, Habermas began to rethink his commitment to Frankfurt. His desire for a change of scenery was furthered by Adorno's death from a heart attack on August 6, 1969—an event likely precipitated by the fact that he had to cancel almost all his classes following the police clearing of the Institute. In a letter to Marcuse, Habermas noted that "since Adorno's death not much has remained [in Frankfurt] that could hold one here, most certainly [there is] no productive potential (*ganz sicher kein produktives Potential*)."[129] During this same period, Habermas's support for Leszek Kołakowski, a Polish scholar of Marx, as Adorno's successor generated further controversy and resulted in even more disruptions to his seminars and lectures; this only reinforced his desire to leave.[130] Habermas was particularly frustrated by opponents of Kołakowski, who seemed to see the "Frankfurt School" and "critical theory" as "the kind of institution that must be preserved by recruiting true believers," thus turning it into an orthodoxy that Adorno himself would have opposed.[131]

The fact that "life at Frankfurt has become very difficult" for Habermas and rumors that he had "already decided to leave" spread quickly in academic circles. As a result, Habermas was inundated with offers of new positions, not only from within Germany—at the University of Konstanz—but also from the United States.[132] In addition to Herbert Gans's invitation to join the sociology department at Columbia University, in 1969 Habermas was also offered a "sanctuary" at Yale University as a guest professor. However, he declined all these offers, noting that he would wait a few years and "if nothing should have changed by then, I would in fact quite like to go to America for a while."[133]

In 1975, only a few months before her death in December, Habermas also declined Hannah Arendt's offer to succeed her at the New School for Social Research. Despite his love for this institution—where he had spent time at a visiting professor in 1967–68—his desire to preserve the tradition of continental philosophy in the United States and his admiration for Arendt, this time his answer was more definitive. In addition to "the very strong hesitation of my wife," Habermas also noted his conviction that "one should not emigrate without real reasons (*ohne wirkliche Gründe*)."[134]

Ultimately, Habermas was lured away from Frankfurt by an offer from the physicist and philosopher Carl Friedrich von Weizsäcker to codirect a Max Planck Institute devoted to the study of the various aspects of life in a scientific and technical world. While Habermas had his doubts about the setup and his abilities as a manager, he was ultimately swayed by the opportunity this position would provide to "get empirical investigations underway for which I do not have the necessary leeway in Frankfurt."[135] This was not an easy decision, and Habermas openly noted that there were a "many good reasons that speak against it."[136]

The media were keen to see this move as rooted in Habermas's break with the students, who accused Habermas of "betraying the project of the critical university" that he had previously defended.[137] Many of his friends also found this explanation plausible, since the act of "running the gauntlet in Frankfurt, where sociology students—radicalized by Adornian theory and disappointed by Adornian practice—are now demanding from the younger generation what Horkheimer and Adorno always promised but never delivered with compound interest, can fray even the strongest of nerves."[138] However, Habermas insisted— both publicly and privately, that his move was based "solely on the motive of finally enjoying the privilege of undisturbed research work after ten years of teaching."[139] On the contrary, he repeatedly insists, "Fear of students is certainly not one of my faults. I did not seek to abscond from them either."[140]

Leaving Frankfurt also clarified for Habermas that he could not be a member of a movement or function as a "partisan professor." Instead, he realized that from here on out he would be on his own. As a result, and in the wake of this period of intense activism and political engagement, he clearly felt the need to devote himself to his theoretical work, so that he could reground it on a firmer foundation.

Writing to Horkheimer to inform him of his decision, Habermas again highlights the role that "the changes in the scene here [in Frankfurt] after Adorno's death" played in this decision, in addition to the fact that moving to Starnberg would allow him "to fill fifteen scientific positions . . . with people I actually want to work with."[141] While many saw this move as the death of critical theory, his friend Marcuse did not. Upon learning of Habermas's move, he noted that rather than seeing this "as the end of the 'Frankfurt School,' " he prefers to interpret it as "a new beginning . . . from an oasis (*von einer Oase aus*)."[142]

CHAPTER 5

Retreat to Starnberg, 1971–1982

Habermas's break with the student movement clearly had a major effect on him. In fact, it probably played a larger role in his second departure from Frankfurt in 1971 than he himself would care to admit. Reflecting on his influence on the students many years later, Habermas notes, "I managed to reach the somewhat older generation . . . with the *Structural Transformation of the Public Sphere* (1962). By that I mean: with an interpretation of the Basic Law based on an aggressive welfare state influenced by the reformist Abendroth."[1]

However, much to his chagrin, "the next 'generation' . . . was already thinking actionistically." Rather than aiming to change the interpretation of the legal order by increasing the quality of discourse in the public sphere, these "young activists saw themselves as the extended arm [*verlängerten Arm*] of Che Guevara in the metropoles."[2] His failure to disabuse the students of what he saw as their violent revolutionary fantasies surely played a role in pushing Habermas to leave the Goethe-University for a directorship at the prestigious Max Planck Institute.

After his clash with the students, Habermas also withdrew from the public sphere to a large extent. When I asked him about this, he insisted that this retreat was due to the fact that a director of a Max Planck Institute—a very prestigious public position—must obey certain rules and should not be an overtly political figure.[3] While his perception of the requirements of this role might indeed have played a part in this change, looking back on this period from the perspective of an observer, this explanation does not fully hold up, at least not on its own. Whereas in the 1960s Habermas often spoke at rallies and protests, during the 1970s he repeatedly turned down invitations to appear in public, noting, "I am . . . absolutely certain that I am not the right person for a big public engagement. . . .

I am not a political speaker (*kein politischer Redner*)."⁴ However, based on his past actions, this is clearly something of an oversimplification.

In addition to pulling back from public appearances, during this period Habermas also largely stopped writing for the public sphere. When turning down invitations from editors to do so, he usually cites both his desire to focus on his research (his vocation or *Beruf*) and his conviction that "one can change the shape of debates with books," as indeed he already had in the 1960s with *Structural Transformation of the Public Sphere*.⁵ The main exceptions to this rule during this period occurred when he was drawn into controversies by personal attacks from outside, most notably accusations that critical theory—and his work in particular—could be used to support terrorism. Interestingly, in light of his own explanation for this retreat, Habermas does not cite his role as director of a Max Planck Institute precluding such engagements as an excuse in his correspondence.

This intellectual withdrawal into "the ivory tower of social scientific research" was accompanied by an institutional retreat as well: from the bustling metropolis of Frankfurt, with its university and active student body, to the sleepy, provincial town of Starnberg.⁶ Starnberg is certainly no peasant village and cannot be compared to Martin Heidegger's famous mountain *Hütte* (cottage) at Totnauberg in the Black Forest. On the contrary, located in rural Bavaria, but connected to downtown Munich by commuter rail (*S-Bahn*), it is an idyllic resort located on the edge of a picturesque lake in the heart of "five lakes country (*Fünfseenland*)" and boasts the highest disposable per capita income in all of Germany.

Although Habermas's name will always be associated with Frankfurt, this move allowed Habermas's five-person household—with their exceedingly large collection of books—to build themselves a house in line with their needs, economic status and modernist aesthetic commitments. Set upon a sloping hillside, the house in which Habermas continues to live was designed in the Bauhaus style by the Munich architects Christoph Sattler and Heinz Hilmer. The fact that Habermas required a loan from his friend and publisher, Siegfried Unseld, to secure the land and build this structure indicates that the move was not meant to be temporary.⁷

In addition to its other virtues, this was also dictated by the fact that it was the location of the Max-Planck-Institut zur Erforschung der Lebensbedingungen der wissenschaftlich-technischen Welt (Max Planck Institute for the Study of the Conditions of Life in the Scientific-Technical World), where Habermas was the director from 1971 until 1981. Besides allowing him a respite from the public controversies that had occupied much of his time in the 1960s, this move to what *Der Spiegel* referred to as "a German Jugendstil-Oxford," or what one of his former students likened to a "German RAND Corporation," also gave him the time and financial support necessary to develop his philosophical paradigm of communication.[8] This research project began with the Christian Gauss lectures that he gave at Princeton University in 1971 and culminated a decade later with the publication of the two-volume *Theory of Communicative Action* in 1981.

Finally, moving to Starnberg allowed Habermas to shake off the symbolic burden he carried as the presumed leader of the Frankfurt School following Horkheimer's retirement and Adorno's untimely death. In his obituary for his mentor, Habermas affirmed not only Adorno's "incomparably brilliant ingeniousness," but also that "[t]here is no substitute for it, however slight."[9] The fact that Habermas saw his connection to the first generation of critical theory more as a curse than a blessing is also visible in his view of the Frankfurt School as not being the kind of institution "that must be maintained by recruiting orthodox believers," and in his conviction that the "traditions that survive are only those that change in order to fit new situations."[10]

Despite Habermas's ambivalence, he continued to develop ideas related to critical theory throughout his career. Although Roman Yos is right that "Habermas cannot simply be considered an epigone of the founders of the Frankfurt school," both the motivations and the thematic content of Habermas's early journalism show that he is an heir to the first generation of critical theorists (see chapter 2).[11] This connection was also clear to the thinkers of what has subsequently come to be seen as the first generation of the Frankfurt School, including Adorno, Horkheimer (who ultimately endorsed Habermas as his successor), and Herbert Marcuse.

Although Habermas's mature conception of the public intellectual as an indirect actor—one who seeks to engage in public discourse at key moments as an "early warning system"—does not appear until the 1980s (as I document in the next chapter), certain features of it gradually start to coalesce during this period. As a result of his experiences with the student movement, in the 1970s he seemingly endorsed Adorno's argument that philosophy "effects change precisely by remaining itself" by committing full-time to his sociological and philosophical *Beruf*.[12]

In the first section of this chapter, I examine Habermas's involvement in letter-writing campaigns on behalf of fellow unorthodox Marxists from behind the Iron Curtain who had fallen afoul of the communist regimes in their homelands, since this is the form that most of his public engagements take during this period. Although it is hard to discern why he chose to intervene in certain cases and not others, in many instances it is clear that intellectual affinities and personal connections played an important role. In the second section, I examine how he was nonetheless drawn into a few public controversies, most notably over the Frankfurt School's alleged connection to terrorism, with which Habermas felt compelled to engage. I conclude by reflecting on how Habermas's experiences of direct engagement, and his subsequent retreat from politics, led him to develop his mature, indirect, and mediated conception of the role of the philosopher as a public intellectual.

SUPPORT FOR PERSECUTED COLLEAGUES

Following his departure from Frankfurt, Habermas repeatedly denied that he had done so out of "fearfulness of students (*Ängstlichkeit vor Studenten*)," a trait that he notes "is certainly not one of my faults."[13] Despite his attempts to downplay the role that his break with the students played in his decision to leave Goethe University in favor of a research position at the Max Planck Institute, it is clear that this experience led Habermas to fundamentally rethink his commitment to writing for the public sphere and his desire for political engagement more generally. Whereas before he had frequently pitched essays to the editors of the feuilletons of major German newspapers, during the 1970s he routinely turned down their invitations to contribute to public debates, often observing, "In recent years, I have not felt the slightest desire (*nicht die geringste Lust*) to get involved in public discussions. This feeling (*diese Stimmung*) continues now."[14]

This reluctance even extends to issues that Habermas is clearly still passionate about, including university reform. Responding to a request to write on this issue, he notes that "my new tasks [at the Max Planck Institute] ... do not, of course, preclude an interest in the problems of higher education policy; they do, however, occupy me to such an extent ... that I simply do not have time for other things."[15] Note that even in this case, where Habermas explicitly mentions his new position, he does not excuse himself based on the fact that this role supposedly requires him to be politically neutral.

His new attitude towards public engagement seems to be driven—at least in part—by a change in Habermas's self-perception of his role in society. Previously, he had seen political involvement as a crucial aspect of his academic profession. Later, in his mature conception of the public intellectual, which coalesces in the 1980s, he interprets involvement in public affairs as his "secondary vocation (*Nebenberuf*)." By contrast, during the 1970s he denies any sense of obligation to the broader reading public, repeatedly observing that "I can't get involved in journalism now. I am being pressured from all sides to do this and that, but after all I still have my profession (*ich habe aber schließlich auch noch meinen Beruf*)."[16]

At this point, it is clear that Habermas had realized he could only speak to the public in his own voice, not on behalf of any party or movement. While this was liberating, at least to a certain extent, it also seems to have pushed him to set his own theory on the firmer foundations necessary to support such solitary stands. For example, in response to an invitation to join a discussion on "The Role of the Intellectual in Class Conflict," he replies, "I like to be addressed as an intellectual, but . . . this time I really can't divide my attention between what I have to do and what I also at some point might quite like to do."[17]

Habermas's decision to step away was clearly visible to many in the West German public sphere. While some—particularly his more radical opponents among the students—welcomed Habermas's retreat, many others did not. For example, at the end of a 1969 letter asking him to grant an interview to *Der Spiegel*, whose goal would be to prevent Habermas being "further stylized as an object of aggression" among the students, Werner Harenberg, senior editor of the prestigious weekly news magazine, asked Habermas to "allow me a personal word: I regret very much that you of all people now apparently want to withdraw (*zurückziehen*) from the public for scientific work."[18] Similarly, the premier of Hessen, Albert Osswald, also wrote to Habermas to thank him for "your active engagement" in discussions of higher education policy, despite the kinds of personal attacks that Habermas was subjected to as a result.[19]

Habermas's retreat from the public sphere is also visible in his bibliography. Whereas over the course of the 1960s he wrote newspaper articles directed to the public sphere on average once every few months, during his time at the Max Planck Institute he pens political contributions only once or twice a year. He also avoids the essay form, which he had previously embraced. Rather, in a move that he recognizes goes "against my custom," he often instead "decide[s] to write a letter to the editor." Although Habermas notes even in this period that "I certainly do not avoid political discussions," his clarification that he only "seek[s] them out when I believe I should help clarify a situation" suggests that he has lost faith in his ability to positively influence debates in the German public sphere.[20]

The main exceptions to Habermas's retreat from political engagement can be found in his vocal support of colleagues who are being subjected to political pressure by the authorities in their homelands. It is unclear exactly how and why Habermas chose to support certain individuals and not others. However, given that most are unorthodox Marxists—much like Habermas himself—it does seem that intellectual affinities play a key role, as does the fact that Habermas had personal connections with many of the individuals in question. The fact that many of them also lived behind the Iron Curtain and had to pay a very high personal price for their scholarly and political views might also have reminded Habermas of his own privileged position.

He was particularly active in defending the Yugoslavian philosophers of the so-called Praxis Group, named after the eponymous journal published between 1964 and 1974. Like Habermas and other thinkers in the tradition of Western Marxism, the members of the Praxis Group read Karl Marx primarily as a social theorist and sought to reinterpret Marxism as "a body of thought which is uncompromising in its rejection of all forms of human alienation, exploitation, oppression and injustice, regardless of the type of society—bourgeois or socialist—in which these phenomena occur."[21] Habermas and many other thinkers associated with the Frankfurt School, including Marcuse, thus saw "the Yugoslav writers associated with the journal *Praxis*" as "kindred souls," whose work "bore the stamp of authenticity, of first-hand experience."[22]

This authenticity came at a high price, however. From 1966 onward, the Praxis Group was subjected to continual critique by Communist Party officials. To bolster their credentials and resist the repression of Marshall Josip Broz "Tito's" regime in Belgrade, they also organized summer "seminar-conferences," first on the island of Korčula and later in Dubrovnik, to which they invited prominent foreign thinkers who could not as easily be censored. Habermas attended these events whenever he could as "a gesture of solidarity with our Yugoslavian colleagues"; later he even helped co-organize the meetings, which for a certain period were "the only place where [the Praxis thinkers] could give public lectures and participate in public discussions in Yugoslavia."[23]

In addition to his participation at the workshops in Korčula and Dubrovnik, Habermas also supported the Praxis thinkers in other ways. From the early 1970s onward, philosophers associated with the group frequently wrote to Habermas to report on their difficulties.²⁴ In response to these reports, Habermas and the German neo-Marxist philosopher Ernst Bloch even penned an open letter to Marshall Tito, in which they praised their colleagues in Yugoslavia "as resolute socialists and outstanding scholars (*hervorragende Wissenschaftler*)" who "had helped Yugoslav philosophy and social theory to achieve international recognition." Bloch and Habermas also noted that they did not understand why the Praxis Group was being prosecuted "in a country that under your leadership wants to realize the prototype of democratic socialism." They concluded with a very Habermasian appeal to Tito, asking him to "please also see to it that in Yugoslavia intellectual disputes can be settled by intellectual means alone (*allein mit intellektuellen Mitteln ausgetragen werden können*)."²⁵

Unfortunately, this letter did not have the desired effect, as the repression of the Praxis Group continued. In 1973, the printing of the international edition of *Praxis* ceased, followed by the Yugoslav edition in 1975. Furthermore, in January of that same year eight members of the group (Mihailo Marković, Ljubomir Tadić, Zagorka Golubović, Svetozar Stojanović, Miladin Životić, Dragoljub Mićunović, Nebojša Popov, and Trivo Inđić) were forcibly expelled from the Faculty of Philosophy in Belgrade. This also led to the cancellation of the Korčula Summer School. As Rudi Supek reported from Zagreb, "The School has been sharply criticised in Yugoslav press and political forums. Some of the most eminent Yugoslav Marxist philosophers and sociologists are presently not able to express their ideas in public. In such circumstances the School couldn't but miss its most important goal: free communication of ideas on vital problems of the modern world."²⁶

The firing of the so-called "Belgrade Eight," which had been predicted for some time, generated a significant response in Habermas's intellectual circle, with many colleagues, including his old friend Karl-Otto Apel, asking him to pen another protest letter.²⁷ Habermas responds to Apel by forwarding a report about the situation that he received from colleagues in the United States. He notes that while he would be willing "to join an initiative starting from Frankfurt," he observes that since he and Bloch had already written to Tito a year and a half earlier, "I do not want to take the initiative for a second time to protest in the same way."²⁸ Yet these concerns did not stop Habermas from signing a second open letter to Tito published in 1975, or from joining the newly created International Committee of Concern for Academic Freedom in Yugoslavia.²⁹

Following their dismissal, a number of the members of the Belgrade Eight wrote to Habermas with updates asking him for support.[30] Habermas invariably promised to do what "what one can do from one's desk (*was man so vom Schreibtisch aus tun kann*)."[31] In response, he often invited these thinkers to give lectures in Starnberg or sought to arrange visiting positions with his colleagues in Germany or elsewhere in the west by mobilizing his academic network.[32] For example, the letter of recommendation he wrote for Milan Kangrga (another member of the Praxis Group who had run into trouble with the regime) for his application for a Humboldt Fellowship in 1975 is preserved in the Habermas Vorlass.[33] He also sought to help Josip Jagar, another Yugoslavian intellectual who had been fired for being "far-left (*ultra-links*)," to extend his stay in Germany when his visa was running out in 1977.[34]

In response to various appeals, Habermas notes that he would like help out however he can in light of the "catastrophic developments" in Yugoslavia, but also observes that he "does not know what to do now that we have shot our powder prematurely.... One cannot write a letter to Tito every time." In brainstorming possible options, Habermas offers to come to Belgrade to give a public lecture that would at least be covered by international correspondents. Although "I am happy to take spectacular steps," he notes that he is not sure if such a mobilization would necessarily be helpful, since "such a lecture in Belgrade is a one-time thing. You should consider whether it would not be better to wait with it."[35]

In addition to these direct forms of assistance, Habermas was also active in helping to mobilize public opinion on behalf of his Yugoslav colleagues, both in Germany and the West more generally. At the initiative of Wolfgang Kraushaar, a German political scientist and historian who was the chairperson of the General Students' Committee (*Allgemeiner Studierendenausschuss*, or AStA), he agreed to participate in an event organized by the students in Frankfurt with "the declared purpose of providing political support for the Praxis Group." The fact that Habermas's relationship with the students is still strained is visible in the fact that he also seeks assurances that the event "will not be instrumentalized for other purposes."[36] Fortunately, things seem to have gone well; in his correspondence with the Finnish philosopher Georg Henrik von Wright, Habermas reports that Dutschke was among those who took part in this event in Frankfurt as well, a sign that his relations with the students was on the mend.[37]

At this time von Wright was coordinating the International Committee of Concern for Academic Freedom in Yugoslavia.[38] Although Habermas is skeptical about "how much use such a committee can be," he still agrees to remain involved and even agrees to help arrange for Bloch to join as well.³⁹ Von Wright expresses sympathy with Habermas's doubts, but notes, "It is to be hoped, however, that the Committee by its sheer existence will be a source of moral support for the intellectuals in Yugoslavia and a <u>memento</u> for the political authorities."⁴⁰

In addition to these other forms of assistance, Habermas also welcomed young students of philosophy from Yugoslavia to join him in Starnberg for research visits. One of these was Zoran Đinđić, a young philosophy student who had run afoul of Yugoslavian authorities in 1974 for attempting to organize an independent student movement.⁴¹ As a result of Chancellor Brandt's intercession on his behalf, Đinđić was allowed to emigrate to the Federal Republic rather than serve his sentence in Yugoslavia. After his arrival, he studied with Habermas, who was sympathetic to this erstwhile student leader. Since Habermas was unable to promote students at the Max Planck Institute, Đinđić officially received his PhD from the University of Konstanz under the supervision of Albrecht Wellmer, one of Habermas's former assistants, in 1979.⁴²

Following the fall of communism Đinđić returned to Serbia and became one of the leaders of the Democratic Party. In 2001, following the overthrow of Slobodan Milošević, he even became Prime Minister. However, his reformist career was brought to a tragic end when he was assassinated on March 12, 2003, due to his advocacy of democratic reforms and his efforts to place Serbia on the path to the European Union.⁴³

The Praxis Group in Yugoslavia were not the only nonorthodox Western Marxist thinkers being repressed by the communist regimes in their homelands. On the contrary, the members of the so-called Budapest School associated with György Lukács, with whom the early Frankfurt School was also connected, were also experiencing considerable difficulties during this period. After hearing reports of their struggles, Habermas wrote to his friend and colleague Ágnes Heller in June 1973, noting that "all of us here are very concerned that independent Marxist thought is now subject to repressive measures in Hungary as well." He also asked her if she would be able to meet with Herbert Gans, a German-born sociologist at Columbia University whom he had met during one of his visits to New York, who would be coming to Budapest in the coming weeks.⁴⁴

In her reply Heller confirms that she, her husband Ferenc Fehér, and the other members of the School had indeed been fired from their university professorships. She also reports that as a result they all "now live on the free market; I translate the works of Rosa Luxemburg, which I enjoy doing from time to time." Despite these difficulties, she writes, "Marxist thinking—like philosophical thinking in general—should remain independent in order to remain true to its function, even if only in possibility. For this one has to pay, and in the history of this discipline greater people have paid higher prices."[45]

In a long letter to Habermas following his visit to Budapest to meet with Heller and Fehér, Gans confirms that the Budapest School is indeed in trouble with the regime "following the death of Lukács, their protector." He reports that while "they wanted help ... because the greatest danger for them was silence from the outside world," he also observes that "they said quite explicitly that they were *not* asking for help ... [since] they presumably do not want also to be charged with having sought help from the West, in addition to their other 'crimes.'"

Based on his conversation, Gans suggests two forms of assistance: 1) invitations to give talks and to contribute to journals, "because it will impress the Central Committee (whose bureaucrats will read the letters before they are delivered by the postman) of the importance and status they have among intellectuals outside Hungary"; and 2) "a public protest letter signed only by Left and liberal intellectuals" that would publicize what was happening to them.[46] In light of Gans's letter, Habermas immediately writes to Heller with a formal invitation for her to come give a talk at the Max Planck Institute in Starnberg.[47] Although Heller appreciates the support, she is forced to decline; the fact that she is currently unemployed means that she cannot travel, since she does not have an employer who can sign the papers she needs to leave the country.[48]

Although Heller was initially hopeful that the repression she and her colleagues were experiencing in Hungary was temporary, it was not. In 1976 she again writes to Habermas to report on their situation and to ask for his assistance. Whereas previously she had noted her enjoyment at having the opportunity to translate Luxemburg's work and had placed her suffering in the broader context of the history of political thought, she now notes that the members of the Budapest School have been reduced to supporting their families "with literary slave labor (*literarischen Sklavenarbeit*)." She also complains to Habermas about the fact that they can "travel neither to the west nor to the east" and "are cut off from all academic contacts." As a result, she notes that many members of the group, including her and her husband, had decided to go into exile—temporarily at least—since it appears that the regime is willing to let them leave.

Since Habermas had previously offered two positions in the past, she asks him to arrange for formal invitations for each individual, so that they can cross the border.[49] In response, Habermas writes, "I would like to say, without mincing any words and without raising false hopes, we will do what we can here." After detailing how he has mobilized his other contacts on behalf of the members of the Budapest School, he writes—with a clear eye to the censors he knows will read his letter before it reaches its recipient—"Dear Mrs. Heller, I hope that you see all the things I do not write (*was ich nicht schreibe*)."[50]

Given György Márkus's work on the analytic philosophy of language—a topic with which Habermas had himself been engaging since delivering the Tanner Lectures at Princeton University in 1971—Habermas was able to arrange a position for him in Starnberg. Unfortunately, Márkus was unable to take it up because his son was soon thereafter called up by the army, and he did not want to leave him behind in Hungary.[51] However, with some help from Habermas, Heller, Fehér, Márkus, his wife Maria, and their son were all able to emigrate to Australia a few years later. Habermas had hoped to organize a meeting in Germany before their departure and had issued formal invitations for them to come to visit him; however, due to problems with their visas, this get-together never took place.

In addition to his sustained engagement in support of the Praxis Group and the Budapest School, Habermas also supported the rights of communists in West Germany, such as the German sociologist Horst Holzer who had been fired for his membership in the German Communist Party (*Kommunistische Partei Deutschlands*, KPD), and the Iranian communist Sascha Haschemi. However, in the latter case he also wanted it to be clear that "I do not share our friend's political beliefs and do not approve of the usual methods of the KPD."[52] He also signs open letters in solidarity with a number of Chilean colleagues, and writes to the Salvadorian President Carlos Humberto Romero protesting, "Since you came to power in July 1977, violations of human rights in El Salvador have increased dramatically."[53] However, especially given the attacks from the right linking him to terrorism, Habermas usually only agreed to add his name to letters of protest with "the reservation that I would first like to see who else signs ... [since] I have made it my maxim not to join the company of false friends of freedom."[54]

During this period Habermas also participated in protests on behalf of the Czechoslovak philosophers Karel Kosik and Jan Patočka.[55] Following the so-called Prague Spring of 1968 these two thinkers were accused of being "corrupters of the youth (*Verderber der Jugend*)" and banned from teaching in Czechoslovakia. Interestingly, Habermas took up the cause of Kosik again in 1992, when he was forcibly retired from his professorship by the democratic regime following the fall of communism in 1989.[56]

Habermas's protests were perhaps most vocal when his friend and longtime editor at the *FAZ*, Karl-Heinz Bohrer, was dismissed from his position as the head of the newspaper's literature division (*Literaturblatt*) by its new publisher, Joachim Fest, who sought to steer the publication in a more conservative direction. In a series of letters voicing his displeasure, Habermas observed that whether this was done for political or "strategic market (*marktstrategischen*)" reasons—"on the grounds that one has to adapt more to the needs of the reader"—it was "either grotesque or a sell-out of the best traditions of the old Frankfurter Zeitung."[57] Given that the FAZ "embodies a piece of the spiritual traditions of the liberal bourgeoisie (*geistigen Traditionen des liberalen Bürgertums*) in Germany," he lamented the potential loss of this resource.[58] He also voices his fear that under Fest's leadership, the *FAZ*'s Feuilleton is now pursuing "an offensive against the left."[59]

After Fest's takeover and Bohrer's firing, Habermas stops publishing in the *FAZ*, preferring to send his commentaries to *Die Zeit*, *Frankfurter Rundschau* or *Süddeutsche Zeitung* (see the introduction for more on where Habermas chooses to publish).[60] Fest and the *FAZ* were also involved in fanning the flames of a controversy that erupted at a meeting organized by the Thyssen Foundation in Munich.[61] In an article the *FAZ* published on this event, Habermas and the Max Planck Institute were accused of politicizing science by bringing together researchers "for whom scientific controversies and political fighting (*politischer Kampf*) go together."

Although Habermas dismisses this accusation as "humbug," he is deeply insulted by the insinuation that he is allowing his political convictions to bias his work and that of the Institute as a whole. He notes that in no way should the notion of fundamental cognitive or "knowledge-constitutive interests (*erkenntnisleitende Interessen*)," a concept he developed in *Knowledge and Human Interests* (1968), be used to condone the idea that researchers should be "guided by an external interest in the application of possible research results." On the contrary, consistent with his developing concept of the separation of theory from practice, Habermas reaffirms in a letter to *Die Zeit*—which also published a report on the incident—that "it is a threat to science (*Wissenschaft*) when scientific criticism is used for the purpose of political discrimination."[62]

In a 1976 letter to the editors of the *FAZ* protesting both this personal attack and the newspaper's broader editorial tone, Habermas wrote, "Mr. Fest may not like the left, but to call leftist what he does not like, that I find illiberal." In the same correspondence, he also accuses Fest of having "contributed to the political neutralization of Hitler in this country."⁶³ The timing of this charge is interesting, as it predates the *Historikerstreit* (Historians' Dispute)—a controversy in which Fest and the *FAZ* published pieces by conservative historians attempting to relativize the uniqueness of the Holocaust—by nearly a decade. Habermas, who later responded forcefully to such revisionist interpretations of Third Reich atrocities as mere reactions to communist crimes, anticipated this revisionist tendency in Fest from the very beginning of his tenure at the *FAZ* (for further discussion, see chapter 6).

ACCUSATIONS OF SUPPORT FOR TERRORISM

In addition to these letter writing campaigns on behalf of persecuted friends and colleagues, Habermas was also involved in a number of smaller controversies. One notable example occurred when he publicly opposed plans for the redevelopment (*Sanierung*) of Heidelberg's old town by signing a petition circulated by the local organization Citizens for Heidelberg (*Bürger für Heidelberg*).⁶⁴ His signature drew the attention of the city council, and one member even wrote to Habermas to question his audacity in signing such a document.⁶⁵ Clearly exasperated, Habermas responded, "I do not need to legitimize my biographical and substantive interest in the fate of Heidelberg's old town: I lived in Heidelberg for many years and taught as a professor at the university there."⁶⁶

Whereas previously Habermas had often commented on the policies of the Social Democrats—as is visible in his objections to the Bad Godesberg program and his support for the SDS—and had also interacted with leftist politicians, these contacts declined in the 1970s as well.⁶⁷ One notable exception is an article that Habermas co-wrote with his assistant, Claus Offe (who had initially accompanied him to Starnberg), and the economists Sigrid Skarpelis-Sperk and Peter Kalmbach; it was published in *Der Spiegel* on February 24, 1975. Writing under the title "A Biedermeier Path Toward Socialism?"—the term *Biedermeier* refers to a mediocre poet of the mid-nineteenth century and is used to label unchallenging artistic styles—they criticize the post-Brandt SPD for its tame approach to socialism, which did not seek to question the capitalist system for fear of alienating its middle class, bourgeois supporters. They call on the SPD to use the state to steer the economy directly, since in their view the rise of large conglomerates and multinational corporations has already replaced the economic laws of supply and demand in favor of "monopolistic pricing behavior."⁶⁸

This intervention turned into a larger controversy when Wilhelm Hennis, a professor of political science at the University of Freiburg, wrote a response calling the idea of using legal means to directly steer the economy "a kind of *levée en masse* plus Enabling Act," referring pejoratively to the *Ermächtigungsgesetz* that granted Adolf Hitler dictatorial powers in 1933.⁶⁹ In a letter to the editor of the *Deutsche Zeitung*, which had published Hennis's critique, Habermas notes, "This, in the vocabulary that Hennis knows so well how to use, is what you call a denunciation." Habermas's irritation was also compounded by the fact that Hennis had not mentioned his article—or its polemical nature—when they had discussed the legitimacy of the state system at an academic conference in Duisburg shortly before its publication.⁷⁰ Klaus von Beyme, who helped organize the debate, was similarly outraged, noting that Habermas had "every right . . . to fire back sharply (*volle Veranlassung . . . scharf zurückzuschießen*)" at Hennis, whom he critiques for his "uncontrolled manner" and labeled both "a conformist and opportunist."⁷¹ In retrospect, however, Habermas has made clear that "I should not have written" his initial piece with Offe, Skarpelis-Sperk, and Kalmbach, since it proved to be too great a distraction to his work at the time.⁷²

Even though Habermas stepped back from the public sphere during his time in Starnberg, his outspokenness and past willingness to take political positions still riled some of his colleagues, leading to a number of disputes that spilled over into the public. For example, in 1974 Habermas wanted to attend the annual meeting of the International Hegel Association in Moscow, but was informed by Wilhelm Raimund Beyer, the head of the association, that, "The International Hegel Society does not want a 'Hegel Prize laureate' in its midst; it remains a philosophical society." Their exchange of letters, in which Habermas accused Beyer of treating him like a "class enemy" rather than a philosophical colleague, was published by *Die Zeit* under the title, "They Will not Be Able to Remain Silent."⁷³

Habermas's unpopularity within the predominantly conservative German academy became particularly evident during a dispute he had with the University of Munich. It was common practice for directors of Max Planck Institutes to apply for and receive honorary professorships at a nearby university. After arriving in Starnberg, Habermas therefore applied for such a position in Munich in 1971. However, rather than leading to a routine appointment, he was again caught up in a controversy, as the Faculty of Philosophy rejected his application.[74] In the aftermath, the Chancellor of Ludwig Maximilian University, Nikolaus Lobkowicz—who had supported Habermas's request—wrote an official letter to Habermas expressing his regret over this decision. Nevertheless, it was clear that Habermas's leftist activism had not won him any friends in the conservative *Bundesland* of Bavaria, where the Christian-Social Union (*Christlich-Soziale Union in Bayern*, CSU) routinely won large majorities.[75]

Habermas was well aware of the political climate in Bavaria and knew that higher education policy there had taken a very different shape to the ideas he had advocated in Hessen.[76] Nevertheless, the rejection still stung—not only because it violated an important norm by denying a Max Planck Institute director such an honor, but also because it meant he would not be able to participate in mentoring the next generation of academics through the supervision of PhD students. On June 13, 1973, the Bavarian minister for culture and education, Hans Maier, wrote to Habermas to dispel the rumors that he was behind this decision, noting, "Your call (*Berufung*) to become an honorary professor would never fail on my account (*wird nie an mir scheitern*)."[77] But Habermas remained skeptical of Maier's excuses and of his moralistic tone. He also rejected the suggestion that "my decision to come here and become more involved in research at the same time oblige me . . . not to accept an honorary professorship."[78]

Interestingly, Robert Spaemann, a professor from Munich with whom he had had a rather testy public exchange in *Merkur* regarding whether his "aim of replacing domination with domination-free consent" was emancipatory, or actually becoming "a theory legitimizing unlimited and uncontrolled domination," supported Habermas's application.[79] In a letter from early 1974 Spaemann wrote to Habermas to apologize for the fact that he had been unable to influence the vote. He also noted his regret that many in Germany today "could not imagine that someone, who once had a substantive controversy with you, would not only vote for you anyway, but would even be happy if the conversation could continue."[80] Although Habermas rarely agreed with Spaemann politically or philosophically, over the course of their exchanges he always recognized him "as a fair discussion partner."[81] A similar story played out again in 1980, when the senate of the Ludwig Maximilian University once again rejected an application for an honorary professorship for Habermas, an application which this time had come from the Institute for Sociology.[82]

While no one involved in the controversy over Habermas's appointment in Munich made this connection explicitly, it is also clear that the broader wave of terrorism sweeping across the FRG at this time—and the conservative accusations linking the Frankfurt School to this violence—also played a role in the outcome. The early 1970s were marked by a wave of political liberalization following the SPD's ascent to the chancellorship of West Germany for the first time in 1969. However, it was also defined by a series of bombings carried out by the Red Army Faction (*Rote Armee Fraktion*, RAF) and the arrest of leading figures in this terrorist group, including Andreas Baader, Gudrun Ensslin, and Ulrike Meinhof.[83] Although Habermas rejected conservative claims that this terrorism was inspired by critical theory, he also recognized the growing fragmentation of the anti-authoritarian protest movement, which he argued had "lost its way, be it on the path toward party-based communism and neo-Stalinism or toward becoming an alternative culture—both leading equally into isolation."[84]

West Germany's confrontation with domestic terrorism reached its height in 1977, when a series of assassinations targeted Germany's top prosecutor, Siegfried Buback, and his security detail; the chairman of the Dresdner Bank board of directors, Jürgen Ponto; and the president of the Confederation of German Employers' Associations, Hanns Martin Schleyer.[85] The so-called "German autumn" culminated with the hijacking of a Lufthansa plane traveling from Palma de Mallorca to Frankfurt.[86] One of the hijackers' demands was the release of members of the RAF group, who had recently been sentenced to life in prison despite repeated complaints about their treatment during their detention. These claims were amplified by France's leading public intellectual, Jean-Paul Sartre, who accused the state of violating the human rights of the RAF prisoners after visiting them in the high-security Stammheim prison.[87]

The government reacted harshly to these events, passing a number of laws, including dragnet searches and a number of other policing measures, that together amounted to a form of emergency rule that bordered on authoritarianism. The German right, including the chairman of the CDU Baden-Württemberg, Hans Karl Filbinger, took advantage of this to attack leftist intellectuals, even going so far as to classify the Frankfurt School as a terrorist organization.[88] In its reporting on these events, in which it warned against the deconstruction of the rule of law in West Germany, the political magazine *Der Spiegel* accused Habermas of being a "negligent enabler of terrorism (*fahrlässiger Wegbereiter des Terrorismus*)" and denounced the Frankfurt School for "providing what serve as justifications for violence."[89]

This controversy extended to academe, pitting leftist liberals and liberal conservatives against one other. More specifically, it set off what could be called a "'civil war (*Bürgerkrieg*)' amongst the '45ers,'" a term often used to refer to the generation that was defined by the rupture of 1945, to which Habermas also belonged.[90] Habermas himself was understandably incensed by these accusations, especially since it was precisely his unequivocal stance *against* violence that had led to his break with the student movement. He was particularly enraged by *Der Spiegel*'s coverage, since the article "Murder Begins with an Evil Word (*Mord beginnt beim bösen Wort*)," failed to provide even a single quotation in which he explicitly condoned violence or offered any other evidence to suggest that support for violence "could be read out of my statements as an unintended consequence. You make no attempt to show that; I maintain that it cannot be shown either." He also rejected the insinuation that his decision to remain silent since 1969 implies support for terrorism, calling it "an absurdity."[91]

Habermas also notes the tendentiousness of trying to link the left to terrorism, given how many right-wing thinkers have explicitly "provided justifications for criminal practices and questionable regimes," including Martin Heidegger, Arnold Gehlen, Carl Schmitt, and Ernst Jünger. He concludes his letter to Walter Busse at *Der Spiegel*'s editorial office by asking, "In the climate of the Federal Republic, it is hardly possible to come to terms with a past of bureaucratic terror (*Vergangenheit des bürokratischen Terrors zu bewältigen*) whose moral connections are quite transparent; today, when the beneficiaries of the desperate terrorism of individuals believe they can target leftists, untenable moral attributions are made overzealously, and at great journalistic expense. Doesn't this cast a strange light on our political culture?"[92] In an interview with the Italian weekly *Rinascita*, he not only rejected attempts to link terrorism in the Federal Republic to the left, but instead argued that attempts by the right to do so were a form of deflection, as this phenomenon "should rather be interpreted as a counterpart to fascism."[93]

However, it was not only conservative agents within political circles that were drawing connections between terrorism and the left; some within the academy were as well. Most notable among these was the German political scientist Kurt Sontheimer, with whom Habermas had maintained a collegial relationship since the 1960s. Whereas Sontheimer had previous identified "resurgent nationalism" as the main threat to West Germany's democratic order, he had now "discovered a greater source of danger—leftist theory (*die linke Theorie*)."

In his unpublished correspondence Habermas admits, "In principle (*grundsätzlich*) I am not a pacifist." However, both in private and in his public statements, he repeatedly rejects any causal connection between critical theory and terrorism. He is particularly disturbed by any attempt "to use Article 18 of the Basic Law [West Germany's constitution] against leftist theorists," which would allow the state to take away the basic rights of the press, teaching, assembly, association, privacy of correspondence and property in order to defend West Germany's basic democratic order. Habermas sees this attempt to apply the principles of militant democracy to those like himself—"who tried to understand the problems of legitimation and motivation" that plagued West Germany—rather to those on the far right who opposed the legitimacy of the postwar Federal Republic as such—as a sign of the "fascistic disintegration of our political culture."[94] He also noted his fear that the attempt to combat terrorism by denying critics their basic rights as citizens would bring about the very degradation of democracy that measures like Article 18 were meant to protect.

Habermas initially published an open letter responding to Sontheimer in *Merkur*. This led to an exchange that later appeared in the *Süddeutsche Zeitung*. In his contribution, Sontheimer recognizes Habermas's democratic credentials and commitment to the *Rechtsstaat* created by the Basic Law but notes that in his support of the student movement he had encouraged the development of a "radical opposition to the bourgeois-democratic system." Quoting the journalist Dieter E. Zimmer, Sontheimer therefore concludes that it would be "deception to deny the left-wing roots of terrorism."[95] Habermas replies that these accusations were no more than unsubstantiated insinuations, especially since the members of the RAF themselves had noted that they could not be considered leftist since the left rejected violence.[96] He also rejects the idea that he had to apologize for positions he had never taken or to distance himself from the left, "from the socialists, who today are slanderously associated with terror."[97]

Habermas commented on these events again in an article in *Der Spiegel*, entitled "A Test for Popular Justice: The Accusations Against the Intellectuals." Here he pushes back on once more on attacks that attempt to link himself and the left to the wave of terrorism that was sweeping West Germany. He finds this accusation absurd given that "between the years 1961 and 1969 I repeatedly spoke out against the use of violence in any form." He sees these attacks, which I address in greater detail below, as reflecting a broader "barbaric animosity toward critical thought" in the CDU and calls on "the intellectual community to wake up from its state of dull passivity."[98] Before her departure to Australia, Heller even sent one last letter to Habermas praising him for this text: "The honesty and sobriety of this text was for many here great evidence (*grosser* [sic] *Beweis*) that German philosophy is worthy of facing the problems of the day (*würdig sich zur heutigen Problemen stellt*) in line with its best traditions."[99]

After this commentary, Habermas had had enough of these debates. He declined an invitation from Michael Theunissen from the University of Heidelberg to participate in a discussion on "Social Criticism and Terrorism."[100] In his reply, he notes that he has to "defend the rest of my ability to concentrate as well as my working time against a trend, which pulls me far too easily into politics as my main pursuit (*Hauptbeschäftigung*)," since "in recent times I have already had to positively respond to too many political inquiries."[101] This is not to say that Habermas was no longer interested in the political situation. In fact, in another sign that many of the protagonists in the student movement had moved past the disagreements sparked by Habermas's accusation of left fascism, Oscar Negt accepted an invitation from Habermas to come to Starnberg to speak to the Institute to "say something here in an internal circle about the situation of the left in the Federal Republic," given that "the political situation [is] so worrying that some of us feel the need to orient ourselves a little more systematically."[102]

Although Habermas had praised the surprisingly liberal political culture that developed in the Federal Republic during the postwar period multiple times at the end of the 1960s and the beginning of the 1970s, by the end of that decade he had become increasingly worried that these gains were being lost. In particular, he worried that the "expansion of authorities for the protection of public opinion (*Gesinnungsschutzbehörden*)" in response to the threat of terrorism—including the application of Article 18 of the *Grundgesetz* and the anti-radical decree, which sought to keep individuals "out of the civil service (*öffentlichen Dienst*) on the basis of their membership in the DKP (*Deutsche Kommunistische Partei*, German Communist Party)"—represented a form of backsliding from liberal democracy that Germany could ill afford given its recent history. In a set of articles he wrote in 1976 and 1978, he opposed the use of *Berufsverbote* (occupational/vocational prohibitions) in the cases of "Mrs. B" and "Mrs. W," who had both been denied teaching positions due to their connections to the DKP.[103]

Habermas's public opposition to such violations of the freedom of opinion of civil servants—a class of employment that includes all university staff in Germany—resulted in an invitation for him to join the third "Russell Tribunal." This "people's tribunal" was originally sponsored by a group of public intellectuals led by Bertrand Russell and Jean-Paul Sartre, and its 1978 edition was to focus on the situation of human rights in Germany. This invitation to join came from his British colleague Steven Lukes, who had agreed to join the tribunal and wrote to Habermas in 1977 to inform him that "I strongly urged [the Russell Foundation] when they approached me that they should invite you as a German participant."[104]

After some consideration and consultation with his colleagues in Starnberg, Habermas turned down Lukes' invitation. Although he recognizes that "We are, indeed, in a situation of growing pressure and even open attack on civil liberties," he fears that "the German groups that are in charge of the preparation of the Russell Tribunal do not give any guarantee that they are sensitive for the chance to produce ill founded [sic] material and weak arguments which then could well be counterproductive." Although Habermas decries the practice of *Berufsverbote* and observes that "the tendency within the CSU and the right wing of the CDU to narrow the range of legitimate opinions and attitudes is frightening," he concludes, "I doubt that the evidence one could gather can be effectively presented within the frame of a tribunal, which probably will mix up hard evidence with soft suspicions and mere propaganda."[105] He affirms, "I still think that your initiative is necessary," but later also refuses to testify because, "I simply do not consider the Russell Tribunal to be the appropriate forum in the Federal Republic today."[106] Rather than relying on outside actors like the Russell Tribunal, during this period Habermas repeatedly insisted that liberals in West Germany should stand up for themselves and their principles on their own.

CONCLUSION

In January 1981 Habermas wrote a letter to Weizsäcker, who had retired a year before, informing him that he would be leaving the Institute as well.[107] This decision had been a long time coming. Soon after Habermas had moved from Frankfurt to the Max Planck Institute, it had become clear he was not cut out for—nor did he enjoy—the bureaucratic obligations that came with running a major research center, a fact that was also visible in growing conflicts with the staff as well.[108]

In December 1972, less than two years after his arrival, he was already complaining that he was "incessantly busy adapting to the surprises of a new way of life." In particular, he seems to have been taken aback by how little time he actually had to focus on his own work. Writing to his British colleague, the historian George Lichtheim, who had written a number of articles analyzing his work, Habermas ruefully observes, "I am such a bad sociologist that I did not know what I could have known: in an institute, you have to live with so many interdependencies that you only experience time from the point of view of a scarce resource."[109]

One of the main reasons he had decided to come to Starnberg in the first place was "the opportunity I now have to go to Starnberg with fifteen research associates," with whom he could work on developing his major new project, which sought to comprehend the crises of late capitalism through the lens of communicative action and its deformations.[110] However, Habermas soon realized that overseeing so many researchers was too laborious and never filled all the positions. Overall, it quickly became clear that "Starnberg was not exactly the research paradise" Habermas had imagined it would be. The working atmosphere was very tense, a situation exacerbated by the significant pressure Habermas put both himself and his coworkers under. The fact that he looked down on the attempts of the other members of the Institute to blow off steam by playing ping-pong in the lecture hall—an activity that Habermas thought was a waste of time—did little to alleviate the conflicts Habermas had with many of his coworkers, even though he and Weizsäcker always treated each other with great respect and admiration.[111]

For a brief period following Weizsäcker's retirement Habermas toyed with the idea of reorienting the Institute completely in line with his own interests. Under this proposal, the relaunched research center would be devoted to the "Comparative Analysis of the Institutionalization and Internalization of Value Systems." He even recruited his old friend Ralf Dahrendorf, whom he had initially met in the summer of 1955 at a meeting of young German sociologists organized by Helmut Schelsky (see chapter 2), to join him as a director.[112] Like Habermas, Dahrendorf was also interested in the relationship between philosophy and the public, though unlike Habermas he had actually run for local office and had sought to shape the system from the inside.[113] However, his reluctance, as well as Habermas's own disillusion with his administrative duties, soon put an end to these plans.

In addition to the failure of these efforts, Habermas's commitment to the Institute was further tested when it became clear that it would be difficult to wind down Weizsäcker's research group; its members were ready to go to court to prevent their termination. This was the last straw, since it took away one of the main benefits Habermas saw in working at the Institute: the ability to choose his collaborators.[114] Habermas writes to his erstwhile codirector that although "I am myself a member of a union and consider labor law to be an historical achievement," he does not want to go through a court battle to ensure "the closing of a unit in compliance with the redundancy plan"—especially in light of the negative press coverage that would result. Given that he also does not feel that he can continue to work with "scientists I have not selected and of whose professional qualifications and proficiency I am, as you know, not able to assure myself," he felt that his only option was to leave.[115]

This is not to say that Habermas's time in Starnberg was a failure. From the point of view of his research, the decade he spent at the Max Planck Institute allowed him to develop his new, linguistic paradigm of critical theory, which appeared in his two-volume *Theory of Communicative Action* (1981). Although this opus retained the focus on communication and discourse that had defined Habermas's work at least since *Structural Transformation*, it abandoned the historical and contextualist approach that defined his early work in favor of a "quasi-transcendental" methodology that grounds "the social sciences in a theory of language."[116]

On one level, this book gave Habermas the opportunity to confront the broader sociological tradition defined by Karl Marx, Max Weber, and Émile Durkheim. More substantively, however, it sought to develop a intersubjective paradigm of rationality that pushed back on the individualistic premises of much of the history of philosophy, to construct a "two-level concept of society" in which this communicative ideal could exist alongside the more functionalist ability of nonsubjective rationality to complete the project of the enlightenment by pushing back on the pathologies of modern life.[117] In a sign of the way Habermas's public engagements shaped academic work, the accusations of terrorism he had to deal with during the German Fall pushed Habermas to finally finish the *Theory of Communicative Action*, which he saw as crucial to showing the key role that linguistically-mediated interaction—not violence—plays in his critical theory.[118]

Interestingly, although the two-volume "blue monster" (as the blue-covered original German edition of the book soon became known) is clearly an academic volume, it also had significant popular appeal. Soon after its publication in 1981, it had to be released in second and third editions, as "almost 10,000 people (another two dozen are added to the count daily), bend over a thick book that they are not allowed to ignore (*nicht ignorieren dürften*)."[119] While not all the reviews were positive, it certainly does seem that Habermas was right to think that this book could help his compatriots make sense of the situation they found themselves in.

Ultimately, the decision to leave Starnberg was made easier by the fact that in 1980 the University of Munich again denied Habermas an honorary professorship. Although he had in large part retreated from the public sphere, he was still viewed in conservative Bavaria as "storm bird of the cultural revolution (*Sturmvogel der Kulturrevolution*)," an allusion to bombers used by the Wehrmacht in World War II, who had contributed to "the pollution of our science" with his public engagements.[120] Despite his earlier conviction that "one should not emigrate without real reasons," at this point Habermas once again considered moving to the United States, where he felt that his ideas and his work were not only more accepted, but where he would not have to "take the blame for anything that is left-wing on his own head," as was the case in West Germany.[121] As a result, he even agreed to "to being considered for a senior chair in sociology" at the University of California, Berkeley.[122]

In the end, however, Habermas decided to return to Frankfurt, this time to a chair in philosophy. This choice occurred soon after the city decided to honor him with the Theodor W. Adorno Prize in 1980. At the award ceremony, the philosopher Michael Theunissen praised Habermas as a suitable successor to Adorno and declared both of them to be "intellectuals who are open to everything lively, within science and philosophy as well as outside it."[123] This event, and this comparison to Adorno the intellectual, may well have helped Habermas to make his decision to stay in Germany, as moving to the United States would have meant that he would have to permanently give up his role as a public intellectual. As the journalist Arno Widmann would later observe, it seems clear that Habermas "believed, indeed knew, that he was needed more here," i.e., in West Germany.[124] In this sense, as a critic from the *FAZ* wrote in his review of the *Theory of Communicative Action* observed, "Insofar as we can speak of the Federal Republic as an experiment, then Habermas's thinking relates to it affirmatively."[125]

Like many "New Left intellectuals," during the 1970s Habermas largely kept "eyes on professional journals, monographs and conferences." However, unlike many of these figures, who disappeared from the public sphere and became "lost in the universities," it was Habermas's return to the Goethe-University in Frankfurt that paved the way for his *Nebenberuf* as a public intellectual.[126] As the debates over terrorism and the Russell Tribunal show, by the end of the 1970s Habermas was becoming increasingly worried about a turn toward illiberalism on the German right. This fear only escalated after the CDU's Helmut Kohl entered the Chancellery in Bonn in 1982—a fear later confirmed by the interventions Habermas felt compelled to make in both the *Historikerstreit* (Historians' Dispute) and the *Vereinigungsdebatte* (Unification Debate), which I address in the next chapter.

One important early signal of Habermas's desire to reengage with the public sphere and with his role as a public intellectual was his decision to create a book series that would bring together his short political writings. Although the first four editions were published together in a single volume under the title *Kleine politische Schriften I-IV*, the contributions republished between its covers spanned Habermas's public interventions from the late 1950s up until the time of its release in 1980. The very fact that Habermas conceptualized this volume as the first in a series hinted that he was thinking about leaving the ivory tower of research that the Max Planck Institute had provided for him over the course of the previous decade.

Although this move back into the West German public sphere was by no means guaranteed—as Habermas's willingness to consider moving to the US makes clear—ultimately he decided in favor of a return to Frankfurt. In fact, it is during the period covered in the next chapter that Habermas develops his mature conception of the public intellectual, which I laid out in chapter 1. His move back to the Goethe University thus signals his commitment to the idea that—as he puts it—"Private edification is of course just one half of the business of philosophical communication. Public commitment is the other, even more important task of philosophy."[127]

CHAPTER 6

Return to the Public Sphere, 1983–1992

After twelve years of relative silence while focusing on his own research as the director of the Max Planck Institute, Habermas forcefully reengaged in the public life of the Federal Republic of Germany (FRG) after his return to the Goethe University in Frankfurt am Main in 1983. As I documented in the previous chapters, his initial retreat from the public sphere was precipitated by his experience with the student movement in the late 1960s. Despite his influence on this movement, he quickly transformed from prophet to pariah after linking the actionism of the students to "left fascism" and defending Adorno after his mentor called the police to clear the Institute of protesting students who had disrupted his classes (despite his own private opposition to this decision). These incidents, which most likely contributed to Adorno's untimely death of a heart attack in 1969, also pushed Habermas to leave Frankfurt for a second time.

This experience also led him to rethink his understanding of the relationship between theory and practice. While Habermas had always maintained a distinction between his private and public use of reason—i.e., between his contracted work in the classroom as a civil servant and his public activities as a citizen—the fallout from his engagement with the students made him wary of associating too closely with concrete social movements. Initially, his newfound reticence caused him to avoid the public spotlight (insofar as this was possible for such a prominent and divisive figure in West Germany) during his time Starnberg.

However, all this changed in 1983. In this chapter, I argue that Habermas's return to Frankfurt for a second time marks the full development of his mature understanding of the public intellectual. In his mature view, the public intellectual is not someone who engages directly in social movements or seeks to influence events behind the scenes; rather, they mediate theory and practice indirectly by openly intervening in public debate "when current events are threatening to spin out of control—but then promptly, as an early warning system" (see chapter 1).[1]

After his return to the "different professional environment" of Goethe University from the Max-Planck Institute, Habermas commented on a number of the most salient political and cultural issues in Germany, mostly related to the growing nationalism he had detected at the end of the 1970s.[2] In a 1978 letter, he observed that "the 'nation' is . . . really no longer a dominant theme in the FRG. But something like this can change overnight, of course."[3] Habermas detected such a change under Helmut Kohl's new government in the mid-1980s. This revival of nationalism pushed Habermas to involve himself in both in the *Historikerstreit* (Historians' Debate or Dispute) and the controversies over the desirability and form of German unification after the fall of the Berlin Wall. These were by far his most significant interventions of the decade, both in terms of the popular attention they generated and their place in the development of Habermas's engaged political thought.

Placing Habermas's seminal contributions to the politics of memory and his self-aware reflections on the role of the public intellectual—both of which shaped his contributions to the *Historikerstreit*—alongside his defensive and reserved reaction to the prospect of unification has the disadvantage of packing two of his most important contributions as a public intellectual into a single chapter. However, it also has advantages, highlighting Habermas's opposition to the reemergence of the nation as a normatively positive ideal in the public discourse of the Federal Republic. Treating the *Vereinigungsdebatte* (unification debate) alongside the *Historikerstreit* further underscores the key role that Habermas's continuing awareness of, and sensitivity to, the politics of memory plays in his interventions as a nonexpert public intellectual.

Examining Habermas's reactions to these two events together also highlights the interaction between what I have labelled the separation thesis, which emphasizes Habermas's role-differentiation between his identity as an academic and as a public intellectual, and the theoretical continuity thesis, which captures the substantive internal consistency between these two parts of his work. The period covered in this chapter is marked by the way in which Habermas draws on his deliberative conception of democratic legitimacy to criticize both attempts by the executive branch to push through a revisionist understanding of history that questioned the uniqueness of the Holocaust in the Germany as well as the use of bureaucratic, constituted powers to achieve the unification of the West German Federal Republic with the East German Democratic Republic (GDR)—a key constitutional issue that Habermas argues should have engaged the constituent power (*pouvoir constituent*) of the German people.[4]

In an accident of history, the English translation of *Structural Transformation of the Public Sphere* appeared in 1989, just as Soviet leader Mikhail Gorbachev was introducing his policy of *glasnost* (гласность), which made "the deliberations within the state visible to all citizens, and hence subject to public criticism."[5] This made Habermas's 1962 analysis of *Öffentlichkeit* (publicness)—the best German translation of this Soviet policy—particularly relevant, highlighting the dynamic, mediated tension that exists between the separation and the theoretical continuity thesis.

The growing relevance of "the most influential of Habermas's signature concepts" was in large part determined by changes to the German political environment. Two factors—one internal and one external—stand out. The first, endogenous change was the inauguration of Helmut Kohl's conservative government in the Federal Republic, which took power after 13 years of Social Democratic Party (SDP) rule under the leadership of Willy Brandt (1969–74) and Helmut Schmidt (1974–82). Habermas had generally supported this social democratic platform. But with its return to power in 1982, the Christian Democratic Union (CDU)—under Kohl's leadership and buttressed by conservative historians in the academy—began a conservative project of revisionism aimed at normalizing the Holocaust so that Germans could once again cultivate a national identity based on pride in their past achievements. These attempts to undermine West German public consensus on the need to "work through the past (*Aufarbeitung der Vergangenheit*)" by keeping collective memories of the atrocities of the Holocaust fresh in German historical conscience drew Habermas's ire and spurred him to fully conceptualize "secondary vocation (*Nebenberuf*)" as a public intellectual.[6]

The second, exogenous factor was the onset of the *Wende* (change or turning point) brought about by the events of November 9, 1989. The fall of the Berlin Wall took everyone by surprise, including the leadership of East Germany, which had triumphantly celebrated its fortieth anniversary just a month earlier. Although Otto Reinhold's argument that "socialism was the sole reason for the existence of the GDR" had been almost universally rejected when the head of the communist east German Academy of Sciences had first presented it earlier that summer, just months later Kohl's rapid movement push to unification had seemingly confirmed the "Reinhold thesis."[7]

Habermas did not harbor any utopian illusions about the emancipatory potential of a reformed East Germany to fulfill the unrealized potential of socialism expressed by some leftist intellectuals on both sides of the border. However, he immediately expressed his concern that the pace of events was impeding public deliberation about the substantive issues at stake.[8] While these developments shaped the issues and intellectual terrain of Habermas's return to the public sphere, he was already predisposed to reengage in the cultural and political life of West Germany. In fact, his reappointment to a teaching chair (*Lehrstuhl*) in 1983, after the relative seclusion of the small, affluent Bavarian resort town of Starnberg, seems to have reinvigorated Habermas. When asked for his views on the political situation in an interview conducted in Frankfurt in 1985, Habermas observed that despite his pessimistic, critical comments, "I am by no means resigned. My first three semesters teaching back here at the local university have given me a lot of encouragement." Although he was worried about the intellectual and political situation of West Germany, recalling Max Weber's famous definition of politics as the "strong and slow boring of hard boards," he noted, "For the patient boring of thick boards one needs to have a tolerance for frustration and a little self-strength (*Ich-Stärke*—literally 'ego-strength')."[9]

In the years immediately following his return to Frankfurt and his reengagement in the public sphere, Habermas's tolerance for frustration and his "*Ich-Stärke*" would be severely tested by West Germany's "weakly developed culture of dealing with political dissenters."[10] The *Historikerstreit* in particular quickly degenerated into a series of ad hominem arguments against Habermas, including the accusation that he had falsified the quotations of his intellectual adversaries.[11] However, despite this, these incidents reestablished Habermas's reputation as a public intellectual and gadfly with an "avantgardistic instinct for relevances," whose contributions to public debate were impossible to ignore.[12]

Additionally, his interventions in the *Historikerstreit*—one of the few major debates where Habermas successfully rallied public opinion to his side (with the assistance of many of his historical colleagues, it must be added)—also provided him with considerable moral and political capital. This newfound status was further enhanced by his participation in the *Vereinigungsdebatte*, where he was one of the few Western intellectuals who took the wishes and desires of many

East Germans seriously, rather than merely assuming that unification under the auspices of West Germany was what all citizens in the soon-to-be "new *Bundesländer*" desired. In this sense, though Habermas had initially established himself as a public intellectual in the nascent public sphere of the old Bonn Republic (a reference to the capital of postwar West Germany), he only became the kind of moral authority expected to issue statements on all major national controversies with the creation of the new Berlin Republic.[13]

Habermas's record in influencing opinion-formation in the Federal Republic's public sphere is mixed. Although unification proceeded—and succeeded—using an administrative, executive-led process that he argued had violated the normative foundations of democratic legitimacy and the principle of self-determination, Habermas is nevertheless usually seen as having prevailed in the Historians' Dispute. But the victory was hardly his alone. As Habermas himself admitted, "The *Historikierstreit*, which was really more of a political dispute, was essentially won by my historian friends (*Historikerfreunden*)," most notably Saul Friedlander and Hans-Ulrich Wehler, whose expert advice Habermas drew on in his own interventions.[14]

While Habermas and his left-wing allies prevailed initially, the longer-term consequences of the Historians' Dispute are less clear. On the one hand, it is true that Habermas isolated his opponents, especially Ernst Nolte, who lost much of his political influence within the CDU.[15] However, on the other hand, Robert Holub points out that what "the conservatives accomplished should not be measured by how much overt support they garnered but by how they managed to determine the public agenda that was discussed." In this sense, they succeeded in placing national pride on the agenda once more by relativizing the Holocaust, even though this topic had been confined to the far right for most of West German history. In retrospect, "If we reread the historians' debate through the filter of German unification, the hastily declared victory for Habermas's position would have to be reversed."[16]

In line with the broader argument of this book, in examining the major public debates in which Habermas participated over the course of the 1980s, I will focus in particular on how they reflect: 1) his understanding of the separate tasks of academic research and public engagement (the separation thesis); and 2) the internal consistency between his legal and political philosophy and his political writings (the theoretical continuity thesis). Dick Howard and much of the existing literature maintain that "the idea that a philosophical theory, whose claims are universal, could be somehow applied to the particular challenges of political life makes no sense."¹⁷ I argue, however, that these interventions are Habermas's attempts to put his theory into practice, albeit in an indirect, mediated way. As such, they are the first examples of his mature understanding of his role as a public intellectual.

I start this chapter by discussing the origins, development and results of the *Historikerstreit*. I then examine some of the smaller controversies in which Habermas involved himself in the 1980s. The third section turns to the *Vereinigungsdebatte* that broke out with the fall of the Berlin Wall in 1989. After a brief conclusion, the epilogue focuses on the "new *Historikerstreit*" that broke out in Germany in the wake of the global Black Lives Matter protests in 2020, as the German public sphere was once again forced to confront the legacy and supposed uniqueness of the Holocaust, this time in comparison to the crimes of imperialism and colonialism.

THE HISTORIANS' DISPUTE

Germany has developed a reputation as a global leader in *Vergangenheitsbewältigung*— that is to say, in confronting the painful, traumatic memories of the recent past. However, for much of the postwar period, there was actually relatively little discussion of these issues, and many of the interventions remained symbolic, prompting Max Czollek to describe Germany's politics of memory as a kind of "reconciliation theater (*Versöhnungstheater*)."¹⁸ Despite Germany's status as a global leader in confronting its recent past, conservative elites in West Germany have long sought to institute revisionist understandings of history behind the public's back.¹⁹

Dating back to the beginning of his career in the 1950s, Habermas's interventions as a public intellectual have been motivated a commitment to "active remembrance—working through (*aufarbeiten*) the past and hoping for a better future."²⁰ Starting with his widely publicized attack on Martin Heidegger for failing to apologize for his collaboration with the Nazis in 1953, Habermas has repeatedly addressed the particular duty Germans have to "learn from catastrophe" as a result of the Holocaust.²¹ In the wake of National Socialism, Habermas argues that "our patriotism . . . cannot deny the fact that in Germany democracy was able to put down roots in the motives and hearts of citizens (at least the younger generations) only after Auschwitz—and in a certain way only through the shock of this moral catastrophe."²² The desire to learn from the past by avoiding the pitfalls of the kinds of "blood and soil" organic conceptions of history and peoplehood propagated by the Nazi regime is a key theme running through almost all of Habermas's interventions as a public intellectual. It is also implicit in much of his theoretical work on democracy and the bonds that bind societies together.

Although these concerns are also present in his early critiques of the political, social, cultural, and economic continuities between the Third Reich and the Federal Republic, they came to the fore in the mid-1980s, when Habermas sparked a public controversy over what he saw as attempts by conservatives to "normalize" the Nazi past by allowing the FRG to "regain national self-confidence through an identification with a past which can be agreed upon."²³ While it is hard to imagine today, at that point there was little consensus in the German public sphere on whether Germany had been "defeated" or "liberated" in 1945. Moreover, even as late as the the mid-1980s no major study of the Holocaust had published in Germany, as most research by historians had focused on issues like Hitler's seizure of power and the course of the war.²⁴ In this sense, this controversy represents an "almost violent return of the historical to the West German consciousness."²⁵

In what became known as the *Historikerstreit*, Habermas reacted to attempts by a number of German historians—most notably Andreas Hillgruber, Michael Stürmer, and Ernst Nolte—to "detoxify" the Holocaust by arguing that it should not be singled out as uniquely evil, but should instead be understood in light of the other mass murders perpetuated over the course of the twentieth century. For instance, Nolte sought to excuse what he called "Hitler's Asiatic act (*'asiatische' Tat*)" by arguing that he merely feared that the Germans would "themselves be potential victims of an 'Asiatic' deed" given that both the gulag and "Bolshevik 'class murder' (*Klassenmord*)" more generally predated the "'racial murder' (*Rassenmord*) of National Socialism." In light of these historical considerations, Nolte and supporters claimed that "the curtain should finally be brought down (*ein Schlussstrich sollte endlich gezogen werden*)" on the history of the Third Reich.²⁶

Led by Habermas, a number of *Linksintellektuellen* (intellectuals of the left) pushed back against this attempt to both relativize and diminish the Nazi past in the FRG's collective memory. Habermas's first published intervention came in "A Kind of Settlement of Damages (*Eine art Schadensabwicklung*)," an essay originally published in the German weekly *Die Zeit* on July 11, 1986. While this text is usually seen as the start of the Historians' Dispute, Habermas had in fact already laid out some of his ideas in a set of comments he delivered on July 2 at an event entitled "Nation as Exhibit: Planning, Criticism and Utopias in the Founding of Museums in Bonn and Berlin (*Nation als Ausstellungsstück. Planungen, Kritik und Utopien zu den Museumsgründungen in Bonn und Berlin*)," which was examining the proposals for the foundation of the new Museum of German History (*Deutsches Historisches Museum*).

Habermas opens his remarks by drawing on his personal experience, noting that new museums are much like new Max Planck Institutes: "Once the directors are in place, they develop an approach, which bears little resemblance to the programmatic statements included in the founding documents." In light of this, rather than focus on the actual proposals for the new museums that were under discussion, he instead offers a "a background understanding that I read from the symbolic actions of the federal government and the publications of some of its advisors." He starts his analysis by arguing that Germany's failure to confront the historical legacy of the *Nazizeit* represents a "loss of history (*Geschichtsverlust*)" that is "causally linked" to the contemporary "weakness in the legitimation (*Legitimationsschwäche*) of the political system." By "banning the vital memory of national history from thought," he argues that the collective memory of West Germany is unable to ground an integrative collective identity.[27]

These initial remarks provide a good summary of Habermas's basic position in the *Historikerstreit*. In the rest of his talk, Habermas provides a brief analysis of the positions of the main conservative historical revisionists, including Michael Stürmer and Ernst Nolte. Since Habermas presents these arguments in more detail in subsequent texts, I will address them in my analysis of these later writings. The key point is that Habermas does not wish "to engage in a methodological debate among historians," but is concerned instead with the desire of these revisionist scholars "to create and disseminate an image of history that is conducive to national consensus," which he identifies as rooted in "a concept of ideological planning that extends beyond the limits of the discipline of history (*die Geschichtswissenschaft überfordern*)."[28] In this sense, as Charles Maier points out, Habermas's intervention is grounded in his belief that "the question of comparability was not just a scholar's issue" or "some recondite argument about a value-free social science (*Wertfreiheit*), but the public use of history."[29]

Not only does Habermas see this attempt to reshape German collective identity in the wake of the Holocaust as ideological; he also argues that it is anachronistic, given the unavoidable pluralism of contemporary societies, which must therefore "draw ambivalent conclusions about their own traditions and educational processes." Rather than seeking to rehabilitate past models of social integration, he advocates a universalistic approach to collective identity based on "constitutional patriotism" and a commitment to the basic principles of the Basic Law. Bringing his argument full circle, he notes that while such a revisionist, ideological conception of history probably subtends the initial proposals for the new Museum of German History, he concludes that this idea—which he welcomes in principle—can still be salvaged by the expert commission and the institution's directors.[30]

As he makes clear during the discussion following his prepared comments, Habermas goes even further, noting that just as modern democratic societies must assume that all citizens can at least understand the basic principles of the constitution, they must also proceed as though citizens can "talk about competing interpretations of history, which of course become all the more important the more they concern one's own traditions, in which one recognizes oneself." This conviction leads him to a markedly different understanding of the role museums should play in public life than that proposed by the government and its revisionist historians. Rather than seeing the museum as an ideological tool designed to create a usable past that can unify the population under a clearly defined understanding of history, Habermas instead argues that it should act as an educational tool that activates the critical faculties of its visitors, encouraging them "to behave reflexively with regard to the information offered to them there."[31]

While these reflections set the foundations for the *Historikerstreit*, the actual debate was set off a week later when Habermas published "A Kind of Settlement of Damages." In it he sought to alert the public to the attempts of these revisionist conservative historians "to provide suitably positive pasts for the legitimation requirements of the present political system." More specifically, he saw them as playing an important "role in the process of ideological planning" in the conservative government of Helmut Kohl, which had adopted a new approach to the politics of memory that not only sought to establish "a Federal Republic firmly anchored in the Atlantic community of value," but also one that would "confirm that we Germans had always been on the right side in the struggle against the Bolshevist enemy."[32]

In his article, Habermas drew the attention of Germany's reading public to a new trend in conservative historical scholarship, which sought to lay the ideological foundations for a new interpretation of postwar memory. His first target was Stürmer, who argues that West Germany needs a more traditional national memory to forge "that higher provision of meaning (*Sinnstiftung*) which only nation and patriotism—after religion—have hitherto been capable of achieving," if it is to avoid the dangers of value pluralism, which leads "sooner or later to social civil war."[33] Stürmer thus treats history not only as a topic of research (*Wissenschaft*), but also a legitimate site of ideological contestation, since "whoever fills the memories, coins the concepts and interprets the past will win the future." Noting West Germany's crucial place in the "arc of the Atlantic system of defense (*Verteidigungsbogen des atlantischen Systems*)," he argues that historical revisionism away from dangerous ideas of guilt and shame both "morally legitimate and politically necessary" in the fight against communism.[34]

For Habermas, such a position is a betrayal of the ethos of academic scholarship, which must be devoted first and foremost to "scientific truth as a form of truth which can be defined only in terms of methodological research."[35] He acknowledges that the distinction between academic work and politics is not "the kind of division of labor in which one thing has nothing to do with the other." Nevertheless, Habermas maintains that research cannot be directly instrumentalized for political ends without undermining its own methodological foundations, which require that "each problem has been examined and pursued in terms of its inner logic" (see also chapter 1).[36]

In a letter to the editor of the *Frankfurter Allgemeine Zeitung* (*FAZ*) on August 11, Habermas also notes that this vision of scholarship—"historical consciousness as vicarious religion" is problematic for the discipline as a whole, which might be overtaxed by this program."[37] As he observes in a later discussion of Daniel Goldhagen's *Hitler's Willing Executioners* (1996), the result of a "union of historicism and nationalism" of the kind seen in the work of Stürmer and his fellow travelers—which blurs the analytic, scientific perspective of the academic with the subjective, ethical-political perspective of the participant—is that "historiographical science degenerates into the politics of history." Instead, the question for Habermas "is not primarily the guilt or innocence of the forefathers," but rather the extent to which historical research conducted independently can aid "the critical self-assurance of their descendants."[38]

Next, Habermas turns to Hillgruber, who earlier that same year had published a short book entitled *Zweierlei Untergang: Die Zerschlagung des Deutschen Reiches und das Ende des europäischen Judentums* (*Two Kinds of Demise: The Shattering of the German Reich and the End of European Jewry*). Habermas saw this monograph as part of the same ideological project inaugurated by Stürmer. His first objection regards the title, which focuses on the active "shattering" of the Third Reich by the Allies but portrays the murder of European Judaism as something that simply passively "came to an end," presumably without any active engagement or effort by the Nazi regime.

In addition to his willful ignorance regarding the perpetrators of the Holocaust and his lack of effort in empathizing with the individual Jews murdered in the death camps, Habermas also takes Hillgruber to task for his identification Germany's interests with the interests of the *Wehrmacht* (the Nazi armed forces). This revisionist perspective allows Hillgruber to praise the military for "protect[ing] the population of the German east from the Red Army's orgy of revenge" by fighting the Red army to the bitter end on the eastern front. The argument is summed up in Hillgruber's attack on the use of the word "liberation" in the context of the end of the Nazi Reich, since this concept "implies an identification with the victors and . . . is inappropriate to the fate of the German nation as a whole."[39]

Habermas is incensed by Hillgruber's decision to describe "events from the point of view of the courageous soldier [and] of the desperate civilian population," a perspective that ignores that of German Jews, Roma and other minorities targeted by the Nazis, as well as of other dissidents and erstwhile Germans made stateless by the Nazi regime.[40] He is also dismayed by Hillgruber's presentation of the noble German soldier, which overlooks the role that the army played in perpetrating the Holocaust. Rather than reflecting on "how a civilized people could allow the monstrous to occur"—the key question for Habermas and much of mainstream postwar German historiography—Hillgruber dismisses this phenomenon as lying outside "the special competence of the overtaxed historian." Instead, he "shov[es it] away uncommittedly into the dimension of the human condition."[41] For Habermas, Hillgruber's methodological decision to identify solely with the limited perspective of participants in the conflict offers no excuse for avoiding broader issues of morality and guilt. This not only does an injustice to the capacities of academic historians, but also reduces them to mere instruments in ideological political battles over collective memory.

Third, Habermas turns to Nolte. Nolte was already a suspect figure for Habermas, having been trained as a philosopher and as a student of Heidegger—i.e., a philosopher whose work was tainted by the fact that he had "never stepped out of the shadow of National Socialism."[42] However, Habermas does not condemn Nolte on this basis. On the contrary, it was the substance of Nolte's article, "The

Past That Will Not Go Away (*Vergangenheit, die nicht vergehen will*)," published in the *FAZ* on June 6, 1986, that prompted Habermas to wade into this debate in the first place. In his piece, directed toward a general audience, Nolte makes a number of claims about how National Socialism functioned as a scapegoat—i.e., "the present enemy in the last form in which it is entirely unmistakable"[43]—for a range of problems in the FRG and served the interests of certain groups, particularly those of Habermas's generation, whose late birth allowed them to carry on an eternal struggle against their fathers.

While Habermas objects to many aspects of Nolte's argument, he focuses on Nolte's attempt to relativize the Holocaust by portraying it as merely building on techniques and ideas developed and deployed during the Armenian genocide in the 1920s and Stalin's brutal purges of millions in the 1930s. As far as Nolte is concerned, the only innovation in the Holocaust was "the technical procedure of gassing." In arguing that the Nazis learned from and responded to these previous annihilations, Nolte even claims that a "causal connection (*kausaler Nexus*) probably exists" between the Gulag and Auschwitz.[44] Going even further, in an academic contribution to an edited collection Nolte even claims that the destruction of Europe's Jews was "a reaction or a distorted copy and not a first act or an original" of the "annihilation therapies" that had been developed on both the right and the left in response to the pathologies of the industrial revolution.[45]

As one might imagine, Habermas wholeheartedly rejects Nolte's apologia for the Holocaust. He is also appalled by Nolte's reference to "the so-called annihilation of the Jews," a statement that borders on Holocaust denial.[46] However, what is ultimately important to Habermas are not Nolte's claims as such, but their political role within the revisionist politics of memory pursued by Kohl's government. As Habermas points out, Nolte's historiography is driven by a desire to reconstruct a national identity that places Germany on the right side of history: "The Nazi crimes lose their singularity by being made comprehensible as the answer to a Bolshevist threat of annihilation (that continues to exist today). Auschwitz is reduced to the format of a technical innovation and is explained as an 'Asiatic' peril by an enemy that is still standing today outside our gates."[47] If the memory of the Jews murdered in the Holocaust has to be sacrificed to achieve these political goals, that is a price that Nolte is more than willing to pay.

The day after Nolte published his article in the *FAZ*, Habermas addressed the issue at the Römerberg Colloquium in downtown Frankfurt. There, he once again expressed grave concern over the ways in which Nolte and his fellow revisionists sought to appropriate the academic discipline of history for political purposes. He was particularly troubled because he associates such "the extensive instrumentalization of historical scholarship for manipulative purposes" with societies suffering "under conditions of political dictatorship." As a West German, he expresses his conviction that "having been torn out of continuities" by the experience of the *Nazizeit*, "we are subject to the constraint of being able to relate to the past only with a reflexive attitude . . . under the premise that the historical consciousness of [our] whole population can only take a decentered form."[48]

Following "A Kind of Settlement of Damages," the *Historikerstreit* quickly degenerated into a series of ad hominem arguments. Much of the discussion was carried out by historians arguing about the scientific merits of Nolte's claims regarding the (non)singularity of Auschwitz. As Holub points out, however, "This focus represents an impoverishment of Habermas's concerns since it reduces his argument to a dispute about historical occurrences and neglects the inherent political aspect of his remarks."[49]

The attempt to bat aside Habermas's arguments by undermining his historical credentials is visible in the fact that Stürmer, Hillgruber, and Nolte all defended themselves by attacking Habermas's qualifications to make judgments about history given his lack of expertise in the area.[50] However, as Maier points out, "True enough, Habermas is not a historian—but historians have never claimed a hermetic discipline."[51] Additionally, Habermas actually sought out the assistance of his friend, Hans-Ulrich Wehler, a historian based in Bielefeld, in drafting his original reply to Nolte. There are a number of letters of support from other prominent West German historians in the Habermas Vorlass as well.[52]

But these reflections miss the crux of Habermas's objections, which are rooted in his understanding of the public intellectual. After all, Habermas admits up front that "as someone without specialist qualifications" he only feels comfortable weighing in on these issues since the texts in question are "obviously aimed at the layman." What gives Habermas the right to comment on this issues is not any disciplinary or academic mandate, but the fact that as a German himself, "I am thus making the self-observations of a patient who undergoes a revisionist operation on his historical consciousness."[53] In other words, the public character of the contributions to which Habermas is reacting—particularly Nolte's, published in one of Germany's leading daily newspapers—and their political instrumentalization means that these issues cannot simply be left to experts, but must be open to public debate and deliberation if they are to meet the standards of democratic legitimation. As Habermas later noted, "The pompous outrage over an alleged mixing of politics and science shunts the issue onto a completely wrong track.... It is not a question of disputes about scientific theory, it is not about questions of value-free analysis—it is about the public use of history."[54]

If Stürmer, Hillgruber, and Nolte had merely been making a historical claim in specialist historical outlets, it is doubtful that Habermas would have even come across their arguments, much less felt the need to comment upon them. His objections are neither disciplinary nor academic in nature; rather, they are based on the fact that it is clear "that the New Revisionism's ideas are also intended to be translated into the shape of exhibits, of display objects with the appropriate effect of a national pedagogics."[55] However, insofar as their arguments are directed towards "question of the inner continuity of the German Republic and of its foreign-political predictability," which Stürmer explicitly states is the "politically necessary" goal of his work, then Habermas argues that these ideas are fair game for non-specialists.[56]

From the perspective of deliberative democratic theory, Habermas argues that debates about the political meaning of the past cannot be based on an "image of history which is closed or indeed ordained by government historians."[57] Instead, the public meaning of the past must be open for debate in the democratic public sphere. While specialists have a role to play in correcting misunderstandings and presenting arguments to the public, they cannot short-circuit the open nature of debate in a public sphere defined by the equality of all voices. Doing so not only delegitimizes the products of public deliberation, in which "there are only participants" and not experts, but "the instrumentalization of scholarship in the public domain" also undermines academic research itself by undercutting its methodological orientation to truth.[58]

Habermas's worries about the political goals and the hidden agendas of these revisionist contributions were not merely products of his imagination or paranoia. On the contrary, Nolte had deep ties and influence within the conservative Christian Democratic Union (CDU), while Stürmer actually served as Chancellor Kohl's speech writer and, in an appointment that generated considerable controversy at the time, even later directed the Ebenhausen Foundation for Science and Policy.[59] The policy influence of their historical interpretations was visible a number of different initiatives that Kohl and the CDU government adopted as part of its revisionist politics of memory.

In the opening paragraphs of "A Kind of Settlement of Damages," Habermas refers to the inscription at the memorial stone at Bonn's North Cemetery as an example of way the view of history defended by Hillgruber, Stürmer and Nolte was being implemented by the government without proper public debate. The problem with its message, which reads "To the Victims of Wars and the Rule of Violence (*Den Opfern der Kriege und der Gewaltherrschaft*)," is that it does not distinguish between the victims of violence and its perpetrators. While Habermas recognizes the legitimacy of remembering all the dead, he notes, "Suffering is always concrete suffering; it cannot be separated from its context." Insofar as such public, state-sponsored memorials help to create traditions that link the "space of experience" in the past to the community's "horizons of expectation" for the future, eliding these differences has important implications.[60] In addition to the injustice involved in the "enforced reconciliation" of victims with their perpetrators, Habermas is also wary, since, "Whoever still insists on mourning collective fates, without distinguishing between culprits and victims, obviously has something else up his sleeve."[61]

His fears that the Kohl government was planning to institute a new memory policy that would present Germany as having "always been on the right side in the struggle against the Bolshevist enemy" by emphasizing the Third Reich's fight against the USSR at the expense of the crimes it committed as part of the "Final Solution (*Endlösung*)," is not rooted in the inscription found on a single memorial stone.[62] On the contrary, it builds on the events of May 5, 1985, when Kohl invited US President Ronald Reagan to join him at the Kolmehöhe Military Cemetery in Bitburg to lay a wreath in remembrance of the dead and the end of the Second World War. This event, which included a handshake between German and American generals, was supposed to signal the reconciliation of the two states that had fought against each other before 1945, but who were now allies in the Cold War. However, the plan backfired after it was revealed that among forty-nine members of the *Schutzstaffel* (SS), some of whom had participated in the massacre of civilians and some of whom might even have worked at concentration camps, were also interred there.

While this might have been an oversight, the fact that the two leaders arrived in Bitburg after visiting the concentration camp at Bergen Belsen made it clear (to Habermas at least) that this action was designed to "[take] away the singularity of the Nazi crimes." The examples of the Bonn North Cemetery and Bitburg taken together signaled that this was part of a broader shift toward "the planning of new memorials and new museum buildings" that would entrench the revisionist perspective in German historical consciousness. In light of this broader background, Habermas saw "the services of historians" like Stürmer, Hillgruber, and Nolte as part of a broader attempt by the government to foster "the bureaucratic production of meaning (*Erzeugung von Sinn*)" through a revisionist politics of memory.[63]

These considerations bring me back to my argument about the necessity of changes to the politics of memory being filtered through debates in the public sphere in order to fulfill the conditions of democratic legitimacy. For Habermas, "The intervention of the state in fostering a nationalist continuity is an illicit attempt to abrogate a process that should occur independently of governmental influence."[64] Thus, despite his substantive concerns about the memorial policies adopted by Kohl's conservative government—and the instrumentalized historical arguments supporting this revisionist approach to the Nazi past—at heart, his objections are procedural.

If these changes had been the product of a broad, open societal debate where all voices were heard, Habermas would not have been satisfied with the result, but he would have accepted it as legitimate. However, this was not the case. Instead, Kohl made an executive decision to deploy symbolic politics to change the country's past without any public deliberation. As Habermas noted in "The Diffusion (*Entsorgung*) of the Past: A Politico-Cultural Tract," originally published in *Die Zeit* in May 1985, "Today the tasks of social integration and self-understanding are no longer matters for the political system. There are good reasons for us not having a Kaiser or a Hindenburg anymore. The public sphere should refuse to tolerate spiritual-moral leadership (*geistig-moralische Führung*) from those in high office."[65]

Habermas's objections in the *Historikerstreit* are thus primarily political, not historical. Although voiced in his capacity as a public intellectual, they are consistent with his philosophical understanding of democracy as fundamentally rooted not in voting or the protection of rights, but in the quality of deliberative opinion-formation in the public sphere. In publishing his objections, he brought this attempt to reshape German historical consciousness—which had been "kept under the covers (*unter der Decke gehalten*)"—out of the back rooms of the executive branch, where historians like Nolte and Stürmer had been able to influence public policy without proper scrutiny, and into the public sphere, where this approach was ultimately rejected.

In this sense, Habermas's participation in the Historians' Debate allowed him to fulfill his role as a public intellectual, intervening by "mobilizing the relevant issues, information and arguments for public disputes," and was also consistent with his theoretical commitment to combatting the depoliticizing tendencies of executive, technocratic politics by ensuring the "active participation of citizens in public life."[66] In this manner, Habermas created a rupture by shaping (West) German memory culture for decades to come. He also reshaped the political landscape. As the German historian of the *Nazizeit*, Ulrich Herbert, observes, following the *Historikerstreit*, "the categories of left and right are determined from then on by the relationship to the Nazi past."[67]

OTHER MINOR INTERVENTIONS

In addition to the *Historikerstreit*, which defines Habermas's public commentaries in the mid-1980s, and the *Vereinigungsdebatte*, which defines the period immediately following the fall of communism in 1989, Habermas involved himself in a number of other debates after his return to Frankfurt. For example, foreshadowing both the *Historikerstreit* itself and his growing interest in political issues beyond the borders of West Germany, during the early 1980s Habermas was already thinking about neo-conservatism as a transnational movement that was working its way across the Atlantic from the US to West Germany. His starting point for these reflections is a conference sponsored by the Konrad Adenauer Foundation—the official thinktank of the CDU—which brought together German and American neoconservatives in September 1981.

In a text that he republished in 1985 in the fifth volume of his "Short Political Writings," Habermas defines neoconservatism as "a response to a disappointment." In the United States—where this movement is defined by individuals like Daniel Bell and Irving Kristol—this dissatisfaction is linked the failure of the war in Vietnam and the rise of identity politics, resulting in both "*inflation of expectations* and *the lack of a willingness to acclaim and obey.*"[68] In order to relieve the resulting cultural crisis that accompanies the heightened legitimation demands that the state simply cannot meet, the neoconservatives call on the state to reduce its burdens by retreating from the economy. This diagnosis reflects the title of this collection, *Die neue Unübersichtlichkeit* (*The New Obscurity*), i.e. "a situation in which the program of the social welfare state ... is losing its capacity to project future possibilities for a collectively better and less endangered way of life."[69]

In West Germany, this phenomenon has a different background, as it is rooted figures like Joachim Ritter, Ernst Forsthoff, and Arnold Gehlen, "who only conditionally accepted social modernity, refusing to affirm cultural modernity." While this constellation welcomes the political goals of the French Revolution, they reject the destruction of cultural hierarchies and the rise of social interests in politics, which drive the creation of the welfare state. Since the "danger lies in cultural transformations, motivational and attitudinal changes, and shifts in patterns of values and identities," they argue that "the legacy of tradition has to be preserved as far as possible."

This involves a rejection of the figure of the "priestly rule of a new class" of intellectuals as well as of new cultural movements like poststructuralism and postmodernism in favor of tradition in the form of "straightforward common sense, historical consciousness, and religion."[70] Although they draw on the decisionist constitutional theory of Carl Schmitt, the conclusions of German neoconservatives regarding the role of the state are similar to the American representatives of this movement: it should restrict itself to guaranteeing the peace against enemies both foreign and domestic. The result is a preference for executive power and technocratic decision-making to "minimize the burden of moral justification incumbent on the political system," since these tasks are better handled by traditional social structures like religion and the family.[71]

Habermas sees the rise of this "neoconservative cultural criticism" as an attempt to backtrack on the postwar opening of the FRG "to the West without reservations" by "reaching back to a German constitutionalism, which reduces democracy to little more than the rule of law, to a Lutheran state ecclesiasticism rooted in a pessimistic anthropology, and to the motifs of a young conservatism, whose heirs could achieve only a half-hearted compromise with modernity."[72] Habermas rejects this not only because he endorses the FRG's opening to the West, but also because he sees this anachronistic "return to before the eighteenth century, which is seen as promising a wondrous regeneration of certainties, a cushion of tradition" as an anti-democratic form of escapism that ignores the achievements of modernity, including not only "the level of subsistence of the masses, but also the democratic and constitutional achievements of citizens."[73]

As he remarks upon receiving the Sonning Prize at the University of Copenhagen in 1987, the key question is thus not so much about *Westbindung* itself, but on its meaning: "whereas the one side stresses the ties to the West's culture of enlightenment, the other conceives of these ties more in terms of power politics and thinks in the first instance of military alliance and foreign policy."[74] In other words, Habermas objects to the purely instrumental use of this "binding to the West" in ways that seek to take advantage of its geopolitical potential without accepting the liberal tradition that comes with it. For him, at its core *Westbindung* is a normative orientation, not merely a position to be used for the enhancement of political power.

Habermas again connects these debates about German constitutionalism and foreign policy in a speech he gave to the Cultural Forum of the German Social Democratic Party (SPD) in September 1983 on civil disobedience. In it, he sought to provide a justification for such consciously illegal forms of protest. The context for this intervention were the mass demonstrations that were being organized in opposition to the stationing of American missiles in Germany, an issue that he had been engaged with since the late 1950s (as the previous chapters have shown). Interestingly, Habermas's opposition, which he argues "was forced upon us," is once again procedural. This ambivalence is visible in his comment, in an interview from 1984, that "the Federal Republic has come so close to being the fifty-first state of the Union that the only thing we still don't have is the right to vote."[75]

In his 1983 speech to the SPD, a shortened version of which was later published in *Die Zeit*, Habermas opposes the position of Kohl's government, which was seeking to tamp down these protests by arguing, "Nonviolent resistance is violence."[76] From Habermas's perspective, this view denies the moral foundations of modern constitutionalism, which are rooted in the individual autonomy of all citizens, in favor of an anachronistic sovereigntism. Habermas associates this kind of "black-and-white thinking [that] seeks security in the false unambiguity of forcibly constructed dichotomies" with the "authoritarian legalism" of Schmitt, whose influence on German constitutional thinking he has long opposed. Rather than seeing civil disobedience as a danger to the peace and unity of society—and therefore demanding the "submission of its citizens to a *higher* sovereign," as Schmitt and the conservative government do—Habermas instead sees the "new" peace, environmental and women's social movements as "offer[ing] the first chance to comprehend civil disobedience even in Germany as an element of a mature political culture . . . that is sure of itself."[77]

Rather than destabilizing society through the threat of revolution or violence, civil disobedience seeks, through its premeditated, public, and announced transgression of legal to communicate its demands to a government that is refusing to heed public opinion. It does so without undermining the rule of law, since civilly disobedient activists accept the legal consequences of their actions. Protesters are compelled to act in this manner in cases where "only the threat of forfeiture of its legitimacy can bring the government around." In this way Habermas argues that civil disobedience serves at a "litmus test" of the maturity of constitutional democracy.[78]

These reflections do not, however, signify that Habermas was unaware of the dangers posed by the peace movement. Yet unlike the government and (neo)conservative jurists, who argue that "illegal protest is not only punishable but also morally reprehensible," he worries that this movement will be beset by "destruction or splitting, which would have the consequence that the protest would overstep the fragile limits of civil disobedience." In contrast to the "German Hobbesianism" of the Schmittians, which decries the illegitimacy of civil disobedience as such, Habermas worries "whether the activists will assess correctly the measure of their success," since "realistically, one cannot expect to prevent the installation of the missiles, but only to make clear to the conservative government that further rearmament is no longer to be carried out."[79]

As I mentioned in the introduction to this chapter, it is during this period that Habermas's mature notion of the public intellectual becomes visible. In fact, as Thomas Biebricher observes, "The concept of the intellectual is largely absent from Habermas' thought until the 1980s."[80] His fullest treatment of this topic is in the context of an lecture he delivered in 1986 in the Maison Heinrich Heine at the Cité internationale universitaire de Paris. In this talk, which was later reprinted in *Merkur* as well as in volume 6 of his *Short Political Writings* under the title "Heinrich Heine and the Role of the Intellectual in Germany," Habermas develops his conception of the public intellectual using the example of the German poet and satirist, who ends up spending many years of his life in political exile in Paris writing political commentaries in the name of public interests.[81] Interestingly, especially considering that Habermas reengaged in the public sphere after a decade of silence devoted to his *Hauptberuf* at the Max Planck Institute, he admitted in a 1989 interview, "I find the role of the intellectual to be disruptive [*störend*] and irritating."[82] And yet, given the frequency of his public interventions, it seems that Habermas simply cannot help himself.

In addition to this essay, Habermas explicitly discusses his conception of the mediated relation of theory to practice in a number of interviews he gives over the course of the 1980s, often contrasting Heine's limited view of the public intellectual to Heidegger's more expansive understanding of the philosopher as an intellectual leader of the nation.[83] These generally reiterate the key aspects of his mature conception of the public intellectual. For example, he repeatedly notes, "Philosophers are not teachers of the nation." While as public intellectuals they can attempt to increase the quality of public debates, "the common business of political discourses among citizens nevertheless stays what it is. It is not a philosophical enterprise."[84] Additionally, he observes that when speaking publicly to their fellow citizens, philosophers have no special insight; on the contrary, "the answers of the intellectuals reflect the same helplessness as do those of the politicians."[85] Given that "critical distance towards and the spontaneous identification with existing practice [define] a halfway functioning [*halbwegs funktionierenden*] constitutional democracy," intellectuals and politicians both play necessary roles.[86]

In another interview reflecting on these themes, Habermas clarifies that while the philosopher as public intellectual must appeal to generalizable interests, this alone is not sufficient to ground universalistic claims to validity. After all, "we are not talking about universalistic rhetoric, but about concrete actions. It is these which must be capable of justification." For example, Habermas mentions that he opposed the 1986 US air strikes against Libya, which were launched in retaliation for the West Berlin discotheque bombing, because they "deliberately and irresponsibly risked the lives of innocent people … which cannot be justified under any circumstances." In fact, he notes that he considered this action "so catastrophic that, for the first time in years, I joined a demonstration."[87]

The key point for Habermas is that intellectuals must recognize that when they enter political debates they are engaging in a separate sphere of life governed by its own internal logic. This is why he rejects the approach of the "mandarin consciousness" of the classic German intellectual, who wants to be left alone on the one hand but expects to be listened to on the other. This "distorted understanding of politics" is evident in Habermas's observation in a 1988 *Frankfurter Rundschau* interview: "Mandarins always speak in the exalted name of science and scholarship. Even when they enter the political public sphere, they are completely unwilling to accept the rules of the game." While Habermas has repeatedly noted his greater comfort in academic waters, he acknowledges, "Anybody who enters the political public sphere and criticizes other people cannot be a crybaby himself."[88]

During this period Habermas also returned to the problems surrounding the "idea of the university," an issue that had interested him since the 1950s and had defined much of his early research at the Institute, as well as his political activities during his first two stays in Frankfurt (as documented in earlier chapters). While Habermas seeks to defend the autonomy of the university (as well as of teaching and research) from both politics and the functional imperatives of the economy, he also pushes back against the degeneration of this neo-humanist intellectual ideal into "an intellectually elitist, apolitical, conformist . . . institution that remained far removed from practice." During the Third Reich, "the demonstrated impotence against (or even complicity with) the Nazi regime" proved that the "sheltered inwardness" enjoyed by these German Mandarins lacked any substance.[89]

Reflecting on these past debates, Habermas openly admits that his proposals for the democratization and participatory self-administration of the university "have not been realized." Yet despite the growing differentiation within scientific disciplines, which makes it even harder to develop a shared conception of the university, he insists that teaching and learning at the university must do more than simply ensure "academic career preparation." On the contrary—restating the core ideas of his research on student political participation in Frankfurt in the late 1950s—he argues, "Going beyond the acquisition of expert knowledge, [university learning processes] contribute to intellectual enlightenment by offering informed interpretations and diagnoses of contemporary events, and by taking concrete political stands."[90]

This conclusion both reflects Habermas's broader theoretical and further reiterates his understanding of the academic's role as a public intellectual. Quoting Friedrich Schleiermacher's 1808 *Idee der deutschen Universität* (*Idea of the German University*), Habermas argues, "The first law of all efforts aimed at knowledge (is): *communication*." Speaking in his own voice, he continues, "I seriously believe that it is the communicative or discursive forms of scientific argumentation which in the final analysis hold the learning processes together in their various functions." Although he "no less faithfully describes the working presuppositions of the more solidly organized operation of a Max Planck Institute than he does that of a philosophy seminar," it is clear that returning to the more communicative atmosphere of the university has reenergized Habermas after his decade of relative isolation in Starnberg.[91]

THE *WENDE* AND THE UNIFICATION DEBATE

While these minor interventions mostly touch on existing themes in Habermas's work as a public intellectual, the debate over the unification of German—and the changes brought about by the fall of communism in 1989—represents the second major strand of his public-facing writing in the 1980s. As I have already demonstrated, the example of the *Historikerstreit* shows how debates about changing the basic orientation of public memory must be discursively legitimated in a democracy. It focuses primarily on the politics of memorialization. While the *Vereinigungsdebatte* is often seen as "a second *Historikerstreit*," the fundamental problem is not Habermas's opposition to "the idea of 'normality' in favor of a form of German exceptionalism based on responsibility for the Nazi past."[92]

Instead, the issue is whether the territories of the former East German Democratic Republic (GDR) could merely be subsumed within the West German FRG, or whether German unification would require a new constitutional settlement to bring together a people that had experienced two separate and distinct political cultures over the previous forty-five years. While this was clearly a German debate, it had broader significance, since the confrontation between Western memory culture, focused on the Holocaust, and Eastern collective memories. dominated by the more recent experience of communist totalitarianism, served as an example "in miniature [of] virtually all of the crisis tendencies of postwar Europe."[93]

The events of November 9, 1989 set off a debate about the future of Germany, especially within the more open media landscape of the Federal Republic. However, nothing could stop the breakneck pace of the *Deutschlandpolitik* (German policy) adopted by Chancellor Helmut Kohl. Less than a year later, at midnight on October 3, 1990, the GDR was absorbed into the FRG.

As the leading public intellectual of West Germany, Jürgen Habermas plays a prominent role in the unification debate. Given his concerns about the dangers of German nationalism, it is understandable that in 1989 "his old fears resurfaced of a rebirth of ideas about being a great nation and power."[94] Unlike many within Kohl's Christian-Democratic Union (CDU), who saw unification as an opportunity for Germany to become a "normal" country in terms of its relation to the past, its willingness to use military force and its right to pursue its sovereign interests, Habermas is concerned about precisely this outcome given his preference for "a form of German exceptionalism based on responsibility for the Nazi past."[95] As a result, his contributions to the *Vereinigungsdebatte* are usually interpreted in light of his observation that "in Germany democracy has taken root in the motives and hearts of the citizens ... after Auschwitz—and in a way only through the shock of the moral catastrophe."[96] Given its propensity to read this debate through the lens of memory politics, the literature generally agrees that Habermas was "mainly concerned with Federal Republican identity."[97]

While his fears regarding the cultural foundations, identity, collective memory, Western orientation and economic power of a united Germany undoubtedly shape Habermas's response to unification, this interpretation is problematic. It is better to see his objections through the prism of his theory of deliberative democracy, in which legitimacy flows from debates within informal spheres of the media and civil society into the formal, decision-making center of parliament. The essence of his critique is actually rooted in Habermas's rejection of Kohl's political approach, which gave primacy to unaccountable executive action—the use of constituted powers—over deliberation in the public sphere and the legislature, whose members are not only more sensitive to public opinion, but who also represent the constituent power (*pouvoir constituant*) of the sovereign. While many scholars contend that Habermas's "criticism does not question the legitimacy of the process" of unification, I argue that in fact it does precisely that.[98]

Following the fall of the Berlin Wall, Kohl quickly decided to follow the path of least resistance by merely subsuming the "new *Bundesländer* (federal states)" of the east into the institutions of the west. Habermas objects because he believed that this approach—and the breakneck pace of unification more generally—violated the fundamental principles of democracy and popular sovereignty. For Habermas, the key question is, "Should the democratic self-determination of the citizens of the GDR or the unification of all Germans in one nation-state take priority?" He concludes that "the principle of self-determination is incompatible with any demand that does not respect the procedural issues required by a transformation of the political system," namely a constitutional convention ratified through a plebiscite in both east and west.[99]

In 1989 Habermas was immediately concerned by how quickly unification under the aegis of the FRG had become the default option for the future of Germany. He was particularly dismayed by the way Kohl was able to the economic power of the West and the perception of a state of emergency to displace substantive public debate about the desirability and conditions of the proposed merger with the east. Although he did not harbor any utopian illusions about how a reformed East Germany could realize socialism's potential, Habermas was concerned that the pace of events was impeding public deliberation about the substantive issues at stake.

He initially only circulated his preliminary thoughts—written two weeks after the fall of the Wall—privately to a small circle of friends. Although its title, "The Hour of National Sentiment: Republican Conviction or Nationalist Consciousness?," makes it appear as though Habermas's concerns are primarily about memory and identity, the text itself shows that for Habermas the issues at hand were already primarily procedural. In particular, he noted that Kohl was seeking to bring about unification through the "annexation (*Anschluss*)" of the GDR, rather than its "accession (*Beitritt*)," thus explicitly invoked the precedent of the Third Reich's absorption of Austria in 1938.[100]

While using nationalist sentiment and economic prosperity to lure East Germany into a quick annexation was the easier option in the short term, Habermas is concerned that this would cause greater political, social and cultural problems in the long run. In particular, he worries that it would undermine the "notion of the constitution as an instrument for realizing a more democratic society."[101] Based on his discursive conception of democracy, he notes that using nationalist sentiment and economic prosperity to justify a quick annexation would undermine the "notion of the constitution as an instrument for realizing a more democratic society."[102] Habermas therefore presents his fellow citizens with a choice: "Either the Federal Republic gives *every* possibility a chance, since the citizens of the GDR want self-determination; or it uses its economic superiority to engage in a politics of carrot-and-stick [*Zuckerbrot und Peitsche*] to dictate the most economically advantageous solution."[103]

His first public comments on unification appeared in *Die Zeit* in March 1990 as "Deutsch-Mark Nationalism." This headline, which Habermas did not like, was chosen by the editors.[104] In the piece, Habermas observes that Kohl was "trying to buy up the GDR" with the offer of a currency union and a one-to-one conversion with the much weaker eastern Mark.[105] Given his longstanding theoretical concerns about the "colonization" of politics by market forces and bureaucratic power, Habermas's objections to the dictates of "economic nationalism" and the "very goal-oriented way" that Kohl was going about the process are clearly consistent with his philosophical commitments. However, ultimately his objections remained the same as they had been in November 1989: that the "republican consciousness" of citizens with the legal right of self-determination was being overwhelmed by economic interests, administrative expediency and the unexamined, dangerous sentiments of a nationalistic "community of fate."[106]

In developing this argument Habermas focuses on three constitutional demands raised by the FRG's Basic Law (*Grundgesetz*). First, he notes that the Preamble's emphasis on the German people's "exercise of their constituent power ... legitimized by popular referendum."[107] Habermas therefore argues that "the principles and the institutions of our constitution" demand "an agenda for reunification which gives priority to the freely exercised right of the citizens to determine their own future by direct vote, within the framework of a non-occupied public sphere that has not already been willed away."[108]

Second, he observes that the Basic Law is not a permanent constitution, but a temporary document designed "for a transitional period" during the division of Germany. The text of the *Grundgesetz* overtly takes its own demise into account in its last article, entitled "The Duration of the Basic Law." This final provision states that it "loses its validity on the day that a new constitution takes effect, chosen by the German people in free determination."[109]

While Habermas admits that preserving the constitutional order of the FRG makes sense given the political success of West Germany, he notes that keeping the *Grundgesetz* after unification would signal one of two things. First, it could mean that "we [are] still waiting for East Prussia and Silesia," i.e. that the territorial conditions for unification demanded by the far-right had not yet been achieved. Second, it might signal that "the last article [i.e., 146] and the preamble of the Basic Law would have to be cut" in order to strip the constitution of its temporary nature. Given that the *Bundestag* had already rejected the irredentism of the former, Habermas sets it aside. As to the latter, he notes that such modifications to the Basic Law "would simply prove that the 'accession' of the GDR cannot fulfill what it is supposed to fulfill: the unification of two parts to one *whole*."[110]

Thirdly, Habermas contends that Kohl's pursuit of "an annexation cleverly initiated but in the final analysis carried through only at the administrative level" is in breach of the constitution.[111] This violation is rooted in the Chancellor's decision to pursue unification under Article 23 rather than Article 146. Although the former does allow for the "accession [*Beitritt*] of other parts of Germany," it was designed to permit the Saarland to join the FRG at the end of its temporary occupation by France following the war (which occurred in 1957).[112] Moreover, Habermas notes that leaving Article 146 in the post-unification constitution would mean that it would "'run itself on empty,' i.e., such a procedure would run counter to the methodological premise of interpreting every single rule with a view to the unity of the constitution."[113] Regardless of its constitutionality, Habermas observes that given the democratic demands of popular legitimacy and sovereign self-determination, "one would at least like to be asked."[114]

In his next contribution, published almost a year later, Habermas addresses concerns about the long-term effects of the normative deficiencies of the quick annexation of East Germany. In this interview, he once again focuses on the importance of the "the mode of the unification process itself (*der Modus des Einigungsprozesses selber*)" highlighting "the instrumental character of the administrative procedure." Although it did not make it into the excerpt published at the time, in the full transcript Habermas concludes, "In retrospect, these depressing aspects have robbed a transformation that anyone would have greeted with enthusiasm of much of its aura."[115]

While he had initially speculated that the damage caused by a normatively deficient form of integration could be long-lasting—"we might wind up paying [the political price] for several generations"—by May 1991 Habermas is able to chart the problems that had already emerged.[116] As he had expected, "using the medium of constitutional law to heave our countrymen into our own boat by the scruff of their necks" had not produced a unified citizenry with a common political culture or a shared sense of being all "in the same boat" and engaged in a common project. On the contrary, the tone of Habermas's comments makes clear that Germans "now distinguished more clearly between 'us'—that is, 'we, in the West'—and 'them' in the former GDR," and vice versa.[117]

In his argument, Habermas repeats his complaint regarding the "land-grabbing territorial fetishism"—which had proceeded without a plebiscite—that he argues had deprived the people of "the chance to make a free choice."[118] He is particularly concerned that this executive-led approach would undermine the Federal Republic's normative foundations. While it produced a process that was "more happening than initiative" and failed to a unified citizenry "who in political self-awareness decided on a common civil union," Habermas's worries now center on the broader damage that has been done to the FRG as a result.[119]

At this point, concerns about the effects of such policies on the quality of debate in the public sphere and the capacity of societal deliberation to generate democratic legitimacy—issues Habermas had already voiced in the *Historikerstreit* nearly a decade earlier—come to the fore. He is particularly concerned that

Kohl's approach will be marked not only by its failure to create a unified populace but also by the structural transformation of the "medium of public communication . . . that is at this moment being allowed to fall into ruins." Habermas sums up his thoughts at the end of this interview with a question: "Is it too much to demand that an effort be made in the medium of public communication, so that a *new* Federal Republic, composed of such unequal parts, can anchor itself in the consciousness of its citizens as something shared—and not experienced just as the byproduct of the forced construction of an expanded currency zone?"[120]

Habermas is also quick to reject the attempts by some conservatives to tar the left and the project of social democracy by equating the legacy of the East Germany with that of the Third Reich. However, he also notes that "the non-communist Left in West Germany . . . cannot pretend that nothing has happened."[121] Habermas sees this controversy as an opportunity to debate the meaning of the past and the differences between the respective legacies of Nazism and communism. In fact, as an intellectual of the left, Habermas devotes a number of essays during this period to exploring the question of what socialism meant following the fall of the Wall.

For Habermas, the failure of the postwar communist experiment in Central and Eastern Europe demonstrates the problem with revolutionary thinking. In its stead, he calls for a "radical reformism" that focuses on ensuring that "the socially integrating force of solidarity should be in a position to stake its claim against the other social forces, money and administrative power, through a wide range of democratic forums and institutions." In his view, such an approach—which builds on the social theory of he developed at Starnberg and published under as *Theory of Communicative Action*—is socialist because it retains a focus on mutual recognition and collective control over the key forces that shape society.[122] Additionally, he urges his readers to keep in mind that while the "substance of those expectations which were connected with the concept of socialism in the workers' movement has not been realized," we should also "not forget what have today become trivial acquisitions—by this I mean not only the level of subsistence of the masses, but also the democratic and constitutional achievements of citizens."[123]

To further his understanding of the differences between his vision of socialism and the recently deposed communist regimes of the East, Habermas also sought to engage intellectuals in the former GDR in conversations about their experiences, aiming to compensate for some of the necessary dialogue that had not occurred during the rushed process of unification. These contacts were particularly important to Habermas, who admitted that he had "no relatives over in the East." Additionally, he noted that he had no contact with that world between 1955, when he was a student, and 1988, when he was invited to give a lecture "under the watchful eye of the chief philosopher of the GDR."[124]

As part of this process, Habermas sought out the East German writer and public intellectual Christa Wolf, who in some senses mirrored his role in the FRG by acting as the public social conscience of the GDR. In 1990 Wolf became embroiled in the *Literaturstreit* (Literature Debate), which raised important issues about the meaning of the communist past similar to those raised about the Nazi past in the West German *Historikerstreit*, in which Habermas had played a central role.[125] Wolf had initially come under fire for her decision to rework and republish a story outlining her difficulties with the *Stasi* (or *Staatssicherheitsdienst*, the East German secret police), even though she had been a well-paid and celebrated intellectual under communism and had not suffered as a dissident under the GDR.[126] In order to learn more—and out of a sense of a certain kind of kinship he felt to his comrade in the East—Habermas and his wife hosted Wolf at their house for dinner. Following this meeting, Wolf thanked Habermas in a letter, remarking: "How little even we know each other, how little we know about each other. That will be a long process, and I shall certainly make sure you remember me by inviting you to the Academy in Berlin."[127]

This mutual lack of knowledge became evident following the promised discussion at the East German Academy of the Arts in Berlin in November 1991, after which Habermas again resumed contact with Wolf. After thanking her for the invitation, he observed that he had felt like an outsider during his visit to the new capital of Berlin, noting that his experience during the debate was "a bit like that of an observer, who looks out from his box at the movement of the scenes on stage."[128] Building on this sense of alienation between "us" and "them," he reaffirmed his pride in the Bonn Republic's attempts to "work though (*aufarbeiten*)" the legacy of fascism and his fear that unification would undermine this achievement. He therefore concluded by pleading for each side to deal with its own history, rather than throwing everything together in a "German casserole (*deutscher Eintopf*)."[129]

Despite their shared disappointment with the process of unification and Wolf's publicly stated sympathy for maintaining a separate socialist state after 1989, she vehemently denied that "intellectuals in the East lacked familiarity with the culture and life of the West." In this sense, she sought to reaffirm the agency of the east Germans, even though Kohl's approach to unification had not given them the opportunity of a "zero hour (*Stunde Null*)."[130] In his reply, Habermas thanked Wolf for her "understanding letter which corrects my perspective somewhat." He also clarified that his apprehensions resulted from "the official practice of the GDR administration, and not at all at the productions of intellectuals whose attitude towards those practices was as critical as mine—and at a time when their situation was much more difficult than ours."[131]

In April 1992, Habermas returns to these issues in a public commentary.[132] Drawing inspiration from Theodor Adorno's concept of "working through the past (*Aufarbeitung der Vergangenheit*)," Habermas expresses his fear of the effects that the rapid absorption of the GDR would have on the politics of memory in Germany. In this piece, entitled "Comments on a Torturous Discussion," he notes that the situation in the former GDR is complicated by the fact that it has to deal with both the recent communist past and the more distant legacy of Nazism. Since he agrees with Adorno that there is no "other Germany" untainted by Nazi appropriation, he argues that the residents of the GDR will also have to address this more distant past as part of the process of unification.[133] While the "bureaucratic net of domination" of the *Stasi* had squelched freedom of expression necessary for public opinion- and will-formation, it was not based on a racist, authoritarian ideology like that of the Nazis, but rather "aroused in each generation a deceptive hope for the democratization of [the] system."[134]

As a result of these important differences, Habermas worries that "tossing everything into the same German pot" would lead to a shift to the right, as "liberals are becoming national-liberals and young conservatives German militants."[135] While he had been able to push back against attempts to "normalize" the German past a few years earlier during the *Historikerstreit*, he notes that with unification "hardly a voice is raised against industrious historians who emphasize, apparently without qualms, the continuity of the Bismarck Reich, or who reckon up, on the other side of the ledger, the measures taken by National Socialism to moderate its mass crimes."[136] In light of these rapid changes in the tenor of public discussion and the positions that soon become *salonfähig*—socially acceptable in polite society—these fears are understandable.[137]

1992 also represents an important rupture in Habermas's thinking and in his public intervention in the *Vereinigungsdebatte*. Whereas he had previously opposed unification, predicting horrible consequences for the political culture of a Germany that had united via executive fiat rather than popular self-determination, two years after the fact he had not only made his peace with unification, but had even come to believe that there was still hope for the new Berlin Republic. Despite its rightward turn and the market-based ideology of Kohl's *Deutschlandpolitik*, he concludes that "the constitutionally established unification signifies that both sides have opted for a common future and a reciprocal understanding with regard to two different postwar histories."

Kohl's unification was clearly not a self-conscious act of republican self-understanding. However, Habermas argues that these weaknesses could be overcome if the new Berlin Republic could seize the "opportunity to learn from the false notes and jarring practices what we can expect from the medium of public communication."[138] In this way, Habermas sought to apply his legal and political philosophy—which is based on the openness of formal, institutional will-formation to the informal, open opinion formation of the public sphere mediated by civil society—to political praxis.

In light of this connection, it is clear that Habermas's concerns were ultimately driven by the fact that the people and their political representatives in the legislative assemblies on both sides of the old border between East and West were not given the opportunity to properly debate the desirability and conditions of bringing the two Germanies together. As a result, a process that should have been guided by open debate and deliberation in the public spheres of both the GDR and the FRG—and which might have helped foster the creation of a new, unified public sphere—was instead pushed through via administrative and legal channels overseen by the executive and judicial branches, sidelining parliamentary decision-making and violating the principle of popular self-determination.[139]

Habermas reiterates these concerns when he spoke to the Commission of Inquiry assembled by the of the German *Bundestag* on "the history and consequences of the SED (*Sozialistische Einheitspartei Deutschlands* or Socialist Unity Party of Germany, the ruling party of East Germany) dictatorship" in 1994. At the start of his testimony, he observes that as a philosopher he could not "assume the role of a scientific expert, but rather will view myself as an intellectual participating in a public discussion." While repressing the past is not a serious option since "[a]wkward truths are hard to control," Habermas also attempts to use the past to construct an affirmative understanding of the present. Instead, he urges the lawmakers and his fellow-citizens to "learn from negative experiences," since "we can only learn from a history that we regard as a critical authority." While such an understanding of the past "can [only] be stimulated, but not brought about by formal means," he encourages his audience to see the lessons of 1989 not as rooted in the restoration of the nation-state, "but rather in the gaining of civil rights and the elimination of at totalitarian regime."[140]

In objecting to the executively administered and judicially approved approach to unification, Habermas is seeking to preserve the notion of democratic legitimacy that he had been developing in his political philosophy since the 1960s—a process culminating in the publication of *Between Facts and Norms* in 1992.[141] Although Habermas began working on what ultimately can be seen as his most complete statement of his political theory in 1985, he only completed it in 1991, i.e. after 1989. As a result, it is "both an epigraph and a manifesto" that "wears a Janus face," looking backward to learn from the achievements of postwar Bonn Republic and also forward to the new FRG with its capital in Berlin.[142]

This timeline is important because it marks Habermas's explicit return to political philosophy for the first time since the 1950s and '60s. While his thinking had developed considerably over the intervening period, his basic theoretical commitments and outlook had not. Just as his early reading of German *Staatsrechtslehre* had led him to prioritize the power of the legislature as the voice of the people over the executive and judicial branches of government (see chapter 3), so too did *Between Facts and Norms* seek to develop a discursive conception of political legitimacy based on the idea that citizens are able to "give themselves their own laws through democratic processes of opinion- and will-formation" mediated through the parliament. In opposition to those who defend an executive or a judicial conception of the constitution, Habermas has consistently argued that there can be "no constitutional state without radical democracy (*kein Rechtsstaat ohne radikale Demokratie*)."[143]

The fact that Habermas's objections to Kohl's *Deutschlandpolitik* were primarily procedural is also backed by his frequent invocations of constitutional patriotism (*Verfassungspatriotismus*) in his political interventions on unification. In his theoretical writings, Habermas adopts this concept to describe a form of "solidarity among strangers" that is not focused on national status or loyalty to the state, but instead "to an orientation to the constitution ... that is inherently abstract and mediated by law."[144] However, such an abstract, procedural notion of political belonging "only endures insofar as the constitution is itself the result of this public debate."

To be sure, the notion of constitutional patriotism—which appears frequently in Habermas's political writings in the 1990s and 2000s—has significant implications for political culture and the politics of remembrance. Ultimately, however, this commitment remains rooted in Habermas's notion of discursive democracy, since it requires that citizens consent "to a political order that is constituted by rights for self-determination in contradistinction to the idea of an order based on an ethnic, cultural, collective 'community of fate' (*Schicksalsgemeinschaft*)."[145] Such a notion of belonging requires that the legal order be justified and ratified through the medium of public debate and deliberation. Through the prism of Habermas's philosophy, a constitution arrived at by any other means, "such as the one being imposed upon the East Germans, is essentially an illegitimate institution."[146]

CONCLUSION

The fall of the Berlin Wall posed a significant challenge to Habermas given his deep-rooted support for the Western, liberal political culture of Federal Republic and his status as the leading public intellectual of the Bonn Republic. Given the profound changes it portended, it is understandable that "Habermas feared that absorption of the former East Germany would jeopardize his life's work."[147] In this sense, there is a certain irony to the fact that Habermas had reestablished himself as the leading public intellectual of the West German Bonn Republic precisely at the time when it was being replaced by the post-1990 Berlin Republic that emerged from the contentious process of unification.

In the words of his friend Ralf Dahrendorf, as the "state philosopher (*Staatsphilosoph*)" of the West German Federal Republic, in 1990 Habermas suddenly found himself "without a state, for which he could philosophize, because the state had changed."[148] In this sense, coming right at the moment when Habermas felt that West Germany had finally "become a contemporary of Western Europe," it is perhaps not surprising that he initially saw unification as "a political catastrophe."[149] However, unlike other prominent West German intellectuals, including Günter Grass, Habermas did not advocate *Zweistaatlichkeit* (a "two state solution") or "German cultural unity, but not political unity."[150] Instead, while he reconciled himself in principle to the possibility of unification, it was the executive-led form the process actually took that lay at the core of his opposition to the West German "annexation (*Anschluss*)" of the East in 1990.

Looking back three decades after these events, Habermas appears to have been correct in arguing that unification should have been a process of reconstruction, not of mere absorption. Rather than "seizing the 'hour of the executive'" to rush reunification "without ever having made the political alternatives into a theme for discussion," there is growing evidence supporting Habermas's theoretically grounded claim that giving public opinion on both sides of the former border—as well as institutional and legislative voices—a greater role in the process would have produced a better long-term outcome. His fear that Kohl's approach would exacerbate divisions between "us" in the West and "them" in the East—and his prediction that a rapid takeover of the GDR by the FRG would produce a general political shift to the right—have also been borne out by the rise of extremist far-right parties in the decades following reunification, whose voting constituencies are almost exclusively located in the territory of the former GDR.

Seen in this light, Habermas's insistence on "an agenda for reunification which gives priority to the freely exercised right of the citizens to determine their own future by direct vote, within the framework of a non-occupied public sphere" is fully consistent with his politically engaged and relevant legal and political philosophy. Moreover, it also demonstrates the sound political judgment subtending the proposals he put forward in his political writings after 1989.[151] If anything, it appears that Habermas's main mistake during this period is to be found in his shift from a position of opposition to *Vereinigung* to acceptance of it in 1992. While at the time he had expressed hope that the Berlin Republic would learn from Kohl's mistakes by developing a more open, unified German public sphere, there is little evidence to suggest that this has occurred.

Reflecting on these changes in a recent reflection entitled "30 Years Later (*30 Jahre danach*)," Habermas observes that insofar as the "'silent acceptance of right-wing violence' is spreading [from east to west], then I do feel reminded of a 'Weimarian' state of affairs."[152] This reference to the bifurcations of the interwar period, which resulted in the rise of Hitler, represents a complete rejection of Habermas's earlier optimism about integration, as he concludes that it is time to abandon any optimistic ideas about a convergence between East and West. What this means for the future and how the deficiencies of unification can now be rectified is unclear.

These considerations make it clear that Habermas's abandonment of his previous optimism regarding the ability of a newly united Germany to overcome foundational challenges has implications beyond this single case. German unification can indeed be seen as an example "in miniature" of the integration of Eastern and Western Europe under the auspices of the EU, a political project that "lies close to his heart (*herzanliegen*)." As a result, the remaining differences between the two Germanies also has implications for the persistent—perhaps even growing—division between the liberal democratic regimes of the postwar West and the "illiberal" states in the postcommunist region.[153]

In his political writings on the EU, Habermas has consistently argued for "the development of a European-wide political public sphere" as a precondition for a supranational democracy in which "European citizens could influence [the EU's] policies through the election of a parliament with its own factions."[154] However, if this strategy of creating a unified public realm between east and west has failed in Germany, is it realistic to expect that it will happen at the European level between twenty-seven member-states? While Habermas's realist critics are clearly wrong in arguing that his theory does not speak to actual politics, they may be right in accusing him of having an overly optimistic view of politics and of using his "normatively highly charged concept of 'discourse' " to overcome fundamental differences that are deeply rooted in historical experiences and collective memory.[155]

In fact, Habermas's support for the EU, which may very well be driven by the crucial role it has come to play in the cosmopolitan political theory he has developed since 1989, has arguably led him to violate his own understanding of the role of the public intellectual by increasingly arguing for concrete positions and even offering a positive program of institutional reform for the EU, which would bring it into line with his philosophy. In this sense, from the perspective I develop in this book, his desire to see the EU succeed can be seen as a victory of the continuity thesis at the expense of the separation thesis. The EU and global politics, the key issues that dominate his political writings over the course of the 1990s and 2000s, are the subject of the next two chapters.

EPILOGUE—*HISTORIKERSTREIT* 2.0

Both the *Historikerstreit* and the *Vereinigungsdebatte* have had long afterlives in the German public sphere. As the controversies that surrounded the 2005 inauguration of the Memorial to the Murdered Jews of Europe (Denkmal für die ermordeten Juden Europas) one block south of the Brandenburg Gate in downtown Berlin clearly show, the debate over the place of the Holocaust in German identity continues, albeit in slightly different form.[156] Far from representing the end of the discussion, in retrospect Habermas's purported victory in the *Historikerstreit*—and his thesis regarding the singularity of the Holocaust—has instead served as the basis for the development of an approach to "cosmopolitan memory" focused on universal human rights.[157]

Habermas's calls for an open engagement with the crimes of the past has led many to call on Germany to build on its *Vergangenheitsbewältigung* of the Third Reich by also recognizing its colonial crimes in Africa, particularly against the Nama and Herero peoples in what was formerly German South West Africa (contemporary Namibia).[158] This move has generated a backlash among those on the right who had finally accepted the previous narrative of the uniqueness of the Holocaust, only to be told now that Germany needed to face up to other further negative chapters that would further delay any form of normalization. It has also helped to fuel far-right nationalism in the former East Germany, where the process of "working through the past" was short-circuited first by the ideology of the GDR and later by its rapid integration into West Germany.

The controversy surrounding this new "specter of comparison" exploded into the FRG's public sphere in 2020. The initial spark was the invitation of the Cameroonian intellectual Achille Mbembe to speak at the Ruhr Triennial festival. Although this event was ultimately cancelled due to the Coronavirus pandemic, accusations of "anti-Semitic 'Israel critique,' Holocaust relativization, and extremist disinformation" leveled by local CDU politician Lorenz Deutsch—and later taken up by Felix Klein, the German Commissioner for Jewish Life in Germany and for the Fight against Antisemitism—resulted in a new controversy. Although these were rather tendentiously based on a handful of citations from Mbembe's work that mentioned Holocaust, apartheid, and the Israeli occupation of Palestine, they were enough to set off what has come to be called *Historikerstreit* 2.0.

Given the changes to German memory culture since the mid-1980s, this second controversy was less about relativizing the Holocaust and more about using this broadly accepted "German catechism (*Katechismus der Deutschen*)" as a way to avoid having to accept accountability for other historical crimes, most notably slavery and colonialism.[159] Given his role in the original controversy, it is not surprising that Habermas ultimately weighed in on the Mbembe affair. Writing in *Philosophie Magazine* in September 2021, he noted the importance of the altered context in which the second *Historikerstreit* was taking place. Pointing to the growing multiculturalism of the FRG as a result of immigration, Habermas observes that these new members of the German public sphere "had acquired the voice of a fellow citizens, which from now on counts in public and can change and expand our political culture."

In light of these demographic and cultural changes, Habermas argues that the concerns of these German citizens whose ancestors did not assist in the perpetration of the Holocaust should be listened to. While Habermas is open to the fact that immigration will change German identity, he has not backed down from his original contention that regarding the importance of the Holocaust for postwar German identity. That being said, he does not see this position as opposed to the attempt to put the crimes of colonialism on the agenda. On the contrary, he concludes that "what is at stake today is not a discharge of this responsibility, but a shift in its weighting (*Verschiebung der Gewichte*)."¹⁶⁰

Despite this shift, Habermas still insists on separating the Holocaust from Germany's colonial crimes, since the former were committed against fellow citizens and the latter against external actors. He has revisited this distinction numerous times, both in the debates around the aforementioned Memorial to the Murdered Jews of Europe in Berlin—which he saw as an issue that needed to be resolved by the heirs of the German perpetrators and the progeny of their victims—as well as in his recent intervention on Germany's obligations vis-à-vis Israel (covered in more detail in the conclusion), since "Jewish life and Israel's right to exist are central elements worthy of special protection in light of the mass crimes of the Nazi era."¹⁶¹ Whether or not this distinction is convincing, it is clear that Habermas does not think that the notion that the Holocaust has a singular, unique place in German national identity should shield Germans from the responsibility of facing up to their other historical crimes.

Reflecting on the debate, one of its main protagonists, Michael Rothberg, observes that he "really welcomed Habermas's intervention," given that it did not display the "rigidity and dogmatism" that defined so much of *Historikerstreit* 2.0. In fact, it was the 2021 translation of Rothberg's book, *Multidirectional Memory* (2009)—in which he argues that memory does not need to be a "zero-sum" game where the recognition of one set of victims requires the forgetting of another—into German that helped to set the intellectual parameters of the Mbembe affair. Building on his own position, Rothberg concludes, "Habermas seemed to 'get it'—to realize that we are not still fighting the 1986 Historikerstreit.... A new memory culture is to be welcomed—and does not have to necessitate the erasure of the gains that were made through grassroots and public sphere struggles in the 1980s and 1990s."¹⁶²

CHAPTER 7

A Turn from Germany to Europe, 1993–2009

Although he retired from his academic post at Goethe University in 1993, Habermas has continued to work as a public intellectual. A long-time observer of events in the German Federal Republic, since the fall of the Berlin Wall he has increasingly brought his experiences as a West German born in 1929—as well as his philosophy—to bear on pan-European problems, even going so far as to call this activity "my main current preoccupation."[1] If previously his work as a public intellectual had been oriented to the political horizon of the Federal Republic, in the wake of the *Wende* Habermas sought to anchor the transformed Berlin Republic in the newly formed European Union (EU), created out of the preexisting European Communities. In contrast to the primacy of domestic politics, which he had implicitly practiced as a public intellectual up to this point, in the 1990s he came to explicitly defend the idea of "the primacy of a *global* domestic policy (*Weltinnenpolitik*)," focused on the EU.[2]

This turn toward Europe is surprising, as Habermas had previously shown little interest in the integration project. Speaking in 1979, he even admitted, "I've never been a fan of the idea of a 'unified Europe,' even when it was very fashionable, and I'm still not one today. But one does have to be glad to see a certain growing integration of the European nations."[3] Although Habermas in many ways became a global, postnational thinker after 1990, his motivations were still rooted in worries about Germany. As he noted in a 1993 interview, "In Germany we need the political union if only to protect us from ourselves. . . . For the same reason, our neighbors should have an interest in binding Germany. . . . But this can be achieved in effect only within the framework of a common European constitution."[4]

This perspective is fitting, since Germany's experience reintegrating after forty-five years of separation mirrors many of the difficulties faced by Europe as a whole after 1989.⁵ However, it is somewhat unusual coming from Habermas. As he himself admits, looking back on this obsession in 2013, "Informed opinions and articulate positions on the direction of European development have to the present remained substantially the monopoly of professional politicians, economic elites and scholars with relevant interests; not even the intellectuals who usually participate in public debates have made this issue their own."⁶ Expanding on these reflections, he notes that many people find the future of the EU "abstract and boring":

> Why should we get worked up about such a tame issue? My answer is simple: if we don't succeed in making the key question of the *finalité*—the ultimate goal—of European unification into the topic of a European-wide referendum . . . then the neoliberal orthodoxy will have decided the future of the European Union.⁷

Given Habermas's intense political interest in these problems—and his participation in the debates surrounding German unification covered in the previous chapter—it is not surprising that between 1993 and 2009, Habermas increasingly "made these debates his own," so to speak. In fact, I argue that his growing philosophical interest in the political effects of multiculturalism and globalization, a set of developments that he collectively refers to as the "postnational constellation," is rooted in his political interest in and commitment to the development of the EU and international law beyond the state. The place of political integration beyond the nation-state in his thought originates in his public-facing works, and speaks to a number of his theoretical interests, including those on the future of human nature and the continuing role of religion in public life, both of which I also address in this chapter.

Throughout these increasingly broad, less German-centric commentaries—which, however, are still fundamentally shaped by Habermas's distinctly Teutonic perspective and his tendency to universalize from the experience of West Germany—he seeks to influence public debate without engaging in the "scorn for 'the masses'" that he associates with the "mandarin" intellectuals of the early twentieth century, who thought they knew better and could tell the people what to think and do.⁸ In contrast to the expansive grand theories of the past, he argues that "today, in our postmetaphysical age, philosophy no longer pretends to have answers to questions regarding the personal, or even the collective, conduct of life."⁹ Speaking in an interview in 1989, Habermas recognizes that intellectuals increasingly appear in public "as experts, who have knowledge about economics, questions of health or atomic energy." However, he notes that even their authority is limited, as they can expect their statements to be met by those of "counter-experts." Additionally, he notes that the category of experts is very different from that of the public intellectual strictly speaking, which is comprised primarily of writers and philosophers, and who act as "someone who feels responsible, regardless of lack of competence [*kompetenzfrei*], for things that matter not just to them personally."¹⁰

Habermas is under no illusions regarding in which category he belongs. In addressing current affairs and the problems of the present he emphasizes his lack of specific expertise—"my competence is at most that of an attentive newspaper reader and of someone interested in the times in which he lives"—and repeatedly rejects the label of an expert.¹¹ Writing in the *Frankfurter Rundschau* he therefore separates what he calls his "roll-up-your-sleeves work [*im Hemdsärmel arbeiten*] by an academic philosopher [trying] to reach a wider public" from his academic publications.¹² Instead of claiming the epistemic superiority of the philosopher, in his public-facing interventions he instead underscores the fact that "I don't know better [than anyone else], of course."¹³

Most of his contributions during the period between 1993 and 2009 address the implications of economic globalization and the multiculturalism it brings with it in the post-Cold War world. His political commitments and theoretical development during this time are defined in important ways by his heartfelt support for continental political integration, an issue that he admitted in 2006 "gets me the most worked up (*am meisten aufregt*)."¹⁴ While this was partly a response to the need to complete the process of binding a unified Germany to the West, it was also a response to growing globalization that, in his view, could only be addressed by the "building out [*Ausbau*] of the European Communities to a political union" in order to make these developments palatable.

In a commentary published in *Der Spiegel* in 1993, he presented his basic normative conclusions to the broader reading public, arguing that the key issues of the post-1989 world can be addressed democratically only insofar as public communication allows "relevant topics and contributions, suitable definitions of problems and proposed solutions to float freely and enter the public consciousness."¹⁵ Despite the fact that he has not taken a direct role in government or led any European political movement, Habermas charts a new course for the EU by meeting and exchanging views with important politicians while also maintaining his independence by influencing public opinion through frequent commentaries in newspapers across the continent. In this way, he has not only theorized the creation of "a transnationalized public sphere" on the continent; his political writings also help to bring into being a discursive space in which "themes are controversially debated at the same time at similar levels of attention across national public spheres."[16]

Habermas's interest in political integration beyond the nation-state speaks to many of his theoretical interests as well as his participation in other debates in the public sphere, including those on gene editing and the future of human nature, and on the continuing role of religion in political life. In *The Structural Transformation of the Public Sphere* (1962), Habermas showed how discourse within the public sphere could legitimize political authority through rational discussion and reasoned agreement. His philosophical work since then has examined the cultural, psychological, and social preconditions and barriers to the realization of deliberative democracy. With the publication of *The Inclusion of the Other* and *Between Facts and Norms* in the 1990s, Habermas elaborated his political "discourse theory" of democracy, where reasons are tested in discourse among free and equal citizens.

Although Habermas's public-facing interventions during this period reflect his mature conception of the public intellectual, in this chapter I also argue that the example of the EU reveals an ongoing process of adjustment, in which real-world political developments force Habermas not only to clarify his political commitments but also to adjust his theory so that it remains consistent with his public-facing works. In this sense, Habermas's writings on the future of Europe are a good example of how what I have called separation thesis coincides with the continuity thesis. The integration of Europe beyond the constitutional architecture of the nation-state is perhaps the paradigmatic example of this phenomenon, as the EU has played an important role in both Habermas's philosophical work as well as in his nonacademic writings. In this sense, following Immanuel Kant, Habermas recognizes that although theory gives an important orientation or direction to political practice, it must be linked by "a middle term ... an act of judgment whereby the practitioner distinguishes instances where the rule applies from those where it does not."[17]

This sentiment expresses itself in the distinction Habermas draws between the "openness" of networks based on rational principles and the "closedness" of lifeworlds that define all human communities.¹⁸ While Habermas had outlined his understanding of the public intellectual in the previous period (see chapter 6), during this time he develops the theoretical architecture to mediate between the separation and continuity theses. To address the increasingly international problems of a globalized world, he argues that the theoretical principles of abstract political order expressed in these international networks and the particular lifeworlds of individuals and communities must "meet halfway (*Entgegenkommen*)."¹⁹

This process of "coming together"—the literal translation of the German word usually rendered as "meeting halfway"—is the philosophical adjustment of theory to practice.²⁰ I argue that the developments of Habermas's thought on the European project can be seen as a process of modification, as his theoretical insights meet concrete, historical, and political developments within the EU "halfway." In this way, his work as a public intellectual fulfills the desiderata of both the theoretical continuity thesis and the separation thesis by mediating theory and practice in an indirect manner.

In charting these transformations, I show how the political development of the Union has opened some possibilities while closing the door on others. Drawing on Habermas's public interventions, I identify four crucial moments in the development of integration up until the onset of the global economic crisis in 2010, which is the subject of the next chapter (chapter 8). In the first period, defined by the disintegration of the Iron Curtain in 1989, the role of Europe is still unclear. In many ways, this initial period can be seen as a continuation of the challenges that Habermas was grappling with in response to the *Wende* and the unification of Germany, which I covered in the previous chapter. By the second, centered on the Treaty of Maastricht and the other major agreements paved the way for the deepening EU integration from 1993–2001, a hope for a common European citizenship emerges.

At this point, the main narrative of this chapter is interrupted by an excursus covering the sudden rise of religion as a topic in Habermas's public interventions. Theoretically, Habermas's interest in faith and secularization culminated with the publication of the two-volume *Also a History of Philosophy* in 2019. Yet this theme had already been occupying Habermas for some time in his theoretical work, largely as a result of his philosophical debates with John Rawls and other liberal thinkers starting in the 1980s. What is interesting, given the focus of this book, is that this issue became a major theme of his public interventions following the terrorist attacks of September 11, 2001. As the crises facing the

EU increased both in number and intensity after 9/11, Habermas prioritized his public-facing work on the EU over his history of philosophy focused on the relationship between faith and knowledge.[21]

Returning to the development of the EU, in the third period Habermas responds to the division between "old" and "new" Europe—brought on most directly by the US invasion of Iraq in 2003—by calling for a common identity based on shared European institutions. By the fourth and final moment, which centers on the rejections of the Constitutional Treaty (2005) and the ratification of the Treaty of Lisbon (2007) as a backup plan, Habermas's pleas for the greater involvement of European citizens in the Union's affairs reach a fever pitch. Although the global financial crisis had already started in the autumn of 2008 in the United States, its effects were not felt in the EU until early 2010. In light of this timeline, this final period lasts until 2009. I detail the effects of the so-called Great Recession on Habermas as a public intellectual in the next chapter.

In reviewing these debates, I show how, over the course of the decade and a half from 1993 to 2009, concrete events forced Habermas both to reevaluate his views of Europe and the EU and to consider how they fit within his theory. This is important not only for our understanding of him as a social commentator but also as an engaged philosopher who seeks to bring his theoretical corpus into harmony with his understanding of current events. While Habermas's forays into issues of religion, secularization, and genetic engineering during this period may appear as a disconnected excursus from his primary interest in the EU, I argue that they are actually intimately connected to his broader emphasis on the need for older, established national lifeworlds to expand beyond what his friend and fellow public intellectual Ulrich Beck refers to as the "container [*Behälter*] of the nation-state."[22]

THE FALL OF COMMUNISM AND THE BERLIN WALL

The events of 1989 changed Germany as an example in "miniature [of] virtually all of the crisis tendencies of postwar Europe."[23] As the previous chapter has already made clear, this was an exciting time for Habermas. His support for the unification of Europe under the aegis of the EU after the fall of communism was clear from the start. In an essay published in 1990, which responds to the dramatic events of the *Wende* in real time, Habermas laid out the basic issues that would occupy him during this later period. He argued that, unlike other great continental regimes, which rose and fell never to rise again, the post-Cold War EU has the opportunity to re-emerge from the ashes of a failed colonialism and a violent imperialism: "The question is whether Europe will use the second chance it now has for the civilizing of the earth, for breaking out of the desperate circulatory process of imperialistic power politics."[24]

These initial impressions return to a number of themes that have remained constant across Habermas's political writings. Most significantly, he seeks to establish the importance of open discourse for democratic legitimacy, noting, "Only through public communication can the institutions of freedom be filled with the substance of a rational process of the formation of political views and political will."[25] These calls for the establishment of open dialogue within political structures, where the better argument is allowed to prevail, are consistent with his philosophy, which is "a protracted examination of, and the barriers to, the implementation of practical discourses."[26]

Although in his later work Habermas expanded on the crisis of the nation-state and the need for policy coordination beyond it, these themes were already present for some time. In a theoretical essay from 1976, Habermas had asked, "Can Complex Societies Develop a Meaningful Identity?" He approaches this issue by rejecting G. W. F. Hegel's contention that modern society has found its identity in the sovereign constitutional state. Instead, even at this early stage Habermas argues that globalization and the declining *de facto* sovereignty of the state have reduced its ability to act as the "binding element" for a "normatively comprehensible lifeworld."[27]

His basic thesis is that publics around the world will have to reconceptualize their collective identities to cope with these new conditions. Though he does not yet know where this new basis will come from, he lays out three basic preconditions for collective identity in complex societies: 1) it can no longer be limited to one territory or organization; 2) it must be grounded in a universal ethics, which remains flexible and open to discussion; and 3) it should not reject all tradition, but appropriate it critically.

Europe, with "its potential for self-criticism, its power of self-transformation," will play an important role in this redefinition. However, in 1990, Habermas is still unsure about what role an integrated Europe would play in this process. He concludes this early intervention on "Europe's Second Chance," when he is still primarily focused on the effects of 1989 on the Federal Republic, with these words:

> What we need is to practice a little more solidarity: without that, intelligent action will remain permanently foundationless and inconsequential. Such practice, certainly, requires rational institutions; it needs rules and communicative forms that don't morally overtax citizens, but rather exact the virtue of an orientation toward the common good in small change.[28]

While the quotation above concerns the EU, Habermas's calls for greater solidarity extend well beyond this transnational perspective. His position is rooted in broader skepticism toward ethnic and cultural definitions of political belonging. In both his theoretical and public writings, he has consistently argued that "the nations, upon which nation-states rely, are highly artificial structures."[29] This stance emerges most strongly in his interventions during the "Asylum Debate," which erupted in Germany soon after unification, when right-wing nationalists sought to amend the German Constitution (Basic Law) to create a legal mechanism for halting the influx of refugees and curtailing the rights of "guest workers" (*Gastarbeiter*). These workers had been invited to Germany to fill temporary labor gap shortages but had ended up making their homes in the country. In a published lecture, Habermas condemned the controversies surrounding these proposals as a "disingenuous debate" that fails to take into account the changing circumstances, in which Germany has been "painfully transformed" from "a country of emigrants" into "a nation of immigrants" due to its growing economic power.[30]

More broadly, Habermas calls for Europe to assume a larger role in setting asylum policy and processing refugees. In a 1993 piece in *Die Zeit*, he also rejects the notion of a "fortress Europe" as outdated and unrealistic—much like the defense of an ethnic or cultural form of belonging, which he deems anachronistic in Germany.[31] The underlying issue, he argues, is that Europe's welfare states—and the EU's normative commitments to human rights—can only be maintained and fulfilled if its inhabitants embrace greater immigration by conceiving of themselves as "a nation of citizens" following the American or French models.[32] Although Habermas's political conception of the future of Europe evolves considerably in the years to come, his insistence on solidarity and on institutional structures capable of fostering coherent, non-national will-formation at the European level—while remaining anchored in the existing public spheres of will formation within the EU's member-states—remains a constant in his public interventions from the 1990s through the early twenty-first century.

EVER DEEPER INTEGRATION—MAASTRICHT, AMSTERDAM, NICE

The Treaty of Maastricht, which came into force in 1993, establishes what Habermas calls "a basis for the development of the European Union beyond the status of a functional economic community." Officially known as the Treaty on European Union, this agreement laid the groundwork for the transformation of the European *Communities* into the European *Union*. It did so by paving the way for the Common Market and granting citizens of member states European citizenship, which brought with it the right to work in any other EU country, along with voting rights in European and local elections. Habermas's hope—expressed in a public commentary published in the *Süddeutsche Zeitung* in 1996—is that these institutional changes, which would require "accepting decisions whose consequences have to be borne equally by all," would also lay the foundations for "a form of abstract solidarity that was first produced during the nineteenth century between citizens of different nation-states."[33]

Only after these concrete political developments does Habermas refer to the EU as an example of a postnational political community, one that could potentially enable the citizens of its member states to once again "assume influence upon the development of worldwide systemic operations through their own political public spheres and their own democratic content."[34] Yet despite this potential, he harbors significant doubts, including the EU's lack of democratic legitimacy and the absence of a commitment by the people of Europe to the "ever closer union" called for by the Treaty of Rome in 1957. Drawing a parallel to his native Germany's struggle with reunification, he notes: "What is evident today is precisely the absence of a union toward a common future made with will and consciousness."[35]

Although concerns about the "will and consciousness" of European citizens reappear in his later writings, in the mid-1990s Habermas's unease focuses on the European Parliament's capacity in Strasbourg and Brussels to oversee the operations of the Common Market. He argues that expanding the powers of this supernational legislature could help to create a unified European people animated by a "democratic attitude" grounded in the conviction "that their decisions can at certain turning points influence a self-enclosed and bureaucratized political world."[36] He rejects the concerns of Dieter Grimm, a professor of constitutional law and former justice of the Constitutional Court of Germany (*Bundesverfassungsgericht*), who is loath to give the EU greater powers and competencies "because there is as yet no European people."[37] Habermas contends that greater political integration through stronger institutions is an important mechanism for the creation of democracy beyond the nation-state.

In his reply to Grimm, Habermas contends that the "no demos thesis" does not hold up to historical scrutiny: in nineteenth-century Europe, territorial and political integration invariably preceded the creation of stable national identities. Recent scholarship supports this view, showing that political unity and a centralized state administration are crucial in identity formation. State-organized projects such as roads, rail lines, universal army conscription, and public schooling provided important avenues for cultivating patriotism and a shared national consciousness.

This claim is also consistent with Habermas's broader theoretical project. In his early work, he traced the emergence of the public sphere as an arena for critical debate on matters of general concern following the consolidation of the European state system in the nineteenth century. Although the concrete features of the bourgeois *Öffentlichkeit* reflected the particular constellation of interests in each country, Habermas maintains that national public spheres fostered group consciousness and legitimized political authority through rational discourse, a concept he elaborated in his two-volume *Theory of Communicative Action* (1981).

Habermas extends his earlier theoretical work—he is in fact forced to expand it beyond the largely statist frame within which it had previously been confined—to argue that open channels of discourse, in the form of "a European-wide integrated public . . . that transcends the boundaries of the until-now limited national public spheres" are crucial to the development of a European people. Such a unified arena for open and critical debate of key social and political issues cannot be expected to develop on its own. Rather, "political institutions to be created by a European constitution would have an inducting effect . . . creat[ing] the politically necessary communicative context as soon as it is constitutionally prepared to do so."[38]

As a result of his observations of current events, Habermas concludes that such a development is necessary not only to ground a European political union but also—and perhaps more importantly—to address "the very global problems today that are now overwhelming us." As he points out in a public lecture delivered at the Paulskirche in Frankfurt in May of 1995, the rising power of international financial markets, coupled with the escalating dual pressures of migration and climate change—none of which can be managed solely by individual nation-states—are "driving us, for reasons of our own self-interest, in precisely this direction."[39] This practical realization, which emerges first in his political writings, will go on to shape his philosophical trajectory during this period, including his growing interest in global governance and international law—topics that were not especially prominent in his earlier legal theory.

Habermas also argues that deeper European integration is necessary for the EU to overcome its inability to act as a single political actor on the world stage. This failure was laid bare in its dithering responses to the massacre at Srebrenica and US intervention in the Yugoslavian wars of succession, which Habermas had endorsed, albeit "with an aching stomach (*mit Bauchschmerzen*)," as he noted in an interview in *Der Spiegel* in 1995.[40] A few years later, writing in *Die Zeit*, he likewise endorsed NATO's military intervention in Kosovo as part of a broader "transition from international to cosmopolitan law"—that is, from a legal order that governs relations between states to one that protects individuals—despite its "paper-thin legitimacy according to international law, the disproportionate use of military force and the unclear political objectives."[41]

While Habermas can hardly be classified as a supporter of liberal interventionism, he clearly maintains that Europe must be able to act decisively in foreign policy if it is to uphold "our shared belief in the value and dignity of the human being." As he noted in a 2007 public letter on the Darfur genocide—cosigned by fellow public intellectuals Umberto Eco, Václav Havel and Bernard Henri-Levy—Habermas grounds this conviction in the continent's own past: "The Europe that allowed Auschwitz and failed in Bosnia must not tolerate the murder in Darfur."[42]

Moving beyond foreign policy, such institutional developments are also necessary to address the EU's internal democratic deficit. From Habermas's perspective, this long-standing problem is rooted in the fact that the "European Parliament . . . equipped with only weak competences" does not have the power to legitimate the executive pronouncements of the European Commission and European Council. This emphasis on the legislature as the branch of government closest to the people—more attuned to the public spheres of its constituents and thus better able to represent their interests faithfully—is in line with Habermas's commitment to the primacy of the legislature as democracy's chief guardian, a position in the German *Staatslehre* that I discussed at length in chapters 3 and 6.

More generally, Habermas argues that if the project of European unification is to succeed in overcoming the crisis of the nation-state, it must develop reliable and legitimate institutions. Given the pressures exerted by globalization, he maintains that action conducted through state-based foreign policies is no longer effective. Building on Kant's *Towards Perpetual Peace* (1795), Habermas argues that while a world state is both unnecessary and undesirable, nation-states no longer have the *de facto* capacity to deal with increasingly globalized problems such as climate change, the financial power of international market forces, and migration. Instead, he argues that "regionally comprehensive regimes like the European Community" must act in line with a "world domestic policy (*Weltinnenpolitik*)" if they are to be able to exercise any political influence in the emerging global system.[43]

The Treaty of Amsterdam (1997) addressed several of Habermas's concerns. In addition to creating a High Representative for EU foreign policy, putting greater emphasis on the rights of individuals and laying the foundations for a Europe without internal borders, the treaty also expanded the powers of the European Parliament. These greater competencies included: 1) subjecting most European legislation to the consultation of the EU's directly elected legislative body through the principle of co-decision; and 2) granting Parliament the authority to approve the individuals nominated to serve in the European Commission, the Union's executive branch.

With these increased powers in place, Habermas returns to the issue of "will and consciousness." In a September 1998 piece described as a political essay and entitled "Postnational Constellation and the Future of Democracy," Habermas fleshes out the effects of globalization on the nation-state and the conditions necessary for the development of solidarity at the supranational level. His central thesis is that "politics has to catch up with globalized markets, and has to do so in institutional forms that do not regress below the legitimacy conditions for democratic self-determination."

Despite democracy's effectiveness in providing legitimacy to political power at the national level, it is unclear whether it can do so at higher levels of aggregation. Within the nation-state, democratic legitimacy is built on a shared national heritage and a common majority culture. Yet if these "pre-established identities have become obsolete," organizations like the EU have to develop new forms of solidarity among citizens of larger political units, allowing them "to take their political destiny into their own hands."[44] The EU and the instrumentally governed systems it administers must find new ways to meet the lifeworlds of their citizens—which Habermas argues act as "the sounding board for crisis experiences"—"halfway," so to speak.[45]

Although a common cultural background was necessary for the development of democracy at the national level, Habermas argues that it need not be so at the supranational level. From a theoretical perspective, Habermas distinguishes between shared national culture and shared political culture. In *Between Facts and Norms* (1992), he argues that political culture "can, at a later point, cut its umbilical links to the womb of the national consciousness of freedom that originally gave it birth."[46] The fact that every state in Europe already has a national political culture makes it possible to establish supranational democracy based on constitutional rule of law and participation in a unified public sphere. There is hope for the EU: "Thanks to its procedural properties, the democratic process has its own mechanisms for securing legitimacy; it can, when necessary, fill the gaps that open in social integration . . . by generating a common political culture."[47]

However, this process has its limits. Habermas argues that institutional integration has proceeded as far as it can without the development of widespread European solidarity through common practices of opinion- and will-formation. In his view, the level of solidarity among EU member states is insufficient both functionally—because postnational institutions require a civic population already bound by more than nation-state solidarity—and normatively—because citizens must recognize that, due to the effects their decisions have on the lives of others, they *ought* to be bound by social ties beyond the nation-state. As a result, Habermas argues that "expanding Europe's political capacity for action has to happen simultaneously with the expansion of the basis of legitimation of European institutions."[48]

The problem is that the EU's economic integration through the Common Market has not been matched by the creation of political institutions capable of overseeing one of the world's most industrialized and developed regions. This is ironic, since the EU was intended to compensate for the nation-state's inability to regulate economic relations in a globalized world. In a February 1999 essay published in German under the title "Euroskepticism, Market Europe, or a Europe of (World) Citizens?," Habermas notes: "Today, the European Union constitutes a broad continental region which is spanned by a dense network of markets in the horizontal dimension, but is subject to relatively weak political regulation by indirectly legitimated authorities in the vertical dimension."[49]

The basic problem, in his view, is that the state has lost much of its capacity for effective governance, while the EU still has not developed enough power and authority to be able to replace it. Speaking to *Die Zeit* in 1998, Habermas observes that this is particularly true in economic affairs, where the power of the state has shrunk in two crucial respects: "[1] The state is increasingly ineffective as a fiscal authority in the domestic economy, while [2] the familiar instruments of macro-economic policy cease to function in an economic space that is no longer a national unit."[50] In addition to its lack of clearly delimited power, the EU also suffers from a deficit of legitimation, as its democratic credentials largely depend on national heads of state or government acting within the European council, rather than on politicians elected by European voters at the transnational level. This critique is related to his rejection of the executive-led, administrative style of politics adopted by the German chancellor Helmut Kohl in the 1980s, which I discussed in the previous chapter in relation to both the Historians' Dispute and the unification debate.

The mismatch between the incomplete political unification of the continent and its relatively high degree of economic integration undergirds Habermas's support "for a European federal state, and that means a European political constitution."[51] In his view, such a development would make it possible to realize democracy at the supranational level by providing an institutional political apparatus beyond the nation-state, a transnational citizenry capable of mobilization, and an economic and social milieu that could be administered legitimately. Only by fulfilling these conditions for democratic governance "would [the EU] acquire the political strength to take market-correcting decisions and impose redistributing regulations."[52]

Yet at the turn of the millennium, discussions of expansion within the EU focused less on the organization's political capacity—i.e., its "deepening"—than on its enlargement to include the post-communist states of the East—that is to say, its "widening." Although it did not occur until 2004, the groundwork for the largest single expansion of the EU was laid in the Treaty of Nice (2001). Despite provisions preparing for enlargement, such as increasing the size of the

European Parliament, the treaty left many of the Union's problems unresolved—in particular, the EU's lack of democratic legitimacy and its insufficient level of social integration.

Habermas decries this lack of focus on the political deficiencies of the Union by once again calling for a European constitution. While he approves of the changes made in the Treaties of Maastricht, Amsterdam and Nice, Habermas notes that they still leave the Union's basic political structure intact, including its executive-led style of politics, which cannot democratically justify or legitimate the Union's competencies. The lecture "Why Europe Needs a Constitution," which he delivered multiple times in 2001, emphasizes that the existing treaties "lack the symbolic power which can only be generated by a political founding act."[53] This is the basis for his argument that there "can be no Europe without a common constitution" as well as his contention that the "opposition between federalists and sovereigntists is sterile."[54]

Although Europe has achieved peace on the continent that started two world wars, it must do more to produce democratic legitimacy at the level above the nation-state. Relying almost exclusively on business interests for continued integration within the Common Market is no longer acceptable. He argues, "The economic advantages of European unification can count as valid arguments for the further expansion of the EU only against the background of the attractive force of a culture extending far beyond the economic sphere."[55] Europe can therefore continue to expand only if the logic of market efficiency is matched by the recognition of common political ties.

Up until 2001, Habermas viewed economic integration as a driving force encouraging the creation of a common social and political structure on the continent. As long as member states were creating common markets through coordination based on non-interference, the intergovernmental legitimacy provided by the Commission and the European Council was sufficient. However, with the increased pressures of globalization and the prospect of trade wars requiring coordination with redistributive effects, "the lack of a pan-European civic solidarity becomes manifest."[56] The solidarity necessary for welfare beyond the nation-state requires the creation of common, recognized, legitimate political structures flowing out of a common identity based on European citizenship.

Habermas stresses that the importance of such a document lies not in its final provisions (i.e., in the positive political program or vision it presents), but in the procedure of drafting and ratifying the text. He enumerates three empirical preconditions for a common, European identity: the existence of a transnational civil society, the construction of a common public sphere, and the creation of a pan-European political culture that all EU citizens can share. He then argues:

> By exerting a kind of catalytic effect, a constitution can accelerate these processes and direct them toward the point of convergence. . . . It would begin with a referendum on the constitution, which would touch off a large-scale debate throughout Europe. For the constitution-founding process itself represents a unique medium of transnational communication which has the potential to become a self-fulfilling prophecy.[57]

There is widespread agreement that common historical narratives or "stories of peoplehood" are crucial in the consolidation of stable political units.[58] If postnational forms of democratic governance like the EU are to take up the political tasks previously reserved for the nation-state, a similar process of identification and self-ascribed unification will also have to occur. However, identity formation at the European level cannot build on differences through the creation of national enemies or a process based on "otherizing" non-Europeans. Instead of being founded on cultural, religious, linguistic or ethnic differences, postnational identities will have to be based on commonalities between citizens with existing national affiliations. As Habermas points out, "Citizens who share a common political life also are others to one another, and each is entitled to *remain* an Other."[59]

Although he recognizes that "the past is not always a good guide (*Ratgeber*) to the future," Habermas nevertheless suggests that Europe build on its shared experience of two world wars and the violent nationalism of the nineteenth and twentieth centuries.[60] Since the 1950s, the European project has rested on the desire to secure peace in Europe: "It is [our] memory of the moral abyss into which the excesses of nationalism led us that lends our current commitment [to peace] the status of an accomplishment." Habermas continues, "This historical background could serve to smooth the transition to a postnational democracy founded on mutual recognition of the differences between proud national cultures."[61]

Instead of building on differences, a European people can be formed through a narrative of learning from history: respecting human rights, abiding by the rule of law, and refraining from violence. These shared historical experiences can provide the basis for solidarity beyond national boundaries. Europeans should focus on their similarities relative to other parts of the world, particularly the United States. Habermas concludes, "Policy differences over the environment, military procurement, and law which are emerging more clearly are contributing to a silent strengthening of European identity."[62]

THE RUPTURE OF 9/11

For most of his career, Habermas has had relatively little to say about religion. Modifying Max Weber's famous statement that he was "unmusical in matters religious," Habermas has usually noted that he is "tone-deaf in the religious sphere."[63] Although he did not engage extensively with the sacred in his early career, when he did so it was through the prism of Marx's critique of faith as "the opium of the people . . . the illusory sun about which man revolves so long as he does not revolve about himself."[64] In the 1980s, however, his theoretical perspective shifted as he took up religious themes explicitly and in a manner more reminiscent of Max Weber and Émile Durkheim, who argued that the "progressive shrinkage and decline of religion" is a byproduct of modernity.[65] Habermas therefore restated Durkheim's thesis in terms of the "linguistification of the sacred (*die Versprachlichung des Sakralen*)," through which the process of modernization gradually translated the basic insights of religion into a secular vocabulary accessible to all, making the further preservation of religion unnecessary.[66]

Habermas began to engage more seriously with religion following the publication of *The Theory of Communicative Action*, largely as a result of his debates with Anglophone philosophers—especially John Rawls and Charles Taylor—regarding the place of religion in public life.[67] In his political writings, this newfound interest is visible in his interventions in debates between the secular and the sacred in the context of genetic research and technology. Initially, his interventions on this topic reflect his conviction that "[t]here is a rational kernel to the archaic revulsion provoked by the vision of cloned human replicas." In a series of articles published in the *Süddeutsche Zeitung* and *Die Zeit* during three consecutive months at the beginning of 1998, Habermas notes that due to its engineered nature, the genetically-engineered clone "is comparable to a slave insofar as he can shift a portion of the responsibility for his actions, which he would otherwise have to bear entirely by himself, onto other persons."[68] He rejects scientistic solutions to this problem, noting, "Biology cannot relieve us of moral reflection."[69]

The key point for Habermas is maintaining the "arbitrary disposition over the genetic makeup" of the human individual, which is disturbed if the "design of one's own genome was carried out neither by the chance of nature, nor by the provision of God."[70] As a result, he turns his attention to the ways in which religion and secular philosophy—or "postmetaphysical thinking," in Habermas's preferred parlance—can come together in reaffirming "the question of the moral status of prepersonal human life." These ideas formed the foundation for a lecture he delivered in Zurich in May 2000, well as for his later 2001 Christian Wolf Lecture at Marburg University, a revised version of which was also published in *Die Zeit*.[71]

In his public interventions on these issues, Habermas focuses on the contingencies and uncertainties of conception and birth, which by virtue of "being a natural fact, meet the conceptual requirement of constituting a beginning we cannot control." This lack of control is important because its inherent "expectation of the unexpected" is "invested with the hope for something entirely other to come and break the chain of eternal recurrence." Although Habermas concludes that an individual created through genetic engineering might be able to come to terms with "the sedimented intention of a third person in one's hereditary factors," he fears that this will undermine the freedom of the child who is able "to see the programmer's intention, reaching through the genome, as a contingent circumstance restricting her scope of action."[72] While this increasing move to religion is surprising in many ways, it can be understood as a response to a question present in the Frankfurt School tradition since the 1940s: where might the resources to save modernity from itself come from?

Habermas's view of religion, as well as his sense that it was a topic that he could avoid, went up in smoke with the destruction of the Twin Towers. As a frequent visitor to the United States—and to New York in particular, where he has held numerous visiting professorships over the years—Habermas was profoundly shaken by the terrorist attacks of September 11. In an interesting and important historical coincidence, Habermas had already planned a two-month visit to the United States—to New York University—for the fall of 2001. Although he had always felt at home there, he notes that upon arriving at the airport less than a month after 9/11 he immediately "felt somehow more foreign than in any of my previous stays." In contrast to the usual American openness to the world that he had previously experienced, he notes that "the impressive generosity toward foreigners" seemed to have given way to an atmosphere of general suspicion.[73] In this sense, after 9/11 "the tension between secular society and religion exploded in an entirely new way."[74] This development, in turn, forced him to address these issues in a new way, both politically and philosophically.

On October 14, a little over a month after the destruction of the Twin Towers, Habermas was awarded the Peace Prize of the German Publishers and Book Sellers' Association (*Friedenspreis des Deutschen Buchhandels*). Although he had a speech already prepared before 9/11, Habermas rewrote it in light of this rupture.[75] As a result, it is possible to date the religious turn in his public-facing work to this intervention, once again demonstrating the connection between real-world events and his political writings.

In this speech, delivered from the lectern of St. Paul's Church (*Paulskirche*) in Frankfurt am Main with the cabinet of the German government in attendance, Habermas makes use of this occasion to conceptualize "fundamentalism as an exclusively modern phenomenon and, therefore, not only a problem of others." Instead, he argues that it is an issue requiring self-reflection in the West as well, where "feelings toward 'secularization' are still highly ambivalent."[76] Rather than blaming the Muslim, Semitic, premodern, fundamentalist "other," he uses this traumatic rupture as a way to reflect on the failures, weaknesses, and pathologies of secular modernity in Europe, i.e., precisely where it is most fully developed.[77] Rejecting the idea that 9/11 represents a "clash of civilizations," he instead warns, "We do not want to be perceived as crusaders of a competing religion or as salespeople of instrumental reason and destructive secularization."[78]

The key insight of Habermas's *Friedenspreisrede* is that secularization is not an either/or choice; the question is not one of "faith *or* knowledge," but of how "faith *and* knowledge" can coexist and learn from one another.[79] In order to overcome what he calls the "inheritance dispute (*Erbstreit*) between philosophy and religion" in a piece published in the *Süddeutsche Zeitung* on September 22, he starts by analyzing the idea of secularization as it developed in Europe.[80] Habermas notes that this concept is typically interpreted either positively as a way of *taming* religious authority, or negatively as a form of unlawful *appropriation*, a meaning tied to the fact that this term initially described the expropriation of Church property by the secular state.

Rejecting his own earlier use of the term, Habermas now argues, "Both readings make the same mistake. They construe secularization as a kind of zero-sum game.... Gains on one side can only be achieved at the expense of the other side, and by liberal rules which act in favor of the driving forces of modernity."[81] He has recently shown such an appreciation for the normative potentials of religion that *la Repubblica* published an interview with Habermas under the title "Only Religion Can Save Us from the Failures of Modernity," a title he did not choose, as it states the case more forcefully than he himself would have put it.[82]

This context makes clear that the underlying motivations for Habermas's growing interest in religion—in both his work as a philosopher and as a public intellectual—are deeply political and driven by his engagement with the real world. His political argument is that 9/11, the second Iraq war, and the so-called "war on terror," as well as Western responses to them, misunderstand secularization and the relationship between faith and knowledge as a dispute rather than an opportunity for mutual learning. After 2001, Habermas therefore devotes a number of public commentaries to transforming what he sees as these "distortion[s] in communication . . . of which terrorism is the most extreme version" into a productive dialogue capable of addressing multiple root causes—those of the violent fundamentalist rejection of modernization, and those of the West's own disenchantment with secularization.[83]

In line with his discourse theory of society—and in contrast to his earlier skepticism that faith still had a place in secular public deliberations—he concludes that "the democratic public sphere must remain open for all contributions, also for religious ones."[84] He now observes that "[t]he mode for nondestructive secularization is translation. This is what the Western world, as the worldwide secularizing force, may learn from its own history."[85] He defends this claim by presenting the European narrative of faith and knowledge as the result of a series of learning processes. He hopes the encourage and promote "a willingness to cooperate (*Kooperationsbereitschaft*) to reach an international agreement on principles of political justice."[86]

Instead of arguing for the replacement of faith by knowledge, he introduces the term "postsecular" to describe his conclusion that even the "largely secularized or 'unchurched' societies" of the West will have to "come to terms with the continued existence of religious communities, and with the influence of religious voices both in the national public sphere and on the global political stage."[87] Although this is in part a sociological description of the actual state of affairs in Europe, as with so much of Habermas's thought, it also contains a normative claim. While the West can no longer count on the disappearance of religion as an empirical matter, he argues that it can benefit from the continued presence of believers, who can salvage (*bergen*) valuable resources for the present from their faith traditions.[88]

This insight forms the basis for Habermas's high-profile public debate with Josef Cardinal Ratzinger—who would become Pope Benedict XVI soon thereafter—at the Catholic Academy of Bavaria in Munich on January 19, 2004. Given the growing awareness that "something is missing" in the ambivalent modern age, Habermas affirms not only that "philosophy must be ready to learn from theology," but also that "religious convictions have an epistemological status that is not purely and simply irrational."[89] This insight, drawn from his political engagement, leads him to recognize that religion is not simply part of the genealogy of reason; it is also a resource of normative inspiration in the present that can help us deal with a number of moral and political issues, including the preservation of conceptions of human freedom in the face of the kinds of determinism seemingly implied by neuroscience.[90] As a result, Habermas argues that a self-consciously and admittedly postsecular society can work with religion not only to combat fundamentalism, but also to "to counteract the insidious entropy of the scarce resource of meaning in its own realm."[91]

THE IRAQ WAR AND THE EXPANSION OF THE EU

Although Habermas had reluctantly endorsed both the Persian Gulf War of 1991 and NATO's intervention in Kosovo in 1999, he found himself unable to support the second Iraq War in 2003. That year, his annual visit to the United States coincided with the buildup to the invasion targeting Saddam Hussein. Reflecting on his experience of these events in the *Frankfurter Rundschau* soon after his return to Germany, he notes, "I felt depressed by the climate of public opinion in that liberal country, where the government was preparing for war against Iraq even in the media."[92]

Habermas expands on the reasons for his depression in a "Letter to America" published in *The Nation* in 2002. He notes that it is difficult "[f]or people like me, who have always sided with the pro-American left" to oppose the second Gulf War while also drawing "a visible boundary between criticizing the policy of the American Administration, on one hand, and the muddy steam of anti-American prejudices on the other." However, he still feels bound to do so in order to work toward "the transition from a soft international law towards a fully implemented human rights regime."[93] As he later points out in the *FAZ*, such a cosmopolitan project cannot be furthered by the invasion of Iraq, since "what the neoconservatives in Washington are actually offering [is] . . . a revolutionary vision: if the regime of international law fails, then the hegemonic imposition of a liberal global order is justified, even when it employs means that violate international law."[94]

The silver lining in this situation—at least from Habermas's perspective—is to be found in the fact that the latent European identity he had previously hoped and called for had seemingly burst onto the world scene in 2003. On February 15 of that year, major cities across Europe hosted the largest simultaneous mass demonstrations since the Second World War, as citizens gathered to protest the US-led attack on Iraq and President George W. Bush's characterization of it as a "crusade," with all the unpleasant historical and religious interpretations that this statement entailed. Reflecting on these protests, Habermas argues that they may "in hindsight, go down in history as a sign of the birth of a European public."[95]

In response to this pan-European expression of opinion-formation against the Iraq war, Habermas convinced a number of European and American intellectuals to respond "as a contribution to prompting the horizontal networking of national public spheres."[96] Habermas notes his surprise at the positive response he received from everyone he contacted—the list of luminaries includes Umberto Eco, Adolf Muschg, Richard Rorty, Fernando Savater, and Gianni Vattimo—with the exception of Paul Ricoeur, "who declined for political reasons."[97] In this way, he demonstrates his awareness that it is—in Pierre Bourdieu's words—"necessary today to invent forms of organization which would give voice to . . . an *Internazionale* of intellectuals."[98]

Leading these contributions was an article by Habermas, cosigned by Jacques Derrida, that appeared simultaneously in both the *FAZ* and *Libération* and was subsequently published and reprinted across Europe. This intellectual broadside prompted wide-ranging debate in the European press about how Europe—and its relationship with the United States—should develop. The article put Habermas's theoretical ideas about the public sphere—and his politically-induced realization that it had to expand beyond the boundaries of the state—into action through the efforts of a broad range of public intellectuals.[99]

In addition to sparking broad-ranging political debate and testing the power of the European public sphere, this essay represents a change in the way he speaks about America—the foreign country that he notes was most important to him intellectually, politically and personally—in his public-facing interventions.[100] Most notably, the invasion of Iraq leads Habermas to conclude that Europe can no longer simply live under the umbrella of US protection through NATO.¹⁰¹ Instead, he urges the member-states of the EU to develop a common foreign and security policy so that they can wield the power necessary to influence events on the world stage. Although Habermas has often voiced his fond feelings for the United States, especially as a West German who lived under American protection during the Cold War, he now appears disillusioned with Washington: "Europe has to throw its weight on the scales to counterbalance the hegemonic unilateralism of the United States."¹⁰²

Previously united by the force that Weber attributed to Western rationality, Habermas now believes that the West is divided between the United States and Europe. He argues that this points to the emergence of a unique and differentiated European identity, concluding that "features of a common political mentality have taken shape, so that others often recognize us as Europeans, rather than as Germans or French—and that happens not just in Hong Kong, but even in Tel Aviv."¹⁰³ Habermas identifies a number of crucial differences between Europe and the United States, including Europe's high level of secularization, its confidence in the capacities of big government, its preference for the welfare state, its skepticism toward markets, its aversion to the use of military force, and its commitment to multilateral diplomacy through the UN. He contends that these features are distinctive markers of "how Europe at large presents itself to non-Europeans."¹⁰⁴

Although these features may form the foundations of a common European identity, such a sense of belonging will not become a political force on its own. Instead, the peoples of Europe must actively appropriate these characteristics and put them into practice. This does not necessarily entail abandoning existing national identities, but it does require a building solidarity within Europe. While such moves are not directly about religion per se, they testify to important differences between the United States and Europe. In his acceptance speech for the Bruno Kreisky Prize for the Advancement of Human Rights, delivered on March 9, 2006, and published a few days later in the Viennese *Der Standard*, Habermas argues that the EU needs "to attain a position where even in a joint military deployment we still remain true to our own conceptions of human rights, the ban on torture and wartime criminal law."¹⁰⁵

To ground this call, Habermas once again argues that the common experience of suffering through the wars of the twentieth century can serve as the common denominator for a European identity grounded in EU citizenship: "A bellicose past entangled all European nations in bloody conflicts. They drew a conclusion from that military and spiritual mobilization against one another: the imperative of developing new, supranational forms of cooperation after the Second World War."[106] While this form of collective identity would be a construction, this is not a problem as long as Europeans actively endorse it: "only what is constructed through an arbitrary choice carries the stigma of randomness.... Historical experiences are only *candidates* for a self-conscious appropriation; without such a self-conscious act they cannot attain the power to shape our identity."[107]

Habermas recognizes that this process of identity formation is complicated. He also realizes that this process of "meeting halfway" may not occur simultaneously in all EU member states. In fact, the internal divisions within Europe—with some members of the EU joining "the coalition of the willing" and others resisting the invasion of Iraq—tempered his optimism. Habermas felt forced to admit to *Die Welt* in 2005 that "Europe is in a miserable state."[108] While Habermas began speaking of a "Europe of different speeds" as early as 2001, the Iraq war and an increasingly militant United States have convinced him than the EU cannot wait any longer to assert itself in international affairs. He therefore calls on "core Europe (*Kerneuropa*)" to serve as a locomotive, endowing the EU with the qualities of a state. Although this is not the ideal solution, a core could advance the European agenda while remaining ready to accept new members at any time. In a 2003 interview entitled "European Identity and Universalistic Action," Habermas himself admits that "the call for a common foreign policy is less an initiative than a reaction born of necessity."[109]

While this appeal (*Plädoyer*) for a united Europe is consistent with aspects of Habermas's theoretical work, it is somewhat in tension with his commitment to universalism. In particular, it is unclear why a broad, political citizenship—grounded in free discussion and the recognition of the dangers of a bloody past—should be limited to Europe. Given the rise of civil conflict worldwide, these conditions seem to apply to many other states around the world. By urging Europeans to form their own identity, Habermas is also asking them to create an outgroup: those excluded from the post-conventional allegiance to Europe and its particular history. As Iris Marion Young observes, "Surely invoking a European identity inhibits tolerance with and solidarity with those far away. Here I fear that Habermas may reinscribe the logic of the nation-state for Europe, rather than transcend it."[110]

I argue that this seeming departure can be understood through the idea of *Entgegenkommen*, in which broad networks like the EU meet the narrow lifeworlds of individuals halfway. The adjustments needed to bring theory and practice together have compelled Habermas to draw on different principles under changing circumstances. The call for a common European identity is part of a broader line of thought regarding continental regimes. In his philosophical works, including *The Inclusion of the Other* (1996), Habermas endorses the development of separate regimes in North America, Asia, and Europe. He envisions these regimes as mechanisms for the unification, rather than the further division, of humanity, since these regimes "could one day provide the requisite infrastructure for the currently rather inefficient United Nations." To be sure, it remains unclear exactly how this would happen.[111]

Habermas believes that the politics of global distribution and similar issues will have to be *negotiated* among such transnational regimes, in contrast to human rights and questions of war and peace, which he assigns to the supranational responsibilities of the UN. While the United States will play a key role in the process given its economic and military might, he argues in a 2000 interview for the Italian outlet *Corriere della Sera* that "the world is too complex" for a Pax Americana to succeed without the support of a truly cosmopolitan law.[112] In this sense, "Habermas . . . is not an unequivocal advocate of *universal* citizenship, for he insists that citizenship can be grounded in *universalist* principles but must be realized in *particular* forms of life."[113] The fact that the nature of these continental regimes remains hazy demonstrates that the process of adjusting theory to practice is a work in progress. Although Habermas believes that the development of solidarity and democracy in postnational federations like the EU is both possible and necessary, much like Kant, he specifically rejects ideas of world government and global community.

THE CONSTITUTIONAL TREATY AND THE TREATY OF LISBON

Habermas's longstanding desire for politics to move to a supranational level above the nation-state received some support from Brussels in 2001, when the EU began the process of drafting a "Treaty Establishing a Constitution for Europe" intended to unify its legal foundations and clarify its end goals and purpose—its "*finalité*," in the Brussels-based jargon of European integration. Writing in the *Süddeutsche Zeitung*, Habermas hoped that the quasi-constitutional convention initiated at the meeting of the European Council in Laeken would yield "a transparent framework of basic norms" that would clarify the "underlying reasons [*Worumwillen*] of the process of unification."[114]

Unfortunately, the draft produced by the so-called convention did little to simply the EU, clarify its basic norms, or argue for its necessity. Instead, after three years of work the legalistic, administrative approach yielded an "unreadable constitution incapable of capturing the imagination."[115] Shortly after its unveiling in 2004, this step in the process of deepening integration was put to the test of popular opinion when both France and the Netherlands announced that they would hold referenda on this document. Although Habermas admired the "courage" it took for both states to put these issues to a vote, he also recognized the danger therein. He was particularly wary of the French left, noting that it would be making "a bad choice if it tried to "bring" capitalism under control by saying 'No' to the European constitution." Instead, in a 2005 piece in the *Nouvel observateur*, he encourages *la gauche* "to regain part of the state's lost capacity for economic regulation" through European policy.[116]

Soon after writing these words, European unification and the possibility of a unified foreign and security policy were dealt a huge blow when both France and the Netherlands rejected the Constitutional Treaty. Not only was this a huge disappointment for the Union politically, it also demonstrated the EU's lack of popular appeal. He addresses these issues in a political essay entitled, "Is the Development of a European Identity Necessary, and Is It Possible?" While the rejection of what was formally known as the Constitutional Treaty was related to concerns about globalization and liberalism, both supposedly furthered by the EU, a dejected Habermas notes, "The mutual mistrust of the nations and member states seems to signal that European citizens lack any sense of mutual political belonging and that the member states are as far away as ever from pursuing a common project."[117] Speaking at the Willy-Brandt-Haus, a foundation run by the German Social Democratic Party (*Sozialdemokratische Partei Deutschlands*, SPD) in Berlin in 2007, Habermas will argue that the only choice left for the EU is either "integration or devolution."[118]

Although discouraged by the rejection of this quasi-constitutional document, Habermas continues to maintain his belief in the European project. He interprets the failure of the treaty as a consequence of the democratic deficit, which had been ignored by leaders of the Union until it began to interfere with their plans. While Habermas acknowledges that the constitutional treaty has not had the catalytic effect he had hoped for, he argues that it could still encourage "solidarity among strangers" by switching the focus of patriotism "from a fixation on the state to an orientation to the constitution . . . that is inherently abstract and mediated by law."[119] This kind of "constitutional patriotism (*Verfassungspatriotismus*)" could replace the desire for a European identity with mutual respect for a common political system, in which minorities could accept being outvoted without fear of democracy turning into a tyranny of the majority.[120]

By this point, Habermas is ready to abandon the grandiose talk of a shared European identity. Instead, he argues, "The question is not whether a European identity 'exists,' but whether the national arenas can be so opened up to each other that a self-propelling process of shared political opinion- and will-formation on European issues can develop above the national level."[121] This narrower goal builds on Habermas's insights into the importance of the public sphere for democracy. However, even the creation of a common public sphere depends on the practices and attitudes of the population—on how far they are willing to adjust their lifeworlds to meet the EU. He further argues that it would require the EU to decide once and for all whether it is merely an economic union, or whether it will truly become a political actor as well.

In both his philosophical and public-facing works, Habermas has consistently made clear where he stands on this question. In contrast to the EU's emphasis on market freedoms and economic prosperity, he notes in the *Süddeutsche Zeitung* that the institutions in Brussels must proceed from the recognition that "voters are not merely consumers."[122] He therefore calls for a more political EU based on the notion of citizenship: "If we cannot succeed in making the polarizing question of the *finalité*, the purpose [*Worumwillen*] of European unification the subject of a Europe-wide referendum . . . then the future of the EU will be decided in favor of neoliberal orthodoxy."[123] Although this inclusion of European citizens would represent "an admittedly risky and unavoidably time-consuming change" in the way European elites are accustomed to doing business, it is the only approach that can help bring about a common public sphere and secure the future of the Union.[124]

A key obstacle standing in the way of Habermas's European vision is the deterioration and marketization of national public spheres. In a 2007 piece in the *Süddeutsche Zeitung* in which Habermas responds to fears that the publication could be taken over by financial investors or a large, for-profit media company, he reaffirms his conviction that the audiences of major media outlets "are not only consumers, that is, market participants, but also citizens who have a right to partake in culture, to follow political events, and to be involved in the formation of political opinions." Without the "discursive vitality" brought about by the equal participation of all citizens in the conflict of opinions enabled by a functioning mass media marketplace, Habermas fears that the "public sphere would no longer offer any resistance to populist tendencies" of the kind seen in debates around the EU's Constitutional Treaty. Although he is writing specifically about Germany, his conclusion holds true both for all EU member states and for the Union as a whole: "Vigilance is required, because no democracy can afford a market failure in this sector."[125]

Habermas's call for a more involved, democratic process in future revisions of EU treaties and operating procedures through the use of referenda was ignored once again in the Treaty of Lisbon. This agreement, intended to push through the most important institutional reforms necessary for the EU to function with 27 members—with less fanfare than the Constitution—was put to a vote only in Ireland. In a 2007 piece in *Die Zeit*, Habermas notes, "A political Constitution should have made the holders of burgundy passports into European citizens. Instead, the pared-down reform Treaty reinforces precisely the elite character of political action, which is withdrawn from the population."[126] Given the opportunity to object, the Irish scuttled the agreement on June 13, 2007, much as the French and Dutch had done with the Constitution four years earlier. As Denis MacShane, a former minister of state for Europe in the United Kingdom, notes, "[The people of Europe] see a bossy Brussels, and when they have the chance of a referendum in France, the Netherlands or Ireland to give their government and Europe a kick, they put the boot in."[127]

On October 2, 2009, as the global financial crisis was already well underway in the United States and was gradually working its way across the Atlantic, the Irish were given a second chance to vote on the Treaty of Lisbon and "get the right answer." Although the Irish cooperated and supplied a "yes" vote, just as they had after their initial rejection of the Treaty of Nice in 2001, they did so in the shadows of a deep recession. Despite their approval, the failure of the European Constitution and the difficulties in passing the Treaty of Lisbon make Habermas's call for a Europe-wide referendum on the EU all the more puzzling.

It is unclear why a Europe-wide referendum would have any more success that the recent votes in France, the Netherlands, and Ireland. In fact, it is precisely because agreements are usually rejected that European elites avoid referenda whenever possible.

Habermas believes that a simultaneous referendum would start a Europe-wide debate. "The national media of each country would merely have to take up and comment on the substance of controversies being conducted in other member countries. Opinions and counterpositions could then develop in parallel around the same kinds of issues, information, and argument in all member countries, regardless of where they originate."[128] However, this hope seems overly optimistic, especially given that fears about globalization, immigration within the EU, and the loss of state powers appear to be the major factors prompting "no" votes in referenda on the EU.

On the contrary, it appears that the leadership of the EU must answer questions of legitimacy and accountability on a smaller scale before holding a Europe-wide referendum, which carries great potential for backfiring. If the recent rejections of EU treaties have shown anything, it is that confidence in the EU must be built up before further voting. The process of aligning the EU with the lifeworlds of European citizens ought to proceed incrementally if they are to meet at any point—halfway or otherwise.

CONCLUSION

At the aforementioned event at the Willy-Brandt-Haus in the fall of 2007, Habermas warned the SPD of the dangers of excluding the EU population from the debate on the Treaty of Lisbon. The leaders of Germany's second-largest party ignored him. The German foreign minister Frank-Walter Steinmeier responded without concern that the Lisbon Treaty was Europe's path forward. As *Die Zeit* reported, "The SPD invited the greatest German philosopher to discuss the future of Europe. However, they did not want to hear him."[129]

Given Habermas's history of support and his hopes for the EU, this setback was not enough to a change either his support of or his hopes for the European project. Habermas's diagnosis of "globalization's valley of tears" and the associated crisis of the nation-state has remained a constant theme in his political writings since the fall of Communism in 1989.[130] Although the multilateral, integrationist vision of the EU once competed with the American approach to international affairs, "The dream of a worldwide hegemonic liberalism, enabled by American patronage, collapsed in Iraq."[131] Thus, the regional integration through organizations like the EU is the only way democratic citizens can once again hope to regain control of their political destinies. As Habermas points out, "A US government that keeps in mind the changes expected in the world by 2030 cannot want a future China that behaves the way the United States does today. It is much more in its interests to try to bind the world powers of the future into a international order, where no more superpowers are needed."[132]

This goal requires the European project to succeed. As one of Europe's most ardent supporters and politically engaged intellectuals, Habermas continues to agitate and propose solutions to global crises through the framework of a more powerful, more democratic EU. In his view, philosophers should confine themselves to abstract principles in an ivory tower—they must also apply their theories in practice. His long-standing engagement with concrete events is not rooted in the idea that intellectuals "are endowed with a form of higher truth or with special powers, but because their task is to influence public debates through arguments and criticism."[133]

The danger is that Habermas's desire to meld his theoretical insights with political practice could lead him to push for greater integration before the people of Europe are ready. It took the EU over fifty years—from its beginnings in the Treaty of Rome and the founding of the European Economic Community in 1957—to get to where it is today. Although leadership from the top will certainly be important in advancing further integration, as Habermas and many European elites desire, it would be unfortunate if the project failed as a result of additional "no" votes on treaties and proposals that seek to move too far, too fast. There is already some evidence of a European identity and a European public sphere. Both should be nurtured and allowed time to develop at the current level of integration before being tested through broad referenda on important structural revisions to the EU.

Unfortunately, the European project that Habermas holds so dear experienced another crisis—and was forced into another round of integration—due to the global financial crisis that started to sweep across international financial markets in the autumn of 2008, starting in the United States and gradually working its way around the world. His initial public interventions in Europe, after the crisis arrived there in early 2010, focused on the EU and its insufficient, overly market-driven response to the problem of sovereign debt and a lack of liquidity. Yet the comprehensive nature of what eventually came to be called the Great Recession soon forced Habermas to expand his vision even more. As a result, his public interventions increasingly addressed the broader problem of the growing ability of market forces to dictate policy to formally sovereign states and the relationship between politics and economics at the beginning of the twenty-first century. It is to these issues—and to their implications for Habermas's late philosophy—that I now turn.

CHAPTER 8

The Colonization of Politics by Economics, 2010–2020

Since his break with the student movement in the late 1960s, Habermas has consistently opposed the model of public philosophy in which theorists seek to influence politics by participating directly in decision-making processes. However, as I show in this chapter, his concerns about the future of the EU in the aftermath of the 2008 financial crisis have led him to violate what I have called the separation thesis. He has done so by choosing to appear on stage with politicians such as French President Emmanuel Macron, and even served as something of an unofficial advisor to pro-European politicians like German Foreign Minister Sigmar Gabriel.[1] Since 2010, Habermas has thus increasingly been recognized as "the unofficial philosopher laureate of the European Union."[2]

Over the period covered by this chapter, I argue, Habermas has increasingly abandoned the model of the public intellectual he developed in the 1980s—one who acts as an external critic and guardian of public debate—in favor of a more direct form of engagement that seeks to advance a more positive political vision. This transformation is also visible in Habermas's political writings during this period. In contrast to his critical commentaries of the 1990s, since the financial crisis he has produced what he admits is "a constant stream of political interventions in support of deeper European unification."[3] Initially, Habermas's interests in the Union focused on building the EU's institutional powers and resolving its democratic deficit. This project led him to develop his ideas regarding the possibility of supranational democracy, the "constitutionalization of international law," and what he calls the "postnational constellation," in which the EU plays a key role as a model of continental integration for other regions to follow.

Habermas's hopeful—if still critical—view of the EU was punctured by the onset of the financial crisis in 2008 and the divisive effects that it had on the *projet européen*. More generally, the concurrent problems in monetary policy, sovereign debt, and globalized economics highlighted the increasing tension between democracy and late capitalism. While this issue had been in the background of Habermas's earlier calls for "politics has to catch up with globalized markets," it took center stage during the Great Recession, as the need "to tame [markets] has re-emerged as a moral and political question with new urgency."[4] As Habermas puts it in a 2012 interview: "Do European citizens really want to commit suicide? The national framework is no longer even sufficient to sustain their cultural wealth or to preserve the substance of their way of life in the welfare state in a museum, let alone to keep it alive."[5]

In his interventions during this period, Habermas gradually abandons his critical stance. Instead, he calls on the EU to use the financial crisis as an opportunity to move from a form of "post-democratic executive federalism" defined by illegitimate emergency politics toward a genuine "transnational democracy."[6] He expressed his hopes in a "rare" 2010 interview, noting:

> Greece's debt crisis has had a welcome political side-effect. . . . Imagine the improbable scenario of a coordination of the economic policies of the eurozone countries which would also lead to an integration of policies in other sectors. Here what has until now tended to be an administratively driven project would also take root in the hearts and minds of the national populations.[7]

Unsurprisingly, however, the leaders of the EU declined to make any fundamental changes in favor of merely "muddling through" without answering any fundamental questions regarding the EU's ultimate ends or *finalité*.[8] Rather than engaging in dialogue about treaty change to move political decision-making and party competition up to the European level where it could deal with global problems, in practice the Eurocrisis instead strengthened the EU's intergovernmental, ad hoc political approach.

Despite the suffering brought about by the succession of crises that have rocked the EU, in his public interventions Habermas argues that it has had the beneficial effect of starting to bring a transnational European public sphere into being "which is no longer tied to a reified body of people such as the nation, but to a latent demos that can be there when time requires it."⁹ Even though addressing the problems of the EU may require institutional transformation as well, Habermas focuses instead "on social movements, and on the civil, cultural, religious, artistic, and political associations of the unofficial public sphere," where regular individuals across all of the member states are increasingly partaking in one common discussion about shared issues and problems.¹⁰ Finally, returning to issues he had originally discussed as part of his critique of positivism, his engagement with the new social movements of the 1960s, and his dispute with Niklas Luhmann regarding systems theory in the 1970s, the first two decades of the twentieth century led Habermas to once again take up the issue of technocracy.

This chapter is organized as follows. I start by outlining Habermas's reactions to the onset of the financial crisis in Europe, where he repeatedly argues that politics must rise to the postnational level to match the power of global markets and criticizes the leaders of the EU for their nationalistic responses to the problems revealed by the Great Recession. In the second section, I examine how this leads Habermas to revisit worries that date back to the 1970s regarding the threats posed to democratic legitimacy by technocratic governance. In the third section, I focus on how he develops similar arguments in response to the migrant crisis of 2015, building on his earlier engagement in the German asylum debate of the 1980s. I conclude by examining his interventions during the Covid-19 pandemic that hit the Western world in March 2020.

THE GREAT RECESSION AND THE CRISIS OF THE EUROZONE

What has come to be known as the Great Recession had its origins in a subprime mortgage crunch in the United States. While it initially appeared as though the EU might escape the worst effects of this crisis, it was soon caught up in the broader collapse of global "financialized capitalism."¹¹ By the time the contagion reached Europe in the winter of 2010, what had started as a problem of private debt and liquidity on one side of the Atlantic had turned into a full-blown economic, banking, and sovereign debt crisis among the member states of the EU that share its common currency, the euro.¹²

The Eurozone Crisis disproportionately affected the new members of the EU's periphery, especially Portugal, Ireland, Greece, and Spain. In contrast to much of the political rhetoric in Germany, which blamed these so-called "PIGS" for their predicament, economic analyses highlighted the divided responsibility between the rich northern core of Europe—where investors financed irresponsible borrowing and whose leaders sought to protect their banking sectors from losses—and the elites of the southern periphery, who took advantage of low interest rates to bankroll unwise investments. As yields on bonds issued by different states in the eurozone began to diverge, an already fragile European unity came apart at the seams. While the crisis-ridden peripheral states demanded cheaper money to service their debts and maintain their competitiveness, those of the fiscally stronger north sought to protect the euro-denominated savings of their citizens. These events, which played out over the following years, clearly demonstrated that "a monetary union which is based on loose rules on budget/tax/economic governance will remain incomplete and unsustainable."[13]

The onset of the Eurozone Crisis had a profound effect on Habermas. Although these events did not lead him to abandon his long-standing support for the EU, they highlighted the growing tension between democratic politics and the material imperatives of late capitalism. Habermas was particularly disturbed by the way that global financial markets, working through institutions like the International Monetary Fund (IMF) and the European "Troika"—an ad hoc constellation composed of the European Commission (EC), the European Central Bank (ECB) and the IMF with "uncertain and ill-defined ties" that had "no basis in the EU treaties"—were able to exercise de facto control over the domestic policy of formally sovereign political communities.[14] Faced with the threat of defaulting on their public debt, states across the EU, but particularly in the south, were forced to liberalize their economies, lower labor standards, rescue overleveraged banks, and sell off public assets at bargain prices in order to placate market interests that operate across borders.[15]

While the crisis can be understood from the micro "point of view of the individual decision-makers," in his political writings Habermas tends to highlight the macro, structural factors at play, focusing in particular on the fact that within the EU as a whole "the mechanisms for controlling speculation and unrestrained capital flows were insufficient."[16] In light of these considerations, Habermas interprets problems of the monetary union as a symptom of a broader "legitimation crisis" within global financial capitalism.[17] Given his preexisting opposition to the takeover of political life by the forces of power (administration) and money (economics), which he laid out in the *Theory of Communicative Action* (1981), his political interventions during this period address the dangers associated with the overexpansion of functional systemic forces, as well as the broader instrumentalization of reason that they promote.[18]

Habermas tackles these issues by discussing the flaws in the EU's response to this crisis, which he argues paid too much attention to the supposed imperatives of the market and too little to the needs and desires of the peoples of Europe. Instead of allowing economic forces to "colonize" politics via processes of reification (*Verdinglichung* or *Vergegenständlichung*), in which social relations "take on the character of a thing," Habermas contends that social and political life *should* be ruled by the deliberative decisions of citizens. Responding to the worrying consequences of the Great Recession in an interview published in *Die Zeit* on November 6, 2008, he observes that the "whole program of subordinating the lifeworld to the imperatives of the market must be subjected to scrutiny."[19]

Building on the arguments highlighted in the previous chapter, Habermas continues to call for the completion of the EU's political project, in which the "negative," market-based integration promoted by changes instituted from the mid-1980s through the end of the twentieth century would be complemented by greater political integration to address Europe's democratic deficit. In making this point, Habermas finds himself in agreement with many influential economists on both sides of the Atlantic, who have argued that no lasting solution is possible without "significantly increasing the degree of political union" through "greater centralization and political unification."[20] However, his later writings go further, contending that the cross-border dynamics of the Eurozone Crisis demonstrate that politics at the level of the nation-state is outdated and no longer fit for purpose.

In this way, Habermas uses the example of the Eurozone Crisis to show how postnational integration can help move politics beyond the nation-state by allowing peoples around the world to wrest control of their destinies away from impersonal economic forces. Institutionally, the global financial crisis demonstrated that the Maastricht model—named after the treaty that laid the legal foundations for the euro, with a central bank but no treasury, and a common market but no common government—was not fit for purpose. However, since many in Brussels and across the Europe saw the common currency as a matter of "destiny" and "an irreversible part of ever-closer European union," these difficulties came to be seen as an existential threat.[21]

In an exchange published in *The Irish Times* in June 2010, Habermas observes that this poses a particular problem for Germany. While giving up the D-Mark was initially a great sacrifice for the FRG, today this is no longer the case. On the contrary, German "politicians can no longer deceive themselves concerning the fact that the Federal Republic is the greatest beneficiary of the single currency." Despite the protestation of leaders across the German political spectrum, Habermas observes, "Self-interest dictates that they support the preservation of the euro zone." For him, the pivotal question for these elites is "whether the Federal Republic is ready to change its European policy before it is too late, and then whether it is also able to co-operate with France in leading the other EU countries in that direction."[22]

In light of the difficulties the leaders of the Eurozone have had in resolving the problems plaguing the common currency, some have argued that these events demonstrate that the broader dreams of the EU as a "special area of human hope" should die along with the euro.[23] Habermas vehemently disagrees with this assessment. In "We need Europe!," published in *Die Zeit* in May 2010, he argues that the creation of a European a bailout fund represents a "paradigm shift" (*Paradigmenwechsel*) that "changes the foundational principles of the European Union."[24] He interprets the need for bailouts as the end of neoliberalism, since the crisis shows that markets cannot function independently of taxpayer support. He sees the crisis is an opportunity to deepen integration, since it proves that "we need institutions capable of acting on a global scale."[25]

Throughout his political commentaries Habermas has argued that politics must catch up with markets. In the afterword to the final volume of his *Kleine politische Schriften*, written during the interregnum between the onset of the financial crisis in the United States and its arrival in Europe, he notes, "My hope is that the neoliberal agenda will no longer be accepted at face value but will be open to challenge. The whole program of subordinating the lifeworld to the imperatives of the market must be subjected to scrutiny."[26] The system of international economic power must meet the lifeworld "halfway," not merely demand its subordination to the logic and efficiency of markets.

In all his writings during this period Habermas is deeply critical of European political elites for failing to use the crisis to create a system of economic governance. He is particularly disappointed in Germany's political leadership. For example, in a May 2010 interview with the *Financial Times*, Habermas criticizes German Chancellor Angela Merkel, who triggered the Eurozone Crisis in February of that year by suggesting that it might be necessary to expel Greece from the Eurozone. While Habermas is aware of the fact that "Merkel's statement was intended at the time for domestic consumption in the run-up to the important regional election in North Rhine-Westphalia," he immediately notes that "there can be no better illustration of the new indifference of the new Federal Republic than her insensitivity to the disastrous impact of her words in the other member states."[27]

Unlike the postwar generation, whose engagement with Europe was normatively anchored and motivated by the horrors of World War II, Habermas sees the current leadership of Germany as "normatively disarmed (*normativ abgerüstet*)," narrow-mindedly obsessed with short-term domestic goals rather than with broader problems. Instead of responding to the issues that arise in an increasingly complex, interdependent society, they "let themselves be bothered only by problems that emerge in day-to-day affairs."[28] In a statement that he will repeat many times over the coming years, he accuses Merkel of having "squandered much of the capital of trust accumulated by her predecessors over four decades."[29] Furthermore, going back to an issue that he had raised as part of the debates around reunification, Habermas notes how Germany's pro-European perspective has changed as a result of the post-1990 desire for normalcy: "since the chancellorship of Gerhard Schroder has pursued an inward-looking national policy. I don't want to overestimate the role of Germany in Europe. But the breach in mentalities that set in after Helmut Kohl has had major significance for Europe."[30]

"In times of crisis, individuals can make history." With this statement, Habermas calls on the European political elite to show some "backbone (*Rückgrat*)" and stop hiding behind Euro-skeptical public opinion surveys as an excuse for inaction. Since these polls are not the result of "a deliberative decision-making process on the part of democratic citizens," Habermas argues that they should be treated as an opportunity for politicians "to change public opinion by going on the offensive."[31] Instead of waiting to see what the people think, European politicians should get up and lead.[32] He argues that cosmopolitans and other supporters of integration beyond the nation-state can only hope that greater political leadership will result in the creation of "a consciousness that reaches beyond national borders to share a common European destiny."[33]

While Habermas was mostly focused effects of the Great Recession on Europe during this period, it was not the only issue that he worried about. In considering the deeper causes for the political failure to resolve the Eurozone Crisis—and building on themes dating back to *Structural Transformation* (1962)—he notes that "the breakdown of public discourse is also progressing quite rapidly" because "national newspapers, which played a decisive role in forming political opinion over the past century and a half, have come under economic pressure and have yet to find a business model that would ensure their survival on the internet."[34] Additionally, writing in the *New York Times* in 2010—that is, five years before the onset of the migration crisis—Habermas had already diagnosed "a quiet but growing hostility to immigrants" in the Federal Republic of Germany.[35] This intervention, published under the title "Leadership and Leitkultur" (leading or guiding culture), was prompted by a book published by Thilo Sarrazin, a politician from the Social Democratic Party who also sat on the Bundesbank board. In his book, *Germany Is Doing Away with Itself* (*Deutschland schafft sich ab*) Sarrazin argued that Germany was undermining itself by accepting the immigrants from the Muslim world, whom he claimed displayed lower levels of intelligence.

For Habermas, the fact that "we are experiencing a relapse into this ethnic understanding of our liberal constitution is bad enough." However, given his ongoing, post-9/11 interest in the relationship between faith and knowledge, he was particularly concerned by the fact that "today *leitkultur* is defined not by 'German culture' but by religion." In line with his other religious writings, Habermas reiterates his view that these issues have nothing to do with faith itself, but instead are "the cumulative effect of a growing uneasiness when faced with a self-enclosed and ever more helpless political system." Returning to his critiques of the leadership of both the EU and Germany, he concludes, "What is needed in Europe is a revitalized political class that overcomes its own defeatism with a bit more perspective, resoluteness, and cooperative spirit."[36]

Habermas's critiques of the EU—and its leadership—during this period did not stop at the structural issues and democratic deficits he identified in the EMU. On the contrary, he was also growing increasingly worried about democratic backsliding within the member states themselves, particularly in Hungary. The proximal cause for his intervention in the *Süddeutsche Zeitung*, published January 2011 under the title "Protect the Philosophers!," was the persecution of a "circle of liberal philosophers" by the self-declared illiberal regime of Victor Orbán. The fact that the targets included Ágnes Heller—whom Habermas had already defended when she lost her professorships in 1973 and had helped to find new positions in the West after her forced emigration from the communist Hungarian People's Republic in 1978 (see chapter 5)—must have sparked déjà vu for Habermas.[37]

As part of his campaign against liberal, cosmopolitan, so-called "Jewish" thought, Orbán had falsely accused these thinkers of misappropriating European research funds after they had publicly criticized the new media law passed in December 2010. This legislation created the National Media and Communications Authority—a body that Orbán's party controlled—that had the power to fine authors of content it deemed objectionable. Habermas coauthored an intervention on this issue with the philosopher, public intellectual, and former State Minister for Culture under Chancellor Schröder, Julian Nida-Rümelin, calling on the EU institutions to review the compatibility of this new legislation with the EU's standards for the protection of democracy and the rule of law. The authors ended their appeal by noting that in addition to calling on China to protect human rights, the EU also had to "keep a close eye on its own fingers. This is the scandal within the scandal."[38]

Writing in September 2011, Habermas points out that the financial crisis had already shattered the German ordoliberal illusion that "mechanisms" such as the supposedly voluntary budget stability criteria could "render the process of reaching joint decisions superfluous." As a result, even the leaders who created these policies had increasingly come to recognize a " 'construction flaw' of a monetary union that lacks the requisite political capacities." Unfortunately, despite this realization, Europe's leaders did not have a plan for what form this should take or how it could be achieved.[39]

This is the background for Habermas's long political essay, *The Crisis of the European Union: A Response*. Although this pamphlet published by Suhrkamp Verlag does not bear the label of a "short political writing," it brings together a number of texts Habermas wrote during and on the financial crisis.[40] *Die Zeit* even compared this volume favorably to one of the most famous essays in the history of philosophy, Immanuel Kant's "Perpetual Peace: A Philosophical Sketch."[41]

Speaking of this "booklet" in a later interview, Habermas notes that he would call "statements in the press, like this one, interventions," but then immediately notes that these are merely his thoughts, since "visions do not belong to the remit of a professor, or among the sidelines of an intellectual."[42] While such figures "may in the best case have a certain influence," Habermas is clear that "they never have power."[43] In a 2010 laudatio to Jan Philipp Reemtsma, Habermas approvingly quotes Reemtsma response to a the question regarding the proper role of the public intellectual: "those who have the privilege of being able to earn their money by thinking should do that as well and as accurately as possible."[44]

The core essay, which takes up about half of the volume, was originally delivered as a lecture at Humboldt University in Berlin on June 16, 2011. It was later excerpted in two of Habermas's favorite public-facing outlets, the *Handelsblatt* and the *Blätter für deutsche und internationale Politik*.[45] Speaking explicitly in his voice as a public intellectual in its preface, he notes that he "would like to use the means at my disposal to try to remove the mental blocks that continue to hinder a transnationalization of democracy."[46]

Despite its critical tone and Habermas's relatively negative outlook regarding the possibility that Europe's leading politicians, who have "long since become a functional elite," will engage "a new mode of politics capable of transforming [existing] mentalities," he still holds out some hope for the future: he believes that "the European Union of the Lisbon Treaty is not as far removed from the form of a transnational democracy as many of its critics assume." However, this encouraging conclusion is tempered by his conviction that "the construction flaw of the monetary union cannot be rectified without a revision of the treaty," as well as by his fear that the existing "executive federalism of a self-authorizing European Council" will result in "a post-democratic exercise of political authority" rather than democratic government at the European level.[47]

The first strand of Habermas's political argument for the EU concerns the changes required to democratically legitimize the Eurozone in view of its growing impact on the daily lives of its citizens. He situates the development of the EU within the broader "constitutionalization of international law," which has advanced the furthest in Europe, where collective memories of World War II created the "preconditions for realizing a more far-reaching goal, namely, the construction of political decision-making capabilities beyond the nation state."[48] This argument is not new; Habermas has been making it since the publication of *The Postnational Constellation and the Future of Democracy* in 1998.[49] Habermas has urged shifting the main site of political contestation from the level of the nation-state to the level of "continental regimes," of which the EU is by far the most developed example. While Habermas does not call for the elimination of nation-states since they "represent the most important source of democratic legitimation for a legally constituted world society," their powers in this system would be rather limited.[50]

The Eurozone Crisis has altered the burden of proof for Habermas's argument. Previously, he had devoted much of his attention to the *need* for politics to move up a level in order to be able to compete with global financial markets. In light of the power wielded by transnational political structures such as the Troika, however, his concerns have now shifted. Rather than pleading with those who "cling to the state-centered tradition of modern political thought" to abandon their anachronistic fetishization of the nation-state, he now observes that recent developments have "inspired fears that the connection between civil rights and democracy vouched for by the nation state could be destroyed and the democratic sovereigns disenfranchised by globally operating independent executive powers."[51]

On the one hand, transnational corporations and international institutions like the WTO (World Trade Organization) and IMF, who contribute greatly to the technocraticization of the EU, can hardly be blamed for this development, as they make no claims to democratic legitimacy in the first place. The bigger problem is the influence these external actors wield on the institutions of the EU, which often seem to be more responsive to these exogenous inputs than they are to the endogenous desires of their own citizens and member states. As a result, Habermas fears that an undemocratic form of executive federalism—a "*Fassadendemokratie* (façade democracy)"—is already a reality.[52]

Changing this will therefore require fundamental changes to the way the EU operates. For Habermas, the Troika exemplifies the illegitimacy and undemocratic nature of most transnational and international politics. However, he does not think that this must always be the case. On the contrary, he encourages his readers not to confuse "popular and state sovereignty" and notes that an "increase in territorial scale alone . . . changes the complexity, but not necessarily the quality, of the process of opinion- and will-formation."[53] As a result, Habermas believes that his existing discourse theory of democracy—where legitimacy originates in political debates in the informal public sphere of civil society and then moves into the formal, institutional public sphere of law-making—is sufficient to ground transnational democracy.

That said, political legitimation beyond the nation-state must address certain differences. Most notably, "whereas here [in the nation state] the institutions which make and enforce the law are bodies of *the same* state, in the European Union law is made and enforced at different levels."[54] In light of this important difference, legitimacy cannot come from either level alone. Instead, within a federated EU, "citizens are involved in a twofold manner in constituting the higher-level political community—directly in their role as future EU citizens and indirectly in their role as members of one of the national peoples."[55]

The legitimation challenges exposed by the management of the Eurozone Crisis after 2010 stem from the fact that Europeans have participated in these debates solely as national citizens, not as EU citizens. Instead of fostering solidarity among members of a shared—if somewhat more distant and attenuated—supranational political community, the intergovernmental approach to the crisis has encouraged national citizens to see themselves as involved in a zero-sum competition with their opponents rather than as partners in a common project. Habermas therefore argues that the main challenge for the EU in the wake of the Eurozone Crisis is to "recover the equal standing and symmetric relation in the distribution of functions and legislative competences which we ascribe reconstructively to the European peoples and EU citizens as construction-founding subjects."[56]

Many critics contend that the European Commission is problematic because, unlike in other federal systems such as the United States, it "actually possesses many legal powers that resemble those of a national government" yet often behaves more like a government agency given that it is not directly "accountable to parliament."[57] However, in an interview with Francis Fukuyama published in *The Global Journal* in 2012, Habermas argues that this comparison is "more ambitious than is necessary or sensible." Instead, he argues that the EC should be "transformed into a government" while "almost all administrative functions can remain with the member states." He concludes, "For the purpose of democratic legitimation it would be sufficient that a European government be responsible in equal measure to the Parliament and the Council in which the national governments are represented."[58]

While this institutional setup would ensure that the peoples of Europe have a place at the table as both citizens of the member states and as *European* citizens, their awareness of the latter function must be strengthened. While this may involve some further institutional tweaking, the key changes would need to be primarily psychological, as a "more abstract and hence comparatively less resilient, civic solidarity would have to [come to] include the members of each of the other European peoples."[59] From a functional perspective, Habermas believes that the peoples of the member states are increasingly recognizing the EU's direct impact on their lives. He argues that the media and educational institutions must also play an active role in fostering this awareness. Such changes will not occur easily or quickly, nor will they leave national identities untouched. Yet, drawing on the historical example of how national identities gradually formed across expanding territories over the course of the nineteenth and early twentieth centuries, Habermas believes that this transformation is possible, especially if it is supported by the further development of a joint public sphere where "European issues are debated as questions of common concern using similar frames of reference."[60]

The central problem for Europe throughout the financial crisis was that the leaders of the member states increasingly saw the EU's difficulties through a narrow, nationalistic lens. During a public address at a panel hosted by the European Council on Foreign Relations and the Mercator Foundation on April 6, 2011, Habermas argued that such narrow-minded opportunism threatened to "sink fifty years of European history" by placing the very project of European integration into question. Since national governments are the primary players, "they perceive the decision-making processes as a zero-sum game in which their own actors must prevail against others. The national heroes compete with 'the others' who are to blame for all the impositions and demands that the Brussels monster places on 'us.'" Building on his existing critiques of the post-1989 German desire for "normality," he was particularly critical of Germany's political elites.[61]

The discussion that followed Habermas's speech, which was published in two parts by the *Blätter für deutsche und internationale Politik*, appeared under the title "Europe and the 'New German Question.'"[62] This debate is interesting, since it is one of the few public appearances that Habermas made with Joschka Fischer of the Green Party, who served as the FRG's foreign minister in Schröder's government from 1998 through 2004. Although Fischer was not formally enrolled as a student in Frankfurt in the 1960s, he attended Habermas's seminars at the university, including the philosophical *Hauptseminar* that Habermas offered on Saturday mornings. From then on, they met regularly to exchange opinions. Their meetings were particularly frequent during Fischer's time in office as part of the coalition government between the Reds (the Social Democrats) and the Greens from 1998 until 2005. These discussions were not strategic but addressed big social questions, such as the future of old-age insurance or of the welfare state. While Habermas was deeply engaged in these debates and had clear views, Fischer praised him for maintaining his role as an engaged thinker: "he was never a political activist; he never confused his role as an intellectual with that of a politician."[63]

Fischer concludes his contribution to the public debate in 2011 by noting that "democracy develops above all through the pressure of crisis."[64] Habermas concurs, noting that if the EU wants to preserve the monetary union, its only opinion is to set out "the institutional preconditions for closer cooperation between member states" by making the choice between further integration or the loss of existing achievements "clear in the public sphere, indeed dramatizing it, so that a broad discussion is initiated." In this sense, before addressing the kinds of formal changes that would require a revision of the treaties that govern the

EU, Habermas instead suggests that debates about the future of the euro—as an issue "that affects the populations of all participating member states"—offers the opportunity for a creation of a common European public sphere. This would not require "to the infrastructure of the national public spheres"; it would merely necessitate "the opening up of national public spheres to one another, so that in Germany, for example, we are informed about the most important discussions in Spain, Greece, Italy, France or Poland—and vice versa."[65]

While opening existing national public spheres to debates in the media of other member states would not require institutional change at either the European or the national level, it could still be potentially transformative. Most notably, it might lead to the development of a more diffuse, yet still politically salient, form of European solidarity. Though weaker than national solidarity, it could reshape EU politics by replacing mutual suspicion between creditors and debtors with "the willingness to make sacrifices based on long-term relations of reciprocity." This would require greater participation by the peoples of Europe as a form of "political integration backed by social welfare" aiming to narrow the differences between the rich and the poor—including among the new member-states from Central-Eastern Europe—while also retaining their specific "way of life (*Lebensform*)."[66] As Habermas wrote in *The Guardian* in November 2011, the development of such a model of European solidarity would require Europe's leaders to replace what he calls "the executive federalism of the Lisbon treaty," which seeks "to transfer the imperatives of the markets to the national budgets without proper democratic legitimation," with true transnational democracy.[67]

Indeed, the issue of solidarity is one that will occupy much of Habermas's public work in the years that followed. Writing in the Italian newspaper *la Repubblica* shortly after the announcement, he interprets the Norwegian Nobel Committee's decision to award the 2012 Peace Prize to the EU as embodying a "double appeal": first, a message to the leaders of the Eurozone, who "must step out from their own shadow and so move the European project forward"; and second, a message to EU citizens broadly speaking—"a call for solidarity among its citizens, who must say what kind of Europe they want."[68]

In a commentary published in 2013 on the public-facing progressive platform *Social Europe*, under the title "Democracy, Solidarity and the European Crisis," Habermas argues that the EU is "trapped in the dilemma between, on the one side, the economic policies required to preserve the Euro and, on the other, the political steps to closer integration."[69] In light of this conclusion, fixing the problems of the Eurozone will require Europeans to expand their conception of the politically possible to include the economically necessary. For Habermas, this is particularly evident in the fact that the euro was originally designed to limit the economic and political influence of a reunified Germany by replacing the continent's dominant currency and central bank—the German Deutschmark and Bundesbank—with European equivalents under joint European control.

The actualization of EMU has failed spectacularly in this regard. Instead of limiting German power, the introduction of the euro has catapulted the Federal Republic "into the position of the undisputed great power in Europe as a whole."[70] The mere fact that it has created a hegemonic "German Europe" is proof enough of the failure of EMU to fulfill its own internal principles, as increased mutual interdependence created by growing crisis loans to finance debt payments and progress on common banking regulation is slowly pushing the sovereign nation-states of the Eurozone toward increased mutuality.

THE SPECTER OF TECHNOCRACY

Habermas's existing fears regarding the EU's democratic deficit were only deepened by the way elites drew on the supposed economic requirements of the moment during the Eurozone crisis justify decisions reached using emergency executive powers. This is a long-standing concern, which is closely related to theoretical work he conducted in the 1960s and 70s, when he criticized the proposals from colleagues like Arnold Gehlen and Helmut Schelsky that sought to "creat[e] a 'technical state' in which major decisions could be made by experts rather than politicians."[71] For Habermas, such conceptions are an ideological misinterpretation of science that truncates reason's discursive potential within the public sphere, in addition to undermining the democratic legitimacy of the decisions made by the coercive apparatus of the state. Instead, he argues that the public sphere must help to bring the technical potential of science into line with the values of the lifeworld in a way that avoids both the Scylla of technocratic rule by scientific-administrative experts and the Charybdis of nihilistic decisionism in the face of pure subjective preference.[72]

The fact that experts in Brussels were once again flirting with technocracy inspired solutions to the EU's difficulties in monetary policy and sovereign debt inspired a new wave of political engagement from Habermas, as well as the publication of a twelfth volume of "short political writings," even through the previous collection had already "presumably" been the last. During the later stages of the Eurozone crisis he is particularly agitated by the way the EU's "political class is being bullied (*kujoniert*) by 'the markets'" into forcing the Greeks to undergo painful reforms demanded by neoliberal financial interests without giving them any say in the matter. If such external demands can be seen as justified, then Habermas agrees with the editor of the FAZ, Frank Schirrmacher, that "democracy is junk (*Demokratie ist Ramsch*)." Habermas is particularly worried that the ability of international market interests to overwhelm the desires of citizens is being portrayed by the EU and the German press not as a coup against democracy, but as the "fortunate victory of expertise (*glückliche Sieg des Sachverstandes*) over the feared ignorance of the people."[73]

This intervention from 2011 thus signals Habermas's growing fear of the discourse of technocracy, which only serves to obscure the fact that "less democracy is better for the markets."[74] This rhetoric enrages Habermas. It also explains the incredibly high volume of his interventions during the height of the crisis of the Eurozone. As he points out in an interview with *Der Spiegel*, "I'm speaking here as a citizen. I would rather be sitting back home at my desk, believe me. But this is too important. Everyone has to understand that we have critical decisions facing us. That's why I'm so involved in this debate."[75]

Habermas's fear of paternalistic, technocratic solutions to the crisis—that justify unpopular, illegitimate policy based on the notion that "there is no alternative" and that the people cannot understand the intricacies of monetary policy and sovereign debt—also explains why he rejects the "plans for an 'institutional solution' to the crisis" that are being cooked up by the EU's leadership in Brussels. As Habermas notes in a public lecture that was later published in *Die Zeit*, the very fact that these reforms "are coming from high-level officials who never have to face the voters" is a sign of their technocratic illegitimacy. Although financial markets are pressuring the EU to develop the kinds of political capacities and economic governance that Habermas actually supports, he argues that these steps must be legitimized by the populations of Europe, not just by the heads of government and the technocrats in Brussels, as this "violate[s] the principle that the legislator that decides on how public money is spent must be identical with the democratically elected legislator that raises taxes for these expenditures."[76]

His principled rejection of technocracy explains why Habermas publicly welcomes political solutions to the crisis, such as the proposal by German Foreign

Minister Sigmar Gabriel of the SPD and French President Emmanuel Macron for the creation of a ministry of finance for the Eurozone overseen by the EP, i.e. by elected politicians, not appointed bureaucrats. His support is visible not only in his writings from this time, which increasingly propose positive political solutions, instead of just exercising critique, but also in his appearances alongside Gabriel and Macron at a joint event in support of this plan. Habermas's willingness to not only endorse these proposals, but also to lobby for them by lending explicit public support to political leaders, demonstrates his increasing transformation from a public intellectual, seeking to improve the quality of public discourse from the outside, to something of a public or even "state" philosopher (insofar as the EU can be considered a state), who engages directly in the political process and seeks to legitimize certain proposals with his philosophical authority.

Despite agreeing to lend it his explicit support, given "the passivity of political actors" in the EU, Habermas is unsurprised that this and other similar proposals subsequently failed.[77] The problem is that these setbacks only increase the likelihood that Europe will pay a "price for a technocratic resolution of the crisis."[78] This outlay will involve further political alienation, the continued divergence between member-states and the strengthening of right-wing populism throughout the continent. In this sense, the reluctance of Europe's leaders to take decisive action to end the crisis—which Habermas refers to as a form of "paralysis"—only further alienates the citizens of Europe from each other.[79]

While Habermas notes that he is "no 'Macronist'" and is wary of the new French President's claim to be "neither right nor left" as well as his "social-liberal promise" to balance social justice and economic productivity," Habermas admires "the *way* he speaks about Europe," Macron's political courage and his desire to subject the EU "to the democratic control of its citizens."[80] The fact that he had finally found a European leader who spoke about the EU in a way that he approved of might help to explain why Habermas chooses to violate the separation thesis by explicitly endorsing some of Macron's proposals and even agreeing to appear at a joint event.

By contrast, for Habermas the fact that Mario Draghi, the technocratic head of the European Central Bank, who under normal circumstances would remain behind the scenes, had to secure the future of the Euro by declaring that he would do "whatever it takes" to defend it, not only testifies to the fact that "the heads of government were incapable of acting in the common European interest," but also to the growing danger of technocracy.[81] The latter fear was further reinforced by the EU's actions in Greece, where institutional actors in the EC, IMF and German—most notably Wolfgang Schäuble—forced "the Greek government to agree to an economically questionable, predominantly symbolic privatisation fund cannot be understood as anything other than an act of punishment against a left-wing government" despite the fact that the Greek people had rejected this agreement in a referendum. Given his previously voiced fears about the FRG's more muscular stance and its desire to return to normality, it is not surprising that Habermas finds the German government's "manifest claim for German hegemony in Europe" unnerving, to say the least.[82]

Ultimately, Habermas's objections to technocratic solutions to the crisis of the Eurozone are deeply rooted in his philosophical conception of markets, which dates back to the 1970s. While he admits that markets can also secure freedom—just like politics—they operate as "self-steered systems for decentrally coordinating a vast number of individual decisions." By contrast, "Politics is the only means by which democratic citizens can *intentionally* influence the fate and social bases of existence of their communities through collective action."[83] In other words, while markets operate "behind the backs" of individuals based on their egoistic decisions as private, self-interested actors, political opinion- and will-formation is the result of debates between citizens, who seek to act together for the common good.

Although Habermas admits that "the complexity of society and of the problems in need of political regulation increases, the less it seems to be possible to cling to the demanding idea of democracy," he is still convinced that voters can "acquire the institutional weight of decisions of co-legislators . . . in conjunction with a vital public sphere," even at the supranational level.[84] However, this will require both politicians and the existing national media to change their existing approach, where "Europe is not a major issue in their discourse."[85]

In fact, Habermas sees this as a crucial moment, because it demonstrates that integration is not fated to move inevitably forward, but can also go in reverse. He points out that in the aftermath of 2008 "for the first time in the history of the EU, we are actually experiencing a dismantling of democracy. I didn't think this was possible." In this 2011 speech at the Goethe Institute in Paris he also made clear that there was a lot at stake in how the crisis was resolved: "If the European project fails, then there is the question of how long it will take to reach the status quo again. Remember the German Revolution of 1848: When it failed, it took us 100 years to regain the same level of democracy."[86] The fact that this has also led to a resurgence of nationalism—a phenomenon that Habermas thought Europe has already "put behind us (*hinter uns haben*)"—only makes matters worse.[87]

While it was clear to everyone that the EMU could not function as a monetary union without a common fiscal policy or as a form of economic governance without a political union, moving more competencies from the member-states to the EU is not the only possible solution. On the contrary, a group of "new sovereigntists" have called for an unwinding of integration, arguing that a return to the nation-state is the proper response to the problems unveiled by the financial crisis.[88] One of the most powerful proponents of this critique is the Wolfgang Streeck, a German economic sociologist who draws on the lessons of the postwar "economic miracle (*Wirtschaftswunder* or *trente glorieuses*)" to argue for the repatriation of economic and monetary policy to the nation-states that enabled Europe's postwar prosperity in the first place. While Streeck laid out his argument in a number of different places—including a number of commentaries in mainstream media—he developed the core arguments for his book *Buying Time* in the course of the Adorno lectures that he delivered at the Institute for Social Research in 2012.[89]

Shortly after it appeared in German, Habermas published a review of Streeck's book in the *Blätter für deutsche und internationale Politik*. Although he agrees with his counterpart's diagnosis of the problems of the Eurozone—he even compares "the eye-opening force of critical factual analysis and telling arguments" to Karl Marx's *The Eighteenth Brumaire of Louis Napoleon*—he is unsparing in his critique of Streeck's choice of the "nostalgic option" of returning to the nation-state.[90] For Habermas, this preference overlooks "the epoque-making transformation undergone by nation states" over the course of the second half of the twentieth century "from states that still exercised control over their territorial markets into disempowered co-players who are themselves embedded in globalized markets."[91] Given developments in the global system of economics and finance, the idea that states could just reimpose the old system of political control that prevailed in the 1960s through an act of will strikes Habermas as completely unrealistic.

Habermas is also wary of Streeck's preference for revolutionary solutions, rather than the kind of radical reformism that he supports. Additionally, while Streeck believes that the coming crises will result in the end of capitalism, to Habermas this seems very unlikely.[92] On the contrary, he argues that since capitalism will persist and since states can no longer exercise control over the global economic system alone, a solution to address the colonization of the lifeworld is still necessary. By turning to the state rather than transnational cooperation across borders, Habermas argues that Streeck and other supporters of national solutions to European problems "on the Left are in the process of repeating their historical error of 1914," when social democrats chose to support the nation in the Great War, rather than voting with their international class interests.⁹³

Given the forcefulness of Habermas's explanation for "why the anti-European Left is wrong," it is perhaps unsurprising that it led to a rancorous public debate between these two intellectuals.⁹⁴ It is safe to say that in this exchange—which is only part of a broader debate about the left's position on sovereignty that often focusing on Brexit and the future of the EU—neither side has succeeded in convincing the other. In any case, as Habermas's speech to a meeting of the German Social Democratic Party in Potsdam shortly after his interaction with Streeck makes clear, he still believes that "the missing national policy space can only be compensated for on the supranational level," a path "which we have trod with the European Union."⁹⁵

It is also visible in a public letter Habermas signed ahead of the EP elections in May 2014. The letter stated that Europe stood before a *"moment of decision"* (English and italics in original), as the voters of Europe finally had the opportunity to decide whether they wanted more or less Europe. Building on Habermas's own arguments about the role that a transnational public sphere could play in closing the EU's democratic deficit, it also noted that the newly implemented *Spitzenkandidat* ("lead candidate") system, where voters had the opportunity to vote for candidates for the President of the EC, was a "political quantum leap forward (*ein politischer Quantensprung*)," since it meant that the peoples of Europe would "be discussing the same topics at the same time across Europe in different languages."⁹⁶ However, this informal system is not written into law, which means that the actual electoral process can produce a different President, as happened in 2019 and almost also occurred in 2014, a fact that drives Habermas crazy given its implications for how the heads of state in the Council view the preferences voiced by the EU's voters.⁹⁷

In light of these events, Habermas begins to seriously consider the possibility that fundamental institutional changes to the architecture of the EU—which he had previously rejected—may be necessary.⁹⁸ In an interview that he later presented in the form of open lectures held at Princeton University and Boston College, he now turns to the US Senate, the upper house of Congress where "the two competing principles of the equality of states and the equality of citizens [are brought] into harmony" as a possible model for the implementation of his two-track conception of Europeans as citizens of their member-states and as European citizens in their own right. While he is not ready to abandon the possibility that a transnational public sphere where individuals "open themselves up sufficiently *to each other*" may also work, by 2014 he is prepared to consider the possibility that "procedures that require agreements between two legislative bodies with equal rights—such as the European Parliament and the Council"—might be necessary.[99]

One of the few things that gives Habermas hope is that "Europe has long since become a matter of course for the younger generations."[100] However, in order to ensure that the EU survives long enough to be able to take advantage of this potential long-term strength, existing political elites will have to ensure that it does not fall apart in the in the short term.[101] Traditionally Habermas and other critical intellectuals have focused on the leaders of Europe in the hope that they might rally public support so that they can actualize immanent goals "by adopting [them] as a conscious aim."[102] This is not the most appealing prospect. As the first cohort born after 1945 to take the reins of power, the leaders in office at the start of the twenty-first century lacks the emotional connection created by memories of war and suffering shared by their predecessors. Habermas therefore point out that the EU's leaders are "preoccupied with a short-winded approach to the day-to-day problems."[103] While political leaders might be able to reach agreement "through the proven neo-functionalist model, without the participation—and possibly even against the will—of the populace," such a development would only generate further popular resentment against the EU.[104]

However, far from leading the way, "Politics seems to be holding its breath and dodging the key issues at the threshold leading from the economic to the political unification of Europe." Since the EU has failed to deliver on its promises of prosperity, Europeans have "let themselves be bothered only by problems that emerge in day-to-day affairs" with an increasingly nationalist focus.[105] Despite Germany's hegemonic position, it is clear that given the democratic nature of all of the member-states, the answer to the question of rule *should* be the citizens of Europe.

This normative realization is reinforced by the fact that the crisis has caused the EU to impinge on the welfare and fiscal policies of member-states, i.e. to issues that are of great interest to the citizens of the EU. Although the vast majority of the effects of the crisis have been profoundly negative, the transnational economic difficulties brought on by the crisis have furthered the creation of a continental public sphere, pushing European citizens to discuss issues relating to monetary and political union across national borders in new processes of transnational opinion-formation.[106] The key question then becomes whether this next round of integration will succeed in pushing democracy up to the European level, or whether it will further alienate the people from an institution increasingly run by technocrats committed to neo-liberal economic principles.

IN THE WAKE OF THE FINANCIAL CRISIS

While it is difficult to say that the fundamental causes of difficulties that faced the Eurozone in the wake of the financial crisis have been addressed, the Eurocrisis was soon displaced by new issues. Most notably, in 2015 the flow of migrants to Europe—by some estimates the largest since the displacements the end of World War II—dominated news headlines across the continent. As individuals fleeing war, political persecution and the effects of a changing climate from the from the Middle East and African began to cross the EU's external borders in previously unprecedented numbers, the EU found itself facing a new set of issues that would divide its member-states. The onset of the novel Coronavirus in March 2020 was thus only the latest in a string of emergencies that wracked the continent.

As migrants displaced by civil conflicts in Afghanistan, Syria and Africa began to push towards Europe's borders on the Mediterranean, the dynamics of this crisis thus mirrored those of the previous one in that they pitted the northern core of the EU against its southern and eastern periphery. After the failure of mandatory resettlement quotas for refugees proposed by the EC, which were designed to share the burden proportionally among all the member-states, it appeared that the same geographical crisis dynamics were destined to replay themselves as states began to close their internal European borders to prevent migrants from taking advantage of the Schengen regime. However, on 31 August 2015 Angela Merkel, seen across Europe as Germany's chief disciplinarian during the Eurozone crisis, surprised both her compatriots and her European partners, by opening Germany's borders unilaterally with the phrase, "*Wir schaffen das* (we can manage this)."

When asked about his reaction in an interview with the *Handelsblatt*, for which he had worked as a freelance contributor in the 1950s, in October 2015 Habermas responded, "I'm as surprised as I am delighted. For years, I haven't been thought as highly of our government as I have since late August." He was particularly taken aback by Merkel's response to her critics, where she noted, "If we also have to apologize for showing a friendly face in emergency situations, then this is not my country." After five years of hesitancy, pragmatism and downright mean-spiritedness, Habermas explains, "What delights me is that once our government finally made a normative statement and took a stand—and then the public reacted in an almost fairy tale way" by cheering migrants at train stations and welcoming them into their homes. As a result, Habermas is pleased to find himself in "rare agreement with both what our government is saying and doing."[107]

In defending her decision to open Germany's borders Merkel, a pastor's daughter, defended using religiously inflected language of welcoming. For Habermas, who by 2015 had been working on his new, two volume book on the relationship between faith and knowledge for well over a decade by this point, this was a sign that modern religious traditions indeed still contained certain normative resources upon which secular thought could continue to draw, especially as most of the migrants arriving in Europe at this time were Muslim. This relatively optimistic spell was broken by three simultaneous attacks by militants inspired by the Islamic State (ISIS) in Paris on November 13, which killed 130 people. These events, particularly given the migrant background of at least some of the attackers, seemed to signal support for Samuel Huntington's predictions of a "clash of civilizations" rather than Habermas's more optimistic story regarding the normative potential of faith in the modern world.

In his response to these events—just as to earlier acts of Islamic terror, like the suicide bombing of the Madrid metro in 2004 and the attacks on the offices of the French satirical magazine *Charlie Hebdo* in 2015—Habermas seeks to interpret them as "fundamentalism [a]s an exclusively modern phenomenon and, therefore, not only a problem of others," but as an issue that requires self-reflection in the West.[108] In addition to examining the West's disastrous legacy of intervention in the Middle East, which encompasses the period of time from colonialism up to the United States's disastrous second invasion of Iraq, he also seeks to draw his fellow Europeans' attention to "the background of failed social integration or faltering social modernisation." This understanding allows him link the various problems Europe has been facing in recent years together; after all, "the terror and the refugee crisis, are—perhaps for the last time—dramatic challenges for a much closer sense of co-operation and solidarity than anything European nations, even those tied up to one another in the currency union, have so far managed to achieve."[109]

Unfortunately for Europe, such solidarity did not seem to be on the horizon. On the contrary, in the aftermath of the UK's decision to end its membership in the EU in a referendum called by Prime Minister David Cameron in 2016, the EU was once again dealing with what was a potentially existential crisis as calls for similar referenda in other member-states proliferated. While Habermas never expected that "that populism would defeat capitalism in its country of origin," given the technocratic, self-interested attitude Europe's leaders have displayed to the EU he is not surprised by the result. In a critique of the failed Remain campaign that applies across Europe, Habermas notes, "How could a pro-European attitude win over the broader population if political leaders behaved for decades as if a ruthlessly strategic pursuit of national interests was enough to keep you inside a supranational community of states." In one sense, Habermas is sympathetic to the desire of the Leave supporters "retake control" given the "technocratic emptying out of the daily agenda with which citizens are confronted." However, rather than return to the nation-state, as the Brexiteers and thinkers like Wolfgang Streeck seek to do, Habermas instead argues that "offsetting the loss of control that citizens feel and complain about" would require a "transnationalisation of democracy."[110]

In the wake of the Brexit referendum and the election of President Donald Trump in 2016, there was much talk of a decline of democracy in the west. Such worries were usually accompanied by diagnoses of the rise of a "new authoritarianism," citing examples like Vladimir Putin in Russia, Recep Tayyip Erdoğan in Turkey and Xi Jinping in China. While Habermas identifies "a variety of structural causes and many coincidences" in these concurrent phenomena, he argues, "What connects them is nationalism in its various shades." In a 2016 interview conducted with the *Blätter*, he therefore argues that the world is not witnessing the birth of an "an authoritarian international"; rather, he argues that these phenomena are the result of a "mobilization of resentment" that has its roots in the failure of the neoliberal agenda, as "the ever-promised 'trickle-down effect' failed to materialise over the decades." In line with his position during the Eurocrisis—and in line with his philosophical arguments dating back to his writings on the "postnational constellation" in the early 1990s—he argues that the left must "go on the offensive against social inequality by embarking on a co-ordinated and cross-border taming of unregulated markets."[111]

At this point Habermas is still convinced that the key problem is that "nation-state's selfishness remains unbroken if not bolstered by misguided considerations of the new International of surging right-wing populism." In a speech that he delivered in Bad Homburg on "New Perspectives for Europe" in September 2018,

Habermas argues that in Germany this resurgence is due to "the psycho-political divisions of an unequally reunited nation" and the "twin issues of immigration and asylum policy" that have dominated the German public sphere since Merkel opened the door to over a million migrants in 2015. By contrast, he contends that "exclusive attention to one's own national fate" in the other member-states dating back to the Eurocrisis—a dynamic which is bolstered by the lack of an opening of national public spheres to each other—has prevented the EU from resolving the problems it faces, from financial speculation and global migration, to rising inequality and declining economic growth and social protection.[112]

Following this intervention Habermas goes silent for a time. However, he once again chose to intervene to comment on the political effects of the Coronavirus pandemic of 2020. It initially appeared that the virus would be contained much like the outbreak of severe acute respiratory syndrome (SARS) between 2002 and 2004, which was largely concentrated in Asia. However, it soon became clear that due to its virulence and airborne transmission patterns, SARS-CoV-2 would become the largest pandemic since the outbreak of the so-called "Spanish flu" in the aftermath of World War I. Its rapid spread, as well as its relatively high mortality, forced governments across the world to return to ancient practices, such as quarantines and *cordons sanitaires*, that had been developed in Europe during the bubonic plagues.

As might be expected, such measures were controversial in much of Western Europe, especially as the pandemic extended across almost two years (in its most acute phases) and across multiple waves of infection. The rapid development of highly effective vaccines failed to put an end to debates about these emergency measure; on the contrary, government vaccination mandates and other official efforts to encourage mass inoculation only fuelled further controversy along "antivax" groups, such as the "*Querdenker* (lateral thinkers)" in Germany, who not only questioned the efficacy of the vaccines themselves, but also saw them as parts of broader conspiracies designed to increase government control of the population.[113]

The shutdown of massive sections of the economy and state-mandated orders to engage in social—or, more accurately, *physical*—distancing turned large parts of the global population into amateur epidemiologists, as everyone sought to understand what was happening and when things would return to normal (if ever). In the piece, entitled "Covid-19 and the protection of life" published in the September 2021 issue of the *Blätter*, Habermas intervenes again not in the guise of the critical public intellectual, but more in the role of a public philosopher to defend the legitimacy of restrictions on civil rights like free movement and assembly in order to reduce SARS-CoV-2 infections. Going even further, Habermas argues that governments were not going far enough to protect the population. By taking as their baseline the availability of intensive care beds, rather than the risk of infection *per se*, he contends that states are failing to observe its constitutional duty to "exclude all courses of action that risk the probable endangerment of the life and physical integrity of a foreseeable number of innocent citizens."[114]

Although Habermas initially frames his argument broadly in terms of the democratic constitutional state, his citations and later discussion reveals that it is primarily addressed to the legal-ethical discourse of the Federal Republic, as so many of his public interventions—particularly before 1989—are. On Habermas's reading, the prohibition on the subordination of individual human life to any other goal is the supreme value not only of Germany's post-war democratic political culture, but of the Basic Law itself. To argue—as some German jurists recently have—that risk to human life could be weighed against other basic rights was therefore not merely unethical; on Habermas's interpretation it was also unconstitutional.[115]

Habermas had foreshadowed his argument in the *Blätter* in a number of previous, shorter public interventions. For example, in an interview in *Le Monde* in April 2020, Habermas notes that while emergency measures posed a number of problems for democratic legitimacy, pandemic states of exception are required to protect "the fundamental right to life and to physical integrity." Despite the understandable pull of the "utilitarian temptation" of growth, he argues that politicians must not trade lives against economic considerations.[116]

This is not to say that Habermas disregards such considerations entirely. On the contrary: in a plea published concurrently in both *Die Zeit* and *Le Monde* two weeks earlier, he and his co-signatories—including Joschka Fisher, Daniel Cohn-Bendit and Axel Honneth—call on the European Commission to set up a "Corona-fund" by borrowing on international financial markets at low interest rates. This, they argue, would enable the EU's members to "shoulder the huge financial burdens of the crisis together." Such a step would not only allow poorer states to care for the economic wellbeing of their citizens without having to lift lockdowns prematurely; it would also take advantage of a new social atmosphere in which it was "popular to show helpfulness, empathy and hope."[117] Interestingly, despite the strident rejection of Eurobonds during the Eurocrisis, the EU ultimately did end up adopting a Corona rescue package based on joint borrowing by the institutions themselves not unlike this proposal.

These earlier interventions highlight the role of solidarity—a common theme in Habermas's recent public commentaries—in democratic politics, especially within states of emergency.[118] In his *Blätter* article, Habermas argues that democracy is incompatible with a purely "negativistic" conception of citizenship based on the assertion of the rights of individuals against their compatriots. Instead, during crisis situations individuals must conceive of themselves as part of a collective able to act for the common good. While the pandemic created a tension in the generally "complementary relationship" between the democratic self-empowerment of citizens to act collectively and the individual rights protected by the constitution, states of exception demand that such conflicts be resolved in favor of the former.[119]

As a result, in situations such as the Coronavirus pandemic, he argues that precedence has to be given to the protection of life as the prerequisite for all other rights. In his interview with *Le Monde*, he therefore notes that the "language of 'value', borrowed from the sphere of economics, encourages quantification. But a person's autonomy cannot be treated in this way . . . there is no 'choosing' one human life over another." It follows that during states of exception politics 'as the means to achieve collective goals' demands priority over the law as 'medium for guaranteeing subjective freedoms.'"[120]

Habermas is sensitive to concerns about the overuse of emergency politics, like those voiced by some critics of his position as well as some other prominent public intellectuals, most notably his Italian colleague Giorgio Agamben.[121] However, he notes that "only Covid deniers could vilify measures justified solely for the duration of the pandemic as an excrescence of biopolitics."[122] In his public comments, Habermas stresses that when the political perspective of the participant is allowed to infringe upon basic rights, citizens must be able to trust the "that the government will not allow the regime of legally mandated common-interest behaviors introduced on health-policy grounds to persist beyond the current hazardous situation."[123]

The source of this trust is difficult to pin down. However, Habermas argues that as the foundation of modern democratic life, the "anarchic, unfettered communicative freedom" of public debate has the ability to fill this gap. The "wild" process of opinion-formation, "in which equal rights of citizenship become socially effective," must be matched by the sensitivity of the government and the institutions of law to public opinion.[124] Such an approach ensures the defence of civil liberties—both through the legal system and the prerequisites of the public sphere itself—and allows citizens to see themselves as co-authors of the laws that bind them. Even the compulsory restrictions imposed by state during the pandemic retain their "unique character as a *voluntary* contribution of the individual towards the collective accomplishment of a universally approved political task."[125]

If an open, functional and politically influential public sphere is the prerequisite for democratic legitimacy, then the presence of such an institution is the origin of citizens' trust that the state will not abuse its powers. Even if governments were to overstep these boundaries, Habermas believes that the public could make use of vibrant national political spheres and the sensitivity of political institutions to public opinion to force a change. Because the modern, digitized public sphere enables both opinion-formation and the mobilization of the people without physical contact, restrictions on mobility and measures to ensure physical distancing no longer impede its functioning.

The situation is very different in illiberal or authoritarian regimes, where the ability of citizens to express themselves is restricted by surveillance, media concentration and other measures designed to tame the "wildness" of the public sphere. So-called "Illiberal democracies" like Poland and Hungary still hold elections and protect constitutional rights at a theoretical level; however, since citizens are no longer empowered to act in a politically autonomous way that would allow them to see themselves as co-authors of the law, these regimes can no longer claim democratic legitimacy. In this regard measures to fight the pandemic are no different than any other political decision, since "without civic common interest to back up mandatory law, the democratic state under the rule of law cannot have a political existence."[126] The pandemic should therefore be seen as an chance to show solidarity and the ability to act collectively, not an opportunity to stubbornly assert one's individual rights in a way that endangers others and further prolongs a pandemic that everyone wishes was already over.

CONCLUSION

Habermas's biographer, Philip Felsch, observes that "since Habermas first stepped on the stage of the German public sphere at the beginning of the 1950s, he appears to have been present in all debates."[127] However, since the end of the Eurocrisis there has been distinct downturn in Habermas's public production. While he has resurfaced to make a number of smaller public interventions, it is clear that following his ninetieth birthday Habermas no longer wields the same sway that he once did.

In part, this decline should not be surprising given his age. Habermas publicly admitted that his age is finally starting to catch up with him when he apologized to his readers for not writing a third (!) volume of *Also a History of Philosophy* that would bring the narrative through the twentieth century, noting that "my strength is simply no longer sufficient for that (*dafür reichen meine Kräfte nicht mehr aus*)."[128] However, other factors are clearly in play as well. While Habermas has often been disappointed by political developments over the course of his "secondary vocation" as a public intellectual, recent developments (or the lack thereof) seem to have had a particularly profound effect on him.

While previously he was able to continue his work as a public intellectual even "when the world from his point of view [was] too stupid or too base for what he wants to offer," it appears that he has found it increasingly difficult to continue, "In spite of [it] all!"[129] In part, this difficulty may demonstrate that despite his increasing transformation from a critical public intellectual into a public philosopher, who lobbies for explicit political positions, Habermas does not actually have what Max Weber—from whom the quotations in the previous sentence come—an actual vocation for politics. In this sense, it may be that Habermas found it easier to deal with disappointments when he was clearly still an outsider. However, after the failure of his many attempts to help to spur further integration more in the role of a public philosopher, he appears resigned to the fact that his hopes will not become a reality. Speaking with uncustomary fatalism in a 2023 interview, he even admitted, "I no longer believe that the EU will play a globally influential role in the future."[130]

Habermas has often been criticized for being overly optimistic and for supposedly seeking to make "even the most unpleasant status quo bearable." However, the disappointment with which Habermas has reacted to recent developments clearly refutes that charge that he practices a form of "legitimatory thinking (*legitimatorisches Denken*) that ... can hardly be distinguished from the attitude (*Gestus*) of a Right Hegelian."[131] It is true that some supporters EU have chosen to interpret the Union's development of "crisis mechanisms, permanent political guidance and a common understanding of its needs" as a welcome "return of politics" that testifies to its growing democratic accountability insofar as the EU is increasingly able "accommodate and bridge differences—by means of compromises and a permanent conversation."[132] However, even as he has increasingly violated the separation thesis—but in line with the theoretical continuity thesis—Habermas has not let his standards of democratic legitimacy slip so that he can continue to endorse the EU's actions.

In the next, concluding chapter, I bring this study to a close by analyzing Habermas's most recent public interventions on Russia's 2022 full-scale invasion of Ukraine and his comments on Israel's offensive in following the Hamas terror attacks of 2023. In line with the theoretical continuity thesis, I read these texts—as well as their reception—alongside the *New Structural Transformation of the Public Sphere and Deliberative Politics* (*Ein neuer Strukturwandel der Öffentlichkeit und die deliberative Politik*), which Habermas published in 2022, to reflect on how the onset of the digital public sphere has impacted the conditions of possibility that made the role of the public intellectual possible in the first place.[133] Building on my analysis of his recent work *on* and *for* the public sphere, I conclude that Habermas, who most fully developed the concept of the philosopher as public intellectual in modern democratic life, may end up being seen as the last public intellectual.

CONCLUSION

The Last Public Intellectual?, 2021–2025

For over seventy years Habermas has worked hard to bring theory and practice into a closer (albeit mediated) relationship with each other in his work. Insofar as the "subject-matter of modern political philosophy . . . is not the polis or its politics, but the relation between philosophy and politics," this desire is understandable.[1] What is unusual, however, is that unlike many other philosophers who have sought to bridge the gap between theory and practice, Habermas has done so without subordinating himself to any political party or movement. For example, when the Spanish newspaper *El País* asked, "Do you think politics and philosophy work well together?," Habermas responded, "For God's sake, spare us governing philosophers!"[2]

In part, this reticence is dispositional; as Habermas has pointed out, "Political consulting was never my thing."[3] More importantly, however, his position is connected to the conviction that "philosophy professors—as well intellectuals in general—have no privileged access to truth," and thus have no special position in public discourse.[4] Furthermore, he argues that philosophy should not seek to influence policy directly. Rather than acting as social engineers, who take advantage of their intellectual capital to gain private access to political leaders behind closed doors, Habermas instead holds that in modern democratic societies philosophers (as well as other nonexpert public intellectuals) can only legitimately influence policy by making their arguments openly in the public sphere. This is doubly true in the German context, where the problematic collaboration of so many leading thinkers with the Nazi regime has permanently tainted philosophical interventions in politics.[5]

Habermas's conception of the public intellectual also affects his understanding of the primary goal of the politically engaged (critical) theorist. For him, such figures should not be driven by the adoption of particular policies; in fact, public intellectuals should not present a positive political program but instead confine themselves to critiquing existing proposals and discourses. In this way their work should seek to ensure that important voices and perspectives that are being ignored, silenced, or devalued are given due consideration. The success of the public intellectual, on his account, is therefore measured by the ability to "improv[e] the *quality* of the decisions" reached by the political system of will-formation, by ensuring that the best possible arguments are put forward in "the vibrant and maximally unregulated circulation of public opinions" in the public sphere.[6]

As the preceding chapters have shown, this indirect approach to public intervention—and to the problem of theory and practice—is in line with the theoretical account of the discursive foundations of democratic legitimacy that Habermas develops in his philosophical work; this is what I have called the theoretical continuity thesis.[7] In light of this commitment, and in opposition to agonistic and "realist" critiques of his work, I have argued that we need to read Habermas's academic (*wissenschaftlich*) works alongside his interventions in the public sphere to truly understand how he mediates the relationship between theory and practice—thus respecting what I have labeled the separation thesis—while also ensuring that these two aspects of his work remain compatible. Although Habermas undoubtedly would have had an easier time of it if he had simply focused on his academic work, he has instead engaged more fully in the "acid bath of relentless public discourse" than any other philosopher in the postwar era.[8] As he himself is well aware, "The professor pays a price in their vocation (*Beruf*) every time they take a political position (*Stellungnahme*)."[9]

Additionally, Habermas's attempts to balance his academic and public-facing work highlight that his mature conception of the public intellectual is not an ethics-first "ideal theory" constructed in the abstract and then applied in practice. Instead, it emerges from his recognition that the internal logics of academic work—oriented toward truth and governed by reasoned debate between opposing positions—are distinct from the "chaotic" political public sphere, which allows for more "robust manifestations (*robuste Manifestationen*)" of disagreement that pit individuals with different ideas and interests against each other as they grapple for power.[10] In mapping Habermas's development as a public intellectual over the course of the preceding chapters, I have also shown that at certain moments Habermas's political engagements have driven his theoretical development, while at others his theoretical ideas have driven his public interventions.

As I have documented over the course of the preceding chapters, Habermas's conception of the relation between theory and practice is itself the product of his own history of engagement in the public sphere and his theoretical reflection on these experiences. As a result—and this is the overarching thesis of this book—I argue that Habermas's political writings reveal how, despite his commitment to the separation thesis, his academic and public facing words are also theoretically consistent with each other. In this way, they mutually inform each other as part of a consistent overall project while also taking into account the boundaries and internal logics of their respective value spheres. Although he repeatedly insisted during our conversation in June 2024 that he did not do this intentionally, I argue (in Habermasian fashion) that the relationship between theory and practice in his work can be reconstructed in this way from the third-person perspective of an external observer, even if he does not recognize it from his own first-person perspective.[11]

In his theoretical work, Habermas often speaks of "learning processes (*Lernprozesse*)" in which agents in a given social system gradually acquire the ability to make better decisions over time by reflecting on past mistakes. For Habermas, while such developments are the product of a gradual rationalization of the decision-making process, they are not motivated by reason alone. Instead, such *Lernprozesse* are driven by past experience, especially by what he refers to "learning from catastrophe," a concept Habermas adapts from Theodor Adorno's critical theory, which seeks to develop a constructive, forward-looking social goal out of the negativistic, backward-looking cataclysm of Auschwitz.[12] The result is a model of social learning in which shared memories—particularly negative ones of experiences individuals and communities would prefer to forget—help actors make better decisions about the future in the present.[13] While Habermas develops this model to explain concrete examples of social learning in theoretical terms, I believe that it can also be applied to his development as a public intellectual.

The backward-looking narrative that I have presented in my chronological reconstruction of Habermas's public-facing work demonstrates that he developed this conception over time as a result of his personal experiences. While he showed an early desire to intervene in public affairs, he was unable to find a theoretically consistent way of doing so during his university studies. In light of this, and the revelations about the widespread collaboration of many of his teachers with the Nazi regime, Habermas chose to pursue a career as a freelance journalist after completing his studies (chapter 2). Though a serendipitous turn of events, Habermas was able to return to academe by becoming Theodor Adorno's assistant, a role through which he was introduced to the Frankfurt School's more politically engaged form of critical theory. However, ultimately his attempts to blend theory and practice at this time were blocked by Horkheimer, who feared what he saw as Habermas's revolutionary instincts and his belief in the possibility of political transformation (chapter 3).

This very well could have been the end of Habermas's academic career. Fortunately, the Wolfgang Abendroth of the University of Marburg agreed to sponsor Habermas's *Habilitation* following Horkheimer's decision to push Habermas out from Frankfurt. In fact, according to Habermas it was Abendroth who first gave him the idea that he could have a career at the university.[14] I argue that Abendroth's engagement as what Habermas would later call—albeit in a somewhat different context—a "partisan professor" aptly describes Habermas's own early activism, particularly within the burgeoning student movement of the 1960s. However, Habermas ultimately found that he could not subordinate himself to the movement, either theoretically or politically, due to his rejection of the students' actionistic, voluntarist belief that they could bring about a revolutionary situation through sheer force of will (chapter 4).

Following this break, Habermas retreated from the public sphere in the 1970s to place his theoretical approach on firmer communicative ground while serving as the director of the Max Planck Institute in Starnberg (chapter 5). It was only after he returned to Frankfurt in the early 1980s that he developed his mature conception of the public intellectual. He then put this role into practice, engaging in debates about German historical consciousness and reunification throughout the 1980s (chapter 6).

In the aftermath of the collapse of the communist regime, Habermas continued to apply his mature conception of the public intellectual to his political interventions. However, these writings increasingly shifted from a focus on democratizing the Federal Republic of Germany to advocating for deeper integration of the European Union (EU) within a postnational constellation capable of constitutionalizing international law (chapter 7). In the aftermath of the global financial crisis of 2008, Habermas's pleas for the EU to develop the kind of constituent power (*pouvoir constituant*) that could ground a European transnational democracy—rather than merely reinforcing an illegitimate executive federalism—become increasingly urgent.[15]

As a result, I argue that following the so-called Great Recession Habermas gradually abandons his own conception of the public intellectual as someone who criticizes developments from the outside. In the first decades of the twenty-first century, he increasingly assumes the role of the EU's "state philosopher," not only seeking to provide public legitimation for European integration but also offering increasingly concrete political proposals and engaging directly with politicians to push for their adoption (chapter 8). In his more recent work, he thus appears to violate the "role-differentiation" between his vocation (*Beruf*) as philosopher and sociologist and his political interventions as a public intellectual (his "secondary vocation" or *Nebenberuf*).[16]

Despite these recent changes, Habermas has consistently sought to avoid the "accusation of moral arrogance or, worse, of a claim to intellectual leadership."[17] While he has "develop[ed] the idea of a theory of society conceived with practical intention" in his academic writings, as part of his public persona he has always rejected the idea of "governing philosophers," even if he may have come closer to it in the 2010s than he himself would care to admit.[18] In any case, it is clear that his position on the relationship between theory and practice is very different from the Platonic notion of a philosopher-king or of organic intellectuals in the Marxist tradition, who represent the interests of a particular political party or social class. It is also at odds with the special place granted to philosophers by political realists, defenders of democratic underlaboring or proponents of public philosophy (see chapter 1).[19] In contrast to these other approaches, Habermas concludes, "When they [intellectuals] take a position regarding practical questions, they do so either in the role of the expert (which I am not), or with the right to participation in the discussions carried on among citizens."[20]

My chronological treatment of Habermas's development as a public intellectual may make it seem like this development had a teleological character. However, far from being the result of a plan or a logical development, his interventions—and the changes in his understanding of theory and practice leading to his mature understanding of role of the public intellectual in contemporary democratic life—have always depended on what issues gain salience in the public sphere. Instead, Habermas's public texts are episodic interventions dictated by the issues already under debate in the public sphere. While it is possible to find narrative connections between these events in hindsight (as I have done in the narrative presented in these pages), such a perspective gives them both an internal coherence and an inevitability that they did not possess for Habermas at the time. As he points out, "A life history consists of many contingencies and few consciously-made decisions (*Weichenstellungen*)."[21]

I ended the previous chapter by engaging with Habermas's interventions on the Coronavirus pandemic that shut down much of the world in March of 2020. In the wake of Covid, Habermas has cut back his public appearances given the threat the virus posed to him. He has also acknowledged his age and the effects it was having on his work in *Also a History of Philosophy*, which was published shortly after his ninetieth birthday in 2019. In its preface he notes that he wanted to bring the narrative up to the present, but had to leave off at the beginning of the twentieth century since going any further "would have required at least another volume, and my strength is simply no longer sufficient for that (*dafür reichen meine Kräfte nicht mehr aus*)."[22]

One can only imagine that his strength has further diminished in the years since. Despite this admission, Habermas has regularly continued to publish articles for German newspapers. Given his advanced age, a growing number of these post–2020 pieces are tributes and remembrances of friends and colleagues, all too often upon the occasion of their deaths.[23]

That being said, Habermas has certainly not limited himself to such laudatios. In September 2022, sixty years after he first released the German edition of *Structural Transformation of the Public Sphere*, Habermas published *A New Structural Transformation of the Public Sphere and Deliberative Politics* (*Ein neuer Strukturwandel der Öffentlichkeit und die deliberative Politik*).[24] This short book is clearly theoretical, not political. However, this "new engagement with an old theme" also signals his continued belief in the importance of the quality of deliberation for democratic legitimacy, especially at a time when "the signs of political regression are there for everyone to see."[25]

Although his production of political texts has gradually slowed, Habermas has continued to comment on the major geopolitical issues, most notably Russia's full-scale invasion of Ukraine, which started on February 24, 2022, and the Israeli offensive in the Gaza Strip following Hamas's devastating terrorist attacks of October 7, 2023. In addition to reading these texts and detailing their reception (see the following two sections of this chapter), I also put them into conversation with Habermas's own philosophical conclusions regarding the broader effects of the rise of the digital public sphere. I thereby identify three new "structural transformations" that have undermined the ability of the public sphere to legitimize democratic politics since he first published the original *Structural Transformation* in 1962. These are: 1) the deterioration of the national public sphere, as the Internet has made the boundaries between publics more porous and increasingly organized them in non-national filter bubbles and echo chambers; 2) the loss of what he calls "leading media," which were able to synthesize debates and present the best arguments on both sides of every issue for public consideration; and 3) the general decline of argumentation in the public sphere as platform-based social media increasingly encourage appearance over argument, self-promotion over engagement, and immediate reactions over deliberation.

Building on my analysis of Habermas's recent work *on* and *for* the public sphere, I suggest that, in retrospect, Habermas—who most fully developed the concept of the philosopher as public intellectual in modern democratic life—may well turn out to be its last representative. This is obviously an overly categorical—perhaps even polemical—claim, especially given the new avenues social media has opened for philosophers to intervene in public discourse. However, given the changes brought about by the digitalization of the public sphere, I conclude that it is unlikely any future figure will be able to use the written word—published in the leading media of the public sphere—to shape public discourse in their native country (and increasingly on their native continent) as powerfully as Habermas has been able to do over the course of his long career.

This argument may seem to undercut the rationale for studying Habermas as a public intellectual. However, in the conclusion to this chapter (and this book), I make the case that the loss of the external preconditions that made the public intellectual possible in the first place actually raise the stakes of contemporary debates about the role of the philosopher in democratic life and the proper relationship of theory to practice in the twenty-first century. While it may no longer be possible to follow Habermas's solution to these problems, his development of both his theory and his practice of the public intellectual is still a valuable source of insights for philosophers who want to engage in public affairs in the new context of the digital public sphere.

HABERMAS'S LEVELHEADEDNESS ON UKRAINE

Given his own experience of World War II and of the rupture that followed in its wake, Habermas, in his interventions as a public intellectual, has not only played a key role in shaping Germany's postwar memory culture but has also been a key supporter of the EU's development of "a multilateral and legally regulated international order" that rejects the "stupid and costly alternative of war."[26] Despite his stated support for the first Iraq war in 1991, which was backed by a UN mandate, as well as NATO's bombing campaign in Yugoslavia in 1999, in general he has held fast to his conclusion regarding "the obsolescence of war as a category of world history."[27] As a result, it is not surprising that the full-scale invasion of Ukraine ordered by Vladimir Putin on February 24, 2022 came as a shock to Habermas.

On April 29, just two months after the start of the invasion, Habermas published a piece entitled "War and Indignation (*Krieg und Empörung*)" in the *Süddeutsche Zeitung*.[28] In it, he bemoans how the conflict "unleashed arbitrarily (*willkürlich*) by Russia" has resulted in "the new scenes of raw destruction and shocking suffering produced each day." While one might assume that such images would have a greater impact on younger cohorts who grew up in an unprecedented era of peace in Europe, Habermas makes the opposite claim. He contends that the impact of Russia's full-scale invasion "may exert a greater impact on the elderly among us," given their that these images were likely to trigger traumatic memories of the conflicts that they experienced in the first half of the twentieth century. Additionally, he notes that while younger cohorts are used to following humanitarian disasters online and on their smartphones, older generations—including his own—are less accustomed to seeing such images broadcast in real time.

This observation about the generational dynamics sets up the rest of his argument, which pushes back against "*the self-assurance* with which the morally indignant accusers in Germany are going after an introspective and reserved federal government" for not immediately providing Ukraine with the weapons it needed to repel its neighbor's invasion. It is explicitly addressed to German Foreign Minister Annalena Baerbock of the Greens, who he sees as the example par excellence of this transformation among younger cohorts, given her strong support for immediately delivering heavier weapons to Ukraine. What is interesting about this critique is—as Philipp Felsch observes in his recent biography—that "it comes from Habermas of all people, since he contributed like no other to formulating the normative guidelines to which Annalena Baerbock's generation refers."[29]

Habermas sympathizes with the plight of the Ukrainians as well as with the widespread desire to assist them. However, given Germany's lamentable historical record of aggression, particularly in the territories of Ukraine and Russia during the Third Reich's 1941 invasion of the Soviet Union, he thinks it is reasonable for German Chancellor Olaf Scholz to take some time to consider his options. In particular, as a self-proclaimed "political pacifist" whose "prime concern is abolishing the set of institutions that enable and perpetuate the existence of war," he worries that the overly aggressive support of Ukraine will not only reinvigorate the nationalist identities that he opposes, but may also "fears that the values and self-understandings that made war normal will return, dragging us back into a more violent time."[30]

This positioning has the added benefit of also allowing the public to form opinions about whether Germany should abandon its longstanding postwar practice of blocking the sale or transfer of lethal weapons to conflict zones. Habermas's support of what many considered to be the chancellor's dithering might even have had an effect on Scholz's thinking: the leader of the Social Democrats has admitted that despite having little use for theory, Marxist or otherwise, "Habermas is the exception, I could always get a lot from him."[31]

In addition to aligning with his procedural account of democratic legitimacy, which requires political leaders to make decisions in a way that is responsive to the open deliberations conducted in the public sphere, this reluctance is also consistent at a substantive level with the positions Habermas took as a public intellectual during the original *Historikerstreit* of the 1980s and in the reunification debates that followed. At that time, Habermas expressed concern that decisions made unilaterally by Chancellor Kohl to relativize the Holocaust and transform the Federal Republic into a "normal" nation-state would lead it to abandon the unique, diplomacy-based, multilateral approach to foreign policy that it had developed through reflection on the meaning of the *Nazizeit* for the present.[32] In 2022, Habermas restated this same concern, noting that sending lethal weapons to Ukraine "heralds a historic shift (*Zeitenwende*) in the German postwar mentality—a hard-won mentality that has repeatedly been denounced from the right—and thus the end of the broad pro-dialogue, peacekeeping focus of German policy."

From this perspective, Habermas's initial intervention in support of Chancellor Scholz's *Besonnenheit* (level-headedness, sobriety) is understandable, given his view of the FRG's unique, historically informed post–World War II approach to foreign policy as "a historical achievement."[33] It is also in line with his position in the "new *Historikerstreit*" that had played out over the previous few years (see the epilogue to chapter 6). As part of that debate, he accepted that greater recognition of Germany's colonial legacy required "not an exculpation (*Entlastung*) of responsibility, but a shift in the balance" that would enable German citizens to incorporate new learning processes based on these other historical crimes into their collective self-understanding without diminishing the lessons—or the unique importance—of the Holocaust for that self-understanding.[34]

In addition to ensuring that the decision to support Ukraine is made in a way that allows sufficient time for debate and fully considers Germany's historical legacy, Habermas also draws on his personal memories of the Cold War, when the nuclear threat hung over the world like the sword of Damocles. He therefore reminds younger readers unfamiliar with this situation "that a war against a nuclear power can no longer be 'won' in any reasonable sense, at least not with the means of military force within the limited timeline of a hot conflict." As a result, he argues that the West must take Putin's indeterminate threats to deploy nuclear weapons—"indeterminate because it depends on Putin's own definition"— seriously if the West interferes too much, given the consequences if it does not.

In light of his commitment to the constitutionalization of international law, part of Habermas would certainly like to see the Russian president put on trial at The Hague for crimes against humanity. However, he notes that current policy must take into account that the "end of the war, or at least a cease-fire, must still be negotiated with him (i.e., Putin)." While distasteful, this is a reality the West cannot ignore. Habermas drives this point home by quoting his friend, the philosopher and filmmaker Alexander Kluge: "War can only teach us to make peace." While Habermas's critics have often accused him of being an idealist, in this case he appears to adopt the kind of realist position he spent much of his career opposing.

Like many of the political writings highlighted in this book, this intervention provoked a "huge brouhaha (*gewaltigen Wirbel*)," including fervent attacks from the left, that is, "from within what he must have thought was his camp."[35] Similarly, as has been the case with much (if not most) of his work as a public intellectual, Habermas's position was received with more rejection than agreement. Ultimately, this uproar appears to have had little effect on public debate in his homeland, as the German government agreed to begin sending lethal weapons to Ukraine shortly thereafter. However, as Felsch observes, "what is remarkable about his comments on the Ukraine war is not their supposed pacifism or defeatism, but the implicit admission that he has completely lost faith in the possibility of a global domestic policy (*Weltinnenpolitik*)," an idea he has consistently defended in his public-facing writings since his turn to European and global affairs in the mid-1990s.[36]

Following this initial salvo, Habermas remained silent for a time. However, as Stefan Müller-Doohm points out, "He simply cannot help himself from speaking out (*Er kann gar nicht anders, als sich zu äußern*)."[37] On February 14, 2023, just ten days before the first anniversary of the conflict, Habermas published another commentary in the *Süddeutsche Zeitung*, this time bearing the title "A Plea for Negotiations."[38] At the start of this second intervention, Habermas notes that "the war started by Putin . . . is a symptom of a regression behind the historically achieved level of civilized interaction between powers . . . that have been able to learn their lesson from the two world wars."

However, despite this admission Habermas's basic position has not changed. On the contrary, he continues to bemoan the fact that "the armament process seems to be acquiring a momentum of its own." He therefore writes again to "add my own voice" to those "making themselves heard not only to defend the Chancellor's stance but also to plead for public reflection on the difficult path to negotiations" to "prevent a prolonged war from claiming even more lives and causing even more destruction."

Even at this point, Habermas continues to maintain that the statement " 'Ukraine must not lose the war!' " is correct. What *has* changed over the course of the first year of the conflict—according to Habermas—is the asymmetry of the nuclear threat. He argues that previously it had been "entirely up to the Russian leadership to define at what point it considers the extent and quality of Western arms deliveries to constitute entering into war." However, after Russia's ally China declared its opposition to the use of nuclear, biological, and chemical weapons in Ukraine in the autumn of 2022, he believes that the one-sided Russian threat has receded. In his view, this opens space for the West to reconsider its position as well. Habermas therefore argues that it is time for Ukraine's supporters to take the initiative by starting to have a serious discussion about the prerequisites for a negotiated settlement to the conflict, since they "share moral responsibility for casualties and destruction caused by [their] weapons."

Given the tenor of public debate at the time—which was buoyed both by Ukraine's surprising success in repelling Russia's armed forces and growing optimism about the prospects of a counteroffensive by new Ukrainian battalions armed by and trained in the West—Habermas's second intervention was met with a response similar to his first. In a subsequent interview, Habermas sought to clarify his position, noting that what "really irked me" were the "bellicose reflexes" and "uninhibited emotional identification with the event of war . . .

[and] the Ukrainians' inflamed national consciousness." While understandable in light of the Ukrainian struggle against what he admits is clearly an unjust and illegal invasion, this metamorphosis shocked Habermas, given both how quickly it had occurred and how little public debate accompanied it. As he points out, in the Federal Republic "we needed half a century to achieve the necessary critical distance from our own nationalistic past," only for what he sees as a fundamental and welcome historical learning process to be reversed almost overnight with the onset of "a highly emotionalized war mentality."[39]

Most recently—at the time of this writing, at least—on March 24, 2025, Habermas published a third essay on Ukraine, entitled "An Appeal for Europe (*Ein Appell für Europa*)" in the *Süddeutsche Zeitung*.[40] Unlike his first two pieces on this conflict, in which he defended Germany's rather halting response to the Russian invasion, in this essay Habermas immediately makes clear that "Europe, with the help of the United States, had to come to the assistance of Ukraine under attack in order to secure its existence as a state quickly enough." However, after this admission, he returns to his conviction that the "flag-waving war cries and full-throated aspirations of 'victory' over a nuclear power like Russia" were a mistake that displayed "a lack of critical awareness" of the situation at hand. Rather than seeking to support Ukraine's aspirations to reclaim all the territory it had lost since the start of the crisis in 2014, including the Crimean peninsula, he observes, "It would also have been in the West's own interest to try to negotiate as quickly as possible with Russia, an irrational imperial power long in decline, an arrangement acceptable to Ukraine, but this time with Western guarantees."

While the situation on the battlefield had changed little since Habermas's previous intervention, this is his first commentary since Donald Trump was sworn in as US president for a second time two months earlier, on January 20. President Trump's inauguration represents a fundamental transformation of geopolitics, as "Trump's unprincipled pandering to Putin is currently dividing the West and calling into question the normatively justified reasons for supporting Ukraine." Building on critiques dating back to the Eurozone Crisis, Habermas takes "European leaders, and especially the German leaders" to task, first for having "turned a blind eye to a convulsion of the democratic system that has been brewing in the United States for some time," and second, for having "repeatedly shirked the long-evident challenge of strengthening the European Union's capacity for international action."

While Habermas does not object to calls for German and European rearmament, he notes that this policy shift should not be primarily directed toward supporting Ukraine: "Rather, the overall goal of this rearmament is the existential self-assertion of a European Union that can no longer count on the protection of the United States in an increasingly unpredictable geopolitical situation." Returning to points he originally made in an article cosigned by Jacques Derrida shortly before Derrida's death during the buildup to the second Iraq War in 2003, Habermas notes that the "member states of the European Union must strengthen and pool their military forces, because otherwise they will no longer count politically in a geopolitically turbulent and disintegrating world." Noting that the United States was now negotiating with Russia over the heads not only of Ukraine but, "irritatingly," also of the EU, he adds that the EU "will only gain geopolitical independence if it is able to act collectively, including in the use of military force."

On one level, as I have already pointed out, the vehement response provoked by Habermas's three commentaries on Ukraine is in line with the public reaction to most of his interventions. However, on another level, these recent texts—and the responses they elicited—display interesting characteristics that point to fundamental transformations in the public sphere. For most of Habermas's career as a public intellectual (and except in some cases where he initially published texts in non-German sources), his political writings appeared in German newspapers. As a result, not only were his contributions primarily directed to the public discourse of the FRG, but this was also the context in which they had their primary effect. While many of these works were later translated, this did not affect their political reception, as the foreign language versions often appeared years later in collections of his writing directed primarily to a scholarly audience.

At first glance, Habermas's interventions on Ukraine follow this trajectory. All were initially published in German in the *Süddeutsche Zeitung*, one of Germany's leading mainstream newspapers. Based in Munich near his home in Bavaria, this progressive-liberal, center-left newspaper, which aligns with the core principles of social democracy, has become Habermas's preferred outlet for his political writings following the Euro-crisis.

The content of these two pieces—as well as the context I outlined above—makes clear that the arguments Habermas presents are directed primarily to readers in Germany. In contrast to most of his previous interventions, however, the *Süddeutsche Zeitung* immediately published an official English-language translation of both of these articles on its website. While this decision allowed a much broader range of readers to access Habermas's arguments, it also removed them from the specifically German milieu for which they were written, transposing them into a global debate about the war in Ukraine that has very different contours from the one Habermas originally addressed.

The effect of this was immediately visible in the emergence of an international reception to Habermas's texts, developing online alongside the German one in real time.[41] However, this response was largely decontextualized—or even *mis*contextualized—as international respondents used Habermas's arguments to intervene in internal debates within their national public spheres, as well as in their own transnational online communities. The international reception then also boomeranged back into the German debate, as some particularly prominent responses to Habermas were subsequently translated and republished in leading German-language media.[42] This might help to explain why, following this debate, Habermas admitted to one of his biographers that "he had the feeling 'for the first time (*zum ersten Mal*)' in his life that he no longer understood the reactions of the German public."[43]

These structural changes in the reception of Habermas's political writings are directly related to the rise of digital technologies and their effects on the public sphere. In line with the first major transformation of the digital public sphere highlighted above, Habermas's sense that he no longer understands the reactions of "the German public" are also likely tied to the increasing porosity of national public spheres with the rise of the Internet. The growth of the digital social media ecosystem has thus not only led to an increasing mixture of local and global discourses, but it has also made it more difficult to address a major issue for a national audience without it being picked up and (mis)used in other contexts.

The fact that German discourses can no longer be isolated from a broader, digitally mediated transnational public sphere is further reinforced by the other two trends identified at the beginning of this chapter. For example, the *Süddeutsche Zeitung*'s decision to simultaneously publish English translations is directly linked to its increasing need to compete for clicks and international advertising revenue at a time when traditional newspapers are under growing threat. Instead of shaping debates by synthesizing arguments and highlighting key points, this previously leading medium of the German public sphere now has to compete for attention online. In doing so, it also feeds online debates that favor immediate reactions—ones that can quickly spread online in the form of selective quotations and sound bites—over the rational argument and deliberation that Habermas highlights as the key democratic function of the public sphere. These dynamics are even more visible when the uproar causes by Habermas's statement is put into conversation with his theoretical work on the *New Structural Transformation*.

A STATEMENT OF PRINCIPLES ON GAZA AND ANTI-SEMITISM

This dynamic of digital decontextualization is even more prominent in the response to Habermas's brief comment on Israel and Palestine. A year and a half after Putin's invasion of Ukraine, the world was shocked again by the unprecedented attack on Israel by Hamas on October 7, 2023. Once more, Habermas could not help himself.

This time, however, rather than writing his own intervention, he instead chose to sign a statement published on the web page of the research center "Normative Orders," which is codirected by his former doctoral student, Rainer Forst. In "Principles of Solidarity (*Grundsätze der Solidarität*)," cosigned by Forst as well as two other leaders of Normative Orders, Nicole Deitelhoff and Klaus Günther, the statement addresses the "rightly understood solidarity with Israel and Jews in Germany."[44] After acknowledging that Israel's justified response to Hamas's attack must abide by the principles of proportionality, the protection of civilians, and the prospect of future peace, the four cosignatories note, "Despite all the concern for the fate of the Palestinian population, however, the standards of judgement slip completely when genocidal intentions are attributed to Israel's actions."

The fact that this universal statement of principles is directed primarily to the German context becomes clear in the third and final paragraph, which notes, "Israel's actions in no way justify anti-Semitic reactions, especially not in Germany." For the cosignatories, "The democratic ethos of the Federal Republic of Germany . . . is linked to a political culture for which Jewish life and Israel's right to exist are central elements worthy of special protection in light of the mass crimes of the Nazi era." As a result, they call on "all those in our country who have cultivated anti-Semitic sentiments . . . and now see a welcome opportunity to express them" to respect the basic protections against racist defamation enshrined in the Germany's Basic Law.

In a manner similar to Habermas's interventions on Russia's invasion of Ukraine, this text addresses a highly specific German debate about Israel and anti-Semitism.[45] In the wake of the Hamas attack on October 7, Germany—like much of the rest of the world—experienced a period of rising anti-Semitic violence, with physical attacks on Jews as well as symbolic acts, including the drawing of swastikas and Stars of David on Jewish businesses and homes, reminiscent of the treatment of Jews during the early stages of the Third Reich. Among the more visible incidents was the attempted firebombing of a Berlin synagogue.[46]

In the birthplace of Nazism and in light of Germany's unprecedented attempts to preserve the collective memory of *Kristallnacht*, such events were particularly shocking to someone like Habermas, given his own commitment to keeping the Holocaust at the center of German historical consciousness and national identity.

This is the specific context in which the statement, whose style and prose suggest it was written by at least one of the other signatories before being cosigned by Habermas, appeared on the Normative Orders website on November 13. Although the fact that he appears not to have been involved in drafting this text does not absolve Habermas from responsibility for its contents, it is important to consider the climate of rising anti-Semitic violence *as well as* the growing Islamophobia and the persecution of pro-Palestinian solidarity communities and intellectuals after October 7. Both are crucial to understanding the volatile moment in which this statement first appeared.

Unfortunately, much like his commentaries on Ukraine, this statement was also immediately divorced from their national context, as the text was simultaneously released in both German and English on the Normative Orders web page, thus inviting commentary from a broader, more international audience. On one level, this decontextualization may not be problematic, since the intervention claims to be a statement of "principles that should not be disputed." Given the Kantian background of the signatories, these principles are presumably universal and applicable in any context.

However, such a universalization is also highly problematic, as the very next sentence of the statement notes that these principles are intended merely to provide "the basis of a rightly understood solidarity with Israel and Jews *in Germany*" (emphasis mine). As a result, unlike many of Habermas's previous interventions in the public sphere, which apply his universalistic philosophy to a concrete local context, this text draws conclusions that are simultaneously ultra-specific and highly universal. To a certain extent, this "dialectic of universalism and particularism" reflects the way Habermas has always sought to put his "timeless-generalistic (*Überzeitlich-Allgemeine*)" philosophy into practice in his interventions as a public intellectual, which are always attuned to the specific historical situation, most often to the "spiritual terrain of the Federal Republic."[47]

In this case, however, I argue that the tension between universality and specificity is too great to be sustainable. In particular, it is unclear how Habermas's longstanding commitment to the constitutionalization of international law, dating back to the 1990s, can be squared with the statement's claim that standards "slip completely when genocidal intentions are attributed to Israel's actions." Most notable among these developments is the International Court of Justice's Order of January 26, 2024, which finds that "at least some of the acts and omissions alleged . . . to have been committed by Israel in Gaza appear to be capable of falling within the provisions of the Convention."[48] Does this conclusion violate the standards of judgment laid out in the Normative Orders statement? Or would the finding of *prima facie* evidence that Israel might have committed acts of genocide in Gaza count as an anti-Semitic statement that violates those standards only if a German court had reached this decision?

Based on the short text, the answer is unclear. However, when asked how he could reconcile this sentiment with his long-standing hopes for a more cosmopolitan condition, Habermas wearily replied, "That is all in the past (*Das ist alles Vergangenheit*)."[49] Combined with his increasing realism regarding Russia's war of choice in Ukraine, this response suggests that he has been affected by a broader loss of hope, bordering on pessimism, though he quickly notes that "defeatism should not be allowed to be the final word!"[50]

In addition to reflecting dynamics of decontextualization within the digital public sphere highlighted above, both this "Statement of Principles" and the reactions to it also display another characteristic that distinguishes online discourses from the virtues of the traditional public sphere: the way they incentivize users to respond immediately, publicly, and tersely to events in real time. The basic problem for Habermas (and his three cosignatories) is that, while social media platforms—like the one formerly known as Twitter—are still primarily textual, they are not modes of communication designed to facilitate dialogue in the public sphere. Instead, they encourage performative engagement, which is not driven by the Habermasian regulative ideal of "the unforced force of the better argument" but by self-promotion measured in clicks and followers.

Habermas is well aware of the role that promotional dynamic despite the fact that he admits to not using or fully understanding these technologies (a fact that is not surprising given his age). He was confronted by this personally in 2025 when Google's Deep Mind research department developed a conflict resolution tool they called the "Habermas machine," which was designed to "improve collective decision-making across various domains" by incorporating dissenting voices into the statements it generates. The creators named it after Habermas, attributing to him claim that "when rational people deliberate under idealized conditions, agreement will emerge in the public sphere."[51]

However, this is a misreading of Habermas's theory, as he never argues that deliberation will lead to agreement. Instead, as he pointed out after learning of the Habermas machine's existence, he does not call on participants in discourse to agree, but instead "to undertake the demanding task of a sensitive mutual adoption of perspectives, from which he or she can assess their own interests and value orientations . . . and, if necessary, adapt them." In an email exchange with the journalist Matthias Pfeffer, later published in the *Süddeutsche Zeitung*, Habermas notes that Google's association of the project with his name was "misleading (*irreführend*)" and "obviously done for the purposes of advertising."[52]

The changes in the design and functioning of digital technology (not the mention the rise of large language models—often spuriously referred to as artificial intelligence) brought about by the rise of the Internet affect not only public discourse more generally but also scholarly debate. On one level, given their desire for attention, it is perhaps not surprising that academics are eager to engage with social media—a forum that encourages participating "in superficial polemic, in games of one-upmanship in what looks like theoretical contestation about sophisticated things but is often a contest for digital charisma."[53] While this may reflect merely an intellectual *déformation professionnelle*, it is also increasingly the result of structural factors. In addition to being good teachers and researchers, scholars around the world are increasingly being asked to engage in publicity.

In part, this response is about individual scholars seeking to build their personal "brand." It is true that Habermas himself has long been identified as a "trademark" in the German public sphere and increasingly internationally as well (as the naming of the Habermas machine makes clear). However, whereas for him this position was associated with his role as a "guardian of rationality," developing a brand on social media is tied more to the number of followers and the amount of engagement a scholar can generate.[54] Rather than serving the social function of improving public debate, as Habermas seeks to do, such activities in online discourse are explicitly geared toward generating new professional opportunities through media appearances and book deals.

This move is further encouraged by universities seeking to demonstrate their influence and the ways their employees "impact" the broader community outside the ivory tower. It is visible in the rising number of media positions available at both the faculty and department levels dedicated to promoting the institution and its members online. The result is that the adage "publish or perish" is increasingly morphing into "promote or perish."[55]

Combined with the short, immediate reactions induced by the structural features of social media, the growing pressure for self-promotion fundamentally alters the incentives that govern how scholars engage in broader social discourse. In contrast to Habermasian public intellectuals, who write long texts in established media in order to improve the quality of opinion-formation by introducing or amplifying important arguments in the public sphere, online self-promotional intellectuals are encouraged to provide controversial, reactionary "hot takes" on whatever topic is trending that day in order to grow their digital profiles.

In an economy where attention is the main currency, this practice replaces the traditional model of generating arguments and counterarguments. Instead, the design features of digital media encourage the production of sound bites that reverberate past each other in competing echo chambers and filter bubbles.[56] The result is that the opportunity to "dunk" on a figure like Habermas in a reactionary, performative mode is almost irresistible, as his prominence increases the likelihood that a comment will "go viral," particularly if the respondent is quick enough to be among the first to post about it.[57]

These issues are not limited to the response to the text; they are also visible within it. While Habermas has no direct presence on social media, "Principles of Solidarity" still exhibits some the features typical of contemporary commentary designed for these platforms. These include not only the immediate translation into English but also the brevity of the text, which makes it easier to repost screenshots of key passages. Yet the ensuing debate also highlights the difficulty of conducting reasoned argument in this medium.

This issue is clearly visible in Deitelhoff's public reaction to the brouhaha over the statement on social media. While the text is clear and makes some good points, it failed to meaningfully affect online discourse. This is partly because it was written in German. Additionally, while Deitelhoff's response might have been clear if published in a traditional newspaper or even a blog, it fell short as a social media post, since reading the thread requires clicking through twenty separate posts whose sentences often break awkwardly from one to the next.[58]

These preliminary reflections highlight how certain design features of the digital public sphere threaten the existence of the Habermasian public intellectual. Interestingly, in addition to commenting on public affairs in this new medium, Habermas has also simultaneously theorized its impact on the public sphere itself. In this sense, just as the 1962 text of the original *Structural Transformation* can be read as a reflection on the conditions of possibility for his own political engagement, the same is true of his 2022 *New Structural Transformation*. Thus, Habermas has not only consistently participated in debate in the public sphere but has also consistently sought to theorize it.

In reflecting on what has changed over the last two decades, Habermas highlights the shift from traditional leading *media* (newspapers, magazines, etc.) to digital *platforms*. Whereas the former curated contributions to the public sphere as a service to readers, the new media serve primarily as stages on which authors can publish, without taking responsibility for the quality or content of these posts. On the one hand, Habermas recognizes that the decline of traditional media, where journalists and editors exercised a "gatekeeper function," is welcome insofar as it opens public debate more directly to new voices. However, it does so in ways that encourage decontextualization and attention-grabbing, reactionary polemic. In this sense, the loss of "the professional selection and discursive examination of contents based on generally accepted cognitive standards," as Habermas points out, "profoundly alters the character of public communication itself."[59] I conclude that these changes pose a fundamental challenge to the conditions of possibly that enabled the rise of the public intellectual.

THE LAST PUBLIC INTELLECTUAL?

In the preceding pages of this book, I have argued that Habermas's *Kleine politische Schriften*—and his work as a public intellectual and engaged critical theorist more generally—should be treated as an integral part of his corpus because his political engagement aligns with his broader theoretical framework.[60] The consistency of his indirect account of the relationship between theory and practice is also what separates him from so many other intellectuals, who are either unwilling or unable to integrate their political commentaries and their academic work into a coherent whole. Habermas's ability to do so forms the basis for my claim that his understudied and underappreciated political writings deserve more attention—both in their own right and as part of his lifelong commitment to acting as "an engaged public intellectual in the very same 'political public sphere' that he theorized as a philosopher."[61]

Over the course of both his equally long *Beruf* as a philosopher/theoretical sociologist and *Nebenberuf* as a public intellectual, Habermas "has shaped political debates in the old Federal Republic like no one else," in large part due to his "positions on the politics of memory (*Vergangenheitspolitischen Positionen*)"[62] Given the nodal role that he has played in shaping postwar Germany's political culture and its public sphere since the end of World War II, it easy to assume in retrospect that the FRG is a something of a Habermasian Republic. However, this is a revisionist perspective that ignores the rejection with which most of his political positions have been met in his homeland.

Although Habermas is accorded a certain respect as the *éminence grise* of the German public sphere, this recognition is more visible in the vehemence with which he is attacked than in the agreement his interventions find. For every word of praise hailing him as the "state philosopher (*Staatsphilosoph*)" or "formative intellectual (*prägende Intellektuelle*)," who shaped the "self-understanding of the Federal Republic," there are many other less complementary voices denouncing him as the "hothead of Frankfurt (*Frankfurter Feuerkopf*)," who seeks to exert a "dictatorship" over the German public sphere.[63] Even the oft-quoted reference to Habermas as the "Hegel of the Federal Republic," which may appear complementary at first glance, really seeks to tar him as a conservative thinker of the status quo who has little to teach the left.[64]

One of his harshest German critics, Peter Sloterdijk, makes this point polemically, arguing that Habermas "practices cultural hegemony."[65] It is true that Habermas's explicit rejection of the "role of a central moral and intellectual authority" and his claims to simply be protecting the quality of argumentation in public debate both stand in tension with "his recurrent attempts to steer the German polity in his preferred left-liberal direction."[66] While he has indeed succeeded in rallying the left in certain cases, most notably in the *Historikerstreit*, he has failed even more frequently across a whole range of issues, including not only German unification, but also rearmament and the democratization of the EU, to name just a few of the most prominent examples. Very often, Habermas has even been rejected by his allies on the left, as the responses to his statements on Ukraine and Gaza make clear.

While Sloterdijk's claim that "whole left-liberal bloc consists of faint Habermasians" is provocative, there is little evidence to back his contention that Habermas maintains "a monologically overstretched concept of truth which takes great pains to appear in dialogical camouflage."[67] It is indeed the case that in his public commentaries Habermas has "frequently and consciously made use of the arsenal of weapons used in ideological warfare" in ways that hardly seem to fit with his philosophical ideal of rational discourse aimed at "mutual understanding

(*Verständigung*)."⁶⁸ However, this contrast is unhelpful, as it compares two different value spheres (public discourse versus academic debate) in which Habermas plays different roles (that of the public intellectual and the researcher, respectively)—each with its own internal logic. Even when narrowing the scope down to his work as a public intellectual, his openness to dialogue and exchange—caustic as some of these interactions may be—makes it probably more accurate to describe him as "a living testimony of the principles of dialogue and communication that are so fundamental in [his] work." This confirms Richard Bernstein's conclusion that in Habermas's case, "The Praxis was [is!—PJV] commensurate with the Theory."⁶⁹

Despite his best attempts to control the reception of his work by choosing where and when he intervenes in political debates, Habermas has never been able to dictate how he is situated within the public sphere. This is even more true today given the changes this institution has experienced since the 1950s. As Joseph Schumpeter predicted in his 1942 "Sociology of Intellectuals," the expansion of education and access to media has indeed led to a dramatic rise in the number of intellectuals.⁷⁰ The development of the Internet has further reinforced this trend, as these digital media do not generate their content centrally in the manner of newspapers, broadcast television and other legacy media, but instead merely provide platforms for would-be intellectuals to share their expertise with the broader public (in addition to contributions by bots and large language models based on machine learning).

However, he was wrong in expecting that this growth of the intelligentsia would lead them to their strengthen their critique of capitalism. On the contrary, as Axel Honneth, points out, the social expansion Schumpeter accurately predicted has instead "produced a normalization of the role of the intellectual not only in a quantitative but also in a qualitative sense." Rather than analyzing and critiquing the way problems are framed within public discourse, Honneth argues that the "normalized intellectuals" of the twenty-first century merely position themselves on questions of day-to-day politics, instead of questioning "the premises of publicly accepted problem descriptions" and interrogating "what can be said in public."⁷¹ As a result, he contends that the link between the work of public intellectuals and social criticism has been decisively ruptured.

While Honneth's basic thesis about the "normalization" of intellectuals in an increasingly digital public sphere may be correct, his claim that the link between public intellectuals and social criticism "is definitively broken" does not apply to Habermas.⁷² While in certain cases Habermas merely positions himself with the already accepted categories of public discourse, in many others he indeed seeks to change the very conversation itself by drawing attention to new topics or framing them in a different light. For example, in calling out Chancellor Kohl for trying to change German memory politics without proper public conversation during the *Historikerstreit*, his work as a public intellectual was also a form of social criticism. By contrast, although Habermas claims to have "criticized the SPD all my life" despite seeing himself "as a left social democrat," his recent defenses of Chancellor Scholz's policy on Ukraine are much more "normalized" in the sense that they merely take a position within an existing public debate.[73]

Despite the fact not all the contributions Habermas has made as a public intellectual qualify as social criticism, a good number of his political writings do indeed try to achieve what Siegfried Kracauer refers to as "the destruction of all mythical powers around and within us." By seeking the "dismantling of natural forces"—i.e. the seemingly inescapably basic assumptions that shape the accepted conceptual frameworks of public discourse and hold it captive—many of Habermas's interventions go beyond the standardized, normalized intellectual discourse of the twenty-first century.[74] The fact that Habermas succeeds in breaking through in this way is surprising, given that he has not fully taken advantage of many of the avenues for impact available in the twentieth century—let alone the twenty-first. For example, although television and radio were established media for most of his career—and were even used by his mentor, Adorno, in his work as a public intellectual—Habermas has remained committed to "the published word" as the "decisive mark" of the public sphere.[75]

Nor has he sought to dumb down his ideas for public consumption. Instead, he builds extensively on the theoretical vocabulary he develops in his philosophical writings. In this way, he draws on what Honneth refers to as the "tool that no doubt most often finds application in social criticism," i.e., "the coining of catchy formulas in which a complex explanation of social processes is compressed and given expression in a single denominator."[76] Examples of such ideas that cross over from Habermas's philosophy into his political writings include not only the aforementioned "colonization of the lifeworld (*Kolonialisierung der Lebenswelt*)," but also "the unforced force of the better argument (*der zwanglose Zwang des besseren Arguments*)," "communication free of domination (*herrschaftsfreie Kommunikation*)" and "constitutional patriotism (*Verfassungspatriotismus*)."

While these ideas indeed act as "advertising slogans (*Werbeslogans*)" for his work, by linking his public statements to social criticism that goes beyond the minutiae of day-to-day politics, Habermas, as a public intellectual, is trying to elevate the quality of public discourse by reframing arguments and exposing fundamental issues that would otherwise remain hidden. He certainly does not always succeed in doing so. But these attempts demonstrate his commitment to enhancing the quality of public discourse in ways that can not only transform social perceptions but also bring about changes in social reality itself. From this perspective, the core goal of Habermas's political writings is to ensure that the public is "in a position to stake its claim against other social forces . . . through a wide range of democratic forums and institutions."[77]

These choices make Habermas something of "an unlikely hero."[78] There can be little doubt, however, that despite these self-imposed disadvantages, as a public intellectual he "represents more th[an] anybody else the tradition of the grand public debate."[79] However, as I already suggested, the ability of the Habermasian public intellectual to improve the quality of public debate is waning, largely due to the "new" structural transformations of public discourse that he reflects on in his recent book revisiting his classic 1962 study of the public sphere.

At first glance, this claim may not appear very interesting or especially controversial. After all, a discourse of decline has accompanied the public intellectual for much of the twentieth century—long before social media influencers replaced the pundit (who putatively replaced the public intellectual in the second half of the century).[80] Similarly, a discourse of deterioration has been a permanent feature of debates about the public sphere, long predating Habermas's own influential accounts of the developments threatening open, public discussion of key principles and values. Writing in 1997, Seyla Benhabib observes:

> theories of the public sphere, from Walter Lippmann to Hannah Arendt, from John Dewey to Juergen Habermas, appear to be afflicted by a nostalgic trope: once there was a public sphere of action and deliberation, participation and collective decision-making, today there no longer is one; or if a public sphere still exists it is so distorted, weakened, and corrupted as to be a pale recollection of what once was.[81]

These premature obituaries highlight the dangers of declaring the age of the intellectual at an end; nevertheless, there are good reasons to believe that this may indeed be the case this time. I have already commented on some of the features that made Habermas a unique figure in the "classical" public sphere of the twentieth century. These include not only his position as both a leading thinker of that sphere and a theorist of the relationship between theory and practice through the concept of *Öffentlichkeit*, but also his commitment to a role separation between his work as a social critic and as an academic—such that his status in the latter domain does not confer undue authority in the former. In his view, allowing influence to seep from one domain to the other would not only blur the distinction between value spheres of politics and science but also undermine fundamental democratic equality of public discourses on concrete social and political issues.

In line with Edward Saïd's understanding of this role, Habermas is "neither a pacifier nor a consensus-builder."[82] Despite the rejection he so often experienced when taking a stand on issues important to him, he nevertheless succeed in becoming a touchstone of the German—and later the European—public sphere. However, given the structure and design of Internet platforms, it no longer appears possible for a public intellectual à la Habermas to develop the same kind of nodal status in today's digital public sphere. On the supply side, there are problems related to the internal pressures faced by increasingly "normalized" intellectuals in universities, who are encouraged to promote their academic work in public rather than approaching participation as part of their calling to think things through—and to help others to do the same. However, perhaps even more importantly, there are also demand-side issues that make the emergence of another Habermas unlikely.

To start with, it is becoming increasingly difficult to separate the signal from the noise. In Habermas's words, the rise of digital communities and platforms "radically alter the pattern of communication that has been dominant in the public sphere until now by *empowering* all potential users . . . to become independent and equally entitled authors." While this development could be seen as emancipatory—since it allows more individuals to join the public conversation—in practice it turns the public sphere into a cacophony of voices talking past one another, as no leading media remain with the ability to select and amplify certain contributions based on their reliability, quality, and general relevance. Instead, users are more likely to participate in like-minded networks, without regard for the inclusiveness and engagement that is required by a democratic public sphere. In this sense, these platforms do not have the ability "to direct the attention of *all* citizens to the *same* problems" in the way that the leading, vintage media were able to do, however imperfectly.[83]

Conclusion 303

This problem is reinforced by the fact that even when the proprietary algorithms that govern what any given user sees online provide content from a figure like Habermas, they do so in ways that are unlikely to promote the kind of substantive engagement necessary for these interventions to "improve the lamentable level of public debates."⁸⁴ Instead of presenting whole arguments for consideration, they are likely to serve up only short extracts, selected by other users to reinforce existing positions. Thus, the "decline in the level of aspiration of the offerings" in the digital public sphere is matched by a decline in "the citizens' receptiveness and intellectual processing of politically relevant news and problems" as well.⁸⁵

This problem is reinforced by the fact that even when users are served up content from a figure like Habermas, this content is unlikely to promote the kind of substantive engagement necessary for such interventions to "improve the lamentable level of public debates."⁸⁶ Instead of finding whole arguments for consideration, users are likely to encounter only short extracts, which have been selected by other users to reinforce their existing positions. Thus, the "decline in the level of aspiration of the offerings" in the digital public sphere is matched by decline in "the citizens' receptiveness and intellectual processing of politically relevant news and problems."⁸⁷

As content shifts from reasoned debate toward entertainment, the role in which the audience is addressed changes as well. Instead of enabling access to "the discursive character of opinion and will formation of *citizens*," the digital public sphere "is adjusting to the commercial services of the platforms that are soliciting the attention of *consumers*." While such "trends towards depoliticization [i.e., addressing individuals not in their political role as citizens but in their economic function as consumers] have been observed in media research since the 1930s," it is clear that they are "evidently intensifying" at the start of the 2020s.⁸⁸

These structural transformations in the kind of content provided by the leading platforms of the digital public sphere—no longer concerned about "the *scope* and the deliberative *quality* of the offerings"—are matched by changes in what users themselves want.⁸⁹ This is evident not only in "the decline in demand for printed newspapers and magazines," but also in the rise and success of platforms like Instagram and TikTok, which focus primarily on providing images and videos to be consumed, not texts to be read.⁹⁰ Unlike Habermas, who has always been defined by "his writing talent" and has favored "the precision afforded by the written word," these new media privilege appearance over deliberation.⁹¹

Even text-based spaces like the platform formerly known as Twitter impose character limits that favor short statements over long-form reasoned argumentation, a change that aligns with the desires of most consumers. The result is that the loss of the space "for *arguments to exert their preference-altering force*" is matched by a "retreat into shielded echo chambers of the like-minded." These developments are accompanied by a decline in "the participants' orientation to reaching a consensus," in which individuals must demonstrate a "willingness to adopt each other's perspectives and to orient themselves to generalizable interests or shared values."[92]

In his lectures on the public intellectual, Saïd points out that the social critic does not seek to "make his/her audiences feel good," but instead aims "to be embarrassing, contrary, even unpleasant" in order to "represent all those people and issues that are routinely forgotten or swept under the rug."[93] This understanding of the role of the public intellectual—which Habermas largely shares—is imperiled when citizens become consumers who are not only unwilling to read texts and engage in deliberation but actively avoid such engagement in favor of entertaining content that confirms their existing opinions. These developments on both the supply and demand side undermine the structural conditions of possibility that make the classical public intellectual possible. They also help to explain why Habermas's recent interventions on both Ukraine and Israel not only failed to improve the quality of public debate, but arguably made it worse.

One of the only potentially positive aspects of the rise of digital platforms is their democratization of the voices that can be heard in public debate. As Habermas points out, "While the invention of the press gave every potential addressee the chance to eventually learn how to read, the digital revolution immediately turned *readers into potential authors*."[94] Yet even this seemingly positive development has been undermined by changes in the epistemic and political attitudes of participants who no longer see themselves as citizens but as promoters of personal brands. As a result, while a "politically appropriate perception of the author role . . . tends to increase the awareness of deficits in one's own level of knowledge," Habermas worries that just the opposite is happening on digital platforms, where users are encouraged to give unpremeditated hot takes rather than engaging in the kind of critical self-reflection that the role of the author requires.[95]

Reflecting on the impact of the printing press—and on what the history of the revolutionary creation of potential readers can teach us about the effects of the digital creation of potential authors—Habermas notes:

In Western countries, it took more or less 300 years until the bulk of the population learned to read and thereby acquired the requisite skill for participating in mass communication. How long will it take us—the educated citizens of the early 21st century and first generation of Internet users—to learn how to organize the new media and use them in the right way?[96]

This is an interesting point. After all, learning to argue well—and to do so on the basis of good evidence—is a skill that can only be acquired with time and effort. The fact that authorship on social media is driven less by quality and more by the amount of attention one is able to draw, as most authors today are paid for clicks by advertisers, means that nuance and good argumentation often take a backseat to snappy phrasing and controvertial positions that go against the grain (*Querdenken* or "lateral thinking" in German).

Perhaps the bigger problem, from the perspective of the future of the public intellectual, is not that the users of digital media platorms have not yet learned how to be authors, but that the very notion of textual authorship as such is in decline at a time when public communication increasingly takes the form of videos or images accompanied (if at all) by only short snippets of text. As a result, it increasingly appears that the role of the author is dissapearing alongside the role of the text—a trend that is only intensified by the rise of large language models that make it even more difficult to discern which contribuitons come from actual human beings and which are merely machine generated. Insofar as this is the case, it constitutes a death sentence for the notion of the classical Habermasian public intellectual, who communicates primarily through the written word.

These difficulties are reinforced by what I refer to as the "individualization of the public sphere."[97] This phenomenon captures two related features of the digital commons. First, it stems from the fact that everyone's experience of the online public sphere is unique. Unlike printed newspapers, which appeared in one or two standard editions available to all, a user's timeline on social and digital media (and increasingly their entire online experience) is specifically tailored to them by an algorithm designed to maximize engagement rather than the quality of the information presented. Since everyone's experience is unique, and thus inaccessible to others, it is becoming more and more difficult for the digital public sphere to serve as the grounding for a common "world" that can "direct the citizens' attention to the relevant issues that need to be decided and, moreover, ensure the formation of competing public opinions."[98]

In a situation where the leading media of the public sphere no longer create the shared space necessary for deliberation, the ability of the public intellectual to improve the quality of public opinion-formation wanes as well. Much has been written (including by Habermas) about the effects of online echo chambers and filter bubbles. However, the kinds of publicly accessible subcultures these terms describe, which thrived in the bygone age of the blog and are preserved in certain spaces like Reddit, are still more likely to promote conversation than the individually curated, private, closed experiences created by the algorithmic timeline that dominate Internet platforms in the second decade of the twenty-first century.[99] The fact that online advertising can be narrowly targeted in ways that are visible only to those for whom it is designed—thus fueling both mis- and disinformation—further reinforces this problem.

Under such conditions, it is not clear how the public intellectual can contribute to democratic opinion-formation once "the integrating power of the communication context . . . established by the press, radio and television" has been lost.[100] It is no exaggeration to claim that most of the reading public in Germany today has read at least some Habermas. In this sense, the label of Habermas as the "Hegel of the Federal Republic" is flawed, insofar as "Hegel could only have dreamed of a comparable public presence during his lifetime and a comparable political influence on the intellectual life of the country."[101] However, recent developments mean that it is unlikely that anyone else will be able to attain such stature based on their written contributions to public debate.

Second, the increasing individualization of the online "public" sphere means that users must decide for themselves what information they consider reliable. While legacy media were able to engage in various processes of quality control (such as vetting and fact-checking) on behalf of citizen-readers before publishing a given contribution, the rise of digital platforms has outsourced this burden to the neoliberal consumer. Moreover, the stakes of engaging with bad information are higher than they initially appear, since a click on an unreliable source activates a negative feedback loop: the algorithm subsequently feeds the user further information that reinforces this claim. As a result, the problem is not so much the loss of "the hitherto customary conceptual distinction between private and public spheres," but the fact that the public sphere is no longer mediated by actors who not only vouch for the quality of the contributions they amplify, but also ensure that this cacophony of voices is distilled into a real conversation in which the opponent address each other and debate the relevant issues at hand.[102]

In light of these fundamental structural transformations of the digital public sphere, the space for the kind of integrative social criticism that ensure that "sharpen[s] our vision for the kinds of problems that can be solved through collective action" by ensuring that "the established parameters of public discussion change to allow new political alternatives to be entertained" has disappeared.[103] This phenomenon has implications beyond the public sphere, given the crucial role that discourse plays in Habermas's political philosophy. Far from enabling the creation of a global public sphere that could move democracy to a supranational level—a move that many international relations theorists and techno-optimists attributed to him—Habermas instead sees the changes brought about by "the libertarian grimace of world-dominating digital corporations" based in Silicon Valley as leading to an " 'abolition of politics' . . . into a mode of corporate management steered by new technologies . . . intended to lead to a new form of technocratic-authoritarian rule, while largely formally retaining a constitution that has in effect been gutted."[104]

It is true that Habermas's stature and his widely recognized status as a public intellectual mean that his work still resonates broadly across the digital platforms that have replaced the leading media of the twentieth-century public sphere. However, as my analysis of his recent contributions on Ukraine and Gaza make clear, even he is no longer able to structure debate around crucial arguments and underrepresented voices in the way he once could. While Habermas himself admits that his conclusions about the digitalization of the public sphere are provisional, given that the Internet "is not my world (*ist nicht meine Welt*)," he concludes: "One thing is clear to me: today it still impossible to have a public sphere without leading media—without this core."[105]

CONCLUDING REFLECTIONS

If I am right in claiming that Habermas is the last public intellectual, then my broader project focusing on this aspect of his work may appear antiquarian at best. Indeed, Habermas himself seems to have become quite pessimistic, not only about the effects of his recent public interventions but about his broader project as a public intellectual, who has long sought to improve the quality of public debate. Speaking in September 2023, Habermas concluded that "everything that had made up his life was currently being lost 'step by step.' "

Habermas's recent calls for Europe to become "a Union capable of independent political action" so that "European countries [can] effectively bring their common global economic weight to bear in support of their normative convictions and interests" demonstrate that at some level he still believes in the European project.[106] This is also visible in his diagnosis of "the urgent need to develop a common European defense policy [that] points toward stronger European integration."[107] However, at other times he has seemingly abandoned his faith in this project. For example, in June 2024 when I asked him about his conviction that the EU could anchor a more democratic "postnational constellation," he replied: "That is all over (*dass ist alles vorbei*). I no longer believe in that."[108]

Commenting on similar statements Habermas has recently made, Felsch notes, "It is dismaying (*bestürzend*) to see Habermas—the last idealist—so fatalistic."[109] Pessimism is certainly one possible response to the interlocking crises of the present. However, the fact that the external conditions have increasingly undermined the Habermasian public intellectual does not mean that his public interventions have nothing to teach philosophers interested in the problem of theory and practice today. On the contrary, his long-standing commitment to bringing theory and practice together—and to do so in a way that does not "supplant or short circuit the democratic process," but instead contributes to it—can still provide important inspiration for contemporary attempts to resolve the social pathologies of the present.[110] I would like to conclude by reflecting on three forward-looking lessons that emerge from this study of Habermas as a public intellectual.

At the theoretical level, I contend that Habermas's ideas can help diagnose the pathologies of the present. In other words, his philosophical insights are valuable insofar as they can help us to understand how and why the rise of social media platforms has distorted not only the possibility of rational discourse guided by the "unforced force of the better argument," but also the ability to generate a truly public conversation. The regulative ideals Habermas identifies in his philosophical work are important not only for conceptualizing the problem but also for highlighting the issues underlying the social and political pathologies of the present. Even if his solution to the problem of theory and practice is no longer fit for purpose given the digitalization of the public realm, at a theoretical level his work can still help define the key normative criteria necessary for a functioning public sphere capable of grounding the legitimacy of a modern democracy, in which the majority of citizens are not and cannot be directly involved in public affairs. In this sense, as Peter Gordon points out, it is still clear that "something like the Habermasian ideal of mundane rationality in public should remain our lodestar."[111]

On a more practical level, Habermas's career as a public intellectual demonstrates that addressing the problem of theory and practice is not easy and cannot be accomplished from the armchair at the philosophical level. As my chronological study of his public interventions makes clear, it not only took Habermas thirty years to develop his mature conception of the public intellectual, but it was also costly—both intellectually and emotionally. As Habermas points out in a 2004 interview, "Taking the opportunity and, above all, making the effort (*Mühe*) to take a public stand on polarizing issues . . . [means] that you have to learn to live with hostility (*Feindseligkeiten*). And sometimes you expose yourself to decades of malice (*Häme*)."[112]

While his activity in the public sphere helped raise his stature and promote his work, it also brought its own difficulties. Habermas does not dwell on these problems, but they are evident in a number of comments he has made about the need to cultivate a certain temperament to participate in public debate. After all, from his perspective, "Anyone who enters the political public sphere and criticizes others people cannot be a crybaby himself."[113] In this sense, it is important to realize—as Habermas himself well knows—that public discourse is a hot furnace that often "burns" those around it, not a closed university seminar where cool rationality prevails.

In this context, it is also important to note that this ideal did not emerge fully formed from theoretical reflection. On the contrary, was the result of practical experimentation with a number of other roles, including that of journalist and partisan professor.[114] While the model of the public intellectual has served Habermas well since he developed it in the mid-1980s, it would be naïve to think that this approach would continue to function indefinitely, given the ever-changing conditions of the public sphere, which itself is the product of a "a unique historical constellation."[115] The fact that we are entering a new historical constellation with its own, "new structural transformation" of the public sphere does not mean that we must start our thinking from scratch. It merely highlights the need for continued reflection on the part of those committed to preserving the power of discourse to legitimate democratic life at a time when elections are increasingly unable to do so on their own (if, indeed, they ever were, as Habermas argues in his democratic theory).

Finally, the contemporary issues undermining the model of the public intellectual do not mean that philosophers interested in public affairs should simply resign themselves to the existing state of affairs. On the contrary, despite his many comments regarding the limits of philosophy in public life, Habermas consistently argues philosophy can "contribute to a *transforming* political practice," even though does not "endow intellectuals who use their philosophical insights with any legitimacy that goes beyond their qualification as citizens."[116] Neither retreating back into the ivory tower nor taking the role of a social engineer, operating behind the backs of citizens within the corridors of power, is the proper philosophical response to the social, cultural, economic, environmental, and political issues facing humanity at the start of the second millennium.

If Habermas the public intellectual has anything to teach us in this moment, it is that resolving these issues must be based on the democratic consensus of citizens committed to exerting control over the external dangers that threaten to "colonize" their lives, to borrow from Habermas's diagnostic terminology.[117] While the model of the public intellectual may no longer be able to fill this role, philosophers, sociologists and other intellectuals can still contribute to public life by continuing to search for ways to rally the public in support of possible solutions to the pathologies of the present that respect the right of citizens to make their own judgements about the best course of action, just as Habermas has sought to do over the course of his long career. If Habermas has anything to teach us in the present, it is that, just like politics itself, making a contribution to political debate as a philosopher or intellectual can also be likened to "a strong and slow boring of hard boards."[118]

Notes

PREFACE

1. Ute Habermas and Jürgen Habermas, "Unser Geschenk: Eine Würdigung des Malers Günter Fruhtrunk, der im Mai 99 Jahre alt geworden wäre und uns einst unter seltsamen Umständen ein Bild vermachte," *Die Zeit*, December 30, 2021.
2. See Peter J. Verovšek, "Meeting Principles and Lifeworlds Halfway: Jürgen Habermas on the Future of Europe," *Political Studies* 60, no. 2 (2012): 363–80.
3. Peter J. Verovšek, *Memory and the Future of Europe: Rupture and Integration in the Wake of Total War* (Manchester University Press, 2020).
4. Jürgen Habermas to Gajo Petrović, January 29, 1975, HV, 31—1975, Band 3 (K–S).

INTRODUCTION: HABERMAS THE PUBLIC INTELLECTUAL

1. Simone Chambers, "Deliberative Democratic Theory," *Annual Review of Political Science* 6 (2003): 308; Jürgen Habermas, *'Es musste etwas besser werden. . . .' Gespräche mit Stefan Müller-Doohm und Roman Yos* (Suhrkamp, 2024), 15. All uncredited translations from the German are my own.
2. Max Pensky, "Historical and Intellectual Contexts," in *Jürgen Habermas: Key Concepts*, ed. Barbara Fultner (Acumen, 2013), 31.
3. Matthew G. Specter, "Habermas in German, European, North Atlantic and Global Perspective," *Los Angeles Review of Books*, August 11, 2019, https://lareviewofbooks.org/article/habermas-german-european-north-atlantic-global-perspective/.
4. Max Pensky, "Universalism and the Situated Critic," in *The Cambridge Companion to Habermas*, ed. Stephen K. White (Cambridge University Press, 1995), 67–68.
5. Matthew G. Specter, *Habermas: An Intellectual Biography* (Cambridge University Press, 2010), 2.
6. Andreas Rosenfelder, "Die Habermas-Diktatur," *Die Welt*, October 11, 2021, https://www.welt.de/kultur/plus234125124/Corona-Politik-Die-Habermas-Diktatur.html; Václav Havel, "The Responsibility of Intellectuals," *New York Review of Books*, June 22, 1995; Jeremy Waldron, "The Vanishing Europe of Jürgen Habermas," *New York Review of Books*, October 22, 2015.

7. Raymond Geuss, *Philosophy and Real Politics* (Princeton University Press, 2008), 98; Jan-Werner Müller, "Rawls in Germany," *European Journal of Political Theory* 1, no. 2 (2002): 163–79; Enzo Rossi and Matt Sleat, "Realism in Normative Political Theory," *Philosophy Compass* 9, no. 10 (2014): 695.
8. Gilles Deleuze, *Die einsame Insel. Texte und Gespräche von 1953 bis 1974* (Suhrkamp, 2003), 377.
9. Philip Felsch, *Der Philosoph: Habermas und Wir* (Propyläen, 2024), 119.
10. Karl Markus Michel, "Über Jürgen Habermas: 'Theorie des kommunikativen Handelns,'" *Der Spiegel*, March 21, 1982; Urs Jaeggi, "Versöhnung als Puzzlearbeit: Nachdenken über Jürgen Habermas: Theorie des kommunikativen Handelns," *Die Zeit*, April 2, 1982.
11. While such pressures on academics are growing worldwide, they are particularly pronounced in the UK. See Richard Watermeyer, "Impact in the REF: Issues and Obstacles," *Studies in Higher Education* 41, no. 2 (2016): 199–214; Robert MacDonald, "'Impact,' Research and Slaying Zombies: The Pressures and Possibilities of the REF," *International Journal of Sociology and Social Policy* 37, nos. 11–12 (2017).
12. Wendy Brown, *Nihilistic Times: Thinking with Max Weber* (Belknap Press of Harvard University Press, 2023), 98, 99, 98–99.
13. Jürgen Habermas, "There Are Alternatives!" *New Left Review*, no. 231 (1998): 8.
14. Brian Leiter, "A More Substantial Response to 'Diversity Sometimes Trumps Academic Freedom' . . . ," *Leiter Reports: A Philosophy Blog*, March 2, 2023, https://leiterreports.typepad.com/blog/2023/03/a-more-substantial-response-to-diversity-sometimes-trumps-academic-freedom.html.
15. John Boswell, Jack Corbett, and Jonathan Havercroft, "Politics and Science as a Vocation: Can Academics Save Us from Post-Truth Politics?" *Political Studies Review* 18, no. 4 (2020): 583.
16. Pierre Bourdieu, "Fourth Lecture. Universal Corporatism: The Role of Intellectuals in the Modern World," *Poetics Today* 12, no. 4 (1991): 656.
17. Jürgen Habermas, "Modernity: An Unfinished Project," in *Habermas and the Unfinished Project of Modernity: Critical Essays on the Philosophical Discourse of Modernity*, ed. Maurizio Passerin d'Entrèves and Seyla Benhabib (Polity, 1996).
18. Joshua Forstenzer, *Deweyan Experimentalism and the Problem of Method in Political Philosophy* (Routledge, 2019), 233.
19. Jürgen Habermas, *Philosophical Introductions: Five Approaches to Communicative Reason* (Polity, 2018), 156.
20. Jürgen Habermas, "An Avantgardistic Instinct for Relevance: The Role of the Intellectual and the European Cause," in *Europe: The Faltering Project*, trans. Ciaran Cronin (Polity, 2009), 55.
21. C. Wright Mills, *The Sociological Imagination* (Oxford University Press, 1959), 6–7.
22. Barbara A. Misztal, *Intellectuals and the Public Good: Creativity and Civil Courage* (Cambridge University Press, 2007), 36–37.
23. Habermas, *Europe: The Faltering Project*, 54.
24. Misztal, *Intellectuals and the Public Good*, 4.
25. Jürgen Habermas, *Politik, Kunst, Religion. Essays über zeitgenössische Philosophen* (Reclam, 1978), 7.

26. Habermas, *Philosophical Introductions*, 152.
27. Havel, "The Responsibility of Intellectuals."
28. Edward W. Said, *Power, Politics and Culture: Interviews with Edward Said*, ed. Gauri Viswanathan (Bloomsbury, 2007), 185; Misztal, *Intellectuals and the Public Good*, 1.
29. Habermas, "An Avantgardistic Instinct," in *Europe: The Faltering Project*; Arthur M. Melzer, "What Is an Intellectual?" in *The Public Intellectual: Between Philosophy and Politics*, ed. Richard M. Zinman, Jerry Weinberger, and Arthur M. Melzer (Rowman & Littlefield, 2004), 5.
30. Neil Walker, "Habermas's European Constitution: Catalyst, Reconstruction, Refounding," *European Law Journal* 25, no. 5 (2019): 509.
31. Wulf Kansteiner, "Losing the War, Winning the Memory Battle: The Legacy of Nazism, World War II, and the Holocaust in the Federal Republic of Germany," in *The Politics of Memory in Postwar Europe*, ed. Richard Ned Lebow, Wulf Kansteiner, and Claudio Fogu (Duke University Press, 2006), 120; Paul Hockenos, "Germany's Public Intellectual No. 1," *Politico*, April 13, 2011, https://www.politico.eu/article/germanys-public-intellectual-no-1/.
32. This magazine is a crucial outlet for German public intellectuals, roughly equivalent to the role of the *New York Review of Books*, *Commentaire*, and *Granta* in other national contexts. Josef Joffe, "The Decline of the Public Intellectual and the Rise of the Pundit" in *The Public Intellectual: Between Philosophy and Politics*, ed. Richard M. Zinman, Jerry Weinberger, and Arthur M. Melzer (Rowman & Littlefield, 2004), 109.
33. "What is MERKUR?," Merkur, accessed April 27, 2020, https://www.merkur-zeitschrift.de/what-is-merkur/. For example, compare the clearly political publication of Habermas, "Auf- und Abrüstung, moralisch und militärisch," *Merkur*, no. 185 (July 1963), which addresses proposals for German rearmament, to his article "Karl Löwiths stoischer Rückzug vom historischen Bewußtsein," *Merkur*, no. 184 (June 1963), a much more academic engagement with Löwith's philosophy. For Habermas's exchange with Sontheimer, see "Die Bühne des Terrors: Ein Brief an Kurt Sontheimer," *Merkur* 31, no. 353 (September 19, 1977).
34. Karl Heinz Bohrer and Kurt Scheel, "Zum fünfzigsten Jahrgang," *Merkur* 50, no. 1 (1996): 1. The description of the journal as "conservative" comes from a private conversation with Habermas on June 7, 2024.
35. Rosenfelder, "Die Habermas-Diktatur"; "Blätter International," *Blätter für deutsche und internationale Politik*, accessed March 12, 2024, https://www.blaetter.de/en.
36. W. G. Regier and H. Peter Reinkordt, "Jürgen Habermas: 'Under the Macroscope,'" *Minnesota Review* 24 (Spring 1985): 122; Dick Howard, "Citizen Habermas," *Constellations* 22, no. 4 (2015): 523.
37. Arnold Gehlen and Odo Marquard, respectively, both cited in Felsch, *Der Philosoph*, 5.
38. Roger Scruton, *Thinkers of the New Left* (Longman, 1985), 120; Howard, "Citizen Habermas," 523; Peter Hohendahl, "Foreword," in *The Past as Future: Vergangenheit als Zukunft*, ed. Jürgen Habermas (University of Nebraska Press, 1994), vi.
39. Jürgen Habermas, "Heinrich Heine and the Role of the Intellectual in Germany," in *The New Conservatism: Cultural Criticism and the Historians' Debate*, trans. Shierry Weber Nicholsen (MIT Press, 1989), 73.

40. Claudia Czingon, Aletta Diefenbach, and Victor Kempf, "Moralischer Universalismus in Zeiten politischer Regression: Jürgen Habermas im Gespräch über die Gegenwart und sein Lebenswerk," *Leviathan* 48, no. 1 (2020): 7–21, here 15.
41. Karl Korn of the *Frankfurter Allgemeine Zeitung* (FAZ) to Habermas, February 14, 1955, Habermas Vorlass (HV), Korrespondenzen 1950er und 1960er Jahre, Folder 1—1954–1958 (A-Z).
42. Karl Korn (FAZ) to Habermas, February 9, 1955, HV, Korrespondenzen 1950er und 1960er Jahre, Folder 1—1954–1958 (A-Z).
43. Jürgen Habermas, *The Philosophical Discourse of Modernity: Twelve Lectures*, trans. Frederick G. Lawrence (MIT Press, 1987).
44. Friedrich V. Kratochwil, "Evidence, Inference, and Truth as Problems of Theory Building in the Social Sciences," in *Theory and Evidence in Comparative Politics and International Relations*, ed. Richard Ned Lebow and Mark Irving Lichback (Palgrave MacMillan, 2007), 42–43.
45. Theodor W. Adorno, "The Essay as Form," *New German Critique*, no. 32 (1984); Peter Uwe Hohendahl, "The Scholar, the Intellectual, and the Essay: Weber, Lukács, Adorno, and Postwar Germany," *The German Quarterly* 70, no. 3 (1997): 224–25.
46. Howard, "Citizen Habermas," 523.
47. For more on the background to the creation of this new series, see Stefan Müller-Doohm, *Adorno: A Biography* (Polity, 2015), 197.
48. Jürgen Habermas, *The Lure of Technocracy* (Polity, 2015), vii.
49. Pauline Johnson, *Habermas: Rescuing the Public Sphere* (Routledge, 2006).
50. Specter, *Habermas: An Intellectual Biography*.
51. Robert C. Holub, *Jürgen Habermas: Critic in the Public Sphere* (Routledge, 1991).
52. Müller-Doohm, *Habermas: A Biography* (Polity, 2016).
53. Roman Yos, *Der junge Habermas: Eine ideengeschichtliche Untersuchung seines frühen Denkens, 1952–62* (Suhrkamp, 2019).
54. Taken from military strategy and marketing, the concept of positioning seeks to capture the way certain features are attributed to an individual or a group or some other entity within a broader field, be it physical or merely representational. See Al Ries and Jack Trout, *Positioning: The Battle for Your Mind* (McGraw-Hill, 1981).
55. Patrick Baert, *The Existentialist Moment: The Rise of Sartre as a Public Intellectual* (Polity, 2015), 165, 169.
56. Private conversation with Jürgen Habermas, June 7, 2024.
57. Jürgen Habermas, *Philosophical-Political Profiles*, trans. Frederick G. Lawrence (MIT Press, 1983), 53–60; Jürgen Habermas, "Mit Heidegger gegen Heidegger denken. Zur Veröffentlichung von Vorlesungen aus dem Jahre 1935," *Frankfurter Allgemeine Zeitung*, July 25, 1953.
58. Christian Lewalter, "Wie liest man 1953 Sätze von 1935? Zu einem politischen Streit um Heideggers Metaphysik," *Die Zeit*, August 13, 1953; Jürgen Habermas, "Eine Art Schadensabwicklung: Die apologetischen Tendenzen in der deutschen Zeitgeschichtsschreibung," *Die Zeit*, July 11, 1986, https://www.zeit.de/1986/29/eine-art-schadensabwicklung/komplettansicht?print; Peter Baldwin, "The Historikerstreit in Context," in *Reworking the Past: Hitler, the Holocaust, and the Historians' Debate*, ed. Peter Baldwin (Beacon, 1990).
59. Jürgen Habermas to Hanjo Kesting (Norddeutscher Rundfunk), November 8, 1977, HV, Korrespondenzen 1970er Jahre, Folder 39—1977, Band 3 (I-M).

60. Bruce Robbins, "The Grounding of Intellectuals," in *Intellectuals: Aesthetics, Politics, Academics*, ed. Bruce Robbins (University of Minnesota Press, 1990), xxiv.
61. For more on Adorno, see Alex Demirović, *Der nonkonformistische Intellektuelle: Die Entwicklung der Kritischen Theorie zur Frankfurter Schule* (Suhrkamp, 1999).
62. One notable exception is: Jürgen Habermas, "Wozu noch Philosophie?" *Hessischer Rundfunk*, January 4, 1971. See René Görtzen, *Jürgen Habermas: Eine Bibliographie seiner Schriften und ser Sekundärliteratur 1952–1981* (Suhrkamp, 1982), 49.
63. Inge Pethran, secretary (on behalf of Habermas) to H. U. Probst (Studio Basel), n.d., HV, Korrespondenzen 1970er Jahre, Folder 17—1972, Band 2 (H-R).
64. For more on these meetings between Habermas and Arendt, see Peter J. Verovšek, "A Case of Communicative Learning? Rereading Habermas's Philosophical Project through an Arendtian Lens," *Polity* 51, no. 3 (July 2019): 606–607.
65. Habermas to Udi Eichler (Thames Television House, "Something to Say"), April 16, 1973, HV, Korrespondenzen 1970er Jahre, Folder 19—1973, Band 1 (A-F).
66. Axel Schildt, *Medien-Intellektulle in der Bundesrepublik* (Wallstein, 2020).
67. Habermas to Klaus Podak (Fernsehen des Hessischen Rundfunks), October 16, 1974, HV, Korrespondenzen 1970er Jahre, Folder 26—1974, Band 4 (O-S).
68. Jürgen Habermas, *The Structural Transformation of the Public Sphere: An Inquiry into a Category of Bourgeois Society* (MIT Press, 1989), 16.
69. Habermas, *Between Naturalism and Religion*, 12.
70. Jürgen Habermas, "Public Space and Political Public Sphere: The Biographical Roots of Two Motifs in My Thought" in *Between Naturalism and Religion* (Polity, 2008), 15, 16.
71. See Régis Debray, *Le pouvoir intellectuel en France* (Ramsay, 1979); Régis Debray, *Teachers, Writers, Celebrities: The Intellectuals of Modern France* (New Left Books, 1981).
72. Jeremy Jennings and Anthony Kemp-Welch, "The Century of the Intellectual: From the Dreyfus Affair to Salman Rushdie," in *Intellectuals in Politics: From the Dreyfus Affair to Salman Rushdie*, ed. Jeremy Jennings and Anthony Kemp-Welch (Routledge, 1997), 15.
73. For a case study of the role of television in the changing intellectual life of France, see Tamara Chaplin, *Turning on the Mind: French Philosophers on Television* (University of Chicago Press, 2007).
74. Shachar M. Pinsker, *A Rich Brew: How Cafés Created Modern Jewish Culture* (New York University Press, 2018), 112.
75. Specter, *Habermas: An Intellectual Biography*, 27.
76. Habermas, "Heinrich Heine and the Role," 73, 75, 74.
77. Pinsker, *A Rich Brew*, 151. The Austrian writer, essayist, and journalist Karl Kraus also famously pronounced that there was "no feuilleton without Heine (Ohne Heine kein Feuilleton)." See Karl Kraus, *Heine und die Folgen* (A. Langen, 1910), 7.
78. Baert, *The Existentialist Moment*, 6, 178–79.
79. Jürgen Habermas, personal conversation, June 7, 2024.
80. For the concept of the "backstage," see Patrick Baert and Marcus Morgan, "A Performative Framework for the Study of Intellectuals," *European Journal of Social Theory* 21, no. 3 (2018): 330.
81. Frank Schirrmacher, "Der Zivilisationsredakteur: 100 Jahre Karl Korn," *Frankfurter Allgemeine Zeitung*, sec. Feuilleton, May 17, 2008, https://www.faz.net/aktuell/feuilleton

/bilder-und-zeiten-1/100-jahre-karl-korn-der-zivilisationsredakteur-1538919.html?print PagedArticle=true#pageIndex_2.

82. Karl Korn (FAZ) to Habermas, July 16, 1953, HV, Korrespondenzen 1950er und 1960er Jahre, Folder 1—1954–1958 (A-Z).
83. Habermas to the editor of the FAZ, May 29, 1973, HV, Korrespondenzen 1970er Jahre, Folder 19—1973 (A-F).
84. Habermas to the editor of the FAZ, May 14, 1973, HV, Korrespondenzen 1970er Jahre, Folder 19—1973 (A-F).
85. Habermas would later break with Bohrer—and with *Merkur*, with which he was also associated—following their disagreements about German unification. Felsch, *Der Philosoph*, 162.
86. Quoted and translated in Müller-Doohm, *Habermas: A Biography*, 276.
87. R. W. Leonhardt (*Die Zeit*) to Habermas, June 4, 1964, HV, Korrespondenzen 1950er und 1960er Jahre, Folder 5—1964 (A-Z).
88. Habermas to R. W. Leonhardt (*Die Zeit*), 16.6.64, HV, Korrespondenzen 1950er und 1960er Jahre, Folder 5—1964 (A-Z).
89. Lewalter, "Wie liest man 1953 Sätze von 1935?"; Martin Heidegger, "Leserbrief," *Die Zeit*, September 24, 1953. See also Richard Wolin, ed., *The Heidegger Controversy: A Critical Reader* (MIT Press, 1993), 187.
90. Michael Funken, "Vom Außenseiter zum geachteten Intellektuellen," in *Über Habermas: Gespräche mit Zeitgenossen*, ed. Michael Funken (Wissenschaftliche Buchgesellschaft, 2009), 15–16.
91. Lewalter, "Wie liest man 1953 Sätze von 1935?"; Habermas, *The New Conservatism*.
92. Michael Funken, "Einleitung," in *Über Habermas: Gespräche mit Zeitgenossen*, ed. Michael Funken (Wissenschaftliche Buchgesellschaft, 2009), 7.
93. Howard, "Citizen Habermas," 523.
94. Habermas, *Between Naturalism and Religion*, 21.
95. Jürgen Habermas, *Autonomy and Solidarity: Interviews*, ed. Peter Dews (Verso, 1992), 127; Leo Löwenthal, *An Unmastered Past* (University of California Press, 1987).
96. Quoted in Martin Joseph Matuštík, *Jürgen Habermas: A Philosophical-Political Profile* (Rowman & Littlefield, 2001), 10; *Frankfurter Allgemeine Zeitung*, January 23, 2003. I have also written elsewhere about the importance of memory in Habermas's work: see Peter J. Verovšek, "Historical Criticism Without Progress: Memory as an Emancipatory Resource for Critical Theory," *Constellations* 26, no. 1 (2019); and Peter J. Verovšek, "Integration After Totalitarianism: Arendt and Habermas on the Postwar Imperatives of Memory," *Journal of International Political Theory* (2018).
97. Jürgen Habermas, personal conversation, June 7, 2024.
98. Habermas, *Autonomy and Solidarity*, 78, 77.
99. Habermas, *Autonomy and Solidarity*, 78. For more on the concept of rupture, see Peter J. Verovšek, "Memory, Narrative, and Rupture: The Power of the Past as a Resource for Political Change," *Memory Studies* 13, no. 4 (2020).
100. Quoted in Claudia Czingon, Aletta Diefenbach, and Victor Kempf, "Moral Universalism at a Time of Political Regression: A Conversation with Jürgen Habermas About the Present and His Life's Work," *Theory, Culture & Society* 37, nos. 7–8 (2020): 20.
101. Quoted in Matuštík, *Jürgen Habermas*, 139.

102. Habermas, *Autonomy and Solidarity*, 126.
103. Habermas, *The New Conservatism*, 234. For an example of how this can occur, see Peter J. Verovšek, *Memory and the Future of Europe: Rupture and Integration in the Wake of Total War* (Manchester University Press, 2020).
104. David Leopold and Marc Stears, "Introduction," in *Political Theory: Methods and Approaches*, ed. David Leopold and Marc Stears (Oxford University Press, 2008), 2.
105. See Quentin Skinner, "Meaning and Understanding in the History of Ideas," *History and Theory* 8, no. 1 (1969): 3–53.
106. Thomas A. McCarthy, "Defending Habermas," *New York Review of Books*, January 20, 1983; Quentin Skinner, "Habermas's Reformation," *New York Review of Books*, October 7, 1982.
107. Skinner quoted in Filip Biały, "Freedom, Silent Power and the Role of an Historian in the Digital Age—Interview with Quentin Skinner," *History of European Ideas* 48, no. 7 (2022): 875.
108. I would like to thank Peter Gordon for making this point to me in his unanonymized report on the full manuscript of this book for Columbia University Press.
109. Ming Kit Wong, "The Cambridge School and the Turn to the Present," *Centre for Intellectual History*, University of Oxford, March 2, 2023, https://intellectualhistory.web.ox.ac.uk/article/cambridge-school-and-turn-present.
110. I borrow these quotations from Peter Gordon, even though he makes them in service of precisely the opposite point—namely, that one should not link "problems of philosophy to questions of political commitment." See Soren Whithed, "Traces of Different Colors: An Interview with Peter E. Gordon," *Platypus Review* 151 (November 2022), https://platypus1917.org/2022/11/01/traces-of-different-colors-an-interview-with-peter-e-gordon/.
111. Müller-Doohm, *Habermas*, xii.
112. See Peter J. Verovšek, "Conclusion: Working in a 'Living' Archive," *PS: Political Science and Politics* 57, no. 1 (2024): 97–99.
113. My thanks to both Roman Yos and Rainer Forst for alerting me to this point.
114. Skinner, "Meaning and Understanding in the History of Ideas," 3.
115. Other scholars, including Roman Yos and Stefan Müller-Doohm, have already done this far better than I ever could.
116. I would like to thank Till van Rahden for providing me with comments that helped me to clarify this point for myself.
117. Peter J. Verovšek, "Meeting Principles and Lifeworlds Halfway: Jürgen Habermas on the Future of Europe," *Political Studies* 60, no. 2 (2012).
118. Jürgen Habermas, *Ein neuer Strukturwandel der Öffentlichkeit und die deliberative Politik* (Suhrkamp, 2022); Jürgen Habermas, *A New Structural Transformation of the Public Sphere and Deliberative Politics* (Polity, 2023).

1. MEDIATING THEORY AND PRACTICE

1. This chapter builds on Peter J. Verovšek, "The Philosopher as Engaged Citizen: Habermas on the Role of the Public Intellectual in the Modern Democratic Public Sphere," *European Journal of Social Theory* 24, no. 4 (2021).
2. Liam Bright, "The End of Analytic Philosophy," *The Sooty Empiric*, May 23, 2021, https://sootyempiric.blogspot.com/2021/05/the-end-of-analytic-philosophy.html; Jeremy Waldron, *Political Political Theory: Essays on Institutions* (Harvard University Press, 2016);

1. Mediating Theory and Practice

Yiannis Kouris and Jonathan Wolff, "Philosophy & Public Policy," *Institute for Alternative Politics Blog*, April 4, 2021.

3. Tom Whyman, "Happy Birthday Habermas, Your Philosophy has Failed Us," *The Outline*, July 30, 2019, https://theoutline.com/post/7734/habermas-failure-political-philosophy; Jürgen Habermas, "Why Europe Needs a Constitution" in *Developing a Constitution for Europe*, ed. Erik Oddvar Eriksen et al. (Routledge, 2004), xl.
4. Fabian Freyenhagen, "Adorno's Politics: Theory and Praxis in Germany's 1960s," *Philosophy & Social Criticism* 40, no. 9 (2014): 878.
5. Jürgen Habermas, "What Theories Can Accomplish—and What They Can't," in *The Past as Future: Vergangenheit als Zukunft*, trans. Max Pensky (University of Nebraska Press, 1994), 116.
6. Habermas, "Theories," 99–120.
7. Steven B. Smith, *Political Philosophy* (Yale University Press, 2012), 7.
8. Helen Small, "Introduction," in *The Public Intellectual*, ed. Helen Small (Wiley-Blackwell, 2002), 4.
9. Max Weber, "Science as a Vocation," in *From Max Weber: Essays in Sociology*, ed. Hans Heinrich Gerth and C. Wright Mills, trans. Hans Heinrich Gerth and C. Wright Mills (Oxford University Press, 1958), 152.
10. Roger Kimball, *Tenured Radicals: How Politics Has Corrupted Our Higher Education* (Ivan R. Dee, 2008).
11. Weber, "Science as a Vocation," 143; Immanuel Kant, "An Answer to the Question: 'What Is Enlightenment?,' " in *Kant: Political Writings*, ed. H. S. Reiss, trans. H. B. Nisbet (Cambridge University Press, 1991), 56.
12. Kant, "An Answer," 56.
13. "Declaration of Support for Adolf Hitler and the National Socialist State (November 11, 1933)," address delivered by Heidegger at a rally held by German university professors in Leipzig in support of the upcoming plebiscite on German withdrawal from the League of Nations held the next day, on November 12. Republished in *The Heidegger Controversy: A Critical Reader*, ed. and trans. Richard Wolin (MIT Press, 1993), 51, 52, emphasis in original.
14. Jürgen Habermas, *Philosophical Introductions: Five Approaches to Communicative Reason* (Polity, 2018), 152; Richard Wolin, *The Seduction of Unreason: The Intellectual Romance with Fascism from Nietzsche to Postmodernism* (Princeton University Press, 2004).
15. Habermas, *Philosophical Introductions*, 152.
16. See John G. Gunnell, "Professing Political Theory," *Political Research Quarterly* 63, no. 3 (2010).
17. David Schmidtz, *The Elements of Justice* (Cambridge University Press, 2006), 27.
18. Habermas, *Philosophical Introductions*, 155.
19. Jürgen Habermas, *'Es musste etwas besser werden. . . .' Gespräche mit Stefan Müller-Doohm und Roman Yos* (Suhrkamp, 2024), 20.
20. Adam Swift and Stuart White, "Political Theory, Social Science, and Real Politics," in *Political Theory: Methods and Approaches*, ed. David Leopold and Marc Stears (Oxford University Press, 2008), 49, 54.
21. William A. Galston, "Realism in Political Theory," *European Journal of Political Theory* 9, no. 4 (2010), 386; Raymond Geuss, *Philosophy and Real Politics* (Princeton University Press, 2008), 98.

22. Alice Baderin, "Political Theory and Public Opinion: Against Democratic Restraint," *Politics, Philosophy & Economics* 15, no. 3 (2016): 209.
23. Geuss, *Philosophy and Real Politics*, 31.
24. Bernard Williams, *In the Beginning Was the Deed: Realism and Moralism in Political Argument*, ed. Geoffrey Hawthorn (Princeton University Press, 2005).
25. Swift and White, "Political Theory," 54, 55.
26. Jo Wolff, quoted in Kouris and Wolff, "Philosophy & Public Policy."
27. Geuss, *Philosophy and Real Politics*, 8.
28. Jürgen Habermas, *The Past as Future: Vergangenheit als Zukunft*, trans. Max Pensky (University of Nebraska Press, 1994), 113, 114; Habermas, quoted in Claudia Czingon et al., "Moral Universalism at a Time of Political Regression: A Conversation with Jürgen Habermas About the Present and His Life's Work," *Theory, Culture & Society* 37, nos. 7–8 (2020): 9.
29. Swift and White, "Political Theory," 49.
30. Jürgen Habermas, "An Avantgardistic Instinct for Relevances: The Role of the Intellectual and the European Cause," in *Europe: The Faltering Project*, trans. Ciaran Cronin (Polity, 2009), 52.
31. Harry F. Dahms, "Theory in Weberian Marxism: Patterns of Critical Social Theory in Lukacs and Habermas," *Sociological Theory* 15, no. 3 (1997): 208.
32. Peter Uwe Hohendahl, "The Scholar, the Intellectual, and the Essay: Weber, Lukács, Adorno, and Postwar Germany," *The German Quarterly* 70, no. 3 (1997): 218, 226.
33. Jürgen Habermas, *Between Facts and Norms: Contributions to a Discourse Theory of Law and Democracy* (MIT Press, 1996), 302–08.
34. Habermas, *Europe: The Faltering Project*, 45.
35. Jürgen Habermas, "Further Reflections on the Public Sphere," in *Habermas and the Public Sphere*, ed. Craig J. Calhoun (MIT Press, 1992), 452.
36. Habermas, *The Past as Future*, 99.
37. Weber, "Science as a Vocation," 147.
38. Hohendahl, "The Scholar, the Intellectual, and the Essay," 218.
39. Habermas, *The Past as Future*, 114.
40. Habermas, *The Past as Future*, 113, 99, 116.
41. John Horton, "What Might It Mean for Political Theory to Be More 'Realistic'?" *Philosophy* 45, no. 2 (2017): 490.
42. Jürgen Habermas, *The Theory of Communicative Action*, vol. 1, *Reason and the Rationalization of Society*, trans. Thomas A. McCarthy (Beacon, 1984–1987), 364.
43. Geuss, *Philosophy and Real Politics*, 8; Jürgen Habermas, *Theory and Practice* (Beacon, 1974), 33.
44. Habermas, *Theory and Practice*, 32.
45. Gerhard Richter and Theodor W. Adorno, "Who's Afraid of the Ivory Tower? A Conversation with Theodor W. Adorno," *Monatshefte* 94, no. 1 (2002): 19.
46. Habermas, *Theory and Practice*, 34.
47. Habermas, *The Past as Future*, 101; Luke Ulaş, "Can Political Realism Be Action-Guiding?" *Critical Review of International Social and Political Philosophy* 26 (June 2020).
48. Habermas, *Theory and Practice*, 33; Geuss, *Philosophy and Real Politics*, 99.
49. Otto Pöggeler, "Den Führer führen? Heidegger und kein Ende," *Philosophische Rundschau* 32, no. 1 (1985).

50. Theodor W. Adorno, *Eingriffe: Neun kritische Modelle* (Edition Suhrkamp, 1963), 32; Jürgen Habermas, *Autonomy and Solidarity: Interviews*, ed. Peter Dews (Verso, 1992), 199.
51. Habermas, *Philosophical Introductions*, 154.
52. Habermas quoted in "The Work of Jürgen Habermas," in *Philosophical Introductions: Five Approaches to Communicative Reason*, ed. Jean-Marie Durand-Gasselin (Polity, 2018), 10.
53. Habermas, *Philosophical Introductions*, 147.
54. Dahms, "Theory in Weberian Marxism," 207.
55. Dahms, "Theory in Weberian Marxism," 195, 206.
56. Raymond Geuss, *Politics and the Imagination* (Princeton University Press, 2010), 3.
57. Habermas, *The Past as Future*, 101, 111; Geuss, *Politics and the Imagination*, 4.
58. Dahms, "Theory in Weberian Marxism," 208.
59. Enzo Rossi, "Reality and Imagination in Political Theory and Practice: On Raymond Geuss's Realism," *European Journal of Political Theory* 9, no. 4 (2010): 510; Habermas quoted in Czingon et al., "Moral Universalism," 9–10.
60. Mark Philp, "What Is To Be Done? Political Theory and Political Realism," *European Journal of Political Theory* 9, no. 4 (October 2010): 482.
61. John Dunn, *Interpreting Political Responsibility: Essays 1981–1989* (Princeton University Press, 2014), 193.
62. Habermas, *Philosophical Introductions*, 56–57.
63. Philp, "What Is To Be Done?" 467.
64. Habermas, *Autonomy and Solidarity*, 127.
65. Immanuel Kant, "An Answer to the Question: What Is Enlightenment?" in *Toward Perpetual Peace and Other Writings on Politics, Peace, and History*, ed. Pauline Kleingeld, trans. David L. Colclasure (Yale University Press, 2006), 55, 57.
66. Kant, "An Answer to the Question," 57, 56.
67. Keith Haysom, "Civil Society and Social Movements," in *Jürgen Habermas: Key Concepts*, ed. Barbara Fultner (Routledge, 2014), 193.
68. Jürgen Habermas, *Towards a Rational Society: Student Protest, Science, and Politics* (Heinemann Educational Books, 1971), 63.
69. Habermas, *Theory and Practice*, 265.
70. Jürgen Habermas, "Über den Begriff der politischen Beteiligung," in *Arbeit, Erkenntnis, Fortschritt: Aufsätze, 1954–1970* (de Munter, 1970), 270.
71. Jürgen Habermas, "Heinrich Heine and the Role of the Intellectual in Germany," in *The New Conservatism: Cultural Criticism and the Historians' Debate*, trans. Shierry Weber Nicholsen (MIT Press, 1989), 87; Habermas, *Europe: The Faltering Project*, 55.
72. Habermas, *Europe: The Faltering Project*, 55.
73. Stefan Collini, " 'Every Fruit-Juice Drinker, Nudist, Sandal-Wearer . . .': Intellectuals as Other People," in *The Public Intellectual*, ed. Helen Small (Wiley-Blackwell, 2002), 210; Karl Mannheim, *Ideology and Utopia* (Routledge, 1960), 9–10.
74. Habermas, *Philosophical Introductions*, 123.
75. Jürgen Habermas, "Produktivkraft Kommunikation. Interview mit Hans Peter Krüger," *Sinn und Form*, 41.6 (1989): 1192–1206; reprinted in Habermas, *Die nachholende Revolution*, vol. 7 of *Kleine politische Schriften* (Suhrkamp, 1990), 96.

76. Michel Foucault, *Power/Knowledge: Selected Interviews and Other Writings, 1972–1977*, ed. Colin Gordon (Pantheon, 1980), 128, 62.
77. Pierre Bourdieu, Gisele Sapiro, and Brian McHale, "Fourth Lecture. Universal Corporatism: The Role of Intellectuals in the Modern World," *Poetics Today* 12, no. 4 (1991): 661.
78. Habermas, *Europe: The Faltering Project*, 55.
79. Michel Foucault, *Foucault Live: Collected Interviews, 1961–1984*, ed. Sylvère Lotringer (Semiotext(e), 1996), 284.
80. Thomas Biebricher, "The Practices of Theorists: Habermas and Foucault as Public Intellectuals," *Philosophy & Social Criticism* 37, no. 6 (2011): 713.
81. Jürgen Habermas, "Political Communication in Media Society: Does Democracy Still Enjoy an Epistemic Dimension?: The Impact of Normative Theory on Empirical Research," *Communication Theory* 16, no. 4 (2006): 412; Simone Chambers, "Balancing Epistemic Quality and Equal Participation in a System Approach to Deliberative Democracy," *Social Epistemology* 31, no. 3 (2017): 270, 271, 273.
82. Jürgen Habermas, "Die neue Unübersichtlichkeit. Die Krise des Wohlfahrtsstaates und die Erschöpfung utopischer Energien," *Merkur* 39, no. 1 (1985): 51.
83. Max Pensky, "Jürgen Habermas and the Antinomies of the Intellectual," in *Habermas: A Critical Reader*, ed. Peter Dews (Blackwell, 1999), 216.
84. Raymond Geuss, *The Idea of a Critical Theory: Habermas and the Frankfurt School* (Cambridge University Press, 1981), 88.
85. Geuss, *Philosophy and Real Politics*, 30, emphasis in original.
86. Benjamin L. McKean, "What Makes a Utopia Inconvenient?: On the Advantages and Disadvantages of a Realist Orientation to Politics," *American Political Science Review* 110, no. 4 (2016): 881.
87. Swift and White, "Political Theory," 54.
88. Baderin, "Political Theory and Public Opinion," 224.
89. Rutger Claassen, "Making Capability Lists: Philosophy Versus Democracy," *Political Studies* 59, no. 3 (2011), 504–05; Jonathan Wolff and Avner de-Shalit, *Disadvantage* (Oxford University Press, 2007), 97.
90. Baderin, "Political Theory and Public Opinion," 224, 217, 225.
91. Jeremy Waldron, "Theoretical Foundations of Liberalism," in *Liberal Rights: Collected Papers 1981–1991*, ed. Jeremy Waldron (Cambridge University Press, 1993), 61; Christopher Bertram, "Political Justification, Theoretical Complexity, and Democratic Community," *Ethics* 107, no. 4 (1997).
92. Dahms, "Theory in Weberian Marxism," 207.
93. Hannah Arendt, "Wahrheit und Politik," in *Zwischen Vergangenheit und Zukunft. Übungen im politischen Denken I* (Piper, 2000), 330.
94. Habermas, *Theory of Communicative Action*, xliii.
95. Habermas, *The Past as Future*, 99; Christian Geyer, "Sein Niveau entzündet," *Frankfurter Allgemeine Zeitung*, June 25, 2008.
96. Pratap Bhanu Mehta, personal communication, September 1, 2019. Mehta was working at the Center for Social Studies at the time and chaired the discussion with Habermas for students at this event.
97. Felsch, *Der Philosoph*, 119.

98. Baderin, "Political Theory and Public Opinion," 225.
99. Dahms, "Theory in Weberian Marxism," 208.
100. Martin Jay, "Habermas and the Light of Reason: On Late Critical Theory," *Los Angeles Review of Books*, August 11, 2019, https://lareviewofbooks.org/article/habermas-light-reason-late-critical-theory/.
101. Habermas, quoted in Matthew G. Specter, *Habermas: An Intellectual Biography* (Cambridge University Press, 2010), 141; Biebricher, "Practices of Theorists," 719.
102. Habermas, *Europe: The Faltering Project*, 162.
103. Max Pensky, "Historical and Intellectual Contexts," in *Jürgen Habermas: Key Concepts*, ed. Barbara Fultner (Acumen Publishing, 2013), 32.
104. Stefan Müller-Doohm, "Theodor W. Adorno and Jürgen Habermas—Two Ways of Being a Public Intellectual: Sociological Observations Concerning the Transformation of a Social Figure of Modernity," *European Journal of Social Theory* 8, no. 3 (2005): 274.
105. Freyenhagen, "Adorno's Politics," 879.
106. Alex Demirović, *Der nonkonformistische Intellektuelle: Die Entwicklung der Kritischen Theorie zur Frankfurter Schule* (Suhrkamp, 1999).
107. Max Horkheimer, "Traditional and Critical Theory," in *Critical Theory: Selected Essays*, trans. Matthew J. O'Connell (Continuum, 1972), 221.
108. Horkheimer, "Traditional and Critical Theory," 215.
109. Freyenhagen, "Adorno's Politics," 875.
110. Karl Marx, letter to Domela Nieuwenhuis, The Hague, London, February 22, 1881, Marxists.org, 2000, https://www.marxists.org.
111. Raymond Geuss, "The Last Nineteenth Century German Philosopher: Habermas at 90," *Verso Blog*, August 14, 2019, https://www.versobooks.com/blogs/4408-the-last-nineteenth-century-german-philosopher-habermas-at-90.
112. Tom Rockmore, *Habermas on Historical Materialism* (Indiana University Press, 1989), 165, 167.
113. Horkheimer, "Traditional and Critical Theory," 198–99.
114. Pensky, "Historical and Intellectual Contexts," 19.
115. Stefan Müller-Doohm, *Habermas: A Biography* (Polity, 2016), 4–5.

2. THE JOURNALISTIC YEARS, 1951–1955

1. I would like to thank Roman Yos for sharing several texts I was having difficulty locating.
2. For more on this period in Habermas's life, see Roman Yos, *Der junge Habermas: Eine ideengeschichtliche Untersuchung seines frühen Denkens, 1952–62* (Suhrkamp, 2019). The best account in English can be found in the opening chapters of Stefan Müller-Doohm, *Habermas: A Biography* (Polity, 2016).
3. Quentin Skinner, "Meaning and Understanding in the History of Ideas," *History and Theory* 8, no. 1 (1969): 25, 26.
4. Habermas quoted in Miguel de la Riva, "Tagung über Habermas: Elektrisierende Lektüre im Zug nach Frankfurt," Feuilleton, *Frankfurter Allgemeine Zeitung*, November 1, 2021, https://www.faz.net/aktuell/feuilleton/debatten/tagung-in-tutzing-habermas-ueber-adorno-17611532.html.
5. Skinner, "Meaning and Understanding in the History of Ideas," 23.

6. Raymond Geuss, *The Idea of a Critical Theory: Habermas and the Frankfurt School* (Cambridge University Press, 1981), 94.
7. Jürgen Habermas, personal conversation, June 7, 2024 (hereafter cited as Habermas, personal conversation).
8. Jürgen Habermas, "Public Space and Political Public Sphere: The Biographical Roots of Two Motifs in My Thought," in *Between Naturalism and Religion* (Polity, 2008), 14, 15.
9. Habermas, *Between Naturalism and Religion*, 12, 16; Jürgen Habermas, *The Structural Transformation of the Public Sphere: An Inquiry Into a Category of Bourgeois Society* (MIT Press, 1989), 16.
10. These paragraphs build on Müller-Doohm, *Habermas: A Biography*, 9–32.
11. Rolf Wiggershaus, *Jürgen Habermas* (Rowohlt Taschenbuch, 2004), 11.
12. Jürgen Habermas, *Kleine politische Schriften I–IV* (Suhrkamp, 1981), 511.
13. Letter from Jürgen Habermas to Hans Paeschke, dated March 15, 1955 (Marbacher Literaturarchiv), quoted in Müller-Doohm, *Habermas: A Biography*, 21.
14. Habermas, *Between Naturalism and Religion*, 17, 18.
15. Habermas, *Between Naturalism and Religion*, 19.
16. Jürgen Habermas, *'Es musste etwas besser werden. . . .' Gespräche mit Stefan Müller-Doohm und Roman Yos* (Suhrkamp, 2024), 11–12.
17. Jürgen Habermas, "Meine gymnasiale Schulzeit: Ausschnitte aus einer geplanten Autobiographie," *Schwarz auf Weiß: Mitteilungen des Vereins der Förderer und ehemaligen Schüler des Städtischen Gymnasiums Moltkestraße in Gummersbach e.V* 26 (December 2002): 52, 53.
18. Habermas, "Meine gymnasiale Schulzeit," 52.
19. Habermas, *Between Naturalism and Religion*, 18, 17.
20. Habermas quoted in Claus Grossner, "Der letzte Richter der Kritischen Theorie," *Die Zeit*, March 13, 1970.
21. Habermas, "Meine Gymnasiale Schulzeit," 51.
22. Habermas, *Kleine politische Schriften I–IV*, 513 ("reeducation" appears in English in the original); Habermas, *Between Naturalism and Religion*, 19.
23. Wiggershaus, *Jürgen Habermas*, 18.
24. Habermas, *Between Naturalism and Religion*, 17.
25. Habermas, "Meine gymnasiale Schulzeit" 52.
26. Jürgen Habermas, "Ein Gespräch über Heimat, Europa und die Zukunft," *Kölnische Rundschau*, July 8, 2019.
27. Jürgen Habermas, "Ist unsere Generation modern?" *Schwarz auf Weiss: Schülerzeitung des Städtischen Gymnasiums in Gummersbach* 1, no. 2 (1951): 7–8.
28. See Till van Rahden, "Die Gummersbacher Schule: Hans Ulrich Wehler inszeniert eine Debatte," *Zeitschrift für Ideengeschichte* 15, no. 3 (2021).
29. Habermas, "Ist unsere Generation modern?," 8.
30. Quoted in Grossner, "Der letzte Richter."
31. Jürgen Habermas, "Wider den moralpädagogischen Hochmut der Kulturkritik," *Die Literatur*, September 15, 1952.
32. Habermas quoted in Grossner, "Der letzte Richter."
33. Jürgen Habermas, "Gottfried Benns neue Stimme," *Frankfurter Allgemeine Zeitung*, June 19, 1952.
34. Heinrich Mann and Thomas Mann, *Letters of Heinrich and Thomas Mann, 1900–1949*, ed. Hans Wysling, trans. Don Reneau (University of California Press, 1998), 367–68.

35. Yos, *Der junge Habermas*, 77.
36. Jürgen Habermas, "Akademische sommerfrische in Erlangen? Internationale Studentenbühnen ohne Mut," *Frankfurter Allgemeine Zeitung*, August 6, 1952.
37. Jürgen Habermas, "Des Hörspiels Mangel ist seine Chance," *Frankfurter Allgemeine Zeitung*, September 15, 1952.
38. Jürgen Habermas, "Die akustische Bühne. Hörspielnotizen zu Adamov, Dürrenmatt und Huber," *Frankfurter Allgemeine Zeitung*, November 27, 1952.
39. Theodor W. Adorno, *Aesthetic Theory*, trans. Robert Hullot-Kentor (Bloomsbury Academic, 2013).
40. For an example of Habermas's admiration of Brecht and his approaches, see Jürgen Habermas, "Noch einmal: Schweyk und die SS," *Frankfurter Allgemeine Zeitung*, June 12, 1959.
41. Jürgen Habermas, "Drei Masken zuviel," *Frankfurter Hefte* 8, no. 3 (1953): 232. Habermas also addresses this "third position" in his review of Thierry Maulniers's "Le Profanateur." See Jürgen Habermas, "Der falsche Prometheus," *Frankfurter Hefte* 8, no. 5 (1953).
42. Jürgen Habermas, "Iphigenie will nicht Sterben. Obeys 'Ein Opfer für Wind' in Bonn," *Frankfurter Allgemeine Zeitung*, November 25, 1953. See also Yos, *Der junge Habermas*, esp. 117–20.
43. Jürgen Habermas, *'Es musste etwas besser werden....' Gespräche mit Stefan Müller-Doohm und Roman Yos* (Suhrkamp, 2024), 39; see Max Horkheimer and Theodor W. Adorno, *Dialectic of Enlightenment: Philosophical Fragments*, trans. Gunzelin Schmid Noerr (Stanford University Press, 2002), 94–136.
44. Jürgen Habermas, "Der musikalische Stil des Films. Ein Vortrag und Zwei Filme von Jean Mitry," *Frankfurter Allgemeine Zeitung*, January 19, 1953.
45. Jürgen Habermas, "Die Ironie der Holz- und Gipsköpfe. Bei Gelegenheit des Internationalen Puppenspielzyklus in Bonn," *Frankfurter Allgemeine Zeitung*, January 29, 1953.
46. Jürgen Habermas, "Die farbigen Schatten aus Szetschuan. Notizen zum zweiten Bonner Puppenspielzyklus," *Frankfurter Allgemeine Zeitung*, July 14, 1953.
47. In this context, *moloch* refers to a mountain devil or similar mythical creature. Jürgen Habermas, "Der Moloch und die Künste. Gedanken zur Entlarvung der Legende von der Technischen Zweckmäßigkeit," *Frankfurter Allgemeine Zeitung*, May 30, 1953.
48. Jürgen Habermas, "Von der heilenden Kraft der Kunst. Ein Vortrag von Erich Rothacker in Bonn," *Frankfurter Allgemeine Zeitung*, December 29, 1953.
49. Habermas makes a similar point in a year later in a review of a guest exhibition of the Compagnia Nazionale Artigiana from Florence hosted in Düsseldorf. Jürgen Habermas, "Im süden nichts Neues? Italienischer Stil vom Kunsthandwerk zur Industrie—Die Ausstellung 'Forme Nuova in Italia'," *Handelsblatt*, December 1, 1954. See also Jürgen Habermas, "'Stil' auch für den Alltag. Die 'Industrieformung' nutzt und hilft dem Konsumenten," *Handelsblatt*, September 23, 1955.
50. Jürgen Habermas, "Martin Heidegger: The Great Influence (1959)," in *Philosophical-Political Profiles*, trans. Frederick G. Lawrence (MIT Press, 1983).
51. Interestingly, Landgrebe's most famous student after his postwar rehabilitation in Kiel was Hans Blumenberg, with whom Habermas would later have a famous debate about the role of religion and secularization in modern political life. See Hans Blumenberg, *The Legitimacy of the Modern Age*, trans. Robert M. Wallace (MIT Press, 1983).

52. Jürgen Habermas, "Im Lichte Heideggers," *Frankfurter Allgemeine Zeitung*, July 12, 1952.
53. Jürgen Habermas, *Autonomy and Solidarity: Interviews*, ed. Peter Dews (Verso, 1992), 192.
54. Habermas, *Between Naturalism and Religion*, 19.
55. For more on Heidegger's Nazism, see Richard Wolin, ed., *The Heidegger Controversy: A Critical Reader* (MIT Press, 1993).
56. Jürgen Habermas, "Martin Heidegger: On the Publication of the Lectures of 1935," *Graduate Faculty Philosophy Journal* 6, no. 2 (1977): 155.
57. Habermas, *Between Naturalism and Religion*, 22.
58. Habermas, *Between Naturalism and Religion*, 20.
59. Habermas, "Martin Heidegger," 156. See also Jürgen Habermas, "The Intellectual and Social Background of The German University Crisis," review of *The Decline of the German Mandarins: The German Academic Community, 1890–1933*, by F. K. Ringer, *Minerva* 9, no. 3 (July 1971): 422–28, esp. 423.
60. Habermas, "Martin Heidegger," 159–60; Habermas, *Between Naturalism and Religion*, 20. Habermas continues: "I gained a clearer understanding of the mindset shared by men such as Martin Heidegger, Carl Schmitt, Ernst Jünger, and Arnold Gehlen. In all of them contempt for the masses and the average was allied . . . with the celebration of the noble individual."
61. Habermas, "Martin Heidegger," 163, 164.
62. Karl Korn (*Frankfurter Allgemeine Zeitung* [FAZ]) to Habermas, July 16, 1953, HV, Korrespondenzen 1950er und 1960er Jahre, Folder 1—1954–1958 (A–Z).
63. Jürgen Habermas, "Mit Heidegger gegen Heidegger denken. Zur Veröffentlichung von Vorlesungen aus dem Jahre 1935," *Frankfurter Allgemeine Zeitung*, July 25, 1953. This is the first—and one of the only—texts from this period that Habermas allowed to be reprinted in German and translated into English.
64. Habermas, "Martin Heidegger," 161. See Habermas, "Mit Heidegger gegen Heidegger denken."
65. Jürgen Habermas, *The Philosophical Discourse of Modernity: Twelve Lectures*, trans. Frederick G. Lawrence (MIT Press, 1987), 155.
66. Quoted in Lutz Hachmeister, *Heideggers Testament. Der Philosoph, der SPIEGEL und die SS* (Propyläen, 2015), 59.
67. Letter from Martin Heidegger to Hannah Arendt, Freiburg, July 15, 1971 in Hannah Arendt and Martin Heidegger, *Letters, 1925–1975*, ed. Ursula Ludz and Thomas Wild, trans. Andrew Shields (Harcourt, 2004), 179.
68. Christian Lewalter, "Wie liest man 1953 Sätze von 1935? Zu einem politischen Streit um Heideggers Metaphysik," *Die Zeit*, August 13, 1953.
69. Karl Korn, "Warum schweigt Heidegger? Antwort auf den Versuch einer Polemik," *Frankfurter Allgemeine Zeitung*, August 14, 1953.
70. Jürgen Habermas, "Freiheit, Anruf und Gewissen," *Frankfurter Allgemeine Zeitung*, August 29, 1953.
71. Habermas, personal conversation,.
72. Ernst Rothacker, "Worauf können wir hoffen?" December 1953, quoted in Yos, *Der junge Habermas*, 108n76.
73. Jürgen Habermas, *Philosophische Texte*, vol. 4, *Politische Theorie* (Suhrkamp, 2009), 9.
74. Gereon Wolters, "Der 'Führer' und seine Denker: Zur Philosophie des 'Dritten Reichs,'" *Deutsche Zeitschrift für Philosophie* 47, no. 2 (1999): 231ff.

75. Gereon Wolters, *Vertuschung, Anklage, Rechtfertigung: Impromptus zum Rückblick der deutschen Philosophie auf das "Dritte Reich"* (Bonn University Press, 2004), 14, 18.
76. Habermas, personal conversation.
77. See Jürgen Habermas, "Das Absolute und die Geschichte: Von der Zwiespältigkeit in Schellings Denken" (PhD diss., University of Bonn, 1954), https://digi.ub.uni-heidelberg.de/diglit/habermas1954/0007/image,info.
78. Manfred Frank, "Schelling, Marx, and the Philosophy of History: Das Absolute und die Geschichte: Von der Zwiespältigkeit in Schellings Denken," in *The Habermas Handbook*, ed. Hauke Brunkhorst et al. (Columbia University Press, 2009), 219.
79. He did later write an article that took up some themes from his dissertation for the centenary of Schelling's death. See Jürgen Habermas, "Schelling und die 'Submission unter das Höhere.' Zum 100 Todestag des Philosophen—Nicht nur in Memoriam," *Frankfurter Allgemeine Zeitung*, August 21, 1954. On the centenary of the death of Søren Kierkegaard, who attended Schelling's lectures, Habermas wrote a lengthy article on how the "father of existentialism" sought "to compensate" for the loss of meaning of religious teachings by turning his gaze inward. See Jürgen Habermas, "Der Pfahl im Fleische . . . Eine verlegene Bemerkung zu Kierkegaards 100. Todestag," *Frankfurter Allgemeine Zeitung*, November 12, 1955.
80. Müller-Doohm, *Habermas*, 56; Jürgen Habermas, *'Es musste etwas besser werden. . . .' Gespräche mit Stefan Müller-Doohm und Roman Yos* (Suhrkamp, 2024), 36.
81. Habermas to Paeschke (*Merkur*), January 12, 1955, HV, Korrespondenzen 1950er und 1960er Jahre, Folder 1—1954–1958 (A–Z).
82. Jürgen Habermas, "Soziologische Notizen zum Verhältnis von Arbeit und Freizeit," in *Konkrete Vernunft. Festschrift für E. Rothacker*, ed. Gerhard Funke (Bouvier, 1958); Stefan Müller-Doohm, *Adorno: A Biography* (Polity, 2015), 46.
83. The reference to the "butcher's block (*Schlachtbank*)" is an allusion to Hegel, who described history this way.
84. Jürgen Habermas, "Demokratie auf der Schlachtbank," *Der Fortschritt. Parteifreie Wochenzeitung Für Neue Ordnung*, August 13, 1953.
85. Habermas, "Demokratie auf der Schlachtbank."
86. Habermas, "Demokratie auf der Schlachtbank."
87. Jürgen Habermas, "'Ohne Mich' auf dem Index," *Deutsche Studentenzeitung* 5, no. 5 (1955): 1.
88. Habermas, "'Ohne Mich,'" 1–2.
89. Korn (FAZ) to Habermas, February 9, 1955, HV, Korrespondenzen 1950er und 1960er Jahre, Folder 1—1954–1958 (A–Z).
90. Korn (FAZ) to Habermas, February 14, 1955, HV, Korrespondenzen 1950er und 1960er Jahre, Folder 1—1954–1958 (A–Z).
91. Habermas to Dr. Sperr (*Süddeutsche Zeitung*), February 14, 1955, HV, Korrespondenzen 1950er und 1960er Jahre, Folder 1—1954–1958 (A–Z).
92. Die Redaktion, "'Ohne Mich' auf dem Index: Notizen zu einer politischen Haltung," *Deutsche Studentenzeitung* 5, nos. 6–7 (1955).
93. Jürgen Habermas, "Die Masse—das sind wir: Bildung und soziale Stellung kein Schutz gegen den Kollektivismus?—Das Gift der Menschenverachtung," *Handelsblatt*, October 29, 1954; Jürgen Habermas, "Irrtum über die Masse. Wider das Gift der Menschenverachtung," *Wiesbadener Kurier*, November 27, 1954.

94. Habermas, "Die Masse."
95. Jürgen Habermas, "Zweihundert 'Eigenschaften' für Vierzehn Völker. Baisse in Nationalen Vorurteilen—Zu einem sozialpsychologischen Versuch mit Berliner Studenten," *Handelsblatt*, August 27, 1954.
96. Jürgen Habermas, "Für und wider den Test. Gegen den Geist der Menschenverachtung," *Frankfurter Allgemeine Zeitung*, September 11, 1954.
97. See also Jürgen Habermas, "Ludwig Klages—Überholt oder Unzeitgemäß? Zum Tode des Deutschen Philosophen," *Frankfurter Allgemeine Zeitung*, August 3, 1956; Yos, *Der Junge Habermas*, 188–92.
98. Theodor W. Adorno et al., *The Positivist Dispute in German Sociology*, trans. Glyn Adey and David Frisby (Harper Torchbooks, 1976).
99. Jürgen Habermas, "Neun Jahre unter die Lupe. Deutschlands geistige Entwicklung seit 1945. Der Versuch einer Bilanz," *Handelsblatt*, November 19, 1954.
100. Habermas, "Neun Jahre unter die Lupe."
101. Jürgen Habermas, "Der Hilfsarbeiter wird angelernter Ingenieur. Die Entwicklung vom Fließband zum Prüfstand—Berufsumschichtung durch die Technik," *Handelsblatt*, October 14, 1954.
102. Jürgen Habermas, "Sie gehören zum 'Staat' oder zum 'Betrieb'. Die unpersönliche Macht der modernen Bürokratie—Ihre Herkunft und Ihre Gefahr," *Handelsblatt*, July 11, 1954.
103. Max Weber, *From Max Weber: Essays in Sociology*, ed. and trans. Hans Heinrich Gerth and C. Wright Mills (Oxford University Press, 1958), 215.
104. Jürgen Habermas, "Beamte müssen Phantasie haben. Gibt es ein Heilmittel gegen die Schwächen der Bürokratie?—Für eine Kontrolle 'von Innen,' " *Handelsblatt*, July 25, 1954
105. Herbert Marcuse, "Some Social Implications of Modern Technology," in *The Essential Frankfurt School Reader*, ed. Andrew Arato and Eike Gerhardt (Urizen Books, 1977), 155.
106. Habermas, " 'Stil' auch für den Alltag. Die 'Industrieformung' Nutzt und Hilft dem Konsumenten," *Handelsblatt*, September 23, 1955.
107. Habermas, " 'Stil' auch für den Alltag."
108. Quoted in Arno Orzessek, "Der Einmischer," *Deutschlandfunk Kultur*, June 18, 2014, https://www.deutschlandfunkkultur.de/geistesgeschichte-der-einmischer-100.html.
109. Jürgen Habermas, "Auto fahren. Der Mensch am Lenkrad," *Frankfurter Allgemeine Zeitung*, November 27, 1954. The translations draw on Müller-Doohm, *Habermas: A Biography*, 71–72. See also Marcuse, "Some Social Implications," 143.
110. Jürgen Habermas, "Poesie, Entschleiert und Eingekellert. Supervielles 'Kinderdieb im Bonner Kontrakreis,' " *Frankfurter Allgemeine Zeitung*, April 17, 1954; Jürgen Habermas, "Kein warten auf Gawdos. Herbert Meiers 'Barke von Gawdos' im Bonner Contrakeller," *Frankfurter Allgemeine Zeitung*, October 18, 1954.
111. Jürgen Habermas, " 'Morgengrauen'—Morgen das Grauen," *Süddeutsche Zeitung*, October 2–3, 1954. Translation of these lines comes from Müller-Doohm, *Habermas: A Biography*, 50, 21–22.
112. Jürgen Habermas, "Mut und Nüchternheit," *Frankfurter Hefte* 9, no. 9 (1954); Jürgen Habermas, "Philosophie ist Risiko," *Frankfurter Allgemeine Zeitung*, June 19, 1954; Jürgen Habermas, "Standpunkt und Existenz," *Frankfurter Allgemeine Zeitung*, November 6, 1954; Jürgen Habermas, "Der metaphysischen Geheimnisse enterbt," *Frankfurter Allgemeine Zeitung*, December 4, 1954; Jürgen Habermas, "Ornament und Maschine," *Frankfurter*

328   2. *The Journalistic Years, 1951–1955*

Allgemeine Zeitung, December 31, 1954; Jürgen Habermas, "Chemische Ferien vom Ich. Huxleys Umgang mit Meskalin," *Frankfurter Allgemeine Zeitung*, December 11, 1954.

113. Jürgen Habermas, "Die letzte Phase der Mechanisierung," *Frankfurter Allgemeine Zeitung*, January 8, 1955; John Diebold, "Automation," *Textile Research Journal* 25, no. 7 (1955): 640.
114. Jürgen Habermas, "Come Back der Deutschen Soziologie," *Frankfurter Allgemeine Zeitung*, July 23, 1955.
115. Jürgen Habermas, "Der Zerfall der Institutionen," *Frankfurter Allgemeine Zeitung*, April 7, 1956.
116. Jürgen Habermas, "Der Aquinate gegen Hegel," *Frankfurter Allgemeine Zeitung*, October 7, 1955.
117. Habermas also published reviews for *Merkur* in this period. See Jürgen Habermas, "Jeder Mensch ist Unbezahlbar," *Merkur* 9, no. 2 (1955); Jürgen Habermas, "Marx in Perspektiven," *Merkur* 9, no. 12 (1955).
118. Habermas to Paeschke (*Merkur*), January 12, 1955, HV, Korrespondenzen 1950er und 1960er Jahre, Folder 1—1954–1958 (A–Z).
119. See, for example, Jürgen Habermas, "Automaten und Gesellschaft. Ein Vortragsabend der Deutschen Forschungsgemeinschaft in Godesberg," *Frankfurter Allgemeine Zeitung*, October 25, 1954. For more on this period in Habermas's life, see Yos, *Der junge Habermas*, esp. 37–272.
120. Jürgen Habermas, "Zufriedene Studentin—Gedrückter Landarbeiter. Junge soziologen untersuchen Probleme von Heute," *Handelsblatt*, June 24, 1955.
121. Jürgen Habermas, "Der Soziologen-Nachwuchs stellt sich vor. Zu einem Treffen in Hamburg unter der Leitung von Professor Schelsky," *Frankfurter Allgemeine Zeitung*, June 13, 1955.
122. These translations from Habermas's report are drawn from Müller-Doohm, *Habermas: A Biography*, 73.
123. Jürgen Habermas, "Der Geist geht zu Fuß . . . Eine Tagung zum Thema Kulturkonsum," *Handelsblatt*, October 28, 1955.
124. Jürgen Habermas, "Notizen zum Missverhältnis von Kultur und Konsum," *Merkur* 10, no. 97 (1956), reprinted in Jürgen Habermas, *Arbeit, Freizeit, Konsum. Frühe Aufsätze* (Eversdijck, 1973), 27–43.
125. Jürgen Habermas, "Konsumkritik—Eigens zum Konsumieren," *Frankfurter Hefte* 12, no. 9 (July 1957), reprinted in Habermas, *Arbeit, Freizeit, Konsum*, 53.
126. Habermas, "Der Geist geht zu Fuß . . ."
127. Yos, *Der junge Habermas*, 244.
128. Jürgen Habermas, "Die Dialektik der Rationalisierung: Vom Pauperismus in Produktion und Konsum," *Merkur* 8, no. 78 (1954): 712; republished in *Arbeit, Erkenntnis, Fortschritt. Aufsätze, 1954–1970* (de Munter, 1970), 7–30.
129. Habermas, "Die Dialektik der Rationalisierung," 712.
130. Habermas, "Die Dialektik der Rationalisierung," 704, 705. The phrases in italics appear in English in the original.
131. Habermas, "Die Dialektik der Rationalisierung," 703.
132. Habermas, "Die Dialektik der Rationalisierung," 715, 713.
133. Habermas, "Die Dialektik der Rationalisierung," 717, 718, 703.
134. Habermas, *Autonomy and Solidarity*, 187.

135. Peter J. Verovšek, "Taking Back Control Over Markets: Jürgen Habermas on the Colonization of Politics by Economics," *Political Studies* 71, no. 2 (2021).
136. Habermas, "Die Dialektik der Rationalisierung," 707, 710, 722.
137. See Gretel Adorno, "Record of a Discussion on the Theory of Needs," *New Left Review* 128 (March–April 2021): 77; see also Theodor Adorno, "Theses on Need," *New Left Review* 128 (March–April 2021).
138. Habermas, "Die Dialektik der Rationalisierung," 722.
139. Habermas, "Die Dialektik der Rationalisierung," 718.
140. Martin Heidegger, *Being and Time*, trans. John Macquarrie and Edward Robinson (Harper, 1962), part 1, chap. 2, para. 12.
141. Habermas, "Die Dialektik der Rationalisierung," 718.
142. Yos, *Der junge Habermas*, 161–62; Joachim Moras to Habermas, May 7, 1954, D: Merkur, DLA Marbach.
143. Helmut Schelsky to Jürgen Habermas, December 3, 1954, HV, Korrespondenzen 1950er und 1960er Jahre, Folder 1—1954–1958 (A–Z); see Helmut Schelsky, "Zukunftsaspekte der industriellen Gesellschaft," *Merkur* 8, no. 1 (January 1954): 13–28.
144. Carl-Göran Heidegren, "Transcendental Theory of Society, Anthropology and the Sociology of Law: Helmut Schelsky: An Almost Forgotten Sociologist," *Acta Sociologica* 40, no. 3 (1997): 286.
145. The manuscript is kept at the Universitäts- und Landesbibliothek Münster, Nachlass Schelsky, 16,012 and 16,015. The reference, as well as this quotation, come from Müller-Doohm, *Habermas: A Biography*, 70n3.
146. Schelsky to Paeschke, October 14, 1954, D: Merkur, DLA Marbach, see Yos, *Der junge Habermas*, 161.
147. Moras to Habermas, February 24, 1955, HV, Korrespondenzen 1950er und 1960er Jahre, Folder 1—1954–1958 (A–Z).
148. Jürgen Habermas to Theodor Adorno, December 20, 1955, HV, Korrespondenzen 1950er und 1960er Jahre, Folder 1—1954–1958 (A–Z).
149. Habermas, "Die Dialektik der Rationalisierung," 724.
150. Adolf Frisé, *Wir leben immer mehrere Leben. Erinnerungen* (Rowohlt, 2004), 238.
151. Habermas to Adorno, December 13, 1955, HV, Korrespondenzen 1950er und 1960er Jahre, Folder 1—1954–1958 (A–Z). See also Habermas to Professor Wagner, December 13 1955, HV, Korrespondenzen 1950er und 1960er Jahre, Folder 1—1954–1958 (A–Z).
152. Theodor Adorno to Jürgen Habermas, December 14, 1955, HV, Korrespondenzen 1950er und 1960er Jahre, Folder 1—1954–1958 (A–Z). See Lorenz Jäger, "Heimsuchung von Heidegger," *Zeitschrift für Ideengeschichte* 15, no. 3 (2021).
153. See Theodor W. Adorno, "Zur Problem der Familie," in *Gesammelte Schriften 20: Vermischte Schriften I* (Suhrkamp, 1986), 302–9; Max Horkheimer, ed., *Studien über Autorität und Familie. Forschungsberichte aus dem Institut für Sozialforschung* (Félix Alcan, 1936).
154. Habermas to Adorno, January 15, 1956, HV, Korrespondenzen 1950er und 1960er Jahre, Folder 1—1954–1958 (A–Z).
155. Jürgen Habermas, *'Es musste etwas besser werden. . . .' Gespräche mit Stefan Müller-Doohm und Roman Yos* (Suhrkamp, 2024), 41.
156. Habermas to Adorno, January 20, 1956, HV, Korrespondenzen 1950er und 1960er Jahre, Folder 1—1954–1958 (A–Z).

157. Habermas to Adorno, January 19, 1956, HV, Korrespondenzen 1950er und 1960er Jahre, Folder 1—1954–1958 (A-Z).
158. Adorno to Habermas, January 26, 1956, HV, Korrespondenzen 1950er und 1960er Jahre, Folder 1—1954–1958 (A-Z).
159. Matthew G. Specter, "From Eclipse of Reason to the Age of Reasons? Historicizing Habermas and the Frankfurt School," *Modern Intellectual History* 16, no. 1 (2019), 322; Judith Butler, "Contingent Foundations," in *Feminist Contentions: A Philosophical Exchange*, eds. Seyla Benhabib et al. (Routledge, 1995), 56n4; Amy R. Allen, *The Politics of Our Selves: Power, Autonomy, and Gender in Contemporary Critical Theory* (Columbia University Press, 2008), 6. See also Raymond Geuss, *The Idea of a Critical Theory: Habermas and the Frankfurt School* (Cambridge University Press, 1981).
160. Skinner, "Meaning and Understanding in the History of Ideas," 27.
161. Tom Rockmore, *Habermas on Historical Materialism* (Indiana University Press, 1989), 41.
162. See Habermas's comments in "Vier Jungkonservative beim Projektleiter der Moderne," *Die Tageszeitung*, October 21, 1980.
163. Jürgen Habermas, "An Avantgardistic Instinct for Relevances: The Role of the Intellectual and the European Cause," in *Europe: The Faltering Project*, trans. Ciaran Cronin (Polity Press, 2009), 55.
164. Habermas quoted in Müller-Doohm, *Habermas: A Biography*, 54. The statistics quoted come from the same source.
165. Rockmore, *Habermas on Historical Materialism*, 166.
166. Müller-Doohm, *Habermas: A Biography*, 54.

3. AT THE INSTITUTE FOR SOCIAL RESEARCH, 1956–1959

1. Habermas, *'Es musste etwas besser werden. . . .' Gespräche mit Stefan Müller-Doohm und Roman Yos* (Suhrkamp, 2024), 35, see also 11.
2. Jürgen Habermas, *The Lure of Technocracy*, trans. Ciaran Cronin (Polity, 2015), 73.
3. Habermas, *Lure of Technocracy*, 73–74.
4. Habermas, *Lure of Technocracy*, 73.
5. Jürgen Habermas, "Jewish Philosophers and Sociologists as Returnees in the Early Federal Republic of Germany: A Recollection," *Journal of Modern Jewish Studies* 13, no. 1 (2014): 115, 116.
6. Jürgen Habermas, *The Structural Transformation of the Public Sphere: An Inquiry into a Category of Bourgeois Society* (MIT Press, 1989), 72, 73.
7. Wulf Kansteiner, "Losing the War, Winning the Memory Battle: The Legacy of Nazism, World War II, and the Holocaust in the Federal Republic of Germany," in *The Politics of Memory in Postwar Europe*, ed. Richard Ned Lebow et al. (Duke University Press, 2006), 120, 111.
8. Karl Jaspers, *The Question of German Guilt* (Fordham University Press, 2001); Dolf Sternberger, "Die Deutsche Frage," *Der Monat* 8–9 (1949): 16–21; Hannah Arendt, "The Aftermath of Nazi Rule: Report from Germany," in *Essays in Understanding, 1930–1954*, ed. Jerome Kohn (Harcourt, Brace & Co., 1994), 248–69.

9. Patrick Bahners, "Theorie und Prazis: Habermas spricht über Unselds Schweigen," *Frankfurter Allgemeine Zeitung*, April 12, 2025.
10. Jürgen Habermas, *Politik, Kunst, Religion. Essays über zeitgenössische Philosophen* (Reclam, 1978), 7.
11. Habermas, "Jewish Philosophers and Sociologists as Returnees," 119, 122.
12. Habermas, "Jewish Philosophers and Sociologists," 120.
13. Jürgen Habermas, "Meine gymnasiale Schulzeit: Ausschnitte aus einer geplanten Autobiographie," *Schwarz auf Weiß: Mitteilungen des Vereins der Förderer und ehemaligen Schüler des Städtischen Gymnasiums Moltkestraße in Gummersbach e.V* 26 (December 2002): 51.
14. Stefan Müller-Doohm, "Theodor W. Adorno and Jürgen Habermas—Two Ways of Being a Public Intellectual: Sociological Observations Concerning the Transformation of a Social Figure of Modernity," *European Journal of Social Theory* 8, no. 3 (2005): 272, 276.
15. Jürgen Habermas, "Public Space and Political Public Sphere: The Biographical Roots of Two Motifs in My Thought," in *Between Naturalism and Religion* (Polity, 2008), 21.
16. Jürgen Habermas, "Reflections and Hypotheses on a Further Structural Transformation of the Political Public Sphere," *Theory, Culture & Society* 39, no. 4 (September 2022): 145.
17. See also Matthew G. Specter, *Habermas: An Intellectual Biography* (Cambridge University Press, 2010).
18. Philip Felsch, *Der Philosoph: Habermas und Wir* (Propyläen, 2024), 26; Stefan Müller-Doohm, "Nation State, Capitalism, Democracy: Philosophical and Political Motives in the Thought of Jürgen Habermas," *European Journal of Social Theory* 13, no. 4 (2010): 443.
19. Jürgen Habermas, "Der Verrat und die Maßstäbe. Wenn Jungkonservative alt werden," *Deutsche Universitätszeitung* 19 (1956).
20. Jürgen Habermas, "Illusionen auf dem Heiratsmarkt," *Merkur* 10, no. 104 (1956);
21. Jürgen Habermas, "Der Zeitgeist und die Pädagogik," *Merkur* 10, no. 96 (1956): 193.
22. See also Jürgen Habermas, "Man möchte sich mitreißen lassen. Feste und Feiern in dieser Zeit," *Handelsblatt*, February 17, 1956.
23. Jürgen Habermas, "Sigmund Freud—Der Aufklärer. Festakt in Frankfurt zum 100. Geburtstag. Wenig Anteilnahme in Wien," *Frankfurter Allgemeine Zeitung*, May 7, 1956.
24. Jürgen Habermas, "Deutschland rehabilitiert Freud," *National Zeitung*, May 13, 1956.
25. Habermas, "Jewish Philosophers and Sociologists," 120.
26. Jürgen Habermas, "Das erste Lächeln. Der Psychiater René A. Spitz über die früheste Kindheit," *Frankfurter Allgemeine Zeitung*, May 17, 1956; Jürgen Habermas, "Versöhnung von Psychoanalyse und Religion," *Frankfurter Allgemeine Zeitung*, June 11, 1956.
27. Jürgen Habermas, "Triebschicksal als politisches Schicksal. Zum Abschluss der Vorlesungen über Sigmund Freud an den Universitäten Frankfurt und Heidelberg," *Frankfurter Allgemeine Zeitung*, July 14, 1956. This contribution was also reprinted in the Basel-based *National Zeitung* on July 20, 1956.
28. Jürgen Habermas, personal conversation, June 7, 2024.
29. Habermas, "Triebschicksal als politisches Schicksal."
30. Jürgen Habermas to Theodor Adorno, January 20, 1956, HV, Korrespondenzen 1950er und 1960er Jahre, Folder 1—1954–1958 (A–Z); Habermas, "Meine gymnasiale Schulzeit: Ausschnitte aus einer geplanten Autobiographie," 51.

31. Jürgen Habermas, "Zur philosophischen Diskussion um Marx und den Marxismus," *Philosophische Rundschau* 5, nos. 3–4 (1957).
32. For more on Habermas's esteem for Marcuse and for the role that his "Heideggermarxism" played in helping Habermas bridge theory and practice, see Habermas to Herbert Marcuse, July 10, 1978, HV, Korrespondenzen 1978 Jahre, Folder 46—Band 4 (L–N).
33. Habermas, "Jewish Philosophers and Sociologists," 121.
34. See Müller-Doohm, "Theodor W. Adorno and Jürgen Habermas."
35. Jürgen Habermas, personal conversation, June 7, 2024.
36. Rolf Wiggershaus, *The Frankfurt School: Its History, Theories, and Political Significance* (MIT Press, 1995), 545.
37. Habermas quoted in Stefan Müller-Doohm, *Habermas: A Biography* (Polity, 2016), 54.
38. Jürgen Habermas, "Konservativer Geist—und die Modernistischen Folgen. Zum Reformplan für die deutsche Schule," *Der Monat* 12, no. 133 (1959). Republished in Habermas, *Kleine politische Schriften I–IV*, 41–57.
39. Habermas, "Konservativer Geist," 41–42, 44.
40. Habermas, "Konservativer Geist," 43–44.
41. Habermas, "Konservativer Geist," 46, 50.
42. In making this point, Habermas draws on a broader discussion within German sociological circles—particularly the work of Arnold Gehlen—as reflected in his coverage of a 1958 meeting of the Wuppertal 'Bund' concerning educational formation. Jürgen Habermas, "Leitbilder in Anführungszeichen. Zu einer Tagung des Wuppertaler 'Bundes'," *Frankfurter Allgemeine Zeitung*, October 22, 1958.
43. Habermas, *Kleine politische Schriften I–IV*, 53–54.
44. Jürgen Habermas, "Das chronische Leiden der Hochschulreform," *Merkur* 11, no. 109 (March 1957). Republished in Habermas, *Kleine politische Schriften I–IV*, 13–40.
45. Habermas, "Das chronische Leiden," 16, 18.
46. Habermas, "Das chronische Leiden," 21.
47. Habermas, "Das chronische Leiden," 22.
48. Habermas, "Das chronische Leiden," 24, 25.
49. Habermas, "Das chronische Leiden," 27, 32, 36; Wiggershaus, *The Frankfurt School*, 546.
50. Habermas, *Kleine politische Schriften I–IV*, 40–41.
51. This quotation, given in the context of the Freiburg University denazification commission, is quoted in Richard Wolin, *Heidegger's Children: Hannah Arendt, Karl Löwith, Hans Jonas, and Herbert Marcuse* (Princeton University Press, 2001), 87.
52. Theodor W. Adorno, *Eingriffe: Neun kritische Modelle* (Edition Suhrkamp, 1963), 32; Jürgen Habermas, *Autonomy and Solidarity: Interviews*, ed. Peter Dews (Verso, 1992), 199.
53. Theodor W. Adorno, *Aspects of the New Right-Wing Extremism* (Polity, 2020), 14; Theodor W. Adorno, *The Jargon of Authenticity* (Northwestern University Press, 1973).
54. Jürgen Habermas, "Die große Wirkung: Eine chronistische Anmerkung zu Martin Heideggers 70. Geburtstag," *Frankfurter Allgemeine Zeitung*, September 26, 1959. Habermas's two essays on Heidegger were republished as Jürgen Habermas, *Philosophisch-Politische Profile* (Suhrkamp, 1987), 65–71 and 72–81. The essay under discussion here was published in English as Jürgen Habermas, *Philosophical-Political Profiles*, trans. Frederick G. Lawrence (MIT Press, 1983), 53–60.

55. Habermas, *Philosophical-Political Profiles*, 53, 54.
56. Habermas, *Philosophical-Political Profiles*, 53.
57. Habermas, *Philosophical-Political Profiles*, 56, 57, 59
58. Habermas, *Philosophical-Political Profiles*, 55, 60.
59. Jürgen Habermas, "Eine anderer Mythos des 20. Jahrhunderts," *Frankfurter Hefte* 14, no. 3 (March 1959). Republished as Jürgen Habermas, *Arbeit, Freizeit, Konsum. Frühe Aufsätze* (Eversdijck, 1973), 97–102.
60. Habermas, *Arbeit, Freizeit, Konsum*, 97; Jürgen Habermas, *The Past as Future: Vergangenheit als Zukunft*, trans. Max Pensky (University of Nebraska Press, 1994), 99–100.
61. Habermas, *Arbeit, Freizeit, Konsum*, 100, 99, 102.
62. Karl Korn (FAZ) to Habermas, November 8, 1955, HV, Korrespondenzen 1950er und 1960er Jahre, Folder 1—1954–1958 (A–Z), "Die Heideggerianer und Hegelianer streiten sich ja um Schelling, vor allem um den alten Schelling"; Jürgen Habermas, "Karl Jaspers über Schelling," *Frankfurter Allgemeine Zeitung*, January 14, 1956.
63. Habermas to Theodor Adorno, January 19, 1956, HV, Korrespondenzen 1950er und 1960er Jahre, Folder 1—1954–1958 (A–Z); Jürgen Habermas, "Philosophie," *Deutsche Universitätszeitung* 23–24 (1956).
64. Jürgen Habermas, "Jaspers und die Gestalten der Wahrheit: Geschichtsphilosophische Betrachtung zu einer Geschichte der Philosophie, zum 75. Geburtstag von Karl Jaspers," *Frankfurter Allgemeine Zeitung*, February 22, 1958. Republished as Habermas, *Philosophisch-Politische Profile*, 87–95, and in English translation as Habermas, *Philosophical-Political Profiles*, 45–52.
65. Habermas, *Philosophical-Political Profiles*, 45.
66. Jürgen Habermas, "Die Grenze in uns—Helmuth Plessner: 'Die verspätete Nation,'" *Frankfurter Hefte* 14, no. 11 (November 1959). Republished in German as Habermas, *Arbeit, Freizeit, Konsum*, 103–11.
67. Jürgen Habermas, "Anthropologie," in *Fischer-Lexikon Philosophie*, ed. Alwin Diemer and Ivo Frenzel (Fischer, 1958). Republished as Habermas, *Arbeit, Freizeit, Konsum*, 164–80.
68. Jürgen Habermas, unpublished interview with Karl-Siegbert Rehberg (2008), quoted in Müller-Doohm, *Habermas: A Biography*, 392.
69. Habermas, "Anthropologie," 18, 19, 20.
70. Habermas, "Anthropologie," 19, 20, 24, emphasis in original.
71. This quotation is from an open letter to Plessner, originally published in *Merkur* in 1972. Quoted in Müller-Doohm, *Habermas: A Biography*, 513–14n130.
72. Habermas, "Anthropologie," 27, 31.
73. Habermas, "Anthropologie," 29, 31, 33–35.
74. Habermas, "Anthropologie," 32.
75. Müller-Doohm, *Habermas: A Biography*, 42.
76. Jürgen Habermas, "Soziologische Notizen zum Verhältnis von Arbeit und Freizeit," in *Konkrete Vernunft. Festschrift Für E. Rothacker*, ed. Gerhard Funke (Bouvier, 1958), 219, 230. See Friedrich Pollock, *Automation: A Study of its Economic and Social Consequences*, trans. W. O. Henderson and W. H. Chaloner (Frederick A. Praeger, 1957).
77. Jürgen Habermas, "Der biographische Schleier. Bei Gelegenheit des Stresemann-Filmes notiert," *Frankfurter Hefte* 12, no. 5 (1957): 357.

78. Habermas, "Der biographische Schleier," 357, 359.
79. Jürgen Habermas, "Können Konsumenten spielen?" *Frankfurter Allgemeine Zeitung*, April 13, 1957.
80. Jürgen Habermas, "Konsumkritik—Eigens zum Konsumieren," *Frankfurter Hefte* 12, no. 9 (July 1957): 641–45. Republished in Jürgen Habermas, *Arbeit, Erkenntnis, Fortschritt. Aufsätze, 1954–1970* (de Munter, 1970), 47–55.
81. Habermas, *Arbeit, Erkenntnis, Fortschritt*, 49.
82. Habermas, *Arbeit, Erkenntnis, Fortschritt*, 55, 52.
83. Habermas, *Arbeit, Erkenntnis, Fortschritt*, 47.
84. Gerhard Schäfer, "Von der nivellierten Mittelstandsgesellschaft zur Risikogesellschaft: Ein Vergleich der soziologischen Zeitdiagnostik Helmut Schelskys und Ulrich Becks," *Geschlossene Gesellschaften. Verhandlungen des 38. Kongresses der Deutschen Gesellschaft für Soziologie in Bamberg 2016* 38 (2017): 2.
85. Jürgen Habermas, "Der Abstraktion gewachsen sein . . . ," *Magnum: Die Zeitschrift für das moderne Leben* (April 1957): 64.
86. Jürgen Habermas, "Für und Wider. Der Mensch zwischen den Apparaten," *Süddeutsche Zeitung*, September 6–7, 1958.
87. Habermas, "Der Abstraktion gewachsen sein . . . ," 64.
88. Yos, *Der junge Habermas*, 470.
89. Saskia Wiedner, "Karl Jaspers: Die Atombombe und die Zukunft des Menschen (1958)," in *Handbuch Nachkriegskultur: Literatur, Sachbuch und Film in Deutschland (1945–1962)*, ed. Elena Agazzi and Erhard Schütz (De Gruyter, 2013).
90. Jürgen Habermas, "Der verschleierte Schrecken: Bemerkungen zu C. F. von Weizsäckers 'Mit der Bombe Leben,'" *Frankfurter Hefte* 13, no. 8 (July 1958): 530–32. Republished in Habermas, *Arbeit, Erkenntnis, Fortschritt*, 92–96.
91. Anthony Buzzard, John Slessor and Richard Lowenthal, "The H-Bomb: Massive Retaliation or Graduated Deterrence?" *International Affairs* 32, no. 2 (1956): 148.
92. Habermas, *Arbeit, Erkenntnis, Fortschritt*, 93, 95.
93. Müller-Doohm, *Habermas: A Biography*, 55.
94. Yos, *Der junge Habermas*, 441.
95. Müller-Doohm, *Habermas: A Biography*, 55.
96. Jürgen Habermas, "Unruhe erste Bürgerpflicht. Römerbergrede gegen die Atombewaffnung der Bundeswehr," *Diskus. Frankfurter Studentenzeitung* 8, no. 5 (May 20, 1958).
97. Habermas, "Unruhe erste Bürgerpflicht."
98. Müller-Doohm, *Habermas: A Biography*, 54.
99. Philipp Lenhard, *Café Marx. Das Institut für Sozialforschung von den Anfängen bis zur Frankfurter Schule* (C. H. Beck, 2024), 219; see also Peter J. Verovšek, "Celebrating Jürgen Habermas and the Institute for Social Research: Reflections on the History of Critical Theory from a Jubilee Year," *European Journal of Political Theory* (2024), https://doi.org/10.1177/14748851241302296.
100. Michael Hofmann, *Reading Habermas: Structural Transformation of the Public Sphere* (Lexington Books, 2023), 47; Jürgen Habermas, *'Es musste etwas besser werden. . . .' Gespräche mit Stefan Müller-Doohm und Roman Yos* (Suhrkamp, 2024), 42.
101. Wiggershaus, *The Frankfurt School*, 547.
102. Habermas, "Unruhe erste Bürgerpflicht."

103. Jürgen Habermas, *Student und Politik; Eine soziologische Untersuchung zum politischen Bewusstsein Frankfurter Studenten* (Luchterhand, 1961), 11–55.
104. Hofmann, *Reading Habermas*, 157, 181.
105. Wiggershaus, *The Frankfurt School*, 548.
106. Yos, *Der junge Habermas*, 382, also 417ff.
107. Jürgen Habermas, *Student und Politik*, 34, 24.
108. Wiggershaus, *The Frankfurt School*, 548.
109. Frieder Günther, "'Staatsrechtslehre' Between Tradition and Change: West-German University Teachers of Public Law in the Process of Westernization, 1949–1970," Conference at the German Historical Institute, Washington, DC, March 25–27, 1999, 6.
110. Erhard Denninger, "Judicial Review Revisited: The German Experience," *Tulane Law Review* 59 (1984–1985): 1013.
111. Günther, "'Staatsrechtslehre' Between Tradition and Change," 1.
112. Michael Hofmann, *Habermas's Public Sphere: A Critique* (Fairleigh Dickinson University Press, 2017), 21n24.
113. Günther, "'Staatsrechtslehre' Between Tradition and Change," 2.
114. Carl Schmitt, *The Crisis of Parliamentary Democracy* (MIT Press, 1985), 45, 43.
115. Günther, "'Staatsrechtslehre' Between Tradition and Change," 4
116. See Denninger, "Judicial Review Revisited."
117. Günther, "'Staatsrechtslehre' Between Tradition and Change," 5.
118. Günther, "'Staatsrechtslehre' Between Tradition and Change," 6, 8.
119. Wolfgang Abendroth, *Antagonistische Gesellschaft und politische Demokratie* (Luchterhand, 1967), 139. English translation quoted in Specter, *Habermas: An Intellectual Biography*, 45.
120. Günther, "'Staatsrechtslehre' Between Tradition and Change," 9.
121. Günther, "'Staatsrechtslehre' Between Tradition and Change," 16.
122. Horst Ehmke, "Prinzipien der Verfassungsinterpretation," *Veröffentlichungen der Vereinigung der Deutschen Staatsrechtslehrer* 20 (1963): 53–102, here 71.
123. Habermas, *Arbeit, Erkenntnis, Fortschritt*, 270.
124. Jürgen Habermas, *A Berlin Republic: Writings on Germany*, trans. Steven Rendall (University of Nebraska Press, 1997), 108.
125. Radbruch, quoted in Specter, *Habermas: An Intellectual Biography*, 54, translation modified.
126. Specter, *Habermas: An Intellectual Biography*, 200; Matthew G. Specter, "From Eclipse of Reason to the Age of Reasons? Historicizing Habermas and the Frankfurt School," *Modern Intellectual History* 16, no. 1 (2019): 117.
127. Specter, *Habermas: An Intellectual Biography*, 20.
128. Habermas, *Student und Politik*, 11.
129. Simone Chambers, "Deliberative Democratic Theory," *Annual Review of Political Science* 6 (2003): 308.
130. Habermas, *Student und Politik*.
131. Adorno to Horkheimer, March 15, 1960. Quoted in Wiggershaus, *The Frankfurt School*, 554.
132. Horkheimer to Adorno, September 27, 1958. Quoted in Wiggershaus, *The Frankfurt School*, 555.
133. Horkheimer to Adorno, September 27, 1958. Quoted in Theodor W. Adorno and Max Horkheimer, *Briefwechsel 1927–1969. Bände I–IV* (Suhrkamp, 2023), 508.

134. Max Horkheimer, "Traditional and Critical Theory," in *Critical Theory: Selected Essays*, trans. Matthew J. O'Connell (Continuum, 1972), 214, 218, 241.
135. Horkheimer to Adorno, September 27, 1958. Quoted in Adorno and Horkheimer, *Briefwechsel*, 516.
136. Max Horkheimer, *Critique of Instrumental Reason*, trans. Matthew J. O'Connell et al. (Continuum, 1974), viii; see also Maeve Cooke, "Forever Resistant? Adorno and Radical Transformation of Society," in *A Companion to Adorno*, ed. Peter E. Gordon et al. (Wiley-Blackwell, 2020), 583–84.
137. Horkheimer to Adorno, Montagnola, at the end of August 1959. Quoted in Wiggershaus, *The Frankfurt School*, 555.
138. Cooke, "Forever Resistant?," 584–85.
139. Philip Lenhard, *Café Marx. Das Institut für Sozialforschung von den Anfängen bis zur Frankfurter Schule* (C. H. Beck, 2024), 497.
140. Müller-Doohm, *Habermas*, 64.
141. Jürgen Habermas, "Mit Heidegger gegen Heidegger denken. Zur Veröffentlichung von Vorlesungen aus dem Jahre 1935," *Frankfurter Allgemeine Zeitung*, July 25, 1953.
142. Habermas, "Meine gymnasiale Schulzeit," 52.
143. Müller-Doohm, *Habermas: A Biography*, 66.
144. Jürgen Habermas, *Theory and Practice*, trans. John Viertel (Beacon Press, 1974), 34.
145. Jürgen Habermas, private conversation, June 7, 2024.
146. These are the adjectives that Habermas himself uses to describe Horkheimer. Personal conversation, June 7, 2024.
147. Müller-Doohm, *Habermas: A Biography*, 80–88.
148. Müller-Doohm, *Habermas: A Biography*, 80.
149. Max Horkheimer, "The Present Situation of Social Philosophy and the Tasks of an Institute for Social Research," in *Between Philosophy and Social Science: Selected Early Writings* (MIT Press, 1993), 11.
150. Müller-Doohm, *Habermas: A Biography*, 80.
151. Jürgen Habermas, "Marx in Perspektiven," *Merkur* 9, no. 12 (1955).
152. Habermas to Hans-Georg Gadamer, January 20, 1956, HV, Korrespondenzen 1950er und 1960er Jahre, Folder 1—1954–1958 (A–Z).
153. Habermas, "Literaturbericht zur philosophischen Diskussion."
154. Hans-Georg Gadamer, "Der Meister der Kommunikation," *Süddeutsche Zeitung*, June 18, 1999.
155. Max Horkheimer, *Gesammelte Schriften*, vol. 18, *Briefwechsel 1949–1973* (Fischer Taschenbuch, 1996), 443, 446, 445.
156. Jürgen Habermas, "Ein Brief," in *Kritische Theorie und Kultur*, ed. Rainer Erd et al. (Suhrkamp, 1989), 392.
157. Letter dated June 11, 1960, Deutsches Literaturarchiv Marbach, Handschriftenabteilung, Briefwechsel Merkur, Mappe 2.
158. Gerhard Richter and Theodor W. Adorno, "Who's Afraid of the Ivory Tower? A Conversation with Theodor W. Adorno," *Monatshefte* 94, no. 1 (2002): 19.
159. Max Horkheimer, "Traditional and Critical Theory," 199.
160. Wiggershaus, *The Frankfurt School*, 543.

4. A PARTISAN PROFESSOR IN THE STUDENT MOVEMENT, 1960-1971

1. Michael J. Thompson, *The Domestication of Critical Theory* (Rowman & Littlefield, 2016).
2. Jürgen Habermas, private conversation, June 7, 2024.
3. Roger Scruton, *Thinkers of the New Left* (Longman, 1985), 126.
4. Dieter Henrich, *Ins denken ziehen. Eine philosophische Autobiographie* (C. H. Beck, 2021), 145.
5. Quoted in Stefan Müller-Doohm, *Habermas: A Biography* (Polity, 2016), 154.
6. Jürgen Habermas, "Meine gymnasiale Schulzeit: Ausschnitte aus einer geplanten Autobiographie," *Schwarz auf Weiß: Mitteilungen des Vereins der Förderer und ehemaligen Schüler des Städtischen Gymnasiums Moltkestraße in Gummersbach E.V* 26 (2002): 52.
7. "Mein Interesse erstreckt sich, wie Sie wissen, auf Philosophie und Soziologie, ein wenig natürlich auch auf zeitkritische und politische Themen." Jürgen Habermas to Dr. Ramseger, January 22, 1964, HV, 4—1963, Band 2 (M–Z). Habermas is responding to an invitation from Jörg Ramseger to contribute to a new publication that styles itself as a German-language version of the *Times Literary Supplement*. While Habermas endorses this idea, he notes that he does not think that he can contribute regularly given his interests, especially since "The new philosophical and sociological publications of German origin are, to be honest, not exciting enough for a person to find something interesting, even if it is only negative, every other month."
8. This description comes from Percy Cohen (LSE) to Jürgen Habermas, September 19. 1969, HV, 11—1969, Band 1 (A–K).
9. Rolf Wiggershaus, *The Frankfurt School: Its History, Theories, and Political Significance* (MIT Press, 1995), 561.
10. Jürgen Habermas, *Autonomy and Solidarity: Interviews*, ed. Peter Dews (Verso, 1992), 79.
11. Robert C. Holub, *Jürgen Habermas: Critic in the Public Sphere* (Routledge, 1991), 2; Pauline Johnson, *Habermas: Rescuing the Public Sphere* (Routledge, 2006), 19.
12. Jürgen Habermas, "Wolfgang Abendroth. Der Partisanenprofessor," *Die Zeit*, April 29, 1966, 24; republished as Jürgen Habermas, "Der Partisanenprofessor (Wolfgang Abendroth)," in *Philosophisch-Politische Profile* (Suhrkamp, 1987), 249–52.
13. Jürgen Habermas, private conversation, June 7, 2024.
14. Jürgen Habermas, private conversation, June 7, 2024.
15. Jürgen Habermas, private conversation, June 7, 2024.
16. Habermas, *Autonomy and Solidarity*, 189.
17. Jürgen Habermas, "Wolfgang Abendroth in der Bundesrepublik," *Düsseldorfer Debatte* 12 (1985): 54–58; reprinted in *Wolfgang Abendroth wissenschaftlicher Politiker. Biobibliographische Beiträge*, ed. Friedrich-Martin Balzer et al. (VS Verlag für Sozialwissenschaften, 2001), 165, 168.
18. Habermas, *Autonomy and Solidarity*, 189.
19. Carl Schmitt, *The Crisis of Parliamentary Democracy* (MIT Press, 1985), 45; Wolfgang Abendroth, *Antagonistische Gesellschaft und politische Demokratie* (Luchterhand, 1967), 139, quoted in Matthew G. Specter, *Habermas: An Intellectual Biography* (Cambridge University Press, 2010), 45.
20. Jürgen Habermas, "Wolfgang Abendroth zum 100. Geburtstag" (lecture, conference "The German social scientist Wolfgang Abendroth", Haus des IG-Metall-Vorstandes,

338   4. A Partisan Professor in the Student Movement, 1960–1971

Frankfurt am Main, May 6, 2006); in *literaturkritik.de* 5 (May 2006); reprinted as Jürgen Habermas, *Ach, Europa*, vol. 11 of *Kleine politische Schriften* (Suhrkamp, 2008), 13.
21. Wiggershaus, *The Frankfurt School*, 561–62.
22. Müller-Doohm, Habermas: *A Biography*, 115.
23. Willy Brandt and Ulrich Lohmar to Jürgen Habermas, September 21, 1963, HV, 3—1963, Band 1 (A–L).
24. "Interview mit Detlef Horster und Willem van Reijen, Starnberg, March 23, 1979", *Intermediair*, June 29, 1979; reprinted in Habermas, *Kleine politische Schriften I–IV*, 511–32; published in English as Detlev Horster et al., "Interview with Jürgen Habermas Starnberg, March 23, 1979," *New German Critique* 18 (1979). See also Jürgen Habermas, "Wissenschaft und Politik," *Offene Welt* 86 (1964): 413–23; Jürgen Habermas, "Wissenschaftliche Politikberatung—Staatliche Forschungspolitik," *Süddeutsche Zeitung*, June 26, 1964.
25. Jürgen Habermas to Ulrich Lohmar, October 22, 1963, HV, 3—1963, Band 1 (A–L).
26. Leo Bauer (*Die Neue Gesellschaft*)—Jürgen Habermas, October 4, 1970, HV, 1970—Band 1 (A–O).
27. Jürgen Habermas to Willy Brandt via Leo Bauer (*Die neue Gesellschaft*), December 8, 1970, HV, 1970—Band 1 (A–O).
28. Müller-Doohm, *Habermas: A Biography*, 139.
29. Jürgen Habermas, "Die Bundesrepublik: Eine Wahlmonarchie?" *Magnum: Die Zeitschrift für das moderne Leben*, special issue "Woher—Wohin: Bilanz der Bundesrepublik," ed. Karl H. Pawek (1961): 28.
30. Jürgen Habermas to Leszek Kolakowski, February 24, 1970, HV, 1970—Band 1 (A–O).
31. Wolfgang Kraushaar, ed., *Frankfurter Schule und Studentenbewegung*, vol. 2, *Dokumente* (Rogner & Bernhard, 1998), 194.
32. Jürgen Habermas, *Eine art Schadensabwicklung*, vol. 6 of *Kleine politische Schriften* (Suhrkamp, 1987), 48.
33. Jürgen Habermas, *Blätter für deutsche und internationale Politik* 4 (1964): 335–40, translation drawn from Müller-Doohm, *Habermas: A Biography*, 117.
34. Jürgen Habermas, "Die fünfte Republik. Was steht hinter de Gaulle?", review of *Die Fünfte Republik. Was steht hinter de Gaulle?* by Armin Mohler. *Die Zeit*, September 18, 1964, translation drawn from Müller-Doohm, *Habermas: A Biography*, 117, also 118.
35. Carl Friedrich von Weizsäcker, "Dankesrede: Bedingungen des Friedens," *Friedenspreis des Deutschen Buchhandels*, Börsenverein des Deutschen Buchhandels, 1963, 10.
36. Jürgen Habermas, "Auf- und Abrüstung, Moralisch und Militärisch," *Merkur* 17, no. 185 (July 1963): 716.
37. Jürgen Habermas, "Vom ende der Politik," *Frankfurter Allgemeine Zeitung*, October 17, 1964, translation drawn from Müller-Doohm, *Habermas: A Biography*, 119.
38. See Jürgen Habermas, "Ein Verdrängungsprozeß wird Enthüllt," *Die Zeit*, June 12, 1964; Jürgen Habermas, "Parteirügen an Schriftsteller—Hüben und Drüben," *Merkur* 17, no. 180 (February 1963): 201–12.
39. See Jürgen Habermas, *Philosophisch-Politische Profile* (Suhrkamp, 1987). Some of these essays also appear in the English edition, published as Habermas, *Philosophical-Political Profiles*.
40. Müller-Doohm, Habermas: A Biography, 118.
41. Jürgen Habermas, '*Es musste etwas besser werden. . . .' Gespräche mit Stefan Müller-Doohm und Roman Yos* (Suhrkamp, 2024), 64.

42. Hans-Georg Gadamer, "Der Meister der Kommunikation," *Süddeutsche Zeitung*, June 18, 1999.
43. Jürgen Habermas, "A Philosophico-Political Profile," *New Left Review* 151 (1985): 76.
44. See also Jürgen Habermas "Von der Schwierigkeit nein zu sagen," *Merkur* 18, no. 201 (December 1964): 1184–88; published in English in Jürgen Habermas, *Religion and Rationality: Essays on Reason, God, and Modernity*, ed. Eduardo Mendieta (MIT Press, 2002), 60–66, esp. 60.
45. Jürgen Habermas, "Diskutieren—was sonst?," *Daten* 2 (1962); reprinted in Habermas, *Kleine politische Schriften I–IV*, 200, 204. See also "Leserbrief," *Civis* 9 (December 1962); reprinted in Kraushaar, *Frankfurter Schule und Studentenbewegung*, 159.
46. See Jürgen Habermas, "Pädagogischer 'Optimismus' vor Gericht einer pessimistischen Anthropologie. Schelskys Bedenken zur Schulreform," *Neue Sammlung* 1, no. 4 (1961): 251–78; reprinted in Habermas, *Kleine politische Schriften I–IV*, 58–100.
47. Jürgen Habermas, "Vom sozialen Wandel akademischer Bildung" (lecture, University of Berlin, January 1963); in *Merkur* 17, no. 183 (May 1963): 413–27; reprinted in Habermas, *Kleine politische Schriften I–IV*, 116, 111.
48. Jürgen Habermas, *Moral Consciousness and Communicative Action* (MIT Press, 1990), 1–20.
49. Holub, *Jürgen Habermas*, 47.
50. Jürgen Habermas to Dr. Büttner (Staatliche Niedersächsische Heimschule Essens), September 19, 1974, HV, 23—1974, Band 1 (A–E).
51. Müller-Doohm, *Habermas: A Biography*, 113.
52. Philip Lenhard, *Café Marx. Das Institut für Sozialforschung von den Anfängen bis zur Frankfurter Schule* (C. H. Beck, 2024), 499.
53. Quoted in Müller-Doohm, *Habermas: A Biography*, 124.
54. Max Horkheimer to Jürgen Habermas, February 26, 1963, HV, 3—1963, Band 1 (A–L).
55. Jürgen Habermas to Hans-Georg Gadamer, January 22, 1964, HV, 3—1963, Band 1 (A–L).
56. Jürgen Habermas to Theodor Adorno, January 16, 1964, HV, 5—1964, Band 1 (A–Z).
57. Jürgen Habermas—Max Horkheimer, January 16, 1964, HV, 3—1963, Band 1 (A–L).
58. Jürgen Habermas—Hans Paeschke, January 24, 1969, HV, 1969—Band 2 (L–Z); Jürgen Habermas to Dr. Werner Becker, November 9, 1973, HV, 19—1973, Band 1 (A–F); Jürgen Habermas to René König, September 13, 1973, HV, 20—1973, Band 2 (G–M).
59. Jürgen Habermas, "Bemerkungen zur Entwicklung des Horkheimerischen Werkes," in *Max Horkheimer Heute: Werk und Wirkung*, ed. Alfred Schmidt and Norbert Altwicker (Fischer, 1986), 163–79, published in English as Jürgen Habermas, "Notes on the Developmental History of Horkheimer's Work," *Theory, Culture & Society* 10, no. 2 (1993): 61–77.
60. Müller-Doohm, *Habermas: A Biography*, 123.
61. See Jürgen Habermas, "Über den Begriff der politischen Beteiligung," in *Arbeit, Erkenntnis, Fortschritt: Aufsätze, 1954–1970* (de Munter, 1970).
62. Jürgen Habermas, "New Social Movements," *Telos* 49 (1981): 33.
63. Jürgen Habermas, "Ich bin alt, aber nicht fromm geworden," in *Über Habermas: Gespräche mit Zeitgenossen*, ed. Michael Funken (Wissenschaftliche Buchgesellschaft, 2009).
64. "Der Marsch durch die Institutionen hat auch die CDU erreicht. Der Frankfurter Philosoph und Soziologe Jürgen Habermas im Gespräch mit Rainer Erd über die politische Kultur in der Bundesrepublik Deutschland nach 1968," *Frankfurter Rundschau*, March 11, 1988; published in English as Jürgen Habermas, "Political Culture in Germany Since

1968: An Interview with Dr. Rainer Erd for the 'Frankfurter Rundschau,'" in *The New Conservatism: Cultural Criticism and the Historians' Debate*, trans. Shierry Weber Nicholsen (MIT Press, 1989), 184.

65. Bericht über neuere amerikanische Forschungen auf Gebieten der Erziehungspsychologie und Soziologie (Spring 1965), HV, 6—1965, Band 1 (A–Z).
66. Jürgen Habermas, "Vier Jungkonservativen beim Projektleiter der Moderne," *Die Tageszeitung* 393 (October 21, 1980): 9.
67. See for example, Jürgen Habermas and Ludwig von Friedeburg, "Offener Brief an den AStA der Freien Universität," May 4, 1967; republished in Jürgen Habermas, *Protestbewegung und Hochschulreform* (Suhrkamp, 1969), 134–36.
68. Jürgen Habermas, "Zwangsjacke für die Studienreform. Die befristete Immatrikulation und der falsche Pragmatismus des Wissenschaftsrates," *Der Monat* 18, no. 218 (November 1966): 7–19; reprinted in Habermas, *Kleine politische Schriften I–IV*, 123.
69. Habermas, *Kleine politische Schriften I–IV*, 130, 131.
70. Habermas, *Protestbewegung und Hochschulreform*, 104.
71. Wiggershaus, *The Frankfurt School*, 617.
72. Jürgen Habermas, "Thesen gegen die Koalition der mutlosen mit den Machthabern," *diskus* 16, no. 8 (1966): 2.
73. Jürgen Habermas, "Offenen Brief an Willy Brandt," *Frankfurter Rundschau*, November 29, 1966; reprinted in Kraushaar, *Frankfurter Schule und Studentenbewegung*, 215. Habermas's comments in the panel discussion are cited in Müller-Doohm, *Habermas: A Biography*, 139 (translation modified).
74. Jürgen Habermas, "Universität in der Demokratie—Demokratisierung der Universität" (lecture, Universität Berlin, January 20, 1967); in *Merkur* 21, no. 230 (May 1967): 416–33, published in English in Jürgen Habermas, *Towards a Rational Society: Student Protest, Science, and Politics* (Heinemann Educational Books, 1971), 2, 3.
75. Habermas, *Towards a Rational Society*, 4, 5–6.
76. Habermas, *Towards a Rational Society*, 10.
77. Jürgen Habermas, "Rede über die politische Rolle der Studentenschaft in der Bundesrepublik" (congress "Hochschule und Demokratie", Hanover, June 9, 1967); in *Der Politologe*, July 23, 1967; reprinted in Habermas, *Kleine politische Schriften I–IV*, 206, 209.
78. Habermas, *Kleine politische Schriften I–IV*, 207, 210–11.
79. Maeve Cooke, "Forever Resistant? Adorno and Radical Transformation of Society," in *A Companion to Adorno*, ed. Peter E. Gordon et al. (Wiley-Blackwell, 2020), 588.
80. Quoted in Müller-Doohm, *Habermas: A Biography*, 141.
81. Habermas, *Kleine politische Schriften I–IV*, 214.
82. Habermas, *Kleine politische Schriften I–IV*, 519–20.
83. Helmut Plessner to Theodor Adorno (cc Jürgen Habermas), no date, HV, HV, 8—1967, Band 1 (A–Z).
84. Jürgen Habermas—Erich Fried (BBC), July 26, 1967, HV, 8—1967, Band 1 (A–Z).
85. Jürgen Habermas—Hans Paeschke, Feburary 10, 1967, HV, 8—1967, Band 1 (A–Z). See also Jürgen Habermas, *Brief [an Claus Grossner]*, May 13, 1968; in Habermas, *Protestbewegung und Hochschulreform*, 151–52.
86. Dr. Jacob Taubes to Jürgen Habermas, June 14, 1968, HV, 10—1968, Band 2 (M–Z).
87. Habermas, *The New Conservatism*, 185.

4. *A Partisan Professor in the Student Movement, 1960–1971*   341

88. Jürgen Habermas, "Zum Tode von Rudi Dutschke: Ein wahrhaftiger Sozialist. Er verband die Kraft zum Visionären mit dem Sinn fürs Konkrete," *Die Zeit*, January 4, 1980, 7; reprinted in Habermas, *Kleine politische Schriften I–IV*, 306.
89. Helmut Plessner to Theodor Adorno (cc Jürgen Habermas), n.d., HV, HV, 8—1967, Band 1 (A–Z).
90. Oscar Negt, "Studentischer Protest—Liberalismus—'Linksfaschismus'," *Kursbuch* 13 (1968); Claus Offe, "Die Bundesrepublik als Schattenriß zweier Lichtquellen," *Ästhetik und Kommunikation* 36 (2005): 153.
91. Joschka Fischer, "Gründungfigur des demokratischen Deutschland," in *Über Habermas: Gespräche mit Zeitgenossen*, ed. Michael Funken (Wissenschaftliche Buchgesellschaft, 2009), 47.
92. See Peter J. Verovšek, "A Case of Communicative Learning?: Rereading Habermas's Philosophical Project through an Arendtian Lens," *Polity* 51, no. 3 (July 2019).
93. "Studentenprotest in der Bundesrepublik" (lecture, Goethe House, New York, November 1967); republished as "Die Proteste der Studenten. Ein Vortrag des Frankfurter Soziologie-Professors Jürgen Habermas in New York," *Frankfurter Allgemeine Zeitung*, December 5, 1967; published in English in Habermas, *Towards a Rational Society*, 15.
94. Habermas, *Towards a Rational Society*, 18, 24–25, 26.
95. Cooke, "Forever Resistant?," 590, 587.
96. Jürgen Habermas, "Einleitung einer Podiumsdiskussion über 'Die Rolle der Studenten in der ausserparlamentarischen Opposition'" (congress "Hochschule und Demokratie," Frankfurt am Main, February 8, 1968), published in Habermas, *Kleine politische Schriften I–IV*, 239, 244.
97. Habermas, *Kleine politische Schriften I–IV*, 239, 244.
98. For more detailed accounts of Habermas's discussions with representatives of the student movement, see Peter Zoller, ed., *Aktiver Streik. Dokumentation zu einem Jahr Hochschulpolitik am Beispiel der Universität Frankfurt am Main* (Joseph Melzer, 1969); Frank Wolff and Eberhard Windaus, eds., *Studenterbewegung 1967–69, Protokolle und Materialen* (Roter Stern, 1977); Wolfgang Kraushaar, ed., *Frankfurter Schule und Studentenbewegung. Von der Flaschenpost zum Molotowcocktail 1946–1995*, vol. 2, *Dokumente* (Rogner & Bernhard, 1998).
99. See Peter J. Verovšek, "Integration After Totalitarianism: Arendt and Habermas on the Postwar Imperatives of Memory," *Journal of International Political Theory* 16, no. 1 (2020).
100. Habermas, *Autonomy and Solidarity*, 231.
101. Philip Felsch, *Der Philosoph: Habermas und wir* (Propyläen, 2024), 33.
102. Jürgen Habermas, "Minister Stoltenberg Diffamiert Bedenkenlos," *Frankfurter Rundschau*, May 9, 1968, 3; republished in Habermas, *Protestbewegung und Hochschulreform*, 186.
103. Jürgen Habermas, "Werden wir richtig Informiert? Zweimal 3 Antworten auf vier Fragen der Zeit," *Die Zeit*, May 31, 1968, 17; reprinted in Habermas, *Kleine politische Schriften I–IV*, 247.
104. Jürgen Habermas, "Die Scheinrevolution und ihre Kinder. 6 Thesen über Taktik, Ziele und Situationsanalysen der oppositionellen Jugend," *Frankfurter Rundschau*, June 5, 1968, 8, also published as "Scheinrevolution unter Handlungszwang. Über Fehldenken und Fehlverhalten der linken Studentenbewegung," *Der Spiegel*, June 10, 1968, 57–59, reprinted in Habermas, *Protestbewegung und Hochschulreform*, 189.

105. Karl Marx, "Letter to Nieuwenhuis," February 22, 1881, quoted in Theodor W. Adorno, *Gesammelte Schriften*, ed. R. Tiedemann, vol. 10, pt. 1 (Suhrkamp, 1972), 291.
106. Jürgen Habermas, "Civil Disobedience: Litmus Test for the Democratic Constitutional State," *Berkeley Journal of Sociology* 30 (1985): 99.
107. Jürgen Habermas to Günter Grass, November 4, 1968, HV, 9—1968, Band 1 (A–N).
108. See Wolfgang Abendroth and Oscar Negt, eds., *Die Linke antwortet Jürgen Habermas* (Europäische Verlagsanstalt, 1968).
109. Holub, *Jürgen Habermas*, 98.
110. Jürgen Habermas to Lorenz Jäger, November 16, 1992, HV, quoted in Müller-Doohm, *Habermas: A Biography*, 156.
111. Jürgen Habermas to Hans Maier, June 15, 1973, HV, 20—1973, Band 2 (G–M).
112. Ralf Dahrendorf to Jürgen Habermas, October 30, 1967, 8—1967, Band 1 (A–Z).
113. Wiggershaus, *The Frankfurt School*, 633.
114. Lenhard, *Café Marx*, 515.
115. Jürgen Habermas, "Erklärung für Studenten (12 Dezember 1968)," in *Protestbewegung und Hochschulreform*, 245. See also Jürgen Habermas et al., "Diskussion mit streikenden Studenten, Walter-Kolb-Studentenwohnung, 16.12.1968," in *Studentenbewegung 67–69. Protokolle und Materialien*, ed. Frank Wolff and Eberhard Windaus (Roter Stern, 1977), 113–32.
116. Jürgen Habermas, "Seminarthesen, 'Probleme einer materialistischen Erkenntnistheorie'" (lecture, Goethe University, Frankfurt am Main, December 14, 1968); published in Habermas, *Protestbewegung und Hochschulreform*, 247–48; see also Jürgen Habermas and A. Wellner, "Zur politischen Verantwortung der Wissenschaftler," in *Das politische Mandat der Studentenschaft*, ed. U. K. Preuss (Suhrkamp, 1969), 133–38.
117. Lenhard, *Café Marx*, 518.
118. See Jürgen Habermas et al., "Wir Unterstützen den Protest unserer Studenten," *Flugblatt*, December 11, 1968, in *Aktiver Streik. Dokumentation zu einem Jahr Hochschulpolitik am Beispiel der Universität Frankfurt am Main*, ed. Jörg Zoller (Darmstadt, 1970), 85.
119. Jürgen Habermas, personal communication, August 17, 2025.
120. Helmut Plessner to Theodor Adorno (cc Jürgen Habermas), no date, HV, 8—1967, Band 1 (A–Z).
121. See Jürgen Habermas to Theodor Adorno, November 29, 1968, HV, 9—1968, Band 1 (A–N); Jürgen Habermas to Herbert Marcuse, November 18, 1968, HV, 10—1968, Band 2 (M–Z). See also Jürgen Habermas et al., "Schreiben an den Rektor der Johann Wolfgang Goethe-Universität," January 10, 1969, in Kraushaar, *Frankfurter Schule und Studentenbewegung*, 540.
122. Habermas sent his proposal to *Der Spiegel* and *Die Zeit*, as well as directly to the Hessisches Kulturministerium. See Jürgen Habermas to Rudolf Augstein (*Der Spiegel*), July 20, 1968, Jürgen Habermas to Gräfin Marion Dönhoff (*Die Zeit*), July 20, 1968, Jürgen Habermas to Frau Staatssekretärin Dr. Hamm-Brücher, July 20, 1968, all HV, 9—1968, Band 1 (A–N). See also Jürgen Habermas et al., "Grundsätze für ein neues Hochschulrecht," *Frankfurter Allgemeine Zeitung*, July 23, 1968, 9–10; Jürgen Habermas, "Heilige Kühe der Hochschulreform. In Hessen könnte die Reform beginnen," *Die Zeit*, September 27, 1968; Jürgen Habermas et al., "Kühne Neuerungen sind Geboten: Frankfurter Professoren zur Hochschulreform," *Der Spiegel*, December 2, 1968, 76–82; Jürgen Habermas, "Empfehlungen zur technokratischen Hochschulreform?" in *Politik, Wissenschaft, Erziehung.*

Festschrift für E. Schüttein, ed. Hans Nicklas (Diesterweg, 1969), 77–82, all republished in Habermas, *Protestbewegung und Hochschulreform*. See also Jürgen Habermas, "Demokratisierung und Hochschule. Politisierung der Wissenschaft?" (lecture, Westdeutsche Rektorenkonferenz, May 28, 1969); in *Merkur* 23, no. 255 (July 1969), 597–604, republished in Habermas, *Arbeit—Erkenntnis—Fortschrift*, 430–38; Jürgen Habermas, "Für eine Handlungsfähige Hochschule. Von einer Bevorstehenden 'Herrschaft der Räte' an den Universitäten Kann Keine Rede Sein," *Frankfurter Rundschau*, December 10, 1969, 3.

123. Max Pensky, "Jürgen Habermas and the Antinomies of the Intellectual," in *Habermas: A Critical Reader*, ed. Peter Dews (Blackwell, 1999), 225. See also Theodor W. Adorno, "Education After Auschwitz," in *Critical Models: Interventions and Catchwords*, trans. Henry W. Pickford (Colombia University Press, 1998).
124. Habermas, *Autonomy and Solidarity*, 186.
125. Jürgen Habermas to Karl-Heinz Bohrer (FAZ), March 19, 1969, HV, 11—1969, Band 1 (A–K).
126. Percy Cohen (LSE) to Jürgen Habermas, September 19, 1969, HV, 11—1969, Band 1 (A–K).
127. Jürgen Habermas, "Wozu noch Philosophie?," Hessischer Rundfunk, RFF, January 4, 1971; published in English as Jürgen Habermas and E. B. Ashton, "Why More Philosophy?" *Social Research* 38, no. 4 (1971), 638, 644.
128. Jürgen Habermas to Rudolf Walter Leonhardt (*Die Zeit*), December 5, 1969, HV, 1969—Band 2 (L–Z).
129. Jürgen Habermas to Herbert Marcuse, April 14, 1971, HV, 15—1971, Band 1 (A–Z).
130. See Jürgen Habermas to Leszek Kolakowski, February 24, 1970, HV, 1970—Band 1 (A–O) and letters that follow.
131. Jürgen Habermas, "Die Antwort von Jürgen Habermas," *Die Zeit*, March 17, 1970.
132. Herbert Gans to Jürgen Habermas, March 17, 1969, HV, 11—1969, Band 1 (A–K).
133. Rolf Meyerson to Jürgen Habermas, March 5, 1969, HV, 11—1969, Band 2 (L–Z) and Habermas's reply on March 31, 1969.
134. Jürgen Habermas to Hannah Arendt, October 28, 1975, HV, 29—1975, Band 1 (A–B).
135. "Leserbrief von Prof. Dr. Jürgen Habermas," *Der Spiegel*, December 14, 1970, 19.
136. Jürgen Habermas, "Ermordung der Theorie?," letter to the editor, *Diskus* 21, no. 3 (1971): 5.
137. Frankfurter Studentensitzung, quoted in Felsch, *Der Philosoph: Habermas und wir* (Propyläen, 2024), 63.
138. Jacob Taubes to Robert Jauss on May 26, 1967, cited by Felsch, *Der Philosoph*, 50.
139. Jürgen Habermas to Hans Maier, May 30, 1973, HV, 20—1973, Band 2 (G–M).
140. "Ängstlichkeit vor Studenten gehört gewiss nicht zu meinen Fehlern. Nun gar Fluch vor meinen Studenten," Jürgen Habermas to Richard Löwenthal, June 8, 1972, HV, 17—1972, Band 2 (H–R). Richard Löwenthal (1908–1991) was a German journalist and professor of political science at the Free University of Berlin, whose work addressed issues of democracy, communism (especially in the Soviet Union), and world politics. He and Habermas clashed in the 1970s, as Löwenthal, who saw the FRG as the most democratic state in Germany's history, pushed back on Habermas's critiques of the Federal Republic, accusing him of utopianism.
141. Jürgen Habermas to Max Horkheimer, April 22, 1971, HV, 15—1971, Band 1 (A–Z).
142. Herbert Marcuse to Jürgen Habermas, January 15, 1971, HV, 15—1971, Band 1 (A–Z).

5. RETREAT TO STARNBERG, 1971–1982

1. Jürgen Habermas, *Die nachholende Revolution*, vol. 7 of *Kleine politische Schriften* (Suhrkamp, 1990), 24.
2. Habermas, *Die nachholende Revolution*, 24.
3. Jürgen Habermas, private conversation, June 7, 2024 (hereafter cited as Habermas conversation).
4. Jürgen Habermas to Walter Bundesmann (Geschäftsführer, BV Oberbayern, der Gewerkschaft Erziehung und Wissenschaft), March 28, 1973, HV, 19—1973, Band 1 (A–F). Walter Bundesmann was the managing director of the Trade Union for Education and Science in Oberbayern at the time. He had previously written to Habermas, in 1971 and again in 1973, inviting him to give a lecture on educational policy for the union.
5. Jürgen Habermas, *Kleine politische Schriften I–IV* (Suhrkamp, 1981), 525.
6. Müller-Doohm, *Habermas: A Biography* (Polity, 2016), 164.
7. Hans Hilmer and Christoph Sattler, *Buildings and Projects; Bauten und Projekte* (Edition Axel Menges, 1999), 77–82.
8. *Der Spiegel* and the sociology student Heinz Bude quoted in Philip Felsch, *Der Philosoph: Habermas und wir* (Propyläen, 2024), 5.
9. Jürgen Habermas, "Odyssee der Vernunft in der Natur. Theodor W. Adorno wäre am 11. September 66 Jahre alt geworden," *Die Zeit*, September 12, 1969; published in English as Jürgen Habermas, *Philosophical-Political Profiles*, trans. Frederick G. Lawrence (MIT Press, 1983), 102, 109.
10. Jürgen Habermas, "Entgegnung. Offener Brief an Ernst Lissner," *Frankfurter Rundschau*, March 14, 1970; reprinted in Wolfgang Kraushaar, *Frankfurter Schule und Studentenbewegung*, vol. 2, *Dokumente* (Rogner & Bernhard, 1998), 718; Axel Honneth et al., "The Dialectics of Rationalization: An Interview with Jürgen Habermas," *Telos* 49 (1981): 96.
11. Roman Yos, "Young Habermas: An Interview with Roman Yos," *JHI Blog*, December 23, 2020, https://jhiblog.org/2020/12/23/young-habermas-interview-roman-yos/.
12. Gerhard Richter and Theodor W. Adorno, "Who's Afraid of the Ivory Tower? A Conversation with Theodor W. Adorno," *Monatshefte* 94, no. 1 (2002): 19.
13. Jürgen Habermas to Richard Löwenthal, July 8, 1972, HV, 17—1972, Band 2 (H–R).
14. Jürgen Habermas to Fritz J. Raddatz (*Die Zeit*), February 7, 1977, HV, 40—1977, Band 4 (N–S).
15. Jürgen Habermas to Dr. Wilhelm Vossenkuhl (Europäische Hochschulgruppe), November 21, 1972, 17—1972, Band 2 (H–R).
16. Jürgen Habermas to Hanjo Kesting (Norddeutscher Rundfunk), November 8, 1977, HV, 39—1977, Band 3 (I–M).
17. Jürgen Habermas to Klaus Pierwoss (Landestheater Württemberg-Hohenzollern), February 21, 1974, HV, 26—1974, Band 4 (O–S). See also Jürgen Habermas to Georg Wolff (*Der Spiegel*), February 19, 1974, HV, 27—1974, Band 5 (T–W); Jürgen Habermas to Rudolf Hartung (*Neue Rundschau*), September 17, 1974, HV, 24—1974, Band 2 (F–H); Jürgen Habermas to Herbert Janssen (FUNK), November 28, 1972, HV, 17—1972, Band 2 (H–R); Inge Pethran (on behalf of Jürgen Habermas) to H. U. Probst (Studio Basel), July 7, 1972, HV, 17—1972, Band 2 (H–R).

18. Werner Harenberg (*Der Spiegel*) to Jürgen Habermas, April 18, 1969, HV, 11—1969, Band 1 (A–K).
19. Albert Osswald (Hessischer Ministerpräsident) to Jürgen Habermas, November 19, 1974, HV, 26—1974, Band 4 (O–S).
20. Jürgen Habermas to Rudolf Walter Leonhardt (*Die Zeit*), December 5, 1969, HV, 1969—Band 2 (L–Z).
21. Gerson S. Sher, *Praxis: Marxist Criticism and Dissent in Socialist Yugoslavia* (Indiana University Press, 1977), 258–59. See also Peter J. Verovšek, "Eastern Praxis and Western Critique: France Bučar's Critical Systems Theory in Context," in *At His Crossroads: Reflections on the Work of France Bučar*, ed. Igor Kovač (Springer International, 2018), 3–14.
22. Garth Massey, "A Final Look at the Critical Perspective of the Yugoslav *Praxis* Group," *Humanity and Society* 15, no. 2 (1991): 228.
23. Richard J. Bernstein, "The Prehistory of the Prague Meetings," *Philosophy & Social Criticism* 43, no. 3 (2017): 272; see also Verovšek, "Eastern Praxis and Western Critique," 6–7.
24. See Mihailo Marković to Jürgen Habermas, November 3, 1972, HV, 17—1972, Band 2 (H–R) and multiple letters from Marković to Habermas in HV, 20—1973, Band 2 (G–M).
25. Jürgen Habermas and Ernst Bloch to Marschall Tito, November 17, 1972, HV, 18—1972, Band 3 (S–Z).
26. Rudi Supek to Jürgen Habermas, June 5, 1975, HV, 31—1975, Band 3 (K–S).
27. Karl-Otto Apel to Jürgen Habermas, February 15, 1974, HV, 23—1974, Band 1 (A–E).
28. Habermas to Apel, February 19, 1974, HV, 23—1974, Band 1 (A–E).
29. Alfred J. Ayer et al., "Letter to Tito," *The New York Review*, February 6, 1975, https://www.nybooks.com/articles/1975/02/06/letter-to-tito/. See also Noam Chomsky, *Yugoslavia: Peace, War, and Dissolution* (PM Press, 2018).
30. See DOKUMENTE des 'Praxis'-Kreises, HV, HV, 31—1975, Band 3 (K–S). See also Jürgen Habermas, "Diskussionsbeitrag auf der Veranstaltung "Solidarität mit der Praxis-Gruppe" (April 9, 1975); reprinted in Kraushaar, *Frankfurter Schule und Studentenbewegung. Band 2: Dokumente*, 792–93.
31. Jürgen Habermas to Gajo Petrović, January 29, 1975, HV, 31—1975, Band 3 (K–S).
32. Habermas to Petrović, January 8, 1974, HV, 26—1974, Band 4 (O–S).
33. Gutachten Milan Kangrga, July 4, 1975, HV, 31—1975, Band 3 (K–S).
34. Jürgen Habermas to Dr. Karl Acham, May 24, 1975, HV, 37—1977, Band 1 (A–D).
35. Habermas to Petrović, November 7, 1974, HV, 26—1974, Band 4 (O–S).
36. Jürgen Habermas to Wolfgang Kraushaar, March 24, 1975, HV, 31—1975, Band 3 (K–S).
37. Jürgen Habermas to Georg Henrik von Wright, April 16, 1975, HV, 32—1975, Band 4 (T–Z).
38. Von Wright to Habermas, March 31, 1975, HV, 32—1975, Band 4 (T–Z).
39. Von Wright to Habermas, May 5, 1975, HV, 32—1975, Band 4 (T–Z). The quotation is from Habermas's letter to Block, which is not contained in the Habermas Vorlass, but which von Wright quotes in his letter back to Habermas.
40. Von Wright to Habermas, June 1975, HV, 32—1975, Band 4 (T–Z), underlining in original. See also Jürgen Habermas, "Wo ist die fünfte Kolonne? Die Intellektuellen der Praxis-Gruppe in Jugoslawien werden verfolgt," *Die Zeit*, January 23, 1981, 34.
41. Robert Thomas, *The Politics of Serbia in the 1990s* (Columbia University Press, 1999), 60.

42. Slawek Magala, *The Management of Meaning in Organizations* (Palgrave Macmillan, 1999), 240.
43. Lenhardt, *Café Marx*, 495.
44. Jürgen Habermas to Agnes Heller, June 14, 1973, HV, 20—1973, Band 2 (G–M).
45. Heller to Habermas, June 28, 1973, HV, 20—1973, Band 2 (G–M).
46. Herbert Gans to Jürgen Habermas, July 26, 1973, HV, 20—1973, Band 2 (G–M).
47. Habermas to Heller, October 4, 1973, HV, 20—1973, Band 2 (G–M).
48. Heller to Habermas, November 5, 1973, HV, 20—1973, Band 2 (G–M).
49. Heller to Habermas, March 15, 1976, HV, 34—1976, Band 2 (F–K).
50. Habermas to Heller, April 6, 1976, HV, 34—1976, Band 2 (F–K).
51. György Márkus to Jürgen Habermas, June 28, 1976, 35—1976, Band 3 (L–S).
52. For Holzer, see Max Planck Society to the State Minister for Education and Cultural Affairs, Prof. Hans Maier, March 5, 1974, HV, 24—1974, Band 2 (F–H). For Haschemi, see Ulrich Enzensberger to Jürgen Habermas, February 17, 1974, HV, 23—1974, Band 1 (A–E); Habermas to Enzensberger, February 26, 1974, HV, 23—1974, Band 1 (A–E).
53. For his signature of a declaration of solidarity vis-à-vis supporting the human rights of Chilean colleagues teaching at the University of Konstanz, see Prof. Dr. U. Sonnemann to Jürgen Habermas, February 28, 1974, HV, 24—1974, Band 2 (F–H); Harry Hermans to Jürgen Habermas, November 8, 1974, HV, 24—1974, Band 2 (F–H). Jürgen Habermas to President Carlos Humberto Romero (El Salvador), November 15, 1978, HV, 45—1978, Band 3 (H–K).
54. Jürgen Habermas to Prof. Dr. Walter Biemel, April 18, 1977, HV, 37—1977, Band 1 (A–D).
55. For the Kosik case, see texts in HV, 34—1976, Band 2 (F–K).
56. Habermas renewed his protests again in 1992, when Kosik was forcibly retired against his will. Jürgen Habermas, "Die nackte Realität neuer Diskriminierung: Karl Kosik gegen seinen Willen in Pension geschickt," *Frankfurter Rundschau*, November 13, 1992. Republished in *Concordia. Internationale Zeitschrift für Philosophie* 24 (1993): 11–12.
57. Jürgen Habermas to the editor of the *Frankfurter Allgemeine Zeitung* (FAZ), May 14, 1973, HV, 19—1973, Band 1 (A–F).
58. Habermas to the editor of the FAZ, May 29, 1973, HV, 19—1973, Band 1 (A–F).
59. This quotation comes from a letter by Marcel Reich-Ranicki responding to the accusation. Marcel Reich-Ranicki to Jürgen Habermas, May 3, 1976, HV, 35—1976, Band 3 (L–S).
60. See Willi Oelmüller to Jürgen Habermas, June 10, 1978, HV, 47—1978, Band 5 (O–S); Habermas to Oelmüller, June 29, 1978, HV, 47—1978, Band 5 (O–S).
61. This was also reported on in *Die Zeit*. See Daniel Bell to Jürgen Habermas, April 29, 1976, HV, 33—1976, Band 1 (A–E).
62. FAZ and Habermas quotations are all from Jürgen Habermas to Dieter E. Zimmer (*Die Zeit*), March 31, 1976, HV, 36—1976, Band 4 (T–Z).
63. Jürgen Habermas to Günther Rühle (editorial office of FAZ), April 20, 1976, HV, 35—1976, Band 3 (L–S).
64. Bürger für Heidelberg in HV, 24, 1974, Band 2 (F–H).
65. Dr. Wanda von Baeyer-Katte (Christian Democratic Union city council member) to Jürgen Habermas, November 26, 1974, HV, 23—1974, Band 1 (A–E).
66. Jürgen Habermas to Dr. Wanda von Baeyer-Katte, December 5, 1974, HV, 23—1974, Band 1 (A–E).

5. Retreat to Starnberg, 1971–1982   347

67. Jürgen Habermas to Dr. Bruno Kreisky (Federal Chancellor of the Republic of Austria), March 24, 1976, HV, 34—1976, Band 2 (F–K).
68. Jürgen Habermas et al., "Ein biedermeierlicher Weg zum Sozialismus?" *Der Spiegel*, February 24, 1975, 44–50. For a similar argument made by Habermas a few years earlier, see Jürgen Habermas, "Demokratie und Planung," *Neues Forum* 20, no. 223 (1973): 34–36.
69. Hennis's response was published in *Deutsche Zeitung*, September 3, 1975. Excerpt quoted from Müller-Doohm, *Habermas: A Biography*, 193.
70. Jürgen Habermas, "Leserbrief zu Hennis, 'Gesellschaft im Visier,' " *Deutsche Zeitung*, October 24, 1975.
71. Klaus von Beyme to Jürgen Habermas, October 16, 1975, HV, 29—1975, Band 1 (A–B).
72. Habermas conversation.
73. Jürgen Habermas, "Sie werden nicht schweigen können," *Die Zeit*, September 13, 1974, 22.
74. Habermas conversation.
75. Müller-Doohm, *Habermas: A Biography*, 178.
76. Prof. Dr. Hermann Krings to Jürgen Habermas, July 23, 1973, HV, 20—1973, Band 2 (G–M).
77. Maier to Jürgen Habermas, July 13, 1973, HV, 20—1973, Band 2 (G–M).
78. Habermas to Maier, June 15, 1973, HV, 20—1973, Band 2 (G–M).
79. Robert Spaemann, "Die Utopie der Herrschaftsfreiheit," *Merkur* 26, no. 291 (1972): 752. See "Die Utopie des guten Herrschers. Eine Diskussion zwischen Jürgen Habermas und Robert Spaemann," *Merkur* 26, no. 296 (December 1972): 1266–78; reprinted in Habermas, *Kleine politische Schriften I–IV*, 318–27.
80. Robert Spaemann to Jürgen Habermas, January 25, 1974, HV, 26—1974, Band 4 (O–S).
81. Jürgen Habermas, "Moralisierende Entrüstung unangebracht, Brief an R. Spaemann," *Die Zeit*, July 21, 1978; reprinted as Jürgen Habermas, "Mut zur Erziehung—Brief an R. Spaemann (1978)," in *Kleine politische Schriften I–IV*, 407.
82. Müller-Doohm, *Habermas: A Biography*, 201–02.
83. For more on this context, see Müller-Doohm, *Habermas: A Biography*, 178.
84. Jürgen Habermas, "Einleitung," in *Stichworte zur "Geistigen Situation der Zeit,"* vol. 1, *Nation und Republik*, ed. Jürgen Habermas (Suhrkamp, 1979), 7–35; reprinted as Jürgen Habermas, "Einleitung zum Band 1000 der edition suhrkamp," in *Kleine politische Schriften I–IV*, 420.
85. See Karrin Hanshew, " 'Sympathy for the Devil?' The West German Left and the Challenge of Terrorism," *Contemporary European History* 21, no. 4 (2012): 511–32.
86. See Jürgen Habermas, "Deutscher Herbst," in *Kleine politische Schriften I–IV*, 346–406. The articles that make up this chapter are cited individually below.
87. See Müller-Doohm, *Habermas: A Biography*, 185–87.
88. See letter of protest: Albrecht Wellmer to Hans Karl Filbinger, October 18, 1977, HV, 42—1977, Band 6 (W–Z).
89. Jürgen Habermas to Walter Busse (*Der Spiegel*), October 20, 1977, HV, 37—1977, Band 1 (A–D); *Der Spiegel*, "Mord beginnt beim bösen Wort," October 16, 1977.
90. Philip Felsch, *Der Philosoph*, 87.
91. Habermas to Busse (*Der Spiegel*), October 20, 1977, HV, 37—1977, Band 1 (A–D).
92. Habermas to Busse (*Der Spiegel*), October 20, 1977, HV, 37—1977, Band 1 (A–D). See also Habermas to Wolfram Schütte (*Frankfurter Rundschau*), October 17, 1977, HV, 40—1977, Band 4 (N–S).

93. Jürgen Habermas, "Interview mit Angelo Bolaffi," in *Kleine politische Schriften I–IV*, 509–10. Translated and republished in English as Jürgen Habermas, "Conservatism and Capitalist Crisis," *New Left Review* 1, no. 115 (May–June 1979): 73–84.
94. Jürgen Habermas, "Die Bühne des Terrors. Ein Brief an Kurt Sontheimer," *Merkur* 31, no. 353 (September 19, 1977): 944–59; reprinted in Habermas, *Kleine politische Schriften I–IV*, 368, 372, 379; Jürgen Habermas to Hannes Feldner, January 25, 1978, HV, 38—1977, Band 2 (E–H).
95. Sontheimer's letter is republished as part of Jürgen Habermas and Kurt Sontheimer, "Linke, Terroristen, Sympathisanten. Ein Briefwechsel mit Kurt Sontheimer," *Süddeutsche Zeitung*, November 26–27, 1977; republished in Habermas, *Kleine politische Schriften I–IV*, 393. Dieter E. Zimmer, *Die Zeit*, October 21, 1977, quoted in Sontheimer, 389.
96. Müller-Doohm, *Habermas: A Biography*, 189.
97. Habermas, *Kleine politische Schriften I–IV*, 397.
98. Jürgen Habermas, "Probe für Volksjustiz: Zu den Anklagen gegen die Intellektuellen," *Der Spiegel*, October 10, 1977, 32; reprinted as Jürgen Habermas, "Volksjustiz," in *Kleine politische Schriften I–IV*, 364–67; published in English as Jürgen Habermas, "A Test for Popular Justice: The Accusations Against the Intellectuals," *New German Critique* 12 (1977): 11, 12–13, translation modified.
99. Heller to Habermas, November 12, 1977, HV, 38—1977, Band 2 (E–H).
100. Michael Theunissen to Jürgen Habermas, December 13, 1977, HV, 41—1977, Band 5 (T–V).
101. Habermas to Theunissen, December 21, 1977, HV, 41—1977, Band 5 (T–V).
102. Jürgen Habermas to Oskar Negt, September 29, 1977, HV, 40—1977, Band 4 (N–S).
103. Jürgen Habermas to Marion Gräfin Dönhoff (*Die Zeit*), April 10, 1978, HV, 43—1978, Band 1 (A–D); published as Jürgen Habermas, "Wo bleiben die Liberalen? Wenn die Gesinnungsschutzbehörden Nebel berbreiten, brauchen wir vielleicht doch ein Russel-Tribunal," *Die Zeit*, May 5, 1978; reprinted as Jürgen Habermas, "Brief an Gräfin Dönhoff," in *Kleine politische Schriften I–IV*, 338; Jürgen Habermas, "Ein Gutachten (1976)," in *Kleine politische Schriften I–IV*, 328–31.
104. Steven Lukes to Jürgen Habermas, October 19, 1977, HV, 39—1977, Band 3 (I–M).
105. Habermas to Lukes, November 8, 1977, HV, 39—1977, Band 3 (I–M).
106. Jürgen Habermas to Kai Dieckmann (Secretariat of the Russell Tribunal), September 26, 1978, HV, 43—1978, Band 1 (A–D).
107. Letter from Jürgen Habermas to Carl Friedrich von Weizsäcker, January 29, 1981, HV, 71—1981, Band 11 (W–Z).
108. See Felsch, *Der Philosoph*, 67.
109. Jürgen Habermas to George Lichtheim, December 21, 1972, HV, 17—1972, Band 2 (H–R).
110. Jürgen Habermas to Herbert Marcuse, April 14, 1971, HV, 15—1971, Band 1 (A–Z).
111. Müller-Doohm, *Habermas*, 176–78. See also Ariane Leendertz, "Ein gescheitertes Experiment—Carl Friedrich von Weizsäcker, Jürgen Habermas und die Max-Planck-Gesellschaft," *Acta Historica Leopoldina* 63 (2014): 243–62.
112. Jürgen Habermas, "Auf die Qualität kommt es an: Warum das Starnberger Institut nicht weitergeführt wird—Ein Gespräch mit Reimar Lüst," *Die Zeit*, May 9, 1980.
113. See Ralf Dahrendorf to Jürgen Habermas, October 30, 1967, HV, 8—1967, Band 1 (A–Z).
114. Jürgen Habermas, "Das Starnberger Debakel. Ein Rücktritt und eine persönliche Erklärung. Jürgen Habermas: 'Warum ich die Max-Planck-Gesellschaft verlasse' ", *Die Zeit*, May 8, 1981, 42.

115. Letter from Habermas to von Weizsäcker, January 29, 1981, HV, 71—1981, Band 11 (W–Z).
116. Jürgen Habermas, *On the Logic of the Social Sciences* (MIT Press, 1988), xiv.
117. Thomas A. McCarthy, *The Critical Theory of Jürgen Habermas* (MIT Press, 1978), iv. See also Jürgen Habermas, "Die Moderne—ein unvollendetes Projekt," *Die Zeit*, September 19, 1980.
118. Felsch, *Der Philosoph*, 90.
119. Karl Markus Michel, "Über Jürgen Habermas: 'Theorie des kommunikativen Handelns,'" *Der Spiegel*, March 21, 1982.
120. See Müller-Doohm, *Habermas: A Biography*, 201.
121. Jürgen Habermas, "Alles linke auf seine Kappe Nehmen: Ein Gespräch mit Jürgen Habermas—aus Anlaß seiner Auszeichnung mit dem Adorno-Preis," interview, *Frankfurter Rundschau*, September 11, 1980.
122. Jürgen Habermas to Robert N. Bellah (UC Berkeley), October 10, 1979, HV, 50—1979, Band 1 (A–C).
123. Quoted in Müller-Doohm, *Habermas: A Biography*, 201. In his acceptance speech entitled "Modernity: An Unfinished Project," Habermas not only sought to defend the aims of the Enlightenment, but also attacked the increasing tendency of conservatives to reject modernity in favor of a return to "religious faith tied to a faith in tradition." Jürgen Habermas, "Die Moderne—ein unvollendetes Projekt" (lecture on the occasion of Habermas's receipt of the Adorno Prize, Frankfurt am Main, September 11,1980); in *Die Zeit*, September 19, 1980, 47–48; reprinted in Habermas, *Kleine politische Schriften I–IV*, 444–64; translated and published in English as Jürgen Habermas and Seyla Ben-Habib, "Modernity Versus Postmodernity," *New German Critique* 22 (1981): 6. See also Jürgen Habermas, "Vier Jungkonservativen beim Projektleiter der Moderne," *Die Tageszeitung* 381 (October 3, 1980): 8–9; and 393 (October 21, 1980): 8–9.
124. Arno Widmann, "Wahrheit und Gesellschaft," *Frankfurter Rundschau*, 26 January 2019.
125. Jürgen Busche, "Sein oder nichtsein—das ist nicht die Frage. Jürgen Habermas und seine 'Theorie des kommunikativen Handelns,'" *Frankfurter Allgemeine Zeitung*, Feburary 27, 1982.
126. Russell Jacoby, "The Last Intellectuals: American Culture in the Age of Innocence," quoted in Jeremy Jennings and Anthony Kemp-Welch, "The Century of the Intellectual: From the Dreyfus Affair to Salman Rushdie," in *Intellectuals in Politics: From the Dreyfus Affair to Salman Rushdie*, ed. Jeremy Jennings and Anthony Kemp-Welch (Routledge, 1997), 14.
127. Jürgen Habermas, *Europe: The Faltering Project*, trans. Ciaran Cronin (Polity, 2009), 13.

6. RETURN TO THE PUBLIC SPHERE, 1983–1992

1. Jürgen Habermas, "An Avantgardistic Instinct for Relevances: The Role of the Intellectual and the European Cause," in *Europe: The Faltering Project*, trans. Ciaran Cronin (Polity, 2009), 55.
2. Jürgen Habermas, "Diskursethik und Gesellschaftstheorie. Ein Interview mit T. Hviid Nielsen," Frankfurt am Main, October 1989, in Jürgen Habermas, *Die nachholende Revolution*, vol. 7 of *Kleine politische Schriften* (Suhrkamp, 1990), 114–45; published in English as Jürgen Habermas, "Discourse Ethics, Law and *Sittlichkeit*," in Jürgen Habermas, "Conservative Politics, Work, Socialism and Utopia Today," in *Autonomy and Solidarity: Interviews*, ed. Peter Dews (Verso, 1992), 246.

3. "'Nation' ist wohl wirklich kein starkes Thema mehr in der BRD. Aber so etwas kann sich natürlich über Nacht ändern," Jürgen Habermas to Henry Patcher, n.d., Habermas Vorlass, 47—1978, Band 5 (O–S). Henry Patcher (1907–1980) was a Marxist libertarian socialist activist and essayist. He taught at the New School and the City University of New York and was also a founder of the magazine *Dissent* after his arrival in the United States following his exile from Nazi Germany. He wrote to Habermas in 1978 asking for a copy of his recent essay on Scholem. As part of their exchange, they also discussed what Patcher saw as a recent German loss of their illusions about reunification. It is in this context that Habermas pushes back on the idea that the nation is still a key topic in the FRG.
4. I would like to thank Peter Niesen for bringing this point to my attention.
5. John Durham Peters, "Distrust of Representation: Habermas on the Public Sphere," *Media, Culture & Society* 15, no. 4 (1993): 10.
6. For a good summary of the relationship between "Habermas and the Historians," see Charles S. Maier, *The Unmasterable Past: History, Holocaust, and German National Identity* (Harvard University Press, 1988), 34–65.
7. Stephen Brockmann, "Introduction: The Reunification Debate," *New German Critique* 52 (1991): 17.
8. Paul Graham, "The Transcendence of a Border: How West German Intellectuals Debated Reunification," *Journal of Communist Studies and Transition Politics* 16, no. 4 (2000): 21–44.
9. Jürgen Habermas, "Eine art Schadensabwicklung: Die apologetischen Tendenzen in der deutschen Zeitgeschichtsschreibung," *Die Zeit*, July 11, 1986, https://www.zeit.de/1986/29/eine-art-schadensabwicklung/komplettansicht?print. For the quotation from Weber, see Max Weber, "Politics as a Vocation," in *From Max Weber: Essays in Sociology*, ed. Hans Heinrich Gerth and C. Wright Mills, trans. Hans Heinrich Gerth and C. Wright Mills (Oxford University Press, 1958), 128.
10. Habermas, "Eine art Schadensabwicklung," 61.
11. See Habermas's response to these accusation in Jürgen Habermas, "Nachspiel," in *Eine art Schadensabwicklung*, in Kleine politische Schriften VI (Suhrkamp, 1987), 149–58; an abridged version translated and republished in English as "Closing Remarks," in *The New Conservatism*, 241–48.
12. Habermas, *Europe: The Faltering Project*, 49–58
13. In this sense, Habermas attained a status not unlike John Dewey in the US from the mid-1890s until his death in 1952. See Robert B. Westbrook, *John Dewey and American Democracy* (Cornell University Press, 2015), ix–x.
14. Quoted in Michael Funken, ed., *Über Habermas: Gespräche mit Zeitgenossen* (Wissenschaftliche Buchgesellschaft, 2009), 204.
15. For example, the CDU president and Chancellor Angela Merkel refused to give a speech in his honor at the right-wing *Deutschland-Stiftung* in 2000. See Michael Funken, "Vom Außenseiter zum Geachteten Intellektuellen," in *Über Habermas: Gespräche mit Zeitgenossen*, ed. Michael Funken (Wissenschaftliche Buchgesellschaft, 2009), 30.
16. Robert C. Holub, *Jürgen Habermas: Critic in the Public Sphere* (Routledge, 1991), 186, 188.
17. Dick Howard, *Between Politics and Antipolitics: Thinking About Politics After 9/11* (Palgrave Macmillan), 124.
18. Max Czolleck, *Versöhnungstheater* (Carl Hanser, 2023).

19. Susan Neiman, *Learning from the Germans: Race and the Memory of Evil* (Farrar, Straus and Giroux, 2019).
20. Martin Joseph Matuštík, *Jürgen Habermas: A Philosophical-Political Profile* (Rowman & Littlefield, 2001), 10.
21. Jürgen Habermas, "The Postnational Constellation and the Future of Democracy," in *The Postnational Constellation: Political Essays*, trans. Max Pensky (MIT Press, 2001), 26–37.
22. Jean-Marc Ferry, "L'Allemagne, la mémoire et l'histoire," interview, *Globe* 30 (July/August 1988); translated and excerpted in Max Czolleck, *Versöhnungstheater* (Carl Hanser, 2023); see also Stephen K. White, "Ethics, Politics and History: An Interview with Jürgen Habermas Conducted by Jean-Marc Ferry," *Philosophy & Social Criticism* 14, nos. 3–4 (1988): 435–36.
23. Jürgen Habermas, "A Kind of Settlement of Damages (Apologetic Tendencies)," *New German Critique* 44 (1988): 27.
24. Philip Felsch, *Der Philosoph: Habermas und wir* (Propyläen, 2024), 125–26.
25. This phrase comes from the critic Gustav Seibt, "Die Formen der Historie. Zu einer Theorie der modernen Geschichtsschriebung," *Merkur* 463–464 (1987): 903–907, 903.
26. Ernst Nolte, "Vergangenheit, die nicht vergehen will. Eine Rede, die Geschrieben, aber nicht gehalten werden konnte," in *'Historikerstreit': Die Dokumentation der Kontroverse um die Einzigartigkeit der Nationalsozialistischen Judenvernichtung*, ed. Rudolf Augstein (Piper, 1987), 45.
27. Jürgen Habermas, "Zum neokonservativen Geschichtsverständnis und zur Rolle der revisionistischen Geschichtsschreibung in der politischen Öffentlichkeit," in *Die Nation als Ausstellungsstück. Planungen, Kritik und Utopien zu den Museumsgründungen in Bonn und Berlin*, ed. Geschichtswerkstatt Berlin (VSA, 1987), 43–49; reprinted in *Deutsches Historisches Museum. Ideen—Kontroversen—Perspektiven*, ed. Christoph Stölzl (Propyläen, 1988), 336.
28. Habermas, "Zum neokonservativen Geschichtsverständnis," 338–39.
29. Maier, *Unmasterable Past*, 60.
30. Habermas, "Zum neokonservativen Geschichtsverständnis," 339.
31. Habermas, "Zum neokonservativen Geschichtsverständnis," 348, 378.
32. Habermas, "A Kind of Settlement of Damages," 28, 27.
33. Michael Stürmer, "Kein Eigentum der deutschen: Die deutsche Frage," in *Die Identität der Deutschen*, ed. Werner Weidenfeld (Schriftenreihe der Bundeszentrale für politische Bildung, 1983), 86, 84.
34. Michael Stürmer, "Geschichte in geschichtslosem Land," in *'Historikerstreit': Die Dokumentation der Kontroverse um die Einzigartigkeit der nationalsozialistischen Judenvernichtung*, ed. Rudolf Augstein (Piper, 1987), 36, 38.
35. Peter Uwe Hohendahl, "The Scholar, the Intellectual, and the Essay: Weber, Lukács, Adorno, and Postwar Germany," *The German Quarterly* 70, no. 3 (1997): 218.
36. Jürgen Habermas, *Autonomy and Solidarity*, 127; Harry F. Dahms, "Theory in Weberian Marxism: Patterns of Critical Social Theory in Lukacs and Habermas," *Sociological Theory* 15, no. 3 (1997): 206.
37. Jürgen Habermas, "Geschichtsschreibung und Geschichtsbewußtsein," *Frankfurter Allgemeine Zeitung*, August 11, 1986; published in English as Jürgen Habermas, "Letter to the Editor of the *Frankfurter Allgemeine Zeitung*, August 11, 1986," in *Forever in the Shadow of*

352   6. Return to the Public Sphere, 1983–1992

        Hitler?: The Dispute about the Germans' Understanding of History, Original Documents of the Historikerstreit, the Controversy Concerning the Singularity of the Holocaust, ed. James Knowlton and Truett Cates (Humanities Press International, 1993), 58.

38. Jürgen Habermas, "Warum ein Demokratiepreis für Daniel J. Goldhagen? Eine Laudatio," Die Zeit, March 14, 1997; republished in Die postnationale Konstellation, 47–64; published in English as Jürgen Habermas, "On the Public Use of History: Why a 'Democracy Prize' for Daniel Goldhagen?," trans. Max Pensky, Common Knowledge 3 (1997): 4, 5.

39. Andreas Hillgruber, Zweierlei Untergang: Die Zerschlagung des Deutschen Reiches und das ende des europäischen Judentums (Corso bei Siedler, 1986), 24.

40. Habermas, "A Kind of Settlement of Damages," 30.

41. Habermas, "A Kind of Settlement of Damages," 33.

42. Jürgen Habermas, "Interview mit Robert Maggiori," in Habermas, Die nachholende Revolution, 30. See also Jürgen Habermas, "Ein Gespräch mit Jürgen Habermas: 'Martin Heidegger? Nazi, Sicher ein Nazi!'" in Die Heidegger Kontroverse, ed. J. Altwegg (Athenaum, 1988), 172–75.

43. Nolte, "Vergangenheit, die nicht vergehen will," 40.

44. Nolte, "Vergangenheit, die nicht vergehen will," 45, 46.

45. Ernst Nolte, "Between Myth and Revisionism? The Third Reich in the Perspective of the 1980s," in Aspects of the Third Reich, ed. H. W. Koch (Macmillan, 1985), 36.

46. Nolte, "Vergangenheit, die nicht vergehen will," 36.

47. Habermas, Autonomy and Solidarity, 131.

48. "En Diskussionsbemerkung", in Gegen den Versuch, Vergangenheit zu verbiegen, ed. Hilmar Hoffmann (Athenäum, 1987), 140–44; reprinted in Eine art Schadensabwicklung (Suhrkamp, 1987), 117–19; published in English as Jürgen Habermas, "Remarks from the Römerberg Colloquium," in The New Conservatism, 209, 210.

49. Holub, Public Sphere, 176.

50. See Rudolf Augstein, ed., 'Historikerstreit': Die Dokumentation der Kontroverse um die Einzigartigkeit der nationalsozialistischen Judenvernichtung (Piper, 1987), 89, 223.

51. Maier, Unmasterable Past, 39.

52. Hans-Ulrich Wehler to Jürgen Habermas, September 1, 1986, HV, Korrespondenzen 1980er Jahre, Folder 109—1986 (T–Z). See also Wolfgang Momsen to Jürgen Habermas, November 18, 1986, HV, Korrespondenzen 1980er Jahre, Folder 106—1986 (L–M); Martin Broszat to Jürgen Habermas, October 8 1986, HV, Korrespondenzen 1980er Jahre, Folder 101—1986 (A–B).

53. Habermas, "A Kind of Settlement of Damages," 29.

54. Jürgen Habermas, "Vom öffentlichen Gebrauch der Historie. Das offizielle Selbstverständnis der Bundesrepublik bricht auf," in 'Historikerstreit': Die Dokumentation der Kontroverse um die Einzigartigkeit der Nationalsozialistischen Judenvernichtung, ed. Rudolf Augstein (Piper, 1987), 251–52. Originally published in Die Zeit, November 7, 1986.

55. Habermas, "A Kind of Settlement of Damages," 36.

56. Stürmer, "Geschichte in geschichtslosem Land," 38.

57. Habermas, "A Kind of Settlement of Damages," 38.

58. Jürgen Habermas, Theory and Practice, trans. John Viertel (Beacon, 1974), 33; Holub, Public Sphere, 176.

59. Maier, The Unmasterable Past, 44–45.

60. I take this language from Reinhart Koselleck, *Futures Past: On the Semantics of Historical Time*, trans. Keith Tribe (MIT Press, 1985).
61. Habermas, "A Kind of Settlement of Damages," 26, 27.
62. Habermas, "A Kind of Settlement of Damages," 27.
63. Habermas, "A Kind of Settlement of Damages," 28.
64. Holub, *Public Sphere*, 164.
65. Jürgen Habermas, "Die Entsorgung der Vergangenheit: Ein kulturpolitisches Pamphlet," *Die Zeit*, May 24, 1985; republished in Jürgen Habermas, "Die neue Unübersichtlichkeit. Die Krise des Wohlfahrtsstaates und die Erschöpfung utopischer Energien," *Merkur* 39, no. 1 (1985): 267.
66. Habermas quoted in Claudia Czingon et al., "Moral Universalism at a Time of Political Regression: A Conversation with Jürgen Habermas About the Present and His Life's Work," *Theory, Culture & Society* 37, no. 7–8 (2020): 9; Fabian Freyenhagen, "Adorno's Politics: Theory and Praxis in Germany's 1960s," *Philosophy & Social Criticism* 40, no. 9 (2014): 879.
67. Ulrich Herbert, "Der Historikerstreit. Politische, wissenschaftliche, biographische Aspekte," in *Zeitgeschichte als Streitgeschichte. Große Kontroversen nach 1945*, ed. Martin Sabrow et al. (C. H. Beck, 2003), 97.
68. Jürgen Habermas, "Die Kulturkritik der Neokonservativen in den USA und in der Bundesrepublik: Über eine Bewegung von Intellektuellen in zwei politischen Kulturen," *Merkur* 36, no. 413 (November 1982): 1047–61; published in English as Jürgen Habermas, "Neoconservative Cultural Criticism in the United States and West Germany: An Intellectual Movement in Two Political Cultures," in *Habermas and Modernity*, ed. Richard Bernstein (MIT Press, 1985), 78, 80, emphasis in original.
69. Jürgen Habermas, "Die neue Unübersichtlichkeit: Die Krise des Wohlfahrtsstaates und die Erschöpfung utopischer Energien," *Merkur* 39, no. 431 (January 1985): 1–14. Published in English as Jürgen Habermas, "The New Obscurity: The Crisis of the Welfare State and the Exhaustion of Utopian Energies," *Philosophy & Social Criticism* 11, no. 2 (1986): 5.
70. Habermas, "Neoconservative Cultural Criticism," 85, 87, 88.
71. Habermas, "Neoconservative Cultural Criticism," 91. See also Jürgen Habermas, "Die Schrecken der Autonomie: Carl Schmitt auf Englisch," *Babylon: Beiträge zur jüdischen Gegenwart*, October 1, 1986; published in English as Jürgen Habermas, "The Horrors of Autonomy: Carl Schmitt in English," in *The New Conservatism: Cultural Criticism and the Historians' Debate*, trans. Shierry Weber Nicholsen (MIT Press, 1989), 128–39.
72. Habermas, "Neoconservative Cultural Criticism," 93. See also Jürgen Habermas, "Interview mit Barbara Freitag," *Tempo Brasileiro* 3 (July–September 1989): 5–21; reprinted in Habermas, *Die nachholende Revolution*, 99.
73. Jürgen Habermas, "Über die Vernunft des Wollens. Einleitung zu: 'Konservative Politik, Arbeit, Utopie und Sozialismus heute'. Gespräch mit Jürgen Habermas" (interview by H. U. Beck, April 2, 1983), *Magazin der Basler Zeitung*, January 7, 1984; published in English as Habermas, "Conservative Politics, Work, Socialism and Utopia Today," in *Autonomy and Solidarity*, 136, 138.
74. Jürgen Habermas, "Geschichtsbewußtsein und posttraditionale Identität: Die Westorientierung der Bundesrepublik," *Frankfurter Rundschau*, May 15, 1987; published in English as Jürgen Habermas, "Historical Consciousness and Post-Traditional Identity: Remarks on the Federal Republic's Orientation to the West," *Acta Sociologica* 31, no. 1 (1988): 4.

354   6. Return to the Public Sphere, 1983–1992

75. Jürgen Habermas, "A Philosophico-Political Profile," interview by P. Anderson and P. Dews, November 1984, in *Autonomy and Solidarity*, 151.
76. Jürgen Habermas, "Ungehorsam mit Augenmaß. Der Rechtsstaat braucht des Bürgers mißtrauen," *Die Zeit*, September 23, 1983. This is an abridged verision of Jürgen Habermas, "Ziviler Ungehorsam—Testfall für den demokratischen Rechtsstaat. Wider den autoritären Legalismus in der Bundesrepublik," in *Ziviler Ungehorsam im Rechtsstaat*, ed. Peter Glotz (Suhrkamp, 1983), 29–53; published in English as Jürgen Habermas, "Civil Disobedience: Litmus Test for the Democratic Constitutional State," *Berkeley Journal of Sociology* 30 (1985): 96.
77. Habermas, "Civil Disobedience," 99.
78. Habermas, "Civil Disobedience," 97, 107. See also Jürgen Habermas, "Das Schicksal der Moderne," *Die Woche*, May 15, 1986; published in English in Habermas, *Autonomy and Solidarity*, 225.
79. Jürgen Habermas, "Recht und Gewalt—ein deutsches Trauma," *Merkur* 38, no. 423 (January 1984): 15–28; published in English as Jürgen Habermas and Martha Calhoun, "Right and Violence: A German Trauma," *Cultural Critique* 1 (1985): 126, 125, 131–34.
80. Thomas Biebricher, "The Practices of Theorists: Habermas and Foucault as Public Intellectuals," *Philosophy & Social Criticism* 37, no. 6 (2011): 711.
81. Jürgen Habermas, "Heinrich Heine und die Rolle des Intellektuellen in Deutschland," *Merkur* 40, no. 448 (June 1986): 453–68; Biebricher, "The Practices of Theorists"; Jürgen Habermas, "Heinrich Heine and the Role of the Intellectual in Germany," in *The New Conservatism: Cultural Criticism and the Historians' Debate*, trans. Shierry Weber Nicholsen (MIT Press, 1989), 71–99.
82. Jürgen Habermas, "Produktivkraft Kommunikation. Interview mit Hans Peter Krüger," *Sinn und Form* 41, no. 6 (1989): 1192–206; reprinted in Habermas, *Die nachholende Revolution*, 97.
83. See Jürgen Habermas, "Sloterdijk zwischen Heine und Heidegger. Ein Renegat der Subjektphilosophie?," *Pflasterstrand* 159 (June 16, 1983); Jürgen Habermas, *Kleine politische Schriften V: Die neue Unübersichtlichkeit* (Suhrkamp, 1985), 209–12.
84. Jürgen Habermas, "Life-Forms, Morality and the Task of the Philosopher," interview by P. Anderson and P. Dews, December 6, 1984, in Habermas, *Autonomy and Solidarity*, 199–200.
85. Jürgen Habermas, "Die neue Unübersichtlichkeit. Die Krise des Wohlfahrtsstaates und die Erschöpfung utopischer Energien," *Merkur* 39, no. 431 (January 1985): 1–14; published in English as Habermas, "The New Obscurity," 2. See also Jürgen Habermas, "Der Intellektuelle ist mit seinem Gewissen nicht allein," *Süddeutsche Zeitung*, November 19–20, 1985; reprinted in Jürgen Habermas, *Eine art Schadensabwicklung: Kleine politische Schriften VI* (Suhrkamp, 1987), 11–17, esp. 15–17.
86. Jürgen Habermas, "Über den doppelten Boden des demokratischen Rechtsstaates" (speech, Verleihung der Wilhelm-Leuschner-Medaille zum hessischen Verfassungstag 1985); reprinted in Habermas, *Eine art Schadensabwicklung*, 20.
87. Habermas, *Autonomy and Solidarity*, 224. See also Jürgen Habermas, "Wider die Logik des Krieges. Ein Plädoyer für Zurückhaltung, aber nicht gegenüber Israel," *Die Zeit*, February 15, 1991, 40.
88. Jürgen Habermas, "Der Marsch durch die Institutionen hat auch die CDU erreicht. Der Frankfurter Philosoph und Soziologe Jürgen Habermas im Gespräch mit Rainer Erd

über die politische Kultur in der Bundesrepublik Deutschland nach 1968," *Frankfurter Rundschau*, March 11, 1988; published in English as Jürgen Habermas, "Political Culture in Germany Since 1968: An Interview with Dr. Rainer Erd for the 'Frankfurter Rundschau,'" in Habermas, *The New Conservatism*, 187.

89. Jürgen Habermas, "Die Idee der Universität—Lernprozesse," *Zeitschrift für Pädagogik* 5 (1986): 703–18; reprinted in Habermas, *Eine art Schadensabwicklung*; published in English as Jürgen Habermas and John R. Blazek, "The Idea of the University: Learning Processes," *New German Critique* 41 (1987): 13.
90. Habermas, "The Idea of the University," 19–20.
91. Habermas, "The Idea of the University," 20, 21.
92. Klaus von Beyme, "The Legitimation of German Unification Between National and Democratic Principles," *German Politics & Society* 22 (Spring 1991): 1; Hans Kundnani, "The Concept of 'Normality' in German Foreign Policy since Unification," *German Politics & Society* 30, no. 2 (2012): 38.
93. Max Pensky, "Editor's Introduction," in *The Postnational Constellation: Political Essays*, ed. Jürgen Habermas (MIT Press, 2001), ix.
94. Stefan Müller-Doohm, *Habermas: A Biography* (Polity, 2016), 269.
95. Kundnani, "The Concept of 'Normality,'" 39, 38.
96. Habermas, *Die nachholende Revolution*, 152. See the essays in *Political Thought and German Reunification: The New German Ideology?*, ed. Howard Williams (St. Martin's Press, 2000).
97. Brockmann, "Introduction," 17.
98. Peter Hohendahl, "Foreword," in *The Past as Future: Vergangenheit als Zukunft*, ed. Jürgen Habermas (University of Nebraska Press, 1994), xix–xx.
99. Habermas, *Die nachholende Revolution*, 160.
100. Jürgen Habermas, "Die Stunde der nationalen Empfindung: Republikanische Gesinnung oder Nationalbewußtsein?," in Habermas, *Die nachholende Revolution*, 157–66.
101. Matthew G. Specter, "From Eclipse of Reason to the Age of Reasons? Historicizing Habermas and the Frankfurt School," *Modern Intellectual History* 16, no. 1 (2019): 103.
102. Specter, "Eclipse of Reason," 103.
103. Habermas, *Die nachholende Revolution*, 161.
104. Habermas, interview.
105. Jürgen Habermas, "Der DM-Nationalismus," *Die Zeit*, March 30, 1990. The quotations are drawn from the English translation: Jürgen Habermas, "Yet Again: German Identity: A Unified Nation of Angry DM-Burghers?," in *When the Wall Came Down: Reactions to German Unification*, ed. Harold James and Maria Stone (Routledge, 1992), 91,
106. Habermas, "Yet Again: German Identity," 91, 86.
107. Excerpts from Basic Law quoted in Habermas, "Yet Again: German Identity," 96.
108. Habermas, "Yet Again: German Identity," 96.
109. Excerpts from Basic Law quoted in Habermas, "Yet Again: German Identity," 96.
110. Habermas, "Yet Again: German Identity," 96–7.
111. Habermas, "Yet Again: German Identity," 96.
112. Excerpts from Basic Law quoted in Graham, "The Transcendence of a Border," 32, also 43n51.
113. Even Dieter Grimm, a justice at the *Bundesverfassungsgericht* (Federal Constitutional Court) in Karlsruhe who accepted the legality of Kohl's approach, noted that he would have

preferred a constitutional convention, "because it is the risk of democracy, and suppressed discussions have a way of avenging themselves." Dieter Grimm, "Das Risiko Demokratie: Ein Plädoyer für einen neuen parlamentarischen Rat," *Die Zeit*, August 17, 1990.

114. Habermas, "Yet Again: German Identity," 96–97.
115. Jürgen Habermas, "Die normativen Defizite der Vereinigung" in *Vergangenheit als Zukunft*, 45–73; published in English as Jürgen Habermas, *The Past as Future: Vergangenheit als Zukunft*, trans. Max Pensky (University of Nebraska Press, 1994), 41, 40. See also Jürgen Habermas, "Die andere Zerstörung der Vernunft," *Die Zeit*, May 10, 1991.
116. Habermas, "Yet Again: German Identity," 97.
117. Habermas, *The Past as Future*, 45–46; Müller-Doohm, *Habermas: A Biography*, 271.
118. Habermas, *The Past as Future*, 36, 52.
119. Habermas, *The Past as Future*, 40, 44.
120. Habermas, *The Past as Future*, 52.
121. Jürgen Habermas, "Nachholende Revolution und linker Revisionsbedarf. Was heißt Sozialismus heute?" in Habermas, *Die nachholende Revolution*, 179–220; translated and republished in English as Jürgen Habermas, "What Does Socialism Mean Today?: The Revolutions of Recuperation and the Need for New Thinking," in *After the Fall: The Failure of Communism and the Future of Socialism*, ed. Robin Blackburn (Verso, 1991), 33.
122. Habermas, "What Does Socialism Mean Today?" 19. See also Jürgen Habermas, *'Es musste etwas besser werden. . . .' Gespräche mit Stefan Müller-Doohm und Roman Yos* (Suhrkamp, 2024), 148.
123. Habermas, *Autonomy and Solidarity*, 138. See also Jürgen Habermas, "Qualche risposta sul post-comunismo," in *Dopo l'utopia. Intervista ad Habermas raccolta da Michael Haller*, ed. W. Privitera (Marsilio, 1992), 123–31.
124. Habermas, *The Past as Future*, 34–35.
125. Andreas Huyssen, "After the Wall: The Failure of German Intellectuals," *New German Critique* 52 (1991): 125.
126. For more on the *Literaturstreit*, see Stephen Brockmann, "The Politics of German Literature," *Monatshefte* 84, no. 1 (1992).
127. Quoted in Müller-Doohm, *Habermas: A Biography*, 479n87. This correspondence is published under the heading "The Leftover Baggage from German History" in Christa Wolf, *Parting from Phantoms: Selected Writings, 1990–1994*, trans. Jan van Heurck (University of Chicago Press, 1997), 109–23. The letter from Habermas can also be found in Jürgen Habermas, *A Berlin Republic: Writings on Germany*, trans. Steven Rendall (University of Nebraska Press, 1997), 95–105.
128. Jürgen Habermas, "Brief an Christa Wolf," in *Die Normalität einer Berliner Republik*, vol. 8 of *Kleine politische Schriften* (Suhrkamp, 1995), 101.
129. Habermas, *Die Normalität einer Berliner Republik*, 109–10.
130. Müller-Doohm, *Habermas: A Biography*, 274.
131. Korrespondenzbestand Vorlass Habermas, quoted in Müller-Doohm, *Habermas: A Biography*, 479n87.
132. Jürgen Habermas, "Bemerkungen zu einer verworrenen Diskussion," *Die Zeit*, April 3, 1992; reprinted in *Die Normalität einer Berliner Republik*, 21–45; published in English as "What Does "Working Off the Past" Mean Today?," in Habermas, *A Berlin Republic* (University of Nebraska Press, 1997), 17–40.

133. Theodor W. Adorno, *Critical Models: Interventions and Catchwords* (Columbia University Press, 1998), 208–9.
134. Habermas, *A Berlin Republic*, 24, 22.
135. Habermas, *A Berlin Republic*, 104; Habermas, *Die Normalität einer Berliner Republik*, 103.
136. Habermas, *A Berlin Republic*, 22.
137. See Holub, *Public Sphere*, 188.
138. Habermas, *A Berlin Republic*, 40, 30.
139. See Jürgen Habermas, "Bemerkungen zu einer verworrenen Diskussion," lecture, Goethe-Institut, Budapest, March 26, 1992, published in *Die Zeit*, April 3, 1992, 82–84; reprinted as "Was bedeutet "Aufarbeitung der Vergangenheit" heute?" in *Die Normalität einer Berliner Republik*, 21–45; published in English as Jürgen Habermas, "What Does "Working Off the Past" Mean Today?," in Habermas, *A Berlin Republic*, 17–40.
140. Jürgen Habermas, "Die Last der doppelten Vergangenheit," *Die Zeit*, April 3, 1994; published in English as Jürgen Habermas, "Burdens of the Double Past," *Dissent* 41, no. 4 (1994): 513, 514, 517, 514. See also Jürgen Habermas," Antworten auf Fragen einer Enquete-Kommission des Bundestags, May 4, 1994," *Deutschland-Archiv*, July (1994): 772–77; reprinted in *Normalität einer Berliner Republik*, 46–62; published in English as Jürgen Habermas, "Replies to Questions from a Bundestag Investigative Commission," in *A Berlin Republic*, 41–58.
141. Howard Williams et al., "German (Re)Unification: Habermas and His Critics," *German Politics* 5, no. 2 (1996): 235.
142. Matthew G. Specter, *Habermas: An Intellectual Biography* (Cambridge University Press, 2010), 171.
143. Habermas, *Die Normalität einer Berliner Republik*, 79.
144. Jürgen Habermas, "Ist die Herausbildung einer europäischen Identität nötig, und ist sie möglich?," in *Habermas—Der gespaltene Westen* (2004), 68–82; published in English as Jürgen Habermas, "Is the Development of a European Identity Necessary, and Is It Possible?" in *The Divided West*, trans. Ciaran Cronin (Verso, 2006), 78, see also 72.
145. Habermas, "Der DM-Nationalismus."
146. Williams, Bishop and Wight, "German (Re)Unification," 235.
147. Specter, *Habermas: An Intellectual Biography*, 25.
148. Quoted in Funken, *Über Habermas*, 138.
149. Jan Philipp Reemtsma, "Erinnerung vergemeinschaften. Ein kurzes Gespräch über Nachteile der Geschichtsschreibung," *Mittelweg 36*, no. 15 (2006): 30; Karl Heinz Bohrer, *Jetzt. Geschichte meines Abenteuers mit der Phantasie* (Suhrkamp, 2017), 287.
150. Graham, "The Transcendence of a Border," 26.
151. Habermas, *The Past as Future*, 41–42; Habermas, "Yet Again: German Identity," 96.
152. Jürgen Habermas, "30 Jahre Danach: Die Zweite Chance," *Blätter für deutsche und internationale Politik* 9 (September 2020); Jürgen Habermas, *Year 30: Germany's Second Chance*, trans. David Gow (Social Europe Publishing, 2020).
153. Christian Geyer, "Sein Niveau entzündet," Feuilleton, *Frankfurter Allgemeine Zeitung*, June 25, 2008.
154. Habermas, *Europe: The Faltering Project*, 87.
155. Raymond Geuss, "The Last Nineteenth Century German Philosopher: Habermas at 90," *Verso Blog*, August 14, 2019, https://www.versobooks.com/blogs/4408-the-last-nineteenth-century-german-philosopher-habermas-at-90.

358   6. Return to the Public Sphere, 1983–1992

156. See Enzo Traverso, "No, Post-Nazi Germany Isn't a Model of Atoning for the Past," *Jacobin*, June 6, 2022.
157. Daniel Levy and Natan Sznaider, "Memory Unbound," *European Journal of Social Theory* 5, no. 1 (2002).
158. See Peter J. Verovšek, "A Burgeoning Community of Justice? The European Union as a Promoter of Transitional Justice," *International Journal of Transitional Justice* 15, no. 2 (July 2021): 367 and citations therein.
159. Michael Rothberg, "Comparing Comparisons: From the 'Historikerstreit' to the Mbembe Affair," *Geschichte der Gegenwart*, September 23, 2020, https://geschichtedergegenwart.ch/comparing-comparisons-from-the-historikerstreit-to-the-mbembe-affair/; A. Dirk Moses, "The German Catechism," *Geschichte der Gegenwart*, May 23, 2021, https://geschichtedergegenwart.ch/the-german-catechism/.
160. Jürgen Habermas, "Der neue Historikerstreit," *Philosophie Magazine* 6 (2021): 11, 10.
161. Nicole Deitelhoff and others, *Grundsätze der Solidarität. Eine Stellungnahme*, 2023, https://www.normativeorders.net/2023/grundsatze-der-solidaritat/. For the English translation, see Nicole Deitelhoff et al., "Principles of Solidarity. A Statement," *Normative Orders*, November 13, 2023, https://www.normativeorders.net/2023/grundsatze-der-solidaritat/.
162. Rothberg quoted in Jonathon Caitlin, "A New German Historians' Debate? A Conversation with Sultan Doughan, A. Dirk Moses, and Michael Rothberg," *JHI Blog*, February 2, 2022, https://www.jhiblog.org/2022/02/02/a-new-german-historians-debate-a-conversation-with-sultan-doughan-a-dirk-moses-and-michael-rothberg-part-i/; See Michael Rothberg, *Multidirectional Memory. Remembering the Holocaust in the Age of Decolonization* (Stanford University Press, 2009).

7. A TURN FROM GERMANY TO EUROPE, 1993–2009

1. Jürgen Habermas, "Ein avantgardischer Spürsinn für Relevanzen. Was den Intellektuellen auszeichnet," lecture given at the ceremony for the Bruno Kreisky Prize, Vienna, March 9, 2006; published in *Blätter für deutsche und internationale Politik* 5 (2006): 551–57; published in English as Jürgen Habermas, *Europe: The Faltering Project*, trans. Ciaran Cronin (Polity, 2009), 56.
2. I borrow this phrase from Philip Felsch, *Der Philosoph: Habermas und wir* (Propyläen, 2024), 168.
3. Detlev Horster et al., "Interview with Jürgen Habermas Starnberg, March 23, 1979," *New German Critique* 18 (1979): 38.
4. Jürgen Habermas, "Ein Gespräch über Fragen der politischen Theorie," *Krisis*, 57 (1994): 77–85; Reprinted in Jürgen Habermas, *Die Normalität einer Berliner Republik*, vol. 8 of *Kleine politische Schriften* (Suhrkamp, 1995), 135–64; published in English as Mikael Carleheden and René Gabriëls, "An Interview with Jürgen Habermas," *Theory, Culture & Society* 13, no. 3 (1996): 16.
5. Martin Joseph Matuštík, *Jürgen Habermas: A Philosophical-Political Profile* (Rowman & Littlefield, 2001), 215.
6. Jürgen Habermas, *The Lure of Technocracy*, trans. Ciaran Cronin (Polity, 2015), 4.
7. Habermas, "An Avantgardistic Instinct for Relevances," in *Europe: The Faltering Project*, trans. Ciaran Cronin (Polity, 2009), 56.

8. Jürgen Habermas, "Die Hypotheken der 'Adenauerschen Restauration,'" June 18, 1994; published in English as Jürgen Habermas, *A Berlin Republic: Writings on Germany*, trans. Steven Rendall (University of Nebraska Press, 1997), 83–93, 83.
9. Jürgen Habermas, "Begründete Enthaltsamkeit. Gibt es postmetaphysische Antworten auf die Frage nach dem 'richtigen Leben'?," *Neue Rundschau Heft* 2 (2001): 93–103; published in English as Jürgen Habermas, *The Future of Human Nature* (Polity, 2003), 1.
10. Jürgen Habermas, "Produktivkraft Kommunikation. Interview mit Hans Peter Krüger, *Sinn und Form* 41, no. 6 (1989): 1192–206; reprinted in Habermas, *Die nachholende Revolution: Kleine politische Schriften VII* (Suhrkamp, 1990), 96.
11. Jürgen Habermas, "National Unification and Popular Sovereignty," lecture, Seoul, South Korea, May 1996; published as Jürgen Habermas, "National Unification and Popular Sovereignty," *New Left Review* 219 (1996): 4.
12. Jürgen Habermas, "Hemdsärmeliges Pamphlet. Erklärung einer Buchempfehlung," *Frankfurter Rundschau*, August 6, 2003.
13. Jürgen Habermas, "Ich weiß es natürlich nicht besser," *Der Tagesspiegel*, June 18, 1999.
14. Quoted in Felsch, *Der Philosoph*, 44.
15. Jürgen Habermas, "Gelähmte Politik," *Der Spiegel* 28 (July 12, 1993): 50, 51.
16. Pauline Johnson, *Habermas: Rescuing the Public Sphere* (Routledge, 2006), 123; Thomas Risse, *A Community of Europeans?: Transnational Identities and Public Spheres* (Cornell University Press, 2010), 11.
17. Immanuel Kant, "On the Common Saying: 'This May Be True in Theory, But It Does Not Apply in Practice,'" in *Kant's Political Writings*, 2nd ed., ed. H. S. Reiss (Cambridge University Press, 1991), 61.
18. Bernhard Peters, *Die Integration moderner Gesellschaften* (Suhrkamp, 1993); Jürgen Habermas, *The Postnational Constellation: Political Essays*, ed. and trans. Max Pensky (MIT Press, 2001), 82.
19. For my previous treatment of this concept, see Peter J. Verovšek, "Meeting Principles and Lifeworlds Halfway: Jürgen Habermas on the Future of Europe," *Political Studies* 60, no. 2 (2012): 363–80.
20. Jürgen Habermas, *Between Facts and Norms: Contributions to a Discourse Theory of Law and Democracy* (MIT Press, 1996), 302; Claus Offe, "Bindings, Shackles, Brakes: On Self-Limitation Strategies," in *Cultural-Political Interventions in the Unfinished Project of Enlightenment*, ed. Axel Honneth et al. (MIT Press, 1992), 62–65.
21. See Stefan Müller-Doohm, *Habermas: A Biography* (Polity, 2016), 361.
22. Ulrich Beck and Edgar Grande, *Das kosmopolitische Europa: Gesellschaft und Politik in der zweiten Moderne* (Suhrkamp, 2004).
23. Max Pensky, "Editor's Introduction," in *The Postnational Constellation: Political Essays*, ed. Jürgen Habermas (MIT Press, 2001), ix.
24. Jürgen Habermas, *The Past as Future: Vergangenheit als Zukunft*, ed. and trans. Max Pensky (University of Nebraska Press, 1994), 96; originally published in Jürgen Habermas, *Vergangenheit als Zukunft* (Pendo, 1990).
25. Habermas, *The Past as Future*, 96.
26. Thomas A. McCarthy, "Kantian Constructivism and Reconstructivism: Rawls and Habermas in Dialogue," *Ethics* 105, no. 1 (October 1994): 48.
27. Jürgen Habermas and Dieter Henrich, "Zwei Reden. Aus Anlaß der Verleihung des Hegel-Preises 1973 der Stadt Stuttgart an Jürgen Habermas am 19. Januar 1974,"

(Suhrkamp, 1974), 25–84; republished as Jürgen Habermas, "Können komplexe Gesellschaften eine vernunftige Identität ausbilden" in *Zur Rekonstruktion des historischen Materialismus* (Suhrkamp, 1976), 110–11.
28. Jürgen Habermas, "Europas zweite Chance," in Habermas, *Vergangenheit als Zukunft*, 96–97; published in English as "Europe's Second Chance" in Habermas, *The Past as Future*, 73–97.
29. Habermas, "Gelähmte Politik," 55.
30. Jürgen Habermas, "Die Asyldebatte," lecture, Paris, January 14, 1993; published in *Vergangenheit als Zukunft* (Pendo, 1990), 121, 122; published in English as Jürgen Habermas, "The Asylum Debate," in *The Past as Future*, 121, 122. See also Jürgen Habermas, "Die zweite Lebenslüge der Bundesrepublik: Wir sind wieder 'normal' geworden," *Die Zeit*, December 11, 1992, 48; published in English as Jürgen Habermas, "The Second Life Fiction of the Federal Republic: We Have Become 'Normal' Again," *New Left Review* 197 (1993): 58–66.
31. Jürgen Habermas, "Die Festung Europa und das neue Deutschland," *Die Zeit*, May 18, 1993, 3. This text is an abridged version of the last part of the essay "Anerkennungskämpfe im demokratischen Rechtsstaat," in Charles Taylor et al., Multikulturalismus und die Politik der Anerkennung (Suhrkamp, 1993), 147–96.
32. Habermas, "Die Asyldebatte," 132.
33. Jürgen Habermas, "Was ist ein Volk?: Bemerkungen zum politischen Selbstverständnis der Geisteswissenschaften im Vormärz, am Beispiel der Frankfurter Germanistenversammlung von 1846," *Süddeutsche Zeitung*, September 26, 1996, 15. Republished in English in Jürgen Habermas, *The Postnational Constellation: Political Essays* (MIT Press, 2001), 17–18.
34. Jürgen Habermas, "Afterword (May 2003)," in *The Past as Future*, 165.
35. Habermas, *The Past as Future*, 149.
36. Jürgen Habermas, "Es gibt doch Alternativen!" *Die Zeit*, October 8, 1998; republished in English as Jürgen Habermas, "There are Alternatives!" *New Left Review* 231 (1998): 3.
37. Dieter Grimm, "Does Europe Need a Constitution?" *European Law Journal* 1, no. 3 (November 29, 1995): 295. As Habermas points out elsewhere, a similar argument was previously also made by another former justice of the Constitutional Court, Ernst-Wolfgang Böckenförde. See Jürgen Habermas, "Toward a European Political Community," *Society* 39, no. 5 (July–August 2002): 59.
38. Jürgen Habermas, "Remarks on Dieter Grimm's 'Does Europe Need a Constitution?'" *European Law Journal* 1, no. 3 (November 1995): 307.
39. Jürgen Habermas, "1989 im Schatten von 1945. Zur Normalität einer künftigen Berliner Republik," lecture, Church of St. Paul, Frankfurt am Main, May 7, 1995, published as "Zur Normalität einer künftigen Berliner Republik. 1989 im Schatten von 1945," *Frankfurter Rundschau*, May 8, 1995; published in English as Habermas, *A Berlin Republic*, 176.
40. Jürgen Habermas, "Ein Abgrund von Trauer," *Der Spiegel*, August 7, 1995, 34.
41. Jürgen Habermas, *Time of Transitions*, trans. Ciaran Cronin and Max Pensky (Polity, 2006), 18. See Jürgen Habermas, "Bestialität und Humanität. Ein Krieg an der Grenze zwischen Recht und Moral," *Die Zeit*, April 29, 1999; republished in Habermas, *Zeit der Übergänge*, 27–39.
42. Jürgen Habermas et al., "Darfur: A Letter from Europe's Leading Writers," *Common Dreams*, March 24, 2007. Habermas later took part in a similar initiative in response to the democracy protests in Iran. See Jürgen Habermas et al., "Open Letter to the UN

Secretary General on the Political Situation in Iran," *Boston Review* (September–October 2009).
43. Habermas, "Remarks on Dieter Grimm's," 303, 305.
44. Jürgen Habermas, *Zur Rekonstruktion des historischen Materialismus* (Suhrkamp, 1976), 115; Jürgen Habermas, "The Postnational Constellation and the Future of Democracy," in *The Postnational Constellation*, 64.
45. Jürgen Habermas, "Das deutsche Sonderbewußtsein regeneriert sich von Stunde zu Stunde," *Frankfurter Rundschau*, June 12, 1993; republished in English in Habermas, *A Berlin Republic*, 71.
46. Habermas, *Between Facts and Norms*, 495.
47. Habermas, *The Postnational Constellation*, 73–74.
48. Habermas, *The Postnational Constellation*, 99–100.
49. Jürgen Habermas, "Euroskepticism, Market Europe, or a Europe of (World) Citizens?" in *Time of Transitions*, trans. Ciaran Cronin and Max Pensky (Polity, 2006), 84; originally published as Jürgen Habermas, "Der Europäische Nationalstaat unter dem Druck der Globalisierung," *Blätter für deutsche und internationale Politik* 42, no. 4 (1999).
50. Habermas, "There are Alternatives!," 5.
51. Habermas, "There are Alternatives!," 7. See also Jürgen Habermas, "Sì, voglio una costituzione per l'Europa federale," *Caffè Europa*, December 14, 2000.
52. Habermas, *Time of Transitions*, 85.
53. Jürgen Habermas, "Why Europe Needs a Constitution?," lecture, University of Warwick, May 5, 2001; University of Madrid, May 17, 2001; Hamburg University, June 16, 2001; Cologne, December 12, 2001; published in English as Jürgen Habermas, "Does Europe Need a Constitution?" in *Time of Transitions*, 90.
54. Jürgen Habermas, "Pas d'Europe sans constitution commune!," *Le Point*, April 13, 2001, 102–103; Jürgen Habermas, "Sur l'Europe de Jospin. L'opposition des fédéralistes et des souverainistes est stérile," *Le Figaro*, June 1, 2001.
55. Habermas, *Time of Transitions*, 93.
56. Habermas, *Time of Transitions*, 98.
57. Habermas, *Time of Transitions*, 101.
58. Rogers M. Smith, *Stories of Peoplehood: The Politics and Morals of Political Membership* (Cambridge University Press, 2003).
59. Habermas, *The Postnational Constellation*, 19, emphasis in original.
60. Jürgen Habermas, "Die Vergangenheit ist nicht immer ein guter Ratgeber," *Die Welt*, January 21, 2004; republished in English in Jürgen Habermas, *The Divided West*, trans. Ciaran Cronin (Polity, 2006), 58.
61. Habermas, *Time of Transitions*, 105.
62. Habermas, *Time of Transitions*, 107.
63. Max Weber, letter to Ferdinand Tönnies (1909), quoted in James T. Kloppenberg, *Uncertain Victory: Social Democracy and Progressivism in European and American Thought, 1870–1920* (Oxford University Press, 1988), 489; Habermas in Joseph Ratzinger and Jürgen Habermas, *Dialectics of Secularization: On Reason and Religion*, ed. Florian Schuller (Ignatius, 2006), 11.
64. Karl Marx, "Contribution to the Critique of Hegel's *Philosophy of Right*: Introduction," in *The Marx-Engels Reader*, 2nd ed., ed. Robert C. Tucker (Norton, 1978), 54, emphasis in original.

362 7. A Turn From Germany to Europe, 1993–2009

65. José Casanova, *Public Religions in the Modern World* (University of Chicago Press, 1994), 20. See Max Weber, *The Protestant Ethic and the Spirit of Capitalism*, trans. Talcott Parsons (Unwin Paperbacks, 1985); Émile Durkheim, *The Elementary Forms of Religious Life*, ed. Mark Sydney Cladis, trans. Carol Cosman (Oxford University Press, 2001); Émile Durkheim, *The Division of Labor in Society*, trans. George Simpson (Free Press, 1968).

66. Jürgen Habermas, *The Theory of Communicative Action*, vol. 2, trans. Thomas A. McCarthy (Beacon, 1984–1987), 77–112. See Seyla Benhabib, *Critique, Norm, and Utopia: A Study of the Foundations of Critical Theory* (Columbia University Press, 1986), 247.

67. See Jürgen Habermas, "Civil Disobedience: Litmus Test for the Democratic Constitutional State," *Berkeley Journal of Sociology* 30 (1985): 95–116; Jürgen Habermas, "Reconciliation Through the Public Use of Reason: Remarks on John Rawls' Political Liberalism," *Journal of Philosophy* 92, no. 3 (1995): 109–31; Jürgen Habermas, "Anerkennung im demokratischen Rechtsstaat," in *Multikulturalismus und die Politik der Anerkennung*, ed. Charles Taylor (Suhrkamp, 1993), 147–96. See also Jürgen Habermas, "Critical Theory, Its Promise and Limitations for a Theology of the Public Realm, Lecture at Divinity School of the University of Chicago," October 7–9, 1988; published as Jürgen Habermas, *Excursus: Transzendenz von innen, Transzendenz ins Diesseits*, in *Texte und Kontexte* (Suhrkamp, 1991), 127–56.

68. Jürgen Habermas, "Genetische Sklavenherrschaft? Moralische Grenzen reproduktionsmedizinischer Fortschritte," *Süddeutsche Zeitung*, January 13, 1998; republished in English in Habermas, *The Postnational Constellation*, 163, 164.

69. Jürgen Habermas, "Nicht die Natur verbietet das Klonen. Wir müssen selbst entscheiden. Eine Replik auf Dieter E. Zimmer," *Die Zeit*, February 19, 1998; published in English in Habermas, *The Postnational Constellation*, 167.

70. Jürgen, Habermas, "Die geklonte Person wäre kein zivilrechtlicher Schadensfall," *Die Zeit*, March 12, 1998; republished in English in Habermas, *The Postnational Constellation*, 170.

71. Jürgen Habermas, "Der Streit um das ethische Selbstverständnis der Gattung," lecture, University of Zürich, September 9, 2000; and Christian Wolff Lecture, University of Marburg, June 28, 2001; published as Jürgen Habermas, "Auf dem Weg zu einer liberalen Eugenetik? Der Streit um das ethische Selbstverständnis der Gattung," in *Die Zukunft der menschlichen Natur. Auf dem Weg zu einer liberalen Eugenetik?* (Suhrkamp, 2001), 34–126; English trans. in Habermas, *The Future of Human Nature*, vii; for the expanded version of the lectures, see 16–74.

72. Habermas, *The Future of Human Nature*, 58, 60.

73. Quoted in Felsch, *Der Philosoph*, 181. For accounts of previous visits, see 44–49.

74. Habermas, *The Future of Human Nature*, 101. Compare to Jürgen Habermas, "Fundamentalismus in Anführungszeichen. Zum Streit um Annemarie Schimmel," *Süddeutsche Zeitung*, September 12, 1995.

75. Jürgen Habermas, '*Es musste etwas besser werden. . . .' Gespräche mit Stefan Müller-Doohm und Roman Yos* (Suhrkamp, 2024), 159.

76. Habermas, *The Future of Human Nature*, 102. The information about the presence of the cabinet at this speech comes from Felsch, *Der Philosoph*, 174.

77. For more on the concept of rupture, see Peter J. Verovšek, "Memory, Narrative, and Rupture: The Power of the Past as a Resource for Political Change," *Memory Studies* 13, no. 4 (2020).

78. Habermas, *The Future of Human Nature*, 103.
79. The end result of this insight in his philosophical research is Jürgen Habermas, *Auch eine Geschichte der Philosophie* (Suhrkamp, 2019). For more, see Peter J. Verovšek, "Habermas's Politics of Rational Freedom: Navigating the History of Philosophy Between Faith and Knowledge," *Analyse und Kritik* 42, no. 1 (2020): 191–218.
80. Jürgen Habermas, "Der Erbstreit zwischen Philosophie und Religion," *Süddeutsche Zeitung*, September 22, 2001.
81. Habermas, *The Future of Human Nature*, 104.
82. Jürgen Habermas, "Solo la religione può salvarci dalle cadute della modernità," *La Repubblica*, January 15, 2005, 50–51. When I asked him about this, Habermas noted "Das klingt nicht nach mir (That doesn't sound like me)." Habermas, interview.
83. Habermas in Giovanna Borradori, "Reconstructing Terrorism—Habermas," in *Philosophy in a Time of Terror: Dialogues with Jürgen Habermas and Jacques Derrida*, ed. Giovanna Borradori (University of Chicago Press, 2003), 64.
84. Jürgen Habermas, "Die demokratische Öffentlichkeit muss für alle Beitrage offenbleiben—auch für religiöse: Eine Antwort auf die Thesen von Paolo Flores d'Arcais," *Die Zeit*, November 29, 2007, 53.
85. Habermas, *The Future of Human Nature*, 114.
86. Habermas, *Auch eine Geschichte*, 1:14.
87. Jürgen Habermas, "Reply to My Critics," in *Habermas and Religion*, ed. Craig J. Calhoun et al. (Polity, 2013), 348.
88. For more, see Peter J. Verovšek, "Habermas's Theological Turn and European Integration," *The European Legacy* 22, no. 5 (2017): 528–48.
89. Jürgen Habermas, "Ein Bewusstsein von dem, was fehlt. Über Glauben und Wissen und den Defaitismus der modernen Vernunft," *Neue Zürcher Zeitung*, February 10, 2007, 71; republished in English as Jürgen Habermas, *An Awareness of What is Missing: Faith and Reason in a Post-Secular Age*, ed. and trans. Ciaran Cronin (Polity Press, 2010), 15–23; Ratzinger and Habermas, *Dialectics of Secularization*, 43, 50.
90. See Jürgen Habermas, "Freiheit und Determinismus," lecture, Tokyo, November 12, 2004; published in part as "Um uns als Selbsttäuscher zu entlarven, bedarf es mehr. Das Ich ist zwar sozial konstruiert, aber deshalb noch keine Illusion: Warum die Hirnforschung einen Kategorien Fehler macht, wenn sie uns die Freiheit abspricht," *Frankfurter Allgemeine Zeitung*, November 15, 2004, 35–36; full English trans. in Jürgen Habermas, *Between Naturalism and Religion: Philosophical Essays* (Polity, 2008), 151–80.
91. Habermas, *The Future of Human Nature*, 114.
92. Habermas, "Hemdsärmeliges Pamphlet."
93. Jürgen Habermas, "Explosive Mischung," *Frankfurter Rundschau*, December 13, 2002; published in English as "Letter to America: An Interview with Habermas," *The Nation*, December 16, 2002. Interestingly, in many public comments, Habermas links antisemitism with anti-Americanism, especially in Germany. See Jürgen Habermas, "El antisemitismo en Alemania es más peligroso que en el resto de Europa," *El País*, January 31, 2004.
94. Jürgen Habermas, "Was bedeutet der Denkmalsturz? Verschließen wir nicht die Augen vor der Revolution der Weltordnung: Die normative Autorität Amerikas liegt in Trümmern," *Frankfurt Allgemeine Zeitung*, April 17, 2003, 33; English trans. in Habermas, *The Divided West*, 27.

95. Jürgen Habermas with Jacques Derrida, "Unsere Erneuerung. Nach dem Krieg: Die Wiedergeburt Europas," *Frankfurter Allgemeine Zeitung*, May 31, 2003, 33–34; published in English as Jürgen Habermas, "February 15, Or: What Binds Europeans," in *Old Europe, New Europe, Core Europe: Transatlantic Relations After the Iraq War*, trans. Max Pensky (Verso, 2005), 4.
96. Ciaran Cronin, "Editor's Preface," in *The Divided West* (Verso, 2006), xx.
97. Jürgen Habermas, "Wege aus der Weltunordnung," *Blätter für deutsche und internationale Politik* 1 (January 2004): 27–45; published in English in Habermas, *The Divided West*, 87.
98. Pierre Bourdieu, "Fourth Lecture. Universal Corporatism: The Role of Intellectuals in the Modern World," *Poetics Today* 12, no. 4 (1991): 667, 665.
99. Daniel Levy et al., "Editor's Introduction," in *Old Europe, New Europe, Core Europe: Transatlantic Relations After the Iraq War*, ed. Daniel Levy et al. (Verso, 2005), xii.
100. Felsch, *Der Philosoph*, 44.
101. Jürgen Habermas, "Hopefully the United States Is Successful in Iraq," *La Vanguardia*, November 4, 2003.
102. Habermas, "February 15," 6.
103. Habermas, "February 15," 9.
104. Habermas, "February 15," 8.
105. Jürgen Habermas, "Towards a United States of Europe," *Sign and Sight*, March 27, 2006.
106. Habermas, "February 15," 12.
107. Habermas, "February 15," 10.
108. Jürgen Habermas, "Europa ist heute in einem miserablen Zustand," *Die Welt*, May 4, 2005.
109. Jürgen Habermas, "Europäische Identität und universalistisches Handeln," *Blätter für deutsche und internationale Politik* 7, no. 7 (2003): 801–6; published in English as Jürgen Habermas, "Core Europe as Counterpower? Follow-Up Questions," in *The Divided West*, 52. See also Jürgen Habermas et al., "Fusion oder Spaltung? Die Kerneuropa-Initiative in der Debatte, Berlin, Akademie der Künste," *Blätter für deutsche und internationale Politik* 7, no. 9 (2003): 935–45.
110. Iris Marion Young, "De-Centering the Project of Global Democracy," in *Old Europe, New Europe, Core Europe: Transatlantic Relations After the Iraq War*, ed. Daniel Levy et al. (Verso, 2005), 156.
111. Jürgen Habermas, *The Inclusion of the Other: Studies in Political Theory*, trans. Ciaran Cronin (MIT Press, 1998), 107.
112. Jürgen Habermas, "Pax americana? Il mondo è troppo complesso," *Corriere della Sera*, August 6, 2003.
113. John P. McCormick, *Weber, Habermas, and Transformations of the European State: Constitutional, Social, and Supranational Democracy* (Cambridge University Press, 2007), 191.
114. Jürgen Habermas, "Über die Köpfe hinweggerollt," *Süddeutsche Zeitung*, June 6, 2005, 15.
115. Habermas, "Europa ist heute in einem miserablen Zustand."
116. Jürgen Habermas, "Le non illusoire de la gauche," *Nouvel observateur*, May 7, 2005; published in English as Jürgen Habermas, "The Illusionary No of the Left," *Voltaire Network*, May 17, 2005.

117. Jürgen Habermas, "Ist die Herausbildung einer europäischen Identität nötig, und ist sie möglich?," in *Der Gespaltene Westen*, vol. 10 of *Kleine politische Schriften* (Suhrkamp, 2004), 68–82; English trans. in Habermas, *The Divided West*, 67.
118. Jürgen Habermas, "Integration oder Devolution. Über die Zukunft Europäischen Union," lecture, Willy Brandt Haus, Berlin, November 23, 2007; published in *Neue Gesellschaft. Frankfurter Hefte* 55, no. 3 (2008): 9–14
119. Habermas, "Integration oder Devolution," 78.
120. See Jan-Werner Müller, *Constitutional Patriotism* (Princeton University Press, 2007).
121. Habermas, *The Divided West*, 78.
122. Jürgen Habermas "Wähler sind nicht nur Kunden. Die nationalstaatliche Politik muss lernen, nicht wie ein Blinder in den globalen Räumen herumzutapsen," *Süddeutsche Zeitung*, June 18, 2004, 15.
123. Jürgen Habermas, "Die avantgardistischer Spürsinn fürs Relevante", *Der Standard*, March 10–11, 2006; reprinted as "Ein avantgardistischer Spürsinn für Relevanzen," *Blätter für deutsche und internationale Politik* 5 (2006): 551–57; reprinted in *Ach, Europa: Kleine politische Schriften* 11 (Suhrkamp, 2008), 85.
124. Jürgen Habermas, "Ist die Herausbildung einer europäischen Identität nötig, und ist sie möglich?," in *Der gespaltene Westen*, 68–82; published in English as Jürgen Habermas, "Is the Development of a European Identity Necessary, and Is It Possible?," in *The Divided West*, 71.
125. Jürgen Habermas, "Medien, Märkte und Konsumenten," *Süddeutsche Zeitung*, May 16, 2007. Republished in English in Habermas, *Europe: The Faltering Project*, 133, 134, 137.
126. Jürgen Habermas, "Erste Hilfe für Europa" lecture, Willy Brandt Haus, Berlin, November 23, 2007); published in *Die Zeit*, December 29, 2007; republished as Jürgen Habermas, "Europapolitik in der Sackgasse: Plädoyer für eine Politik der abgestuften Integration," in *Ach, Europa*, 99; English trans. in Habermas, *Europe: The Faltering Project*, 78–105.
127. Quoted in Sarah Lyall and Stephen Castle, "Irish Voters Reject EU Treaty," *International Herald Tribune*, June 13, 2008, http://www.iht.com/bin/printfriendly.php?id=13702436.
128. Habermas, *Time of Transitions*, 103.
129. Kai Biermann, "Fern Jeder Vision," *Die Zeit*, November 29, 2007, http://www.zeit.de/online/2007/48/habermas-spd.
130. Jürgen Habermas, "Crossing Globalization's Valley of Tears," *New Perspectives Quarterly* 17, no. 4 (2000): 51–57. This text is an abridged version of "Der europäische Nationalstaat unter dem Druck der Globalisierung," *Blätter für deutsche und internationale Politik* 4 (1999): 425–36; published in English as Jürgen Habermas, "The European Nation-State and the Pressures of Globalization", *New Left Review* 235 (May–June 1999): 46–59.
131. Habermas, "Europapolitik in der Sackgasse," 118.
132. Habermas, "Europapolitik in der Sackgasse," 120. For more on Habermas's view of China and its relations to the West, see Jürgen Habermas, "Das Geht ans Eingemachte," *Der Spiegel*, April 30, 2001.
133. Peter Hohendahl, "Foreword," in *The Past as Future: Vergangenheit als Zukunft*, ed. Jürgen Habermas (University of Nebraska Press, 1994), x.

8. THE COLONIZATION OF POLITICS BY ECONOMICS, 2010–2020

1. See Philip Felsch, *Der Philosoph: Habermas und wir* (Propyläen, 2024), 174.
2. Matheson Russell, *Habermas and Politics: A Critical Introduction* (Edinburgh University Press, 2019), 1.
3. Jürgen Habermas, *The Lure of Technocracy*, trans. Ciaran Cronin (Polity, 2015), 65.
4. Jürgen Habermas, "The Postnational Constellation and the Future of Democracy," in *The Postnational Constellation: Political Essays*, trans. Max Pensky (MIT Press, 2001), 84; Timo Jütten, "Habermas and Markets," *Constellations* 20, no. 4 (2013): 588.
5. Jürgen Habermas et al., "Wollen europäische Bürger Suizid begehen?," *Der Standard*, May 23, 2012.
6. Jürgen Habermas, *The Crisis of the European Union: A Response*, trans. Ciaran Cronin (Polity, 2012), 12.
7. Stuart Jeffries, "A Rare Interview with Jürgen Habermas," *Financial Times*, April 30, 2010.
8. Dimitar Lilkov, "Muddling through: Towards an EU Federal Response to the Crisis," *Wilfried Martens Centre for European Studies Blog*, March 20, 2020, https://www.martenscentre.eu/blog/muddling-through-towards-an-eu-federal-response-to-the-crisis/.
9. Klaus Eder, "Making Sense of the Public Sphere," in *Handbook of Contemporary European Social Theory*, ed. Gerard Delanty (Routledge, 2005), 342.
10. Seyla Benhabib, *The Claims of Culture: Equality and Diversity in the Global Era* (Princeton University Press, 2002), 21.
11. Michel Aglietta, "The European Vortex," *New Left Review* 75 (2012): 15.
12. This chronology follows the analysis of Jean-Claude Trichet, former head of the European Central Bank, in "The State of the Euro," lecture at the Center for European Studies, Harvard University, Cambridge, MA, October 16, 2013. For a broader summary of these events, see also Costas Lapavitsas, "Financialised Capitalism: Crisis and Financial Expropriation," *Historical Materialism* 17, no. 2 (June 2009): 114–48.
13. Jean-Claude Piris, *The Future of Europe: Towards a Two-Speed EU?* (Cambridge University Press, 2012), 42.
14. Jonathan White, *Politics of Last Resort: Governing by Emergency in the European Union* (Oxford University Press, 2020), 17, 18.
15. For a thorough account of the economic crisis and its political implications, see Adam Tooze, *Crashed: How a Decade of Financial Crises Changed the World* (Viking, 2018).
16. Hans-Werner Sinn, *Casino Capitalism: How the Financial Crisis Came About and What Needs to Be Done Now* (Oxford University Press, 2010), 20; David Lizoane and Matthias Ecke, "European Youth Need a Change from a New German Government," *Social Europe Journal*, November 14, 2013, 2.
17. Jürgen Habermas, *Legitimation Crisis* (Beacon, 1975); Nancy Fraser, "Legitimation Crisis? On the Political Contradictions of Financialized Capitalism," *Critical Historical Studies* 2, no. 2 (2015).
18. For more on these ideas, see Peter J. Verovšek, "Taking Back Control Over Markets: Jürgen Habermas on the Colonization of Politics by Economics," *Political Studies* 71, no. 2 (2021).
19. Jürgen Habermas, *Europe: The Faltering Project*, trans. Ciaran Cronin (Polity, 2009), 186. Originally published as Jürgen Habermas, "Nach dem Bankrott. Ein Interview," interview by Thomas Assheuer, *Die Zeit*, November 6, 2008, 46.

20. Paul De Grauwe, "The Governance of a Fragile Eurozone," *Centre for European Policy Studies*, May 4, 2011; Michael Spence, "Five Steps to Fix the World," *Newsweek*, January 31, 2011; Lagarde quoted in Jeanna Smialek, "IMF Chief Lagarde Calls Merkel 'Unchallenged Leader' in Germany," *Bloomberg*, April 10, 2013.
21. Chris Bowlby, "European Central Bank Calls for 'Quantum Leap,' " *BBC News*, June 29, 2010, http://news.bbc.co.uk/2/hi/business/10453433.stm.
22. Jürgen Habermas, "Merkel Has Depleted Her Capital of Trust Within EU," *The Irish Times*, June 12, 2010.
23. Alessandro Ferrara, "Europe as a 'Special Area for Human Hope,' " *Constellations* 14, no. 3 (2007); Christopher Hitchens, "Is the Euro Doomed? The Dreams of European Union Could Die Along with It," *Slate*, April 26, 2010, http://www.slate.com/id/2251986.
24. Jürgen Habermas, "Wir brauchen Europa!," Ausland, *Die Zeit*, May 20, 2010, http://www.zeit.de/2010/21/Europa-Habermas.
25. Jürgen Habermas, "The Cost and Challenge of the Eurozone Debt Crisis," FT Magazine, *Financial Times*, May 1, 2010.
26. Jürgen Habermas, "Afterword: Lessons of the Financial Crisis," in *Europe: The Faltering Project*, trans. Ciaran Cronin (Polity, 2009), 184–85.
27. Habermas, "Cost and Challenge." See also Jürgen Habermas, "Merkel's European Failure: Germany Dozes on a Volcano," *Der Spiegel*, September 8, 2013, http://www.spiegel.de/international/germany/juergen-habermas-merkel-needs-to-confront-real-european-reform-a-915244-druck.html.
28. Habermas, "Wir brauchen Europa!."
29. Habermas, "Merkel Has Depleted Her Capital."
30. Habermas, "Cost and Challenge." This is a consistent refrain in Habermas's work. See Jürgen Habermas, "Sind wir noch gute Europäer?," lecture delivered at the awarding ceremony of the Franco-German Media Prize, Berlin, 2018; published in English as Jürgen Habermas, "Are We Still Good Europeans?" *Zeit Online*, July 6, 2018, https://www.zeit.de/kultur/2018-07/european-union-germany-challenges-loyalty-solidarity/komplettansicht.
31. Habermas, "Wir brauchen Europa!."
32. See also Jürgen Habermas, "Für eine engere politische Union," *Die Zeit*, June 22, 2011. This was an open letter cosigned by Habermas and a number of other influential thinkers, and also published in English with the collective byline "Jürgen Habermas and 18 others" under the title "The EU Needs Leadership to Tackle this Crisis, Not Repeated Doses of Austerity," *The Guardian*, June 22, 2011, https://www.theguardian.com/commentisfree/2011/jun/22/eu-leadership-tackle-crisis-austerity.
33. Habermas, "Wir brauchen Europa!."
34. Habermas, "Merkel Has Depleted Her Capital."
35. Jürgen Habermas, "Leadership and Leitkultur," Opinion, *New York Times*, October 28, 2010, http://www.nytimes.com/2010/10/29/opinion/29Habermas.html. The concept of Leitkultur comes from the work of one of Adorno's students, Bassam Tibi. See Bassam Tibi, *Europa ohne Identität?: Die Krise der multikulturellen Gesellschaft* (C. Bertelsmann, 1998).
36. Habermas, "Leadership and Leitkultur."
37. When Ágnes Heller passed away in 2019, Habermas wrote a heartfelt tribute. See Jürgen Habermas, "Abschied von einer Philosophin," *Die Zeit*, July 21, 2019; published in English as Jürgen Habermas, "Farewell to a Philosopher," *Constellations* 26, no. 3 (2019).

38. Jürgen Habermas and Julian Nida-Rümelin, "Schützt die Philosophen!," *Süddeutsche Zeitung*, January 25, 2011.
39. Habermas, *The Crisis of the European Union*, vii.
40. Jürgen Habermas, *Zur Verfassung Europas: Ein Essay* (Suhrkamp, 2011). During this period Habermas was also involved in a dispute regarding the future of the publishing house with which his work is so closely connected. See Jürgen Habermas et al., "Eigentum Verpflichtet! A Call for a Solution of the Suhrkamp Conflict," *Frankfurter Allgemeine Zeitung*, January 4, 2013.
41. Georg Diez, "A Philosopher's Mission to Save the EU," *Der Spiegel*, November 25, 2011, https://www.spiegel.de/international/europe/habermas-the-last-european-a-philosopher-s-mission-to-save-the-eu-a-799237.html.
42. Habermas, *The Lure of Technocracy*, 64. Originally published as Jürgen Habermas, "Der nächste Schritt. Ein Interview," interview by Hans-Ch. Ehalt and Claus Reitan, *Die Furche*, May 23, 2012.
43. Jürgen Habermas, "Vom schwinden der Solidarität," interview by L. Schröder, *Rheinische Post*, December 10, 2012.
44. Jürgen Habermas, "Wie konnte es dazu kommen?," laudatio for Jan Phillip Reemtsma, delivered at the Award Ceremony for the Prize for Understanding and Tolerance, Jüdischen Museum Berlin, November 13, 2010); published in *Mittelweg 36* (2010): 60–63; reprinted in Jürgen Habermas, *Im Sog der Technokratie*, vol. 12 of *Kleine politische Schriften* (Suhrkamp, 2013), 174–79.
45. See Jürgen Habermas, "Die Krise der Europäischen Union im Lichte einer Konstitutionalisierung des Völkerrecht," lecture delivered at Humboldt-Universität Berlin, June 16, 2011; see also Jürgen Habermas, "Das Europa der Staatsbürger," *Handelsblatt*, June 17–18, 2011, 12–13; reprinted as Jürgen Habermas, "Wie demokratisch ist die EU?" *Blätter für deutsche und internationale Politik* 8 (2011): 37–48.
46. Habermas, *The Crisis of the European Union*, x.
47. Habermas, *The Crisis of the European Union*, x, ix, vii.
48. Habermas, *The Crisis of the European Union*, x–xi.
49. Jürgen Habermas, *The Postnational Constellation: Political Essays*, ed. and trans. Max Pensky (MIT Press, 2001), 58–112; originally published in Jürgen Habermas, *Die postnationale Konstellation: Politische Essays* (Suhrkamp, 1998), 91–169.
50. Jürgen Habermas, "The Constitutionalization of International Law and the Legitimation Problems of a Constitution for World Society," *Constellations* 15, no. 4 (2008): 447.
51. Habermas, "Constitutionalization," 444; Habermas, *The Crisis of the European Union*, 12.
52. Jürgen Habermas et al., "Einspruch gegen die Fassadendemokratie," *Frankfurter Allgemeine Zeitung*, August 3, 2012.
53. Habermas, *The Crisis of the European Union*, 16, 19.
54. Habermas, *The Crisis of the European Union*, 24.
55. Habermas, *The Crisis of the European Union*, 35.
56. Habermas, *The Crisis of the European Union*, 43.
57. Christoph Möllers, *The Three Branches: A Comparative Model of Separation of Powers* (Oxford University Press, 2015), 182.
58. Jürgen Habermas and Francis Fukuyama, "The European Citizen: Just a Myth?," *The Global Journal*, May 18, 2012.

59. Habermas, *The Crisis of the European Union*, 46.
60. Thomas Risse, *A Community of Europeans?: Transnational Identities and Public Spheres* (Cornell University Press, 2010), 5; Gerard Delanty and Chris Rumford, *Rethinking Europe: Social Theory and the Implications of Europeanization* (Routledge, 2005), 79.
61. Jürgen Habermas, "A Pact for Or Against Europe," in *The Crisis of the European Union*, 135. Originally published as Jürgen Habermas, "Ein Pakt für oder gegen Europa?," lecture at the conference "Europe and the Rediscovery of the German Nation-State," European Council on Foreign Relations, Berlin, April 6, 2011; partially in *Süddeutsche Zeitung* 81, April 7, 2011, 11.
62. Jürgen Habermas, "Der Konstruktionsfehler der Währungsunion," *Blätter für deutsche und internationale Politik* 56, no. 5 (2011): 64–66; see also Jürgen Habermas et al., "Europa und die neue deutsche Frage," *Blätter für deutsche und internationale Politik* 56, no. 5 (2011): 45–63; published in English as Jürgen Habermas et al., "Europe and the New German Question," *Eurozine*, August 26, 2011.
63. Joschka Fischer, "Gründungfigur des demokratischen Deutschland," in *Über Habermas: Gespräche mit Zeitgenossen*, ed. Michael Funken (Wissenschaftliche Buchgesellschaft, 2009), 49.
64. Habermas et al., "Europe and the New German Question," 5.
65. Habermas et al., "Europe and the New German Question," 11.
66. Jürgen Habermas, "Europe's Post-Democratic Era," *The Guardian*, November 10, 2011, https://www.theguardian.com/commentisfree/2011/nov/10/jurgen-habermas-europe-post-democratic. Originally delivered as a lecture titled "Die Krise der Europäischen Union im Lichte einer Konstitutionalisierung des Völkerrecht," Humboldt-Universität Berlin, June 16, 2011; republished in part as "Das Europa der Staatsbürger," *Handelsblatt*, June 17–18, 2011, 12–13; and Jürgen Habermas, "Schluss mit der Feigheit der Politiker," *Vorwärts*, January 31, 2012, 8.
67. Habermas, "Europe's Post-Democratic Era."
68. Jürgen Habermas, "Nobel per la pace: Oslo chiama l'Europa," *la Repubblica*, October 13, 2012; English trans. in Jürgen Habermas, "Oslo's Call to Europe," *Presseurop*, October 15, 2012, http://www.presseurop.eu/en/content/article/2875321-oslo-s-call-europe.
69. Jürgen Habermas, "Democracy, Solidarity and the European Crisis," *Social Europe Journal*, May 7, 2013, 5.
70. Ulrich Beck, *German Europe* (Polity, 2013), 3.
71. John McIntyre, *The Limits of Scientific Reason: Habermas, Foucault, and Science as a Social Institution* (Rowman & Littlefield, 2021), 43.
72. Jürgen Habermas, *Towards a Rational Society: Student Protest, Science, and Politics* (Heinemann Educational Books, 1971), 60
73. Jürgen Habermas, "Rettet die Würde der Demokratie," *Frankfurter Allgemeine Zeitung*, November 4, 2011; Frank Schirrmacher, "Demokratie ist Ramsch," *Frankfurter Allgemeine Zeitung*, November 1, 2011.
74. Habermas, "Rettet die Würde."
75. Jürgen Habermas, "Schluss jetzt! Der Philosoph Jürgen Habermas hat seinen Schreibtisch Verlassen, weil er die Idee von Europa retten will: vor Unfähigen Politikern, vor der sunklen Macht der Märkte," interview by Gisela Diez, *Der Spiegel*, November 21, 2011, 134–18; published in English as Diez, "A Philosopher's Mission to Save the EU," *Der*

Spiegel, November 25, 2011, https://www.spiegel.de/international/europe/habermas-the-last-european-a-philosopher-s-mission-to-save-the-eu-a-799237.html.
76. Jürgen Habermas, "Politik und Erpressung," lecture delivered at the awarding ceremony for the Georg-August-Zinn Prize, Wiesbaden, September 6, 2012; originally published in *Die Zeit*, September 6, 2012; English trans. in Habermas, *The Lure of Technocracy*, 75, 76.
77. Sigmar Gabriel, Jürgen Habermas and Emmanuel Macron, "Europa neu denken. Eine Diskussion zwischen Jürgen Habermas, Sigmar Gabriel und Emmanuel Macron," *Blätter für deutsche und internationale Politik* 3 (2017): 41–54, published in English as Sigmar Gabriel et al., "Rethinking Europe: A Discussion Between Jürgen Habermas, Sigmar Gabriel and Emmanuel Macron," *Eurozine*, April 4, 2017, 2. See also Jürgen Habermas, "Europas zögerliche Liebhaber," *Die Zeit*, March 1, 2018.
78. Habermas, *The Lure of Technocracy*, 76.
79. Jürgen Habermas, "L'Europe actuelle, entre paralysie et distraction" (interview by N. Weill), *Le Monde*, November 8, 2014, 13.
80. Jürgen Habermas, " '. . . . was das uns Deutsche wieder kostet!' Ist das die Antwort auf den französischen Präsidenten?" *Der Spiegel*, October 21, 2017, 134–36; published in English as Jürgen Habermas, "What Macron Means for Europe: 'How Much Will the Germans have to Pay?,' " *Spiegel Online*, October 26, 2017, https://www.spiegel.de/international/europe/juergen-habermas-on-the-european-vision-of-emmanuel-macron-a-1174721.html; Jürgen Habermas, "Eine Umgruppierung der Kräfte ist überfällig," *Die Zeit*, April 20, 2017, 17. For more on Habermas's views of Macron, see Jürgen Habermas, "Nous n'avons pas besoin d'un Macron allemand," *Le Point*, February 15, 2018.
81. Jürgen Habermas, "Warum Merkels Griechenland-Politik ein fehler ist," *Süddeutsche Zeitung*, June 22, 2015; published in English as Jürgen Habermas, "Why Angela Merkel Is Wrong on Greece," *Social Europe Journal*, June 25, 2015.
82. Jürgen Habermas, "Jürgen Habermas's Verdict on the EU/Greece Debt Deal," *The Guardian*, July 16, 2015. See also Jürgen Habermas, "La réaction abrupte de l'Allemagne a été indigne," interview by Odile Benyahia-Kouider, *L'Obs*, July 30, 2015, 24–27.
83. Jürgen Habermas, "Drei Gründe für 'Mehr Europa,' " address at the sixty-ninth "Deutscher Juristentag," Munich, September 21, 2012; published in *Süddeutsche Zeitung*, September 22–23, 2012, 15; English trans. in Habermas, *The Lure of Technocracy*, 81.
84. Jürgen Habermas, "Recht und Demokratie in der postnationalen Konstellation," masterclass on international law, Max Planck Institute for Comparative Public Law and International Law, Heidelberg, February 11, 2013; English trans. in Habermas, *The Lure of Technocracy*, 46, 47.
85. Jürgen Habermas, "Europa is niet langer een eliteproject," interview by L. Meyvis, *Campuskrant* 24, no. 8 (May 2, 2013).
86. Diez, "A Philosopher's Mission."
87. Habermas, "Schluss mit der Feigheit," 8. See also Jürgen Habermas, "En Europe, les nationalismes sont de retour," *L'Express*, November 12, 2014, 14–18.
88. Seyla Benhabib, "The New Sovereigntism and Transnational Law: Legal Utopianism, Democratic Scepticism and Statist Realism," *Global Constitutionalism* 5, no. 1 (2016).
89. Wolfgang Streeck, *Buying Time: The Delayed Crisis of Democratic Capitalism*, trans. Patrick Camiller (Verso, 2014). See also Wolfgang Streeck, "Wenn die EU untergeht, wird keiner

weinen," Feuilleton, *Die Zeit*, October 13, 2016; Martin Höpner et al., "Europa braucht die Nation," Wirtschaft, *Die Zeit*, September 15, 2016.
90. See also Habermas, "Jürgen Habermas's Verdict."
91. Jürgen Habermas, "Demokratie oder Kapitalismus? Vom Elend der nationalstaatlichen Fragmentierung in einer kapitalistisch integrierten Weltgesellschaft," *Blätter für deutsche und internationale Politik* 5 (2013): 59–70; English trans. in Habermas, *The Lure of Technocracy*, 85, 89.
92. See Wolfgang Streeck, *How Will Capitalism End?: Essays on a Failing System* (Verso, 2016).
93. Habermas, "Demokratie oder Kapitalismus?, 102.
94. Jürgen Habermas, "Vi spiego perché la sinistra anti-Europa sbaglia," *Reset* 9 (2013). See also Wolfgang Streeck, " 'Vom DM-Nationalismus zum Euro-Patriotismus? Eine Replik auf Jürgen Habermas,' " *Blätter für deutsche und internationale Politik* 58, no. 9 (2013); Wolfgang Streeck, "Small-State Nostalgia? The Currency Union, Germany, and Europe: A Reply to Jürgen Habermas," *Constellations* 21, no. 2 (2014).
95. Jürgen Habermas, " 'Für ein starkes Europa'—aber was heißt das?," speech, Potsdam, February 2, 2014; published in *Blätter für deutsche und internationale Politik* 59, no. 3 (2014): 85–94; published in English as Jürgen Habermas, " 'In Favour of a Strong Europe'—What Does This Mean?," *Juncture*, March 12, 2014.
96. Jürgen Habermas et al., "Wählt Europa! Aufruf europäischer Intellektueller zur Europawahl," *Blätter für deutsche und internationale Politik*, February 26, 2014. See also Jürgen Habermas, "Nationalistische Gespenster rumoren," *Kölner Stadt-Anzeiger*, June 14, 2014; published in English as Jürgen Habermas, "Internet and Public Sphere," *Reset Dialogues on Civilizations*, July 24, 2014.
97. Jürgen Habermas, "Europa wird direkt ins Herz getroffen," *Frankfurter Allgemeine Zeitung*, May 30, 2014; Jürgen Habermas et al., "Juncker Is the Democratic Choice to Head the EU Commission," *The Guardian*, June 6, 2014.
98. Jürgen Habermas, "Democracy in Europe," lecture delivered at symposium on "The Conditions for Democracy," University of Stavanger, Norway, September 11, 2014; republished as Jürgen Habermas, "Democracy in Europe: Why the Development of the European Union into a Transnational Democracy Is Necessary and How It Is Possible," *European Law Journal* 21, no. 4 (2015).
99. Jürgen Habermas, "Das eigentliche Ziel ist die Transnationalisierung der Demokratie," interview by Thomas Meyer, *Neue Gesellschaft/Frankfurter Hefte* 4 (2014): 14–20; Jürgen Habermas, "Transnationalization of Democracy: A European Experiment," lecture given at Princeton University, May 1, 2014, and at Boston College Law School, May 7, 2014; English trans. in Habermas, *The Lure of Technocracy*, 36, 39 (emphasis in original), 40.
100. Habermas and Fukuyama, "The European Citizen."
101. Peter J. Verovšek, "The EU is Muddling Through Another Crisis—Which May Be Good Enough," *Social Europe Journal*, July 2, 2020, https://www.socialeurope.eu/the-eu-is-muddling-through-another-crisis-which-may-be-good-enough.
102. Seyla Benhabib, *Critique, Norm, and Utopia: A Study of the Foundations of Critical Theory* (Columbia University Press, 1986), 7.
103. Habermas, *The Crisis of the European Union*, 124. For more on these generational dynamics, see Peter J. Verovšek, "Memory and the Euro-Crisis of Leadership: The Effects of Generational Change in Germany and the EU," *Constellations* 21, no. 2 (2014): 239–48.

104. Wolfgang Streeck, "Markets and Peoples: Democratic Capitalism and European Integration," *New Left Review* 73 (2012): 66.
105. Habermas, *The Crisis of the European Union*, 7; Jürgen Habermas "Wir Brauchen Europa!,"; English trans. in Habermas, *The Crisis of the European Union*, 119–26.
106. Jürgen Habermas, "Zur Prinzipienkonkurrenz von Bürgergleichheit und Staatengleichheit im Supranationalen Gemeinwesen. Eine Notiz aus Anlass der Frage nach der Legitimität der ungleichen Repräsentation der Bürger im Europäischen Parlament," *Der Staat* 53, no. 2 (2014): 184–85. See also Jürgen Habermas, "Dalla crisi economica può nascere l'Europa politica," interview by Donatella Di Cesare, *MicroMega*, November 19, 2012.
107. Habermas and Merkel quoted in Moritz Koch, "Rare Praise from a Philosopher," *Handelsblatt*, October 10, 2015.
108. Jürgen Habermas, *The Future of Human Nature* (Polity, 2003), 102.
109. Jürgen Habermas, "Le djihadisme, une forme moderne de réaction au déracinement," *Le Monde*, November 21, 2015; published in English as Jürgen Habermas, "The Paris Attack and Its Aftermath," *Social Europe*, November 26, 2015, https://socialeurope.eu/habermas-paris-attack.
110. Jürgen Habermas, "Die Spieler treten ab," *Die Zeit*, July 7, 2016, 37; published in English as Jürgen Habermas, "The Players Resign—Core Europe to the Rescue," *Die Zeit Online*, July 12, 2016, https://www.zeit.de/kultur/2016-07/juergen-habermas-brexit-eu-crises-english/komplettansicht.
111. Jürgen Habermas, "Für eine demokratische Polarisierung. Wie man dem Rechtspopulismus den Boden entzieht," *Blätter für deutsche und internationale Politik* 11 (2016): 35–42; published in English as Jürgen Habermas, "For a Democratic Polarization," *Eurozine*, November 22, 2016. See also Jürgen Habermas, "Aufruf: Wir sind in tiefer Sorge um die Einigung Europas und die Zukunft Deutschlands," *Handelsblatt*, October 22, 2018; published in English as Jürgen Habermas et al., "We Are Deeply Concerned About the Future of Europe and Germany," *Handelsblatt Global*, October 25, 2018, https://www.handelsblatt.com/english/opinion/time-to-wake-up-we-are-deeply-concerned-about-the-future-of-europe-and-germany/23583722.html.
112. Jürgen Habermas, "New Perspectives for Europe," address at conference on "New Perspectives for Europe", Bad Homburg, September 21, 2018; published as Jürgen Habermas, "New Perspectives for Europe," *Social Europe*, October 22, 2018.
113. Peter J. Verovšek, "Experts, Public Intellectuals and the Coronavirus," *Duck of Minerva*, March 29, 2020, https://www.duckofminerva.com/2020/03/experts-public-intellectuals-and-the-coronavirus.html.
114. Jürgen Habermas, "Corona und der Schutz des Lebens: Zur Grundrechtsdebatte in der pandemischen Ausnahmesituation," *Blätter für deutsche und internationale Politik* 9 (September 2021): 74.
115. See also Jürgen Habermas and Klaus Günther, "Kein Grundrecht gilt grenzenlos," *Die Zeit*, May 6, 2020, https://www.zeit.de/2020/20/grundrechte-lebensschutz-freiheit-juergen-habermas-klaus-guenther/komplettansicht?print.
116. Jürgen Habermas, "Dans cette crise, il nous faut agir dans le savoir de notre non-savoir," *Le Monde*, April 15, 2020.
117. Peter Bofinger et al., "Europa kann nur weiterleben, wenn die Europäer jetzt füreinander Einstehen," *Die Zeit*, April 2, 2020, https://www.zeit.de/2020/15/europa-kann-nur

-weiterleben-wenn-die-europaeer-jetzt-fuereinander-einstehen; Peter Bofinger et al., "Nous appelons la Commission européenne à créer un fonds corona pour aider les etats membres," *Le Monde*, April 2, 2020, https://www.lemonde.fr/idees/article/2020/04/02/nous-appelons-la-commission-europeenne-a-creer-un-fonds-corona-pour-aider-les-etats-membres_6035262_3232.html.

118. Peter J. Verovšek, "Habermas on the Legitimacy of Lockdown," *Eurozine*, February 14, 2022.
119. Habermas, "Corona und der Schutz des Lebens," 76.
120. Habermas, "Dans cette crise."
121. Andreas Rosenfelder, "Die Habermas-Diktatur," Meinung (Opinion), *Die Welt*, 2021, accessed October 12, 2021, https://www.welt.de/kultur/plus234125124/Corona-Politik-Die-Habermas-Diktatur.html; Giorgio Agamben, "L'invenzione di un'epidemia," *Quodlibet*, February 26, 2020, https://www.quodlibet.it/giorgio-agamben-l-invenzione-di-un-epidemia.
122. Habermas, "Corona und der Schutz des Lebens," 78.
123. Habermas, "Corona und der Schutz des Lebens," 76.
124. Jürgen Habermas, *Between Facts and Norms: Contributions to a Discourse Theory of Law and Democracy* (MIT Press, 1996), 186, 307–8.
125. Habermas, "Corona und der Schutz des Lebens," 74.
126. Habermas, "Corona und der Schutz des Lebens," 77.
127. Felsch, *Der Philosoph*, 7.
128. Jürgen Habermas, *Auch eine Geschichte der Philosophie*, vol. 1 (Suhrkamp, 2019), 10.
129. Max Weber, "Politics as a Vocation," in *From Max Weber: Essays in Sociology*, ed. and trans. Hans Heinrich Gerth and C. Wright Mills (Oxford University Press, 1958), 128.
130. Jürgen Habermas, "Europe's Mistake," *Granata*, November 23, 2023, https://granta.com/europes-mistake/.
131. Felsch, *Der Philosoph*, 172.
132. Luuk van Middelaar, "The Return of Politics—The European Union After the Crises in the Eurozone and Ukraine," *Journal of Common Market Studies* 54, no. 3 (2016): 501, 504.
133. Jürgen Habermas, *Ein neuer Strukturwandel der Öffentlichkeit und die deliberative Politik* (Suhrkamp, 2022), 7; published in English as Jürgen Habermas, *A New Structural Transformation of the Public Sphere and Deliberative Politics* (Polity, 2023).

CONCLUSION: THE LAST PUBLIC INTELLECTUAL?, 2021–2025

1. Robert D. Cumming, *Human Nature and History: A Study of the Development of Liberal Political Thought* (Chicago University Press, 1969), 216.
2. Jürgen Habermas, "For God's Sake, Spare Us Governing Philosophers!," interview by Borja Hermoso, *El País*, May 25, 2018, https://english.elpais.com/elpais/2018/05/07/inenglish/1525683618_145760.html.
3. Jürgen Habermas, "Europe's Mistake," *Granata*, November 23, 2023, https://granta.com/europes-mistake/.
4. Jürgen Habermas, *Die neue Unübersichtlichkeit* (Suhrkamp, 1985), 268.
5. For more, see Peter J. Verovšek, "The Philosopher as Engaged Citizen: Habermas on the Role of the Public Intellectual in the Modern Democratic Public Sphere," *European Journal of Social Theory* 24, no. 4 (2021): 526–44.

6. Jürgen Habermas, *Europe: The Faltering Project*, trans. Ciaran Cronin (Polity, 2009), 143.
7. Peter J. Verovšek, "Direct Engagement or Discursive Impact?: Public Philosophy in the United Kingdom and Germany," *Angermion* 14, no. 1 (2021): 193–216.
8. Jürgen Habermas, *Time of Transitions*, trans. Ciaran Cronin and Max Pensky (Polity, 2006), 45.
9. Jürgen Habermas, conversation with the author, June 7, 2024 (hereafter cited as Habermas coversation).
10. Jürgen Habermas quoted in Claudia Czingon et al., "Moralischer Universalismus in Zeiten politischer Regression: Jürgen Habermas im Gespräch über die Gegenwart und sein Lebenswerk," *Leviathan* 48, no. 1 (2020): 15.
11. Habermas coversation.
12. Jürgen Habermas, *The Postnational Constellation: Political Essays* (MIT Press, 2001, 38–57. For more on the debate about the nature of Adorno's negativism, see Fabian Freyenhagen, *Adorno's Practical Philosophy: Living Less Wrongly* (Cambridge University Press, 2013); Peter E. Gordon, *A Precarious Happiness: Adorno and the Sources of Normativity* (University of Chicago Press, 2024).
13. See Peter J. Verovšek, "Historical Criticism Without Progress: Memory as an Emancipatory Resource for Critical Theory," *Constellations* 26, no. 1 (2019), 132–47.
14. Habermas conversation.
15. See Peter Niesen, "Constituent Power in Global Constitutionalism," in *Handbook on Global Constitutionalism*, ed. Anthony F. Lang and Antje Wiener (Edward Elgar, 2023).
16. Jürgen Habermas, *Autonomy and Solidarity: Interviews*, ed. Peter Dews (Verso, 1992), 127.
17. Habermas, *Die neue Unübersichtlichkeit*, 268.
18. Jürgen Habermas, *Theory and Practice*, trans. John Viertel (Beacon, 1974), 1; Habermas, "For God's Sake, Spare Us Governing Philosophers!"
19. For a summary of these debates, see Haig Patapan, *Modern Philosopher Kings: Wisdom and Power in Politics* (Edinburgh University Press, 2023).
20. Habermas, *Die neue Unübersichtlichkeit*, 268. For more on these other movements in the applied turn, see chapter 1.
21. Jürgen Habermas, *'Es musste etwas besser werden. . . .' Gespräche mit Stefan Müller-Doohm und Roman Yos* (Suhrkamp, 2024), 27.
22. Jürgen Habermas, *Auch eine Geschichte der Philosophie*, vol. 1, *Die Okzidentale Konstellation von Glauben und Wissen* (Suhrkamp, 2019), 10.
23. See Jürgen Habermas, "Literatur und Leben als Lebensthema: Erinnerung an Karl Heinz Bohrer," *Frankfurter Allgemeine Zeitung*, August 11, 2021; Jürgen Habermas, "Der Elektrisierende: Meine Erinnerung an den Schriftsteller und Gefährten Hans Magnus Enzensberger," *Süddeutsche Zeitung*, November 25, 2022; Jürgen Habermas, "Die Vielen Farben des Eigensinns; Meinem Freunde Alexander Kluge zum 90.," *Die Zeit*, February 10, 2022; Ute Habermas and Jürgen Habermas, "Unser Geschenk; Eine Würdigung des Malers Günter Fruhtrunk, der im Mai 99 Jahre alt geworden wäre und uns einst unter seltsamen Umständen ein Bild vermachte," *Die Zeit*, December 30, 2021; Jürgen Habermas, "Die vielen Farben"; Jürgen Habermas, "Bildung als Erfahrung: Erinnerung an Oskar Negt," *Sociopolis*, February 12, 2024.
24. Jürgen Habermas, *Ein neuer Strukturwandel der Öffentlichkeit und die deliberative Politik* (Suhrkamp, 2022); Jürgen Habermas, *A New Structural Transformation of the Public Sphere and Deliberative Politics* (Polity, 2023).

25. Habermas, *Ein neuer Strukturwandel*, 7; Jürgen Habermas, "Reflections and Hypotheses on a Further Structural Transformation of the Political Public Sphere," *Theory, Culture & Society* 39, no. 4 (2022): 158.
26. Jürgen Habermas and Jacques Derrida, "February 15, or What Binds Europeans Together: A Plea for a Common Foreign Policy, Beginning in the Core of Europe," *Constellations* 10, no. 3 (2003): 295, 293.
27. Jürgen Habermas, "Wider die Logik des Krieges. Ein Plädoyer für Zurückhaltung, aber nicht gegenüber Israel," *Die Zeit*, February 15, 1991.
28. Jürgen Habermas, "Krieg und Empörung," *Süddeutsche Zeitung*, April 29, 2022, published in English as Jürgen Habermas, "War and Indignation," *Süddeutsche Zeitung*, April 28, 2022, accessed April 29, 2022, https://www.sueddeutsche.de/projekte/artikel/kultur/the-dilemma-of-the-west-juergen-habermas-on-the-war-in-ukraine-e032431/.
29. Felsch, *Der Philosoph*, 184.
30. Michael Haiden, "Jürgen Habermas: A Political Pacifist?" *Res Philosophica* 101, no. 2 (2024): 193, 210. Habermas accepts Haiden's characterization of his position during our conversation. See also Jürgen Habermas, *'Es musste etwas besser werden. . . .' Gespräche mit Stefan Müller-Doohm und Roman Yos* (Suhrkamp, 2024), 150.
31. Quoted in Nils Minkmar and Nicolas Richter, " 'Ab und an lese ich auch Comics.' Olaf Scholz im Interview," *Süddeutsche Zeitung*, July 28, 2023.
32. See Peter J. Verovšek, " 'One Would at Least Like to Be Asked': Habermas on Popular Sovereignty, Self-Determination, and German Unification," *German Politics and Society* 41, no. 3 (2023): 22–43.
33. Habermas and Derrida, "February 15," 294.
34. Jürgen Habermas, "Der neue Historikerstreit," *Philosophie Magazine* 6 (2021): 10.
35. Karl Korn (*Frankfurter Allgemeine Zeitung*) to Habermas, July 16, 1953, Habermas Vorlass, Korrespondenzen 1950er und 1960er Jahre, 1—1954–1958 (A–Z); Wolfgang Streeck, "Getting Closer," *Sidecar*, November 7, 2022, https://newleftreview.org/sidecar/posts/getting-closer.
36. Felsch, *Der Philosoph*, 183.
37. Stefan Müller-Doohm, "Habermas-Biograph: 'Er kann gar nicht anders, als sich zu äußern,' " *Frankfurter Rundschau*, February 20, 2023, https://www.fr.de/kultur/gesellschaft/habermas-biograph-er-kann-gar-nicht-anders-als-sich-zu-aeussern-92099059.html. For more on Habermas's constructivist international political theory, see Thomas Risse, " 'Let's Argue!': Communicative Action in World Politics," *International Organization* 54, no. 1 (2000): 1–39; Peter J. Verovšek, "Integration After Totalitarianism: Arendt and Habermas on the Postwar Imperatives of Memory," *Journal of International Political Theory* 16, no. 1 (2020): 2–24.
38. Jürgen Habermas, "Ein Plädoyer für Verhandlungen," *Süddeutsche Zeitung*, February 14, 2023, https://www.sueddeutsche.de/projekte/artikel/kultur/juergen-habermas-ukraine-sz-verhandlungen-e159105/?reduced=true; published in English as Jürgen Habermas, "A Plea for Negotiations," *Süddeutsche Zeitung*, February 14, 2023, https://www.sueddeutsche.de/projekte/artikel/kultur/juergen-habermas-ukraine-sz-negotiations-e480179/?reduced=true.
39. Habermas, "Europe's Mistake."
40. Jürgen Habermas, "Ein Appell für Europa," *Süddeutsche Zeitung*, March 24, 2024, https://www.sueddeutsche.de/projekte/artikel/kultur/juergen-habermas-gastbeitrag-europa

-e943825/; published in English as Jürgen Habermas, "An Appeal for Europe," *Süddeutsche Zeitung*, March 24, 2025, https://www.sueddeutsche.de/projekte/artikel/kultur/juergen-habermas-essay-europa-e494414/.

41. Thomas Gregersen, Political Theory—Habermas and Rawls (blog), accessed February 16, 2023, http://habermas-rawls.blogspot.com. See collections of responses posted April 30, 2022, February 14, 2023, and February 16, 2023.
42. For a particularly prominent example, see Timothy Snyder, "Germans Have Been Involved in the War, Chiefly on the Wrong Side," *Frankfurter Allgemeine Zeitung*, June 27, 2022, https://www.faz.net/-gq5-asmiu.
43. Philip Felsch, *Der Philosoph: Habermas und wir* (Polypläen, 2024), 16.
44. Nicole Deitelhoff et al., *Grundsätze der Solidarität. Eine Stellungnahme* (2023), https://www.normativeorders.net/2023/grundsatze-der-solidaritat/. An English translation is available: Nicole Deitelhoff et al., "Principles of Solidarity: A Statement," *Normative Orders*, November 13, 2023, https://www.normativeorders.net/2023/grundsatze-der-solidaritat/.
45. Thomas Gregersen, "Habermas on the Hamas Massacre, Israel's Response, and Anti-Semitic Sentiments," *Political Theory—Habermas and Rawls*, November 14, 2023, habermas-rawls.blogspot.com/2023/11/on-hamas-massacre-and-israels-response.html.
46. See Kirsten Grieshaber, "The German Chancellor Condemns a Firebomb Attack on a Berlin Synagogue and Vows Protection for Jews," *AP News*, October 18, 2023, https://apnews.com/article/germany-berlin-synagogue-antisemitism-fdd10f32f7d5efc6da973f-00c9a8b030. My thanks to Peter Gordon for highlighting the need to include more of this specific context at this point in the narrative.
47. Felsch, *Der Philosoph*, 17.
48. International Court of Justice, *Summary 2024/1: Summary of the Order of 26 January 2024*, https://www.icj-cij.org/sites/default/files/case-related/192/192-20240126-sum-01-00-en.pdf, 4.
49. Quoted in Felsch, *Der Philosoph*, 187.
50. Habermas, 'Es musste etwas besser werden. . . .,' 168.
51. Michael Henry Tessler, et al. "AI Can Help Humans Find Common Ground in Democratic Deliberation," *Science* 386, no. 6719 (2024).
52. Jens-Christian Rabe, "Habermas vs. Google; Nicht in seinem Namen," *Süddeutsche Zeitung*, April 25, 2025.
53. Soren Whited, "Traces of Different Colors: An Interview with Peter E. Gordon," *Platypus Review* 151, November 2022, https://platypus1917.org/2022/11/01/traces-of-different-colors-an-interview-with-peter-e-gordon/#_ftn1.
54. Karl Markus Michel, "Karl Markus Michel über Jürgen Habermas' 'Theorie des kommunikativen Handelns' ", *Der Spiegel*, March 21, 1982; Jürgen Habermas, *Moral Consciousness and Communicative Action* (MIT Press, 1990), 3.
55. Jeffrey J. Williams, "The Rise of the Promotional Intellectual," *Chronicle of Higher Education*, August 5, 2018, https://www.chronicle.com/article/the-rise-of-the-promotional-intellectual/.
56. Peter J. Verovšek and Maruša Gorišek, "Experts in Times of Pandemic: Reframing the Debate in the Context of Structural Transformations of the Public Sphere," *Javnost—the Public* 30, no. 4 (2023): 496–512.
57. See, for example, Adam Tooze (@adam_tooze), "This statement by @NDeitelhoff und Rainer Forst, Klaus Günther und Jürgen Habermas should," Twitter (now X), November

15, 2023, https://twitter.com/adam_tooze/status/1724565111107436576. Capitalization in original.
58. Nicole Deitelhoff (@NDeitelhoff), "Dunkle Zeiten. Ein Thread in 20," Twitter (now X), November 17, 2023, https://twitter.com/NDeitelhoff/status/1725538516224884864.
59. Habermas, "Reflections and Hypotheses," 160, 159.
60. See also Peter J. Verovšek, "Jürgen Habermas and the Public Intellectual in Modern Democratic Life," *Philosophy Compass* 17, no. 4 (2022): e12818.
61. Max Pensky, "Historical and Intellectual Contexts," in *Jürgen Habermas: Key Concepts*, ed. Barbara Fultner (Acumen, 2013), 31.
62. Felsch, *Der Philosoph*, 8, 7.
63. Joschka Fischer, "Gründungfigur des demokratischen Deutschland," in *Über Habermas: Gespräche mit Zeitgenossen*, ed. Michael Funken (Wissenschaftliche Buchgesellschaft, 2009), 52; Stefan Müller-Doohm, *Habermas: A Biography* (Polity, 2016), viii; Andreas Rosenfelder, "Die Habermas-Diktatur," *Die Welt*, October 11, 2021, https://www.welt.de/kultur/plus234125124/Corona-Politik-Die-Habermas-Diktatur.html.
64. Jan Ross, "Der Hegel der Bundesrepublik," *Die Zeit*, October 11, 2001, accessed February 20, 2010, http://www.zeit.de/2001/42/200142_habermas.xml.
65. Sloterdijk quoted in Müller-Doohm, *Habermas: A Biography*, 316.
66. Quoted in Stefan Müller-Doohm, *Habermas: A Biography* (Polity, 2016), 320; Matthew G. Specter, "From Eclipse of Reason to the Age of Reasons? Historicizing Habermas and the Frankfurt School," *Modern Intellectual History* 16, no. 1 (2019): 323.
67. Sloterdijk quoted in Müller-Doohm, *Habermas: A Biography*, 316; Müller-Doohm, *Habermas: A Biography*, 425.
68. Müller-Doohm, *Habermas: A Biography*, 262.
69. Dick Bernstein to Jürgen Habermas, November 14, 1972, HV, 16—1972, Band 1 (A–G).
70. Joseph Schumpeter, *Capitalism, Socialism and Democracy* (Harper and Row, 1950), 145–55.
71. Axel Honneth, *Pathologies of Reason: On the Legacy of Critical Theory* (Columbia University Press, 2009), 181, 182.
72. Honneth, *Pathologies of Reason*, 182.
73. Habermas, "Europe's Mistake."
74. Siegfried Kracauer, "Minimalforderung an die Intellektuellen" in *Der verbotene Blick: Beobachtungen, Analysen, Kritiken*, ed. Johanna Rosenberg (Reclam), 249.
75. Habermas, *A New Structural Transformation*, 16.
76. Honneth, *Pathologies of Reason*, 190.
77. Jürgen Habermas, "What Does Socialism Mean Today?: The Revolutions of Recuperation and the Need for New Thinking" in *After the Fall: The Failure of Communism and the Future of Socialism*, ed. Robin Blackburn (Verso, 1991), 25–46, 42.
78. Peter E. Gordon, "A Lion in Winter," *The Nation*, September 14, 2016, https://www.thenation.com/article/a-lion-in-winter/.
79. Hans J. Kleinstüber, "Habermas and the Public Sphere: From a German to a European Perspective," *Javnost - The Public* 8, no. 1 (2001): 102.
80. Josef Joffe, "The Decline of the Public Intellectual and the Rise of the Pundit" in *The Public Intellectual: Between Philosophy and Politics*, ed. Richard M. Zinman et al. (Rowman & Littlefield, 2004).

81. Seyla Benhabib, "The Embattled Public Sphere: Hannah Arendt, Juergen Habermas and Beyond," *Theoria: A Journal of Social and Political Theory* 90 (1997): 1.
82. Edward W. Said, *Representations of the Intellectual: The 1993 Reith Lectures* (Pantheon Books, 1994), 23.
83. Habermas, *New Structural Transformation*, 37, 53.
84. Habermas, *Europe: The Faltering Project*, 52.
85. Habermas, *New Structural Transformation*, 44.
86. Habermas, *Europe: The Faltering Project*, 52.
87. Habermas, *New Structural Transformation*, 44.
88. Habermas, *New Structural Transformation*, 49, 50.
89. Habermas, "Reflections and Hypotheses," 156.
90. Habermas, *New Structural Transformation*, 48.
91. Felsch, *Der Philosoph*, 80; Habermas, *Between Naturalism and Religion* (Polity, 2008), 16.
92. Habermas, *New Structural Transformation*, 65, 45, 67.
93. Said, *Representations of the Intellectual*, 12, 11.
94. Jürgen Habermas, "Foreword," *Habermas and the Crisis of Democracy: Interviews with Leading Thinkers*, ed. Emilie Prattico (Routledge, 2022), xviii.
95. Habermas, "Reflections and Hypotheses," 160.
96. Habermas, "Foreword," xviii.
97. Peter J. Verovšek, "Authorship and Individualization in the Digital Public Sphere," *Constellations* 30, no. 1 (2023): 39.
98. Habermas, "Reflections and Hypotheses," 167.
99. See Katharine Dommett and Peter J. Verovšek, "Promoting Democracy in the Digital Public Sphere: Applying Theoretical Ideals to Online Political Communication," *Javnost - The Public* 28, no. 4 (2021): 358–74.
100. Habermas, "Reflections and Hypotheses," 152.
101. Florian Meinel, "Die Feindortung klappte immer," Feuilleton, *Frankfurter Allgemeine Zeitung*, March 8, 2024.
102. Habermas, "Reflections and Hypotheses," 165.
103. Jürgen Habermas, *Philosophical Introductions: Five Approaches to Communicative Reason* (Polity, 2018), 155.
104. Habermas, *New Structural Transformation*, 38; Habermas, "An Appeal for Europe." For the way Habermas has been misappropriated in IR theory, see Matthew Specter, "A Great Misrecognition: How *Between Facts and Norms* Was Conflated With (But Resists) the Cosmopolitan Moment in 1990s International Relations Theory," in *Critical Encounters with Habermas's Legal and Political Theory*, ed. John Abromeit et al. (Brill, forthcoming).
105. Habermas conversation.
106. Habermas, "An Appeal for Europe."
107. Quoted in Daniel Steinmetz-Jenkins, "Jürgen Habermas Still Believes in Modernity," *The Nation*, July 7, 2025, https://www.thenation.com/article/culture/jurgen-habermas-qa/.
108. Quoted in Peter J. Verovšek, "Celebrating Jürgen Habermas and the Institute for Social Research: Reflections on the History of Critical Theory from a Jubilee Year," *European Journal of Political Theory*, December 8, 2024, https://doi.org/10.1177/14748851241302296.
109. Felsch, *Der Philosoph*, 187.

110. Adam Swift and Stuart White, "Political Theory, Social Science, and Real Politics," in *Political Theory: Methods and Approaches*, ed. David Leopold and Marc Stears (Oxford University Press, 2008), 55. See also Peter J. Verovšek, "Social Criticism as Medical Diagnosis? On the Role of Social Pathology and Crisis within Critical Theory," *Thesis Eleven* 155, no. (2019): 109–26.
111. Quoted in Soren Whithed, "Traces of Different Colors."
112. Jürgen Habermas, "Amerika ist auf Abwegen," *Kölnische Rundschau*, June 17, 2004.
113. Jürgen Habermas, "Political Culture in Germany Since 1968: An Interview with Dr. Rainer Erd for the 'Frankfurter Rundschau,'" in Habermas, *The New Conservatism*, 187.
114. See Peter J. Verovšek, "Habermas the Freelance Journalist: The Relationship between Theory and Practice in Habermas's Early Career," *New German Critique* 51, no. 2 (August 1, 2024).
115. Jürgen Habermas, *Structural Transformation*, 79.
116. Habermas, *Philosophical Introductions*, 155, 156.
117. See Peter J. Verovšek, "Taking Back Control Over Markets: Jürgen Habermas on the Colonization of Politics by Economics," *Political Studies* 71, no. 2 (2023): 398–417.
118. Max Weber, "Politics as a Vocation," in *From Max Weber: Essays in Sociology*, ed. and trans. Hans Heinrich Gerth and C. Wright Mills (Oxford University Press, 1958), 128.

Bibliography

ARCHIVES

Habermas Vorlass (HV), Na. 60, Sonstige Nachlässe und Autographen, Universitätsbibliothek Johann Christian Senckenberg, Goethe-Universität, Frankfurt am Main, Germany.

BOOKS AND ACADEMIC ARTICLES BY HABERMAS

Due to space constraints, this bibliography is somewhat abridged. A more complete bibliography is Luca Corchia, *Jürgen Habermas: A Bibliography*. Vol. 1 of *Works of Jürgen Habermas (1952–2018)*. Department of Political Science, University of Pisa; Società Italiana di Teoria Critica [SITC], n.d. See also Thomas Gregersen, *Jürgen Habermas's Works 1992–2023: A Bibliography*. https://www.academia.edu/36360233/Bibliography_of_J%C3%BCrgen_Habermas_1951_2024.

Habermas, Jürgen. "Das Absolute und die Geschichte: Von der Zwiespältigkeit in Schellings Denken." PhD diss., Universität Bonn, 1954. https://doi.org/10.11588/diglit.41402#0007.
——. *Ach, Europa*. Vol. 11 of *Kleine politische Schriften*. Suhrkamp, 2008.
——. "Anthropologie." In *Fischer-Lexikon Philosophie*, ed. Alwin Diemer and Ivo Frenzel. Fischer, 1958.
——. "Eine Antwort auf die Kommentare." In *Okzidentale Konstellationen zwischen Glauben und Wissen. Beiträge zu Jürgen Habermas' "Auch eine Geschichte der Philosophie"*, ed. Rudolf Langthaler and Hans Schelkshorn. wbg Academic, 2024.
——. *Arbeit, Erkenntnis, Fortschritt: Aufsätze, 1954–1970*. Munter, 1970.
——. *Arbeit, Freizeit, Konsum. Frühe Aufsätze*. Eversdijck, 1973.
——. *Eine Art Schadensabwicklung: Kleine politische Schriften VI*. Suhrkamp, 1987.
——. *Auch eine Geschichte der Philosophie*. Suhrkamp, 2019.
——. *Autonomy and Solidarity: Interviews*. Ed. Peter Dews. Verso, 1992.
——. *An Awareness of What Is Missing: Faith and Reason in a Post-Secular Age*. Ed. Ciaran Cronin. Polity, 2010.
——. *A Berlin Republic: Writings on Germany*. Trans. Steven Rendall. University of Nebraska Press, 1997.

———. *Between Facts and Norms: Contributions to a Discourse Theory of Law and Democracy*. MIT Press, 1996.

———. *Between Naturalism and Religion*. Trans. Ciaran Cronin. Polity, 2008.

———. "Ein Brief." In *Kritische Theorie und Kultur*, ed. Rainer Erd, Dietrich Hoss, Otto Jacobi, and Peter Noller. Suhrkamp, 1989.

———. "Civil Disobedience: Litmus Test for the Democratic Constitutional State." *Berkeley Journal of Sociology* 30 (1985): 95–116. http://www.jstor.org.proxy-ub.rug.nl/stable/41035345.

———. "Conservatism and Capitalist Crisis." *New Left Review* 115 (May–June 1979): 73–84.

———. "The Constitutionalization of International Law and the Legitimation Problems of a Constitution for World Society." *Constellations* 15, no. 4 (2008): 444–55.

———. *The Crisis of the European Union: A Response*. Trans. Ciaran Cronin. Polity, 2012.

———. "Democracy in Europe: Why the Development of the European Union Into a Transnational Democracy Is Necessary and How It Is Possible." *European Law Journal* 21, no. 4 (2015): 546–57.

———. *The Divided West*. Trans. Ciaran Cronin. Polity, 2006.

———. '*Es musste etwas besser werden. . . .*' *Gespräche mit Stefan Müller-Doohm und Roman Yos*. Suhrkamp, 2024.

———. "Der europäische Nationalstaat unter dem Druck der Globalisierung." *Blätter für deutsche und internationale Politik* 42, no. 4 (1999): 425–36.

———. *Europe: The Faltering Project*. Trans. Ciaran Cronin. Polity, 2009.

———. "Farewell to a Philosopher." *Constellations* 26, no. 3 (2019): 353–54.

———. "February 15, or: What Binds Europeans." In *Old Europe, New Europe, Core Europe: Transatlantic Relations After the Iraq War*, ed. Daniel Levy, Max Pensky, and John Torpey, trans. Max Pensky. Verso, 2005.

———. "Foreword." In *Habermas and the Crisis of Democracy: Interviews with Leading Thinkers*, ed. Emilie Prattico. Routledge, 2022.

———. "Further Reflections on the Public Sphere." In *Habermas and the Public Sphere*, ed. Craig J. Calhoun. MIT Press, 1992.

———. *The Future of Human Nature*. Polity, 2003.

———. "Heinrich Heine and the Role of the Intellectual in Germany." In *The New Conservatism: Cultural Criticism and the Historians' Debate*, trans. Shierry Weber Nicholsen. MIT Press, 1989.

———. "Historical Consciousness and Post-Traditional Identity: Remarks on the Federal Republic's Orientation to the West." *Acta Sociologica* 31, no. 1 (1988): 3–13.

———. "Ich bin alt, aber nicht fromm geworden." In *Über Habermas: Gespräche mit Zeitgenossen*, ed. Michael Funken. Wissenschaftliche Buchgesellschaft, 2009.

———. *Im Sog der Technokratie*. Vol. 12 of *Kleine politische Schriften*. Suhrkamp, 2013.

———. *The Inclusion of the Other: Studies in Political Theory*. Trans. Ciaran Cronin. MIT Press, 1998.

———. "Jewish Philosophers and Sociologists as Returnees in the Early Federal Republic of Germany: A Recollection." *Journal of Modern Jewish Studies* 13, no. 1 (2014): 115–22.

———. "A Kind of Settlement of Damages (Apologetic Tendencies)." *New German Critique* 44 (1988): 25–39.

———. *Kleine politische Schriften I–IV*. Suhrkamp, 1981.

———. *Knowledge and Human Interests*. Trans. Jeremy J. Shapiro. Beacon, 1971.

———. "Konservativer Geist—und die modernistischen Folgen. Zum Reformplan für die deutsche Schule." *Der Monat* 12, no. 133 (1959): 41–50.

———. "Der Konstruktionsfehler der Währungsunion." *Blätter für deutsche und internationale Politik* 56, no. 5 (2011): 64–66.
———. *Legitimation Crisis.* Beacon, 1975.
———. "Letter to the Editor of the *Frankfurter Allgemeine Zeitung*, August 11, 1986." In *Forever in the Shadow of Hitler?: The Dispute About the Germans' Understanding of History, Original Documents of the Historikerstreit, the Controversy Concerning the Singularity of the Holocaust*, ed. James Knowlton and Truett Cates. Humanities Press International, 1993.
———. *The Lure of Technocracy.* Trans. Ciaran Cronin. Polity, 2015.
———. "Martin Heidegger: On the Publication of the Lectures of 1935." *Graduate Faculty Philosophy Journal* 6, no. 2 (1977): 155–64.
———. "Modernity: An Unfinished Project." In *Habermas and the Unfinished Project of Modernity: Critical Essays on the Philosophical Discourse of Modernity*, ed. Maurizio Passerin d'Entrèves and Seyla Benhabib. Polity, 1996.
———. *Moral Consciousness and Communicative Action.* MIT Press, 1990.
———. "National Unification and Popular Sovereignty." *New Left Review* 219 (1996): 3–13.
———. *Die nachholende Revolution.* Vol. 12 of *Kleine politische Schriften.* Suhrkamp, 1990.
———. "Neoconservative Cultural Criticism in the United States and West Germany: An Intellectual Movement in Two Political Cultures." In *Habermas and Modernity*, ed. Richard Bernstein. MIT Press, 1985.
———. *Ein neuer Strukturwandel der Öffentlichkeit und die deliberative Politik.* Suhrkamp, 2022.
———. *Die neue Unübersichtlichkeit.* Vol. 5 of *Kleine politische Schriften.* Suhrkamp, 1985.
———. *The New Conservatism: Cultural Criticism and the Historians' Debate.* Trans. Shierry Weber Nicholsen. MIT Press, 1989.
———. "The New Obscurity: The Crisis of the Welfare State and the Exhaustion of Utopian Energies." *Philosophy & Social Criticism* 11, no. 2 (1986): 1–18.
———. "New Social Movements." *Telos* 49 (1981): 33–37.
———. *A New Structural Transformation of the Public Sphere and Deliberative Politics.* Polity, 2023.
———. *Die Normalität einer Berliner Republik.* Vol. 13 of *Kleine politische Schriften.* Suhrkamp, 1995.
———. "Notes on the Developmental History of Horkheimer's Work." *Theory, Culture & Society* 10, no. 2 (1993): 61–77.
———. *On the Logic of the Social Sciences.* MIT Press, 1988.
———. *The Past as Future: Vergangenheit als Zukunft.* Trans. Max Pensky. University of Nebraska Press, 1994.
———. *The Philosophical Discourse of Modernity: Twelve Lectures.* Trans. Frederick G. Lawrence. MIT Press, 1987.
———. *Philosophical-Political Profiles.* Trans. Frederick G. Lawrence. MIT Press, 1983.
———. "A Philosophico-Political Profile." *New Left Review* 151 (1985): 75–105.
———. "Philosophie." *Deutsche Universitätszeitung* 23–24 (1956): 29.
———. *Philosophische Texte. Band 4: Politische Theorie.* Suhrkamp, 2009.
———. *Philosophical Introductions: Five Approaches to Communicative Reason.* Polity, 2018.
———. *Philosophical-Political Profiles.* Trans. Frederick G. Lawrence. MIT Press, 1983.
———. *Philosophisch-politische Profile.* Suhrkamp, 1987.
———. "Political Communication in Media Society: Does Democracy Still Enjoy an Epistemic Dimension? The Impact of Normative Theory on Empirical Research." *Communication Theory* 16, no. 4 (2006): 411–26.

———. *Politik, Kunst, Religion. Essays über zeitgenössische Philosophen*. Reclam, 1978.
———. *The Postnational Constellation: Political Essays*. Ed. and trans. Max Pensky. MIT Press, 2001.
———. *Die postnationale Konstellation. Politische Essays*. Suhrkamp, 1998.
———. "Produktivkraft Kommunikation. Interview mit Hans Peter Krüger." *Sinn und Form* 41, no. 6 (1989): 1192–206.
———. *Protestbewegung und Hochschulreform*. Suhrkamp, 1969.
———. "Reconciliation Through the Public Use of Reason: Remarks on John Rawls' Political Liberalism." *Journal of Philosophy* 92, no. 3 (1995): 109–31.
———. "Reflections and Hypotheses on a Further Structural Transformation of the Political Public Sphere." *Theory, Culture & Society* 39, no. 4 (September 2022): 145–71.
———. *Religion and Rationality: Essays on Reason, God, and Modernity*. Ed. Eduardo Mendieta. MIT Press, 2002.
———. "Remarks on Dieter Grimm's 'Does Europe Need a Constitution?'" *European Law Journal* 1, no. 3 (November 1995): 303–7.
———. "A Reply." In *Communicative Action: Essays on Jürgen Habermas's Theory of Communicative Action*, ed. Axel Honneth and Hans Joas. MIT Press, 1991.
———. "Reply to My Critics." In *Habermas and Religion*, ed. Craig J. Calhoun, Eduardo Mendieta, and Jonathan VanAntwerpen. Polity, 2013.
———. "Soziologische Notizen zum Verhältnis von Arbeit und Freizeit." In *Konkrete Vernunft. Festschrift für E. Rothacker*, ed. Gerhard Funke. Bouvier, 1958.
———. *The Structural Transformation of the Public Sphere: An Inquiry Into a Category of Bourgeois Society*. MIT Press, 1989.
———. *Student und Politik: Eine soziologische Untersuchung zum politischen Bewusstsein Frankfurter Studenten*. Luchterhand, 1961.
———. "A Test for Popular Justice: The Accusations Against the Intellectuals." *New German Critique* 12 (1977): 11–13.
———. *Texte und Kontexte*. Suhrkamp, 1991.
———. *Theorie und Praxis. Sozialphilosophische Studien*. Suhrkamp, 1978.
———. *Theory and Practice*. Vol. 489. Beacon Press, 1974.
———. *The Theory of Communicative Action*. Trans. Thomas A. McCarthy. Beacon, 1987.
———. "There are Alternatives!" *New Left Review* 231 (1998): 3–12.
———. *Time of Transitions*. Trans. Ciaran Cronin and Max Pensky. Polity, 2006.
———. *Toward a Rational Society: Student Protest, Science, and Politics*. Heinemann Educational Books, 1971.
———. *Vergangenheit als Zukunft*. Pendo-Verlag, 1990.
———. "What Does Socialism Mean Today?: The Revolutions of Recuperation and the Need for New Thinking." In *After the Fall: The Failure of Communism and the Future of Socialism*, ed. Robin Blackburn. Verso, 1991.
———. "Why More Philosophy?" *Social Research* 38, no. 4 (1971): 633–54.
———. *Year 30: Germany's Second Chance*. Trans. David Gow. Social Europe Publishing, 2020.
———. "Yet Again: German Identity: A Unified Nation of Angry DM-Burghers?" In *When the Wall Came Down: Reactions to German Unification*, ed. Harold James and Maria Stone. Routledge, 1992.
———. *Zeit der Übergänge*. Vol. 9 of *Kleine politische Schriften*. Suhrkamp, 2001.

———. "Zur philosophischen Diskussion um Marx und den Marxismus." *Philosophische Rundschau* 5, nos. 3–4 (1957): 165–235.
———. *Zur Rekonstruktion des historischen Materialismus*. Suhrkamp, 1976.
———. *Zur Verfassung Europas. Ein Essay*. Suhrkamp, 2011.
Habermas, Jürgen, and Seyla Ben-Habib, "Modernity Versus Postmodernity." *New German Critique* 22 (1981): 3–14.
Habermas, Jürgen, and John R. Blazek. "The Idea of the University: Learning Processes." *New German Critique* 41 (1987): 3–22.
Habermas, Jürgen, and Martha Calhoun. "Right and Violence: A German Trauma." *Cultural Critique* 1 (1985): 125–39.
Habermas, Jürgen, and Jacques Derrida. "February 15, or What Binds Europeans Together: A Plea for a Common Foreign Policy, Beginning in the Core of Europe." *Constellations* 10, no. 3 (2003): 291–97.

NEWSPAPER AND OTHER PUBLIC-FACING ARTICLES BY HABERMAS

Carleheden, Mikael, and René Gabriëls. "An Interview with Jürgen Habermas." *Theory, Culture & Society* 13, no. 3 (1996): 1–17.
Deitelhoff, Nicole, Rainer Forst, Klaus Günther, and Jürgen Habermas. "Grundsätze der Solidarität. Eine Stellungnahme." *Normative Orders*, November 13, 2023. https://www.normativeorders.net/2023/grundsatze-der-solidaritat/.
———. "Principles of Solidarity. A Statement," *Normative Orders*, November 13, 2023. https://www.normativeorders.net/2023/grundsatze-der-solidaritat/.
Gabriel, Sigmar, Jürgen Habermas, and Emmanuel Macron. "Rethinking Europe: A Discussion between Jürgen Habermas, Sigmar Gabriel and Emmanuel Macron." *Eurozine*, April 4, 2017. http://www.eurozine.com/rethinking-europe/.
Habermas, Jürgen. "30 Jahre Danach: Die zweite Chance." *Blätter für deutsche und internationale Politik* 9 (September 2020): 41–46.
———. "Der Abstraktion gewachsen sein . . ." *Magnum: Die Zeitschrift für das moderne Leben* (April 1957): 64.
———. "Akademische Sommerfrische in Erlangen? Internationale Studentenbühnen ohne Mut." *Frankfurter Allgemeine Zeitung*, August 6, 1952.
———. "Die akustische Bühne. Hörspielnotizen zu Adamov, Dürrenmatt und Huber." *Frankfurter Allgemeine Zeitung*, November 27, 1952.
———. "Alles linke auf seine Kappe nehmen: Ein Gespräch mit Jürgen Habermas—aus anlaß seiner Auszeichnung mit dem Adorno-Preis." Interview, *Frankfurter Rundschau*, September 11, 1980.
———. "Amerika ist auf Abwegen." *Kölnische Rundschau*, June 17, 2004.
———. "An Appeal for Europe." *Süddeutsche Zeitung*, March 24, 2025. https://www.sueddeutsche.de/projekte/artikel/kultur/juergen-habermas-essay-europa-e494414/.
———. "Ein Appell für Europa." *Süddeutsche Zeitung*, March 24, 2024. https://www.sueddeutsche.de/projekte/artikel/kultur/juergen-habermas-gastbeitrag-europa-e943825/.
———. "Are We Still Good Europeans?" *Zeit Online*, July 6, 2018. https://www.zeit.de/kultur/2018-07/european-union-germany-challenges-loyalty-solidarity/komplettansicht.

———. "Eine art Schadensabwicklung: Die apologetischen Tendenzen in der deutschen Zeitgeschichtsschreibung." *Die Zeit*, July 11, 1986. https://www.zeit.de/1986/29/eine-art-schadensabwicklung/komplettansicht?print.

———. "Auf die Qualität kommt es an: Warum das Starnberger Institut nicht Weitergeführt wird—ein Gespräch mit Reimar Lüst." *Die Zeit*, May 9, 1980.

———. "Auto fahren. Der Mensch am Lenkrad." *Frankfurter Allgemeine Zeitung*, November 27, 1954.

———. "Automaten und Gesellschaft. Ein Vortragsabend der Deutschen Forschungsgemeinschaft in Godesberg." *Frankfurter Allgemeine Zeitung*, October 25, 1954.

———. "Der Aquinate gegen Hegel." *Frankfurter Allgemeine Zeitung*, October 7, 1955.

———. "Beamte müssen Phantasie haben. Gibt es ein Heilmittel gegen die Schwächen der Bürokratie?—Für eine Kontrolle 'von Innen.' " *Handelsblatt*, July 25, 1954.

———. "Der biographische Schleier. Bei Gelegenheit des Stresemann-Filmes Notiert." *Frankfurter Hefte* 12, no. 5 (1957): 357–61.

———. "Die Bundesrepublik: Eine Wahlmonarchie?" *Magnum: Die Zeitschrift für das Moderne Leben*, special issue, "Woher—Wohin: Bilanz der Bundesrepublik" (1961): 26–29.

———. "Chemische Ferien vom Ich. Huxleys Umgang mit Meskalin." *Frankfurter Allgemeine Zeitung*, December 11, 1954.

———. "Das chronische Leiden der Hochschulreform." *Merkur* 11, no. 109 (March 1957): 265–84.

———. "Come Back der deutschen Soziologie." *Frankfurter Allgemeine Zeitung*, July 23, 1955.

———."Corona und der Schutz des Lebens: Zur Grundrechtsdebatte in der pandemischen Ausnahmesituation." *Blätter für deutsche und internationale Politik* 9 (September 2021): 65–78.

———. "The Cost and Challenge of the Eurozone Debt Crisis." *Financial Times*, sec. FT Magazine, May 1, 2010.

———. "Dans cette crise, il nous faut agir dans le savoir de notre non-savoir." *Le Monde*, April 15, 2020.

———. "Democracy, Solidarity and the European Crisis." *Social Europe* (May 2013): 1–21. http://www.social-europe.eu/2013/05/democracy-solidarity-and-the-european-crisis-2/.

———. "Demokratie auf der Schlachtbank." *Der Fortschritt. Parteifreie Wochenzeitung für neue Ordnung*, August 13, 1953.

———. "Demokratie und Planung." *Neues Forum* 20, no. 223 (1973): 34–36.

———. "Deutschland rehabilitiert Freud." *National Zeitung*, May 13, 1956.

———. "En Diskussionsbemerkung." In *Gegen den Versuch, Vergangenheit zu verbiegen*, ed. Hilmar Hoffmann. Athenäum, 1987.

———. "Drei Masken zuviel." *Frankfurter Hefte* 8, no. 3 (1953): 231–34.

———. "Die Dialektik der Rationalisierung: Vom Pauperismus in Produktion und Konsum." *Merkur* 8, no. 78 (1954): 701–24.

———. "Der Elektrisierende: Meine Erinnerung an den Schriftsteller und Gefährten Hans Magnus Enzensberger." *Süddeutsche Zeitung*, November 25, 2022.

———. "Die Entsorgung der Vergangenheit: Ein kulturpolitisches Pamphlet." *Die Zeit*, May 24, 1985.

———. "Das erste Lächeln. Der Psychiater René A. Spitz über die Früheste Kindheit." *Frankfurter Allgemeine Zeitung*, May 17, 1956.

———. "Europa wird direkt ins Herz getroffen." *Frankfurter Allgemeine Zeitung*, May 30, 2014.

———. "Europe's Mistake." *Granata*, November 23, 2023. https://granta.com/europes-mistake/.

———. "Europe's Post-Democratic Era." *The Guardian*, November 10, 2011. https://www.theguardian.com/commentisfree/2011/nov/10/jurgen-habermas-europe-post-democratic.

———. "Der falsche Prometheus." *Frankfurter Hefte* 8, no. 5 (1953): 398–400.

———. "Die Farbigen Schatten aus Szetschuan. Notizen zum zweiten Bonner Puppenspielzyklus." *Frankfurter Allgemeine Zeitung*, July 14, 1953.

———. "For a Democratic Polarization." *Eurozine*, November 22, 2016. https://www.eurozine.com/for-a-democratic-polarization-an-interview-with-jurgen-habermas/.

———. "For God's Sake, Spare Us Governing Philosophers!" *El País*, May 25, 2018. https://english.elpais.com/elpais/2018/05/07/inenglish/1525683618_145760.html.

———. "Freiheit, Anruf und Gewissen." *Frankfurter Allgemeine Zeitung*, August 29, 1953.

———. "Freud—der Aufklärer. Festakt in Frankfurt zum 100. Geburtstag. Wenig Anteilnahme in Wien." *Frankfurter Allgemeine Zeitung*, May 7, 1956.

———. "Fundamentalismus in Anführungszeichen. Zum Streit um Annemarie Schimmel." *Süddeutsche Zeitung*, September 12, 1995.

———. "Für und wider den Test. Gegen den Geist der Menschenverachtung." *Frankfurter Allgemeine Zeitung*, September 11, 1954.

———. "Für und wider. Der Mensch zwischen den Apparaten." *Süddeutsche Zeitung*, September 6–7, 1958.

———. "Der Geist geht zu Fuß... Eine Tagung zum Thema Kulturkonsum." *Handelsblatt*, October 28, 1955.

———. "Merkel's European Failure: Germany Dozes on a Volcano." *Der Spiegel*, September 8, 2013. http://www.spiegel.de/international/germany/juergen-habermas-merkel-needs-to-confront-real-european-reform-a-915244-druck.html.

———. "Geschichtsschreibung und Geschichtsbewußtsein." *Frankfurter Allgemeine Zeitung*, August 11, 1986.

———. "Ein Gespräch über Heimat, Europa und die Zukunft." *Kölnische Rundschau*, July 8, 2019.

———. "Die Grenze in uns—Helmuth Plessner: 'Die verspätete Nation'." *Frankfurter Hefte* 14, no. 11 (November 1959): 826–31.

———. "Gottfried Benns neue Stimme." *Frankfurter Allgemeine Zeitung*, June 19, 1952.

———. "Die große Wirkung: Eine chronistische Anmerkung zu Martin Heideggers 70. Geburtstag." *Frankfurter Allgemeine Zeitung*, September 26, 1959.

———. "Der Hilfsarbeiter wird angelernter Ingenieur. Die Entwicklung vom Fließband zum Prüfstand—Berufsumschichtung durch die Technik." *Handelsblatt*, October 14, 1954.

———. "Des Hörspiels Mangel ist seine Chance." *Frankfurter Allgemeine Zeitung*, September 15, 1952.

———. "Illusionen auf dem Heiratsmarkt." *Merkur* 10, no. 104 (1956): 996–1004.

———. "Im Lichte Heideggers." *Frankfurter Allgemeine Zeitung*, July 12, 1952.

———. "Im süden nichts neues? Italienischer Stil vom kunsthandwerk zur Industrie—Die Ausstellung 'Forme Nuova in Italia.'" *Handelsblatt*, December 1, 1954.

———. "Internet and Public Sphere: What the Web Can't Do." Interview by Markus Schwering. *Reset Dialogues on Civilizations*, July 24, 2014. https://www.resetdoc.org/story/internet-and-public-sphere-what-the-web-cant-do/.

———. "Iphigenie will nicht Sterben. Obeys 'Ein Opfer für Wind' in Bonn." *Frankfurter Allgemeine Zeitung*, November 25, 1953.

———. "Die Ironie der Holz- und Gipsköpfe. Bei Gelegenheit des internationalen Puppenspielzyklus in Bonn." *Frankfurter Allgemeine Zeitung*, January, 29, 1953.

———. "Irrtum über die Masse. Wider das Gift der Menschenverachtung." *Wiesbadener Kurier*, November 27, 1954.

———. "Ist unsere Generation modern?" *Schwarz auf Weiss. Schülerzeitung des Städtischen Gymnasiums in Gummersbach* 1, no. 2 (1951): 7–8. https://lindengymnasium.de/media/schwarz_auf_weiss/1951a.pdf.

———. "Jaspers und die Gestalten der Wahrheit: Geschichtsphilosophische Betrachtung zu einer Geschichte der Philosophie, Zum 75. Geburtstag von Karl Jaspers." *Frankfurter Allgemeine Zeitung*, February 22, 1958.

———. "Jeder Mensch ist unbezahlbar." *Merkur* 9, no. 2 (1955): 994–98.

———. "Jürgen Habermas's Verdict on the EU/Greece Debt Deal." *The Guardian*, July 16, 2015.

———. "Karl Jaspers über Schelling." *Frankfurter Allgemeine Zeitung*, January 14, 1956.

———. "Kein Warten auf Gawdos. Herbert Meiers 'Barke von Gawdos' im Bonner Contrakeller." *Frankfurter Allgemeine Zeitung*, October 18, 1954.

———. "Konsumkritik—Eigens zum Konsumieren." *Frankfurter Hefte* 12, no. 9 (July 1957): 641–45.

———. "Können Konsumenten spielen?" *Frankfurter Allgemeine Zeitung*, April 13, 1957.

———. "Krieg und Empörung." *Süddeutsche Zeitung*, April 29, 2022.

———. "Leadership and Leitkultur." *New York Times*, sec. Opinion, October 28, 2010. http://www.nytimes.com/2010/10/29/opinion/29Habermas.html.

———. "Leitbilder in Anführungszeichen. Zu einer Tagung des Wuppertaler 'Bundes.' " *Frankfurter Allgemeine Zeitung*, October 22, 1958.

———. "Leserbrief zu Hennis, 'Gesellschaft im Visier.'" *Deutsche Zeitung*, October 24, 1975.

———. "Die letzte Phase der Mechanisierung." *Frankfurter Allgemeine Zeitung*, January 8, 1955.

———. "Literatur und Leben als Lebensthema: Erinnerung an Karl Heinz Bohrer." *Frankfurter Allgemeine Zeitung*, August 11, 2021.

———. "Ludwig Klages—Überholt oder unzeitgemäß? Zum Tode des deutschen Philosophen." *Frankfurter Allgemeine Zeitung*, August 3, 1956.

———. "Man möchte sich mitreißen lassen. Feste und feiern in dieser Zeit." *Handelsblatt*, February 17, 1956.

———. "Eine anderer Mythos des 20. Jahrhunderts." *Frankfurter Hefte* 14, no. 3 (March 1959): 206–9.

———. "Marx in Perspektiven." *Merkur* 9, no. 12 (1955): 1180–83.

———. "Die Masse—das sind wir: Bildung und soziale Stellung kein Schutz gegen den Kollektivismus?—das Gift der Menschenverachtung." *Handelsblatt*, October 29, 1954.

———. "Meine gymnasiale Schulzeit: Ausschnitte aus einer geplanten Autobiographie." *Schwarz auf Weiß: Mitteilungen des Vereins der Förderer und ehemaligen Schüler des städtischen Gymnasiums Moltkestraße in Gummersbach e.V* 26 (December 2002): 51–53. https://lindengymnasium.de/media/schwarz_auf_weiss/2002.pdf.

———. "Merkel Has Depleted Her Capital of Trust Within EU." *The Irish Times*, June 12, 2010.

———. "Der metaphysischen Geheimnisse enterbt." *Frankfurter Allgemeine Zeitung*, December 4, 1954.

———. "Mit Heidegger gegen Heidegger denken. Zur Veröffentlichung von Vorlesungen aus dem Jahre 1935." *Frankfurter Allgemeine Zeitung*, July 25, 1953.

———. "Die Moderne—ein unvollendetes Projekt." *Die Zeit*, September 19, 1980.

———. "Der Moloch und die Künste. Gedanken zur Entlarvung der Legende von der Technischen Zweckmäßigkeit." *Frankfurter Allgemeine Zeitung*, May 30, 1953.

———. " 'Morgengrauen'—Morgen das Grauen." *Süddeutsche Zeitung*, October 2–3, 1954.

———. "Der musikalische Stil des Films. Ein Vortrag und zwei Filme von Jean Mitry." *Frankfurter Allgemeine Zeitung*, January 19, 1953.

---. "Mut und Nüchternheit." *Frankfurter Hefte* 9, no. 9 (1954): 702–4.
---. "Nachspiel." In *Eine art Schadensabwicklung*. Suhrkamp, 1987.
---. "Die nackte Realität neuer Diskriminierung: Karl Kosik gegen seinen Willen in Pension geschickt." *Frankfurtez Rundschau*, November 13, 1992.
---. "Zum neokonservativen Geschichtsverständnis und zur Rolle der revisionistischen Geschichtsschreibung in der politischen Öffentlichkeit." In *Die Nation als Ausstellungsstück. Planungen, Kritik und Utopien zu den Museumsgründungen in Bonn und Berlin*, ed. Geschichtswerkstatt Berlin. Hamburg: VSA Verlag, 1987).
---. "Der neue Historikerstreit." *Philosophie Magazine* 6 (2021): 10–11.
---. "Die neue Unübersichtlichkeit. Die Krise des Wohlfahrtsstaates und die Erschöpfung Utopischer Energien." *Merkur* 39, no. 1 (1985): 1–14.
---. "Neun Jahre unter die Lupe. Deutschlands geistige Entwicklung seit 1945. Der Versuch einer Bilanz." *Handelsblatt*, November 19, 1954.
---. "New Perspectives for Europe." *Social Europe Journal*, October 22, 2018.
---. "Noch einmal: Schweyk und die SS." *Frankfurter Allgemeine Zeitung*, June 12, 1959.
---. "Notizen zum Missverhältnis von Kultur und Konsum." *Merkur* 10, no. 97 (1956): 212–28.
---. "'Ohne mich' auf dem Index." *Deutsche Studentenzeitung* 5, no. 5 (1955): 1–2.
---. "'Ohne mich' auf dem Index: Notizen zu einer politischen Haltung." *Deutsche Studentenzeitung* 5, nos. 6–7 (1955): 14.
---. "Ornament und Maschine." *Frankfurter Allgemeine Zeitung*, December 31, 1954.
---. "Oslo's Call to Europe." *Presseurop*, October 15, 2012. http://www.presseurop.eu/en/content/article/2875321-oslo-s-call-europe.
---. "The Paris Attack and Its Aftermath." *Social Europe*, November 26, 2015. https://socialeurope.eu/habermas-paris-attack.
---. "Der Pfahl im Fleische . . . Eine verlegene Bemerkung zu Kierkegaards 100. Todestag." *Frankfurter Allgemeine Zeitung*, November 12, 1955.
---. "Philosophie ist Risiko." *Frankfurter Allgemeine Zeitung*, June 19, 1954.
---. "The Players Resign—Core Europe to the Rescue." *Die Zeit Online*, July 12, 2016. https://www.zeit.de/kultur/2016-07/juergen-habermas-brexit-eu-crises-english/komplettansicht.
---. "A Plea for Negotiations." *Süddeutsche Zeitung*, February 14, 2023. https://www.sueddeutsche.de/projekte/artikel/kultur/juergen-habermas-ukraine-sz-negotiations-e480179/?reduced=true.
---. "Ein Plädoyer für Verhandlungen." *Süddeutsche Zeitung*, February 14, 2023. https://www.sueddeutsche.de/projekte/artikel/kultur/juergen-habermas-ukraine-sz-verhandlungen-e159105/?reduced=true.
---. "Poesie, Entschleiert und Eingekellert. Supervielles 'Kinderdieb im Bonner Kontrakreis.'" *Frankfurter Allgemeine Zeitung*, April 17, 1954.
---. "Rettet die Würde der Demokratie." *Frankfurter Allgemeine Zeitung*, November 4, 2011.
---. Schluss mit der Feigheit der Politiker. *Vorwärts*, January 31, 2012.
---. "Schelling und die 'Submission unter das Höhere.' Zum 100 Todestag des Philosophen—Nicht Nur in Memoriam." *Frankfurter Allgemeine Zeitung*, August 21, 1954.
---. "Sie Gehören zum 'Staat' oder zum 'Betrieb'. Die unpersönliche Macht der modernen Bürokratie—Ihre Herkunft und Ihre Gefahr." *Handelsblatt*, July 11, 1954.
---. "Sie werden nicht schweigen können." *Die Zeit*, September 13, 1974.
---. "Der Soziologen-Nachwuchs Stellt Sich vor. Zu einem Treffen in Hamburg unter der Leitung von Professor Schelsky." *Frankfurter Allgemeine Zeitung*, June 13, 1955.

———. "Standpunkt und Existenz." *Frankfurter Allgemeine Zeitung*, November 6, 1954.
———. "Das Starnberger Debakel. Ein Rücktritt und eine persönliche Erklärung. Jürgen Habermas: 'Warum ich die Max-Planck-Gesellschaft Verlasse.'" *Die Zeit*, May 8, 1981.
———. "'Stil' auch für den Alltag. Die 'Industrieformung' nutzt und hilft dem Konsumenten." *Handelsblatt*, September 23, 1955.
———. "Triebschicksal als politisches Schicksal. Zum Abschluss der Vorlesungen über Sigmund Freud an den Universitäten Frankfurt und Heidelberg." *Frankfurter Allgemeine Zeitung*, July 14, 1956.
———. "Towards a United States of Europe." *Sign and Sight*, March 27, 2006. http://www.signandsight.com/features/676.html.
———. "Unruhe erste Bürgerpflicht. Römerbergrede gegen die Atombewaffnung der Bundeswehr." *Diskus. Frankfurter Studentenzeitung* 8, no. 5 (May 20, 1958).
———. "Der Verrat und die Maßstäbe. Wenn Jungkonservative alt werden." *Deutsche Universitätszeitung* 19 (1956): 8–11.
———. "Der verschleierte Schrecken: Bemerkungen zu C. F. von Weizsäckers 'Mit der Bombe leben.'" *Frankfurter Hefte* 13, no. 8 (July 1958): 530–32.
———. "Versöhnung von Psychoanalyse und Religion." *Frankfurter Allgemeine Zeitung*, June 11, 1956.
———. "Die vielen Farben des Eigensinns; Meinem Freunde Alexander Kluge zum 90." *Die Zeit*, February 10, 2022.
———. "Vier Jungkonservativen beim Projektleiter der Moderne." *Die Tageszeitung* 381 (October 3, 1980): 8–9; no. 393 (October 21, 1980): 8–9.
———. "Von der heilenden Kraft der Kunst. Ein Vortrag von Erich Rothacker in Bonn." *Frankfurter Allgemeine Zeitung*, December 29, 1953.
———. "War and Indignation." *Süddeutsche Zeitung*, April 28, 2022. https://www.sueddeutsche.de/projekte/artikel/kultur/the-dilemma-of-the-west-juergen-habermas-on-the-war-in-ukraine-e032431/.
———. "Warum ein Demokratiepreis für Daniel J. Goldhagen? Eine Laudatio." *Die Zeit*, March 14, 1997.
———. "What Macron Means for Europe: 'How Much Will the Germans Have to Pay?'" *Spiegel Online*, October 26, 2017. https://www.spiegel.de/international/europe/juergen-habermas-on-the-european-vision-of-emmanuel-macron-a-1174721.html.
———. "Why Angela Merkel Is Wrong on Greece." *Social Europe Journal*, June 25, 2015.
———. "Wider den moralpädagogischen Hochmut der Kulturkritik." *Die Literatur*, September 15, 1952.
———. "Wir Brauchen Europa!" *Die Zeit*, sec. Ausland, May 20, 2010. http://www.zeit.de/2010/21/Europa-Habermas.
———. "Wo ist die Fünfte Kolonne? Die Intellektuellen der Praxis-Gruppe in Jugoslawien werden verfolgt." *Die Zeit*, January 23, 1981.
———. "Der Zeitgeist und die Pädagogik." *Merkur* 10, no. 96 (1956): 189–93.
———. "Der Zerfall der Institutionen." *Frankfurter Allgemeine Zeitung*, April 7, 1956.
———. "Zufriedene Studentin—gedrückter Landarbeiter. Junge Soziologen untersuchen Probleme von heute." *Handelsblatt*, June 24, 1955.
———. "Zur Prinzipienkonkurrenz von Bürgergleichheit und Staatengleichheit im supranationalen Gemeinwesen. Eine Notiz aus Anlass der Frage nach der Legitimität der ungleichen Repräsentation der Bürger im Europäischen Parlament." *Der Staat* 53, no. 2 (2014): 167–92.

———. "Zweihundert 'Eigenschaften' für vierzehn Völker. Baisse in nationalen Vorurteilen—Zu einem sozialpsychologischen Versuch mit Berliner Studenten." *Handelsblatt*, August 27, 1954.

Habermas, Jürgen, Christian Calliess, Henrik Enderlein, Joschka Fischer, and Ulrike Guérot. "Europa und die neue Deutsche Frage." *Blätter für deutsche und internationale Politik* 56, no. 5 (2011): 45–63.

Habermas, Jürgen, Stefan Collignon, Simon Hix, Roberto Castaldi, Costas Simitis, Lorenzo Bini-Smaghi, et al. "Juncker is the Democratic Choice to Head the EU Commission." *The Guardian*, June 6, 2014.

Habermas, Jürgen, Hans Eichel, Roland Koch, Friedrich Merz, Bert Rürup, and Brigitte Zypres. "We Are Deeply Concerned About the Future of Europe and Germany." *Handelsblatt Global*, October 25, 2018. https://www.handelsblatt.com/english/opinion/time-to-wake-up-we-are-deeply-concerned-about-the-future-of-europe-and-germany/23583722.html.

Habermas, Jürgen, Christian Calliess, Henrik Enderlein, Karsten Fischer, and Ulrike Guérot. "Europe and the New German Question." *Eurozine*, August 26, 2011, 1–16.

Habermas, Jürgen, Alexandra Föderl-Schmid, and Ronald Pohl. "Wollen Europäische Bürger Suizid begehen?" *Der Standard*, May 23, 2012.

Habermas, Jürgen, and Francis Fukuyama. "The European Citizen: Just a Myth?" *The Global Journal*, May 18, 2012.

Habermas, Jürgen, Amato Giuliano, Zygmunt Bauman, Ulrich Beck, Peter Bofinger, Stefan Collignon, et al. "The EU Needs Leadership to Tackle This Crisis, Not Repeated Doses of Austerity." *The Guardian*, June 22, 2011. https://www.theguardian.com/commentisfree/2011/jun/22/eu-leadership-tackle-crisis-austerity.

Habermas, Jürgen, and Klaus Günther. "Kein Grundrecht gilt grenzenlos." *Die Zeit*, May 6, 2020. https://www.zeit.de/2020/20/grundrechte-lebensschutz-freiheit-juergen-habermas-klaus-guenther/komplettansicht?print.

Habermas, Jürgen, and Julian Nida-Rümelin. "Schützt die Philosophen!" *Süddeutsche Zeitung*, January 25, 2011.

Habermas, Jürgen, S. Skarpelis-Sperk, P. Kalmbach, and C. Offe. "Ein biedermeierlicher Weg zum Sozialismus?" *Der Spiegel*, February 24, 1975.

Habermas, Ute, and Jürgen Habermas. "Unser Geschenk; Eine Würdigung des Malers Günter Fruhtrunk, der im Mai 99 Jahre alt geworden wäre und uns einst unter seltsamen Umständen ein Bild vermachte." *Die Zeit*, December 30, 2021.

SECONDARY LITERATURE

Abendroth, Wolfgang. *Antagonistische Gesellschaft und politische Demokratie*. Luchterhand, 1967.

Adorno, Gretel. "Record of a Discussion on the Theory of Needs." *New Left Review* 128 (March–April 2021): 73–78.

Adorno, Theodor W. *Aspects of the New Right-Wing Extremism*. Polity, 2020.

———. *Aesthetic Theory*. Trans. Robert Hullot-Kentor. Bloomsbury Academic, 2013.

———. *Critical Models: Interventions and Catchwords*. Trans. Henry W. Pickford. Columbia University Press, 1998.

———. *Eingriffe: Neun kritische Modelle*. Edition Suhrkamp, 1963.

———. "The Essay as Form." *New German Critique* 32 (1984): 151–71.

———. *Gesammelte Schriften Band 1: Philosophische Frühschriften*. Suhrkamp Verlag, 2003.

———. *The Jargon of Authenticity*. Northwestern University Press, 1973.
———. *Minima Moralia: Reflections on a Damaged Life*. Trans. E. F. N. Jephcott. Verso, 2005.
———. "Theses on Need." *New Left Review* 128 (March–April 2021): 79–82.
———. "Zur Problem der Familie." In *Vermischte Schriften I*. Vol. 20 of *Gesammelte Schriften*. Suhrkamp Verlag, 1986.
Adorno, Theodor W., Hans Albert, Ralf Dahrendorf, Jürgen Habermas, Harald Pilot, and Karl R. Popper. *The Positivist Dispute in German Sociology*. Trans. Glyn Adey and David Frisby. Harper Torchbooks, 1976.
Adorno, Theodor W., and Max Horkheimer. *Briefwechsel 1927–1969*. Vols. 1–4. Suhrkamp Verlag, 2023.
Aglietta, Michel. "The European Vortex." *New Left Review* 75 (2012): 15–36.
Allen, Amy R. *The Politics of Our Selves: Power, Autonomy, and Gender in Contemporary Critical Theory*. Columbia University Press, 2008.
Anderson, Perry. "Arms and Rights: Rawls, Habermas and Bobbio in an Age of War." *New Left Review* 31 (January–February 2005): 5–40.
Arendt, Hannah. "The Aftermath of Nazi Rule: Report from Germany." In *Essays in Understanding, 1930–1954*. Ed. Jerome Kohn. Harcourt, Brace, 1994.
Arendt, Hannah. "Wahrheit und Politik." In *Zwischen Vergangenheit und Zukunft. Übungen im politischen Denken I*. Piper Verlag, 2000.
Arendt, Hannah, and Martin Heidegger. *Letters, 1925–1975*. Ed. Ursula Ludz. Trans. Andrew Shields. Harcourt, 2004.
Augstein, Rudolf, ed. '*Historikerstreit*': *Die Dokumentation der Kontroverse um die Einzigartigkeit der Nationalsozialistischen Judenvernichtung*. Piper Verlag, 1987.
Ayer, Alfred J., Noam Chomsky, Robert S. Cohen, Dagfinn Follesdal, Juergen Habermas, Jaakko Hintikka, et al. "Letter to Tito." *The New York Review*, February 6, 1975. https://www.nybooks.com/articles/1975/02/06/letter-to-tito/.
Blumenberg, Hans. *The Legitimacy of the Modern Age*. Trans. Robert M. Wallace. MIT Press, 1983.
Baderin, Alice. "Political Theory and Public Opinion: Against Democratic Restraint." *Politics, Philosophy & Economics* 15, no. 3 (2016): 209–33.
Baerbock, Annalena. "Rede von Außenministerin Annalena Baerbock zur Vorstellung der Leitlinien zur feministischen Außenpolitik." Speech, March 1, 2023. https://www.auswaertiges-amt.de/de/newsroom/baerbock-leitlinien-ffp/2585138.
Baert, Patrick. *The Existentialist Moment: The Rise of Sartre as a Public Intellectual*. Polity, 2015.
Baert, Patrick, and Marcus Morgan. "A Performative Framework for the Study of Intellectuals." *European Journal of Social Theory* 21, no. 3 (2018): 322–39.
Bahners, Patrick. "Theorie und Prazis: Habermas spricht über Unselds Schweigen." *Frankfurter Allgemeine Zeitung*, 12 April 2025.
Baldwin, Peter. "The Historikerstreit in Context." In *Reworking the Past: Hitler, the Holocaust, and the Historians' Debate*, ed. Peter Baldwin. Beacon, 1990.
Beck, Ulrich. *German Europe*. Polity, 2013.
Beck, Ulrich, and Edgar Grande. *Das kosmopolitische Europa: Gesellschaft und Politik in der zweiten Moderne*. Suhrkamp, 2004.
Benhabib, Seyla. *The Claims of Culture: Equality and Diversity in the Global Era*. Princeton University Press, 2002.

———. "The Embattled Public Sphere: Hannah Arendt, Juergen Habermas and Beyond." *Theoria: A Journal of Social and Political Theory* 90 (1997): 1–24.

———. *Critique, Norm, and Utopia: A Study of the Foundations of Critical Theory*. Columbia University Press, 1986.

———. "The New Sovereigntism and Transnational Law: Legal Utopianism, Democratic Scepticism and Statist Realism." *Global Constitutionalism* 5, no. 1 (2016): 109–44.

Bernstein, Richard J. "The Prehistory of the Prague Meetings." *Philosophy & Social Criticism* 43, no. 3 (2017): 272–73.

Bertram, Christopher. "Political Justification, Theoretical Complexity, and Democratic Community." *Ethics* 107, no. 4 (1997): 563–83.

Białý, Filip. "Freedom, Silent Power and the Role of an Historian in the Digital Age—Interview with Quentin Skinner." *History of European Ideas* 48, no. 7 (2022): 871–78.

Biebricher, Thomas. "The Practices of Theorists: Habermas and Foucault as Public Intellectuals." *Philosophy & Social Criticism* 37, no. 6 (2011): 709–34.

Biermann, Kai. "Fern jeder Vision." *Die Zeit*, November 29, 2007. http://www.zeit.de/online/2007/48/habermas-spd.

Blyth, Mark. *Austerity: The History of a Dangerous Idea*. Oxford University Press, 2013.

Bofinger, Peter, et al. "Europa kann nur Weiterleben, Wenn die Europäer jetzt füreinander Einstehen." *Die Zeit*, April 2, 2020. https://www.zeit.de/2020/15/europa-kann-nur-weiterleben-wenn-die-europaeer-jetzt-fuereinander-einstehen.

———. "Nous appelons la Commission Européenne à créer un fonds corona pour aider les etats membres." *Le Monde*, April 2, 2020. https://www.lemonde.fr/idees/article/2020/04/02/nous-appelons-la-commission-europeenne-a-creer-un-fonds-corona-pour-aider-les-etats-membres_6035262_3232.html.

Bohrer, Karl Heinz. *Jetzt. Geschichte meines Abenteuers mit der Phantasie*. Suhrkamp Verlag, 2017.

Bohrer, Karl Heinz, and Kurt Scheel. "Zum fünfzigsten Jahrgang." *Merkur* 50, no. 1 (1996): 1–3.

Borradori, Giovanna, ed. *Philosophy in a Time of Terror: Dialogues with Jürgen Habermas and Jacques Derrida*. University of Chicago Press, 2003.

———. "Reconstructing Terrorism—Habermas." In *Philosophy in a Time of Terror: Dialogues with Jürgen Habermas and Jacques Derrida*, ed. Giovanna Borradori. University of Chicago Press, 2003.

Boswell, John, Jack Corbett, and Jonathan Havercroft. "Politics and Science as a Vocation: Can Academics Save Us from Post-Truth Politics?" *Political Studies Review* 18, no. 4 (2020): 575–90.

Bourdieu, Pierre. "Fourth Lecture. Universal Corporatism: The Role of Intellectuals in the Modern World." *Poetics Today* 12, no. 4 (1991): 655–69.

Bowlby, Chris. "European Central Bank Calls for 'Quantum Leap.'" *BBC News*, June 29, 2010. http://news.bbc.co.uk/2/hi/business/10453433.stm.

Bright, Liam. "The End of Analytic Philosophy." *The Sooty Empiric*, May 23, 2021. https://sootyempiric.blogspot.com/2021/05/the-end-of-analytic-philosophy.html.

Brockmann, Stephen. "Introduction: The Reunification Debate." *New German Critique* 52 (1991): 3–30.

———. "The Politics of German Literature." *Monatshefte* 84, no. 1 (1992): 46–58.

Brown, Wendy. *Nihilistic Times: Thinking with Max Weber*. Belknap Press of Harvard University Press, 2023.

Bull, Hedley. "Civilian Power Europe: A Contradiction in Terms?" *Journal of Common Market Studies* 21, no. 2 (1982): 149–64.
Busche, Jürgen. "Sein oder nichtsein—das ist nicht die Frage. Jürgen Habermas und seine 'Theorie des kommunikativen Handelns.'" *Frankfurter Allgemeine Zeitung*, Feburary 27, 1982.
Butler, Judith. "Contingent Foundations." In *Feminist Contentions: A Philosophical Exchange*, eds. Seyla Benhabib, Judith Butler, Drucilla Cornell, and Nancy Fraser. Routledge, 1995.
Buzzard, Anthony, John Slessor, and Richard Lowenthal. "The H-Bomb: Massive Retaliation or Graduated Deterrence?" *International Affairs* 32, no. 2 (1956): 148–65.
Caitlin, Jonathon. "A New German Historians' Debate? A Conversation with Sultan Doughan, A. Dirk Moses, and Michael Rothberg." *JHI Blog*, February 2, 2022. https://www.jhiblog.org/2022/02/02/a-new-german-historians-debate-a-conversation-with-sultan-doughan-a-dirk-moses-and-michael-rothberg-part-i/.
Casanova, José. *Public Religions in the Modern World*. University of Chicago Press, 1994.
Chambers, Simone. "Balancing Epistemic Quality and Equal Participation in a System Approach to Deliberative Democracy." *Social Epistemology* 31, no. 3 (2017): 266–76.
———. "Deliberative Democratic Theory." *Annual Review of Political Science* 6 (2003): 307–26.
Chaplin, Tamara. *Turning on the Mind: French Philosophers on Television*. University of Chicago Press, 2007.
Chomsky, Noam. *Yugoslavia: Peace, War, and Dissolution*. PM Press, 2018.
Claassen, Rutger. "Making Capability Lists: Philosophy Versus Democracy." *Political Studies* 59, no. 3 (2011): 491–508.
Cohn-Bendit, Daniel, and Claus Leggewie. "Europe's Second Chance." *Eurozine*, July 14, 2023. https://www.eurozine.com/europes-second-chance/.
Collini, Stefan. "'Every Fruit-Juice Drinker, Nudist, Sandal-Wearer . . .': Intellectuals as Other People." In *The Public Intellectual*, ed. Helen Small. Wiley-Blackwell, 2002.
Cooke, Maeve. "Forever Resistant? Adorno and Radical Transformation of Society." In *A Companion to Adorno*, ed. Peter E. Gordon, Espen Hammer, and Max Pensky. Wiley-Blackwell, 2020.
———. *Re-Presenting the Good Society*. MIT Press, 2006.
Corchia, Luca. *Jürgen Habermas: A Bibliography*. Department of Political Science, Società Italiana di Teoria Critica, University of Pisa, 2019.
Cronin, Ciaran. "Editor's Preface." In *The Divided West*, ed Jürgen Habermas. Verso, 2006.
Cumming, Robert D. *Human Nature and History: A Study of the Development of Liberal Political Thought*. Chicago University Press, 1969.
Czingon, Claudia, Aletta Diefenbach, and Victor Kempf. "Moralischer Universalismus in Zeiten politischer Regression: Jürgen Habermas im Gespräch über die Gegenwart und sein Lebenswerk." *Leviathan* 48, no. 1 (2020): 7–21.
———. "Moral Universalism at a Time of Political Regression: A Conversation with Jürgen Habermas About the Present and His Life's Work." *Theory, Culture & Society* 37, nos. 7–8 (December 2020): 11–36.
Czolleck, Max. *Versöhnungstheater*. Carl Hanser Verlag, 2023.
Dahms, Harry F. "Theory in Weberian Marxism: Patterns of Critical Social Theory in Lukacs and Habermas." *Sociological Theory* 15, no. 3 (1997): 181–214.
de la Riva, Miguel. "Tagung über Habermas: Elektrisierende Lektüre im Zug nach Frankfurt." *Frankfurter Allgemeine Zeitung*, sec. Feuilleton, November 1, 2021. https://www.faz.net/aktuell/feuilleton/debatten/tagung-in-tutzing-habermas-ueber-adorno-17611532.html.

Debray, Régis. *Le pouvoir intellectuel en France*. Ramsay, 1979.
———. *Teachers, Writers, Celebrities: The Intellectuals of Modern France*. Trans. David Macey. New Left Books, 1981.
Deitelhoff, Nicole (@NDeitelhoff). "Dunkle Zeiten. Ein Thread in 20." Twitter, November 17, 2023. https://twitter.com/NDeitelhoff/status/1725538516224884864.
Delanty, Gerard, and Chris Rumford. *Rethinking Europe: Social Theory and the Implications of Europeanization*. Routledge, 2005.
Deleuze, Gilles. *Die einsame Insel. Texte und Gespräche von 1953 bis 1974*. Suhrkamp Verlag, 2003.
Demirović, Alex. *Der nonkonformistische Intellektuelle: Die Entwicklung der Kritischen Theorie zur Frankfurter Schule*. Suhrkamp, 1999.
Denninger, Erhard. "Judicial Review Revisited: The German Experience." *Tulane Law Review* 59 (1984–85): 1013–31.
Diebold, John. "Automation." *Textile Research Journal* 25, no. 7 (1955): 635–40.
Diez, Georg. "A Philosopher's Mission to Save the EU." *Der Spiegel*, November 25, 2011. https://www.spiegel.de/international/europe/habermas-the-last-european-a-philosopher-s-mission-to-save-the-eu-a-799237.html.
Dommett, Katharine, and Peter J. Verovšek. "Promoting Democracy in the Digital Public Sphere: Applying Theoretical Ideals to Online Political Communication." *Javnost - The Public* 28, no. 4 (2021): 358–74.
Dullien, Sebastian, and Ulrike Guérot. "The Long Shadow of Ordoliberalism: Germany's Approach to the Euro Crisis." *ECFR Policy Brief* 49 (2012): 1–15.
Dunn, John. *Interpreting Political Responsibility: Essays 1981–1989*. Princeton University Press, 2014.
Durand-Gasselin, Jean-Marie. "The Work of Jürgen Habermas." In *Philosophical Introductions: Five Approaches to Communicative Reason*, ed. Jürgen Habermas. Polity, 2018.
Durham, John Peters. "Distrust of Representation: Habermas on the Public Sphere." *Media, Culture & Society* 15, no. 4 (1993): 541–71.
Durkheim, Émile. *The Division of Labor in Society*. Trans. George Simpson. Free Press, 1968.
———. *The Elementary Forms of Religious Life*. Ed. Mark Sydney Cladis. Trans. Carol Cosman. Oxford University Press, 2001.
Eder, Klaus. "Making Sense of the Public Sphere." In *Handbook of Contemporary European Social Theory*, ed. Gerard Delanty. Routledge, 2005.
Feenberg, Andrew. *The Philosophy of Praxis: Marx, Lukács and the Frankfurt School*. Verso, 2014.
Feldenkirchen, Markus, Matthias Gebauer, Kevin Hagen, Christoph Hickmann, Dirk Kurbjuweit, Veit Medick, Laura Meyer, et al. "Germany's Greens Have Transformed in the Face of Russia's War." *Der Spiegel*, sec. International, May 6, 2022. https://www.spiegel.de/international/germany/from-peaceniks-to-hawks-germany-s-greens-have-transformed-in-the-face-of-russia-s-war-a-19bd95f6-fcbc-497d-8ad9-12767be205f1.
Felsch, Philipp. *Der Philosoph: Habermas und wir*. Propyläen, 2024.
Ferrara, Alessandro. "Europe as a 'Special Area for Human Hope.'" *Constellations* 14, no. 3 (2007): 315–31.
Fischer, Joschka. "Gründungfigur des demokratischen Deutschland." In *Über Habermas: Gespräche mit Zeitgenossen*, ed. Michael Funken. Wissenschaftliche Buchgesellschaft, 2009.
Forstenzer, Joshua. *Deweyan Experimentalism and the Problem of Method in Political Philosophy*. Routledge, 2019.

Foucault, Michel. *Foucault Live: Collected Interviews, 1961–1984*. Ed. Sylvère Lotringer. Trans. Lysa Hochroth and John Johnston. Semiotext(e), 1996.
——. *Power/Knowledge: Selected Interviews and Other Writings, 1972—1977*. Ed. Colin Gordon. Pantheon, 1980.
Frank, Manfred. "Schelling, Marx, and the Philosophy of History: Das Absolute und die Geschichte: Von der Zwiespältigkeit in Schellings Denken." In *The Habermas Handbook*, ed. Hauke Brunkhorst, Regina Kreide, and Cristina Lafont. Columbia University Press, 2017.
Fraser, Nancy. "Legitimation Crisis? On the Political Contradictions of Financialized Capitalism." *Critical Historical Studies* 2, no. 2 (2015): 157–89.
——. "The Theory of the Public Sphere: The Structural Transformation of the Public Sphere (1962)." In *The Habermas Handbook*, ed. Hauke Brunkhorst, Regina Kreide, and Cristina Lafont. Columbia University Press, 2017.
Fraser, Nancy, and Rahel Jaeggi. *Capitalism: A Conversation*. Ed. Brian Milstein. Polity, 2018.
Freyenhagen, Fabian. "Adorno's Politics: Theory and Praxis in Germany's 1960s." *Philosophy & Social Criticism* 40, no. 9 (2014): 867–93.
——. *Adorno's Practical Philosophy: Living Less Wrongly*. Cambridge University Press, 2013.
Frisé, Adolf. *Wir Leben immer mehrere Leben. Erinnerungen*. Rowohlt Verlag, 2004.
Funken, Michael. "Einleitung." In *Über Habermas: Gespräche mit Zeitgenossen*, ed. Michael Funken. Wissenschaftliche Buchgesellschaft, 2009.
——, ed. *Über Habermas: Gespräche mit Zeitgenossen*. Wissenschaftliche Buchgesellschaft, 2009.
——. "Vom Außenseiter zum geachteten Intellektuellen." In *Über Habermas: Gespräche mit Zeitgenossen*, ed. Michael Funken. Wissenschaftliche Buchgesellschaft, 2009.
Galston, William A. "Realism in Political Theory." *European Journal of Political Theory* 9, no. 4 (2010): 385–411.
Gehrke, Christian, and Heinz D. Kurz. "Karl Marx on Physiocracy." *The European Journal of the History of Economic Thought* 2, no. 1 (1995): 53–90.
Geyer, Christian. "Sein Niveau entzündet." *Frankfurter Allgemeine Zeitung*, sec. Feuilleton, June 25, 2008.
Geuss, Raymond. *The Idea of a Critical Theory: Habermas and the Frankfurt School*. Cambridge University Press, 1981.
——. "The Last Nineteenth Century German Philosopher: Habermas at 90." *Verso Blog*, August 14, 2019. https://www.versobooks.com/blogs/4408-the-last-nineteenth-century-german-philosopher-habermas-at-90.
——. *Philosophy and Real Politics*. Princeton University Press, 2008.
——. *Politics and the Imagination*. Princeton University Press, 2010.
Gordon, Peter E. "A Lion in Winter." *The Nation*, September 14, 2016. https://www.thenation.com/article/a-lion-in-winter/.
——. *A Precarious Happiness: Adorno and the Sources of Normativity*. University of Chicago Press, 2024.
Görtzen, René. *Jürgen Habermas: Eine Bibliographie seiner Schriften und der Sekundärliteratur 1952–1981*. Suhrkamp Verlag, 1982.
Graham, Paul. "The Transcendence of a Border: How West German Intellectuals Debated Reunification." *Journal of Communist Studies and Transition Politics* 16, no. 4 (2000): 21–44.
Gregersen, Thomas. *Jürgen Habermas's Works 1992–2023—A Bibliography*. https://www.academia.edu/7913989/Jürgen_Habermass_Works_1992_2023_A_Bibliography.

Grieshaber, Kirsten. "The German Chancellor Condemns a Firebomb Attack on a Berlin Synagogue and Vows Protection for Jews." *AP News*, October 18, 2023. https://apnews.com/article/germany-berlin-synagogue-antisemitism-fdd10f32f7d5efc6da973f00c9a8b030.

Grimm, Dieter. "Does Europe Need a Constitution?" *European Law Journal* 1, no. 3 (November 29, 1995): 282–302.

———. "Das risiko Demokratie: Ein Plädoyer für einen neuen parlamentarischen Rat." *Die Zeit*, August 17, 1990.

Grossner, Claus. "Der letzte Richter der Kritischen Theorie." *Die Zeit*, March 13, 1970.

Gunnell, John G. "Professing Political Theory." *Political Research Quarterly* 63, no. 3 (2010): 674–79.

Günther, Frieder. "'Staatsrechtslehre' Between Tradition and Change: West-German University Teachers of Public Law in the Process of Westernization, 1949–1970." Paper delivered at the German Historical Institute, Washington, DC, March 25–27, 1999. www.ghi-dc.org/conpotweb/westernpapers/guenther.pdf.

Hachmeister, Lutz. *Heideggers Testament. Der Philosoph, der SPIEGEL und die SS*. Propyläen, 2015.

Haiden, Michael. "Jürgen Habermas: A Political Pacifist?" *Res Philosophica* 101, no. 2 (2024): 191–217.

Hanshew, Karrin. "'Sympathy for the Devil?': The West German Left and the Challenge of Terrorism." *Contemporary European History* 21, no. 4 (2012): 511–32.

Havel, Václav. "The Responsibility of Intellectuals." *New York Review of Books*, June 22, 1995. https://www.nybooks.com/articles/1995/06/22/the-responsibility-of-intellectuals/.

Haysom, Keith. "Civil Society and Social Movements." In *Jürgen Habermas: Key Concepts*, ed. Barbara Fultner. Routledge, 2014.

Heidegren, Carl-Göran. "Transcendental Theory of Society, Anthropology and the Sociology of Law: Helmut Schelsky: An Almost Forgotten Sociologist." *Acta Sociologica* 40, no. 3 (1997): 279–90.

Heidegger, Martin. *Being and Time*. Trans. John Macquarrie and Edward Robinson. Harper, 1962.

Henrich, Dieter. *Ins Denken ziehen. Eine philosophische Autobiographie*. C. H. Beck, 2021.

Herbert, Ulrich. "Der Historikerstreit. Politische, wissenschaftliche, biographische Aspekte." In *Zeitgeschichte als Streitgeschichte. Große Kontroversen nach 1945*, ed. Martin Sabrow et al. C. H. Beck, 2003.

Hilmer, Hans, and Christoph Sattler. *Buildings and Projects; Bauten und Projekte*. Edition Axel Menges, 1999.

Hillgruber, Andreas. *Zweierlei Untergang: Die Zerschlagung des Deutschen Reiches und das Ende des europäischen Judentums*. Corso bei Siedler, 1986.

Hitchens, Christopher. "Is the Euro Doomed? The Dreams of European Union Could Die Along with It." *Slate*, April 26, 2010. http://www.slate.com/id/2251986.

Hockenos, Paul. "Germany's Public Intellectual No. 1." *Politico*, April 13, 2011. https://www.politico.eu/article/germanys-public-intellectual-no-1/.

Hofmann, Michael. *Reading Habermas: Structural Transformation of the Public Sphere*. Lexington Books, 2023.

———. *Habermas's Public Sphere: A Critique*. Fairleigh Dickinson University Press, 2017.

Hohendahl, Peter. "Foreword." In *The Past as Future: Vergangenheit als Zukunft*, ed. Jürgen Habermas. University of Nebraska Press, 1994,

Hohendahl, Peter Uwe. "The Scholar, the Intellectual, and the Essay: Weber, Lukács, Adorno, and Postwar Germany." *The German Quarterly* 70, no. 3 (1997): 217–32.

Holub, Robert C. *Jürgen Habermas: Critic in the Public Sphere*. London: Routledge, 1991.
Honneth, Axel. *Pathologies of Reason: On the Legacy of Critical Theory*. Columbia University Press, 2009.
Honneth, Axel, Eberhard Knödler-Bunte, and Arno Widmann. "The Dialectics of Rationalization: An Interview with Jürgen Habermas." *Telos* 49 (1981): 5–31.
Horkheimer, Max. *Between Philosophy and Social Science: Selected Early Writings*. MIT Press, 1993.
———. *Critical Theory: Selected Essays*. Trans. Matthew J. O'Connell. Continuum Publishing, 1972.
———. *Critique of Instrumental Reason*. Trans. M. O'Connell et al. Continuum, 1974.
———. *Briefwechsel 1949–1973*. Vol. 18 of *Gesammelte Schriften*. Fischer Taschenbuch, 1996.
———, ed. *Studien über Autorität und Familie. Forschungsberichte aus dem Institut für Sozialforschung*. Félix Alcan, 1936.
Horkheimer, Max, and Theodor W. Adorno. *Dialectic of Enlightenment: Philosophical Fragments*. Trans. Gunzelin Schmid Noerr. Stanford University Press, 2002.
Horster, Detlev, Willem van Reijen, Jürgen Habermas, and Ron Smith. "Interview with Jürgen Habermas Starnberg, March 23, 1979." *New German Critique* 18 (1979): 29–43. http://www.jstor.org.proxy-ub.rug.nl/stable/487849.
Horton, John. "What Might It Mean for Political Theory to Be More 'Realistic'?" *Philosophy* 45, no. 2 (2017): 487–501.
Howard, Dick. "Citizen Habermas." *Constellations* 22, no. 4 (2015): 523–32.
———. *Between Politics and Antipolitics: Thinking About Politics After 9/11*. Palgrave Macmillan, 2016.
Höpner, Martin, Fritz Scharpf, and Wolfgang Streeck. "Europa braucht die Nation." *Die Zeit*, sec. Wirtschaft, September 15, 2016.
Huyssen, Andreas. "After the Wall: The Failure of German Intellectuals." *New German Critique* 52 (1991): 109–43.
Jay, Martin. "Habermas and the Light of Reason: On Late Critical Theory." *Los Angeles Review of Books*, August 11, 2019. https://lareviewofbooks.org/article/habermas-light-reason-late-critical-theory/.
———. *Immanent Critiques: The Frankfurt School Under Pressure*. Verso, 2023.
Jäger, Lorenz. "Heimsuchung von Heidegger." *Zeitschrift für Ideengeschichte* 15, no. 3 (2021): 11–13.
Jaeggi, Urs. "Versöhnung als Puzzlearbeit: Nachdenken über Jürgen Habermas: Theorie des kommunikativen Handelns." *Die Zeit*, April 2, 1982.
Jaspers, Karl. *The Question of German Guilt*. Fordham University Press, 2001.
Jeffries, Stuart. "A Rare Interview with Jürgen Habermas." *Financial Times*, April 30, 2010
———. *Grand Hotel Abyss: The Lives of the Frankfurt School*. Verso, 2017.
Steinmetz-Jenkins, Daniel. "Jürgen Habermas Still Believes in Modernity." *The Nation*, 7 July 2025, https://www.thenation.com/article/culture/jurgen-habermas-qa/.
Jennings, Jeremy, and Anthony Kemp-Welch. "The Century of the Intellectual: From the Dreyfus Affair to Salman Rushdie." In *Intellectuals in Politics: From the Dreyfus Affair to Salman Rushdie*, ed. Jeremy Jennings and Anthony Kemp-Welch. Routledge, 1997.
Joffe, Josef. "The Decline of the Public Intellectual and the Rise of the Pundit." In *The Public Intellectual: Between Philosophy and Politics*, ed. Richard M. Zinman, Jerry Weinberger and Arthur M. Melzer. Rowman & Littlefield, 2004.
Johnson, Pauline. *Habermas: Rescuing the Public Sphere*. Routledge, 2006.
Jütten, Timo. "Habermas and Markets." *Constellations* 20, no. 4 (2013): 587–603.

Kansteiner, Wulf. "Losing the War, Winning the Memory Battle: The Legacy of Nazism, World War II, and the Holocaust in the Federal Republic of Germany." In *The Politics of Memory in Postwar Europe*, ed. Richard Ned Lebow, Wulf Kansteiner, and Claudio Fogu. Duke University Press, 2006.

Kant, Immanuel. "On the Common Saying: 'This May Be True in Theory, But It Does Not Apply in Practice.'" In *Kant's Political Writings*, 2nd ed. Ed. and trans. H. S. Reiss. Cambridge University Press, 1991.

———. *Toward Perpetual Peace and Other Writings on Politics, Peace, and History*. Ed. Pauline Kleingeld, trans. David L. Colclasure. Yale University Press, 2006.

Kimball, Roger. *Tenured Radicals: How Politics Has Corrupted Our Higher Education*. Ivan R. Dee, 2008.

Kleinstüber, Hans J. "Habermas and the Public Sphere: From a German to a European Perspective." *Javnost - The Public* 8, no. 1 (2001): 95–108.

Kloppenberg, James T. *Uncertain Victory: Social Democracy and Progressivism in European and American Thought, 1870–1920*. Oxford University Press, 1988.

Koch, Moritz. "Rare Praise from a Philosopher." *Handelsblatt*, October 10, 2015.

Korn, Karl. "Warum schweigt Heidegger? Antwort auf den Versuch einer Polemik." *Frankfurter Allgemeine Zeitung*, August 14, 1953.

Koselleck, Reinhart. *Futures Past: On the Semantics of Historical Time*. Trans. Keith Tribe. MIT Press, 1985.

Kouris, Yiannis, and Jonathan Wolff. "Philosophy & Public Policy." *Institute for Alternative Politics Blog*, April 24, 2021. https://www.enainstitute.org/en/publication/philosophy-public-policy-interview-with-jonathan-wolff/.

Kracauer, Siegfried. "Minimalforderung an die Intellektuellen." In *Der verbotene Blick: Beobachtungen, Analysen, Kritiken*, ed. Johanna Rosenberg. Reclam-Verlag, 1992.

Kraushaar, Wolfgang. *Frankfurter Schule und Studentenbewegung. Band 2: Dokumente*. Rogner & Bernhard, 1998.

Kratochwil, Friedrich V. "Evidence, Inference, and Truth as Problems of Theory Building in the Social Sciences." In *Theory and Evidence in Comparative Politics and International Relations*, ed. Richard Ned Lebow and Mark Irving Lichback. Palgrave MacMillan, 2007.

Kundnani, Hans. "The Concept of 'Normality' in German Foreign Policy since Unification." *German Politics & Society* 30, no. 2 (2012): 38–58.

Lapavitsas, Costas. "Financialised Capitalism: Crisis and Financial Expropriation." *Historical Materialism* 17, no. 2 (June 2009): 114–48. http://search.ebscohost.com/login.aspx?direct=true&db=aph&AN=41786263&site=ehost-live&scope=site.

Leendertz, Ariane. "Ein gescheitertes Experiment—Carl Friedrich von Weizsäcker, Jürgen Habermas und die Max-Planck-Gesellschaft." *Acta Historica Leopoldina* 63 (2014): 243–62.

Leiter, Brian. "A More Substantial Response to 'Diversity Sometimes Trumps Academic Freedom'. . . ." *Leiter Reports: A Philosophy Blog*, 2 March 2023. https://leiterreports.typepad.com/blog/2023/03/a-more-substantial-response-to-diversity-sometimes-trumps-academic-freedom.html.

Leopold, David, and Marc Stears. "Introduction." In *Political Theory: Methods and Approaches*, ed. David Leopold and Marc Stears. Oxford University Press, 2008.

Lenhard, Philip. *Café Marx. Das Institut für Sozialforschung von den Anfängen bis zur Frankfurter Schule*. C. H. Beck, 2024.

Levy, Daniel, Max Pensky, and John C. Torpey. "Editor's Introduction." In *Old Europe, New Europe, Core Europe: Transatlantic Relations After the Iraq War*, ed. Daniel Levy, Max Pensky, and John C. Torpey. Verso, 2005.
Levy, Daniel, and Natan Sznaider. "Memory Unbound." *European Journal of Social Theory* 5, no. 1 (2002): 87–106.
Lewalter, Christian. "Wie liest Man 1953 Sätze von 1935? Zu einem politischen Streit um Heideggers Metaphysik." *Die Zeit*, August 13, 1953.
Lilkov, Dimitar. "Muddling Through: Towards an EU Federal Response to the Crisis." *Wilfried Martens Centre for European Studies Blog*, March 20, 2020. https://www.martenscentre.eu/blog/muddling-through-towards-an-eu-federal-response-to-the-crisis/.
Lizoane, David, and Matthias Ecke. "European Youth Need a Change from a New German Government." *Social Europe Journal*, November 14, 2013. http://www.social-europe.eu/2013/11/european-youth-need-new-german-government/.
Löwenthal, Leo. *An Unmastered Past*. University of California Press, 1987.
Lyall, Sarah, and Stephen Castle. "Irish Voters Reject EU Treaty." *International Herald Tribune*, June 13, 2008. http://www.iht.com/bin/printfriendly.php?id=13702436.
MacDonald, Robert. "'Impact,' Research and Slaying Zombies: The Pressures and Possibilities of the REF." *International Journal of Sociology and Social Policy* 37, nos. 11–12 (2017): 696–710.
Magala, Slawek. *The Management of Meaning in Organizations*. Palgrave Macmillan, 1999.
Maier, Charles S. *The Unmasterable Past: History, Holocaust, and German National Identity*. Harvard University Press, 1988.
Mann, Heinrich, and Thomas Mann. *Letters of Heinrich and Thomas Mann, 1900–1949*. Ed. Hans Wysling. Trans. Don Reneau. University of California Press, 1998.
Manners, Ian. "Normative Power Europe: A Contradiction in Terms?" *Journal of Common Market Studies* 40, no. 2 (2002): 235–58.
Mannheim, Karl. *Ideology and Utopia*. Routledge, 1960.
Marcuse, Herbert. "Some Social Implications of Modern Technology." In *The Essential Frankfurt School Reader*, eds. Andrew Arato and Eike Gerhardt, 138–62. Urizen Books, 1977.
———. *Studies in Critical Philosophy*. Beacon Press, 1972.
Marx, Karl. "Capital, Volume One." In *The Marx-Engels Reader*. 2nd ed. Ed. Robert C. Tucker. W. W. Norton, 1978.
———. "Contribution to the Critique of Hegel's *Philosophy of Right*: Introduction." In *The Marx-Engels Reader*. 2nd ed. Ed. Robert C. Tucker. W. W. Norton, 1978.
———. "Economic and Philosophical Manuscripts of 1844." In *The Marx-Engels Reader*. 2nd ed. Ed. Robert C. Tucker. W. W. Norton, 1978.
———. "Marx to Domela Nieuwenhuis in the Hague, London, February 22, 1881." Marxists.org, 2000. Accessed December 29, 2020. https://www.marxists.org/archive/marx/works/1881/letters/81_02_22.htm.
Massey, Garth. "A Final Look at the Critical Perspective of the Yugoslav *Praxis* Group." *Humanity and Society* 15, no. 2 (1991): 223–38.
Matuštík, Martin Joseph. *Jürgen Habermas: A Philosophical-Political Profile*. Rowman & Littlefield, 2001.
McCarthy, Thomas A. *The Critical Theory of Jürgen Habermas*. MIT Press, 1978.
———. "Kantian Constructivism and Reconstructivism: Rawls and Habermas in Dialogue." *Ethics* 105, no. 1 (October 1994): 44–63.

———. "Defending Habermas." *New York Review of Books*, January 20, 1983.
McCormick, John P. *Weber, Habermas, and Transformations of the European State: Constitutional, Social, and Supranational Democracy*. Cambridge University Press, 2007.
McIntyre, John. *The Limits of Scientific Reason: Habermas, Foucault, and Science as a Social Institution*. Rowman & Littlefield, 2021.
McKean, Benjamin L. "What Makes a Utopia Inconvenient?: On the Advantages and Disadvantages of a Realist Orientation to Politics." *American Political Science Review* 110, no. 4 (2016): 876–88.
Meinel, Florian. "Die Feindortung klappte immer." *Frankfurter Allgemeine Zeitung*, Feuilleton, March 8, 2024.
Melzer, Arthur M. "What Is an Intellectual?" In *The Public Intellectual: Between Philosophy and Politics*, ed. Richard M. Zinman, Jerry Weinberger, and Arthur M. Melzer. Rowman & Littlefield, 2004.
Michel, Karl Markus. "Karl Markus Michel über Jürgen Habermas' 'Theorie des kommunikativen Handelns.'" *Der Spiegel*, March 21, 1982.
Mills, C. Wright. *The Sociological Imagination*. Oxford University Press, 1959.
Minkmar, Nils, and Nicolas Richter. "'Ab und an lese ich auch Comics.' Olaf Scholz im Interview." *Süddeutsche Zeitung*, July 28, 2023.
Misztal, Barbara A. *Intellectuals and the Public Good: Creativity and Civil Courage*. Cambridge University Press, 2007.
Möllers, Christoph. *The Three Branches: A Comparative Model of Separation of Powers*. Oxford University Press, 2015.
Moses, A. Dirk. "The German Catechism." *Geschichte der Gegenwart*, May 23, 2021. https://geschichtedergegenwart.ch/the-german-catechism/.
Müller, Jan-Werner. *Constitutional Patriotism*. Princeton University Press, 2007.
———. "Rawls in Germany." *European Journal of Political Theory* 1, no. 2 (2002): 163–79.
Müller-Doohm, Stefan. *Adorno: A Biography*. Polity, 2015.
———. *Habermas: A Biography*. Polity, 2016.
———. "Habermas-Biograph: 'Er kann gar nicht anders, als sich zu äußern'." *Frankfurter Rundschau*, February 20, 2023. https://www.fr.de/kultur/gesellschaft/habermas-biograph-er-kann-gar-nicht-anders-als-sich-zu-aeussern-92099059.html.
———. "Nation State, Capitalism, Democracy: Philosophical and Political Motives in the Thought of Jürgen Habermas." *European Journal of Social Theory* 13, no. 4 (2010): 443–57.
———. "Theodor W. Adorno and Jürgen Habermas—Two Ways of Being a Public Intellectual: Sociological Observations Concerning the Transformation of a Social Figure of Modernity." *European Journal of Social Theory* 8, no. 3 (2005): 269–80.
Negt, Oscar. "Studentischer Protest—Liberalismus—'Linksfaschismus.'" *Kursbuch* 13 (1968): 179–89.
Neiman, Susan. *Learning from the Germans: Race and the Memory of Evil*. Farrar, Straus and Giroux, 2019.
Niesen, Peter. "Constituent Power in Global Constitutionalism." In *Handbook on Global Constitutionalism*, ed. Anthony F. Lang and Antje Wiener. Edward Elgar Publishing, 2023.
Nolte, Ernst. "Between Myth and Revisionism? The Third Reich in the Perspective of the 1980s." In *Aspects of the Third Reich*, ed. H. W. Koch. Macmillan, 1985.
———. "Vergangenheit, die nicht vergehen will. Eine Rede, die Geschrieben, aber nicht gehalten werden konnte." In *'Historikerstreit': Die Dokumentation der Kontroverse um die Einzigartigkeit der nationalsozialistischen Judenvernichtung*, ed. Rudolf Augenstein. Piper Verlag, 1987.

Offe, Claus. "Bindings, Shackles, Brakes: On Self-Limitation Strategies." In *Cultural-Political Interventions in the Unfinished Project of Enlightenment*, ed. Axel Honneth, Thomas A. McCarthy, Claus Offe, and Albrecht Wellmer. MIT Press, 1992.
——. "Die Bundesrepublik als Schattenriß zweier Lichtquellen." *Ästhetik und Kommunikation* 36 (2005): 149–60.
Oltermann, Philip. "Israel–Hamas War Opens Up German Debate Over Meaning of 'Never again.'" *The Guardian*, November 22, 2023. https://www.theguardian.com/world/2023/nov/22/israel-hamas-war-opens-up-german-debate-over-meaning-of-never-again.
Orzessek, Arno. "Der Einmischer." *Deutschlandfunk Kultur*, June 18, 2014. https://www.deutschlandfunkkultur.de/geistesgeschichte-der-einmischer-100.html.
Outhwaite, William. "Reviews: Habermas: A Biography." *Studies in Social and Political Thought* 26 (2017): 126–33.
Patapan, Haig. *Modern Philosopher Kings: Wisdom and Power in Politics*. Edinburgh University Press, 2023.
Pensky, Max. "Editor's Introduction." In *The Postnational Constellation: Political Essays*, ed. Jürgen Habermas. MIT Press, 2001.
——. *The Ends of Solidarity: Discourse Theory in Ethics and Politics*. State University of New York Press, 2008.
——. "Historical and Intellectual Contexts." In *Jürgen Habermas: Key Concepts*, ed. Barbara Fultner. Acumen Publishing, 2013.
——. "Jürgen Habermas and the Antinomies of the Intellectual." In *Habermas: A Critical Reader*, ed. Peter Dews. Blackwell, 1999.
——. "Two Cheers for the Impunity Norm." *Philosophy & Social Criticism* 42, nos. 4–5 (2016): 487–99.
——. "Universalism and the Situated Critic." In *The Cambridge Companion to Habermas*, ed. Stephen K. White. Cambridge University Press, 1995.
Peters, Bernhard. *Die Integration Moderner Gesellschaften*. Suhrkamp, 1993.
Philp, Mark. "What Is to Be Done? Political Theory and Political Realism." *European Journal of Political Theory* 9, no. 4 (October 1, 2010): 466–84.
Pinsker, Shachar M. *A Rich Brew: How Cafés Created Modern Jewish Culture*. New York University Press, 2018.
Piris, Jean-Claude. *The Future of Europe: Towards a Two-Speed EU?* Cambridge University Press, 2012.
Pollock, Friedrich. *Automation: A Study of its Economic and Social Consequences*. Trans. W. O. Henderson and W. H. Chaloner. Frederick A. Praeger, 1957.
Pöggeler, Otto. "Den Führer führen? Heidegger und kein Ende." *Philosophische Rundschau* 32, no. 1 (1985): 26–67.
Putin, Vladimir. "On the Historical Unity of Russians and Ukrainians." *The Kremlin*, July 12, 2021. http://en.kremlin.ru/events/president/news/66181.
Rabe, Jens-Christian. "Habermas vs. Google; Nicht in seinem Namen." *Süddeutsche Zeitung*, April 25, 2025.
Ratzinger, Joseph, and Jürgen Habermas. *Dialectics of Secularization: On Reason and Religion*. Ed. Florian Schuller. Ignatius Press, 2006.
Reemtsma, Jan Philipp. "Erinnerung vergemeinschaften. Ein kurzes Gespräch über Nachteile der Geschichtsschreibung." *Mittelweg 36*, no. 15 (2006): 29–36.

Regier, W. G., and H. Peter Reinkordt. "Jürgen Habermas: 'Under the Macroscope.'" *Minnesota Review* 24 (Spring 1985): 121–32.

Rensmann, Lars. "Radical Right-Wing Populists in Parliament: Examining the Alternative for Germany in European Context." *German Politics and Society* 36, no. 3 (2018): 41–73.

Richter, Gerhard, and Theodor W. Adorno. "Who's Afraid of the Ivory Tower? A Conversation with Theodor W. Adorno." *Monatshefte* 94, no. 1 (2002): 10–23.

Ries, Al, and Jack Trout. *Positioning: The Battle for Your Mind*. McGraw-Hill, 1981.

Risse, Thomas. *A Community of Europeans?: Transnational Identities and Public Spheres*. Cornell University Press, 2010.

———. "'Let's Argue!': Communicative Action in World Politics." *International Organization* 54, no. 1 (2000): 1–39.

Robbins, Bruce. "The Grounding of Intellectuals." In *Intellectuals: Aesthetics, Politics, Academics*, ed. Bruce Robbins. University of Minnesota Press, 1990.

Rockmore, Tom. *Habermas on Historical Materialism*. Indiana University Press, 1989.

———. "Theory and Practice Again: Habermas on Historical Materialism." *Philosophy & Social Criticism* 13, no. 3 (1987): 211–25.

Rosenfelder, Andreas. "Die Habermas-Diktatur." *Die Welt*, sec. Meinung, October 11, 2021. https://www.welt.de/kultur/plus234125124/Corona-Politik-Die-Habermas-Diktatur.html.

Rossi, Enzo. "Reality and Imagination in Political Theory and Practice: On Raymond Geuss's Realism." *European Journal of Political Theory* 9, no. 4 (2010): 504–12.

Rossi, Enzo, and Matt Sleat. "Realism in Normative Political Theory." *Philosophy Compass* 9, no. 10 (2014): 689–701.

Rothberg, Michael. "Comparing Comparisons: From the 'Historikerstreit' to the Mbembe Affair." *Geschichte Der Gegenwart*, September 23, 2020. https://geschichtedergegenwart.ch/comparing-comparisons-from-the-historikerstreit-to-the-mbembe-affair/.

———. *Multidirectional Memory: Remembering the Holocaust in the Age of Decolonization*. Stanford University Press, 2009.

Russell, Matheson. *Habermas and Politics: A Critical Introduction*. Edinburgh University Press, 2019.

Said, Edward W. *Power, Politics and Culture: Interviews with Edward Said*. Ed. Gauri Viswanathan. Bloomsbury, 2007.

———. *Representations of the Intellectual: The 1993 Reith Lectures*. Pantheon Books, 1994.

Schäfer, Gerhard. "Von der nivellierten Mittelstandsgesellschaft zur Risikogesellschaft: Ein Vergleich der soziologischen Zeitdiagnostik Helmut Schelskys und Ulrich Becks." *Geschlossene Gesellschaften. Verhandlungen des 38. Kongresses der Deutschen Gesellschaft für Soziologie in Bamberg 2016* 38 (2017): 1–7.

Schelsky, Helmut. "Zukunftsaspekte der industriellen Gesellschaft." *Merkur* 8, no. 1 (January 1954): 13–28.

Schildt, Axel. *Medien-Intellektulle in der Bundesrepublik*. Wallstein Verlag, 2020.

Schirrmacher, Frank. "Demokratie ist ramsch." *Frankfurter Allgemeine Zeitung*, November 1, 2011.

———. "Der Zivilisationsredakteur: 100 Jahre Karl Korn." *Frankfurter Allgemeine Zeitung*, sec. Feuilleton, May 17, 2008. https://www.faz.net/aktuell/feuilleton/bilder-und-zeiten-1/100-jahre-karl-korn-der-zivilisationsredakteur-1538919.html?printPagedArticle=true#pageIndex_2.

Schmidtz, David. *The Elements of Justice*. Cambridge University Press, 2006.

Schmitt, Carl. *The Crisis of Parliamentary Democracy*. MIT Press, 1985.

Schumpeter, Joseph. *Capitalism, Socialism and Democracy*. Harper and Row, 1950.
Scruton, Roger. *Thinkers of the New Left*. Longman, 1985.
Seibt, Gustav. "Die Formen der Historie. Zu einer Theorie der modernen Geschichtsschreibung." *Merkur* 463/64 (1987): 903–7.
Sher, Gerson S. *Praxis: Marxist Criticism and Dissent in Socialist Yugoslavia*. Indiana University Press, 1977.
Skinner, Quentin. "Habermas's Reformation." *New York Review of Books*, October 7, 1982.
———. "Meaning and Understanding in the History of Ideas." *History and Theory* 8, no. 1 (1969): 3–53.
Sinn, Hans-Werner. *Casino Capitalism: How the Financial Crisis Came About and What Needs to Be Done Now*. Oxford: Oxford University Press, 2010.
Small, Helen. "Introduction." In *The Public Intellectual*, ed. Helen Small. Wiley-Blackwell, 2002.
Smith, Rogers M. *Stories of Peoplehood: The Politics and Morals of Political Membership*. Cambridge University Press, 2003.
Smith, Steven B. *Political Philosophy*. Yale University Press, 2012.
Snyder, Timothy. "Germans Have Been Involved in the War, Chiefly on the Wrong Side." *Frankfurter Allgemeine Zeitung*, June 27, 2022. https://www.faz.net/-gq5-asmiu.
Specter, Matthew G. "From Eclipse of Reason to the Age of Reasons? Historicizing Habermas and the Frankfurt School." *Modern Intellectual History* 16, no. 1 (2019): 321–37.
———. "A Great Misrecognition: How *Between Facts and Norms* Was Conflated With (But Resists) the Cosmopolitan Moment in 1990s International Relations Theory." In *Critical Encounters with Habermas's Legal and Political Theory*, ed. John Abromeit, Matt Dimick, and Paul Linden-Retek. Brill, forthcoming.
———. *Habermas: An Intellectual Biography*. Cambridge University Press, 2010.
———. "Habermas in German, European, North Atlantic and Global Perspective." *Los Angeles Review of Books*, August 11, 2019. https://lareviewofbooks.org/article/habermas-german-european-north-atlantic-global-perspective/.
Steinbaum, Marshall. "Thomas Piketty Takes on the Ideology of Inequality." *Boston Review*, March 25, 2020. http://bostonreview.net/class-inequality/marshall-steinbaum-thomas-piketty-takes-ideology-inequality.
Streeck, Wolfgang. *Buying Time: The Delayed Crisis of Democratic Capitalism*. Trans. Patrick Camiller. Verso, 2014.
———. "Germans to the Front." *Sidecar*, March 16, 2023. https://newleftreview.org/sidecar/posts/germans-to-the-front.
———. "Getting Closer." *Sidecar*, November 7, 2022. https://newleftreview.org/sidecar/posts/getting-closer.
———. *How will Capitalism End?: Essays on a Failing System*. Verso, 2016.
———. "Markets and Peoples: Democratic Capitalism and European Integration." *New Left Review* 73 (2012): 63–71.
———. "Small-State Nostalgia? The Currency Union, Germany, and Europe: A Reply to Jürgen Habermas." *Constellations* 21, no. 2 (2014): 213–21.
———. "'Vom DM-Nationalismus zum Euro-Patriotismus? Eine Replik auf Jürgen Habermas.'" *Blätter für deutsche und internationale Politik* 58, no. 9 (2013): 75–92.
———. "Wenn die EU untergeht, wird keiner weinen." *Die Zeit*, sec. Feuilleton, October 13, 2016.

Sternberger, Dolf. "Die deutsche Frage." *Der Monat* 8–9, (1949): 16–21

Stürmer, Michael. "Geschichte in geschichtslosem Land." In *'Historikerstreit': Die Dokumentation der Kontroverse um die Einzigartigkeit der nationalsozialistischen Judenvernichtung*, ed. Rudolf Augstein. Piper Verlag, 1987.

———. "Kein Eigentum der Deutschen: Die deutsche Frage." In *Die Identität der Deutschen*, ed. Werner Weidenfeld, 83–101. Bonn: Schriftenreihe der Bundeszentrale für politische Bildung, 1983.

Swift, Adam, and Stuart White. "Political Theory, Social Science, and Real Politics." In *Political Theory: Methods and Approaches*, eds. David Leopold and Marc Stears. Oxford University Press, 2008.

Tessler, Michael Henry et al. "AI can help humans find common ground in democratic deliberation." *Science* 386, no. 6719 (2024).

Thomas, Robert. *The Politics of Serbia in the 1990s*. Columbia University Press, 1999.

Thompson, Michael J. *The Domestication of Critical Theory*. Rowman & Littlefield, 2016.

Tibi, Bassam. *Europa ohne Identität?: Die Krise der multikulturellen Gesellschaft*. C. Bertelsmann, 1998.

Tooze, Adam. *Crashed: How a Decade of Financial Crises Changed the World*. Viking, 2018.

Tooze, Adam, Samuel Moyn, Amia Srinivasan, Nancy Fraser, Alice Crary, Linda Zerilli, et al. "The Principle of Human Dignity Must Apply to all People." *The Guardian*, November 22, 2023. https://www.theguardian.com/world/2023/nov/22/the-principle-of-human-dignity-must-apply-to-all-people.

Traverso, Enzo. "No, Post-Nazi Germany Isn't a Model of Atoning for the Past." *Jacobin*, June 6, 2022. https://jacobin.com/2022/06/post-nazi-germany-colonialism-holocaust-israel-atonement

Ulaş, Luke. "Can Political Realism Be Action-Guiding?" *Critical Review of International Social and Political Philosophy* 26 (June 2020): 1–26.

van Middelaar, Luuk. "The Return of Politics—The European Union After the Crises in the Eurozone and Ukraine." *Journal of Common Market Studies* 54, no. 3 (2016): 495–507.

van Rahden, Till. "Die gummersbacher Schule: Hans Ulrich Wehler inszeniert eine Debatte." *Zeitschrift für Ideengeschichte* 15, no. 3 (2021): 6–10.

Verovšek, Peter J. "A Case of Communicative Learning?: Rereading Habermas's Philosophical Project Through an Arendtian Lens." *Polity* 51, no. 3 (July 2019): 597–627.

———. "Authorship and Individualization in the Digital Public Sphere." *Constellations* 30, no. 1 (2023): 34–41.

———. "A Burgeoning Community of Justice?: The European Union as a Promoter of Transitional Justice." *International Journal of Transitional Justice* 15, no. 2 (July 2021): 351–69.

———. "Celebrating Jürgen Habermas and the Institute for Social Research: Reflections on the History of Critical Theory from a Jubilee Year," *European Journal of Political Theory*, forthcoming (2024).

———. "Conclusion: Working in a 'Living' Archive." *PS: Political Science and Politics* 57, no. 1 (2024): 97–99.

———. "Direct Engagement or Discursive Impact?: Public Philosophy in the United Kingdom and Germany." *Angermion* 14, no. 1 (2021): 193–216.

———. "Eastern Praxis and Western Critique: France Bučar's Critical Systems Theory in Context." In *At His Crossroads: Reflections on the Work of France Bučar*, ed. Igor Kovač. Springer International, 2018.

———. "The EU is Muddling Through Another Crisis—Which May Be Good Enough." *Social Europe Journal*, July 2, 2020. https://socialeurope.eu/the-eu-is-muddling-through-another-crisis-which-may-be-good-enough.
———. "Experts, Public Intellectuals and the Coronavirus." *Duck of Minerva*, March 29, 2020. https://www.duckofminerva.com/2020/03/experts-public-intellectuals-and-the-coronavirus.html.
———. "Habermas on the Legitimacy of Lockdown." *Eurozine*, February 14, 2022. https://www.eurozine.com/habermas-on-the-legitimacy-of-lockdown/.
———. "Habermas's Politics of Rational Freedom: Navigating the History of Philosophy Between Faith and Knowledge." *Analyse und Kritik* 42, no. 1 (2020): 191–217.
———. "Habermas's Theological Turn and European Integration." *The European Legacy* 22, no. 5 (2017): 528–48.
———. "Historical Criticism Without Progress: Memory as an Emancipatory Resource for Critical Theory." *Constellations* 26, no. 1 (2019): 132–47.
———. "Integration After Totalitarianism: Arendt and Habermas on the Postwar Imperatives of Memory." *Journal of International Political Theory* 16, no. 1 (2018): 2–24.
———. "Jürgen Habermas and the Public Intellectual in Modern Democratic Life." *Philosophy Compass* 17, no. 4 (2022): e12818. https://doi.org/10.1111/phc3.12818.
———. "Meeting Principles and Lifeworlds Halfway: Jürgen Habermas on the Future of Europe." *Political Studies* 60, no. 2 (2012): 363–80.
———. "Memory and the Euro-Crisis of Leadership: The Effects of Generational Change in Germany and the EU." *Constellations* 21, no. 2 (2014): 239–48.
———. *Memory and the Future of Europe: Rupture and Integration in the Wake of Total War*. Manchester University Press, 2020.
———. "Memory, Narrative, and Rupture: The Power of the Past as a Resource for Political Change." *Memory Studies* 13, no. 4 (2020): 208–22. http://dx.doi.org/10.1177/1750698017720256.
———. "Meeting Principles and Lifeworlds Halfway: Jürgen Habermas on the Future of Europe." *Political Studies* 60, no. 2 (2012): 363–80.
———. "'One Would at Least Like to be Asked': Habermas on Popular Sovereignty, Self-Determination, and German Unification." *German Politics and Society* 41, no. 3 (2023): 22–43.
———. "The Philosopher as Engaged Citizen: Habermas on the Role of the Public Intellectual in the Modern Democratic Public Sphere." *European Journal of Social Theory* 24, no. 4 (2021): 526–44.
———. "Social Criticism as Medical Diagnosis? On the Role of Social Pathology and Crisis Within Critical Theory." *Thesis Eleven* 155, no. 1 (2019): 109–26.
———. "Taking Back Control Over Markets: Jürgen Habermas on the Colonization of Politics by Economics." *Political Studies* 71, no. 2 (2021).
Verovšek, Peter J., and Maruša Gorišek. "Experts in Times of Pandemic: Reframing the Debate in the Context of Structural Transformations of the Public Sphere." *Javnost - The Public* 30, no. 4 (2023): 496–512.
von Beyme, Klaus. "The Legitimation of German Unification Between National and Democratic Principles." *German Politics & Society* 22 (Spring 1991): 1–17.
Waldron, Jeremy. *Political Political Theory: Essays on Institutions*. Harvard University Press, 2016.
———. *Liberal Rights: Collected Papers 1981–1991*. Cambridge University Press, 1993.

———. "The Vanishing Europe of Jürgen Habermas." *New York Review of Books*, October 22, 2015. https://www.nybooks.com/articles/2015/10/22/vanishing-europe-jurgen-habermas/.

Walker, Neil. "Habermas's European Constitution: Catalyst, Reconstruction, Refounding." *European Law Journal* 25, no. 5 (2019): 508–14.

Watermeyer, Richard. "Impact in the REF: Issues and Obstacles." *Studies in Higher Education* 41, no. 2 (2016): 199–214.

Weber, Eugen. *Peasants into Frenchmen: The Modernization of Rural France, 1870–1914*. Stanford University Press, 1976.

Weber, Max. *From Max Weber: Essays in Sociology*. Ed. and trans. Hans Heinrich Gerth and C. Wright Mills. Oxford University Press, 1958.

———. "Politics as a Vocation." In *From Max Weber: Essays in Sociology*, ed. and trans. Hans Heinrich Gerth and C. Wright Mills. Oxford University Press, 1958.

———. *The Protestant Ethic and the Spirit of Capitalism*. Trans. Talcott Parsons. Unwin Paperbacks, 1985.

———. "Science as a Vocation." In *From Max Weber: Essays in Sociology*, ed. and trans. Hans Heinrich Gerth and C. Wright Mills. Oxford University Press, 1958.

Westbrook, Robert B. *John Dewey and American Democracy*. Cornell University Press, 2015.

White, Jonathan. *Politics of Last Resort: Governing by Emergency in the European Union*. Oxford University Press, 2020.

White, Stephen K. "Ethics, Politics and History: An Interview with Jürgen Habermas Conducted by Jean-Marc Ferry." *Philosophy & Social Criticism* 14, nos. 3–4 (1988): 433–39.

Whithed, Soren. "Traces of Different Colors: An Interview with Peter E. Gordon." *Platypus Review* 151 (November 2022). https://platypus1917.org/2022/11/01/traces-of-different-colors-an-interview-with-peter-e-gordon/.

Whyman, Tom. "Happy Birthday Habermas, Your Philosophy Has Failed Us." *The Outline*, July 30, 2019. https://theoutline.com/post/7734/habermas-failure-political-philosophy?zi=pdlstmhz&zd=5.

Widmann, Arno. "Wahrheit und Gesellschaft." *Frankfurter Rundschau*, January 26, 2019.

Wiedner, Saskia. "Karl Jaspers: Die Atombombe und die Zukunft des Menschen (1958)." In *Handbuch Nachkriegskultur: Literatur, Sachbuch und Film in Deutschland (1945–1962)*, ed. Elena Agazzi and Erhard Schütz. De Gruyter.

Wiggershaus, Rolf. *The Frankfurt School: Its History, Theories, and Political Significance*. MIT Press, 1995.

———. *Jürgen Habermas*. Rowohlt Taschenbuch Verlag, 2004.

Williams, Bernard. *In the Beginning Was the Deed: Realism and Moralism in Political Argument*. Ed. Geoffrey Hawthorn. Princeton University Press, 2005.

Williams, Howard, Catherine Bishop, and Colin Wight. "German (Re)Unification: Habermas and His Critics." *German Politics* 5, no. 2 (1996): 214–39.

Williams, Howard, Colin Wight, and Norbert Kapferer, eds. *Political Thought and German Reunification: The New German Ideology?* St. Martin's Press, 2000.

Wittenberg, Jason. *Crucibles of Political Loyalty: Church Institutions and Electoral Continuity in Hungary*. Cambridge University Press, 2006.

Williams, Jeffrey J. "The Rise of the Promotional Intellectual." *Chronicle of Higher Education*, August 5, 2018. https://www.chronicle.com/article/the-rise-of-the-promotional-intellectual/.

Wolf, Christa. *Parting from Phantoms: Selected Writings, 1990–1994*. Trans. Jan van Heurck. University of Chicago Press, 1997.

Wolff, Frank, and Eberhard Windaus, eds. *Studentenbewegung 1967–69, Protokolle und Materialen*. Roter Stern, 1977.
Wolff, Jonathan, and Avner de-Shalit. *Disadvantage*. Oxford University Press, 2007.
Wolin, Richard, ed. *The Heidegger Controversy: A Critical Reader*. MIT Press, 1993.
——. *Heidegger's Children: Hannah Arendt, Karl Löwith, Hans Jonas, and Herbert Marcuse*. Princeton University Press, 2001.
——. *The Seduction of Unreason: The Intellectual Romance with Fascism from Nietzsche to Postmodernism*. Princeton University Press, 2004.
Wolters, Gereon. "Der 'Führer' und seine Denker: Zur Philosophie des 'Dritten Reichs'." *Deutsche Zeitschrift für Philosophie* 47, no. 2 (1999): 223–52.
——. *Vertuschung, Anklage, Rechtfertigung: Impromptus zum Rückblick der Deutschen Philosophie auf das 'Dritte Reich'*. Bonn University Press, 2004.
Wong, Ming Kit. "The Cambridge School and the Turn to the Present," *Centre for Intellectual History*, University of Oxford, March 2, 2023. https://intellectualhistory.web.ox.ac.uk/article/cambridge-school-and-turn-present.
Young, Iris Marion. "De-Centering the Project of Global Democracy." In *Old Europe, New Europe, Core Europe: Transatlantic Relations After the Iraq War*, ed. Daniel Levy, Max Pensky, and John C. Torpey. Verso, 2005.
Yos, Roman. *Der junge Habermas: Eine ideengeschichtliche Untersuchung seines frühen Denkens, 1952–62*. Suhrkamp, 2019.
——. "Young Habermas: An Interview with Roman Yos." *JHI Blog*, December 23, 2020. https://jhiblog.org/2020/12/23/young-habermas-interview-roman-yos/.
Zoller, Peter, ed. *Aktiver Streik. Dokumentation zu einem Jahr Hochschulpolitik am Beispiel der Universität Frankfurt am Main*. Joseph Melzer, 1969.

Index

Abendroth, Wolfgang, 26, 120–21, 128, 131–34, 137, 141, 147–48, 150, 156, 281; model of the partisan professor, 141; political influence and model of partisan professor, 132–34; reformism, 156; sponsorship of Habermas's habilitation, 132–33

Adenauer, Konrad, 59, 72–73, 114, 116–17, 135, 136, 140, 149; criticism of technocratic leadership, 116–17, 135, 149; described by Habermas as heading an elective monarchy, 135, 140; rearmament, 72–73, 114

Adorno, Theodor W., 10, 14, 16, 23, 26, 41, 51–52, 53, 55–56, 63–65, 78, 81, 84–99, 92–96, 107, 109, 112, 117–18, 122–28, 130, 132, 135, 138–39, 140, 145, 147, 152–55, 181–82, 209, 219, 266; art and cultural criticism, 63–65; clash with students, 145, 152–55, 180; continued influence on Habermas's democratic theory, 219; continuing influence on public role, 186, 209, 280–81; contrast with Heller's Marxism, 158; contrast with Horkheimer, 96, 109, 122–28; death, 158; on the essay form, 10; intellectual desire for authority, 41; invoked in Habermas's reflections on critical theory, 181–82; as a media intellectual, 14, 46, 51–52; mentorship of Habermas, 55–56, 81, 92–96, 122–28, 139; ongoing influence on Habermas, 149–50, 158; Positivism dispute, 75, 138–39; shared themes with Habermas, 54–56, 78, 84–99, 149; support for Habermas's public role, 26, 95–96, 300

Adorno Prize, 178
Agamben, Giorgio, 275
Alexander the Great, 33
Alexander, Franz, 98
Amsterdam Treaty, 225–31
Anders, Günther, 81–82
anthropology, philosophical, 80, 108–9, 197
Apel, Karl-Otto, 66, 162
Arendt, Hannah, 14–15, 28, 56, 68, 82, 146, 154, 301; declines television appearance, 14, 82; memory of Nazism, 93; on philosopher's pursuit of truth versus power, 49; on totalitarianism and public action, 15–16; public sphere, 301; student mobilizations, 146; words and deeds, 56
Aristotle, 33
Armenian genocide, 191
art and aesthetics, 61–64, 137–38, 157; as social critique, 63–64, 137–38; film and music, 63; puppet theater, 63; radio theater and critical potential, 62–63
asylum debate, 224, 250, 272
austerity policies, 250–55, 258–59; effects on European democracy, 253–55; Habermas's critique of fiscal discipline, 250–53; linked to rise of populism, 258–59. *See also* democracy; European Union (EU)

Auschwitz, 58, 60, 108, 128, 136, 153, 185, 191–92, 203, 227, 280
Außerparlamentarische Oposition (APO, extra-parliamentary opposition), 130–31, 147

Baerbock, Annalena, 285
Bahrdt, Hans Paul, 80
Barth, Karl, 9
Basic Law (*Grundgesetz*), 59, 131, 135, 147–48, 174, 205; defense of constitutional democracy, 135; realization of democratic aims of, 148
Becker, Oscar, 70
Bednarik, Karl, 112
Belgrade eight (Mihailo Marković, Ljubomir Tadić, Zagorka Golubović, Svetozar Stojanović, Miladin Životić, Dragoljub Mićunović, Nebojša Popov, and Trivo Inđić), 27, 161–63
Bell, Daniel,
Benhabib, 301
Benn, Gottfried, 61–62
Bergen Belsen, 194
Berlin Wall, fall of 11, 28, 136–37, 181–82, 185, 198–200; 203–4, 207, 212, 217, 222
Bernsdorf, Wilhelm, 80
Bernstein, Richard, 299
Berufsverbote (employment bans), 174–75
Between Facts and Norms, 28, 211, 220, 229,
Beyer, Wilhelm Raimund, 169
Beyme, Klaus von, 169
Biebricher, Thomas, 199
Bismarck, Otto von, 209
Bloch, Ernst, 162, 164
Böhm, Franz, 115–17
Bohrer, Karl-Heinz, 17, 153, 167
Bolte, Karl Martin, 80
Bourdieu, Pierre, 4–5, 46, 238; concept of "bidimensional being," 5; on defenders of the universal, 46
Boveris, Margret, 96
Brandt, Willy, 134–35, 164, 168, 182, 242
Brehms, Bruno, 79

Brexit, 267–71
Bröcker, Walter, 106
Brown, Wendy, 4, 6
Bubak, Siegfried, 171
Bülow, Friedrich, 80
Burke, Edmund, 33
Bush, George W., 238
Buzzard, Anthony, 115

Cambridge School, 22–24. See also Skinner, Quentin
Cameron, David, 271
Christlich Demokratische Union Deutschlands (Christian Democratic Union, or CDU), 115–16, 143, 148, 152, 171, 174–75, 179, 182–84, 193, 196, 202, 215. See also Kohl, Helmut
civil disobedience, 142, 149–50, 198–99
Cohn-Bendit, Daniel 273
colonization, 20, 38, 51, 84, 102, 204, 248ff, 300, 310; of the lifeworld, 20, 38, 51, 84, 102, 300, 310; of politics by economics, 204, 248ff
constitutional patriotism (*Verfassungspatriotismus*), 20, 185, 188–89, 211, 220–22, 238–40, 243, 300
Coronavirus (SARS-CoV-2), 215, 269. 272–75, 283
COVID-19 pandemic, 277–79
Czollek, Max, 185

Dahrendorf, Ralf, 80, 162–63
de Tocqueville, Alexis, 33
Debray, Réne, 15
Deitelhoff, Nicole, 292, 296
democratic underlaborer (also, democratic underlabourer), 31, 40, 42–43, 48–50, 282
democracy, 4–6, 38–39, 43–44, 47–48, 52–53, 180–82, 193–95, 199–201, 217–21, 225–28, 238–40, 243–46, 248–49, 253–55, 254–58, 258–61, 277–79, 283–85, 291–94, 301–3; defined in context of technocracy, 248–49; defended in globalization debates, 243–46; endangered by technocracy

and austerity, 248–49, 253–55; global
challenges to, 291–94; Habermas's
response to depoliticization, 254–58;
linked to European constitutionalism,
220–21, 225–26; postnational form of,
217–18, 238–40; reaffirmed as
communicative project, 283–85;
reflections during COVID-19, 277–79;
relation to populism and legitimacy,
258–59; revitalized through European
solidarity, 258–61; role of digital media
and public sphere, 301–3
Derrida, Jacques, 238, 290
Deutsch, Lorenz, 215
Dialectic of Enlightenment (*Dialektik der
Aufklärung*), 63, 86, 123
Diebold, John, 79
Dutschke, Rudi, 145–46, 148, 163; clashes with
Habermas, 145–46; reconciliation and
later correspondence, 146, 163
Durkheim, Émile, 177, 233
Đinđić, Zoran, 164
Draghi, Mario, 264

Eco, Umberto, 227, 238
education and universities, 7–8, 99–104,
137–43, 152–53; democratic function of,
7; link to student participation, 143;
Habermas's critique of institutionalized
planning of, 142–43; Habermas's critiques
of reform plans, 100–103;
Einsiedel, Wolfgang von, 75
Engels, Friedrich, 98
Erdoğan, Recep Tayyip, 271
Erhard, Ludwig, 136
Erikson, Erik H., 97
European Central Bank (ECB), 250–53,
257–58
European citizenship, 221, 231, 239–43, 274
European integration, 220–30, 237–40,
248–50, 253–58, 268–70; advocacy of
stronger EU institutions, 237–40; analysis
of Maastricht and Amsterdam Treaties,
224–26; challenges during Eurozone crisis,
248–50; Habermas's defense of deeper
integration, 253–55
European public sphere, 228–30, 239–40,
243–45; linked to global communication,
243–45; Habermas's concept of, 228–30;
expanded through media and civil society,
239–40
European Union (EU), 2, 9–10, 220–30,
237–40, 243–45, 248–50, 253–58,
268–70, 290–92; challenges during
Eurozone crisis, 248–50; criticism
of intergovernmentalism, 256–58;
democratic legitimacy debates, 225–26,
239–40; effects of Brexit, 268–70;
expanded through media and civil
society, 239–40; Habermas's concept
of, 228–30; Habermas's defense of
democratic legitimacy, 248–49, 253–55;
Habermas's engagement with, 220–24;
Lisbon Treaty discussions, 237–38;
linked to global communication, 243–45.
See also European integration; austerity
policies
eurocrisis, 271–75. *See also* Eurozone crisis
Eurozone crisis, 2, 29, 248–69, 289. *See also*
eurocrisis.

Fehér, Ferenc, 27, 164
Felsch, Philip, 275, 285, 287, 308, 312–13
Fest, Joachim, 17, 167–68
Fetcher, Irving, 143
Feuilleton, 10, 15–19, 159, 167
Filbinger, Hans, 171
Fischer, Joschka, 146, 260
Flügge, Johannes, 79
Forst, Rainer, 292
Forsthoff, Ernst, 119, 197
Foucault, Michel, 44–47, 112
Freud, Sigmund, 52, 97–98, 125, 149
Friedeburg, Ludwig von, 143
Friedländer, Saul, 184
Frisé, Adolf, 75, 86
Fukuyama, Francis, 259
Fürstenau, Peter, 106

Gabriel, Sigmar, 248, 263–64
Gadamer, Hans-Georg, 126–28, 137, 140
Gans, Herbert, 154, 164–65
Gaulle, Charles de, 136
Gehlen, Arnold, 61, 65, 79–81, 109–10, 172, 197, 262
genetic engineering, 230–33
Gentile, Giovanni, 18
Geuss, Raymond, 40
Glazer, Nathan, 118
Goethe House, 146
Goethe Institute, 255
Goethe, Johann Wolfgang von, 61
Goethe Prize, 97
Goethe-University, 28, 115, 139, 156, 159, 178–81, 217
Goldhagen, Daniel, 189
Google, Deep Mind, 294–95
Gorbachev, Mikhail, 182
Gordon, Peter, 309
Grass, Günther, 150, 212, 216
Grimm, Dieter, 226
Guevara, Che, 156
Gulag, 186, 191
Günther, Frieder, 119–20
Günther, Klaus, 292

Habermas, Ernst (father of Jürgen Habermas), 57
Habermas, Hans-Joachim (brother of Jürgen Habermas), 57
Hamas, 30, 277, 283, 292
Harenberg, Werner, 160
Haschemi, Sascha, 166
Hasenclever, Walter, 61
Havel, Václav, 7, 227
Haysom, Keith, 44
Hegel, G.W.F., 41, 61, 66, 94, 106–106, 119, 169, 223, 278, 298, 306
Heidegger, Martin, 2–3, 13, 17–18, 26, 34, 41, 54–56, 63, 65–70, 73, 84–85, 90, 94, 103–7, 109–10, 124, 132, 137, 157, 172, 185, 190, 200
Heine, Heinrich, 16, 199–200
Heller, Ágnes, 27, 120, 164–66, 174, 255

Heller, Hermann, 120
Hennis, Wilhelm, 169
Henri-Levy, Bernard, 227
Herbert, Ulrich, 196
Herder, Johann Gottfried, 108
Heuss, Theodor, 97
Hillgruber, Andreas, 186, 189–95
Hindenburg, Paul von, 195
Historikerstreit (Historians' Debate), 11, 18–19, 168, 179, 181, 183–96, 230
Hitler, Adolf, 41, 57, 61–62, 73, 102, 103–4, 108, 111, 121, 135, 168–69, 186, 213; seizure of power (*Machtergreifung*), 57, 103–4, 121, 169, 186
Hitler Youth, 21
Hobbes, Thomas, 33
Holocaust, 19–20, 60, 95, 168, 181–82, 184–87, 190–91, 202, 214–16, 286–87, 293
Hölderlin, Friedrich, 106
Holub, Robert, 12, 184, 192
Holzer, Horst, 166
Homer, 106
Honneth, Axel, 273, 299–300
Horkheimer, Max, 26, 52–53, 64–65, 86–89, 91–92, 95–97, 109, 116–17, 122–32, 138–40, 152, 155, 158, 281; conflict with Habermas over political activism, 129–30; contrast with Adorno, 96, 109; opposition to Habermas's activism, 96; support for Frankfurt appointment, 138–39
Howard, Dick, 184
Huntington, Samuel, 270
Huxley, Aldous, 79

IMF (International Monetary Fund), 251, 258, 265
Imhoff, Hans, 151
Instagram, 303
Institute for Social Research (*Institut für Sozialforschung*), 14, 16, 26, 52, 87–91, 92ff, 129–31, 137, 138–40, 149, 152–54, 201, 266,
Iraq War, 222, 236–38, 240, 243–46, 270, 285, 290
Israel–Gaza conflict, 30, 283, 292–97

Jagar, Josip, 163
Jaspers, Karl, 93, 101, 103, 106–7, 124; as public intellectual, 124; on the German university, 101, 103, 106–7; views on German guilt, 93, 114
Jones, Morris, 118
Jünger, Ernst, 172

Kaiser, Georg, 61
Kalmbach, Peter, 168–69
Kangrga, Milan, 163
Kant, Immanuel, 4, 33–35, 41, 43–44, 83, 93, 108, 220, 226–28, 241, 256, 293; influence on Habermas's cosmopolitanism, 226–28; influence on Habermas's democratic theory, 4; on public use of reason, 43–44
Kirchheimer, Otto, 120
Klein, Felix, 215
Kluge, Alexander, 287
Knowledge and Human Interests, 11, 140, 167
Kohl, Helmut, 28, 179, 181–83, 188–98, 202–123, 230, 254, 286, 300
Kołakowski, Leszek, 135, 154
Korn, Karl, 10, 17–18, 67–69, 73, 106, 132; early supporter of Habermas's publications, 17–18; support for Habermas's attack on Heidegger, 68–69
Kosík, Karel, 166
Kracauer, Sigfried, 300
Krapf, Eduardo, 98
Kraushaar, Wolfgang, 163
Kristol, Irving, 196

Lakebrink, Berhard, 80
Landgrebe, Ludwig, 65
left fascism, 26, 34, 131, 145–48
Leitkultur (leading culture), 255
Leonhardt, Rudolf Walter, 18
Leninism, 40–41
Lersch, Philipp, 75
Lewalter, Christian, 68
Lichtheim, George, 176

lifeworld (*Lebenswelt*), 20, 38–39, 41, 51, 84, 102, 110, 138, 221–23, 229, 243, 245, 252–53, 262, 266, 300
Lippmann, Walter, 74, 301
Lipps, Hans, 79
Lisbon Treaty, 237–38
Lobkowicz, Nikolas, 170
Loewenstein, Karl, 120
Luhmann, Niklas, 250
Lukács, György, 164–65
Lukes, Steven, 175
Luxemburg, Rosa, 164–65

MacShane, Denis, 244
Maastricht Treaty, 221, 224–25, 231, 252
Machiavelli, Niccolò, 33
Macron, Emmanuel, 248, 263–64
Maier, Charles, 187, 192
Maier, Hans, 170
Mannheim, Karl, 45
Marcuse, Herbert, 23, 77–78, 98–99, 109, 138, 149, 152, 154–55, 158–59, 161; correspondence with Adorno and Habermas, 152; divergence over student radicalism, 158–59; influence on Habermas's synthesis of Marx and Freud, 98–99, 138
Márkus, György, 166
Marx, Karl, 26–29, 43, 39–41, 52, 68–69, 75–76, 83–84, 86, 88, 94, 98–99, 109–11, 122, 126, 129–35, 141, 149–51, 157–59, 161–62, 164–65, 176–77, 233, 266, 282, 286; influence on Abendroth's and Habermas's thought, 133; influence on critical theory, 52; mediated through Lukács and Heller, 157–58; on practice and theory, 39–40; philosophical influence on Habermas, 98–99; relation to critical theory, 99; reinterpreted within communicative framework, 176–77
Max Planck Institute (Starnberg), 27, 114, 136, 156–62, 164–65, 167, 169, 170, 175, 177, 179, 181, 187, 199, 201, 281
Mbembe, Achille, 215–16

Menzel, Walter, 115
memory, collective, 19–22, 28, 90, 93–95, 135–36, 146, 148, 181, 185–96, 202–4, 209, 214–16, 232, 284, 293, 298, 300
Merkel, Angela, 253–55, 269–70, 272
Merkur (journal), 8–9, 57, 75, 80–82, 85–86, 97, 99, 126, 136–38, 143, 145, 170, 173, 199
Mill, John Stuart, 33
Mills, C. Wright, 6
Mitscherlich, Alexander, 97, 143
Mitry, Jean, 63
Mohler, Armin, 136
Moras, Joachim, 85–86
Müller-Doohm, Stefan, 12, 53, 90, 95, 116, 124–25, 134, 288
Muschg, Adolf, 238

Nagy, Imre, 114
nationalism, 258–60, 265–70; connection to Brexit, 268–70; critique of populist rhetoric, 265–67; resurgence during Eurozone and migration crises, 258–60
NATO (North Atlantic Treaty Organization), 72, 113, 135, 227, 237, 239, 273, 285, 292–94, 300
Negt, Oskar, 146, 174
neoconservatism, 196–97, 238
neoliberalism, 218, 242–44, 253, 263, 271; critique of economic globalization, 242–44; linked to democratic legitimacy, 243–44
Nida-Rümelin, Julian, 256
Nobel Peace Prize, 261
Nolte, Ernst, 13, 184–87, 190–95
normalization, 19, 27–28, 182, 186, 202, 209, 215, 260, 265, 299–300; in reference to German foreign policy, 19, 215, 260, 265; in reference to German memory politics, 27–28, 182, 186, 202, 209; normalized intellectuals, 299–300

Oevermann, Ulrich, 119, 130
Offe, Claus, 146, 168
Ohnesorg, Benno, 144

Orbán, Viktor, 255–56
Ordoliberalism, 256
Osswald, Albert, 160

Paetschke, Hans, 57, 85, 145
Patočka, Jan, 166
Pfeffer, Matthias, 295
Plato, 33
plebiscite, 116, 203, 206. *See also* referendum
Plessner, Helmut, 79, 107–9
Pollock, Friedrich, 110
Ponto, Jürgen, 171
Popitz, Heinrich, 80
Popper, Karl, 138–39
Positivism dispute (*Positivismusstreit*), 138–39
postnational constellation, 28–29, 217–18, 220–24, 228–29, 232, 241, 248, 250, 252, 257, 271, 281; European path beyond nation-state, 217–18, 223–24; title of Habermas's 1998 work, 220–22;
postnational identity, 199–202
postsecularism, 234–36
Praxis Group (Yugoslavia), 27, 52, 81, 131, 161–66. *See also* Tito, Josip Broz
public philosophy, 31, 36, 43, 51, 248, 272, 276
Putin, Vladimir, 271, 285–89, 292. *See also* Ukraine, full scale invasion of

Radbruch, Gustav, 121
Rahden, Till van, 60
Ratzinger, Joseph (Pope Benedict XVI), 235–36
Rawls, John, 221, 233
Reagan, Ronald, 194
realism (political theory), 31–32, 35–37, 39–41, 48–49, 50–52, 279, 282, 294; critique of Habermas, 35–36, 39–40; Habermas's response to, 40–41, 48–49, 50–52
Red Army Faction (*Rote Arme Fraktion*, RAF), 171 (Andreas Baader, Gudrun Ensslin, and Ulrike Meinhof)
Reddit, 306
Reemtsma, Jan Philipp, 256

referendum, 205, 232, 242–46, 265, 271; as part of German unification, 205; in reference to EU, 232, 242–46, 265, 271. *See also* plebiscite.
Reinhold, Otto, 182–83
Riesman, David, 118
Ritter, Joachim, 197
Romero, Carlos Humberto, 166
Rorty, Richard, 238
Rossman, Mike, 142
Rothacker, Ernst, 64, 66, 69–71, 75, 80, 84, 107–10, 132
Rothberg, Michael, 216
Rousseau, Jean-Jacques, 33
Rüegg, Walter, 151
Russell, Bertrand, 175
Russell Tribunal, 175, 179
Russia–Ukraine war, 2, 30, 277, 283–94, 298, 300, 304, 307

Saïd, Edward, 7, 302, 304
Sarrazin, Thilo, 255
Sartre, Jean-Paul, 46, 61, 63, 105, 175
Savater, Fernando, 238
Schäuble, Wolfgang, 264–65
Schelling, Friedrich Wilhelm Joseph, 70, 88, 106–7; subject of Habermas's PhD dissertation, 70
Schelsky, Helmut, 80–81, 85–86, 100, 132, 138, 176, 262
Schirrmacher, Frank, 18
Schleiermacher, Friedrich, 201
Schleyer, Hanns Martin, 171
Schluchter, Wolfgang, 187–88
Scholz, Olaf, 286, 300
Schmidt, Helmut, 182
Schmitt, Carl, 18, 41, 119–21, 132, 172, 197–99
Schröder, Gerhard, 256, 260
Schulenburg-Kehnert, Friedrich Wilhelm Graf von der, 116
Schumpeter, Joseph, 299
Skarpelis-Sperk, Sigrid, 168–69
Skinner, Quentin, 22, 24, 55
Sloterdijk, Peter, 298

Socrates, 7, 42, 148
Sontheimer, Kurt, 8, 172–73
Sozialdemokratische Partei Deutschlands (Social Democratic Party of Germany, or SPD), 132–35, 143, 152, 168, 171, 198, 242, 245, 264, 300; exchange on SPD reform and social democracy, 134–35; internal debates and Bad Godesberg program, 133–34, 168; meetings with Habermas, 134, 198, 242, 245, 264; participation in grand coalition, 143, 152; relations with Habermas and student groups, 134–35
Spaemann, Robert, 170
Spitz, René A., 98
Smend, Rudolf, 120–21, 132
Staatslehre (also *Staatsrechtslehre*, state or constitutional theory), 26, 28–29, 95, 119–21, 128, 132, 208, 211, 228, 298
Stalin, Joseph, 171, 191; Stalinism, 191
Stoltenberg, Gerhard, 148
Steinmeier, Frank-Walter, 245
Sternberger, Dolf, 93, 124
Strauss, Franz Joseph, 143
Streeck, Wolfgang, 266–67, 271
Stresemann, Gustav, 110–11
Structural Transformation of the Public Sphere, 5, 14–16, 25–26, 38, 72, 91, 93, 95, 112, 114, 117, 121, 125, 127–28, 130–32, 135, 138–40, 149, 156, 177, 182, 197, 220, 254
student movement, 129–31, 140–53; conflicts with Adorno and Horkheimer, 152–53; critique of violence and actionism, 145–47, 149–50; role in democratizing public sphere, 129–30, 149–50. *See also* Dutschke, Rudi
Stürmer, Michael, 186–95
Supek, Rudi, 162

Taylor, Charles, 233
technocracy, 149, 250, 262–64
Theodor Heuss Visiting Professorship, 14, 146
Theunissen, Michael, 174
Tito, Josip Broz, 161–63
Todorov, Tzvetan, 185;

terrorism, 27, 144, 157, 159, 166–74, 177, 179, 236; Habermas's distinction between violence and protest, 167–70; public debate over, 168–70; state response to left-wing violence, 166–67
Theory of Communicative Action, 27, 29, 84, 102, 158, 177, 207, 226, 233, 251
Theunissen, Michael, 174, 178
TikTok, 303
Tolstoy, Leo, 98
Tourjanski, Viktor, 79

Ukraine, full scale invasion of 2, 30, 277, 283–94, 298, 300, 304, 307. *See also* Putin, Vladimir
Unseld, Siegfried, 94, 157

Vattimo, Gianni, 238
Vereinigungsdebatte (Unification Debate), 28, 179, 181, 183, 196, 202, 209, 214
Vietta, Egon, 63
violence, 66, 129–30, 145–47, 171–73, 188, 194, 198, 213, 232, 293; debate with student radicals over legitimacy of, 145–47; Habermas's critique of revolutionary violence, 129–30, 145–47

Weber, Alfred, 45
Weber, Max, 4, 33–35, 39–45, 46–47, 50–52, 76, 84, 94, 177, 183, 233, 239, 276; distinction between science and politics, 34–35, 43–44; influence on Habermas's conception of value spheres, 33–35, 39–41, 50–51; influence on Habermas's distinction between scholarship and politics, 4
Weber, Werner, 119
Wedekind, Frank, 61
Wehler, Hans-Ulrich, 60, 184, 192
Weimar Republic, 20–21, 56, 93, 110, 121, 135, 213
Weizsäcker, Carl Friedrich von, 27, 114–15, 155, 175–77
Wellek, Albert, 75
Wesselhoeft, Ute, 67, 69, 71
Widman, Arno, 178
Wiggershaus, Rolf, 118
Willy-Brandt-Haus, 242, 245
Wolf, Christa, 208–9
Wright, Georg Henrik von, 163–64
WTO (World Trade Organization), 258

Xi, Jinping, 271

Yos, Roman, 12, 158
Young, Iris Marion, 240

Zimmer, Dieter E., 173
Zinn, Georg August, 97
Zullinger, Hans, 98

GPSR Authorized Representative: Easy Access System Europe, Mustamäe tee 50, 10621 Tallinn, Estonia, gpsr.requests@easproject.com